CENSORSHIP, SECRECY, ACCESS, and OBSCENITY

Readings from
COMMUNICATIONS AND THE LAW

Edited by
The Honorable Theodore R. Kupferman

1. Defamation: Libel and Slander
ISBN 0-88736-507-8 CIP 1990

2. Privacy and Publicity
ISBN 0-88736-508-6 CIP 1990

3. Censorship, Secrecy, Access and Obscenity
ISBN 0-88736-509-4 CIP 1990

4. Advertising and Commercial Speech
ISBN 0-88736-510-8 CIP 1990

CENSORSHIP, SECRECY, ACCESS, and OBSCENITY

Readings From *Communications and the Law, 3*

Edited by
The Honorable Theodore R. Kupferman

Meckler
Westport • London

Citations to the original appearance of articles collected in this volume appear at the back of this book.

Library of Congress Cataloging-in-Publication Data

Censorship, secrecy, access, and obscenity / edited by Theodore R. Kupferman.
    p. cm. -- (Readings from Communications and the law ; 3)
  ISBN 0-88736-509-4 (alk. paper) : $
  1. Freedom of the press-- United States. 2. Censorship--United States. 3. Secrecy--Law and legislation--United States.
I. Kupferman, Theodore R. II. Series.
KF 4775. A75C46   1990
342.73 ' 0853 -- dc20
[347.302853]   89-31994
                                                       CIP

British Library Cataloguing in Publication Data

Censorship, secrecy, access, and obscenity: readings from Communications and the law.
1. United States. Freedom of information. Law 2.
United States. Censorship. Law
I. Kupferman, Theodore R. II. Communications and the law
347. 302 ' 853

ISBN 0-88736-509-4

Copyright © 1990 Meckler Corporation. All rights reserved.
No part of this publication may be reproduced in any form by any means without prior written permission from the publisher, except by a reviewer who may quote brief passages in review.

Meckler Corporation, 11 Ferry Lane West, Westport, CT 06880.
Meckler Ltd., Grosvenor Gardens House, Grosvenor Gardens, London SW1W 0BS, U.K.

Printed on acid free paper.
Printed and bound in the United States of America.

CONTENTS

Preface — vii

Open Justice: The Threat of *Gannett*
    JAMES C. GOODALE — 1

Introduction: The *Snepp* Case —
    Government Censorship Through
    The "Back Door"
    HENRY R. KAUFMAN — 13

First Amendment Implications
    For Secondary Information Services
    PAUL G. ZURKOWSKI — 41

Obscene/Indecent Programming: The FCC and WBAI
    STANLEY D. TICKTON — 57

Heightened Judicial Scrutiny: A Test
    for the First Amendment Rights of Children
    DENISE M. TRAUTH and JOHN L. HUFFMAN — 71

Obscenity and the Supreme Court:
    A Communication Approach to a
    Persistent Judicial Problem
    JOHN KAMP — 91

Shield Laws and the Separation of Powers Doctrine
    LOUIS A. DAY — 133

Attitiudes of Media Attorneys Concerning
    Closed Criminal Proceedings
    F. DENNIS HALE — 149

TV in the Courtroom: Right of Access
    MARY KAY PLATTE — 157

The Trials and Tribulations of Courtroom Secrecy and
 Judicial Craftsmanship: Reflections on Gannett
 and Richmond Newspapers
  DAVID M. O'BRIEN ——————————————— 177

The Right to Know: Whose Right and Whose Duty?
  EUGENIA ZERBINOS ——————————————— 209

Government Lawyers and the Press
  ANTHONY GREEN ———————————————— 227

"Consistent with Security" . . . A History of
 American Military Press Censorship
  JACK A. GOTTSCHALK ———————————— 259

Abating Obscenity As a Nuisance: An Easy
 Procedural Road for Prior Restraints
  ROBERT L. HUGHES ——————————————— 277

The Cost of Prior Restraint: *U.S. v.The Progressive*
  JOHN SOLOSKI and
  CAROLYN STEWART DYER ———————————— 289

State Press Law Provisions and State Demographics
  F. DENNIS HALE ———————————————— 311

Political Speech or Obscenity
  DEBRA M. ZIGELBAUM ——————————————— 319

The Irrelevant First Amendment
  STEVE BACHMANN ———————————————— 331

Indecent Broadcast: An Assessment of *Pacifica*'s Impact
  JAMES C. HSIUNG ———————————————— 355

Open Meetings in Higher Education
  JON DILTS ———————————————————— 371

Freedom of Expression: The Warren and Burger Courts
  F. DENNIS HALE ———————————————— 383

An Affirmative First Amendment Access Right
  TRACIEL V. REID ———————————————— 403

PREFACE

The four subjects for which articles are included together in this volume have an affinity.

While Censorship is by no means confined to Obscenity, it is naturally pervasive in that area, and secrecy and lack of access is a form of Censorship

Our first article, from Volume 1, No. 1, authored a decade ago by James C. Goodale and reprinted herein, considered the problem of closed courts — a version of censorship — in the framework of fair trial. The public's right to know with access to court trials, in their various ramifications, was considered vis á vis a party's right to have a matter decided only on the evidence actually introduced and allowed in court without public clamor.

The *Kaufman* article in the next issue considered the *Snepp* case, prior to the Supreme Court decision 444 U.S. 507 and the problem of supposed national security needs versus the need for public truth.

Freedom for secondary sources in an information bank is the theme of *Zurkowski* as, in the author's words, we move "from a predominatly industrial age to an information age . . . "

Obscenity comes to the fore in articles by *Tickton, Kamp, Hughes, Zigelbaum,* and *Hsiung,* although other aspects are considered.

While we started with *Goodale* on "Open Justice," aforementioned, the problem continues to be with us and was well thought out in the *Day* and *O'Brien* articles.

Throughout all the articles runs a First Amendment thread. The underpinnings thereof are considered by *Bachman* and *Reid* in their writings.

Specific aspects are covered by *Trauth* and *Huffman* considering the "Rights of Children" under the First Amendment; by *Green* for "Government Lawyers"; by *Platte* for the move toward "TV in the Courtroom," which is an access question; by *Dilts* for "Open Meetings in Higher Education"; by *Soloski* and *Dyer* on "The Cost of Prior Restraint"; by *Hale*, a prolific writer, on comparing "The Warren and Burger Courts" in this area and on "State Press Law Provisions."

Zerbinos takes on the linchpin words, "The Right to Know: Whose Right and Whose Duty?"

While the definitive rules are still to some extent in the future, we have gathered from these articles a much better understanding of derivation and substantiation, a fine groundwork.

JAMES C. GOODALE

Open Justice:
The Threat of *Gannett*

Mr. Goodale, Executive Vice President of
The New York Times Co., is a visiting
Lecturer of Law at Yale Law School, a
member of the New York City Bar
Association, and serves on its
communication and corporate law
committees. He is also a member
of the ANPA/ABA Task Force
Committee and the ANPA Press-Bar
Relations Committee.

The latest chapter in this country's lengthy history of tension between the right of a defendant to a fair trial and the right of the public to a free press will be written during the next year. In its 1978-79 Term, the Supreme Court will decide for the first time, in the case of *Gannett v. De Pasquale*,[1] whether it is constitutional to bar the press and the public from a pre-trial hearing in a criminal case. In *Gannett,* a New York trial court, acting at the request of defense counsel, closed a pre-trial hearing on the admissibility of confessions in a murder case, and this action was upheld by a 4-2 vote in New York's highest court. The approach taken by

1. Gannett Co. v. De Pasquale, 43 N.Y.2d 370, 401 N.Y.S.2d 756, 372 N.E.2d 544 (1977), *cert. granted,* 46 U.S.L.W. 3679 (May 1, 1978).

the New York courts in dealing with the fair trial-free press problem, denying access by the press to judicial proceedings, is somewhat novel. But the many other fair trial-free press cases decided in the past provide a clue how the Court will, or at least should, decide this one.

In the past, the courts have attempted to deal with perceived press violations of fair trial rights through (a) punishing the press in summary contempt or other proceedings and (b) issuing prior restraints. An examination of this earlier history suggests that to affirm the decision in the *Gannett* case would be to limit substantially the First Amendment rights established by the cases of the last 35 years.

A.   Summary Contempt Proceedings

For roughly the first 150 years of the history of this country, until 1941, the fair trial-free press battle was fought out in state courts in summary contempt proceedings. What happens in such a proceeding is this: A newspaper publishes putatively prejudicial information about a trial and thereafter it is hauled into court and ordered to show cause why it should not be held in contempt. The same judge who is responsible for the trial decides whether the newspaper is in contempt. If he concludes it is, then the paper pays a fine; if an individual—such as a reporter, editor, or publisher—is found in contempt, he or she may be jailed.

This summary contempt procedure is as violative of First Amendment rights as it is of the elementary requirements of due process. There is no notice to the news media of the possible offense to the court, and the judge is prosecutor, judge, and jury to determine whether he or his court has been offended. This is the way fair trial-free press matters are handled in England. But of course there is no First Amendment in that country, and just how much difference this makes can be seen from the array of restrictions on the British press. For instance, a British newspaper may be held in contempt for describing an arrested person as a "crank" or for printing a photograph of a defendant in a case where identification is an issue.[2] Although such heavy-handed use of the contempt power would be unthinkable in the United States today, for 150 years this country had such a system of restrictions on the press. Many state courts adopted the English procedure, and it was not seriously limited by the Supreme Court until 1941.

Long before then, however, the summary contempt procedure had become the subject of severe criticism. In the late 1820's, the United States Senate was in an uproar over the summary contempt proceeding

2. See Gillmor, *Free Press and Fair Trial in English Law,* 22 Washington and Lee L. Rev. 17 (1965).

conducted by Judge Peck against one Luke Lawless, an attorney. Peck had rendered a decision adverse to a client of Lawless. Lawless then wrote a newspaper article criticizing Peck, and Peck held him in contempt, having Lawless imprisoned for a day and suspended from practice for 18 months. The resulting storm of controversy led to an impeachment effort in the Senate in order to unseat Peck. Senator James Buchanan, later President, managed the drive, but it lost by one vote.[3] Undaunted, Buchanan then drafted an amendment to the Judiciary Act to outlaw the use of summary contempts to punish out-of-court publications. The section is in force today as 18 U.S.C. § 401. It generally limits the power of a federal court to punish contempts to cases of the "misbehavior of any person in its presence or so near thereto as to obstruct the administration of justice."

With this history, one would have thought that the use of summary contempts in the fair trial-free press context was dead. But when the Supreme Court got around to interpreting the section, nearly 100 years later, it held that the provision meant exactly the opposite of what Buchanan had intended it to mean. The case was *Toledo Newspaper Company v. United States*.[4] There, a newspaper's publications had challenged the right of a federal district court to issue certain injunctions in a pending controversy over the Toledo street railways. A summary contempt proceeding was brought, and the conviction was upheld by the Supreme Court. The Court held that the statute did not curtail previous powers to summarily punish for contempt, and that if it could be shown that the acts complained of *tended* to endanger the fair administration of justice, then they could be punished. Holmes and Brandeis dissented, one of several instances where they disagreed with the application of the mere tendency test.[5]

The crabbed approach of *Toledo Newspaper* was repudiated in 1941, when the Supreme Court killed summary contempt proceedings against the media forever in the federal courts and gave them a mortal wound in the state courts. In *Nye v. United States*,[6] the high Court reversed *Toledo Newspaper* and concluded that section 401 meant what it said: A federal court had no summary contempt power unless the contempt was committed in its presence. Since newspapers and magazines were not published in courtrooms, they could not be held in contempt for what they published about federal court proceedings. Later that year, the Court decided *Bridges v. California*,[7] a state court case which arose after

3. *See* Committee on the Judiciary, House of Representatives, 93rd Cong., 1st Sess., *Impeachment, Selected Materials* 136-139 (Comm. Print 1973).
4. Toledo Newspaper Co. v. United States, 247 U.S. 402 (1918).
5. Ultimately, of course, they articulated the clear and present danger test which was accepted by the Court in Schenck v. United States, 249 U.S. 47 (1919).
6. Nye v. United States, 313 U.S. 33 (1941).
7. Bridges v. California, 314 U.S. 252 (1941).

the *Los Angeles Times* was held in contempt for writing editorials lambasting union members convicted of assault and warning the sentencing judge that he would "make a serious mistake if he grant[ed] probation."[8] Although section 401 did not apply to the states, the Court ruled that the state courts could not bring summary contempt proceedings against the news media unless there was a showing that the publication in question created a clear and present danger to the fair administration of justice. The publications at issue in *Bridges* were held not to meet that test.

With that decision, state summary contempt proceedings virtually disappeared. Although three cases involving publications punished by summary contempt went to the Supreme Court in the next decades, *Pennekamp* v. *Florida*,[9] *Craig* v. *Harney*,[10] and *Wood* v. *Georgia*,[11] the Court held in each instance that the clear and present danger test had not been met. The result was that state courts simply stopped bringing summary contempt proceedings against the press, having discovered that it is virtually impossible to show that a publication in fact created a clear and present danger to the trial. Since *Wood,* no case has gone to the Court, nor am I aware of any such proceedings in the lower courts since that date.

Bridges did leave open, however, the issue of whether a state could achieve through legislation the result which it could not achieve through its courts.[12] But in May 1978 the Supreme Court held in *Landmark Communications, Inc.* v. *Virginia*[13] that having a statute did not make any difference. In *Landmark,* a Norfolk newspaper, the *Virginian-Pilot,* was convicted and fined under a Virginia statute for "divulging" (*i.e.,* publishing) the name of a judge whose fitness was being investigated by a judicial commission. Under Virginia law, the proceedings would remain confidential unless and until charges were filed by the commission. The Virginia courts found that the statute setting up these proceedings represented a binding legislative determination that publication of the judge's name constituted "a clear and present danger" to the "orderly administration of justice."

The Supreme Court reversed, in a 7-0 opinion by Chief Justice Burger. The Court held that a state could never penalize the press for reporting on proceedings of the kind in question, saying, "the publication Virginia seeks to punish under its statute lies near the core of the First Amendment."[14] Chief Justice Burger pointed out that it was important to

8. Id., 314 U.S. at 272, n.17.
9. Pennekamp v. Florida, 328 U.S. 331 (1946).
10. Craig v. Harney, 331 U.S. 367 (1947).
11. Wood v. Georgia, 370 U.S. 375 (1962).
12. *See* Bridges v. California, 314 U.S. at 260.
13. Landmark Communications, Inc. v. Virginia, 98 S.Ct. 1535 (1978).
14. Id., 98 S.Ct. at 1541.

encourage discussion of judicial administration and that "[t]he article published by Landmark provided accurate factual information about a legislatively authorized inquiry pending before the Judicial Inquiry Commission, and in so doing clearly served those interests in public scrutiny and discussion of governmental affairs which the First Amendment was adopted to protect."[15] Since the Court found that this type of publication was so heavily protected, it was not required to discuss the question of whether the Virginia court had correctly applied the clear and present danger test; but it did so nevertheless. After noting that the test may not be relevant to this type of case, the Court held that the judiciary may not defer to a legislative finding on the point. A court is required to make the judgment for itself.

It is important to emphasize that *Landmark* is a fair trial-free press case. A proceeding before the Virginia Judicial Inquiry Commission is a judicial proceeding for all practical purposes, and commentary on pending charges can influence the commission. Further, the proceeding is one which is held in private to protect the defendant's rights. Yet the Supreme Court held that a publication concerning such a proceeding could not be penalized unless it constituted at least a clear and present danger to the proceeding.[16]

B. Prior Restraints

Once *Bridges* had undermined summary contempt procedures as a way of dealing with the perceived fair trial-free press conflict, courts turned to the imposition of prior restraints as a way of coping with the problem.

Strangely enough, this movement was given an impetus by the famous case of *Sheppard* v. *Maxwell*,[17] and for a period of time there was a wave of such restraints until in 1976 *Nebraska Press Assn.* v. *Stuart*[18] put an end to them. I say "strangely" because *Sheppard* was not a prior restraint case at all. Justice Clark discussed the steps a trial judge could take to limit prejudicial publicity, and said that they included control of the seating and general decorum of members of the press in the courtroom, but also noted, "Of course, there is nothing that proscribes the press from reporting events that transpire in the courtroom."[19] Clark did suggest, however, that the trial court might proscribe extrajudicial state-

---

15. Id., 98 S.Ct. at 1542.
16. For a more extensive discussion of Landmark, see Goodale, "News Media and the Law," N.Y.L.J. May 25, 1978 at 1, col. 1.
17. Sheppard v. Maxwell, 384 U.S. 333 (1966).
18. Nebraska Press Assn. v. Stuart, 427, U.S. 539 (1976).
19. Sheppard v. Maxwell, 384 U.S. at 362-363.

ments by the participants in legal proceedings.[20] In other words, *Sheppard* held that the decorum of the press may be controlled in and around the courtroom, a concept consistent with 18 U.S.C. § 401, but not that prior restraints could be directed to the press. Yet despite the clear distinction in the *Sheppard* opinion between restraints on the press and restraints on others, state courts began to impose restraints on the press. What began as a trickle in the late 1960's became a veritable deluge by the mid 1970's. As will be shown briefly below, the issue of prior restraints against trial participants is still undecided, but the issue of restraints against the press has been decided—and decided against the validity of the restraints.

Scholarly thinking on freedom of the press has long made a sharp distinction between prior restraints, *i.e.*, court orders not to publish certain information, such as those involved in the Pentagon Papers case,[21] and subsequent punishments, such as those sought to be imposed in summary contempt cases. The Supreme Court has approved the conclusion of Alexander Bickel, who argued the Pentagon Papers case for *The New York Times*, that "[i]f it can be said that a threat of criminal or civil sanctions after publication 'chills' speech, prior restraint 'freezes' it at least for the time."[22] In other words, a prior restraint is simply censorship; it means that there can be no publication whatsoever. If, on the other hand, sanctions are limited to "subsequent punishment," the offending material can at least see the light of day so that a determination can be made as to whether it is indeed libelous or otherwise offensive.[23] Since prior restraint is the greater evil, it follows that the standard which the government must meet to justify the imposition of such a restraint is greater than that which it must meet to justify the imposition of a subsequent punishment. We have already seen that at least the clear and present danger test must be met before imposing subsequent punishment, and in *Nebraska Press* the Supreme Court correctly held that the standard to be met in prior restraint cases was stricter still. Indeed, the presumption against prior restraints is so great as to be virtually impossible to overcome.

Nebraska Press involved an episode of mass murder and sexual assault in a small town in Nebraska. A suspect confessed to the crimes, and the confession was read in open court in a preliminary hearing. The trial court enjoined publication of the confession and the injunction was upheld by the Nebraska courts. The Supreme Court unanimously reversed. Four Justices (Brennan, Stewart, Marshall, and Stevens) voted for the

20. Id., 384 U.S. at 361.
21. New York Times Co. v. United States, 403 U.S. 713 (1971).
22. Nebraska Press Assn. v. Stuart, 427 U.S. at 559, citing A. Bickel, *The Morality of Consent* 61 (1975).
23. For an expanded discussion of these points, see Goodale, "News Media and the Law," N.Y.L.J., May 26, 1977 at 1, col. 1.

proposition that there should be an absolute ban against prior restraints in the fair trial context, while the majority, in an opinion by Chief Justice Burger, held that prior restraints could be imposed in such circumstances only if the state could meet a strict three-part test. In fact, I believe this test is so strict that it can never be met,[24] for reasons which bear directly on the question before the Court in *Gannett.*

Under the majority's test in *Nebraska Press,* a court may enter a prior restraint only after making specific findings that: (1) pre-trial publicity is likely to be so pervasive that it will probably have an effect on jurors; and (2) there are no alternative methods of dealing with the problem; and (3) the prior restraint will be effective. It is quite clear from Chief Justice Burger's opinion in *Nebraska Press* that the required findings may not be made *a priori.* In meeting the first part of the test, for instance, a court may not simply speculate on the effect publicity will have on jurors; it must have proof. The *Nebraska Press* trial judge was chastised for his failings on this point, the Court writing that "[h]is conclusion as to the impact of such publicity on prospective jurors was of necessity speculative, dealing as he was with factors unknown and unknowable."[25]

The effect of this strict standard is to undermine in large part the major premise which has hitherto supported judicial intervention in fair trial-free press cases. Typically, most analyses of this highly complex issue have begun by noting that the Sixth Amendment grants a defendant the right to a fair trial, while the First Amendment gives the press the right to publish reports of judicial proceedings. Since neither right is absolute, qualifications must be made to each so that the two rights may be accommodated. Implicit in this approach is the belief that there is always a conflict between the two rights, and that a totally free press will always effect the outcome of a trial. But Chief Justice Burger's opinion in *Nebraska Press* assumes, to the contrary, that there is no effective conflict that requires restriction of press rights during the pre-trial period. *Nebraska Press* explicitly requires that pre-trial publicity must be *shown* to have affected the attitude of jurors; if it has, then veniremen can be disqualified or chosen jurors sequestered. Chief Justice Burger is therefore willing to assume that there will in every case be some potential jurors who, although exposed to pre-trial publicity, will be able to judge the case on the evidence presented in court. But if there are always such jurors to be found, then the pre-trial publicity problem disappears. This leaves only the question of publicity during a trial. But since it seems very likely that the second part of the *Nebraska Press* test requires the trial judge to

24. For a more detailed explication of this view, see Goodale, *The Press Ungagged: The Practical Effect on Gag Order Litigation of* Nebraska Press Association v. Stuart, 29 Stan.L.R. 497 (1977).
25. Nebraska Press Assn. v. Stuart, 427 U.S. at 563.

make use of the highly effective alternative method of sequestering the jury, instead of imposing restrictions on the press, a prior restraint imposed to protect an ongoing trial would almost certainly be invalid.

If this reading of *Nebraska Press* is correct, then prior restraints on parties, lawyers, and witnesses would seem to be virtually eliminated.[26] Allegedly prejudicial statements by such persons may be dealt with only through subsequent punishment, which means under *Bridges* and *Landmark* that the statements must be shown at the least to create a clear and present danger to the fair administration of justice. While there is little law on this subject, because the concept of restricting the speech of the people listed above is a fairly novel one, the view presented here has found a certain amount of support recently. Following the *Sheppard* case, the American Bar Association adopted a series of rules curtailing the extrajudicial speech of lawyers about their cases.[27] But the rules were deemed overbroad and vague, and were held unconstitutional in a 1975 declaratory judgment in *Chicago Council of Lawyers* v. *Bauer*.[28] In *Bauer*, the Seventh Circuit held that no restraint could be imposed on a defense lawyer's speech unless the speech posed a serious and imminent danger to the trial. In 1978, a special committee of the ABA amended the earlier ABA rules to take account of the *Bauer* case and recommended to the ABA House of Delegates that new rules with higher standards be adopted. The House of Delegates approved these amendments on August 9, 1978.

Thus there has begun to be recognition of the fact that the Supreme Court has set very high standards indeed before there can be interference with speech in the fair trial-free press context.[29] Because the New York Court of Appeals decision in *Gannett* falls afoul of the policies behind these standards, it should be reversed.

26. Possibly, a more restrictive standard could properly be applied to out-of-court statements by prosecutors, since they are a part of the government.
27. Disciplinary Rule 7-107 of the American Bar Association's Code of Professional Responsibility.
28. Chicago Council of Lawyers v. Bauer, 522 F.2d 242 (7th Cir. 1975).
29. However, it should also be noted that in its 1977-78 Term the Court denied certiorari in two cases where courts had imposed restraints on participants in a trial. In Society of Professional Journalists v. Martin, 556 F.2d 706 (4th Cir. 1977), cert. denied, 46 U.S.L.W. 3437 (Jan. 10, 1978), a South Carolina trial court had enjoined extrajudicial statements by "lawyers, parties, witnesses, jurors and court officials, which might divulge prejudicial matter not of public record in the case." The Fourth Circuit Court of Appeals approved the lower court opinion, 431 F.Supp. 1182 (D.S.C. 1977), which had applied the test of whether there was "a reasonable likelihood" that the speech would prejudice the trial. In the second case, Leach v. Sawicki, summarized at 46 U.S.L.W. 3377 (Dec. 6, 1977) cert. denied, 46 U.S.L.W. 3436 (Jan. 10, 1978), which involved an unreported order of the Ohio Supreme Court, witnesses, jurors and lawyers were forbidden to talk to the press without any finding—as far as I can determine—of a clear and present danger to the trial or even a reasonable likelihood of such danger. In other words, the Court may have applied no test whatsoever in restraining speech. From what has been already said, it would seem clear that both the Ohio and South Carolina cases were wrong.

C.   Closing the Courtroom

Gannett involved the murder of a former town policeman in upstate New York who had last been seen in the company of two youths. Two youths were subsequently arrested in Michigan driving the victim's pick-up truck, and made incriminating statements. The defense moved to suppress the statements and also asked that the pre-trial suppression hearing be held *in camera* to minimize the prejudicial effects of further disclosures. The trial judge granted the closure motion, and local press representatives took the matter to New York's highest court. That court concluded that the trial judge had the right to close pre-trial hearings, saying that "[a]t the point where press commentary on the hearings would threaten the impaneling of a constitutionally impartial jury in the county of venue, pre-trial evidentiary hearings in this State are presumptively to be closed to the public."[30]

This holding presents an approach to the fair trial-free press problem that seems quite different from those we have observed to this point. The standard announced by the Court of Appeals is one of restriction where publication "would threaten" the trial. Is this the same as the tests used for prior restraints or as the clear and present danger test used in the subsequent punishment cases? Are we indeed talking about prior restraint, or subsequent punishment, or neither?

Strictly speaking, closing a courtroom is neither a prior restraint nor a subsequent punishment. Rather, it is a limitation on access to information. When a courtroom is closed, the press has no access to it but may still publish what it learns; hence, there is no prior restraint. Thus, the press in *Landmark* was barred by statute from attending certain judicial proceedings, but the Supreme Court found that such a bar could not operate to prevent the press from reporting what had happened at those proceedings. And while such reports could presumably form the basis for subsequent punishment under some appropriate standard, closing the courtroom door does not itself impose such a punishment. Moreover, the press' right of access to the news is generally thought to be less expansive than its right to be free of either prior restraint or subsequent punishments, because the right of the public to receive information (which as a practical matter is directly related to the amount of access the press has) is subject to well-recognized exceptions in order to safeguard personal privacy, the safety of witnesses, and the like.[31]

Yet when dealing with the concept of access in the fair trial-free press context, the policies behind the prior restraint and subsequent punishment cases are of direct relevance. The assumption inherent in *Ne-*

30. Gannett v. De Pasquale, 43 N.Y.2d at 380.
31. *See,* e.g. United States ex. rel. Smallwood v. LaValle, 377 F.Supp. 1148 (E.D.N.Y. 1974), *affirmed,* 408 F.2d 837, *cert. denied,* 421 U.S. 920; People v. Hagan, 24 N.Y.2d 395, 300 N.Y.S.2d 835, 248 N.E.2d 588 (1969), *cert. denied,* 396 U.S. 886.

braska Press is that there are jurors who can decide cases fairly no matter how pervasive and outrageous pre-trial publicity is. After all, what could be more prejudicial than the disclosure in a town of 750 people that one neighbor has confessed that he murdered five other neighbors because he was caught in a sexual act with yet another neighbor? The effect of the holdings in *Bridges* and *Landmark* is that publications before or during a trial cannot be punished except under the most egregious circumstances—so egregious, in fact, that they probably do not exist. Thus, taken together, *Nebraska Press, Bridges,* and *Landmark* create an almost absolute right to publish during trials, reaching this result not only because of the general policies surrounding the First Amendment, but also because extrajudicial publications will be discounted by an objective juror and their effects can generally be lessened through such other means as sequestration and change of venue.

It seems to me that these considerations are fully applicable to the situation which will be before the Supreme Court in *Gannett*. The "would-threaten-the-trial" test applied by the Court of Appeals is perhaps intended to connote a standard of clear and present danger to the fair administration of justice. Yet how can a confession in a pre-trial hearing in upstate New York be any different than such a confession in Nebraska? If the assumption of the *Nebraska Press* case is that a defendant can have a fair trial notwithstanding unrestrained press reports—and therefore a prior restraint is inappropriate—how is it permissible to seal off a courtroom at the mere threat of prejudicial publicity? Publication of the confession "threatened" a fair trial in *Nebraska Press* no less than in *Gannett*. If that threat was not sufficient for the imposition of restrictive measures in *Nebraska Press*, it should be equally insufficient in *Gannett*. To hold otherwise would be to allow trial courts to avoid the clear holding of *Nebraska Press* through the simple device of issuing closure orders rather than gag orders.[32]

Only a fraction of the criminal cases brought ever go to trial. The real courtroom for most criminal trials in the United States is the pre-trial hearing, where proceedings of vital public concern often take place. For instance, in order to meet Fourth Amendment standing requirements, a defendant may establish in great detail the chain of custody of a particular piece of evidence, say a suitcase of heroin, as part of his motion to suppress the evidence. If the motion is denied, the defendant may be on the stand the next day denying any knowledge of the suitcase. Clearly the public must be privy to both proceedings if it is to know how accurately the jury system is functioning. To take another common situa-

---

32. "The guidelines expressed by the majority signal the common, if not certain, locking of the courtroom door virtually whenever requested in pretrial hearings." Gannett v. De Pasquale, 43 N.Y.2d at 386 (Cooke, J., dissenting).

tion, a successful suppression motion will probably mean that an account of the improper methods the police used to extract a certain confession will be brought out only at the pre-trial hearing, and nowhere else. Again, this is information which the public needs to have if its public officers are to be accountable. Without multiplying examples, we need only remember the shocking trials of Ginzburg and Shcharansky behind closed doors in Russia in the summer of 1978 to realize that criminal trials in this country must remain open.

Simply put, without open trials we will never be able to know how justice is being administered. For this reason, the justifications advanced for closing the courts should be held to be as ineffectual in this chapter of fair trial-free press history as the justifications advanced for the imposition of parallel restraints have been held to be in previous chapters of this lengthy struggle.

HENRY R. KAUFMAN

Introduction: The *Snepp* Case—Government Censorship Through The "Back Door"

Mr. Kaufman is Vice President-General Counsel of the Association of American Publishers. He was the principal author of the Association's *amicus curiae* brief, being reprinted in full herewith. The opinions stated in this introduction are Mr. Kaufman's and not necessarily those of the AAP or of PEN American Center or the Radio Television News Directors Association, co-signatories of the AAP brief.

The law, it often seems, has a front door and a back door. That is, it provides alternative means to accomplish the same result—one direct, and if that be foreclosed, one indirect.

For some reason, this duality develops not infrequently in the field of communications law. Copyright proprietors are familiar with the "back door to Berne," securing the broader international copyright protection of the Berne treaties through the fiction of "simultaneous" publication of United States works in Canada or some other Berne signatory nation even though the United States has adhered only to the narrower Universal Copyright Convention.

Other back doors of a different and more insidious kind have been cultivated by those who wish to circumvent the established limits of government power to encroach upon the freedom of the press. For example, the landmark 1976 Supreme Court decision in *Nebraska Press Association* v. *Stuart*[1] seemed to spell the death knell for "gag orders" of the kind which had increasingly been issued by courts to bar press coverage of controversial cases. *Nebraska Press Association* imposed a stringent—some said impossible—burden of justification for such "prior restraints" against the press. However, since the *Nebraska Press Association* case, a legal back door has sprung open, introducing new forms of prior restraint. Now, instead of orders against the media, gag orders are directed at parties and lawyers. Combined with a rash of courtroom closings and the frequent sealing of records, these modified "gag" procedures threaten to clamp a lid of secrecy over judicial proceedings perhaps tighter than existed before the *Nebraska Press Association* case was decided.[2]

Last year, in *Stanford Daily* v. *Zurcher*,[3] the Supreme Court kicked open yet another legal backdoor when it ruled that officials could seize, by means of warrants to search pressrooms issued *without notice,* the same confidential information many state statutes and court opinions have held cannot be subpoenaed from the press *with notice* for fear of violating the journalist's privilege to protect confidential sources.

The back door with which we are here concerned arises in the context of recent controversies over the publication of alleged "national security" information. Here again, a landmark Supreme Court decision, affirming press liberties and striking down a prior restraint, has been undermined by the development of a new and indirect means to achieve the same result. In this instance, in the noted Pentagon Papers case—*New York Times Co.* v. *United States*[4]—a clear majority of the high Court appeared to approve strict limits upon the government's power to restrain publication of any but the most sensitive national security information and only then if the publication threatened grave and immediate harm to the very survival of the nation.

Yet today, less than a decade later, the government has won a series

1. 427 U.S. 539 (1976).
2. A case now pending before the Supreme Court may become the landmark precedent on the issue of Courtroom closings. *Gannett Co.* v. *DePasquale,* 372 N.E. 2d 544 (New York 1977), *cert. granted* 435 U.S. 1006 (1978).
3. 436 U.S. 547 (1979).
4. 403 U.S. 713 (1971).

Introduction: The Snepp Case—Government Censorship

of court cases, the latest of which was brought by the United States against Frank Snepp, that have cut off national security information at its source and by so doing may effectively hide the operations of government from needed public scrutiny. To fully understand the significance of the *Snepp* case and the context in which the AAP *amicus* brief was written it is essential to review these developments since the Pentagon Papers case.

It was less than ten months after the Supreme Court had issued its landmark opinions in *New York Times Co.* v. *United States* when, on April 18, 1972, government lawyers appeared in the chambers of Judge Albert Bryan, Jr. in Alexandria, Virginia to begin the search for a back door around the rule in the Pentagon Papers case. In an *ex parte* application the United States sought what had so recently been denied to them against *The New York Times* and the *Washington Post*—an injunction against Victor Marchetti seeking to prevent publication of a book he was planning to write about the CIA.[5]

Significantly, the government did allege in *Marchetti,* as the Pentagon Papers case seemed minimally to require, that publication of the planned book "would result in grave and irreparable injury to the interests of the United States." In the Pentagon Papers case, attempted proof of this kind of grave injury was a focus of the intensely concentrated, albeit hurried, proceedings in the courts. Although the courts were presented with the massive collection of secret materials contained in the volumes of the Defense Department study of the Vietnam conflict that came to be known as the Pentagon Papers, they were unable to find in the proposed publication of these volumes the kind of immediate injury to the nation that, they held, the First Amendment prior restraint standard required. Actually, the trial judge found no such threat in the Pentagon Papers; only the threat of official "embarrassment." And while a majority of the Supreme Court Justices did credit the Government's contention that some harm to United States' national security interests was a possibility, a majority was unable to conclude that this harm rose to the level of irreparable danger that, in their view, the Constitution requires before a breach in the First Amendment armor could be justified.

Evidentiary developments in the *Marchetti* case stand in stark contrast to the punctillious judicial deference to constitutional constraints shown in *New York Times Co.* v. *United States*. In the *Marchetti* case the courts stayed publication by Marchetti, first temporarily and then permanently, based upon the mere outline of a book and a brief magazine article which, the government was apparently able to prove,

---

5. Much of the historical background that follows is traced in V. Marchetti and J. Marks, *The CIA and The Cult of Intelligence* (Knopf, 1974).

Censorship, Secrecy, Access, and Obscenity 15

had revealed information previously classified by CIA bureaucrats. Indeed, despite the holding of the Pentagon Papers case, the U.S. Court of Appeals for the Fourth Circuit held that this injunction could be issued without any attempt by the court to look behind CIA classifications to explore whether, in fact, publication would "result in direct, immediate and irreparable damage" to national security interests.[6]

How could the Fourth Circuit Court sanction this blatant violation of a recent Supreme Court ruling? Quite simple—another "back door" was being opened. The key to the door—Marchetti's status as a former CIA official and the fact that he had signed "secrecy agreements" as a condition of employment with the CIA. These agreements promised that Marchetti would never "divulge any classified information, intelligence or knowledge except in the performance of (his) official duties . . . unless specifically authorized in writing . . . by the (CIA)." Entirely setting aside the rigorous standards of proof and strict limitations seemingly established in the Pentagon Papers case, the Fourth Circuit held that this secrecy agreement, without more, gave the government the right to prevent publication of classified materials obtained by Marchetti during the course of his CIA employment. No need, according to the Fourth Circuit, to impose the *New York Times* burden upon the government. Indeed, so it at first held, the validity of the "classification" was itself "beyond the scope of judicial review." So long as information to be revealed bore a classification stamp, and had not been previously made public, the Fourth Circuit Court held, the government's request to enjoin publication would be honored.

This was hardly a standard calculated to advance the public's "right to know" about the operations of its government, since massive abuse of the classification process is widely conceded. Indeed, the *Marchetti* rule invited continued over-classification as a judicially unreviewable means of controlling the disclosure of information government bureaucrats wished to hide from public scrutiny, regardless of the information's true relationship to significant "national security" interests. The Fourth Circuit later drew back somewhat from this extreme position, holding in *Knopf* v. *Colby*,[7] a second, related case brought by Marchetti and his publisher to challenge the CIA's censorship of the actual book manuscript, that the classification of such information *is* judicially reviewable. However, the kind of judicial review permitted in *Knopf* was exceedingly narrow, with government classification subject to a broad presumption of "regularity" and with the burden of proof of improper classification placed squarely upon the proponent of publication.

6. *United States* v. *Marchetti,* 466 F.2d 1309 (4th Cir. 1972), *cert. denied,* 409 U.S. 1063 (1972).
7. *Alfred A. Knopf* v. *Colby,* 509 F.2d 1362 (4th Cir.), *cert. denied,* 421 U.S. 992 (1975).

Introduction: The Snepp Case—Government Censorship

Despite the grave impairment of First Amendment freedoms implicit in the two *Marchetti* rulings, the Supreme Court twice refused to accept appeals from the Fourth Circuit's decisions. In *Marchetti* I Justices Douglas, Brennan and Stewart indicated that they would have granted *certioriari*. In *Marchetti* II only Justice Douglas recorded his dissent to the Court's refusal to hear the case. Just why the Supreme Court refused to hear the Marchetti appeals is not known. Certainly the case raised important constitutional issues. Undeniably, the injunction issued against Marchetti was unprecedented and appeared to violate the rule established in the Pentagon Papers case. Perhaps the Justices voting to deny "certiorari" (it takes the votes of four Justices to place this kind of appeal on the Supreme Court's docket) were convinced that Marchetti's status as a former CIA employee made a difference—either legally, as the Fourth Circuit had held, or as a matter "cosmetics" with Marchetti's arguably self-serving violation of a promise of confidentiality seen as an unattractive case in which to expend judicial prestige in opposing actions of the Executive Branch.

In any event, the Supreme Court's refusal to hear the case left the Fourth Circuit's prior restraint in effect as the law of the case. Thus, when Marchetti finally completed his manuscript he was required to submit it, under pain of judicial contempt, for prior review and censorship by the CIA. And indeed, when the Marchetti book, *The CIA and The Cult of Intelligence,* was ultimately published it appeared—for the first time in the nation's history—with 168 government-imposed deletions indicated by blank spaces in the Knopf edition.

It was with the *Marchetti* precedent established that the Government could seek to validate yet another, and still more expansive, theory of national security censorship in order to stem what some officials apparently viewed, in the post-Watergate era, as a disturbing increase in leaks and whistleblowing by present or former government employees. Frank Snepp provided one opportunity when, in November of 1977, he beat the intelligence bureaucracy at its own game. With Random House (parent of Marchetti's publisher Alfred A. Knopf) as his publisher, Snepp secretly and dramatically brought out an uncensored book on his CIA activities in Vietnam without prior submission to the CIA. A new and expanded censorship theory was needed because, by the government's own admission, the content of Snepp's book, *Decent Interval,* posed no threat to national security interests. Indeed, far from revealing information endangering the nation's security if not survival, as was alleged in the Pentagon Papers case, and far from revealing merely "classified" information, as was alleged and apparently proven in the *Marchetti* case, *Decent Interval* revealed no classified information whatsoever. Snepp's only discernible transgression, as later proceedings would clearly establish, was his decision not to submit to the administrative procedures established by the CIA ostensibly to censor the classified information that the *Marchetti* case held it had the right to suppress. No matter that such prior review of the Snepp book would have been a meaningless formality since the book contained nothing that could have been censored by the CIA under the Marchetti guidelines. Instead, the government insisted in *Snepp,* that a mere violation of the CIA's system of censorship, in actuality harmless vis-à-vis national security information, could itself justify sanctions against the freedom to write and publish information otherwise protected by the First Amendment. How long a road, indeed, had been travelled since those memorable days of crisis, in the summer of 1971, when the government sought to justify suppression of the Pentagon Papers on a theory of imminent risk to the nation's very survival!

With the Snepp book already published, a prior injuction against distribution was obviously a moot issue. So the government's case against Snepp sought a different—and unique—remedy. The United States claimed that Snepp's actions represented a violation of his secrecy agreement—a civil breach of "contract" and "fiduciary duty" that justified the imposition of civil sanctions. Money damages were claimed, to be measured by Snepp's profits from his book. An injunction against future violations was also sought. United States District Judge Oren Lewis agreed, and in August, 1978 he entered judgment in favor of the United States, ordering Snepp to pay over all royalties and advances earned on his book and enjoining Snepp, for a lifetime, from speaking and/or writing about anything he learned while employed by the CIA without prior review and censorship by the CIA. It was in support of the appeal from that ruling that the accompanying friend-of-the-court brief was prepared by the AAP and two cooperating organizations and filed with the United States Court of Appeals for the Fourth Circuit.

The dangerous impact that the *Snepp* ruling would have—if ultimately upheld—upon a range of persons, groups and constitutional interests is explored at length in the AAP brief. In particular, the direct economic effect of the ruling upon government employees is readily apparent. Hardly less apparent is the impact upon book publishing because of its usual reliance upon independent authors—often primary sources of information such as knowledgeable current and former government employees—as the sources for publishable manuscripts. Authors share in any profits derived from book publication and most would be thoroughly chilled in their book writing activities if their entire remuneration could be seized by the Government. In contrast, media such as newspapers and broadcast news generally employ independent professional journalists who secure information from primary sources such as government

Introduction: The Snepp Case—Government Censorship

"leakers" and "whistleblowers," and then prepare news stories that are published or broadcast to the public. Payment to sources is rare and is usually considered improper.

It is this distinction between book publishing and the journalistic media that has led some members of the fourth estate to view the *Marchetti* and *Snepp* cases as limited in their application. It is argued that the journalistic media will continue to have access to information and, because the independent publisher will have no contractual obligation to the government agency, no effective control can be asserted against the publisher. With regard to the impending civil remedies against Snepp, a similar argument is made. That is, since the government has no economic leverage against the independent journalist and publisher, the imposition of damages against Snepp is irrelevant to the operations of the news press.

This kind of reasoning has in turn led a substantial segment of the news media to underestimate the potential impact of these recent, troubling rulings. Surely, a similar direct attack upon the news media would have yielded a far more vociferous response in the editorial pages of the nation's press. This obvious political fact is not lost on the federal government. Certainly it has scored a significant tactical victory by concentrating security efforts against isolated members of the intelligence community rather than against the media establishment.

But those who minimize the impact of these developments have overlooked the very real possibility that, in addition to their intrinsic harm to First Amendment doctrine, the *Marchetti* and *Snepp* rulings could eventually be turned against all press media. First, as argued in the AAP brief, it is not beyond imagining that this doctrine of contractual or fiduciary confidentiality, if rigorously enforced and extended to its logical limits, could impose a stifling network of secrecy obligations upon the agents of government. Such an expansion of government secrecy would surely represent a most significant setback for "freedom of information" policy. It is difficult to believe that the nation's press would sit silently by as the fundamental underpinnings of open government are systematically attacked in this manner.

Perhaps equally dangerous is the potential application of the *Marchetti-Snepp* rules to persons and entitites not directly in "privity"—i.e. not contractually-bound—to the government. Indeed, this is the grave and obvious danger that much of the press has either misunderstood or else simply wished to ignore. For if Marchetti and Snepp can be held to have breached their secrecy contracts in seeking to publish government data, then are not their publishers—at least to the extent they are aware of the existence of such contractual limitations, which are well known—aiders, abettors, or inducers of the breach? And, if so, would it not be logical to hold publishers liable to the same extent as their sources of information?

Even putting aside the contract theory, the broad judicial restraining orders that have been issued against Marchetti and Snepp would also seem to form the basis for a post-injunction action against any person or firm that publishes information received from Marchetti or Snepp—again, at least if the publisher were aware of the restraining order and published the information without prior review and censorship by the government agency.

Neither of these theories are nearly as speculative as they might sound. It is known, for example, that in connection with the *Snepp* case the United States gave serious consideration to adding Snepp's publisher, Random House, as a co-party-defendant in the action. Perhaps more significantly, it is reported that the Government even considered joining CBS as a party for its role in breaking the story of the Snepp book on its "60 Minutes" telecast. By the same reasoning, *The New York Times* and Seymour Hersch, who broke the Snepp story in print, could also have been made parties-defendant in the case. The theory for adding these defendants would presumably have been that Random House or CBS or *The Times* either induced, or aided and abetted, Snepp in actions violative of his secrecy "contract."

Of course, for sound tactical reasons the government chose not to procede against these powerful representatives of the Fourth Estate. However, it is a shaky freedom, indeed, that rests exclusively upon the forebearance of government, particularly a government bent upon shielding many of its operations from public scrutiny. Predictably—perhaps inevitably—some publisher will sooner or later find itself at the wrong end of a government action premised upon the same theory that supports the *Marchetti* and *Snepp* rulings. The first case may not be brought against *The Times*, or CBS or even Random House. But the message will then be clear and at that point it may be too late easily to reverse the pernicious legal doctrine that sanctions such unwarranted government censorship.

Of course, as always, there is still some hope. The *Snepp* case, at this writing, is still pending on appeal. But even if the *Snepp* decision were reversed, the rule of the *Marchetti* case might still be left intact since *Snepp*—which implicates no classified information—could be distinguished from *Marchetti* by a court that wished to limit *Marchetti* to its own factual setting. If *Snepp* is lost in the Fourth Circuit there is still the possibility of an appeal to the Supreme Court, although there is little reason to believe that the Court, having lost Justice Douglas (one of the three dissenters on the *Marchetti* petition for *certiorari*) and having revealed an increasingly anti-press attitude in the past two or three years, would reach out to decide such a controversial matter.

Perhaps a more realistic hope is held out by another closely related case—*McGehee* v. *Turner*[8]—pending in the more liberal District of Columbia Circuit that challenges enforcement of CIA's secrecy agreement against another ex-agent who wishes to publish a book. *McGehee* raises issues almost identical to those presented in the *Snepp* case. A ruling against the government in the District of Columbia Circuit could create a conflict of law among the Circuits that might form the basis of a renewed application to the Supreme Court to consider these consquential issues.

In the interim, let the AAP brief in *Snepp* speak for itself—and let the publishing community beware.

ADDENDUM: THE FOURTH CIRCUIT DECISION IN THE SNEPP CASE

On March 20, 1979, after this introduction had been prepared but before it went to press, The United States Court of Appeals for the Fourth Circuit decided the *Snepp* case. The Fourth Circuit panel (Judges Winter, Phillips and Hoffman) unanimously affirmed District Judge Lewis' decision enforcing Snepp's secrecy "agreements" and permanently enjoining Snepp from speaking or writing about the CIA without prior CIA review and possible censorship. However, by a two to one vote, the panel reversed Judge Lewis' award of damages equal to Snepp's entire earnings from his book. The Fourth Circuit's decision represents a significant additional setback for the AAP position against the enforcement of government secrecy agreements in the absence of a direct and immediate threat to the nation's security. The Court rejected AAP's first amendment arguments and refused to reconsider the *Marchetti* cases. The Court not only reaffirmed *Marchetti,* but extended *Marchetti* in at least two respects. It made clear for the first time that *Marchetti* could be used to require pre-submission of *all* CIA-related material, whether or not classified. Second, it upheld the validity of a civil breach of contract remedy for violation of a CIA-type secrecy agreement. While the majority ruled that the seizure of all book proceeds was inappropriate absent disclosure of classified information, it did uphold the government's right to compensatory and possibly punitive damages based upon the mere failure to submit to the prior review process. Moreover, it confirmed that disclosure of classified information would justify the seizure of all proceeds from publication.

8. Civil Action No. 78-2407, filed on December 22, 1978.

UNITED STATES COURT OF APPEALS
FOR THE FOURTH CIRCUIT

UNITED STATES OF AMERICA,
    Plaintiff-Appellee,

v.   No.: 78-1651

FRANK W. SNEPP, III,
    Defendant-Appellant.

BRIEF OF ASSOCIATION OF AMERICAN PUBLISHERS, INC., P.E.N. AMERICAN CENTER AND RADIO TELEVISION NEWS DIRECTORS ASSOCIATION, AS *AMICI CURIAE,* IN SUPPORT OF DEFENDANT-APPELLANT

Preliminary Statement

This brief is submitted on behalf of the Association of American Publishers, Inc., P.E.N. American Center and the Radio Television News Directors Association, as *amici curiae,* urging reversal of the judgment below.[1]

In *United States* v. *Marchetti* this Court issued an unprecedented injunction against publication of *The CIA and The Cult of Intelligence,* by Victor Marchetti, pending pre-publication review of the book manuscript and censorship by the CIA.[2] Upon review, numerous portions of the Marchetti book were found to reveal classified information whose release was said to threaten substantial harm to the national security. As a result, the Marchetti book was published with deletions coerced by government censors. Albeit grounded on such asserted risks to the national security, the *Marchetti* decision nonetheless unquestionably

---

1. Consents from both parties to the filing of this brief are being submitted herewith.
2. 466 F.2d 1309 (4th Cir.), *cert. denied,* 409 U.S. 1063 (1972). *See also Alfred A. Knopf, Inc.* v. *Colby,* 509 F.2d 1362 (4th Cir.), *cert. denied,* 421 U.S. 992 (1975) (enforcement of injunction).

sanctioned one of the most far reaching judicially-enforced prior restraints in our nation's history.

Now, in this civil action by the United States against former CIA agent Frank Snepp, the government seeks significantly to expand the already unprecedented prior restraint power won in *Marchetti* and to add a new weapon to its arsenal—confiscatory civil damage penalties subsequent to publication.

Where in *Marchetti* the injuction against publication was limited to *classified* information, in this case a broad prior restraint has been entered applicable to publication of *unclassified* information as well.

Where in *Marchetti* this Court's ruling was based upon proven past, and imminent future, publication of classified information presumptively implicating significant national security interests, here coercive and compensatory relief has been granted by the District Court not to prevent or punish the direct compromise of national security information—indeed the government stipulates that such information is not implicated—but solely to punish an alleged failure to honor an administrative system of pre-publication review whose sole legitimate purpose is to screen out information of a kind not published by Snepp.

Where in *Marchetti* this Court reflected a sensitivity to the grave First Amendment implications of a prior restraint against free expression, in this case the District Court systematically excluded any consideration of the First Amendment. It, therefore, ignored the very substantial burden its rulings would impose upon the constitutional rights of current and former government employees, authors, publishers and broadcasters, as well as members of the public at large, to act free of chilling prior and subsequent restraints upon their freedom to speak, to write, to publish, to broadcast and, generally, to receive information related to issues of undisputed public moment concerning the operations of their government.

Interests of the Amici

Amici, trade and professional associations representing the nation's leading book publishers and many of its leading authors, editors and broadcast news directors, have a substantial stake in the outcome of this litigation, particularly regarding the significant dilution of First Amendment rights implicit in the government's claims in this case and threatened by the ruling of the District Court below. *Amici* believe that they can be of assistance to this Court in resolving the vitally important constitutional issues here presented in the broader context of the practical and potentially devastating impact of their resolution on the free exercise of authors', publishers' and broadcasters' First Amendment rights.

The Association of American Publishers, Inc. is the major national association for publishers of general and educational books in the United States. Its more than 325 members include large commercial book publishers and smaller or non-profit publishers, university presses and scholarly associations.[3] Association members publish numerous books by current and former government officials and employees about their government activities and the activities of the agencies with which they are or were associated. The Association has previously filed *amicus curiae* briefs before this Court in the *Marchetti* cases, urging recognition of First Amendment considerations.

P.E.N. American Center, the United States chapter of International P.E.N.,[4] is a non-profit association of 1,500 leading American poets, playwrights, essayists, editors, novelists and translators. The charter of International P.E.N. affirms that P.E.N. stands for the principle of unhampered transmission of thought within each nation and between all nations, and members pledge themselves to oppose any form of suppression of freedom of expression in the country and community to which they belong.

The Radio Television News Directors Association includes approximately 1,500 members who are active in the supervision, gathering, reporting and editing of news and other information of public affairs broadcast throughout the nation.

Summary of Argument

Hamlet was played in the Court below without the Prince of Denmark.

Thus, a First Amendment case starkly presenting troubling conflicts between the constitutional guarantee of freedom of expression and the government's asserted need for secrecy was tried by the Court below without reference to the First Amendment as if it were a simple contract case governed by the Uniform Commercial Code. The result of this one-sided championship of government secrecy, irrespective of First Amendment rights, was a grievously truncated and skewed District Court proceeding, and an outcome at odds with the First Amendment.

The District Court initially failed to recognize and be bound by established and controlling First Amendment principles. Prior restraints against speech are generally forbidden by the First Amendment. Only a

---

3. Random House, Mr. Snepp's publisher, is a member of the Association.
4. International P.E.N. has voted to support and endorse the actions of P.E.N. American Center as a friend of the Court in this case.

grave and imminent threat to the very survival of the nation could possibly justify the result reached by the District Court here. Yet, the government's concessions in this case establish that no such threat is presented here. (Point I)

Having improperly excluded First Amendment principles from consideration, the District Court necessarily failed to recognize the potential implications of its ruling upon the free speech rights of current and former government employees, of publishers, authors and broadcasters, and of the public in general. The First Amendment mandates the broadest possible non-interference with the rights of all citizens—even former government employees—to discuss and debate the workings of government. (Point II)

For similar reasons, the District Court misconstrued this Court's ruling in *Marchetti*. *Marchetti* reflects a recognition that the First Amendment does indeed strictly limit the extent to which the government may, by contract or otherwise, impose secrecy upon its current or former employees or those acting in concert with them. Indeed, in *Marchetti*, this Court squarely held that the government could not censor a book of the kind Frank Snepp has published here. Thus, *Marchetti* itself requires reversal of the judgment below. Were this not so, then in *amici's* view, the case of Frank Snepp demonstrates that *Marchetti* was wrongly decided and that it should now be reconsidered and, upon reconsideration, overruled. (Point III)

ARGUMENT

I.

GENERALLY-ESTABLISHED FIRST AMENDMENT PRINCIPLES PRECLUDE THE RELIEF SOUGHT BY THE GOVERNMENT AND AWARDED BY THE DISTRICT COURT IN THIS CASE

The District Court ruled below that Frank Snepp, a former official of the CIA who had signed "secrecy" agreements as a condition of his employment, had breached those agreements by publishing a book, *Decent Interval*, containing information Snepp obtained while with the government, without first having submitted the manuscript to the Agency for pre-publication review and possible censorship. This ruling was made despite the government's concession that Snepp revealed no classified information and that, therefore, the process of pre-publication review could not in this case have resulted in the modification or censorship of any aspect of the Snepp book.

The lower court determined that the appropriate penalties for "one who breaches his trust and secrecy agreement" with the CIA in such a fashion were the forfeiture of all monies derived from sale of the uncensored book and adherence to a broad injunction forbidding "any further violation of the secrecy agreement." As recently construed by the District Court, its injunction requires Snepp, for the rest of his life, to submit to the CIA for pre-publication review any manuscript containing information obtained by him during the course of his employment for the Agency, whether or not related to classified or confidential material or to the security interests of the nation.[5] In this recent ruling, the District Judge held that even fiction and personal opinion come within the scope of the all-encompassing restraining order.

Indisputably, such procedures and penalties constitute a prior restraint on First Amendment expression and have a broadly "chilling" impact on the exercise of speech and press freedoms. Yet, despite such effects and such impact, the lower court staunchly refused to entertain defenses, discovery, offers of proof and legal arguments bearing upon the serious First Amendment issues at stake in this case.

Treating the case as it would any breach of contract suit, the District Court utterly failed to consider the impact of established and controlling First Amendment principles on its decision. And ignoring the clear mandate of these constitutional dictates, the Court failed to require the government to meet its heavy burden in overcoming the presumption against the validity of measures which have such devastating impact on expression protected under the First Amendment.

At least since *Near v. Minnesota*, 283 U.S. 697, 716 (1931), where it was noted that "liberty of the press" has historically included "immunity from previous restraints or censorship," the Supreme Court has made clear the "heavy presumption against [the] constitutional validity" of "prior restraints of expression," *Bantam Books, Inc. v. Sullivan*, 372 U.S. 58, 70 (1963), and the "heavy burden" upon the government "of showing justification for the imposition of such a restraint." *Organization for a Better Austin v. Keefe*, 402 U.S. 415, 419 (1971). As was most recently noted by the Court:

> "The thread running through all these cases is that prior restraints on speech and publication are the most serious and least tolerable infringement on First

---

5. The District Court's injunctive relief is broadly framed to cover not only Snepp but also "those persons in active concert or participation with him," suggesting the possibility that a publisher or broadcaster who might choose to disseminate any of Snepp's works or information prior to their submission to the Agency for pre-review and censorship could arguably be subjected to judicial contempt sanctions.

Amendment rights." *Nebraska Press Ass'n v. Stuart,* 427 U.S. 539, 559 (1976).

It is thus clear from the cases that, to uphold any system of prior restraint, a court must conclude that the government has met its heavy burden and has overcome the presumed invalidity of the requested prior restraint. In discharging its burden, moreover, the government must establish that the restraint falls "within one of the narrowly defined exceptions to the prohibition against prior restraints." *Southeastern Promotions, Ltd. v. Conrad,* 420 U.S. 546, 559 (1975).

This showing has rarely been made. Even in the area of potentially grave threats to the national security of the kind which assertedly lie behind efforts of agencies like the CIA to shield highly classified intelligence information from unauthorized disclosure, the Supreme Court has rejected attempts to restrain publication despite an awareness that publication might well do substantial damage to public interests.

Thus, in *New York Times Co. v. United States,* 403 U.S. 713 (1971) (the Pentagon Papers Case), the leading and controlling case in this area, a majority of the Justices reaching the merits made clear that the scope of the exceptions to the bar on prior restraints is to be confined to the truly extraordinary situation when disclosure ". . . will *surely result in direct, immediate, and irreparable damage* to our Nation or its people," *id.* at 730 (Stewart, J., joined by White, J., concurring) (emphasis added), or when there is "governmental allegation *and proof* that publication must inevitably, *directly and immediately* cause the occurrence of an event kindred to imperiling the safety of a transport already at sea . . . . [But] [i]n no event may mere conclusions be sufficient." *Id.* at 726-727 (Brennan, J., concurring) (emphasis added).[6]

In short, it has been noted that, "even within the sole possible exception to the prohibition against prior restraints on publication of constitutionally protected materials [*i.e.,* relating to the protection of the national security], the obstacles to issuance of such an injunction are formidable." *Nebraska Press Ass'n v. Stuart, supra,* 427 U.S. at 593-94 (Brennan, J., concurring).

In the instant case, the government utterly failed to make the required showing in justification of the imposition of prior restraints and, indeed, the District Court failed to demand that such a showing be made. The injunctive relief afforded by the District Court, in the form of a restraint on future publication by Snepp pending prior review and possible censorship, together with the punitive confiscation of monies received

---

6. *See also id.* at 730-731 (White, J., joined by Stewart, J., concurring) (concededly extraordinary protection against prior restraints enjoyed by the press under our constitutional system is not overcome even by a showing that revelation of these documents will do substantial damage to public interests).

by him from his already published book, clearly contravene the established First Amendment doctrine summarized above. The sanctions ordered constitute the very kinds of "prior restraints" and coercive penalties to secure compliance with a system of prior restraints which have long been subjected to the closest judicial scrutiny and viewed with the greatest disfavor.[7] Because the District Court failed completely to weigh the fundamental First Amendment interests at stake in this litigation, and because a weighing of those interests conclusively compels the conclusion that the judgment below runs afoul of the First Amendment, *amici* respectfully submit that that judgment must be reversed or, at the very least, remanded for consideration with due deference to established constitutional principles.

II.

THE DISTRICT COURT SHOULD HAVE CONSIDERED THE ADVERSE IMPACT OF ITS RULING ON RECOGNIZED FIRST AMENDMENT RIGHTS AND INTERESTS

In deciding a case with a potential bearing on First Amendment rights, a court should consider the impact of its decision not only on the rights of the parties, but also on the rights of those who could be directly affected or indirectly chilled by the court's ruling.[8] Unfortunately, the District Court not only failed to give meaningful consideration to Frank Snepp's constitutional claims, but also apparently gave no thought to the impact of its decision on other First Amendment interests not represented before it.

---

7. Even were the civil penalties imposed on Snepp subsequent to publication of *Decent Interval* viewed as something short of effective "prior restraints" on speech—and *amici* do not view them as such—the courts have made clear that punitive measures of the type here invoked are also disfavored, in recognition of the potential of such a "system of liability" to "inhibit the vigorous exercise of First Amendment freedoms," and to "punish expressions of unpopular views." *Gertz* v. *Robert Welch, Inc.*, 418 U.S. 323, 349, 350 (1974). *See also Curtis Publishing Co.* v. *Butts*, 388 U.S. 130, 160 (1967); *Rosenbloom* v. *Metromedia, Inc.*, 403 U.S. 29, 83, 84 (1971) (Marshall, J. dissenting) (unbridled discretion to award damages in a First Amendment case allows the trier of fact "to penalize heavily the unorthodox and the unpopular" and "presents obvious and basic threats to society's interest in freedom of the press"). The "chilling" impact on Snepp's and others' speech arising out of the confiscatory penalties imposed by the District Court may be seen to be identical to that brought about by the District Court's injunctive measures, and must equally be condemned under the First Amendment.
8. *See generally* Note, *The First Amendment Overbreadth Doctrine*, 83 Harv. L. Rev. 844 (1970).

In the sections below, *amici* briefly explore some of the constitutionally-relevant factors which the District Court refused to consider, namely, the heavy burdens that Court's ruling, if left to stand, will surely impose on the rights of other government employees not only at the federal but at the state and local levels as well (IIA); on the rights of the public at large (IIB); and on the rights of the press in general and on *amici's* members in particular (IIC). Finally, the District Court's failure, at the very least, to minimize the impact of its ruling on such rights by searching for "less drastic means" to enforce the governmental interests it upheld, is also explored (IID).

A. The Ruling Below Unduly Encumbers the Constitutional Rights of Government Employees.

In contrast to the special circumstances presented in the *Marchetti* case, there is nothing in this case, at least as it was decided by the District Court, to prevent its application to justify similar prior restraints upon a multitude of government employees, however far removed from classified national security information.[9]

Thus, as previously noted, where the rule in *Marchetti* was narrowly limited in its applicability to individuals in possession of *classified* information who had revealed or threatened to reveal such classified information, the ruling of the Court below in this case is not so delimited. Here, the District Court not only enforced the CIA "secrecy" agreements with respect to *unclassified* information, but the Court also found a potentially far broader implied "fiduciary duty" of "trust" arising out of the general need for confidentiality related "to the public's interest in the effective functioning of government." (Memorandum Opinion, pp. 10-11)

Amici fear that it is but a short step, indeed, from the breach of "fiduciary duty" found in this case by the District Court based on an otherwise harmless (in the national security sense) asserted violation of an administrative system of prior review, to the establishment of an all-encompassing network of written contracts and implied fiduciary obligations effectively clamping a lid on information of all sorts at all

---

9. The District Judge purported, in part, to rest his ruling against Frank Snepp upon the notion that government employment is "a privilege—not a right." (Memorandum Opinion, page 5) But surely this assertion of government employment as a "privilege," from which a waiver of constitutional rights may be implied, has long ago been put to rest by the Supreme Court. *See generally* Van Alstyne, *The Demise of the Right-Privilege Distinction in Constitutional Law*, 81 Harv. L. Rev. 1440 (1968). The question here, ultimately, is whether it is sound—either as a matter of constitutional law or public policy—to attempt to extract as a condition of government employment a waiver of First Amendment rights. For the reasons stated throughout this brief, *amici* strongly believe such a policy to be unwise as well as in violation of the First Amendment.

levels of government.[10] For, certainly, at all levels of government a colorable claim can be laid for the need to maintain the confidentiality of operations and information. Indeed, *amici* do not dispute the legitimacy of administrative efforts to assure a modicum of confidentiality regarding facets of governmental deliberations and activities.

But *amici* do question whether coercive or confiscatory judicial restraints upon free expression, publication or broadcast of unclassified information—and, therefore, potentially of *all* government information—are either necessary or appropriate, as a matter of constitutional law or sound public policy, to secure this degree of confidentiality. Doubtless at times "breaches" of confidentiality through the dissemination of unclassified information may embarrass or even in a sense hinder the ongoing operations of government. But, in *amici's* view, such revelations—at least absent proof of grave and imminent harm to a truly vital national interest—are a part of the "risks" of "open and robust" public debate that our democracy requires and that the First Amendment was designed to guarantee.

As between the potential risks of the overexposure, and the inherent dangers in underexposure, of the important operations of government, it is *amici's* firm belief that the First Amendment decidedly favors the

---

10. *Amici* understand that many federal agencies already require employees to sign "secrecy" agreements of one kind or another and that such agreements are not unique to intelligence and defense agencies. Thus, agreements requiring pre-publication review similar to the ones signed by Frank Snepp at the CIA are required by the FBI, the Defense Intelligence Agency and possibly the National Security Agency/Central Security Service (NSA's agreements are themselves classified and not generally accessible). Many other agencies require secrecy agreements with regard to classified information that expressly carry over into the post-employment period. These include the Department of State, AID, the International Communications Agency (formerly the USIA), the Bureau of Intelligence and Research, the Department of Treasury, the Department of Energy and various branches or components of the Department of Defense. Still other agencies utilize varying types of "Security Acknowledgements," "Security Agreements," "Security Briefing Statements," "Security Termination Statements," "Nondisclosure Agreements" or similar forms of oaths, affirmations or agreements acknowledging obligations of secrecy or confidentiality with regard to classified information. Some of these include the Nuclear Regulatory Commission, the Department of Justice, Energy Research and Development Administration, and the Defense Intelligence Service. Finally, most other federal agencies that do not require such formalities do maintain policies—some more stringent than others—affecting private publication by government employees of information acquired while working for the government. In sum, the foundations for an all-encompassing network of enforceable prior restraints is already in place within the federal bureaucracy should such agreements, oaths, etc., carry with them—as found by the District Court—express or implied lifelong obligations of silence and/or pre-screening by the government.

former and provides an enforceable barrier against those who would push the desire for secrecy too far. Indeed, our national experience over the past several years clearly suggests—if the mandate of the First Amendment has not already decreed—that it is open and not closed government that is, ultimately, most likely to assure the national security.[11]

Needless to say, in stark contrast to the First Amendment's preference for a free flow of information, the District Court, in its excessive solicitude for an administrative procedure protective of clandestine governance violation of which it found to represent a grave "breach of trust", revealed a marked preference for silence about the workings of government, with its necessary resulting lid on the exposure of error, mismanagement and, possibly, corruption. *Amici* question whether the District Court's perception of the "duties" implicit in the government employment relationship—a silent loyalty to the bureaucracy—is either a wise one or one which comports with the First Amendment.[12]

---

11. "The choice between the dangers of suppressing information and the dangers arising from its free flow was seen as precisely the choice 'that the First Amendment makes for us.' [citing *Virginia State Bd. of Pharmacy* v. *Virginia Citizens Consumer Council*, 425 U.S. 748 (1976)]. See also *Linmark Associates, Inc.* v. *Willingboro*, 431 U.S. 85, 97 (1977)." *Bates* v. *Arizona*, 433 U.S. 350, 365 (1977).

12. It is noteworthy that within recent days Congress has passed, and the President has signed, a new law applicable to government employees which includes provisions specifically designed to protect the so-called government "whistleblower" from harassment and reprisals. Section 208, Title II, Civil Service Reform Act of 1978, P.L. 95-454 (95th Cong., 2d Sess.) (signed by President Carter on October 13, 1978). The testimony of its Senate sponsor, Patrick Leahy, stands in marked contrast to the District Court's views:

> "At the core of the whistleblower issue is ... the Federal Government's responsibility to the people. The disclosure of waste and abuse by government officials should be seen as a sincere commitment to make this government more responsive to people's needs and more worthy of their trust. Taken in this light, these disclosures can be used to strengthen and improve the government, not to weaken or disrupt it.
>
> * * *
>
> The responsibility of a Federal employee to work toward the elimination of governmental malfeasance, misfeasance, abuse, and inefficiency should not be a discretionary one. However, an employee who discharges his duty to expose abuse cannot be subjected to the harassment and reprisals which have become standard operating procedure."

Testimony of Sen. Patrick Leahy (D-Vt.) concerning S. 2640 (Civil Service Reform Act of 1978) before the Senate Committee on Governmental Affairs, April 19, 1978. While the provisions of the new law would not be directly applicable to the CIA, which is exempted from its coverage, they are highly pertinent to the District Court's theory of "fiduciary duty" to the extent it applies—as *amici* read it to apply—to potential "whistleblowers" in many, if not all, agencies of government.

B. **The Ruling Below Erroneously Neglects the Public's Need and Constitutional Right to Receive an Uncensored Flow of Available Information About the Workings of Government.**

The Supreme Court has consistently recognized that the protection the First Amendment affords "is to the communication, to its source *and to its recipients both.*" *Virginia State Bd. of Pharmacy* v. *Virginia Citizens Consumer Council,* 425 U.S. 748, 756 (1976) (emphasis added). In other words, the public possesses a right to receive information that is entitled to a protection similar to that which the First Amendment guarantees to the freedom of speech. *See, e.g., Kleindienst* v. *Mandel,* 408 U.S. 753, 762-63 (1972); *Red Lion Broadcasting Co.* v. *FCC,* 395 U.S. 367, 390 (1969); *Stanley* v. *Georgia* 394 U.S. 557, 564 (1969); *Griswold* v. *Connecticut,* 381 U.S. 479, 482 (1965); *Lamont* v. *Postmaster General,* 381 U.S. 301 (1965); *Marsh* v. *Alabama,* 326 U.S. 501, 505 (1946); *Thomas* v. *Collins,* 323 U.S. 516, 534 (1945); *Martin* v. *Struthers,* 319 U.S. 141, 143 (1943).

The District Court was wholly insensitive to the impact of its ruling on the rights of the public to receive information, particularly to receive uncensored information, publication of which would present no legally-cognizable risk to a legitimate governmental interest. *Amici* urge, without further lengthy discussion, that the District Court's failure to weight this important, indeed fundamental, interest compounds the error committed below.

C. **The Ruling Below Improperly Burdens The Press' Right to Secure and Publish or Broadcast Uncensored Information About the Operations of Government.**

The public's right to know can only be fully effectuated if the press is able to perform its assigned function of securing and then publishing or broadcasting uncensored information about the operations of government. And, of course, the press is expressly granted constitutional protection from governmental interference at least to the same extent that freedom of speech in general is protected under the First Amendment.

Within this tradition of a free and uncensored press, innumerable first-hand accounts have been published or broadcast by or with the assistance of current and former government employees often in the best position to write informatively and authoritatively about the inner workings of government. Indeed, it is hardly necessary to compile long lists of the many employees and officials, at all levels of government, who have in the past published, presumably without any pre-publication review, information about their government service, or the agencies for which they worked. Prominent figures who had access to classified and confidential information and who have so published come readily to mind, including Richard Nixon, Theodore Sorensen, Arthur Schlesinger, George Ball, George Kennan, John Kenneth Galbraith, Dean Acheson, Henry Stimson, and Harry Hopkins. There are, of course, many, many more.

The publication or broadcast of such information by high-ranking officials and other government employees has historically been viewed as an entirely proper, indeed salutary, undertaking that has surely not brought the nation to its knees. On the contrary, much of this information, and the far greater bulk of practical information provided in more pedestrian works by those working at lower levels of government, has been of assistance in assuring a public knowledgeable—or at least more knowledgeable than it otherwise might have been—concerning their government.

Despite this proven capacity of current and former government employees—even those who have worked with highly sensitive, classified information—to write and speak from their experience without compromising the security of the nation, the Court below nonetheless felt compelled to issue its restraining order and impose damages for failure to submit yet one other unclassified manuscript to an agency of government which now insists that it needs to impose a rigid system of pre-publication review in order to assure the ability of the agency to operate or, indeed, to survive. The Court below accepted these representations while evidencing no apparent concern for the damage that such a judicially-enforced system of pre-publication review and censorship might well pose to the operations of the press within the system of free expression which the First Amendment jealously guards.

D. The Court Below Failed to Search For Means to Minimize the Drastic Impact of Its Ruling on First Amendment Rights and Interests

The same considerations which impose the heavy burden to justify a prior restraint of the press demand that any judicial curtailment of First Amendment freedoms "accomplish the pin-pointed objective" of the justification asserted. *Carroll* v. *President & Commissioners of Princess Anne,* 393 U.S. 175, 183 (1968). For even if the justification proferred "be legitimate and substantial, that purpose cannot be pursued by means that broadly stifle fundamental personal liberties when the end can be more narrowly achieved." *Wooley* v. *Maynard,* 430 U.S. 705, 716 (1976), *quoting Shelton* v. *Tucker,* 364 U.S. 479, 488 (1960). Whether legislative or judicial, the abridgment of First Amendment rights "must be viewed in the light of less drastic means for achieving the same basic purpose." *Id.* Here, *amici* submit, there are surely "less drastic means" available to prevent the release of classified information than the harsh remedies imposed by the Court below to punish the release of unclassified information protected by the First Amendment.

(i) The Forfeiture of All Royalties

The unprecedented civil damage and equitable remedies imposed by the District Judge to punish Snepp's alleged violation of his pre-publication submission obligation were not only unduly punitive, but must also be seen to have the effect of chilling—indeed freezing—speech at its source. As earlier noted, such Draconian penalties in connection with the punishment of speech, which invite self-censorship, cannot be sanctioned by the courts. Were the District Court's penalties to stand, no author subject to an administrative system of prior review and who is dependent on royalties to earn a livelihood could henceforth risk publishing materials without submitting them for pre-publication review, even were he to conclude that such review would violate his rights or would otherwise be improper.[13]

(ii) Pre-Publication Review of All Materials

The breadth of the District Judge's order requiring submission of all future manuscripts for pre-publication review, whether or not they contain materials of a classified nature, and whether or not national security interests are implicated, represents an overbroad application of the prior restraint power (assuming *arguendo* that such power was properly invoked at all). It is fundamental that any system of prior restraints, if permitted at all, must be narrowly tailored to minimize the burden on First Amendment rights and bring within its ambit only those materials which are not subject to First Amendment protection. *Freedman v. Maryland*, 380 U.S. 51 (1965). Moreover, even permissible restraints must be accompanied by strict procedural safeguards. (*Id.*)

The scope of the District Court's order, sweeping within the government's review power every manner of information, together with

---

13. The District Judge seemed to be influenced by what he perceived as Snepp's desire "for personal financial gain," commenting critically concerning Snepp's receipt of "some sixty thousand dollars in advance payments and the contract with Random House . . . for royalties and other potential profits." (Memorandum Opinion, page 6.) But First Amendment protection has never been held to be limited—even before the recent application of First Amendment coverage to so-called "commercial speech"—by the fact that speakers or publishers have been paid. See, e.g., *Joseph Burstyn, Inc.* v. *Wilson*, 343 U.S. 495 (1952); *Smith* v. *California*, 361 U.S. 147 (1959); *New York Times* v. *Sullivan*, 376 U.S. 254 (1964).

the inevitable delay, cost and uncertainty inherent in the CIA's essentially standardless administrative pre-publication review procedure can only exacerbate the potential burdens upon First Amendment rights inherent in the District Court's order requiring submission for prepublication review of *all* materials, whether or not classified, and however far removed from national security interests. Indeed, the overbroad scope of this order has already been demonstrated by the District Court's ruling that even fiction and personal opinion in essay form must be reviewed.

Finally, it would seem clear that even if the CIA's prior review could be kept within narrow bounds not subject to overreaching—and there are grounds for concluding otherwise[14]—any system of pre-submission to the government is inherently at odds with our system of freedom of expression. Systems of government censorship, however clothed or however narrowly confined by court interpretation, are seldom tolerated under the First Amendment, no doubt because of their inevitable tendency to operate crudely and to overreach their stated objectives and limitations. In the process, those who wish to speak out about their government, when faced with the immediate prospect of ridicule from their superiors, job sanctions, other harassment or even outright efforts to suppress exposure of the information which may attend submission of materials to the government prior to their release generally, may well be deterred in this ambition. In such event, the government censorship apparatus will have succeeded in chilling, indeed stifling, valuable expression, to the loss of society.

In sum, the sweeping scope of the District Court's order, mandating as it does the submission of all materials whether properly censorable or not, makes that order overbroad, and constitutionally impermissible.

(iii) Application to Third-Party Publishers or Broadcasters

Among the most significant burdens on free expression implicit in the District Court's restraining order is its potential impact on the rights of independent, third-party publishers or broadcasters. (See [footnote 5], *supra*.) Such an extension of the Court's prior restraint so to cover the activities of third parties would not only further chill free expression, but also would bring about even more anomalous results than already invited by other aspects of the District Court's rulings.

Thus, a citizen who has had no connection with the government and

---

14. Thus, there is evidence, based on the CIA's own published materials, that in *Marchetti* the CIA requested the deletion of more than one hundred items from the book manuscript solely as a bargaining chip for future negotiations. Warner, "The Marchetti Case: New Case Law" published in *Studies in Intelligence* (CIA, 1977), pages 6-7.

who comes into possession of unclassified or publicly disclosed information—or, indeed, of classified information that does not meet the strict standards set forth in *New York Times Co. v. United States, supra,*—may freely exercise his First Amendment right to speak or write about that information. Yet, under the government's and District Court's view of this case, the disclosure of the very same information by an ex-government employee who has signed agreements of the type here involved warrants the invocation of the kinds of drastic penalties imposed in this case by the District Court.

Equally troublesome, the District Court's order is susceptible to interpretation such that the publisher or broadcaster of such information in the one case may also freely exercise its First Amendment prerogatives, while in the other (under the District Court's order in this case) it could arguably face contempt sanctions for acting "in concert with" the former government employee. Such a result, in *amici*'s view, is entirely unwarranted under the First Amendment.

III.

MARCHETTI ITSELF REQUIRES REVERSAL OF THE DECISION BELOW

The preceding discussion establishes that generally-recognized First Amendment principles, and the policies underlying those principles, preclude the invocation of prior restraints or the award of civil damages with respect to the publication of unclassified materials of the type involved in this case. As detailed above, the District Court's disposition of the case reflects a total insensitivity to these principles and, if left to stand, would be seriously detrimental to the right of authors, publishers, broadcasters and citizens generally to inform and be informed on matters of public moment. The right of the press to disseminate and of the public to receive such vital information, free of encumbrances and in uncensored form—particularly in the absence of any clearly demonstrated, significant corollary detriment to the security interests of the United States—should now be affirmed by this Court.

In fact, in *amici's* judgment, the decision of this court in *Marchetti* already requires the application of the constitutional principles which *amici* have set forth above to the facts at issue in this case. For the *Marchetti* case explicitly recognized that "the First Amendment limits the extent to which the United States, contractually or otherwise, may impose secrecy requirements upon its employees and enforce them with a system of prior censorship." 466 F.2d at 1313. This Court further made clear that the First Amendment "precludes such restraints with respect to information which is unclassified or officially disclosed"—concededly the only form of information published here by Snepp. (*Id.*)

In refusing to be bound by such established First Amendment principles, the District Court relied exclusively on a single passage in *Marchetti* that the Court contended supports the conclusion that *Marchetti* blanketly validates government secrecy agreements such as those imposed by the CIA—no matter what their intended scope or application—as against constitutional attack. (See Memorandum Opinion at p. 8.)[15] By reaching this conclusion of *per se* validity despite the significant distinctions between this case and *Marchetti*, the District Court ignored both the context in which this Court upheld the injunction against Marchetti and all of the other language in *Marchetti* which leads, in *amici's* view, to precisely the opposite conclusion.

Thus, the District Court not only failed to address the already-cited language in *Marchetti* clearly reflecting this Court's awareness of the limiting impact of the First Amendment on such secrecy agreements, as well as its preclusive effect on efforts to restrain the dissemination of unclassified or already disclosed materials, but also ignored the following language, to the same effect:

> "Marchetti by accepting employment with the CIA and by signing a secrecy agreement did not surrender his First Amendment right of free speech. The agreement is enforceable only because it is not a violation of those rights. *We would decline enforcement of the secrecy oath signed when he left the employment of the CIA to the extent that it purports to prevent disclosure of unclassified information, for, to that extent, the oath would be in contravention of his First Amendment rights.*" (466 F.2d at 1317) (emphasis added)

A clearer statement of the unquestionable applicability of the First Amendment to government secrecy agreements is hard to imagine. Equally clear is the rule enunciated by this Court with respect to the non-enforceability of secrecy agreements that purport "to prevent disclosure of unclassified information": Such agreements are "in contravention of ... First Amendment rights," and will not be judicially enforced. (*Id.*)

Perhaps most significantly, the Court below failed to recognize that the sole basis on which this Court enforced—and could constitutionally have enforced—the secrecy agreement in *Marchetti,* even in the face of

15. The District Judge flatly concluded without any reference to the factors that distinguish the *Marchetti* case from this case that "Marchetti . . . does not invalidate CIA's secrecy agreement," citing only a portion of concluding section VI of *Marchetti,* 466 F.2d at 1318.

acknowledged First Amendment considerations, was the Court's assessment that "the risk of harm from disclosure [of *classified* information obtained during the course of employment] is so great and maintenance of the confidentiality of the information so necessary" that relief in the government's favor was warranted. 466 F.2d at 1317. While *amici* do not agree with the outcome of the balancing process engaged in by this Court in *Marchetti* that led it to affirm the prior restraint there imposed, in light of the First Amendment principles and policies set forth above, it is of the utmost significance that the Court nevertheless recognized that such a balancing process must take place. Although clearly required to do so by *Marchetti*, the Court below failed to apply a similar balancing test to the circumstances of this case.

In any event, it is clear that the unavoidable result of this Court's balancing process, had Marchetti been writing not about classified, non-public information but instead—like Snepp—about concededly unclassified information and information in the public domain, would have been a denial of the requested relief. As this Court has properly stated, in such circumstances Marchetti would have had the "right to speak and write about the CIA and its operations, and to criticize it as any other citizen may . . .," *i.e.*, Marchetti could have acted free of governmental interference or prior review and censorship. 466 F.2d at 1317.

In short, this case presents the very fact situation cited in *Marchetti* as warranting the full application of the First Amendment to permit a former government employee to speak, write and inform free of restraint or retribution—even though, while in government employ, he had signed a secrecy agreement. Thus, were Snepp here to have submitted his manuscript to the CIA for pre-review, the Agency has implicitly conceded that it could *not,* consistent with this Court's ruling in *Marchetti,* have withheld approval of publication of any portion of the manuscript.

What all of this suggests, therefore, is that Snepp's "sin," in the eyes of the government, and the only possible reason for this action, was not the disclosure, or even threatened disclosure, of classified information; it was, simply, that Snepp had failed to abide by the CIA's system of prior restraints, albeit without the resultant harm of unauthorized disclosure of classified information. The guarantees of the First Amendment are far too important to permit their displacement by so casual a government interest, *amici* believe. This Court so recognized in *Marchetti* and such recognition warrants reversal of the judgment below.

Finally, in the event that, the foregoing analysis notwithstanding, this Court determines that *Marchetti* can be read to support the judgment issued by the Court below, then *amici* respectfully submit that such a result would emphatically demonstrate the inadequacy of the balancing process undertaken in *Marchetti* in safeguarding First Amendment interests. In such event, *Marchetti* should be reconsidered and, upon such reconsideration, reversed.[16] For, if *Marchetti* mandates the chilling burden on free speech (detailed above) implicit in the District Court's judgment, then surely *Marchetti* has created standards unjustifiably inimical to the established First Amendment principles discussed herein. A proper sensitivity to such interests would place a far more demanding burden on an agency of government that purports, by any means, so significantly to impede freedom of expression.

CONCLUSION

As discussed herein, fundamental First Amendment principles, and the policies underlying those principles, together with this Court's ruling in *Marchetti*, mandate reversal of the judgment below.

October 23, 1978

> Respectfully submitted,
> HENRY R. KAUFMAN
> *Attorney for Amici Curiae*
> Association of American
>   Publishers, Inc.
> One Park Avenue
> New York, New York 10016

IRA M. MILLSTEIN
R. BRUCE RICH
WEIL, GOTSHAL & MANGES
Of Counsel

---

16. Indeed, the *Marchetti* rulings have been criticized by numerous legal scholars for the manner in which the required balancing of interests was resolved. *See, e.g.,* Edgar and Schmidt, *The Espionage Statutes and Publication of Defense Information,* 73 Colum. L. Rev. 929, 1078-79 (1973); Hill, *Defamation and Privacy Under the First Amendment,* 76 Colum. L. Rev. 1205, 1294-95 (1976); Ryan, *United States v. Marchetti and Alfred A. Knopf, Inc. v. Colby: Secrecy 2; First Amendment 0,* 3 Hastings Const. L.Q. 1073 (1976); Note, *Constitutional Law—Prior Restraint Enforced Against Publication of Classified Material by CIA Employee,* 51 N. C. L. Rev. 865 (1973); *Cf.* F.O. Wilcox and R.A. Frank, eds., *The Constitution and the Conduct of Foreign Policy: An Inquiry by a Panel of the American Society of International Law* 9-10 (1976).

PAUL G. ZURKOWSKI

First Amendment Implications
For Secondary Information Services

Mr. Zurkowski is President and Acting
Counsel of the Information Industry
Association.

Freedom of expression is a good in itself. It is essential to all other freedoms. It is essential to self fulfillment, the acquisition of knowledge and the discovery of truth. The good society is not competent to judge whether individual *expression* promotes good or evil, justice or injustice, equality or inequality. *Conduct* or *action,* however, can be controlled by society to achieve its goals.[1]

The First Amendment is the principle support for the freedom of expression. The fundamental meaning of the Constitutional guarantee: "Congress shall make no law . . . abridging the freedom of speech, or of the press, or the right of the people peaceably to assemble, and to petition the Government for a redress of grievances," is to guarantee an effective system of freedom of expression.

---

1. *The System of Freedom of Expression,* Thomas I. Emerson, Random House, 1970, 754 pp. The definitions and theory underlying this brief discussion of the First Amendment are derived from this indepth treatise.

It guarantees the right to hear as well as to speak.[2]

Individuals need these freedoms to form their judgments. Taken together these judgments constitute our culture, direction and intellectual achievement.

These well accepted principles face severe testing in the information age.

Secondary information services have been with us for some time. When Samuel Johnson was questioned about his ". . . desire to look at the backs of books," he replied:

> "Sir, the reason is very plain. Knowledge is of two kinds. We know a subject ourselves, or we know where we can find information upon it. When we inquire into any subject, the first thing we have to do is to know what books have treated of it. This leads us to look at catalogs, and the backs of books in libraries."[3]

Johnson's reference to two kinds of knowledge led Eric Boehm, President, ABC-Clio, to coin the phrase "Second Knowledge," meaning, to quote Johnson, "Where we can find information upon." What Boehm calls Second Knowledge are reference tools, abstracts, indexes, archival finding tools. But he would also include dictionaries, thesauri, almanacs, encyclopedias, yellow pages, etc.[4]

But Secondary information services extend beyond these largely literary tools.

In "Death Comes as the End," Agatha Christie pointed beyond such tools to a concept of information equivalents of real things in the following excerpt:

> "By and by," she said dreamily, "It would be interesting to know how to write on papyrus. Why doesn't everyone learn?"
>
> "It isn't necessary."
>
> "Not necessary, perhaps, but it would be pleasant."
>
> "You think so, Renisenb? What difference would it make to you?"

---

2. Lamont v. Postmaster General, 381 US 301 (1965). The U.S. Supreme Court held invalid a law authorizing the Postmaster General to detain "communist political propaganda" as in conflict with the First Amendment.
3. Hill, George B., ed., Boswell's *Life of Johnson* (6 vols.), Vol. 2, *Life,* 1765-1776, (NY: Harper, 1891), pp. 414 and 417-419.
4. Boehm, E. H., *Second Knowledge Education, A Long Range View,* Remarks at a conference on Bibliographic Instruction, College of Wooster, Wooster, OH, April 24-25, 1975.

First Amendment Implications For Secondary Information Services

Renisenb considered for a moment or two. Then she said slowly, "When you ask me that, truly I do not know, Hori."

Hori said, "At present a few scribes are all that are needed on a large estate, but the day will come, I fancy, when there will be armies of scribes all over Egypt. We are living at the beginning of great times. . . . It is so easy and it costs so little labor to write down ten bushels of barley, or a hundred head of cattle, or ten fields of spelt—and the thing that is written will come to seem like the real thing. . ."

The information age arrived when more transactions occurred in such information equivalents than occurred in the real thing. A recent U.S. Department of Commerce Study, based on 1967 Census of Business Figures, reported that 46% of the U.S. Gross National Product was informational in nature.[5]

In the past ten years a whole new industry, the information industry, has grown up creating and marketing information equivalents of every event and artifact of human existence past, present, and future. Many companies focus on abstracting and indexing published materials. Others create machine-readable equivalents of economic trends, events and time series. (Econometric modeling of national economies is dependent on these capabilities). Still others perform a distribution function by storing many varied data banks on their computers and by providing access to their computers via telephone lines and computer terminals. Still others perform a retail function, offering users answers (developed by the retailers through performing searches of data bases, manual library searches, telephoning sources and in other ways tracing down wherever they can "information about it.").[6]

The growth and experience of this industry on the front line of the emerging information age points up some serious First Amendment implications of the information age.

THE INFORMATION AGE

What will the mature information age look like? How will it differ from the industrial age we live in today?

It will be increasingly electronic. For example, today over 300 published data bases exist in electronic or machine-readable form, cover-

---

5. Porat, M. V., *The Information Economy,* 9 Volumes, OT Special Report 77-12, May 1977, GPO Stock Number 003000-00513-5.
6. For further detailed information about this industry see: *Information Sources,* Information Industry Association Membership Directory, pp. 245 (1978), IIA, 316 Pennsylvania Ave. SE, Suite 502, Washington, DC 20003.

ing 80 to 100 million documents.[7] In these data bases information equivalents of events and artifacts are stored, organized, processable and retrievable. *The New York Times* Information Bank covers every article carried in *The Times* since 1970, plus the content of sixty other serial publications. The International Data Corporation data files cover computer locations in the nation including who owns and operates what computer at what location with what peripheral equipment with how many programmers, systems analysts, and managers. Congressional Information Service covers all the bills, hearings and reports of the Congress dating back to 1969. Its American Statistics Index covers all government documents with statistical content. Economic Information System files cover manufacturing data on most of the industrial capacity of the U.S. based on an "input/output" model enabling suppliers of raw materials, for example, to identify users, large and small, of their raw materials in the manufacturing process.

The ability to create these files and to provide access to them from a central computer is as well established and documented as the assembly line process on which our industrial strength is based. This information industry process is the result of the ingenious combination of sophisticated information technologies like computers, microfilm, computer composition, computer programming, systems design, and sound publishing and marketing techniques. The major hurdle the information industry process faced ten years ago, and one it faces but to a lesser degree today, is the assumption that information, like air, is and should be free. It has taken ten years or more to begin establishing in the mind of the user that information starts out in life as raw data and that for it to be useful value must be added to it. The information industry process adds value and it is that value, tested in the competitive marketplace, that determines the price of the product or service. Upon the recognition of this value added depends the viability of competitive services of information and ultimately of the individual's freedom to choose other than the government's report of what it does.

This is a relatively new business. Some companies like R. R. Bowker, H. W. Wilson, Dun and Bradstreet, (you can tell the older companies because they bear the founder's name), have been around for seventy-five to 100 years. The evolution of the process into a growth industry was set in motion, however, by third generation computers capable of processing alpha-numerics. The ability of computers to compare, sort and array vast quantities of word information, as opposed to simply numerical data, stimulated many minds to applying that capability to the highly visible information explosion that, strangely enough, coincided in time with the third generation computer.

---

7. Thousands of other data bases are maintained on a completely proprietary basis for internal use only.

A Matrix Illustrating the Multitudinous Dimensions of Information

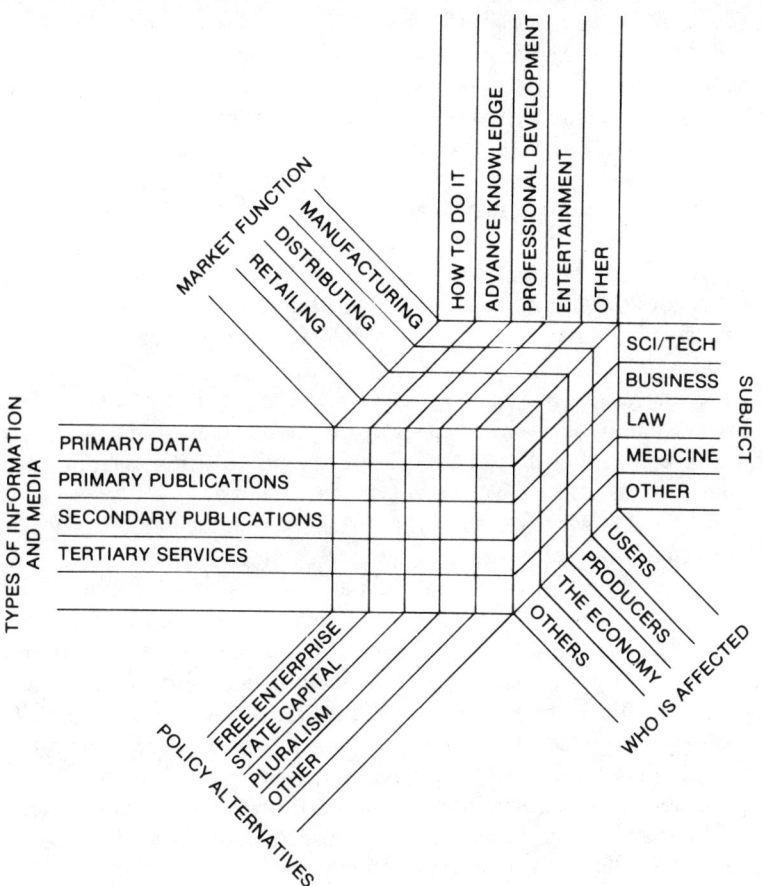

Information means many things to many people. Unfortunately, this is usually true when only two people are discussing it. This figure illustrates that it is possible to identify precisely what it is we are talking about at a given moment when discussing information policy. The example cited of the MEDLINE data base involved the Distribution *(Market Functions) of* Secondary Publications *(Type of information) for* Medical Applications *(Intended Purpose) in* Medicine *(Subject Area) affecting the* Economic *(Who is affected) relationship of MEDLINE to commercially available services based on* Pluralism *(As a Policy Alternative). By identifying the information subject under consideration that precisely it is possible to have a fairly reasonable discussion. Without such precise definition, the people involved begin discussing the manufacture of primary publications for professional development of doctors and its affect on patients. That, too, of course, is a valid subject but it is different from the subject addressed in this article and should be treated separately. The purpose of inserting this illustration is to determine how broad the subject is and how we have only begun to understand it.*

PAUL G. ZURKOWSKI

Roger Summit was instrumental in developing computer programs for searching and retrieving bibliographic information from computer data bases. Dr. Eugene Garfield applied citation indexing to scientific literature, enabling his company to graphically display an "invisible college" of scientists working in a particular area of research by identifying which scientist cited research of other scientists in the published literature. John Rothman was central to the development of the Information Bank at *The New York Times*. Innumerable others have made similar contributions to the capacity of society to handle information in electronic form in their respective areas. Thus, vast quantities of environmental information, petroleum information, celebrity information, information on literature, energy information, chemical, biological, engineering information and much, much more can now be accessed electronically.

An analysis of our age soon to be published is entitled *The Invisible Industry*. The book is the product of the ten years or more of work by Harding Vowles, inventor of the belt press, a printing process for printing one book at a time, of Toronto, Canada.

Harding Vowles draws a comparison between the industrial age and the information age in terms of their respective visibility.

In the industrial age every human's senses are constantly bombarded by urgent visible and audible indications of the age we live in.

In the information age, however, there are no supersonic aircraft, suspension bridges, skyscrapers, Indianapolis 500 auto races, or super highways as there are testifying to the power of the industrial age. The business of the information age is performed quietly. Yet it is no less powerful. This is because the "thing that is written" is communicated over telephone wires, satellites, microwave or other electronic means. The "armies of scribes" involved in the process are invisibly revolutionizing how we live and how society functions.

This invisibility should raise our level of concern over the question of who controls the switches of information. In the information age, whoever controls the switches of information will literally control the freedom of expression allotted to us.

Who Will Control the Switches of Information?

In Babylonia 2,000 years before Christ, the culture enjoyed 1,000 years of stability. Throughout that thousand years the medium of expression was clay tablets. Molds were formed and clay was poured into the molds. The tablets were allowed to dry and were then used to communicate ideas. Ideas remain fairly static when required to be communicated in a medium which is created so laboriously. The process did

First Amendment Implications For Secondary Information Services

not permit many "new" or "frivolous" ideas to be "run up the flag pole." When leather and papyrus arrived as new communications media the stability of the society was undermined and lost. In this case control over the switches of information was inherent in the media.

The next historical object lesson for the information age and the question of who controls the switches of information came with Gutenberg's invention. In that case and since control has been political.

It is significant that the people who controlled the switches of information as Gutenberg began producing the first printed Bible were the guilds, the banks and the monks.

To learn a trade, a worker had to join a guild since there were no "how to do it" books available.

Capital was controlled by the banks. And the monks, being literate, were able to deal with their contemporaries on the basis of the Gospel of St. John, which begins, "In the beginning was the word."

On the strength of their ability to read and write, these literate monks convinced their illiterate contemporaries that they, by dealing in the word, could affect the world hereafter. Control was based on a mystique.

The Turks invaded Cyprus about this same time and Pope Nicholas V authorized the massive sale of indulgences to raise money to assist the Christian Greeks in repelling the heathen invaders. With so many indulgences to be produced (up to that time each indulgence form had been hand-lettered) and without the benefit of the Xerox machine, the monks sought out Gutenberg. The result is that the first piece of dated printing is a thirty-one-line indulgence form dated 1454. It precedes the Gutenberg Bible.

These printed forms ultimately debunked the monk's mystique.

This must have contributed to the decline in the sale of indulgences since (1) the same printed form is not likely to be as effective for one sinner as it is for another and (2) there must have arisen a question whether a temporal document containing a date (1454) could have any eternal significance.

Martin Luther followed Gutenberg in Mainz, Germany by half a century or more. Luther tried to reform the Catholic Church from within. He attacked the practice of selling indulgences, but more importantly he authored the first Catechism through which he hoped to "internalize" the Catholic religion.

This is another example of a new medium drastically affecting who controls the switches of information.

Years after the Gutenberg Bible and indulgence experience, Henry VIII demonstrated, in a more overt way, a concern for the control over the switches of information.

After Henry VIII and William Tindale, Henry's translator of the

Bible, had a falling out over the translation of the New Testament, Tindale left England. He went to the Continent seeking a printer to publish the Tindale version of the New Testament. Henry VIII declared a war on books. In order to keep Tindale's Bible out of England, he had every book coming into England from the continent seized and dumped in the harbor. He also had Tindale run to earth and burnt at the stake as a heretic.

The need to control what people said in print led subsequent British monarchs to create the Stationers Company. Later the Statute of Queen Anne created a right in the Crown to grant copyrights, i.e., the right to make copies or to publish. This grew into a kind of property right in the Crown which is the source of Crown copyright in Britain today.

It is said our copyright law derives from the statute of Queen Anne. A reading of the Federalist Papers and the reports of various deliberations over the Constitution, however, sheds no direct light on the source of Article 1, Section 8, Clause 8 of the Constitution.

> Clause 8: The Congress shall have power... to promote Progress of Science and useful Arts, by securing for limited times to Authors and Inventors the exclusive right to their Respective Writings and Discoveries.

In the light of the colonists' experience with the Stationers Company and the need to obtain from the King a license to publish, it was quite logical for the Founding Fathers to cast our copyright language in directly opposite terms. Thus, a principle of our form of government, so basic as to not require any discussion and so important as to appear in the 1st Article of the Constitution, gives ownership in expression of thought and ideas to the individual. It is an additional underpinning to our system of freedom of expression. It gives control over the switches of information, in one respect, to the individual creator of the information. It assures him the right to speak out and through the use of his copyright to get publishers to invest in producing and distributing those ideas. At the same time it assures the rest of us the right to hear what those thoughts are and to create and publish our own responses.

Universal Access

The information age will also be known for the phenomenon of "Universal Access." It is technologically feasible today for every person to have access to electronic records of everything that is known or knowable.[8]

8. Obviously society's experience dictates that there be limits on what is accessable by whom. Rights of privacy, proprietary information of various kinds, security information, and many others are likely to be considered inappropriate for universal access.

First Amendment Implications For Secondary Information Services

Of the 300 or more machine-readable data bases, more than half are available for searching by the public today. SDC Search Service, Lockheed Information Systems, Bibliographic Research Service, each have stored forty to fifty or more data bases on their respective computers and have offered "dial-up" access for online searching of those data bases to the public.

That means that anyone can lease a terminal for use at home or office. The terminal can be connected to the SDC or Lockheed computer by telephone.[10] Once connected the user questions the data base seeking to identify those parts of the data base which are relevant to the user's questions.

The computer answers by having the user's terminal print out the information desired. This "online" method of searching large files of information is extremely cost-effective, reducing the time formerly needed to do manual and less complete searches of library files.

Although this has been applied primarily to scientific, technical and business information, and tends to serve the research and business communities, a whole new application has been developed for those technologies dealing with more day to day information.

The British Post Office has created Viewdata, a system for utilizing computerized data bases, the telephone and the television set operating as the equivalent of a computer terminal.

This system enables a user to communicate with the computer by use of a slightly expanded "Touch Tone" telephone "Keyboard," roughly the size of a simple hand calculator. When the user asks a question and the computer identifies the "page" of information containing the answer, the "page" of information is transmitted over the telephone line to the user's TV set. The TV set needs to have a buffer unit added to receive these "pages" and to cause the TV set to display them.

The significance of Viewdata is that it relies on equipment already in the home, telephone and television.

It encourages the application of the information industry process to many fields of information needed by individuals in the course of their every day lives. Train, air and bus schedules, restaurant and entertainment information, repair services, advertising, and many more. In its first year of operation in Great Britain, it has more than 150 suppliers of data bases.

Several other systems are also being introduced. CEEFAX is a

---

9. Martha Williams Report, *Computer-Readable Bibliographic Data Bases—A Directory and Data Source Book;* October 1976; American Society for Information Science.
10. This has been made economically feasible by the development of "Packet switching" technologies which, in effect, transmit data messages in, around, and between voice messages across the nation's phone system on a time sharing basis.

system that broadcasts a "menu" of constantly updated information of interest to subscribers. The "menu" takes several minutes per cycle displaying brief items sequentially. The items are updated periodically. The service has particular appeal in the financial community where there is a high coincidence of interest in specific items of financial information throughout the day.

The concept of "Universal Access" is an appealing one. It suggests a cerebral age. Much that we travel to find out can be delivered to us in its information equivalent form. In many respects the "television games" being marketed today suggest a direction for entertainment and education in the information age. Where industrial age activities are physical—in effect energy intensive—activities in the information age will be cerebral and energy conservative.[11]

Centralization

A third aspect of the information age is its trend toward centralization. Obviously, if the system of freedom of expression this nation developed during the Gutenberg era—that of dispersed, decentralized printing capability—is to survive, we must begin considering how to protect that system when the media involved require centralization. If the media of the information age is electronic, largely invisible in operation, and depends on a central computer facility accessible through a centrally controlled communication system, it becomes imperative to address the question of who controls the switches of information if a system of freedom of expression is to survive. The answer will ultimately be found in First Amendment terms.

FIRST AMENDMENT EXPERIENCES

In print media the application of the first amendment is fairly clear. The apparatus for implementing the freedom of expression is dispersed. Printing presses and photocopying machines are distributed among many owners. Case law has eliminated one restraint after another on the operations of the press. Newspapers in colonial America needed a license to operate. *The Boston News-letter,* America's first newspaper, was

11. It also is a little disturbing to consider the effect of the temporary evanescent character of the media today in comparison with the clay tablet. If the clay tablet contributed to a stable society, what effect will the temporary, erasable magnetic impulses stored on magnetic tape contribute to the stability or instability of our society?

denied its license to publish when the Crown determined it to be a seditious newspaper. No such "prior restraints" are permitted today. Nor has the Supreme Court permitted taxes on the press that do not apply equally to any business.

Ithiel de Sola Pool in the Spring 1978 issue of *The Key Reporter*,[12] compares print media, broadcast media and common carriers. In contrast to print media where the necessary apparatus is widely distributed, broadcast media is controlled and limited by the scarcity of radio spectrum. As a result, the broadcaster must prove that it serves "the public necessity, interest and convenience" in order to obtain and retain a license.

Similarly, in communications the common carriers, telephone, telegraph and the postal system, a different set of policies has applied.

Pool outlines a long series of cases illustrating how the postal service has progressed, on the one hand, from a crown franchise selling services to the public and distributing free of charge the franchisee's newspapers, or other products to, on the other, a more or less neutral highway on which all sorts of views may travel at will and on equal terms.

Pool argues that an inherently central system depends on a common carrier principle to protect freedom of expression. He elaborates this pattern in the history of the Postal Service as evidence of a temptation to use the central system for political control, to spread the monopoly over activities that might otherwise be diffused. The control of the postal service by government encouraged it to restrict what the system could be used for.

Pool sees a three-act freedom of expression drama being reenacted in our time:

1) In Act 1, a monopoly is created for reasons of expanding, rather than controlling speech;

2) In Act 2, a temptation emerges to use the resulting power to control citizens;

3) In Act 3, the Supreme Court, as hero, rescues the Constitution.

Often citing many of the activities of the information industry, Pool concludes:

> As publishing becomes an electronic activity, will the producers of text find themselves under the same regulation as that govern the electronic communications? Inadvertently, a few decades hence, publishing may have ceased to be a realm free of government regulation. Publishers may end up like broadcasters today, with one eye constantly on government agencies.

12. *From Gutenberg to Electronics: Implications for the First Amendment,* "The Key Reporter", Vol. XLIII, Number 3, Spring 1978, p. 2.

PAUL G. ZURKOWSKI

In secondary information it is not a matter of "a few decades hence," but an immediate problem already drastically reducing dispersed and disaggregated activities and substituting for them a centralized government-funded information apparatus.

At first blush this may appear to be a logical development. It can be argued that computerized systems function more efficiently as centralized activities. Such a concept does not take into account each individual's right to hear, however.

Each of us has developed a finely tuned cognitive screen which permits us to screen out material not germane to our current interests. Each reader will get a different message out of this article because each has unique, personal cognitive screens conditioned to permit certain ideas to get through and to keep other ideas out.

It is essential, therefore, to the successful communication of information that it be creatively packaged and available from multiple sources. A centralized system, originally created to serve all, ends up monopolizing and limiting access to information. No single source can possibly imagine and create all the various packages of information needed to penetrate the cognitive screens of people for whom the information has value and importance.

Government funded research will generate one report. Who will repackage that report to communicate its content to everyone for whom the information has value?

The answer lies not so often in rewriting the report, but in creating information equivalents of the literature. An abstract of one article prepared for biologists will emphasize things in the report different from those emphasized in an abstract prepared for chemists.

It is easy to overlook the value of such finding tools as abstracts and indexes. Yet, the fact of the information explosion, the doubling of recorded knowledge every eight to ten years, gives rise to the need for such finding tools. Without the means to find precisely the bit of information you need, if you have all the information in the world you really have nothing. Control over these finding tools has far reaching significance for our democracy.

An example of the importance of indexing to the information age was provided in the late 1960's in the midst of the Viet Nam War demonstrations in Washington. The Department of the Army was reprimanded by Congress for photographing and keeping records on activities of civilians participating in the demonstrations. The Secretary of the Army at first agreed to the destruction of records relating to civilians. When he looked into it, however, he discovered that those records were mixed in with all the other records and had been microfilmed in random sequence and indexed. He offered, instead of destroying the files, to destroy the index, arguing that without the index nothing could be found. Congress agreed.

The experience of the information industry in secondary information services parallels the drama Pool suggested.

In Act 1, a centralized service is created for reasons of expanding access of information.

Item: The National Library of Medicine has created Medline, providing on-line computerized access to abstracts of thousands of journal articles. Its purpose was to apply information technologies to the task of making medical information rapidly and readily available to doctors and others in the healing professions.

In Act 2, we see the temptation to use the resulting power.

Item: NLM priced this article service at first at $8 per connect computer hour and then at $15 per connect hour. It offered to lease the computer tapes at $50,000 per year. The real, and intended, effect of underpricing online access and overpricing the tapes was to preclude anyone else from being able to offer such services. The result is that in the medical field there is a single source of online information—the government.[13] Obviously, this service costs far in excess of $15 per hour. If priced in that fashion by a private company, it would be easy to characterize that as "predatory" and anti-competitive pricing.

The Director of NLM has stated that this pricing was calculated to "ensure" that no private company ever profited from the Medline file. Regardless of the merits of that economic policy view, government control over the switches of medical information gives NLM the power to impose it on citizens.

This is a pattern oft repeated in the government. The underlying rationale is that the taxpayers have paid once for this information; why should they pay a second time?

The result, however, is the creation of a state-owned and operated secondary information press.

In fact, in secondary information services electronic, invisible and centralized government operated information services have created a de facto state-press to the exclusion of the competitive non-government services.

The pattern has become fixed in the past decade. Literature relevant to a particular field is gathered, abstracted and indexed by a government agency. Secondary finding tools are prepared and distributed free of charge or on a subsidized basis to the specialists primarily concerned with that field.

The result is a kind of cream skimming. If you happen to be a

---

13. Excerpta Medica, a product of Elsevier in the Netherlands, has recently become available at $55.00 per connect computer hour.

specialist in the particular field involved you are provided information relevant to that field. If you are not part of that field, you will probably not be served.

The government agency involved probably will not be funded to serve the general public. By virtue of the existence of a government subsidized service preempting the market by supplying services to people directly involved in the field, no alternative service will be economically feasible to serve the rest of the public who may be interested in the information but not eligible for the government service.

It is difficult to see how Pool's Act 3 will be realized in this situation. It may not be the Supreme Court which rescues the Constitution. It may require Congress itself to recognize the need to protect the system of freedom of expression from being overwhelmed by a government created state press in secondary information services.

The fact that a private sector capability exists offers some hope that the situation can be dealt with while actually increasing public access to information.

The need exists today for government to exercise self restraint in the performance of these secondary information services.

Information can be both a public good and a private good at the same time. Information is the primary function of government. It collects it, it creates it. It uses it . . . in unbelievably large amounts.

But it does not have to be the sole distributor of it.

Cognitive screens being what they are requires that information gathered by the government have value added to it in the form of packaging and related efforts necessary to make it useful to all the myriad cognitive screen audiences for which it has value.

This calls for the creation of a new kind of institution in government and a new approach to the distribution of government information. The institution called for would perform a broker function identifying all the information that is available in government and making it available for distribution through competitive commercial channels.

Government agencies would thus be free to utilize all the exciting new electronic information technologies in the performance of their respective government functions without at the same time monopolizing the dissemination of information to the public about how the public is being governed.

A current example of the need for a new approach is the impending decision of the Commerce Department to release the data base containing key data elements on all patents granted by the U.S. Patent Office. There is fairly wide interest in this data base. Standing alone it could be a valuable "property" for an information company to have the rights to market.

Mindful of the cognitive screen phenomena, however, it is dubious that any one company or government agency could package and repackage the content to serve all of the users for whom that data base has potential value.

At the same time it is necessary to recognize that the cost of adding value to government information will be undertaken only if there is some degree of certainty the costs can be recovered. In the absence of some confidence on this point the work of adding value will not be undertaken.

In the past, government agencies facing these difficult problems have usually opted for one of two choices:

1) do the distribution entirely with government funds, or
2) contract with a private firm to do the distribution with government funds.

In either case the government controls the switches of information, and a single source of the information involved is established. If the agency chose to restrict access to some information or to "push" certain information there was no alternative source for users to go to.

A system of freedom of expression requires that we develop an alternative method for utilizing the alternate and varied means for communicating ideas in this country.

Congress could rescue our First Amendment rights directly. Instead of directing each agency to "create a data base," Congress could direct each agency (1) to develop an inventory of the alternative channels available for communicating its information output to people for whom it has potential value; (2) to establish an inventory of the information to be communicated to various audiences, requiring the application of multiple information repackaging efforts; and (3) to adopt a standard "common carrier" type understanding or agreement between the agency and its channels of communication providing fair and equitable treatment to all.

CONCLUSION

We are indeed at several crossroads. We are moving from a predominantly industrial age to an information age; from decentralized publishing and information dissemination activities to electronic centralized networks; from a free enterprise system to increased government controls especially in the industrial environment.

It is time we stopped to take stock of what this means for the free marketplace of ideas and our cherished freedom of expression. There is a clearly marked trend toward the growth of a centralized state press in secondary information activities. Such a regime, in the words of Justice Douglas "is at war with the 'uninhibited, robust and wide-open' debate and discussion that are contemplated by the First Amendment."

Fortunately, there is no conspiracy of forces assembled for the express purpose of gaining control of the switches of information. For the most part government interests are still focusing on better information service to their respective constituencies. In the process, however, the reality of a government controlled centralized information system is rapidly being put together. The opportunity for control will then exist—and then it may be too late to rescue our First Amendment rights.

STANLEY D. TICKTON

Obscene/Indecent Programming: The FCC and WBAI

Dr. Tickton is an Associate Professor,
Mass Communications Department,
Norfolk State University.

The regulation of alleged obscene, indecent, or profane programming has by no means been a contemporary activity.[1] What follows is an update of the situation.[2]

WBAI-FM

In February 1975, the Federal Communications Commission (FCC), under increasing pressure from Congress and the public, sent a report to Congress on the broadcast of violent, indecent, and obscene material.[3] The Commission stated that, in its view, governmental action

1. For background, see Feldman and Tickton *Obscene/Indecent Programming: Regulation of Ambiguity*, J. BROADCASTING 20, no. 2 (Spring 1976): 273-282, and Feldman, *Broadcast Obscenity and Indecency—A Research Bilbiography: 1927-1976*, CLIENT 4, no. 1 (Fall 1976): 15-20.
2. Feldman and Tickton, *Obscene/Indecent Programming*, pp. 273-282.
3. Report on the Broadcast of Violent, Indecent and Obscene Material, 51 FCC 2d 418 (1975).

was required by statute, and that the Commission would, therefore, meet its responsibility.

On 21 February 1975, one week before sending its report to Congress, the Commission acted upon the complaint (3 December 1973) of one listener—John R. Douglas; and issued a declaratory ruling concerning Pacifica Foundation's WBAI-FM (New York City) afternoon broadcast (30 October 1973) of a segment entitled "Filthy Words" contained in the George Carlin comedy album, "George Carlin—Occupation Foole."[4] The Commission wanted to clarify its position on indecent materials and did not impose any forfeiture on WBAI-FM. According to the Commission:

> ... the concept of "indecent" is intimately connected with the exposure of children to language that describes, in terms patently offensive as measured by contemporary community standards for the broadcast medium, sexual or excretory activities and organs, at times of the day when there is a reasonable risk that children may be in the audience.[5]

Finally, in December 1975, the FCC assessed a $2,000 fine against the Board of Trustees of the University of Pennsylvania as licensee of WXPN-FM (Philadelphia) for broadcasting obscene and indecent language on the program, "The Vegetable Report."[6] The broadcasts were found obscene under the decision in *Miller* v. *California*, 414 U.S. 881 (1973), and as a "pandering approach to the description of sexual acts."[7] The *Illinois Citizens* decision was cited in support of the Commission's actions to review the program material per se rather than in the context of the program's entirety.[8] The problem of children in the audience was also of prime concern to the Commission.[9]

THE FCC'S PROPOSED LEGISLATION

The issues in regulating the broadcast of obscene and/or indecent materials have been numerous and perplexing. How does society protect

---

4. Carlin repeatedly (106 times in 12 minutes) said the words "cock-sucker," "piss," "mother-fucker," "fuck," "cunt," and "shit." Pacifica Foundation, Memorandum Opinion and Order, 51 FCC 2d 430 (1975). *See also* Feldman and Tickton, *Obscene/Indecent Programming*, p. 278.
5. 51 FCC 2d at 433.
6. Board of Trustees, University of Pennsylvania (WXPN-FM), 57 FCC 2d 782 (1975) and 57 FCC 2d 793 (1976).
7. 57 FCC 2d at 790. *See also* Miller v. California, 414 U.S. 881 (1973).
8. Illinois Citizens Committee for Broadcasting et al. v. FCC, 515 F. 2d 317 (1975). *See also* Feldman and Tickon, *Obscene/Indecent Programming*, pp. 277-278.
9. 57 FCC 2d at 790-791.

impressionable children without infringing upon the First Amendment rights of the Constitution? Can acceptable standards for content be defined and applied? Given the case history, the FCC believed that a more definitive standard was needed in governing morally offensive materials in broadcasting and cable, than those general standards set down by the United States Supreme Court in its *Miller* decision and in other related cases.

Thus, in June 1976, the Commission submitted to the Ninety-fourth Congress a proposed amendment to the Communications Act of 1934 (Section 511),[10] and also proposed the deletion of the current Section 1464 of the United States Criminal Code.

The Commission's basic rationales for the proposed legislation were: (1) the traditional "scarcity" argument, (2) a "federal interest" in broadcasting, (3) the "intrusive nature" of the electronic media, and (4) the concern for children in the audience.

The traditional "scarcity of available frequencies" argument, which had been cited by the FCC and the courts in the past, logically led the Commission into its second rationale—that of having a federal interest in broadcasting. The United States Supreme Court indicated in *Miller* that the so-called federal interest for regulation of morally offensive materials was less urgent than in the past. However, the Commission believed that the *Miller* decision should be interpreted by taking into consideration the same court's decisions in *Red Lion*[11] and *CBS* v. *DNC*[12] which recognized and advocated such a federal interest in broadcasting. Any incompatibility regarding the federal interest in the court's decisions was thought by the Commission to rest on the fact that *Miller* and other related cases had not dealt with the electronic media.

The federal interest concept was also necessary, in the FCC's view, because of the third rationale which dealt with the intrusive nature of the electronic media. The Commission was concerned about the automatic and unabridged intrusion of the electronic media into the home, compared to the volitional act of an individual purchasing printed matter or movie tickets and then reading or viewing such materials.[13] The intrusion

10. S. 3858, 94th Cong., 2nd Sess. (1976). The Commission started drafting its proposal several months earlier, in September 1975. *See* Feldman and Tickton, *Obscene/Indecent Programming*, p. 279; *FCC Drafts Harsh New Law on Obscene or Indecent Programming*, BROADCASTING (September 15, 1975), pp. 47-48; and *FCC Sends Message to Congress on Obscenity and Indecency*, BROADCASTING (June 7, 1976), pp. 19-20.
11. 395 U.S. 367 (1969).
12. 412 U.S. 94 (1973).
13. The "intrusion argument" has been debatable to the point that some say the public can select what to listen to or watch from newspaper broadcast logs and *TV Guide,* which in many instances have printed warnings in addition to the usual warning given by stations and/or networks before a program is broadcast. Needless to say, if one has not read the print listings, or tunes in after the start of the program, no such warning will have been received.

argument, therefore, had validity as far as the Commission was concerned.

The intrusion argument led the Commission to its final, and perhaps most important, rationale for submitting the proposed legislation—the concern for children. Concern for children in the audience, as noted above, was expressed in the Commission's decision in *Illinois Citizens* and in its more recent 1975 Pacifica *WBAI* and University of Pennsylvania *WXPN* decisions.[14] The Commission expressed concern in *Illinois Citizens* over the effect of such materials on children as members of a captive audience without the ability to control the receiver, or the capacity for individual choice, concerning materials which could thus intrude into the home unabridged. In *WBAI*, the Commission was not only concerned with children, but also noted that different standards should be applied when children were not in the listening/viewing audience. The Commission's logic in *WBAI* and *WXPN* was partly based on the reasoning that the materials broadcast were "indecent" by virtue of the fact that children were most likely part of the afternoon audience. The Commission was aware of the fact that definitions and criteria would be needed.

In the *Miller* decision, the court suggested that the term "obscenity" be specifically defined. Therefore, the Commission, in its proposed legislation (Section 511), itemized what it believed to be patently offensive descriptions or depictions of sexual conduct.

> The term "obscene material" means a patently offensive representation or verbal description of an act of sexual intercourse, including genital-genital, anal-genital, or oral-genital intercourse, whether between human beings or between a human being and an animal; of masturbation; or lewd exhibition of a human genital or excretory organ; and which taken as a whole, appeals to the prurient interest of the average person applying contemporary community standards for radio communication or cable television and, taken as a whole, lacks serious literary, artistic, political, or scientific value.[15]

The Commission's "obscenity" criteria were basically those put forth by the Department of Justice in its proposed legislation to amend the United

---

14. The Commission felt, however, that there should be different standards when children are not likely to be in the audience; hence, an affirmative defense was built into the proposal.
15, 1975), pp. 47-48; and *FCC Sends Message to Congress on Obscenity and Indecency*, BROADCASTING (June 7, 1976), pp. 19-20.

States Criminal Code, submitted to both the Ninety-third and Ninety-fourth Congress.[16]

The Commission's definition of indecent in its legislative proposal was based upon its ruling in the *WBAI* case.

> The term "indecent material" means a representation or verbal description of a human sexual or excretory organ or function, which under contemporary community standards for radio communication or cable television is patently offensive.[17]

Moreover, the Commission developed a double standard whereby dissemination of such materials was possible when the risk of exposure of such materials to children under twelve years of age was minimized.[18] In terms of programming, age twelve was the general industry and Commission age-level standard. The age of eighteen was ruled out because the Commission realized that it would be almost impossible to limit the risk of exposure to those who were eighteen years old. Generally, the Commission felt that any dissemination which minimized the risk of exposure—such as a locked box or pay-cable channel, or the broadcast of such materials between the hours of 11 P.M. and 7 A.M.—would be adequate compliance with its standards and free from First Amendment complications. The Commission noted that there were 10 percent fewer children under twelve years of age in the audience Monday-Friday after 11 P.M. than during the previous hour (compared to figures of 19 to 32 percent depending on the day of the week).[19] Using the 11 P.M. to 7 A.M. time frame, the Commission was of the opinion that the number of children exposed, and the number of other people who would or could be offended, would be greatly reduced. Permitting dissemination on this basis to consenting adults would avoid First Amendment complications since such materials would not be totally suppressed.

The Commission indicated that application of its proposal would occur in four ways: (1) it would apply to both the person who disseminates obscene/indecent materials, and the person who is the performer or speaker, (2) it would apply to all cable-controlled channels, (3) it would not apply to cable public access channels in which cable operators have no power of censorship, but (4) it could and would apply

---

16. S. 1400 (§ 1851), 93rd Cong., 1st Sess. (1973); and S. 1 (§ 1847), 94th Cong., 1st Sess. (1975).
17. S. 3858, p. 2.
18. *Id.*, pp. 3-4.
19. *Television in Day-to-Day Life: Patterns of Use, A Technical Report*, TELEVISION AND SOCIAL BEHAVIOR REPORTS AND PAPERS: VOLUME IV, (Washington: GPO) 1972, p. 143.

to the performer's or speaker's conduct on a cable public access channel.[20]

In its legislative proposal, the Commission purposefully chose to define its terminology. Using dictionary definitions, the proposal stated that a "person" violates the law if that person "disseminates" obscene or indecent materials. The Commission chose to use the word "disseminates" rather than the words "language" and "utter," used in Section 1464 of the United States Criminal Code. The Commission apparently believed that the term "disseminates" could be applied to offensive conduct and language. Since the Commission wanted its proposed legislation to ban morally offensive conduct as well as language, the Commission believed the phrase "disseminates obscene or indecent materials" was broader than the words used in Section 1464, "utter" and "language." The Commission also deleted the word "profane," as it was used in Section 1464, since it had never been adequately defined by the courts.

Although the Commission believed that the contemporary "community standard" concept should be applied with respect to its proposal, it actually wanted the courts to decide whether this standard should be based on local, state, or national standards and by whom it should be applied. Since the constitutionality of the Commission's power in this area had not yet been clearly tested in the courts, the Commission did not attempt to define contemporary community standards. (Since *Miller* and other related cases addressed themselves to local community standards concerning the print media, but not the electronic media as previously indicated, the Commission was not sure whether the local community standard would apply as outlined in *Miller* and other recent print media cases.) Although the courts have acted on this question and others, as discussed below, to date the Congress has not acted on the Commission's legislative proposal.

WBAI OVERTURNED

The FCC's *WBAI* ruling on 21 February 1975 was appealed by the Pacifica Foundation to the United States Court of Appeals for the District of Columbia. Just prior to the oral argument of the case, the Commission—in response to a petition submitted by the Radio-Television News Directors Association—clarified its opinion to indicate that a broadcaster would not be held to account for the broadcast of instantaneous or ad-lib obscene or indecent materials during live on-the-spot bonafide news events coverage.[21]

20. S. 3858, pp. 2-5.
21. Pacifica Foundation, 59 FCC 2d 892 (1976).

Obscene/Indecent Programming

On 16 March 1977, the court of appeals in a 2-to-1 decision, overturned the Commission's decision in the Pacifica *WBAI* case in which the Commission tried to make a distinction between the electronic and the print media for First Amendment purposes, and to protect children in the audience.[22] Writing for the majority, Judge Edward A. Tamm said the Commission's order in the *WBAI* case violated the no-censorship provision (Section 326 of the Communications Act), was "overbroad," and "sweepingly forbids any broadcast of the seven words (from the George Carlin album) irrespective of context or however innocent or educational they may be."[23] Judge Tamm noted that the Commission's ruling would therefore prohibit the broadcast of certain Shakespearean plays, passages from the Bible, and the works of numerous prominent authors. He also said that the ruling was "vague in that it fails to define children."[24] Furthermore, Judge Tamm indicated that the Commission had failed to prove its case by distinguishing between the media, whereby such material would be protected in other (print) media, but subject to regulation in the broadcast media.[25]

Concurring with Judge Tamm was Chief Judge David Bazelon, who stated that it was not up to the federal government to engage in censorship on the rationale of aiding those parents who would like to restrict their children's programs.[26] Moreover, Judge Bazelon said the Commission "incorrectly assumes that material regulatable for children can be banned from broadcast."[27]

The court's decision also furthered discussion of the terms "obscenity" and "indecent." Judge Tamm felt it was not necessary to define "indecent" more narrowly than the term "obscenity."[28] He noted that the FCC's stance in the *WBAI* case was that "indecent" language was different from "obscenity" in that it lacked the element of appealing to a prurient interest, and when children are present, such language can not be held to have literary, artistic, political, or scientific value as outlined in the *Miller* case.[29] Judge Tamm reasoned that if the words which were prohibited by the Commission were "merely crude" or vulgar, but not obscene, they could "quite possibly have literary, political or artistic

---

22. Pacifica Foundation v. Federal Communications Commission, 181 U.S. App. D.C. 132, 556 F.2d 9 (1977). *See also, FCC Thrown Out of Censorship Business by D.C. Court,* BROADCASTING (March 21, 1977), pp. 27-28; and *Court Overturns FCC on "Dirty" Lingo,* VARIETY (March 23, 1977), pp. 53 and 72.
23. 181 U.S. App. D.C. 132, 556 F.2d at 19-23.
24. *Id.,* at 22.
25. *Id.,* at 19-23.
26. *Id.,* at 24-30. It is also interesting to note that unlike the figures used by the Commission in forming its legislative proposal concerning fewer children in the audience after 11:00 P.M. *(see note 19 above),* Judge Tamm cited a report that there were a large number of children present in the audience until 1:30 A.M.
27. 181 U.S. App. D.C. 132, 556 F.2d at 24-30.
28. *Id.,* at 19.
29. *Id.,* at 19-20.

value. Therefore, the non-obscene speech is entitled to First Amendment protection."[30]

The court's decision also referred to the contemporary community standards concept. Judge Bazelon noted that the Commission did not use the local community standards concept of the *Miller* decision, and admitted that only a national standard would be feasible for the Commission.[31]

Judge Leventhal dissented by stating that the only issue was whether or not the Commission could regulate the language "as broadcast."[32] He concluded, on the basis of protecting children from exposure to such language or of indicating that such language has any form of official approval, that the Commission was correct in determining such a daytime broadcast as indecent.[33]

CERTIORARI GRANTED

The Commission appealed the decision to the United States Supreme Court, which granted certiorari in early January 1978. From the granting of certiorari until the oral argument of the case before the court on 18 April 1978, there was a ground swell of support for *WBAI* which its licensee, the Pacifica Foundation, had not enjoyed in previous battles with the Commission.[34]

30. *Id.*, 20-21.
31. *Id.*, at 28.
32. *Id.*, at 31.
33. *Id.*, at 37 and note 18.
34. The "establishment" within the broadcasting industry in the past did not condone or support the rather free programming policies and formats of the Pacifica Foundation stations. Moreover, the industry did not support Pacifica when programming policies similar to those in the WBAI case were under FCC fire, such as in 1964. See Pacifica Foundation 36 FCC 147 (1964). The situation in 1978, however, was markedly different. BROADCASTING, in its 16 January 1978 issue, editorialized in support of Pacifica Foundation's WBAI. WBAI was also supported, in friend-of-court briefs by the CBS, NBC, ABC, and PBS networks; National Association of Broadcasters; National Radio Broadcasters Association; Radio-Television News Directors Association; Reporters' Committee for Freedom of the Press; Writers Guild of America-West; Authors League; Motion Picture Association of America; American Civil Liberties Union; and others. The Pacifica Foundation mounted a fund-raising campaign with a full-page advertisement in one industry publication entitled "Let's Hear It for the First Amendment (While We Still Can)," and the National Association of Broadcasters Television Code Board adopted, as a measure of self-regulation, a new provision (IV-8) for the TV Code during its January 17-20, 1978 meeting. See "Common Interest," BROADCASTING (January 16, 1978), p. 82; "All for One," BROADCASTING (February 20, 1978), p. 26; "Establishment Rushes to Side of Pacifica in WBAI Case," BROADCASTING (April 3, 1978), p. 42; "Let's Hear It for the First Amendment," BROADCASTING PROGRAMMING AND PRODUCTION (March/April 1978), p. 43; and "TV Board Affirms Code Obscenity Language, Ratifies Revised Provision on Gambling," CODE NEWS 11, nos. 1 and 2 (January-February 1978), p. 1.

The Supreme Court was faced with deciding whether the scope of any judicial review encompassed more than the FCC's declaratory ruling in *WBAI* that the George Carlin monologue was indecent "as broadcast"; whether such broadcast was "indecent" within the meaning of Section 1464 of the United States Criminal Code; whether the FCC's ruling was a violation of the no-censorship provision of Section 326 of the Communications Act of 1934; and whether the FCC's ruling violated the First Amendment.

On 3 July 1978, the final day of the court's 1977-1978 term, the Justices overturned the lower court ruling in a 5-to-4 vote and sustained the FCC's actions in the *WBAI* case.[35] The majority opinion was written by Justice Stevens for himself, Chief Justice Burger, and Justices Blackmun, Powell, and Rehnquist. In deciding whether the scope of judicial review encompassed more than the Commission's *WBAI* declaratory ruling that the Carlin monologue was indecent as broadcast, Justice Stevens stated in very specific language:

> The general statements in the Commission's memorandum opinion do not change the character of its order. Its action was an adjudication under the U. S. C. [Criminal Code]. . . . it did not purport to engage in formal rulemaking or in the promulgation of any regulations. The order "was issued in a special factual context"; questions concerning possible action in other contexts were expressly reserved for the future. The specific holding was carefully confined to the monologue "as broadcast."[36]

The court was blunt on the issue of whether the broadcast was indecent within the meaning of Section 1464:

> Because neither prior decisions nor the language or history of paragraph 1464 supports [Pacifica] . . . there is no basis for disagreeing with the Commission's conclusion that indecent language was used in the broadcast.[37]

Since the Commission took action in the form of its declaratory ruling after-the-fact, and did not engage in prior censorship, Justice Stevens concluded for the majority that the Commission had not violated Section 326 of the Communications Act. He also emphasized that Section 326 in no way limited "the Commission's authority to impose sanctions on

---

35. Federal Communications Commission v. Pacifica Foundation et al., U.S. Supreme Court Opinion No. 77-528, July 3, 1978; FCC v. Pacifica Foundation, 438 U.S. 726, 98 S. Ct. 3026 (1978).
36. Opinion No. 77-528, July 3, 1978 at 6.
37. *Id.,* at 13.

licensees who engage in obscene, indecent or profane broadcasting."[38]

The narrow construction by the court also led to its holding that the Commission had not violated the First Amendment:

> When the issue is narrowed to the facts of this case, the question is whether the First Amendment denies government any power to restrain the public broadcast of indecent language in any circumstances, for if the government has any such power, this was an appropriate occasion for its exercise. The words of the Carlin monologue are unquestionably "speech" within the meaning of the First Amendment. . . . Our past cases demonstrate, however, that no such absolute rule is mandated by the Constitution.
>
> . . . the question . . . is whether a broadcast of patently offensive words dealing with sex and excretion may be regulated because of its content. Obscene materials have been denied the protection of the First Amendment because their context is so offensive to contemporary moral standards. *Roth* v. *United States,* 345 U.S. 476.
>
> In this case it is undisputed that the context of Pacifica's broadcast was "vulgar," offensive and "shocking." . . . content of that character is not entitled to absolute constitutional protection in all circumstances.[39]

Finally, Justice Stevens set forth two major bases for the majority opinion which indicated the court's agreement with the Commission's rationales for its action. Justice Stevens concluded by stressing the narrowness of the court's holding.

> . . . First, the broadcast media have established a uniquely pervasive presence in the lives of all Americans. Patently offensive, indecent materials presented over the airways confronts the citizen, not only in public, but also plainly outweighs the First Amendment rights of an intruder.
>
> Because the broadcast audience is constantly tuning in and out, prior warnings cannot completely protect the listener or viewer from unexpected program content. . . . Second, broadcasting is uniquely accessible

38. *Id.,* at 10.
39. *Id.,* at 15-19.

to children, even those too young to read.... The ease with which children may obtain access to broadcast material... justify special treatment of indecent broadcasting.

It is appropriate in conclusion to emphasize the narrowness of our holding. This case does not involve a two-way radio conversation between a cab driver and dispatcher, or a telecast of an Elizabethan comedy. We have not decided that an occcasional expletive in either setting would justify any sanction, or, indeed, that this broadcast would justify a criminal prosecution. The Commission's decision rested entirely on a nuisance rationale under which context is all-important [time of day, audience composition].... As Mr. Justice Sutherland wrote, a "nuisance may be merely a right thing in the wrong place—like a pig in the parlor instead of the barnyard."... We simply hold that when the Commission finds that a pig has entered the parlor, the exercise of its regulatory power does not depend on proof that the pig is obscene.[40]

The dissents of Justices Brennan, Marshall, Stewart, and White were largely based on First Amendment principles and letting the public "choose those communications worthy of its attention from a market place unsullied by the censor's hand."[41] Justice Brennan responded to Justice Steven's animal metaphor by stating that to follow the majority's opinion would be "to burn the house to roast the pig."[42] A petition for rehearing, filed by *WBAI* and other groups, was denied on 2 October 1978.[43]

DISCUSSION

Although the court's decision was by no means unanimous, and the majority opinion narrow, some interpretations have been drawn:
  (1) Based on the pervasiveness, intrusion, audience composition, federal interest, and scarcity of frequency arguments, prior to judicial review, if any, the FCC has been empowered to use guidelines based on *Miller* and other related cases in making

---

40. *Id.,* at 20-21.
41. 77-528 (dissent) at 11.
42. *Id.,* at 5.
43. NAB Legal Dept., *Broadcasting and Government: Review of 1978 and Preview of 1979,* (Washington, D.C. NAB), 1979, p. 33.

judgments on alleged obscene or indecent program material.
(2) Such judgments will depend on the facts of each case, as in *WXPN, WBAI,* and *WGBH* (discussed below). In the absence of a total set of criteria, Commission decisions and any judicial review will remain on an ad hoc basis.
(3) In the specific instance of Pacifica Foundation's *WBAI,* the Commission's judgments were correct and upheld by the court. Moreover, the Commission's definition of "indecent" in *WBAI* (and its legislative proposal) was supported by the court.
(4) As a result of the *Illinois Citizens, WXPN,* and *WBAI* cases, there appear to be some established and interrelated criteria that can be employed by the Commission and accepted by the court. These criteria are the amount of material, time of broadcast, audience composition, and type of broadcast (free, cable, or pay-cable). Indeed, the first three criteria were employed just three weeks after the court's *WBAI* decision. On 20 July 1978, the Commission rejected the complaint of Morality in Media of Massachusetts (MMM) concerning alleged obscene and indecent material in episodes of "Vision," "Monty Python's Flying Circus," and "Masterpiece Theatre" broadcast on WGBH-TV in Boston.[44] The Commission held that the examples provided by MMM did not meet the court's definition of obscenity, and that certain words were broadcast only twice in one program after 11:00 P.M. and only once in another program broadcast at 5:30 P.M., rather than in a "concentrated and repeated assault," such as the Carlin monologue.[45] Therefore, the broadcast of a little or a lot of alleged obscene or indecent material at 4:00 P.M., as opposed to 4:00 A.M., could yield a multitude of different judgments based on the facts of each case.
(5) Since the amount of material broadcast is one of the criteria, a few minutes or one particular segment of an entire program could be judged indecent. Therefore, the concept of "material taken as a whole" in *Miller* does not necessarily apply.
(6) While the Supreme Court in *WBAI* did not address the issue of "local" community standards (enunciated in *Miller*) versus "national" standards, it appears to be in agreement with Judge Bazelon's view that the concept of national standards should apply for broadcasting. The fact that the majority in *WBAI* indicated that the FCC was empowered to make judgments on

---

44. *In re:* Application of WGBH Educational Foundation, FCC 2d 1250 (1978). *See also* "Which Way the Wind Blows at the FCC," BROADCASTING (July 24, 1978), pp. 31-32.
45. Id.

alleged obscene or indecent program material would seem to advocate a national standard, in contrast to the court's clarification of *Miller* in its 1974 decision in *Jenkins v. Georgia,* 418 U.S. 153 (1974), in which the court stated that a jury was by definition a legitimate body which reflected the "local" community standards in which it served.[46]

Thus some problems previously outlined[47] are again posed. In establishing national standards, the FCC is subject "to the political and budgetary pressures which are exerted by both the executive and legislative branches of government"[48] and the general public. Even though the federal courts are not subject to such pressures and "have a more stable composition over time,"[49] there is no guarantee of judicial review of any FCC decision. Moreover, since the court's decision in *WBAI,* the Commission has indicated that it intends to stay out of programming as much as possible and has re-emphasized the narrowness of the *WBAL* ruling informally and in its *WGBH-TV* decision.

Furthermore, instead of tenaciously holding onto the First Amendment—whereby the broadcaster "would rather fight than switch"—those in the past who have been recipients of a Section 1464 violation and have been fined, have preferred to pay rather than fight.[50] Citizens groups such as those in Illinois, or licensees like the Pacifica Foundation, have been the exceptions.

In conclusion, future FCC decisions in the area of obscenity and indecency will apparently be few. Unless those future decisions are appealed to the courts, or until Congress acts on the Commission's legislative proposal, more definitive guidelines will elude us. Regulation of obscene or indecent programming, although somewhat clearer, still remains cloudy.

---

46. 418 U.S. 153 (1974).
47. Feldman and Tickton, p. 280.
48. *Id.*
49. *Id.*
50. In both the WUHY-FM Eastern Educational Media, 24 FCC 2d 408 (1970), and the WGLD-AM Sonderling Broadcasting, 41 FCC 2d 777 (1973), cases the broadcasters paid their $500 and $2000 fines respectively to the Commission, rather than go through the expense of an appeal.

DENISE M. TRAUTH
JOHN L. HUFFMAN

Heightened Judicial Scrutiny: A Test for the First Amendment Rights of Children

Dr. Denise M. Trauth is Assistant Professor of Speech Communication and chair of the Radio-Television-Film Program at Bowling Green State University. She teaches in the area of broadcast regulation.
Dr. John L. Huffman is Associate Professor of Journalism and a teacher of Mass Communication Law at Bowling Green State University.

INTRODUCTION

The legal area of children's* rights under the First Amendment to the Constitution of the United States is unexplored and judicially un-

This study was made possible in part by a grant from the Faculty Research Committee, Bowling Green State University (Ohio).

*"Children" is used generically to refer to all persons who have not reached the age of majority. "Minors" is used interchangeably with "children."

developed. An initial analysis of the area reveals two basic facts. First, the courts have not yet articulated any special factors that might determine *how* existing legal mechanisms for analyzing the First Amendment rights of *adults* can be applied to minors. Second, the constitutional tests of equal protection traditionally used to determine if an adult has been afforded civil rights are themselves, as will be shown, in a state of flux.

In order to delineate and provide a means of discussing the First Amendment rights of children, this paper proposes a test, the "heightened judicial scrutiny test," which can be used as a legal litmus in the area of children and the First Amendment; various laws and court decisions concerning minors can be measured against the test with the goal of developing a unified approach to the First Amendment rights of children.

THE CONSTITUTIONAL RIGHTS OF CHILDREN

An examination of the rights that adhere particularly to children quickly reveals that the notion of a special legal status for minors and the attendant protectionist attitude that our society takes toward them is a relatively recent phenomenon. Until the seventeenth century no special emphasis was given to childhood as a separate phase of the life cycle. "Obviously infants needed special care and attention, but once they had been weaned and had achieved a minimum of ability to take care of themselves, they became "small adults"—mingling, working and playing with mature people."[1] As the French intellectual historian Phillip Aries has pointed out:

> In the middle ages . . . and for a long time after that in the lower classes, children were mixed with adults as soon as they were considered capable of doing without their mothers or nannies, not long after a tardy weaning (in other words at about the age of seven). They immediately went straight into the great community of men, sharing in the work and play of their companions, old and young alike.[2]

In the seventeenth century, attitudes toward children changed. Clergymen and humanitarians of this time encouraged the separation of

---

1. *See* P. Mussen, J. Conger & J. Kagan, Child Development and Personality, at 7 (1969) [hereinafter cited as Mussen, Conger, & Kagan]. *See also* J. Pikunas, *Fundamental Child Psychology,* at 6-11 (1965).
2. Phillipe Aries, Centuries of Childhood: A Social History of Family Life, at 411, (1962).

children from adults, and, as these thinkers influenced parents, a whole new attitude toward the child resulted. The child emerged as a special person—primitive, irrational, and innocent.[3]

This increase in concern for the welfare of children had as a corollary the legal notion that minors were the charges of the family and the state and were legally unable to act for themselves.

> In colonial America children were treated as servants, owing strict obedience to their parents and holding positions of complete subservience within the family unit. The common law did not distinguish between the infant and the mature teenager, categorizing both as minors and generally treating them as the "property" of their parents, who could make any and all decisions affecting them.[4]

Although this view of children has been rejected by the United States Supreme Court in recent years,[5] the Court has still not analyzed the "totality of the relationship of the minor and the State."[6]

The Court has recognized that children "are 'persons' under our Constitution,"[7] and that they "are possessed of fundamental rights which the state must respect."[8] Similarly, it has stated that "constitutional rights do not mature and come into being magically only when one attains the state-defined age of majority. Minors, as well as adults, are protected by the Constitution and possess constitutional rights."[9]

But other than these very general statements, the Court has provided little commentary regarding how and to what extent the rights of adults apply to children. Recently, in dealing with minor's attempts to receive medical services without parental consent, the Court has taken the opportunity to comment somewhat more specifically on the rights of children. For this reason the case containing these comments, *Bellotti* v. *Baird*,[10] invites examination.

The issue the Court faced in this case, which was decided in July 1979, was the constitutionality of a Massachusetts statute that required

---

3. MUSSEN, CONGER, & KAGAN at 7.
4. *Parental Consent Requirements and Privacy Rights of Minors: The Contraceptive Controversy*, 88 HARV. L. REV. 1001, 1008 (1975) [hereinafter cited as *Parental Consent Requirements*].
5. *See* Tinker v. Des Moines, 393 U.S. 503 (1969), and *In re* Gault, 387 U.S. 1 (1967).
6. Ginsberg v. N.Y., 390 U.S. 629, 636 (1968).
7. 393 U.S. 503, 511 (1969).
8. *Id.*
9. Planned Parenthood of Cent. Mo. v. Danforth, 428 U.S. 52, 74 (1976).
10. 61 L.Ed. 2d 797 (1979).

unmarried minor girls desiring an abortion to first attempt to gain approval of both parents and subsequently to petition a judge if one or both parents refused consent.

The Court began its eight-to-one majority opinion, written by Justice Powell, with a statement about the rights of children: "A child, merely on account of his minority, is not beyond the protection of the Constitution. . . . Whatever may be their precise impact, neither the Fourteenth Amendment nor the Bill of Rights is for adults alone."[11]

But the Court went on to quote Justice Frankfurter's 1953 statement that "legal theories and their phrasing in other cases readily lead to fallacious reasoning if uncritically transferred to determination of a state's duty toward children."[12]

Why can the rights of children be limited? The Court articulates three reasons that make the limitation acceptable. First is the peculiar vulnerability of children. The Court points out that this factor has led to the establishment of a system of juvenile courts, an arrangement that is constitutionally permissible: "The State is entitled to adjust its legal system to account for children's vulnerability and their needs."[13]

The second reason for such limitations is the "inability of children to make critical decisions in an informed, mature manner."[14] Here the Court referred to past decisions in which it has held that "the States validly may limit the freedom of children to choose for themselves in the making of important, affirmative choices with potentially serious consequences."[15]

The last reason is the importance of the parental role in child rearing. The Court noted that the tradition of parental authority, long accepted by our legal system, "is not inconsistent with our tradition of individual liberty."[16]

Having thus outlined the rights of children and the instances in which these rights may be limited, the Court held the Massachusetts law unconstitutional because it failed to provide an alternative permission procedure for those minors who did not want to seek parental authorization. The Court felt that the state law unduly burdened the minor's fundamental right to abortion, especially in light of the time factor: "A pregnant adolescent . . . cannot preserve for long the possibility of aborting, which effectively expires in a matter of weeks from the onset of pregnancy."[17]

11. *Id.* at 807.
12. *Id.*
13. *Id.* at 808.
14. *Id.* at 807.
15. *Id.* at 808.
16. *Id.* at 810.
17. *Id.* at 813.

Because of the unique nature and consequences of an abortion decision, the Court was loathe "to give a third party an absolute, and possibly arbitrary, veto over the decision...."[18] Wading further into the delicate issue of the parent's right to make such a decision for his or her child, the Court admonished the state "to act with particular sensitivity when it legislates *to foster parental involvement in this matter.*"[19] (Emphasis added.)

To summarize *Bellotti,* the case would seem to yield three important points: (1) the rights of children may be different from those of adults in arrangements such as the juvenile court system, in instances in which children could make critical decisions that could result in their harm, and in cases that defer to parental authority; (2) when a right may effectively expire due to a time factor, the state must use extreme care in the exercise of its authority; and (3) although the Court accords great respect to the role of parents in the upbringing of their children, the state must be sensitive when it fosters parental involvement in the exercise of rights of the minor.

With *Bellotti* as a backdrop, it is productive to examine two instances in which the Court has specifically dealt with the involvement of children in First Amendment issues.

THE FIRST AMENDMENT RIGHTS OF CHILDREN

Ginsberg v. *New York*[20] tested the constitutionality of a state law which prohibited the sale to minors under seventeen years of age material defined to be obscene on the basis of its appeal to children. At the outset of the case, New York determined that the "girlie" magazines sold to a minor in this case would not be considered obscene for adults. Thus, the issue the Court faced was not whether such material could be sold to adults but, rather, if a state could apply different standards for determining what is obscene for children.

In determining that the state does have the power to adopt what has been termed "variable obscenity" standards,[21] the Court pointed out the general authority of legislatures:

> That the State has power to make that adjustment [i.e., differing standards for obscenity] seems clear, for we have recognized that even where there is an invasion of protected freedoms "the power of the state to control

18. *Id.*
19. *Id.* at 812.
20. 390 U.S. 629 (1968).
21. "Variable obscenity" is the name given to laws such as that of New York.

the conduct of children reaches beyond its authority over adults."[22]

This authority derives from two interests. The first is the right of parents to control their children:

> [C]onstitutional interpretation has consistently recognized that parents' claims to authority in their own households to direct the rearing of their children is basic in the structure of our society. . . . The legislature could properly conclude that parents and others, teachers, for example, who have this primary responsibility for children's well-being are entitled to the support of laws designed to aid discharge of that responsibility. . . . Moreover, the prohibition against sales to minors does not bar parents who so desire from purchasing the magazines for their children.[23]

The second interest promoted by this law is the concern of the state itself for the well-being of its youth:

> [T]he knowledge that parental control or guidance cannot always be provided and society's transcendent interest in protecting the welfare of children justify reasonable regulation of the sale of material to them. It is, therefore, altogether fitting and proper for a state to include in a statute designed to regulate the sale of pornography to children special standards . . .[24]

Finally, the Court pointed out that since "obscenity is not within the area of protected speech and press,"[25] this statute does not invade constitutional rights. For this reason, the Court rejected the assertion by New York that the sale of such material to minors poses "a clear and present danger to the people of the state,"[26] and noted that such a test is not required where unprotected speech is at issue.

Application of the "clear and present danger"[27] doctrine would

---

22. 390 U.S. 629, 638 (1968).
23. *Id.* at 639.
24. *Id.* at 640.
25. *Id.* at 635.
26. *Id.* at 641.
27. Justice Holmes authored the clear and present danger doctrine in Schenck v. United States, 249 U.S. 47 (1919), as a guide to the boundaries of protected speech. Under the doctrine, political expression can be punished when the circumstances are such that they "create a clear and present danger that they will bring about the substantive evils that Congress has a right to prevent."

compel the state to demonstrate a showing of circumstances which could lead to violence. The Court was skeptical about this link and registered doubt that "this finding by New York expressed an accepted scientific fact."[28] Nevertheless, the law is upheld because the test is *not* required and because the law promotes the legitimate interest of the state in its youth.

In his concurring opinion, Justice Stewart sums up the underlying philosophy of the majority:

> I think a State may permissibly determine that, at least in some precisely delineated areas, a child ... is not possessed of that full capacity for individual choice which is the presupposition of First Amendment guarantees. It is only upon such a premise, I should suppose, that a State may deprive children of other rights—the right to marry, for example, or the right to vote—deprivations that would be constitutionally intolerable for adults.[29]

In contemplating the implications of *Ginsberg,* two factors must be kept in mind. The first is that in using obscenity doctrine to hold the statute valid, and not some other ground, such as the Fourth Amendment, the Court was in a sense, since obscenity is not protected speech, making this a non-First Amendment issue; therefore the ability of the states to regulate the reading matter of minors is a limited one. "*Ginsberg* should not be read to support broad state restrictions on the access of minors to nonobscene material such as violent films even if the state reasonably judges them to be injurious to minors."[30] The second factor is that the New York statute was very narrowly drawn. It only restricted visual material of a specific nature and said nothing whatever about the publication of ideas.[31]

The next case under review, *Tinker* v. *Des Moines Independent School District,*[32] dealt with communication, which was very clearly within the ambit of the First Amendment. This case grew out of a ruling by public school officials that prohibited students from wearing black armbands as symbols of their sentiments against the Vietnam war. In its adjudication of the case, three facts were emphasized by the Supreme Court: first, only seven out of eighteen thousand Des Moines schoolchildren chose to wear the armbands; second, the administrators' contention

---

28. 390 U.S. 629, 641 (1968).
29. *Id.* at 649–50.
30. *The Supreme Court: 1967 Term,* 82 HARV. L. REV. 63, 127 (1968).
31. *Id.* at 127–28.
32. 393 U.S. 503 (1969).

that a disturbance which would interfere with school discipline would result from the display was not realized; and third, students in the schools prior to this incident had been allowed to war political symbols such as the Nazi Iron Cross and national political campaign buttons.

In its opinion, which held unconstitutional the ruling of the school administrators, the Court took the opportunity to emphasize the First Amendment rights of children:

> First Amendment rights, applied in light of the special character of the school environment, are available to teachers and students. It can hardly be argued that either students or teachers shed their constitutional rights to freedom of speech or expression at the schoolhouse gate. This has been the unmistakable holding of this Court for almost 50 years.[33]

The Court displayed its respect for the authority of the states and school officials to control conduct in the schools, but pointed out that this case deals not with conduct "that intrudes upon the work of the school or the rights of other students"[34] but, rather, with "direct, primary First Amendment rights akin to 'pure speech.' "[35] A simple fear on the part of school officials that a disturbance may erupt is not sufficient ground to deny First Amendment rights:

> [I]n our system, undifferentiated fear or apprehension of disturbance is not enough to overcome the right to freedom of expression. Any departure from absolute regimentation may cause trouble. Any variation from the majority's opinion may inspire fear.... But our Constitution says we must take this risk ...[36]

The Court went on to reinforce the full constitutional rights of children:

> Students in school as well as out of school are "persons" under our Constitution. They are possessed of fundamental rights which the State must respect, just as they themselves must respect their obligations to the State. In our system, students may not be regarded as closed-circuit recipients of only that which the State chooses to communicate.... In the absence of a specific

33. *Id.* at 506.
34. *Id.* at 508.
35. *Id.*
36. *Id.*

showing of constitutionally valid reasons to regulate their speech, students are entitled to free expression of their views.[37]

This reference to an "absence of a specific showing of constitutionally valid reasons to regulate their speech" suggests that in *Tinker* the Court was applying the clear and present danger doctrine. There was no showing by officials that the speech in question might lead to violence. In fact, the officials' position was based on the feeling that "schools are no place for demonstrations."[38] Since there was no danger of violence, under the clear and present danger test, the speech could not be proscribed.

It should be noted that in this case the Court made no attempt to differentiate between the First Amendment rights of adults and minors as Justice Stewart did in his concurring opinion in *Ginsberg*. Since the Court chose not to qualify its opinion, it "appears to have concluded either that minors do in fact possess the necessary capacity for claiming and exercising First Amendment rights or that the level of capacity is not crucial to making the threshold determination whether such rights are applicable to minors."[39]

The apparent differences in the holdings of *Ginsberg* and *Tinker*, which were decided within a year of each other, can be explained in terms of the nature of the expression involved; one dealt with obscenity (a form of communication not protected by the First Amendment) and the other with political speech (the very type of communication some commentators believe the First Amendment was expressly written to protect).[40]

However, at least one member of the Court was confused enough by the distance between the two holdings to remark: "I cannot share the Court's uncritical assumption that . . . the First Amendment rights of children are co-extensive with those of adults. Indeed, I had thought the Court decided otherwise just last term in *Ginsberg* . . ."[41]

This confusion, unmitigated by scholarly inquiry into the area, suggests that what is needed is a general theory of the First Amendment rights of children, a theory that might provide a test that could be applied to a variety of factual situations and still yield a unified approach to this complex area.

---

37. *Id.* The notion that children have obligations to the state adds emphasis to the Court's determination that children have constitutional rights. To have responsibilities to the state suggests that one is a participating, respected citizen. *See* Karst, *The Supreme Court: 1976 Term*, 91 HARV. L. REV. 1, 8–11 (1977).
38. *Id.* at 509 note 3.
39. *Parental Consent Requirements,* at 1009.
40. *See generally* A. MEIKLEJOHN, POLITICAL FREEDOM (1948).
41. 393 U.S. 503 (1969).

Such a theory is especially crucial at a time when administrative agencies, such as the Federal Trade Commission and the Federal Communications Commission, are enacting administrative laws in the belief that children must be protected from various types of communication.

In his book, *The System of Freedom of Expression,* Thomas Emerson refers to the need for such a test, at least when questions of obscenity are involved:

> [T]he full protection theory of the First Amendment cannot be applied. Nor, in view of the present lack of knowledge about the subject, can the clear and present danger test be employed, or any test based on the effect of obscenity on children. Even a balancing test would not be feasible. We are left then, at least for the time being, with little more than a due process test—that the restriction be a reasonable one.[42]

This paper suggests that a refined Fourteenth Amendment equal protection test is most suitable to determine the First Amendment rights of children.[43]

FOURTEENTH AMENDMENT AND EQUAL PROTECTION

The Fourteenth Amendment to the U.S. Constitution, ratified in 1868, was passed in reaction to President Johnson's veto of the Civil Rights Bill of 1866, which was to guarantee blacks the same civil rights as whites.

Although constitutional historians debate the many purposes of the framers of the amendment, there is no doubt that, whatever else they may have wished to do, they did intend to validate the 1866 act and thereby ensure that blacks had equality of legal status and voting rights.[44]

---

42. T. Emerson, *The System of Freedom of Expression,* at 502 (1970).
43. The first specific transfusion of First Amendment rights into the Fourteenth Amendment by way of the due process clause was achieved in Gitlow v. N.Y., 268 U.S. 652 (1925). In dicta in the case, Justice Stanford "offhandedly extended the limitations on legislation curtailing freedom of expression binding on the federal government by reason of the First Amendment to the states . . . " (D. Gillmor, & J. Barron, Mass Communication Law, at 21 [1979]). In Gitlow the Court said that "for present purposes" freedom of speech and of the press are among the fundamental rights and liberties protected by the due process clause of the Fourteenth Amendment from impairment by the states. 268 U.S. 652, 666 (1925).
44. Karst, at 11–12.

Nevertheless, the language of the amendment does go beyond the prohibition of racial discrimination:

> All persons born or naturalized in the United States, and subject to the jurisdiction thereof, are citizens of the United States and of the State wherein they reside. No state shall make or enforce any law which shall abridge the privileges or immunities of citizens of the United States; nor shall any State deprive any person of life, liberty, or property, without due process of law; nor deny to any person within its jurisdiction the equal protection of the laws.[45]

By choosing language that went beyond the tangible harm they were seeking to redress, that is, unequal treatment of blacks, the drafters of the Fourteenth Amendment provided generations of jurists and legal scholars with words that do not assert a specific rule but, rather, state a principle capable of a wide range of meaning.

One hundred years of interpretation of the amendment and of its final Equal Protection Clause has pumped solidity into the abstract principle that application of the amendment usually begins when a group or classification has been drawn by the state or by some agency thereof and people in the group claim that this grouping or "discrimination" denies them equal protection of the law.

A determination of whether equal protection has been denied must take into account the fact that "all legislation involves classification of some sort."[46] Even the most noncontroversial statutes, such as those punishing persons convicted of murder, divide people into groups according to conduct and motivation, and treat various groups differently. Accordingly, when applying equal protection, courts have operationalized "equal" to mean similar and "protection" to mean treatment. Thus the Fourteenth Amendment does not require that every single person be dealt with in exactly the same way but rather that similar persons be treated similarly.

The first step then, and the central one for equal protection analysis, involves determining which lines or classifications are permissible.[47] The key concept here is that of "relatedness." A continuum exists with "completely related" or "reasonable" at one end and "completely un-

---

45. U.S. CONST. amend. XIV, § I.
46. E. CORWIN, THE CONSTITUTION AND WHAT IT MEANS TODAY (revised by H. Chase, C. Ducat, 1974), at 403.
47. Fiss, *Groups and the Equal Protection Clause,* 5 PHIL. and PUB.AFF.107, 108–109 (1976).

related" or "arbitrary" at the other. A grouping is deemed "arbitrary" if the criterion upon which it is based is unrelated to the state's purpose for the legislation at issue. For example, if a state, for the purpose of curbing juvenile crime, imposed a curfew on all blue-eyed minors, the state would be guilty of an "arbitrary" grouping since no relationship exists between blue-eyed juveniles and a tendency toward criminal conduct. On the other hand, a grouping is reasonable if its criteria are related to the state's purpose. For example, if a state imposed a fine on all convicted juveniles, the grouping of juveniles would be considered reasonable because a manifest relationship exists between convicted juveniles and crime.

An oversimplification results from using obvious examples: these illustrations suggest that relatedness and unrelatedness are discrete qualities when in fact they are not. It is usually not a question of whether the criterion and the end are related or unrelated but, rather, one of how well they are related. A criterion can be considered arbitrary even when related to the purpose of the law if the relationship is distant. The Supreme Court and its commentators have labeled this distant relationship "ill-fit."[48]

Ill-fit is the consequence of two types of legislation: overinclusive and underinclusive. The former occurs when a statute picks out or affects more people than it should. Underinclusiveness results when a statute affects fewer people than it should. For example, if Congress, upon a finding that saccharin is carcinogenic, prohibited the sale of soda pop containing saccharin, the law could be termed underinclusive since soda pop is only one of many foods containing the sweetener. If, on the other hand, the law prohibited the sale of all artificially sweetened soda pop, it would be overinclusive since saccharin is only one of many artificial sweeteners, some of which may not be carcinogenic.

It should be apparent that a state could use this process of fitting a means to an end to defend legislation of dubious quality. For example, if a state's purpose were to subordinate women to men rather than to choose the best students for admission to professional schools, then gender would be well-suited for deciding who should be admitted to the state's law and medical schools. Under the means-end test, this classification would be related and permissible. Thus, in equal protection analysis it is necessary to go beyond a mere test of fit to a second step: identifying the state's purpose for the law and determining whether this purpose is legitimate.

In the great bulk of the cases it decides, the Supreme Court has

---

48. *Id.* at 111.

deferred to the wisdom of state legislatures and assumed that these bodies, when legislating to protect the health, welfare, and safety of their citizens, were guided by legitimate state purposes.[49] As the Court noted in a case questioning the limits of a state's police power,

> [A] State has the same undeniable and unlimited jurisdiction over all persons and things within its territorial limits, as any foreign nation, where that jurisdiction is not surrendered or restrained by the Constitution of the United States. That, by virtue of this, it is not only the right, but the bounden and solemn duty of a state to advance the safety, happiness and prosperity of its people . . . by any and every act of legislation which it may deem to be conducive to these ends . . .[50]

However, there have been instances when the Court determined that a state's purpose was not legitimate.

In *Loving v. Virginia*[51] the Court pronounced as illicit the purpose of a state law and went on to explain that this examination of purpose is appropriate since the Equal Protection Clause requires more than a simple showing that all persons in a given class are treated similarly. In 1967, Virginia enforced a miscegenation statute, the purpose of which was to preserve the racial integrity of its white citizens. Virginia contended that the statute did not violate the Fourteenth Amendment because it punished equally both the white and black participants in the interracial marriage.

In repudiating Virginia's contention that the Equal Protection Clause requires only equal treatment, the Court stated: "[W]e reject the

---

49. The principle of separation of powers among our three branches of government is not specifically declared in the federal Constitution; it is implicit in the organization of the first three articles: (1) "All legislative powers herein granted shall be vested in the Congress of the United States," (2) "The executive power shall be vested in the President of the United States," (3) "The judicial power shall be vested in one Supreme Court and in such inferior courts as the Congress shall . . . ordain and establish."
    From this separation is derived the doctrine that certain functions, such as the legislative one may properly be exercised by only a particular branch of government and that one branch may not interfere with another by usurping its powers. Because of this separation of powers, augmented by the authority of the Tenth Amendment that "All powers not delegated to the United States by the Constitution . . . are reserved to the States respectively . . .," the Supreme Court routinely defers to the wisdom of state legislatures and assumes that these bodies are guided by legitimate state purposes.
50. Mayor of New York v. Miln, 36 U.S. 102, 139 (1837).
51. 388 U.S. 1 (1967).

notion that the mere 'equal application' of a statute containing racial classifications is enough to remove the classification from the Fourteenth Amendment's proscription of all invidious racial discrimination."[52]

Then the Court went on to reject the stated intent of the law: "There is patently no legitimate overriding purpose independent of invidious racial discrimination which justifies this classification."[53]

This two-step test of the application of equal protection—determination first of a proper legislative purpose and second of a rational relationship between means and end—is termed the rational basis test. In addition to giving a presumption of validity to state purposes under the rational basis test, the Court also "rather generously defers to legislative judgment on classification."[54] This deferral is necessary since some measure of overinclusiveness and underinclusiveness can be discovered in any law. It is up to the courts to decide how ill-fit the relationship between the criterion and the end must be before it is considered arbitrary; the rational basis test gives wide latitude to the states in this respect. This latitude appeared to wane in the late 1960s as the Supreme Court evolved a more stringent Fourteenth Amendment and thus developed what has been called the "new equal protection."

The new test—called "close scrutiny"—is based on two doctrines: that of suspect classification and of fundamental rights. These two doctrines are essentially standards for determining the degree of fit required between means and ends. In contrast to the looser "rational basis test" which tolerates broad margins of overinclusiveness and underinclusiveness, these two doctrines require a tighter fit.

A fundamental right is one which is either directly guaranteed in the Bill of Rights or emanates from one of these rights.[55] The Court has termed these to be "the basic civil rights of man, fundamental to our very existence and survival."[56] The right to vote,[57] to marry,[58] to marital privacy,[59] to procreation,[60] to abortion,[61] and to travel,[62] are some of the rights regarded as fundamental by the Court.

52. Id. at 8.
53. *Id.* at 11.
54. A. MASON & W. BEANEY, AMERICAN CONSTITUTIONAL LAW, at 461 (1978).
55. As the Court pointed out in Griswold v. Conn., "[S]pecific guarantees in the Bill of Rights have penumbras, formed by emanations from those guarantees that help give them life and substance." 381 U.S. 479, 484 (1965). In this case, the Court viewed privacy as emanating from the First, Third, Fourth, Fifth, and Ninth Amendments.
56. Loving v. Va., 388 U.S. 1, 12 (1967).
57. Harper v. Va. Bd. of Elections, 383 U.S. 663 (1966).
58. 388 U.S. 1 (1967).
59. Griswold v. Conn., 381 U.S. 479 (1965).
60. Skinner v. Okla. 316 U.S. 535 (1942).
61. Roe v. Wade, 410 U.S. 113 (1973).
62. Shapiro v. Thompson, 394 U.S. 618 (1969).

The suspect classification doctrine grew out of the Court's recognition that classifications drawn along racial lines are inherently suspect and carry "a very heavy burden of justification."[63] Once the suspect classification principle had become clearly established in race cases, other forms of discrimination began to be attacked on the ground that they too were suspect. Race[64] and alienage[65] have been firmly established as suspect classifications. Whether or not illegitimacy,[66] sex,[67] and poverty[68] are suspect classifications has been debated.

Under the "new equal protection" strict scrutiny test, whenever either a suspect classification or a fundamental right is involved, a higher standard than that of the rational basis test must be used. This stricter standard requires that in order to survive review, the state law at issue must further a "compelling state interest" and must be less restrictive of federally protected rights than any alternative means of promoting that interest.[69]

Strict scrutiny can be contrasted with rational basis as follows: rational basis requires a proper legislative purpose, strict scrutiny requires a compelling state interest; rational basis requires a rational relationship between the means and the end, strict scrutiny requires that the state use the best and narrowest method available. Finally, while rational basis gives a presumption of validity to the state, strict scrutiny places the burden of proving a compelling state interest on the state.[70]

This two-tiered approach to equal protection was very much the product of the Warren Court. Since the establishment of the Court of Chief Justice Burger, the strict scrutiny test seems reserved for a very few cases—usually those involving racial discrimination. In its place the Court has adopted a test that is less demanding than strict scrutiny but more stringent than rational basis.

---

63. Loving v. Va., 388 U.S. 1, 9 (1967).
64. *Id.*
65. Graham v. Richardson, 403 U.S. 365 (1971).
66. Levy v. La., 391 U.S. 68 (1968).
67. Reed v. Reed, 404 U.S. 71 (1971).
68. San Antonio Ind. School Dist. v. Rodriguez, 411 U.S. 1 (1973).
69. Gunther, *In Search of an Evolving Doctrine on a Changing Court: A Model For a Newer Equal Protection,* 86 HARV. L. REV. 1, 105–106 (1972).
70. *Groups and the Equal Protection Clause,* at 116. A compelling state interest is a purpose "so important that it excuses imperfect means. This doctrine seems to have its roots in the *Japanese Relocation Cases* [Korematsu v. United States, 323 U.S. 214 (1944)] where the Supreme Court permitted the use of a racial or national-origin criterion (clearly a suspect one) for determining who should be relocated and otherwise confined. The state purpose—self-preservation of the nation in time of war—was deemed to be of sufficient importance to excuse the overinclusiveness (not all Japanese were security risks) and the underinclusiveness (those of German origin might be as much of a security risk)."

In two recent cases[71] the Court has applied this test. Both dealt with groups that, while not conclusively suspect, do represent classifications about which the Court has remained skeptical: gender and illegitimacy. This test would seem to have two parts. The first involves a determination that the group, while not suspect, "is analogous in many respects to the personal characteristics that have been held suspect when used as a basis of statutory differentiations."[72] The second part involves a judicial awareness that these classifications are subject to scrutiny under the Equal Protection Clause."[73] Although "classifications based on [this analogy] . . . fall into a realm of less than strictest scrutiny . . . [we] also establish that the scrutiny is not a toothless one."[74] In order to withstand a challenge, the classification "must serve important government objectives and must be substantially related to the achievement of those objectives."[75]

The essential differences between this test (which can be termed "heightened judicial scrutiny") and the close scrutiny test are that the former test involves "scrutiny," the latter "close scrutiny"; the former test involves a group "analogous" to suspect, the latter suspect; and the former test requires that legislation serve "important government objectives," and the latter a "compelling state interest."

The Court has provided some commentary regarding what are *not* important government objectives: avoiding intrafamily controversy[76]; reducing the workload on courts[77]; and administrative ease and convenience.[78]

"HEIGHTENED JUDICIAL SCRUTINY" APPLIED TO CHILDREN

As we suggested above, the development of a unified approach to children's First Amendment rights requires that a test be developed which can be applied to a number of legal issues involving freedom of

---

71. Craig v. Boren, 429 U.S. 190 (1976), and Trimble v. Gordon, 430 U.S. 762 (1977). Craig involved a gender-based classification and Trimble dealt with a state law that made different provisions for legitimate and illegitimate children inheriting by intestate succession. In Craig the Court used the test outlined in Reed v. Reed, 404 U.S. 71 (1971), as its guide.
72. 430 U.S. 762, 767 (1977).
73. 429 U.S. 190, 197 (1976).
74. 430 U.S. 762, 767 (1977).
75. 420 U.S. 190, 197 (1976).
76. Reed v. Reed, 404 U.S. 71 (1971).
77. *Id.*
78. Stanley v. Ill., 405 U.S. 465 (1972).

speech vis-à-vis minors. The heightened judicial scrutiny test would seem appropriate because it provides a mechanism for discussing the exercise of a fundamental right by a group that, although not suspect, is regularly classified on the basis of personal characteristics.

Why should children constitute a classification that is at least suspicious if not suspect? Kenneth Karst[79] has suggested that there are two factors relevant in determining the degree to which a classification is suspect: one emphasizes the value of respect—classification on the basis of a trait that is immutable and highly visible leads to a system of thought dominated by stereotypes which often imply the inferiority of the person so categorized. The other emphasizes the value of participation. This factor may seem unrelated to children since their ostensible participation in the democracy is precluded. But the First Amendment protection for freedom of expression is not limited to political expression. As Thomas Emerson has pointed out: "The principle also carries beyond the political realm. It embraces the right to participate in the building of the whole culture, and includes freedom of expression in religion, literature, art, science, and all areas of human learning and knowledge."[80] If the ability to actively participate in the democracy were a criterion for suspectness, then alienage, for example, could not constitute. But the Court has gone to great lengths to stipulate that although aliens may not vote, their categorization is suspect and they must be allowed to participate in institutions such as the state bar[81] and the civil service.[82]

Perhaps the strongest reason in favor of considering children suspect in this context is because discrimination against children, and the attendant limit on their right to receive information, invades one of the most fundamental interests of children: the interest in becoming an informed member of the adult society.[83]

Given that for the sake of the present argument, the classification of children is suspect enough to trigger the heightened judicial scrutiny test, two questions must be answered: (1) *Does the regulation at issue serve an important government objective?* and (2) *Is the regulation substantially related to the achievement of that objective?*

In order to apply these two criteria, it is instructive to look at a factual situation that the Supreme Court faced recently in *Federal Communications Commission* v. *Pacifica Foundation*.[84] At two o'clock in the

---

79. Karst, at 22–25.
80. Emerson, at 7.
81. *In re* Griffiths, 413 U.S. 717 (1973).
82. Sugarman v. Dougall, 413 U.S. 634 (1973).
83. This reasoning parallels that of Karst at 33.
84. 438 U.S. 726 (1978).

afternoon a noncommercial radio station in New York City played the recording "Filthy Words," taped by satiric humorist George Carlin. The recording was played during a program about contemporary society's attitude toward language. Because the recording contained, according to Carlin, "the words you couldn't say on the public airwaves," listeners were advised immediately before its broadcast that it included "sensitive language that might be regarded as offensive to some."

A man who had heard the recording while driving with his fifteen-year-old son[85] complained to the FCC. In its response, the station explained that "Carlin is not mouthing obscenities, he is merely using words to satirize as harmless and essentially silly our attitudes toward those words."[86]

The issue the Court faced in this case, of importance to this discussion, is whether speech that is concededly not "obscene" may be restricted as "indecent." The answer of the Court was affirmative: although the words used are not categorically excluded from radio, indecent speech could be proscribed[87] because of the presence of children in the audience. The ruling in this case is that the use of speech which is deemed indecent may be prohibited from daytime radio programing when children are presumed to be in the audience. Since the Court went to great length to define "obscene" as separate from "indecent" speech,[88] the assumption can be made that indecent speech is not outside First Amendment protection. Thus we reach the question of why the fundamental First Amendment rights of children can be so limited.

Under the heightened judicial scrutiny test, the two questions that must be answered pertain to the government objective and the relationship of the regulation to that objective. The objective of both the FCC and the Supreme Court in *Pacifica* would seem to be to protect children from a certain type of language.

According to the dicta of *Bellotti,* there are three circumstantial government objectives which may lead to the circumscription of children's constitutional rights: if a system makes a child particularly vulnerable, such as the adult court system would; if a child, through a decision, could cause himself harm; and if the reinforcement of parental authority so requires. The first objective is clearly not related to *Pacifica*.

---

85. The issue of a "mature" versus an "immature" minor is not discussed here although it may be pertinent given the age of the youth involved in *Pacifica*. See Bellotti v. Baird, 61 L.Ed. 2d 797, 803 (1979).
86. 438 U.S. 726, 730 (1978).
87. *Id.* at 750.
88. "Prurient appeal is an element of the obscene, but the normal definition of 'indecent' merely refers to nonconformance with accepted standards of morality." *Id.* at 740.

Neither is the third, for truly this ruling removes all discretion from parents and gives it to a regulatory commission.

The second objective may pertain, for one could argue, although not strongly, that a child could unwittingly do himself some undefined harm by choosing to listen to a recording such as Carlin's. Assuming that this is the objective of the ruling, it must now be determined if there is a substantial relationship between the regulation and the achieving of this objective.

What is the meaning of "substantial" in this context? The guideline falls somewhere between the reasonable relationship of the rational basis test and the requirement of the narrowest and best alternative of the strict scrutiny test. The question may be posed in this manner: Is proscribing indecent language from daytime radio an effective way to keep children from doing themselves this undefinable harm? In the total absence of persuasive evidence, the substantialness of this relationship pales. Since this question cannot be answered strongly in the affirmative, it is apparent that the objective does not meet the heightened judicial scrutiny test of substantial relationship, and that, when this test is applied, the FCC ruling considered in *Pacifica* violates the First Amendment rights of children.

CONCLUSION

A number of court cases are being decided and laws being passed which have an impact upon the First Amendment rights of children.[89] In addition, citizens' groups such as the national PTA and Action for Children's Television[90] and professional organizations such as the Council on Dental Health of the American Dental Association and the American Public Health Association[91] are lobbying Congress for legislation which would limit the types of communication available to children. Congress, in turn, is pressuring federal agencies like the Federal Communications Commission and the Federal Trade Commission to make rules defining material permissible for children's consumption.

89. Much of this litigation revolves around the rights of high school journalists. For a discussion of such cases *see* J. NELSON, THE REPORT OF THE COMMISSION OF INQUIRY INTO HIGH SCHOOL JOURNALISM (1974). State and local laws have been upheld which zone "adult" material to keep children away from it, even when such material is not obscene. *See* Young v. Am. Mini Theatres, Inc., 427 U.S. 50 (1976).
90. *See, e.g., Children's Television Report and Policy Statement,* 31 R.R. 2d 1228 (1974).
91. *See Federal Trade Commission Staff Report on TV Advertising to Children,* 49 ADV. AGE 73 (February 23, 1978).

Although this trend seems to be gathering momentum,[92] there is as yet no mechanism for defining what the rights of children are and no approach which allows for the uniform application of those rights.

The heightened judicial scrutiny test would give lawmakers and judges alike guidelines to be used in insuring society's interest in the protection of children and the child's interest in becoming an informed member of the adult society.

---

92. For example, the number of complaints regarding programing to children brought to the FCC and reported in *Pike and Fisher Radio Reports* is as follows: two in 1974, one in 1975, three in 1976, and three in 1977. *See Id.* for groups petitioning FTC for regulation of advertising of sugared products aimed at children. *See generally* Writers Guild of America West, Inc. v. FCC, 423 F. Supp. 1064 (C.D. Calif. 1976) for a discussion of the pressure put on the FCC with regard to the "family hour."

JOHN KAMP

Obscenity and the Supreme Court: A Communication Approach to a Persistent Judicial Problem

John Kamp, Ph.D., J.D., is an assistant professor, Faculty of Communication, University of Tulsa and chairperson of the Mass Media News (Print and Broadcast Journalism) Program. He is currently on leave working with the Broadcast Bureau of the Federal Communications Commission.

I. INTRODUCTION

This article uses the concept of communication as the basic theoretical background from which to analyze the continuing debate over the role of government in the censorship of sexually explicit material. It focuses on the Supreme Court's adjudication of obscenity cases and proposes a set of principles consistent with the United States Constitution as an alternative framework for such adjudication. The focus on sex censorship is appropriate because it leads to the very core of the nature of man and his relationship to his government, and because the Court has been unsuccessful in its attempts to develop a consistent set of constitutional principles of adjudication in the area.

A. The Concept of Communication

This article views communication as *the* basic social process, the process through which people continuously recreate themselves and their societies.[1] Communication originates in the process of symbolic thinking wherein humans are able to isolate certain aspects of their environments, concentrate on them, and assign them meanings.[2] This activity is endemic to social life,[3] and enables humans to control their responses to their environments and manipulate them in ways which enhance survival.[4]

Two aspects of the human communication process are especially important here: it is both active and social.[5] It is active in that people impose meaning and value on elements of their environment; people must actively participate in constructions of reality or fall back into the reflex-

---

1. This view is accepted by many in the social sciences, especially those of the "symbolic interactionist" school. For a general introduction: *see* BERGER and LUCKMANN, THE SOCIAL CONSTRUCTION OF REALITY (1953).
2. A general introduction is contained in MONTAGU, THE HUMAN REVOLUTION (1965). He says: "Man is the toolmaking animal, and he is so only because he is the symbol-using animal . . . . Signals differ from symbols in belonging more strictly to the physical world, and the meanings they convey are derived from the physical form they take in the external world. Most of the communication between animals is of the signaling variety. It is man alone who communicates virtually exclusively through symbols." *Id.* at 3
3. John Dewey has suggested that it is the sharing of common experience, common perception and common purpose that makes communication and social existence possible. His most direct statement on the issue may be the following: "Men live in a community in virtue of the things which they have in common; and communication is the way in which they come to possess things in common. What they must have in common in order to form a community or society are aims, beliefs, aspirations, knowledge . . . ." DEWEY, DEMOCRACY AND EDUCATION (1916), 4.
4. "Life, to our way of thinking, is more than mere change. It involves an interesting relationship between parts of our universe wherein one part, the living creature, is able to bring himself around to represent another part, his environment . . . . Because he can represent his environment, he can place alternative constructions upon it and indeed, do something about it if it doesn't suit him." KELLY, A THEORY OF PERSONALITY (1963), 8.
5. Although this dual aspect of the communication process has been most directly explicated in the study of the "symbolic interactionists" who worked in the tradition of John Dewey and George Herbert Mead, it has roots in the sociology of Georg Simmel. Simmel saw a dynamic dualism between "the autonomous life of the individual and the life of society, a dualism which is often harmonized in experience, but which in principle, is irreconcilable." SIMMEL, THE SOCIOLOGY OF GEORG SIMMEL, ed. Kurt Wolf (1950), 240. Simmel thus thought of life as a process of dealing with this fundamental ambiguity by participating in social life through communication: "The individual can never stay within a unit which he does not at the same time stay outside of, he is not incorporated into any order without also confronting it." *Id.*

response existence of other beings.⁶ The active quality of human communication presupposes an environment encouraging reflexive and creative activity.

Communication is social in that people develop mind and humanness in interaction with others. Communication requires participation in reality construction and the propensity for its reconstruction to meet changing human needs. Communicating beings are compounds of individual and social reality; each person is the product of a continuous interactive relationship between society and his own creative consciousness. At the same time a person is both alone and immersed in a continuous set of human relationships which maintain his humanity. In and through the creative experience of communication, people cope with this dual nature; they continually create and test their own conceptions of reality and thereby participate in the collective decision-making process.

One of the products of the communication process is the creation of the social order wherein people provide for themselves the continuity and stability necessary for the organization and direction of ongoing society. This habituation, or "institutionalization," allows people to develop patterns of behavior and thus benefit from cumulative experience and carry on further social experimentation. Though most institutionalized ways of behaving are informal, some attain formal and codified status. Often the most institutionalized aspects of a society are its governmental structures and the laws contained in them.

The relationship of communication between individuals and their government is illuminated by the political and social philosophy of John Dewey, which stresses the communicative nature of democratic government. According to Dewey's view, people derive their citizenship in democratic government through their participation in the collective creation and use of the material goods and the social meanings of the society.⁷ Thus, democracy, and education for it, requires an environment of social experimentation; that is, an environment that, through com-

---

6. Lewis Mumford suggests that the reconceptualization of man's dreams and the communication of those dreams to others is the essence of the humanizing process: "..... man became man by formalizing, ritualizing, symbolizing, dramatizing every natural act he performed; and in time this facility permitted him to transform his entire environment, bring it closer to his self by giving it the same attributes. This capacity for projection brought forth a second self, one in accord with man's still unstated and unfathomed possibilities." MUMFORD, THE TRANSFORMATION OF MAN (1956), 20.
7. According to Dewey, communities are democratic by virtue of the common interests of its members and the participation of its members in the "continuous readjustment" process. Clusters of communities existing in communication constitute democracy. Thus, democracy is not so much a form of government as a "mode of associated living, of conjoint communicated experience." DEWEY, DEMOCRACY AND EDUCATION 40.

munication, encourages social inquiry and creative participation. Accordingly, the social institution of government must reflect this requirement; it must maintain the creative social environment, and its laws must be continually reappraised and revitalized to meet the changing needs of the social system.[8]

The private and public dimensions of the communication process further illuminate the proper relationship of individuals to their government. Private communication involves rather specific, intimate, and largely self-determined personal relations and is exemplified by intrafamily relations. Public communication involves more general, institutionalized, and largely pre-determined formal communication and is exemplified by the relations of individuals to their government.[9] Private relations are considered the source and staging area for mature participation in the communication process, while public relations provide the cultural background, social cooperation, and individual protection necessary for maintenance and continued growth of all the people in the system.[10] In this scheme, private relations are considered primary while

8. In one book Dewey clearly states the nature of the "democratic ideal" in its generic sense: "From the standpoint of the individual, it consists in having a responsible share according to capacity in forming and directing the activities of the groups to which one belongs and in participating according to need in the values which the groups sustain. From the standpoint of the groups, it demands liberation of the potentialities of members of a group in harmony with the interests and goods which are common. Since every individual is a member of many groups, this specification cannot be fulfilled except when different groups interact flexibly and fully in connection with other groups .... Regarded as an idea, democracy is not an alternative to other principles of associated life. It is the idea of community itself." DEWEY, THE PUBLIC AND ITS PROBLEMS (1927), 147-48.

9. This division of public and private communication follows the distinction of Ferdinand Tönnies, a 19th century German theorist, who divided social relations into *Gemeinschaft* and *Gesellschaft*, roughly translated community and society. The distinction has been very influential among those who discern a relational difference between groups which operate in an atmosphere of mutual commitment and respect, and groups which operate on a more mechanical or contractual basis. See TÖNNIES, GEMEINSCHAFT AND GESELLSCHAFT, trans. Charles P. Lomis, (1957). The relationship of these ideas of Tönnies and those of Dewey and Mead has been suggested by Hanno Hardt, who extends the dichotomy to deal directly with communication using the concepts *Gemeinschaftkommunikation* and *Gesellschaftkommunikation*. See Hardt, *The Dilemma of Mass Communication: An Existential Point of View*, PHILOSOPHY AND RHETORIC 5 (1972).

10. The analogy to the theater has been detailed by Erving Goffman who suggests that social encounters can be conceived as performances in which individuals play roles in the presence of others. For the individual to have a successful "onstage" performance he must have "backstage" areas for preparation, rehearsal, and rest, out of the purview of the usual audience. The association of fellow actors is seen as beneficial for future performances. See GOFFMAN, THE PRESENTATION OF SELF IN EVERYDAY LIFE (1959); and RELATIONS IN PUBLIC, (1971). Robert Ardrey's popular book on animal territoriality suggests that a need for social insulation has roots in the animal world. See ARDREY, THE TERRITORIAL IMPERATIVE (1966).

others are considered secondary or ancillary, with the government being the most institutionalized of the latter type.[11]

B. Legal Protection of Communication

In this essay the system of liberty is viewed as having been initiated in the Constitution and as having evolved in the interpretations of it by the Supreme Court, the major social institution in this society[12] responsible for protecting the process of communication. As interpreter of the Constitution and its amendments, the Court has emphasized fundamental rights in many of its cases, and has operated as the major social institution to balance the forces between individuals and their government; thus maintaining a constitutional system of liberty.[13] Further, the principles applied by the Court in several other areas involving fundamental liberties, which are consistent with the process of human communication, suggest the proper framework for the adjudication of cases involving sexually explicit material.

This framework begins with the founding documents of the United States which posit the communicative activity of citizens as the operational principle of the social order. The Declaration of Independence and the Constitution respect the right and capacity of men to govern their own affairs; that is, to create, use, and change their government to reflect their desires and needs. The new government created a system of ordered liberty, bestowing on individuals the rights of thought and action in order that truth and self-determination could prevail and the corresponding responsibility to respect the rights of others in order to establish equal liberty for all.

The founding fathers thus instituted a system with broad protections of the process of human communication. The first amendment of the Constitution, for example, specifically prohibits government abridgement of the rights to believe, speak, publish, and assemble. Other provisions provide for election of leaders, strict separation of powers, and direct limitations on the extent of public power. These and other such provisions protect both individuals and the social system. From the

---

11. *See* especially: BERGER and LUCKMANN, THE SOCIAL CONSTRUCTION OF REALITY (1953). A classic statement of the importance of the dynamics required in interpretation of the law is contained in: CARDOZO, THE NATURE OF THE JUDICIAL PROCESS (1921).
12. Law is a social institution and so is the judicial process of interpretation of law. As elements of the social order, laws are the formal codification of those social institutions which participating individuals have found necessary and useful for the development of the social order. For further discussion *see* BERMAN and GREINER, THE NATURE AND FUNCTION OF LAW (1966).
13. *See* generally: HAND, THE BILL OF RIGHTS (1958).

standpoint of individuals, they protect the opportunity for people to become human and to act in a human manner in society. From the standpoint of the social order, they protect the process of social participation which keeps the society viable.

C. The Constitutional History of Obscenity

The notion that some sexually explicit material is obscene and thus can be suppressed by government action has had a tortuous history in United States courts. Following the common law of Victorian England which presumed that such material tended to corrupt the morals of youth,[14] United States courts generally upheld government suppression through the first half of the twentieth century. The United States Supreme Court did not directly decide the issue until 1957, although scattered dicta of earlier decisions indicated support for such suppression.[15] In its earliest decision, the Court rejected complete suppression of such material but left open the possibility of its regulation. In the landmark *Roth v. United States* decision, the Court declared that obscenity had no social value and therefore did not require constitutional protection.[16] To protect non-obscene material, the Court fashioned the first of a long series of definitions of obscenity predicated on its dominant theme and on community standards of prurience.

In the years that followed, the issue generated judicial discord, which some members of the Court considered unparalleled in constitutional adjudication, and a jumble of precedent, much of which was barely comprehensible to those affected by the law. The core of the problem has been the insistence by majorities of the Court that obscenity is outside the protection of the Constitution, which has resulted in the Court's concentration on definitions of obscenity rather than on the rights of individuals and the needs of the society.

---

14. The English landmark case is Regina v. Hicklin, L.R. 3 Q.B. 360 (1868). Sir Alexander Cockburn deferred to the most susceptible members of the community and handed down the decision that became the standard in both England and America for decades: "The test of obscenity is whether the tendency of the matter charged as obscenity is to deprave and corrupt those whose minds are open to such immoral influences and into whose hands a publication of this sort may fall." L.R. 3 Q.B. 360, 370 (1868).
15. See for examples: Chaplinsky v. New Hampshire, 315 U.S. 568, 571-2 (1942) and; Near v. Minnesota, 283 U.S. 697, 716 (1931).
16. The first major obscenity decision was Butler v. Michigan, 315 U.S. 568 (1957). Soon thereafter, the Supreme Court announced Roth v. United States, 354 U.S. 476 (1957).

II. THE ALTERNATIVE FRAMEWORK

The primary assertion of this article is that the Supreme Court should consider sexually explicit communication to be within the system of liberty, and should, therefore, apply rigorous constitutional principles derived from other fundamental rights cases to "obscenity" cases.[17] More specifically, the Supreme Court should follow two broad postulates for adjudicating cases involving sexually explicit material: (1) substantial bans aimed at communication content should be presumed unconstitutional; and (2) the presumption should be rebuttable only in certain narrowly defined circumstances where fundamental rights are endangered, and then the regulation should be no broader than necessary to rectify that danger. As will be demonstrated below, these two postulates undergird the Supreme Court decisions in other areas involving fundamental rights, especially the first amendment rights, and they provide a suitable framework for cases concerning sexually explicit material. From the standpoint of communication, the first postulate protects the possibility of the human social activity which allows individuals to become human and the society to remain viable, and the second postulate allows the society to keep individuals within bounds which maintain the system of human communication. From the standpoint of the Constitution, postulate one protects the legal right of the individuals to participate in the social/political process, and postulate two protects the system which makes that participation possible. Taken together, the opportunity to participate in the social process is assumed as a basic right of each individual in the society, but the society maintains the power of selective regulation in order to insure that exercise of individual rights do not infringe on similar exercise by others.

The following sections view the adjudication of "obscenity" cases in light of these postulates and the social and legal principles which undergird them: first, a summary and critique of the principles now imposed by the Supreme Court in obscenity cases, focusing on the majority opinions in the important 1973 cases;[18] then, a presentation of the principles applied in other areas affecting fundamental rights and illustration of their use in obscenity cases.

17. The term "obscenity" is most often applied to cases involving sexually explicit communication. This paper, however, does not accept the assumption that there is a reasonably identifiable subset of communication that can be labeled obscene, and thus be given an automatic exclusion from usual constitutional protections. The term obscenity is used here, therefore, only to identify those cases where the Supreme Court has made such a distinction.
18. Although the Supreme Court has decided several cases since 1973, Miller v. California, 413 U.S. 15 (1973), and the accompanying cases remain the important symbolic center of this controversy, and thus the appropriate point of departure here.

III. THE CURRENT PRINCIPLES OF ADJUDICATION

A. The *Miller* test

The most important current principles of adjudication of "obscenity" cases are contained in a series of related cases decided in 1973, principally *Miller v. California*[19] and *Paris Adult Theatre I v. Slaton*.[20] Although at least two later decisions involving sexually explicit material have bypassed these holdings and sustained additional content-related restrictions,[21] the *Miller* guidelines have remained the most important precedent since their announcement, and their theoretical basis has not yet been successfully challenged before the Supreme Court.

The *Miller* case reaffirmed the holding of *Roth v. United States*[22] that "obscenity" is not protected by the first amendment. Then, speaking through Chief Justice Warren Burger, the majority reformulated the *Roth* definition of obscenity, dividing it into three parts:

> The basic guidelines for the trier of fact must be: (a) whether "the average person, applying contemporary community standards would find that the work, taken as a whole, appeals to the prurient interest . . .;" (b) whether the work depicts or describes, in a patently offensive way, sexual conduct specifically defined by the applicable state law; and (c) whether the work, taken as a whole, lacks serious literary, artistic, political, or scientific value.[23]

The decision requires that laws, as written or construed by the courts, impose specific standards and that these be limited to "representation or descriptions of ultimate sexual acts, normal or perverted, actual or simulated" or "of masturbation, excretory functions and lewd exhibi-

---

19. 413 U.S. 15 (1973).
20. 413 U.S. 49 (1973).
21. The two most important cases are Young v. American Mini Theatres, 427 U.S. 50, (1976); and Federal Communications Commission v. Pacifica Foundation, 438 U.S. 726, (1978). In Young a plurality affirmed a Detroit zoning ordinance dispersing specified businesses, including bookstores and movie theaters specializing in "adult" sexual material. Relying on a nuisance theory supported by the zoning power, the plurality found adequate power for the regulations and ignored the possible applicability of the Miller test. In Pacifica another plurality affirmed the power of the F.C.C. to regulate "indecent" broadcasts which were not found "obscene" under the Miller test. The Court upheld the regulation relying not only on a nuisance analogy but also on the "special First Amendment problems" posed by broadcasting because of: (1) the licensing process; (2) its "uniquely pervasive presence in the lives of all Americans"; and (3) the fact that it is "uniquely accessible to children."
22. 354 U.S. 476 (1957).
23. 413 U.S. 15, 24 (1973). (Quoting Roth, 354 U.S. 476, 489).

tion of the genitals."[24] *Miller* involved a conviction for mailing unsolicited sexually explicit material, presenting an issue of nonconsensual intrusion of offensive material into one's enclave or privacy. But *Paris* extended the holding, affirming a conviction under the *Miller* standard, to an adult's fully informed and consensual access to such material. The Court thus seems to have limited *Stanley v. Georgia*,[25] a 1969 case invalidating a statute prohibiting the possession and private use of such material, to its facts. Censorship is allowed under *Miller* when the allegedly obscene material is without "serious value,"[26] thus overruling the requirement of previous holdings that the term "obscenity" was confined to that material the prosecutor could prove as "utterly without redeeming social value."[27] Furthermore the test incorporates local standards of prurience, permitting varying constitutional standards in different judicial jurisdictions. At base then, the Supreme Court's present position regarding the circulation and use of sexually explicit materials relies on two important propositions: (1) that judges and juries can appropriately find such material without value, and enforce that finding on their geographical communities, and (2) that there is a distinguishable class of communication content that can be labeled "obscene." Neither of these propositions bears critical analysis.

Empirical evidence does not clearly support the assertion that sexually explicit material is without value.[28] On the contrary, empirical studies, including many conducted by the President's Commission on Obscenity and Pornography, indicate that sexually explicit material has significant value for many individuals.[29] These studies also indicate that this material may have significant societal value as well, inasmuch as its

---

24. 413 U.S. 15, 25 (1973).
25. 394 U.S. 557 (1969).
26. 413 U.S. 15, 24.5 (1973).
27. *See also* Jacobellis v. Ohio, 378 U.S. 184, 192-93 (1964).
28. The most comprehensive collection of data concerning the effects of sexually explicit material is contained in: UNITED STATES COMMISSION ON OBSCENITY AND PORNOGRAPHY, REPORT OF THE COMMISSION ON OBSCENITY AND PORNOGRAPHY (1970). Works predating the REPORT OF THE COMMISSION include: Cairns, Paul and Wishner, *Sex Censorship: The Assumptions of Anti-Obscenity Laws and the Empirical Evidence*, MINN. L. REV. 46 (1962), 1009; Jahoda, THE IMPACT OF LITERATURE: A PSYCHOLOGICAL DISCUSSION OF SOME ASSUMPTIONS IN THE CENSORSHIP DEBATES (1954); and Murphy, *The Value of Pornography*, WAYNE L. REV. 19 (1964), 165. Material updating the REPORT OF THE COMMISSION in this regard include: Money and Anthanasion, *Pornography: Review and Bibliographic Annotations*, AMER. J. OF OBSTETRICS AND GYNECOLOGY 115 (1973), 143-46; GAGNON and SIMON, SEXUAL CONDUCT (1973), 265-75; and Wilson, *Facts Versus Fears: Why Should We Worry about Pornography?* ANNALS OF THE AMER. ACAD. OF POLIT. AND SOC. SCI. 397 (1971), 105-17.
29. *See* GOLDSTEIN and KANT, PORNOGRAPHY AND SEXUAL DEVIANCE (1973), 147-53; REPORT OF THE COMMISSION, 128-34; and Polsky, HUSTLERS, BEATS AND OTHERS (1967), 186-202.

use serves as a catharsis for those otherwise inclined toward anti-social sexual behavior. Perhaps more important, in saying that so-called obscene materials are not constitutionally protected, the Court allows majority standards of prurience to be imposed on minority and majority alike in the delineated communities. As such, the Supreme Court violates the principle that majority attitudes per se are not a constitutionally valid basis for suppression of individual communication.[30] Another way of addressing this latter point is to note that the Court's obscenity decisions are political,[31] and that, therefore, they violate the ideal of neutral principles of constitutional adjudication.[32] This society is in the midst of what has been termed a "sexual revolution," meaning, at least, that there is an ongoing debate over many questions of sexual morality.[33] Some of these questions have surfaced in major constitutional decisions.[34] Longstanding and deep-seated conventions of personal morality and proper sexual activity are being seriously challenged, and significant constitutional arguments are being asserted to invalidate laws regulating adult consensual sexual behavior.[35] Part of the debate is a re-evaluation of the right of the majority to ban sexually explicit communication through legal institutions.[36] Considering this current social debate over sexual morality and the Supreme Court's repeated support of the "uninhibited marketplace of ideas,"[37] it is difficult to sustain the asser-

30. Perhaps the most compelling statement against the use of majority standards in obscenity cases is that of Justice Hugo Black in Roth: "Any test that turns on what is offensive to the community's standards is too loose, too capricious, too destructive of freedom of expression to be squared with the First Amendment. Under this test, jurors can censor, suppress and punish what they don't like . . . ." Roth v. United States 354 U.S. 476, 511-12, (1957).
31. See Rosenfield, Politics and Pornography, QUAR. J. OF SPEECH 59 (1973), 413. For a contrasting view see Anastaplo, Obscenity and Common Sense, ST. LOUIS UNIV. LAW J. 16 (1972), 527.
32. See Wechsler, Toward Neutral Principles of Constitutional Law, HARV. LAW REV. 73 (1959), 1; BICKEL, THE LEAST DANGEROUS BRANCH (1962); Black, The Lawfulness of the Segregation Decisions, YALE LAW J. 69 (1960), 421; Henkin, Some Reflections of the Current Constitutional Law Controversy, UNIV. OF PA. LAW REV. 109 (1961), 637; Wright, Professor Bickel, the Scholarly Tradition and the Supreme Court, HARV. LAW REV. 84 (1971), 769.
33. See, for examples of discussions of the topic: PETRAS, SEXUALITY IN SOCIETY (1973); FIRESTONE, THE DIALECTIC OF SEX (1970); and KENNEDY, THE NEW SEXUALITY: MYTHS, FABLES AND HANG-UPS (1971).
34. See, for example: Roe v. Wade, 410 U.S. 113 (1973) (abortion); Griswold v. Connecticut, 381 U.S. 479 (1965) (contraception).
35. See, for example: BARNETT, SEXUAL FREEDOM AND THE CONSTITUTION (1973) (challenging the constitutionality of laws against consensual homosexual acts).
36. Note, for example, the formation and use of the President's Commission of Obscenity and Pornography. See also: BARBER, PORNOGRAPHY AND SOCIETY (1972); RIST, THE PORNOGRAPHY CONTROVERSY: CHANGING MORAL STANDARDS IN AMERICAN LIFE (1975); OBOLER, FEAR OF THE WORD: CENSORSHIP AND SEX (1974).
37. Reaffirmed repeatedly since introduced as legal theory by Justice Oliver Wendell Holmes in Abrams v. United States, 205 U.S. 616 (1919). See for example Miami Herald Publishing Company v. Tornillo, 418 U.S. 214 (1974).

tion that some communication can be labeled "obscene" by the majority and thus withheld from the marketplace.

Meanwhile, the assertion that "obscenity" is a distinct class of communication lacks adequate support. Efforts by the Supreme Court to define obscenity have repeatedly faltered,[38] as the chronology of the term's definition and redefinition indicates. These definitions have often failed because of their dependence upon dogmatic and rigid attitudes toward proper communication concerning the use of human sexual organs.[39] Different cultures, and different groups and individuals within cultures, have a broad range of beliefs and attitudes in these matters.[40] The diverse material available and the controversy which surrounds the obscenity issue are testimony to the variety of viewpoints and, thus, the impossibility of a satisfactory delineation of obscenity through a government standard.

It is apparent that obscenity laws are implicit political expressions of the broad popular attitudes toward the proper thoughts about and use of the body.[41] Other such laws have been tested by the Supreme Court and have been stricken, including laws against the distribution of contraceptive information and devices,[42] and the suspension of a woman's right to control her own body.[43] Inasmuch as judicial application of obscenity laws indirectly impose a particular attitude about the proper use of the body, even according to a "community standard," it contradicts a central notion of liberty inscribed in the Constitution—to secure the greatest possible liberty of communication compatible with a like liberty for all.

The first amendment rests on the fundamental liberties of belief, conscience, and expression; these are necessary conditions for the integrity and competence of a person in mastering the mind and sharing that mastery with others.[44] In essence, the first amendment enables mature communicative activity. The available evidence does not prove that the freedom to determine the sexual content of one's communication is any less important to self-mastery than that freedom is in other areas

---

38. *See*, note, *Obscenity: The Definitional Dilemma*, GA. STATE BAR J. 10 (1973), 327.
39. *See* Henkin, *Morals and the Constitution: The Sin of Obscenity*, COLUMBIA LAW REV. 63 (1963), 390; CLOR, OBSCENITY AND PUBLIC MORALITY (1969); Richards, *Free Speech and Obscenity Law: Toward a Moral Theory of the First Amendment*, UNIV. OF PA. LAW REV. 123 (1974), 45.
40. *See* GICHNER, EROTIC ASPECTS OF CHINESE CULTURE (1957); RAWSON, EROTIC ART THE EAST (1968); KRONHAUSEN and KRONHAUSEN, PORNOGRAPHY AND THE LAW (1959).
41. *See* Richards, *Free Speech*, 72.
42. Griswold v. Connecticut, 381 U.S. 479 (1965).
43. Roe v. Wade, 410 U.S. 113 (1973).
44. For a summary of the premises upon which the First Amendment is based *see* EMERSON, THE SYSTEM OF FREEDOM OF EXPRESSION (1970), 6-9.

of communication content. On the contrary, developing methods of sexual therapy in our culture have helped people in "learning to communicate . . . in an area that heretofore in our culture has been denied the dignity of freedom of communication."[45] Obscenity laws have been used to deny such sex education and instruction,[46] contracting the spectrum of knowledge concerning the varieties of sexual pleasure and debasing the human capacity to master one's own sexual life.[47] The ability of self-determination in these matters is essential to mature communication. Without a suitable social context, people cannot adequately come to grips with themselves in relation to their environments and, thus, participate in the ongoing social process.

B. The Assumptions and the Evidence

In the 1973 obscenity cases Justice Burger justified the suppression of sexually explicit materials through the power of the state to protect the general quality of life and also the right of individuals to protect their own moral standards. This section examines these and similar justifications of obscenity laws and finds them unsupportable in light of legal theory and in contradiction with the communicative needs of individuals and society.

In *Paris* the Chief Justice justified the conviction because of the "interest of the public in the quality of life and total community environment, [and] the tone of commerce in the great city centers . . ."[48] To the

---

45. MASTERS and JOHNSON, HUMAN SEXUAL INADEQUACY (1970), 204.
46. The text of the substantive section of the Comstock Act § 2, ch. 258, § 2, 17 Stat. 598, 599 (1873), as amended, 18 U.S.C.A. 1461 (1970) reads as follows: "[N]o obscene, lewd, or lascivious book, pamphlet, picture, paper, print, or other publication of an indecent character, or any particle or thing designed or intended for the prevention of conception or procuring of abortion, nor any article or thing intended or adapted for any indecent or immoral use or nature, nor any written or printed card, circular, book, pamphlet, advertisement or notice of any kind giving information, directly or indirectly, where, or how, or of whom, or by what means either of the things before mentioned may be obtained or made, nor any letter upon the envelope of which, or postal-card upon which indecent or scurrilous epithets may be written or printed, shall be carried in the mail. . . ." *See also* United States v. Dennett, 39 F.2d 564 (2d Cir. 1930).
47. The President's Commission on Obscenity and Pornography supported its proposal for the liberalization of obscenity laws in light of the need for better sex education. *See* REPORT OF THE COMMISSION, 47-48, 58, 265-279. Note also that popular sex manuals have recommended the use of the type of materials prosecuted under obscenity laws including: COMFORT, JOY OF SEX (1972), 208-9. Note also the similar suggestion in: RUSSELL, MARRIAGE AND MORALS (1929), 93-117.
48. 413 U.S. 49, 58 (1973).

extent that this is a valid justification for a commercial regulation, it would, at best, support some limited control over the sale of sexually explicit material—such as in commercial zoning—or limit on the obtrusiveness of such advertising.[49] But the justification fails in the area of substantive law because the prescription doesn't fit the problem. In constitutional terms, such laws are invalid because their means are overbroad in light of their ends, and because there is no verifiable evidence to prove that the laws solve the problem to which they are addressed.[50]

Suppose, for example, the government could prove the assertion of Anthony Comstock that the publication and use of sexually explicit material is a "social poison,"[51] leading directly to disease, death, crime, and social disorder.[52] If this were verifiable, the system of liberty might be shown to be threatened by the presence of such materials. Then, consistent with similar decisions and postulate two above, the state could justifiably regulate the circulation of such material. The social poison idea was prevalent during the Victorian era,[53] but appears to rest basically on intuition and is not supported by major medical, psychological, or sociological research.[54] Regardless, Justice Burger advanced the argument as justification in *Paris*, citing the Hill-Link minority report of the President's Commission on Obscenity and Pornography which posits "at least an arguable correlation between obscene material and crime."[55] Justice Burger ignored the fact that the minority

---

49. Such a suggestion has been made by KUH in FOOLISH FIGLEAVES (1967), 269-79. Recent cases suggest that such regulations will still meet significant first amendment challenges. *See* Landmark Communications v. Virginia, 435 U.S. 829 (1978); and Smith v. Daily Mail, 5 MED. L. RPTR. 1305 (1979).
50. A discussion of the law of substantive due process in this regard appears below in this article.
51. The metaphor of poison pervades the writing of Anthony Comstock. For example, he noted the case of the thirteen-year-old girl, in whose bureau he "found a quantity of the most debasing and foul-worded matter. The last heard from this child she was in a dying condition, the result of habits induced by this foul reading." COMSTOCK, TRAPS FOR THE YOUNG, ed. Robert Bremmer (1967), 139.
52. The "social poison" approach is an informal application of the "Stimulus-Organism-Response" model of effects often used in the physical sciences, and sometimes used in the social sciences. The idea as applied to studies of effects of mass communication messages is often referred to as the "hypodermic needle" model of effects, because it assumes that communication messages are somehow "injected" into the communication system of the receiver, and have rather predictable effects. This model has been largely rejected by modern social scientists, including those who did research for the President's Commission on Obscenity and Pornography. *See* REPORT OF THE COMMISSION, 132. *See also* notes 28 and 29.
53. *See* COMFORT, THE ANXIETY MAKERS (1970); HALLER and HALLER, THE PHYSICIAN AND SEXUALITY IN VICTORIAN AMERICA (1974); and Hare, *Masturbational Insanity: The History of an Idea*, J. OF MENTAL SCI. 108 (1962), 6-9.
54. *See* notes 9 and 10.
55. 413 U.S. 49, 58 (1973).

report is based on a conviction that obscenity ought to be suppressed to protect religious standards,[56] and ignored the main body of the commission report which concludes that there is no empirical evidence to support the social poison concept.[57]

Justice Burger also posited the general argument that society can forbid all access to pornographic materials in order to protect moral standards. The opinion extensively quotes Alexander Bickel's assertion that the consensual and unobtrusive use of so-called obscene materials by consenting adults intrudes upon the liberty of all members of the society. The argument of Bickel was presented as independent justification of the suppression of such materials:

> *Quite apart from sex crimes,* however, there remains one problem of large proportions aptly described by Professor Bickel: "It concerns the tone of society . . . [If a man] demands a right to obtain the books and pictures he wants in the market, and to foregather in public places—discreet, if you will, but accessible to all—with others who share his tastes, *then to grant him his right is to affect the world about the rest of us, and to impinge on other privacies.* Even supposing that each of us can, if he wishes, effectively avert the eye and stop the ear (which, in truth, we cannot), what is commonly read and seen and heard and done intrudes upon us all, want it or not" (emphasis added).[58]

This justification requires examination, for its substance appears to be that allowing any form of disapproved conduct among consenting adults violates the right of privacy of others who disapprove of that conduct. Thus, knowledge of the existence of disapproved conduct is sufficient justification for the use of law to prohibit that conduct. In *Miller* the Chief Justice did not require that the material at issue cause crime or invade the rights of specific persons. Rather, the effects of the material and the result ng power of the state to suppress it was assumed *arguendo.*

The Burger/Bickel justification appears to be an extension of the traditional argument by John Stephen[59] against John Stuart Mill[60] and

---

56. *See* REPORT OF THE COMMISSION, 383, 385-386.
57. *Id.,* 215-243. In fact, the experience in Denmark was after the repeal of its obscenity statutes, as applied to the consensual behavior of adults, the rate of sex crimes actually lowered. *See Id.,* 230-232; UNITED STATES COMMISSION ON OBSCENITY AND PORNOGRAPHY, TECHNICAL REPORT, Vol. VII, 254.
58. 413 U.S. 49, 59 (1973).
59. STEPHEN, LIBERTY, EQUALITY, FRATERNITY(1968).
60. MILL, ON LIBERTY, ed. Currin Shields (1956).

the modern argument by Patrick Devlin[61] against H. L. A. Hart,[62] although both Stephen and Devlin assume that condemned conduct weakens the structure of society. The Burger/Bickel argument assumes that mere existence of offensive activity is an invasion of rights; the logical extension of which would be that no one in the society would be allowed to do anything to which others have serious objection.[63] Widespread application of this idea would transform the concept of liberty from one favoring individual diversity, participatory democracy, and social dynamism to one enforcing conformity, social homogeneity, and rigidity. It would allow legal institutions to reify majoritarian morality and prejudice in an area affecting fundamental rights.[64] Such a modus operandi on the part of the Supreme Court would counter its traditional role as protector of individual rights, which was developed in the first half of the twentieth century and more recently extended to issues such as abortion,[65] contraception for married[66] and unmarried persons,[67] miscegenation,[68] and segregated education.[69] Further, it could counter the constitutional principles of substantive due process, traced below, which require specific and narrow regulation according to rational means in areas affecting fundamental liberties.

The Burger/Bickel argument also ignores the needs of a viable system of human communication. If applied as constitutional principle, the argument would empower the majority, through the social institution of law, to create an objective social order which would suspend the communicative, participatory capacity of individuals in the society concerning matters within its scope. The result would be to deny to individuals the capability of self-determination, and thus maturity, confining them to a state of adolescence. Conversely, it would deny the society the benefits of an active, participatory communication system thereby limiting experimentation, innovation, and progress. This, in turn, would limit the capability of the social system to adapt to the environment, thus threatening its survival. From the point of view of the legal and political system as well as that of a viable system of communication, the argument

---

61. DEVLIN, THE ENFORCEMENT OF MORALS (1965).
62. HART, LAW, LIBERTY, AND MORALITY (1963). *See also* BAY, THE STRUCTURE OF FREEDOM (1958).
63. HART, 46-47.
64. *See* Barnett, *Corruption of Morals*, J. OF LAW AND SOCIAL ORDER 2 (1971), 189-243; and Dworkin, *Lord Devlin and the Enforcement of Morals*, YALE LAW J. 75 (1966), 986.
65. Row v. Wade, 410 U.S. 113 (1973).
66. Griswold v. Connecticut, 381 U.S. 479 (1965).
67. Eisenstadt v. Baird, 405 U.S. 438 (1972).
68. Loving v. Virginia, 388 U.S. (1967).
69. Brown v. Board of Education, 347 U.S. 483 (1954).

stated by Professor Bickel and elevated to legal principle in *Paris* by Justice Burger is unsound.

Although not explicit in the 1973 decisions, there is a form of the Burger/Bickel justifications for obscenity laws which deserves attention here.[70] The argument stems from a moral perspective of the Constitution. As such it considers the libertarian protections in the Constitution as basically moral statements of principle which presuppose responsible exercise of those liberties by citizens. As a statement of principle, this moral argument is consistent with the communication and legal perspective of this article. But the argument sometimes is taken one step further to contend that there are certain character traits based on religious virtues which citizens under the Constitution must have, and that sexually explicit communication necessarily undermines these virtues, thereby undermining the constitutional order. From this extended moral position the suppression of "obscenity" is justified, perhaps necessary.[71]

The general form of the argument is plausible and especially attractive to those with moral principles based on religious doctrine.[72] But the argument is circular, not supported by evidence, and raises serious independent questions under the establishment of the religion clause of the first amendment. Its circularity stems from two co-dependent assumptions: (1) that religious and constitutional virtues are equivalent, and (2) that constitutional responsibility and sexually explicit communication are mutually exclusive. More directly, it equates the responsibilities of constitutional citizenship with the responsibilities of a specific set of religious principles regarding the sex.[73] But the assumptions are not sup-

70. Following the Bickel quote in Paris, Chief Justice Burger implied the argument by saying: "As Chief Justice Warren stated there is a 'right of the Nation and of the States to maintain a decent society....'" 413 U.S. 49, 59-60 (1973). Quoting the Chief Justice Warren from Jacobellis v. Ohio, 378 U.S. 184, 199 (1964).
71. For statements of this view *see* CLOR, OBSCENITY AND PUBLIC MORALITY: CENSORSHIP IN A LIBERAL SOCIETY (1969); and Berns, *Pornography vs. Democracy: The Case for Censorship,* PUBLIC INTEREST 22 (1971), 1. For a contrary view *see* Richards, *Free Speech.*
72. For example, the Canon Law of the Roman Catholic Church states "... as a basic and cardinal fact, that complete sexual activity and pleasure is licit and moral only in a naturally completed act in a valid marriage. All acts which, of their psychological and physical nature, are designed to be preparatory to the complete act, take their licitness and their morality from the complete act. If, therefore, they are entirely divorced from the complete act, they are distorted, warped, meaningless, and hence immoral." Quoted from Gardiner, *Moral Principles Toward a Definition of the Obscene,* LAW AND CONTEMPORARY PROBLEMS 20 (1965), 564. Charles Keating, a member of the President's Commission, claims that obscenity is against the law of God and is thus justifiably suppressed. *See* REPORT OF THE COMMISSION, 511, 515, 547.
73. This view derives from the classic teaching of St. Augustine that the only proper sexual thoughts and acts are those directly aimed at reproduction. *See* ST. AUGUSTINE, THE CITY OF GOD, trans. W. J. Wand (1963). For a contrary view *see* MASTERS and JOHNSON, SEXUAL INADEQUACY, 189-99.

ported by adequate evidence or argument. One cannot clearly equate the conventional virtues of democratic citizenship—responsible voting, public activity, democratic tolerance, and so on—with the religious virtue of strict avoidance of unorthodox sexual material.[74] There is no consensus in this society that such avoidance is a virtue,[75] and some religious leaders have found religious value in its use.[76] Moreover, there is increasing support among medical and psychological professionals for the use of sexually explicit material to aid patients integrate their physical and mental lives, and thereby communicate more effectively with others.[77]

If the Court accepted this extended moral argument as constitutional fact, it would again run headlong into the problem of determining what is and what is not obscene. Different behaviors and different forms of communication appeal to different tastes and produce varying responses from people of differing moralities.[78] But suppose that some sexually explicit material were definable in terms of their expressed opposition to constitutional principles; for example, that sadism undermines the mutual self-respect implied in the Constitution. In that case the material would well be construed as an expression of ideology,[79] and not suppressible under present first amendment theory, in the absence of evidence of incitement to imminent lawless action.[80] But the evidence is,

74. *See* McKeon, Merton and Gelhorn, The Freedom to Read (1957), 23-24.
75. *See* Petras, Sexuality; Sherman, A History of the Sex Revolution (1973); Daily, The Anatomy of Censorship (1973).
76. *See* Memoirs v. Massachusetts, 383 U.S. 413, 433 (1966). (Appendix to the opinion of Justice Douglas, consisting of an address by a clergyman urging that *Fanny Hill* was a moral book.) *See also* Report of the Commission, 378.
77. A significant number of couples in a survey reported by William Lockhart noted that exposure to sexually explicit materials produced increased openness and satisfaction in their marriages. *See* Lockhart, *The Findings and Recommendations of the Commission on Obscenity and Pornography: A Case Study of the Role of Social Science in Formulation Public Policy*, Okla. Law Rev. 24 (1971), 218. *See also* note 45.
78. Note, for examples, the differing views on the same material by the Justices of the Supreme Court in its many obscenity decisions.
79. Kingsley Pictures most directly illustrates the Supreme Court position on ideological obscenity. There the majority construed the conviction as resting on the proposition that the film "alluringly portrays adultery as proper behavior," and responded that it had thus "struck at the very heart of constitutionally protected liberty." Kingsley International Pictures v. Regents, 360 U.S. 684, 688 (1959). *See also* Cohen v. California, 403 U.S. 15 (1971). For other decisions construing the role of the first amendment in the protection of ideas *see* Gertz v. Robert Welch, Inc., 418 U.S. 323 (1974); and Madison v. Wisconsin Employment Relations Commission, 429 U.S. 167 (1978).
80. The constitutional guarantees of free speech and free press do not permit a state to forbid or proscribe advocacy of the use of force or of law violation "except where such advocacy is directed to inciting or producing imminent lawless action and is likely to incite or produce such action." Brandenburg v. Ohio, 395 U.S. 444, 447 (1969). *See also* the general discussion of the clear and present danger doctrine as applied to obscenity below.

at best, mixed, indicating that such material may even decrease antisocial behavior.[81] To the extent such material serves as a catharsis, as a harmless outlet for aggressive fantasy, it contributes to the health of the constitutional system and ought to be protected by the courts.

What is left of the moral argument supporting suppression of obscene materials is based on religious conviction that obscenity undermines the social order. But special religious convictions of this type are not constitutionally admissible justification for limitation of the fundamental rights expressed in the Constitution.[82] Specifically, two major provisions of the first amendment prohibit such state interference; the free speech and press clause and the establishment of religion clause.[83]

In summary, there is no clear evidence of a generally accepted empirical nature that access to and use of sexually explicit materials such as those most often suppressed by obscenity laws have an adverse effect on the virtue of democratic citizenship. Nor is there significant evidence that such materials cause social and cultural breakdown. The Constitution creates a system where communication is given the presumption of protection, and the accepted empirical evidence does not support a general refutation of that presumption in the case of sexually explicit materials.

IV. THE CONCEPT OF LIBERTY AND THE PROTECTION OF FUNDAMENTAL RIGHTS

A. Introduction

A more suitable framework for the adjudication of obscenity cases stems from the concept of liberty inscribed in the Declaration of Independence and the Constitution and since interpreted by the Supreme Court. The concept of liberty emerged from this country's social and legal heritage and has evolved over the two centuries of experience and adjudication. Liberty is an operational principle of democratic govern-

---

81. Gorer notes that de Sade himself experienced such a release and, during some times of his life, displayed considerable tolerance and sympathy. *See* GORER, THE DANGER OF EQUALITY (1966), 210.
82. The outstanding obscenity case of this type is Burstyn, where a city wished to ban a movie because of alleged "sacrilegious" content. The response of the Supreme Court was direct and terse: "[T]he state has no legitimate interest in protecting any or all religions from views distasteful to them ... It is not the business of government in our nation to suppress real or imagined attacks upon a particular religious doctrine, whether they appear in publications, speech or motion pictures." Burstyn v. Wilson, 343 U.S. 495, 502 (1952).
83. Epperson v. Arkansas, 393 U.S. 97 (1968); Barnett, 74-93; and Henkin, 391.

ment and a necessary condition for the process of communication and, as such, provides a suitable framework for this analysis. In cases involving sexually explicit material, this framework would avoid definitions of obscenity and instead encourage systematic consideration of the context of each case and the needs of the social and political system. Thus, rather than centering on obscenity *vel non,* Supreme Court decisions would center on the system of liberty and the appropriate actions necessary to optimize the operation of that system.

It is important to remember that although the system of liberty does not require absolute protection of fundamental rights, it does provide a presumption of protection and requires that the government demonstrate a compelling need to rebut that presumption. Libertarian democracy is based on the notion that the people control the government, not vice versa. Thus, the protection of liberty includes the rights to think, to speak, to congregate, to travel, and to vote according to individual determination.[84] In other words, it guarantees several rights of self-determination, so long as these do not infringe upon the similar rights of others.[85] In short, the principle of liberty protects responsible participation in the social process.

In this parlance, it is the task of the United States Supreme Court to protect liberty through the cases it adjudicates, including those involving sexually explicit material. In the following two sections an outline of the constitutional principles developed and applied to other areas involving fundamental rights by the United States Supreme Court is presented along with outlines of their use in obscenity cases. To the extent that they can be so delineated, the first group of principles emphasizes the freedom of communication of acting individuals, and the second group of principles emphasizes contexts where limited regulations might be appropriate to protect the maximum liberty for all.

B. Principles Emphasizing Communication Freedom

In broad form three basic areas of law which emphasize communicational freedom are outlined in the following section: the prior restraint doctrine, the clear and present danger doctrine, and the substantive due process protections of fundamental liberties. Each of these has been used extensively by the Supreme Court in this century, and each has a well elaborated and widely recognized set of rules and rationales which

---

84. A comprehensive summary of these rights is contained in: TRIBE, AMERICAN CONSTITUTIONAL LAW (1978), 564-1135.
85. The classic statement of the libertarian principle is contained in MILL, ON LIBERTY (1859).

surround its application. The cases cited below are exemplary and suggestive of the principles of communication protection recognized by the Supreme Court which could be used in the adjudication of obscenity cases. These cases should not be viewed as binding precedent because the definitional test allowing for exclusion of "obscenity" from the realm of protected communication is often incorporated in their holdings. So, too, the following cases and broad areas of law discussed below should not be considered an exclusive list of appropriate precedent.

1. Clear and Present Danger

The clear and present danger test was announced by Justice Oliver Wendell Holmes in the first major free expression case in 1919 and has remained an important defense of liberty to the present. Although the test has undergone several stages of evolution since Holmes announced it in *Schenck v. United States*,[86] it has remained an important defense against governmental action abridging any expression which does not pose "a clear and present danger of illegal action the state has a right to prevent."[87] The test is used most often with cases which involve public advocacy of illegal activity, and the most important recent application of the test came in *Brandenburg v. Ohio*,[88] involving a televised report of a Ku Klux Klan rally. There the Supreme Court summarized and applied the modern version of the Holmes test:

> These ... decisions have fashioned the principle that the constitutional guarantees of free speech and free press do not permit a State to forbid or proscribe advocacy of the use of force or of law violation except where such advocacy is directed to inciting or producing imminent lawless action and is likely to incite or produce such action.[89]

---

86. 249 U.S. 47 (1919).
87. *Id.* at 52.
88. 395 U.S. 444 (1969). The clear and present danger test enjoyed a period of general acceptance in the wake of Schenck but was significantly weakened in the 1950s in American Communication Association v. Douds, 339 U.S. 382 (1950), and Dennis v. United States, 341 U.S. 494 (1951). It was later strengthened in Yates v. United States, 354 U.S. 298 (1957). In the 1960s the test was not generally used, prompting Harry Kalven to announce its demise, but it was resurrected by the Supreme Court in Brandenburg. See Kalven, *The New York Times Case: A Note on "The Central Meaning of the First Amendment,"* SUP. CT. REV. 1964 (1964), 213-214. Other important discussions of the clear and present danger tests are reported in: Strong, *Fifty Years of Clear and Present Danger*, SUP. CT. REV. 1969 (1969), 41; SHAPIRO, FREEDOM OF SPEECH: THE SUPREME COURT AND JUDICIAL REVIEW (1966), 121-35.
89. 395 U.S. 444, 447 (1969).

Fashioned in this manner, the clear and present danger test applies to both the content and the context of the communicative activity; the proscribable communication must be (1) directed to inciting or producing imminent lawless action, *and* (2) must be likely to incite or produce such action. Thus in cases where there is a threat of physical violence, the Supreme Court requires that its historical concerns with content[90] and context[91] coalesce. Thus stated and applied the clear and present danger doctrine supports the two postulates stated in this article.

The *Brandenburg* principle underlines the Supreme Court's traditional distaste for general bans on communication.[92] The government is specifically prohibited from suppressing the advocacy of violence, the speech content, without reference to the circumstances within which the advocacy occurs. *Brandenburg*, in fact, specifically overruled an early free expression decision which allowed such suppression.[93] Thus, the clear and present danger test as formulated in *Brandenburg* prohibits a general ban on advocating violence by stipulating that such a ban can only be applied in circumstances of imminent lawless action.

A 1978 case has also made it apparent that the clear and present danger doctrine cannot be avoided by an unproven legislative assumption that a presumed evil will automatically create a "clear and present danger." In *Landmark Communications* v. *Virginia*,[94] the Court struck the conviction of a publisher for violating a state law making it a crime to breach the confidentiality of judicial disciplinary proceedings. Purportedly, the state legislature in passing the law had determined that a clear and present danger to the orderly administration of justice would be created by any divulgence of such proceedings. Chief Justice Burger rejected the idea that the judiciary automatically defer to legislative judgment when fundamental rights are at stake:

> The judicial function commands analysis of whether the specific conduct charged falls within the reach of the

90. *See* Whitney v. California, 274 U.S. 357 (1927); and Gitlow v. New York, 268 U.S. 652 (1925).
91. *See* Abrams v. United States, 250 U.S. 616 (1919); Debs v. United States, 249 U.S. 211 (1919); Frohwerk v. United States, 249 U.S. 204 (1919); and Schenck v. United States, 249 U.S. 47 (1919).
92. A classic such statement comes in Lovell v. Griffin, 303 U.S. 444 (1938): "The ordinance prohibits the distribution of literature of any kind at any time, at any place, and in any manner without a permit from the City Manager. We think the ordinance is invalid on its face. Whatever the motive which induced its adoption, its character is such that it strikes at the very foundation of the freedom of the press by subjecting it to license and censorship." *Id.* at 449.
93. 395 U.S. 444, 449 (1969). The case was Whitney v. California, 274 U.S. 357 (1927).
94. 435 U.S. 829 (1978).

statute and if so whether the legislation is consonant with the Constitution. *Were it otherwise, the scope of the freedom of speech and of the press would be subject to legislative definition and the function of the First Amendment as a check on legislative power would be nullified* (emphasis added).[95]

Applying the test, the Court found that although disclosure posed some risk to the judge under inquiry, the investigative process of the commission, and to the system of justice, the danger of such risk was not "clear and present," and what risk there was could be mitigated through less restrictive means not infringing on the rights of speech and press.[96]

The Supreme Court's distaste for bans on communication stems directly from those constitutional provisions which protect the rights of free expression and political action. Principally, it is supported by the notion that an open system of social participation is the operational principle of democracy, and that the legal institutions must be especially vigilant to protect that system. As such, the notion protects communication as *the* social process within which people form themselves into individuals and continually form and reform their communities and social order. The importance of communication to democratic self-government has been given considerable legal expression since the *Schenck* opinion, much of it following a dissent in *Abrams* v. *United States*,[97] where Holmes presented the "marketplace of ideas" analogy. This famous characterization of the freedom of communication compared the search for truth to the economic marketplace and offered an impassioned argument against any unwarranted state interference in the ideological marketplace:

> ... when men have realized that time has upset many fighting faiths, they may come to believe even more than they believe the very foundations of their own conduct that the ultimate good desired is better reached by free trade in ideas—that the best test of truth is the power of the thought to get itself accepted in the competition of the market ....[98]

Holmes noted that many forms of speech content can endanger vital interests of society, but maintained that "we should be eternally vigilant" against attempts to suppress expressions "we loathe and believe to be

95. *Id.* at 844.
96. *Id.* at 845.
97. 250 U.S. 616 (1919).
98. *Id.* at 630.

fraught with death, unless they so imminently threaten immediate interference with the lawful and pressing purposes of the law that an immediate check is required to save the country."[99] In the years since the *Abrams* dissent, the majority of the Court has come to accept this view[100] and has generally proceeded on the assumption that censorship is more dangerous to the public order than "the principle that debate on public issues should be uninhibited, robust, and wide-open."[101] The argument loses no force when it is applied to sexually related communication. Bans aimed at any specific type of communication clearly diminish the marketplace of ideas by limiting access to it and participation in it. Conversely, total bans have the indirect effect of creating an ideological orthodoxy by leaving some areas open for free communication and foreclosing others. Furthermore, if the Constitution requires that the advocacy of violence be included in the marketplace of ideas and, therefore, protected from total suppression, as the *Brandenburg* case mandates, then it appears a breach of judicial reasoning to hold that the Constitution requires a lesser status for obscenity.[102]

But the clear and present danger doctrine allows *regulation* of some communication.[103] The principle is that in certain narrowly defined circumstances where the danger is clear and present and the state interest is compelling, the government can rebut the presumption of unconstitutionality to uphold a narrowly drawn law. The test specifies both the content and the context wherein such communication can be regulated. In *Brandenburg* the specified content is the advocacy of violence, which would harm individuals and the public order and which is prohibited by statutes. The context is also specified; the right of com-

99. *Id.*
100. *See,* for examples, C.B.S. v. Democratic National Committee, 412 U.S. 94 (1973); and Miami Herald Publishing Company v. Tornillo, 418 U.S. 241 (1974).
101. New York Times v. Sullivan, 376 U.S. 254, 170 (1969).
102. Note that the suppression of obscenity is based largely on the dicta from cases predating Roth v. United States, 354 U.S. 476 (1957). Significantly, the Court has retreated from much of the dicta concerning other exemptions to fundamental liberties stated with obscenity in these cases. Note also that the Court's reliance in Roth on the quoted portion of Chaplinsky v. New Hampshire, 34 U.S. 568, 571-72 (1948), which in turn relies on Zechariah Chafee is misplaced. Chafee viewed obscenity as justifying application of the clear and present danger test, or some variation thereof, but not as putting obscenity outside the first amendment altogether. *See* CHAFEE, GOVERNMENT AND MASS COMMUNICATIONS (1947), 49-61.
103. One of the persistent criticisms of clear and present danger has been that it does not, of itself, offer a rationale for regulation. *See,* for example, DuVal, *Free Communication of Ideas and the Quest for Truth: Toward a Teleological Approach to First Amendment Adjudication,* GEO. WASHINGTON LAW REV. 41 (1972), 166-178. This section views the test in the context of its use by the Supreme Court, but does not present it as the exclusive test for obscenity adjudication.

munication can be suspended where the specified content produces the likelihood of "imminent lawless action."

Thus, the United States Supreme Court is not neutral to all communication under all circumstances. The reason for this is illustrated in part by those who argue that some communication is "absolutely" protected. For example, Thomas Emerson defines the concept of the right of communication along an action/expression dichotomy wherein "expression" is absolutely protected while "action" is not.[104] This dichotomy is unfortunate because it denies the role of all communication as full-fledged *social action,* subject to both the limitations and the protections of the Constitution.[105] To posit, as Emerson does, that "expression" requires absolute constitutional protection implies that it is somehow disembodied from the context of the right of communication and constitutional self-government. But the freedom to communicate—be it specified in the first amendment or not—requires constitutional protection precisely because it enables social action and because it is important to the social order.[106]

Again, an opinion of Justice Holmes, in an early free speech case involving advocacy to overthrow the government, illustrates the point. Holmes' dissent in *Gitlow* v. *United States*[107] began with an affirmation of the majority assumption that first amendment rights are due the protection of the due process clause of the fourteenth amendment: "The general principle of free speech, it seems to me, must be taken to be included in the Fourteenth Amendment, in view of the scope that has been given to the word 'liberty' as there used . . ."[108] But Holmes refused to

104. *See* especially: EMERSON, SYSTEM, 14-20. The absolutist position of Justice Hugo Black follows a similar pattern. Compare the Black opinions in obscenity cases to those involving demonstrations and protests. For examples, *see:* Adderley v. Florida, 385 U.S. 39 (1966); and Tinker v. Des Moines Independent School District, 393 U.S. 503 (1969).
105. Tribe also finds such distinctions troublesome: "No satisfactory jurisprudence of free speech can be built upon such partial or compromised notions of the bases for expressional protection or the boundaries of the conduct to be protected. However tempting it may be to resist governmental claims for restricting speech by retreating to an artificially narrowed zone and then defending it without limit, any such course is likely in the end to sacrifice too much to strategic maneuver: the claims for suppression will persist, and the defense will be no stronger for having withdrawn to arbitrarily constricted territory. Any adequate conception of freedom of speech must instead draw upon several strands of theory in order to protect a rich variety of expressional modes." TRIBE, 579.
106. "Those who won our independence believed that the final end of the state was to make men free to develop their faculties, and that in its government the deliberative forces should prevail over the arbitrary. They valued liberty both as an end and a means. They believed liberty to be the secret of happiness and courage to be the secret of liberty." Whitney v. California, 274 U.S. 357, 375 (1927) (Brandeis, concurring).
107. 268 U.S. 652 (1925).
108. *Id.* at 672.

join in the conviction of Gitlow for participating in the debate on social questions by printing and distributing a revolutionary pamphlet:

> It is said that this manifesto was more than a theory, that it was an incitement. *Every idea is an incitement.* It offers itself for belief and if believed it is acted on unless some other belief outweighs it or some failure of energy stifles the movement at its birth (emphasis added).[109]

Emerson is right in his contention that *some* communication ought to be protected by the first amendment from abridgment from state action, but that point has been categorically settled by the Court. The problem is how to regulate some communication in light of the reasons for doing so, rather than resorting to a definitional dichotomy such as obscenity/free speech or action/expression.[110] In other words, the problem is not that some communication can be regulated, but *how* to regulate communication of specified content without resorting to general censorship of any one type of communication. The clear and present danger test does so by limiting the context of such regulation to those circumstances which would clearly violate the system of ordered liberty. The Constitution establishes a system of liberty which by its very existence denies a constitutional right to incite or produce imminent lawless action. In those circumstances where the advocacy of lawless action is very likely to produce such action, the clear and present danger doctrine allows the government to protect the system of liberty. In such circumstances the countervailing interest of the integrity of the social order is considered sufficiently compelling to justify a selective governmental regulation of communication content.

When invoked and actually applied, the clear and present danger doctrine imposes a very heavy practical burden of proof on the government. First, the right of the individual to participate in the social process through communication is presumed and the doctrine is stated in terms of the *protection* of that right. Second, the contervailing state interest is not granted a similar presumption of validity, but must be demonstrated

---

109. *Id.* at 673.
110. Emerson objects to the defining element of the Supreme Court's adjudication of obscenity cases, but similarly applies his own dichotomy. "There remains, then, the task of analyzing the obscenity problem in terms of the expression-action theory of the First Amendment here being proposed. Clearly most communication alleged to be obscene constitutes 'expression.' It appears in oral, written or pictorial form, as speech, a book, picture, film, play, or the like There are, however, some areas in which the conduct alleged to be obscene, or to contain obscenity, would be classified as 'action.' Thus most of what may be called 'live conduct' falls into the category of action . . . Admittedly these are difficult lines to draw at times. The result reached may on the surface sometimes appear arbitrary or nonsensical." EMERSON, SYSTEM, 495.

by the state; the danger from the content of the expression must be proven to be both clear and present in light of the extrinsic circumstances of the case. Applied to sexually explicit material, the clear and present danger doctrine would provide great deference to exercise of the individual's right to communicate, but would permit regulation in circumstances where the countervailing interests of society are clear and compelling.

In the third major section of this article, the broad outlines of some of the circumstances in which the social interest might be regarded as sufficient for purposes of regulating sexually explicit material are developed. It is important to note that careful adjudication under a clear and present danger doctrine permits government regulation in those circumstances where government interest is clear and compelling, but would preserve the liberty of individual choice in other areas.

2. Prior Restraint

The prior restraint doctrine provides extensive protection of the rights of self-determination of communication. Like clear and present danger, the doctrine supports the two postulates presented in this article; it is a principle presuming freedom from government interference in communication, and it allows selective exceptions to maintain the system of liberty.

Although not usually expressed in this way, the prior restraint doctrine for purposes of this essay is best construed as having both a procedural and a substantive aspect. As a procedural right, the doctrine disallows censorship in all but the most extreme circumstances and then in conformity with strict procedural guidelines. Under this procedural aspect of the doctrine, all materials are presumably protected by the first amendment and prior restraints on publication are not allowed without a showing of extreme danger or the institution of judicial procedures, which presumably guarantee that only non-protected communication will be restrained. As a substantive right, on the other hand, the prior restraint doctrine prohibits prior restraint of all protected communication. If a legally compensable harm results because of such publication, the proper parties are then allowed to pursue compensation or penalty based on the consequences of the publication.

In obscenity decisions since *Miller*, the procedural aspect of the doctrine has been one of the important legal impediments to official censorship of sexually explicit materials. The doctrine checks the power of police and censorship boards by requiring strict adherence to the principles of procedural due process.[111] As such, sexually oriented materials have been presumed to be protected until demonstrated otherwise in a judicial or quasi-judicial proceeding. But as a matter of substantive law the definitional approach to sexual explicit material has prevailed to exclude all "obscenity" from the system of constitutionality protected liberty.

The prior restraint doctrine has roots in the English system of licensed printers. Beginning about the time of the introduction of the printing press, the British civil and ecclesiastical governors by law retained the power of prior approval over all printers. These laws expired in 1695 and thereafter freedom from licensing and prior approval became a recognized right in the common law.[112] The most famous historical statement of the principle came in Sir William Blackstone's eighteenth century *Commentaries:*

> The liberty of the press is indeed essential to the nature of a free state; but this consists of laying no *previous* restraints upon publications, and not the freedom from censure for criminal matter when published. Every freeman has an undoubted right to lay what sentiments he pleases before the public; to forbid this, is to destroy the freedom of the press; but if he publishes what is improper, mischievous, or illegal, he must take the consequence of his own temerity.[113]

The framers of the first amendment clearly intended to outlaw prior restraint and the basic system has never been seriously challenged.[114] In 1931, in *Near* v. *Minnesota,*[115] the Supreme Court formally endorsed the broad concept and presented it as a working principle of constitutional law. The case involved an attempt to stop all further publication of a newspaper pursuant to a state law. The newspaper had been found guilty

---

111. *See,* for example: Roaden v. Kentucky, 413 U.S. 496 (1973), reversing an obscenity conviction for the lack of adequate judicial determination of probable obscenity before official restraint of further sale of sexually explicit material. For discussion of the prior restraint doctrine as a protection of alleged obscenity predating the Miller decisions *see* EMERSON, SYSTEM, 503-512.
112. A more comprehensive study of the English history of press restraint is contained in SIEBERT, FREEDOM OF THE PRESS IN ENGLAND, 1476-1776, (1952).
113. Quoted from GUNTHER and DOWLING, CONSTITUTIONAL LAW CASES AND MATERIALS (1970), 1260.
114. Note the opinion of Justice Black in New York Times v. United States, 403 U.S. 713 (1971). More recent cases involving the doctrine include: National Socialist Party of America v. Village of Skokie, 432 U.S. 43 (1977) (involving an injunction against a street demonstration); and Lo-Ji Sales v. New York, 5 MED. L. REPR. 1177 (1979) (involving an invalid search of an adult bookstore).
115. 283 U.S. 697 (1931).

of publishing "malicious, scandalous and defamatory"[116] materials. The Supreme Court disallowed the injunction and, through Chief Justice Charles E. Hughes, stated that the prior restraint doctrine was subject to limitation "only in exceptional cases."[117] The exceptions, unfortunately, included "obscenity," but otherwise paralleled those of the clear and present danger doctrine. Generally, the exceptions included direct threats to a war effort and incitements to violence or to overthrow the government by force.

The Court in *Near* relied almost exclusively on the historical basis of the prior restraint doctrine and did not develop a functional rationale for either the decision or the exceptions laid out in dicta. This failure was crucial in regard to sexually explicit material. Whereas other exceptions had already been given significant protection by that time under clear and present danger, precedent regarding sexually explicit material was virtually absent.

The first application of the prior restraint doctrine to an "obscenity" case came in *Kingsley Books* v. *Brown*,[118] decided on the same day as *Roth*. There the justices all agreed, contrary to *Near*, that the prior restraint doctrine did apply to "obscenity" cases, but disagreed on the construction of the facts and, thus, left the situation unresolved.[119] In 1961 the Court faced the issue in its "baldest form" in *Times Film Corp.* v. *Chicago*,[120] and decided five to four that the prior restraint doctrine did not require "complete and absolute freedom to exhibit, at least once, any and every kind of motion picture."[121] Writing for the majority, Justice Tom Clark carefully limited the scope of the decision to the facts, saying, "We are dealing only with the motion pictures and, even as to them, only in the context of the broadside attack presented on this record."[122] The four dissenters, led by Chief Justice Earl Warren, vigorously protested that the ordinance was a prior restraint and created a system of licensing and "censorship in its purest and most far-reaching form."[123]

In 1965 the Supreme Court decided another movie censorship case and revived the prior restraint doctrine in this area by melding it with

116. *Id.* at 702.
117. *Id.* at 715.
118. 354 U.S. 436 (1957).
119. The case dealt with a complex regulation which was construed by some justices to be more like a prior restraint, and by others to be more like subsequent punishment for commission of a crime.
120. 365 U.S. 43 (1961).
121. *Id.* at 46. On the history of motion picture censorship *see* Kupferman and O'Brien, *Motion Picture Censorship—The Memphis Blues*, Cornell Law Quar. 36, 273.
122. *Id.* at 50.
123. *Id.* at 49.

notions of procedural due process. In *Freedman* v. *Maryland*[124] the Court struck down the state movie censorship statute for lack of adequate safeguards for protected expression. Justice William Brennan noted that "a noncriminal process which requires the prior submission of a film to a censor avoids constitutional infirmity only if it takes place under procedural safeguards designed to obviate the dangers of a censorship system."[125] The requirements stated there and since applied elsewhere include (1) placing on the censor the burden of proving that the film is unprotected expression, (2) a judicial determination in an adversary hearing to impose a final restraint, and (3) prompt final judicial decisions. In subsequent cases the Court has demanded strict conformity with the rules laid down in *Freedman*. In *Teitel Film Corp.* v. *Cusack*[126] it struck, *per curiam*, a Chicago film ordinance for lack of adequate judicial procedures, including fatal judicial delays. Similar ordinances were struck by the Supreme Court in 1968 in *Interstate Circuit* v. *Dallas*[127] and *Rabeck* v. *New York*[128] for prior restraints imposed without sufficiently specific standards. In the shadow of the *Miller* cases, the Court struck, *per curiam*, a conviction for obscenity in *Roaden* v. *Kentucky*[129] for lack of a proper preliminary determination of probable obscenity, and in 1975 the Court disallowed the prior restraint of a theater production in *Southeastern Promotions* v. *Conrad*.[130]

Two 1971 cases demonstrate the use of the prior restraint doctrine in other areas of communication law. In *Organization for a Better Austin* v. *Keefe*[131] the Court disallowed an injunction sought by Keefe prohibiting the organization from "passing out pamphlets, leaflets, or literature of any kind, and from picketing anywhere in the City of Westchester, Illinois."[132] Through Chief Justice Burger, eight members of the Court affirmed the use of the *Near* doctrine and noted that Keefe had not met the "heavy presumption" against the constitutional validity of such restraints, despite a claim of invasion of privacy. Six weeks later the Court decided *per curiam* the famous and complicated "Pentagon Papers" case, *New York Times* v. *United States*,[133] wherein the prior restraint doctrine was generally upheld. Each of the justices wrote in the decision and each affirmed use of the prior restraint doctrine, but disagreed in its application to the particular facts. Most important here,

124. 380 U.S. 51 (1965).
125. *Id.* at 60.
126. 390 U.S. 139 (1968).
127. 390 U.S. 676 (1968).
128. 391 U.S. 462 (1968).
129. 413 U.S. 496 (1973). *See also* note 111.
130. 420 U.S. 526 (1975).
131. 402 U.S. 415 (1971).
132. *Id.* at 417.
133. 403 U.S. 713 (1971).

the decision favored the unrestrained publication of the documents in question in spite of the United States Attorney General's claim that publication would bring about "irreparable injury" to the defense interests of the United States.

The efficacy of the prior restraint doctrine in regard to sexually explicit material is as clear as in other areas of communication law. At bottom, the prior restraint doctrine imputes a prior presumption of governmental protection upon communication. Somewhat like the presumption of innocence of crime, the prior restraint doctrine puts a very heavy burden of proof on the accuser. The prior restraint doctrine allows free communication until the exceptionable quality of the communication has been established by the censor. As in clear and present danger, the prior restraint doctrine is a principle of protection; it begins with the assumption that communication ought to be protected and requires that the censor demonstrate otherwise. As such it is an important principle of constitutional law which ought to be applied as vigorously to obscenity as to other areas of communication law.

3. Substantive Due Process

The doctrine that the Constitution imposes restrictions on government action affecting fundamental human liberty is a basic bulwark of substantive law. The Bill of Rights specifies several of the rights construed under this constitutional guarantee of liberty, but is not generally considered an exclusive statement of those rights. To protect the fundamental rights, the Supreme Court has developed the rules of substantive due process which demand that whenever a state action infringes on a fundamental right the state must bear a substantial burden of justification. Similar to clear and present danger and prior restraint, the Court requires that the reason for such action be compelling and demonstrable. Further, the Supreme Court applies "close scrutiny" to determine whether fundamental freedoms have been unwarrantedly abridged, and whether the government's objective could be reached with a less restrictive law.[134]

The fundamental freedoms doctrine is most often traced to *United States* v. *Carolene Products*,[135] a 1938 case involving a federal statute concerned with economic regulation. There Chief Justice Harlan Stone stated in his opinion for the Court that in commercial regulation the courts presumed the constitutionality of laws, but added a famous foot-

---

134. *See* TRIBE, 564-574.
135. 304 U.S. 144 (1938).

note indicating that in matters involving fundamental freedoms the presumption of constitutionality is reversed. In the wake of the *Carolene Products* footnote, the Supreme Court developed substantive due process principles protecting political and civil liberties, and has continued that protection through the present.[136]

The essence of substantive due process is that state action restricting substantive rights requires more severe and exact judicial review than that required in most other areas of constitutional law. These substantive due process principles are also consistent with the concept of communication presented here which views communication as the operational activity of democracy. The rationale is based upon judicial responsibility to protect citizen participation in the self-governing process. Conversely, government action which does not involve fundamental freedoms is given the presumption of constitutionality because it is the product of the political participation process; that is, it is the expression of the will of the people. But if government action disenfranchises a segment of the electorate by restraining liberty, especially the process of communication, it potentially inhibits the ability of citizens to rationally engage in the collective decision-making process and, thus, is extended no presumption of constitutionality. In the latter case, constitutionality must be proven before the action is sustained by the Supreme Court; the government action must withstand "close scrutiny."[137]

To withstand this close judicial examination, the government must make the usual showing that the law has a proper societal purpose and that it is reasonably related to the accomplishment of that purpose; the government must also demonstrate that the societal objective is a *compelling* subordinating interest to the fundamental freedom, and that the law is necessary to the accomplishment of the stated objective. In effect, this part of substantive due process is similar to clear and present danger and prior restraint. But the requirements have two additional dimensions when applied to fundamental freedoms: (1) the law must not sweep more broadly than absolutely necessary; and (2) the law must be sufficiently specific to give adequate warning as to what is proscribed. Specific constitutional authority for these requirements is derived from the due process clauses of the fifth and fourteenth amendments, the equal protec-

---

136. A comprehensive statement of that protection with regard to sexual freedom is contained in BARNETT, SEXUAL FREEDOM.
137. Substantive due process is similar to a related principle under the "equal protection clause" of the fourteenth amendment. As such it is used to insure that suspect classifications; e.g., those regarding race, religion, and national origin, are protected from unequal treatment under the law. *See*, for example: Shapiro v. Thompson, 394 U.S. 618 (1969).

tion clause of the fourteenth amendment, and the doctrine of unenumerated rights of the ninth amendment.

Several of the early fundamental rights cases were decided under these principles, including the early voting rights cases and the seminal *Skinner v. Oklahoma*[138] case where the Court found procreation a fundamental right. The outstanding case in the recent history of the Court is *Griswold v. Connecticut*,[139] the landmark case, which established privacy as a fundamental constitutional right and aggressively protected the right of individuals to communication involving sexual matters. The *Griswold* case is especially relevant because it involved a ban on communication concerning birth control devices. Specifically, the litigants were prosecuted for giving information, instruction, and medical advice to married persons as to the prevention of conception. The Supreme Court emphatically overturned the conviction, noting that the law was a direct and unwarranted intrusion into the intimate sexual relations of husbands and wives. The constitutional authority rested in the recognition, according to the majority opinion written by Justice William O. Douglas, that the "specific guarantees in the Bill of Rights have penumbras, formed by emanations from those guarantees that help give them life and substance."[140] The right of privacy was thus implicit from a number of specific provisions, including the first, third, fourth, fifth, and ninth amendments. The recognition of the protection of the first amendment has the most direct relevance here:

> .... the State may not, consistently with the spirit of the First Amendment, contract the spectrum of available knowledge. The right of freedom of speech and press includes not only the right to utter or to print, but the right to distribute, the right to receive, the right to read .... and freedom of inquiry, freedom of thought, and freedom to teach ....[141]

Griswold underlines the requirement that state action be narrowly tailored so not to interfere with the fundamental rights of those who are not part of the compelling problem. Generally, the over inclusiveness principle protects citizens from laws with a proper legislative purpose, but which are overly broad either as written or as applied. The classic "obscenity" case is *Butler v. Michigan*,[142] where the state forbade the sale

---

138. 316 U.S. 535 (1942).
139. 381 U.S. 479 (1965). *See also* Carey v. Population Services International 431 U.S. 678 (1977), and Bigelow v. Virginia, 421 U.S. 809 (1975).
140. *Id.* at 484.
141. *Id.* at 482.
142. 352 U.S. 380 (1957).

to the general public of books which were thought to have a deleterious effect on children. The legislative means clearly outstripped the problem, prompting Justice Felix Frankfurter to say, "Surely, this is to burn the house to roast the pig."[143] Thus, Frankfurter declared for the unanimous Court that the reading rights of the general public could not be suspended in light of a specific intention to protect children.

Substantive due process as applied to state action involving fundamental freedoms is strikingly similar to the more specific clear and present danger and prior restraint doctrines. Each of these begin with the assumption that important liberties are involved, and therefore the Court must place a heavy burden of proof on the government to justify the abberation. Each test requires a showing of grave state interest and specific and narrow tailoring of the state action in protection of that interest. But substantive due process is a more general provision, which leads the Court to concentrate upon the entire system of liberty rather than on specific elements, as in clear and present danger and prior restraint. *United States v. O'Brien*,[144] a draft card burning case, illustrates the difference. The Supreme Court adjudicated that case according to the principles of substantive due process and applied close scrutiny to the provision under which O'Brien was prosecuted. The law was found to serve a compelling state interest without unwarranted intrusion upon fundamental rights. The conviction was thus upheld. Had the Court concentrated on the first amendment challenge and applied the clear and present danger doctrine, as O'Brien suggested, it is unlikely that the government could have made the required showing of either imminent lawless action or clear danger to the security of the country.

Application of the substantive due process principles to the question of sexually explicit material is profoundly consistent with the needs of the system of human communication, and would provide a body of judicial precedent successfully applied in other areas of liberty. The rationale for inclusion of the right to control communication concerning sexual materials exists in several of the cases, including those above. Even if the Court continues to persist in the notion that such material is not protected by the specific provisions of the first amendment, expanded protection could be granted under substantive due process principles. Extended use of substantive due process in obscenity cases would be supported by the Court's careful application of the prior restraint doctrine in these cases and decisions like *Griswold* which grant constitutional protection of the rights to distribute, receive, and read sexual materials, and the freedoms of inquiry, thought, and teaching such matters.

143. *Id.* at 383.
144. 391 U.S. 367 (1968).

It is important to emphasize that the principles of clear and present danger, prior restraint, and substantive due process do not bestow "absolute" liberty upon individuals to pursue their self-determined activity regardless of the social context. Instead, these principles elevate the system of liberty to a primary constitutional position and allow the weighing of all factors relevant to the preservation of that system. As such, they are consistent with the notion that communication is inextricably associated with the social process, and that individual freedom is continually bounded by social reality. The principles, therefore, support the process of human communication and allow the incorporation of legal consideration of all the relevant factors. Some factors of compelling importance to the maintenance of the system of liberty are sketched in the next section.

C. Contexts Suggesting Special Consideration

The system of liberty, based on human communication, protected by constitutional government requires that primary group associations (especially the family) and privacy be carefully considered in the adjudication of cases involving sexually explicit material. A recurrent theme in the Court's "obscenity" decisions has been the protection of the family and of other self-determined communicative environments. Sufficient precedent and functional rationale exists to treat these as compelling social interests which can sometimes be countervailing, and thus be recognized by the Supreme Court as sufficient to rebut the presumption of unconstitutionality.

It is important to note that human communication implies the capacity of men to make value judgments from human experiences; that is, to operate rationally. Likewise, liberty presupposes rationality and socially responsible exercise of that capacity; the liberty of communication correlates with the liberty of others to choose to participate or not in specific aspects of the social process. Thus, the principles of liberty may not apply to children or the insane.[145] Furthermore, the society protects

---

145. Minors for example were excluded by the classic libertarian thinkers. Sir Henry Maine compared the rights of children "before the age of discretion" to those of "the adjudged lunatic" because "they do not possess the facility of forming a judgment on their own interests; in other words . . . they are wanting in the first essential to engagement by Contract." MAINE, ANCIENT LAW (1870), 163-64. Likewise, John Stewart Mill, often identified as the founder of the modern libertarian ideal, excluded children and tied that exclusion to the ability of children to participate in classic first amendment activities: "Liberty as a principle has no application to any state of things anterior to the time when mankind have become capable of being improved by free and equal discussion." MILL, 14-15. See also EMERSON, p. 91.

enclaves of communicative stability and support where humans can develop and sustain their system of rationality, where they can selectively choose what will and will not enter their communicative environment.[146] The need of humans to communicate and the libertarian spirit of the Constitution support selective regulation of communication consistent with these concerns.

1. Primary Group Communication

The Supreme Court has given considerable support to the leaders of primary groups; namely, parents, in order that children can organize themselves in the enclaves of communicative support necessary for maturation. The decision of Justice William Brennan in *Ginsberg v. New York*[147] contains one of the most direct statements of such support:

> First of all, constitutional interpretation has consistently recognized that parents' claims to authority in their own households to direct the rearing of their children is basic in the structure of our society .... [P]arents and others, teachers for example, who have this primary responsibility for children's well being are entitled to the support of law designed to aid discharge of that responsibility.[148]

Accordingly, Brennan reasserted the position that "the power of the state to control the conduct of children reaches beyond the scope of its authority over adults,"[149] and used that power to sustain a New York law regulating the sale of sexually explicit material to children.

This position of the Supreme Court supports primary group association, a necessary element for mature communication. The importance of primary group association stems from its function as a generative base for the communicative process in children. Children create their first ordered and unified conceptions of the world in primary group association and eventually learn to integrate the larger world outside into a mature conceptual scheme. As such, it is the source of mature communicative action and of compelling importance to the system of democratic living.[150]

---

146. An extensive discussion of this is contained in Willard, "Privacy and Communication: A Conceptual Approach for Law and Social Science," (Ph.D. diss., University of Iowa, 1975).
147. 390 U.S. 629 (1968).
148. *Id.* at 639.
149. *Id.* at 638. (Citing Prince v. Massachusetts, 231 U.S. 158, 170 [1944]).
150. *See* PIAGET, THE CONSTRUCTION OF REALITY IN THE CHILD, (1952); and BERGER and LUCHMANN.

These considerations permeate American law; children never automatically have the full rights of adults, and most often attain their rights vis-à-vis their parents.[151] Correlatively, the protective power of the government over youth is greater than the protective power of government over adults.[152] The assumption is apparent in several areas, including restrictions on child labor, jury duty, marriage, and military service.[153]

In the "obscenity" area the pattern is quite different. Chief Justice Burger prefaced his announcement of the "serious value" test in *Miller* by saying that it was presented against the background of obtrusive exposure to unwilling audiences and to juveniles,[154] although these were not part of the facts in *Paris* and the related cases decided that day. In *Ginsberg* the Court held that a state statute prohibiting the dissemination of obscenity to minors was valid when sufficiently specific and selective. *Redrup v. New York*[155] stated that a "specific and limited state concern for juveniles" was a permissible factor in obscenity regulation. The primary dissents in the 1973 decisions were filed by Justice Brennan, author of *Ginsberg*. Though Brennan expressly refused to consider the issue of children, he noted no dissatisfaction with his *Ginsberg* opinion

---

151. The most difficult unresolved questions in this regard have to do with in whom the legal rights are vested, the parents or the children, and against whom these rights can be enforced. Two 1977 Supreme Court decisions indicate that children are protected by the due process clause against at least some forms of state interference with family relationships because of their interest in receiving parental guidance. *See* Smith v. Organization of Foster Families for Equality and Reform (OFFER), 431 U.S. 816, 850-54 (1977); and Moore v. City of East Cleveland, 431 U.S. 494, 499, 503-4, (1977). One commentator suggests that the right of autonomy is the proper frame of analysis for the question, and that autonomy should be considered to reside in the children and the family against the government. Garvey, *Child, Parent, State and the Due Process Clause: An Essay on The Supreme Court's Recent Work*, Southern Calif. Law Rev. 51 (1978), 769. *See also* Garvey, *Children and the First Amendment*, Texas Law Rev., 57 (1979).
152. Prince v. Massachusetts, 321 U.S. 158 (1944) illustrates the greater power of the government over children than over adults as regards to constitutional rights. In Prince, the Court upheld a Massachusetts law prohibiting any girl under eighteen from selling periodicals in "any street or public place" (at 161). The law was upheld against a claim of the right, under the free exercise clause of the first amendment, to sell religious literature. Had the law had the effect of a general ban of the sale of periodicals, as in Lovell, the Court would have most likely struck it. Because of the fact that in Prince the law was limited to children, the Court favored the state interest in protection of the safety and health of children over first amendment values.
153. Such restriction appears both in federal and state laws. For example, the federal government exercises the power to control the voting age in federal elections, and states in state elections. *See* Oregon v. Mitchel, 400 U.S. 112 (1970).
154. 413 U.S. 12, 24 (1973).
155. 386 U.S. 767 (1967).

and intimated continued recognition of the state power in the area.[156] Thus, all members of the Court at the time of *Miller*, except Justice Douglas, appear to agree that the government has the constitutional authority to support parents in the selective regulation of their children's exposure to obscenity. The regulatory rationale is consistent with a comprehensive understanding of human communication and is perhaps most succinctly stated by Justice Potter Stewart in his *Ginsberg* concurrence:

> I think a State may permissibly determine that at least in some precisely delineated areas, a child—like someone in a captive audience—is not possessed of that full capacity for individual choice which is the presupposition of the First Amendment guarantees.[157]

The Supreme Court decision in *Tinker v. Des Moines Independent Community School District*[158] helps illustrate some of the important issues. In *Tinker* the Court upheld the right of school children to wear black armbands as part of a peaceful political protest; the justices supported the right of the children to use the school as a secondary socialization institution for education in political participation. In *Ginsberg* and similar cases the justices have taken the converse of the *Tinker* position, protecting children from unregulated communication environments. The opinion of Justice Abe Fortes clarifies the distinction by noting that schools "may not be enclaves of totalitarianism," nor should "students be regarded as closed-circuit recipients"[159] of communication in such environments.

The decision thus supports the position that arbitrarily restricting the right of children to participate in the ideological marketplace of ideas would have a stultifying effect on individual growth, and would disregard the function of schools as preparatory institutions for democratic decision makers. The process of education and communication implies regulated exposure to ideas of ever increasing complexity and diversity. The schools, as the churches and other secondary socialization institutions, are the logical extensions of the family. Thus, the notion that the state has a compelling interest in the protection of youth has a double

---

156. Brennan said: "The opinions in *Redrup* and *Stanley v. Georgia* reflected our emerging view that the state interests in protecting children and in protecting unconsenting adults may stand on a different footing from the other asserted state interests." (413 U.S. 49, 106 (1973)). For further discussion of the Brennan view *see* Meiklejohn, *The Reconciliation of First Amendment Freedoms with Local Control Over the Moral Development of Minors*, SUFFOLK LAW REV, 13 (1978), 1205.
157. 390 U.S. 629, 649-650 (1968).
158. 393 U.S. 503 (1969).
159. *Id.* at 511.

edge which recognizes the right of youth to preliminary participation in the social process, but under the guided supervision of those responsible for their communicative environment.[160] It proceeds from the fundamental fact of human communication that the capacity of imparting value on experience requires the attainment of maturity in a relatively stable communication environment. Rational decision-making is usually acquired during late adolescence and, although exceptions to that norm exist, the norm reflects the social reality, and society has an important interest in laws that reflect those social facts.[161]

As a constitutional principle, the use of youth as a classification does not pose the problems under the equal protection clause of the fourteenth amendment associated with "suspect" classifications.[162] Youth as a state in life is neutral as to race, national heritage, religion, and sex; it is a state through which all must pass and is not permanent. Furthermore, restrictions on children would create only a partial ban on sexually oriented matter, leaving consenting adults' rights unimpeded.

Such regulation adds a positive dimension to the system of liberty; it operates to strengthen the capability of parents to choose for their children the type of material which will enter their primary communication environments. In addition, such regulation is functionally similar to laws which allow adults to control their own communication under the law of privacy discussed below.

---

160. Donald Meiklejohn suggests that the crucial question is who shall censor, and that the alternative answers are not limited to the official censor, the police, and the commercial pornographer: "A genuinely liberal policy imposing controls on matters touching manners and customs ought to locate such authority in nonlegal agents—family, friends, or the church. To the extent that 'Thou Shalt Not' must be promulgated, both intellectual and emotional freedom requires not mere censoriousness but also sympathy and tolerance." MEIKLEJOHN, 1223.
161. Generally the President's Commission on Obscenity and Pornography "recommends the adoption by the States of legislation . . . prohibiting the commercial distribution or display for sale of certain sexual materials to young persons." REPORT OF THE COMMISSION, 70. The Commission make the recommendation with these comments: "In view of the limited amount of information concerning the effects of sexually explicit materials on children, other considerations have assumed primary importance in the Commission's deliberations. The Commission has been influenced, to a considerable degree, by its finding that a large majority of Americans believe that children should not be exposed to certain sexual materials. In addition, the Commission takes the view that parents should be free to make their own conclusions regarding the suitability of explicit sexual materials for their children, and that it is appropriate for legislation to aid parents in controlling the access of their children to such materials during their formative years." *Id.* at 63. For a general discussion on the subject, *see* Trauth and Huffman, *Heightened Judicial Scrutiny: A Test for the First Amendment Rights of Children*, COMM AND THE LAW 2, no. 2 (Spring 1980): 39-58.
162. *See* note 137.

2. Privacy

The notion of privacy explored earlier in this essay also has a correlative dimension which requires careful consideration by the Supreme Court in these cases.[163] Privacy in light of *Griswold* is essentially a fundamental right of persons to access to materials of a private nature without the interference of the state. This aspect of privacy directly supports the first postulate of this article that would impose a presumption against the constitutionality of restrictions by censors. A correlative aspect of the privacy notion is that there is a very important sphere of human communication which must necessarily remain private; that is, beyond the purview and control of the larger society. This private sphere allows individuals to maintain essential control over their own communicative behavior, and to preserve and continually develop their own identities. In essence, privacy is the functional corollary of primary group associations, and legal institutions might well be used to protect it.

Accordingly, freedom from invasion of privacy has been asserted in several recent decisions of the Supreme Court which have elevated privacy to clear constitutional status. For example, the right has been used to protect a woman's right to make the abortion decision in consultation with her personal physician,[164] an association's right to maintain the secrecy of its membership list,[165] and a person's right not to have private information published in a newspaper feature article.[166] The issues of privacy and obscenity met in *Stanley* v. *Georgia*,[167] which upheld the right of Stanley to view obscene materials in his home, and *Rowan* v. *Post Office*,[168] which upheld a homeowner's right to block sexually offensive mail from entering his home. These cases grant extensive protection to individuals in their pursuit of a zone of privacy and indicate the permissible posture of the state vis-à-vis the individual control of that zone.

The justification of the right of privacy pervades the spirit of the Constitution.[169] In fact, one of the functional bases of the constitutional system of government by, for, and of the people is the presumption of the ability of citizens to choose in the ideological marketplace. Not only

---

163. *See* the discussion of Willard which considers privacy as a constituent aspect of the process of communication, a point of view not inconsistent with this article. WILLARD, 277-322.
164. Roe v. Wade, 410 U.S. 113 (1973).
165. NAACP v. Alabama, 357 U.S. 449 (1958).
166. Cantrell v. Forest City Publishing, 419 U.S. 245 (1974).
167. 294 U.S. 557 (1969).
168. 397 U.S. 728 (1970).
169. For a comprehensive account of the development of privacy law in the United States *see* WILLARD, 115-182.

should the government be prohibited from invading this zone, as in *Stanley*, but the government should help individuals protect this zone from the intrusion of unwanted ideas, as in *Rowan*. In reference to the second postulate of this article, the state has a compelling interest in the ability of individuals to maintain enclaves within which the communication process can prosper. Implicit in the "marketplace of ideas" analogy is the notion that once persons have made their selection, they can retreat to savor and use it; perhaps even improve it and reintroduce it into the market. But without a human mind developed and maintained in the privacy of one's personal enclave, the marketplace would have few buyers. Thus, if an individual desires to block certain materials from his private communication environment, it appears proper for the government to aid him in that quest. While vigorous competition in the marketplace may be essential for the survival of the right to communicate, the competition need not be ubiquitous. Or as Justice Brandeis noted in his famous concurrence in *Whitney* v. *California*:[170] "Those who won our independence believed that the final end of the state was to make men free to develop their facilities . . . . They valued liberty both as an end and as a means."[171]

This right of the state to assist people in this regard is outlined by the Supreme Court's traditional respect for those who are in a so-called "captive audience." In *Saia* v. *New York*[172] in 1948 and *Kovacs* v. *Cooper*[173] in 1949, the Court allowed the regulation of sound trucks so long as that regulation was not based on the content of the ideas and the regulation was not vague and overbroad. In other cases, such as *Public Utilities Commission* v. *Pollak*,[174] the Court has noted that persons do not have unlimited rights to an enclave of privacy, especially when a person leaves home. In *Pollak* the Court refused to sustain an injunction against the broadcasting of news, music, and advertising in a public bus system, maintaining that an individual's zone of privacy is not unlimited and must be weighed against the concomitant rights of others.

One potentially troublesome element in the protection of privacy is the proper role of the government in the quest for individual privacy. Perhaps the best example of a successful resolution of this is the statute upheld in *Rowan* which allowed a person to "require that a mailer remove his name from its mailing lists and stop all future mailings . . ."[175] Writing the majority opinion Chief Justice Burger noted

170. 274 U.S. 357 (1927).
171. *Id.* at 375-6.
172. 334 U.S. 558 (1948).
173. 336 U.S. 77 (1949).
174. 343 U.S. 414 (1952).
175. 397 U.S. 728, 729 (1970).

that the Court has traditionally respected the right of householders to bar people from their homes, and that it is appropriate to "make the householder the final judge of what will cross his threshhold" in spite of the fact that such power impeded the flow of ideas.[176] The Chief Justice noted the law specifically escaped a constitutional challenge in this regard because the individual was making the determination, not the government.

> Both the absoluteness of the citizen's right under [the law] and its finality are essential; what may not be provocative to one person may well be to another.... Congress provided this sweeping power not only to protect privacy but to avoid possible constitutional questions that might arise from vesting the power to make any discretionary evaluation of the material in a government official.[177]

The notions expressed by the Chief Justice in the *Rowan* case provide firm positive precedent in the area of sexually explicit material. Vesting the power of control of communication in mature individuals, both as individuals and as leaders of primary groups, keeps significant power of self-determination of communication in the hands of citizens. Meanwhile those who do not wish particular material are assisted by the state in exercising their power against it. The government acts only to assist people in their exercise of constitutional rights and does not limit the right of access to such materials.

3. Summary

Deriving its power from the direction of individuals, the government could be allowed the power to regulate communication selectively. In the areas of youth and privacy, the government may conclude that the state has a compelling interest in protecting the system of liberty and thus in certain narrowly defined situations may assist the exercise of that liberty by individuals by carefully restricting the sale and use of sexually oriented materials.

One important aspect to consider here is the narrowness of permissible regulation. As in *Butler* above, regulation designed to protect the compelling state interest in primary group association and individual

---

176. *Id.* at 736.
177. *Id.* at 737.

enclaves of privacy must be clearly, on its face,[178] as construed by the courts or applied by the law enforcement agencies, related only to those interests and not sweep unnecessarily into the compelling interests of liberty of adults. The state's power cannot be used as a covert tool for placing a substantial ban on the dissemination of obscenity to consenting adults, nor can it have that practical effect. A functional test for detecting such an abuse of state power might be: does the regulatory scheme in question restrict the spectrum of materials available to consenting adults?[179] If the scheme does not do so and is otherwise constitutional, it could be upheld as a valid exercise of governmental power.

---

178. *See* Broadbeck v. Oklahoma, 413 U.S. 601 (1973). There the Supreme Court appeared to weaken the "overbreadth" doctrine: "[T]he overbreadth of [the] statute must not only be real, but substantial as well, judged in relation to the statute's plainly legitimate sweep." *Id.* at 615.
179. The President's Commission on Obscenity supports this type of test and "recommends that federal, state, and local legislation prohibiting the sale, exhibition, or distribution of sexual materials to consenting adults should be repealed." REPORT OF THE COMMISSION, 51.

LOUIS A. DAY

Shield Laws and the
Separation of Powers Doctrine

Louis A. Day is Associate Professor of Journalism at the School of Journalism and Mass Communication, University of Oklahoma (Norman).

INTRODUCTION

Few first amendment issues have generated as much controversy in recent years as "newsman's privilege"—the right of a reporter to protect the names of his or her confidential sources from the interrogations of legislative, judicial, or other official investigatory bodies. The increase in reporters' subpoenas during the late 1960s and early 1970s, the incarceration of reporters, and the Supreme Court's *Branzburg* decision[1] prompted a new round of "shield" legislation at the state level. Over half the jurisdictions now have shield laws in effect,[2] and there has been some Congressional interest in a federal shield law.[3]

---

1. Branzburg v. Hayes, 408 U.S. 665 (1972).
2. However, in 1976 the New Mexico supreme court declared that the state's shield law was an unconstitutional encroachment on the authority of the court. Ammerman v. Hubbard Broadcasting, Inc., 551 P.2d 1354 (1976).
3. In 1973, the year following the Branzburg decision, more than sixty bills creating various forms of a journalists' privilege were introduced in the 93d Congress. However, only one made it out of subcommittee, and it died at the committee

Such statutes represent an attempt to fill a vacuum left by the absence of any common law or constitutional privilege. Not unexpectedly, the enactment of shield laws has resulted in mixed reviews. Proponents claim that protection of news sources is essential to the journalistic newsgathering process. Source confidentiality is the cornerstone of investigative reporting. Indeed, there is even some empirical evidence that loss of privilege may "poison the atmosphere" between reporters and their sources.[4] But opponents, some of whom come from the ranks of the journalistic profession itself, argue that testimonial privileges have an adverse effect on the administration of justice because they withhold relevant evidence from the trier of fact. In short, a privilege is an impediment to the search for truth.[5]

The literature in this area is voluminous, and the pros and cons of the controversy have been explored in great detail.[6] But one legal issue that needs further investigation is the extent to which these privileges embodying legislative policy judgments impose such burdens on the judiciary as to constitute a violation of the separation of powers doctrine.[7] This is not merely a hypothetical question. In recent years courts in two states, California and New Mexico, have severely narrowed or declared unconstitutional their states' privilege statutes.[8] The prospects of a federal shield law magnifies the significance of this question. This article examines the nature of shield laws and their relationship to the separation of powers doctrine.

---

level. *See* S. Ervin, *In Pursuit of a Press Privilege*, 11 HARV. J. LEG. 233, 255-61 (1974). There has been a renewed interest in some form of federal statutory privilege following the Supreme Court's ruling that news media are not exempt from searches under the Fourth Amendment. See Zurcher v. Stanford Daily, 436 U.S. 547 (1978).

4. V. Blasi, *The Newsman's Privilege: An Empirical Study*, 70 MICH. L. REV. 229 (1971).
5. See United States v. Nixon, 418 U.S. 683, 710 (1974).
6. *See, e.g.,* A. Pickerell, *Newsmen's Shield Laws and Subpoenas: California's Farr and the Fresno Four*, 1 COMM/ENT 101, note 2 (1977); M. Neubauer, *The Newsman's Privilege After Branzburg: The Case For a Federal Shield Law*, 24 U.C.L.A. L. REV. 160 (1976); note, *Newsman's Source Privilege: A Foundation In Policy For Recognition At Common Law*, 26 U. FLA. L. REV. 453 (1974); J. Cades, *The Power of the Courts To Protect Journalists' Confidential Sources of Information: An Examination of Proposed Shield Legislation*, 11 HAW. B. J. 35 (1974); J. Beaver, *The Newsman's Code, The Claim of Privilege and Everyman's Right To Evidence*, 47 ORE. L. REV. 243 (1968).
7. One article that has explored this issue is T. Shomaker and P. Zesk, *A Study In Governmental Separation of Powers: Judicial Response To State Shield Laws*, 66 GEO. L. J. 1273 (1978).
8. Rosato v. Superior Court, 51 Cal. App. 190 (1975), *cert. denied*, 427 U.S. 912 (1976); Farr v. Superior Court, 22 Cal. App. 3d 60 (1971), *cert. denied*, 409 U.S. 1011 (1972); Ammerman v. Hubbard Broadcasting, Inc., 551 P.2d 1354 (1976).

HISTORICAL BACKGROUND OF SHIELD LAWS

American journalists have a long history of protecting the confidentiality of their news sources. In fact, the issue predates the founding of the republic itself. In 1722, Benjamin Franklin's half-brother, James, was hauled before a committee of the Assembly and asked to reveal the name of an author of an article in his newspaper, the *New England Courant*. Franklin refused and was imprisoned for a month.[9]

The first officially reported newsman's privilege case occurred in 1848. In that year the Senate went into secret session to debate the treaty to end the Mexican-American War. A reporter for the *New York Herald* obtained a confidential draft of the treaty and other secret documents. The Senate subpoenaed the reporter, John Nugent, and demanded that he reveal his source. Nugent refused and was jailed for contempt of Congress after failing to secure a writ of *habeas corpus*.[10]

Until the 1930s the issue received little legislative or judicial attention. Claims of privilege occasionally arose out of stories dealing with political corruption, stories that resulted in a libel suit, or reports of supposedly secret grand jury proceedings.[11] But the courts consistently refused to find any privilege in the common law.

Maryland adopted the nation's first shield law in 1896,[12] which met with a chilly reception from the legal profession. There were even predictions that this legislative precedent would remain unique.[13] Indeed, it did remain unique until the 1930s when seven states enacted shield laws.[14] In the ensuing years other states followed suit and by 1972—the year that the Supreme Court handed down the *Branzburg* decision—eighteen states had passed shield legislation.

It was not until 1958 that the question of a constitutional privilege was considered by the federal judiciary. In a libel action, actress Judy Garland sought to discover the source of allegedly defamatory statements about her printed in an article by columnist Marie Torre. Torre refused to identify her source on first amendment grounds. The court recognized a qualified privilege but refused to grant the privilege

---

9. Ervin, *supra* note 3, at 233.
10. *Ex parte* Nugent, 18 F. Cas. 471 (D.C. Cir. 1848).
11. *See, e.g., Ex parte* Lawrence, 48 P. 124 (1897); *In re* Grunow, 85 A. 1011 (1913); Brogan v. Passaic Daily News, 123 A.2d 473 (1956); *Ex parte* Holliway, 199 S.W. 412 (1917); *In re* Shortridge, 34 P. 227 (1893); Herbert v. Lando, 73 F.R.D. 387 (S.D.N.Y. 1977), *aff'd* by U.S. Supreme Court, 4 M ED. L. RPTR. 2575 (1979).
12. Md. Ann. Code, art. 35, sec. 2 (1957), Replacement 1971.
13. 5 J. WIGMORE, EVIDENCE, sec. 2286 (1923).
14. These were New Jersey (1933), Alabama (1935), California (1935), Arkansas (1936), Kentucky (1936), Arizona (1937), and Pennsylvania (1937).

when the identity of the source goes to the "heart of the plaintiff's claim."[15]

During the next several years some courts endorsed the recognition of a first amendment privilege,[16] but a majority of courts refused to accord reporters a privilege in any form.[17] One such case received national attention when a student newspaper editor at the University of Oregon refused to answer grand jury questions regarding sources of an article on marijuana use. She was cited for contempt and fined $300.[18]

Despite these inconsistencies in lower court rulings and the dramatic increase in subpoenas issued against reporters in the late 1960s, the Supreme Court declined to review the issue. But in the early 1970s the Court, reacting to public pressure to decide the question, granted *certiorari* in four cases involving the claim of a first amendment privilege.[19] Journalists had hoped for at least a qualified privilege from official investigations. But in *Branzburg* v. *Hayes*[20] the Court, in a 5–4 decision, held that reporters have no first amendment privilege to refuse to appear before a grand jury or to refuse to answer the relevant and material questions posed during a "good faith" grand jury investigation.[21] Although the ruling was a narrow one and raised as many questions as it answered, the majority emphasized that its decision did not preclude Congress or state legislatures from enacting statutory privileges, nor did it prevent state courts from construing state constitutions to recognize a journalist's privilege.[22]

Following the 1972 *Branzburg* decision, nine states accepted the Court's invitation and enacted shield legislation.[23] This brought to twenty-six the total number of states which provide some statutory protection for reporters' sources. But the continued viability of statutory privileges for journalists must be questioned in light of the issues raised by the separation of powers doctrine and the distribution of power between the legislative and judicial branches of government.

---

15. Garland v. Torre, 259 F.2d 545 (2d Cir. 1958), *cert. denied,* 358 U.S. 910 (1958).
16. See, *e.g.,* Adams v. Associated Press, 46 F.R.D. 439 (S.D. Tex. 1969).
17. *In re* Goodfader, 367 P.2d 472 (1961); *In re* Taylor, 193 A.2d 181 (1963).
18. State v. Buchanan, 436 P.2d 729, *cert. denied,* 392 U.S. 905 (1968).
19. Branzburg v. Pound, 461 S.W. 2d 345 (1970); Branzburg v. Meigs, 503 S.W. 2d 748 (1971); *In re* Pappas, 266 N.E. 297 (1971); Caldwell v. United States, 434 F.2d 1081 (9th Cir. 1970).
20. 408 U.S. 665 (1972).
21. *Id.* at 708.
22. *Id.* at 706.
23. Shomaker and Zesk, *supra* note 7, at 1276.

SHIELD LAWS AND THE SEPARATION OF POWERS

The separation of powers doctrine is a fundamental principle of American constitutional government, both at the national[24] and state levels.[25] Although the states vary in their implementation of the doctrine, the separation of powers concept has four goals: (1) protection of the individual from absolute majority rule and government tyranny; (2) independence of the judiciary; (3) checks and balances between the departments of government; and (4) efficiency in government.[26] In order to provide substance to these goals, the founding fathers realized that a physical separation was insufficient. There must be a clearly defined distribution of powers. As James Madison wrote in *The Federalist:*

> It is agreed on all sides, that the powers properly belonging to one of the departments ought not to be directly and completely administered by either of the other departments. It is equally evident, that none of them ought to possess, directly or indirectly, an overriding influence over the others, in the administration of their respective powers.[27]

This political philosophy has been given judicial recognition by the Supreme Court, which held in the 1933 case of *O'Donoghue v. United States* that the acts of each department "shall never be controlled by, or subjected directly or indirectly to the coercive influence of, either of the other two departments."[28] At both the federal and state levels the legislative "sphere of influence" includes the responsibility for making substantive law, which prescribes the duties and rights under our system of government.[29] Judicial authority has been defined as the power to determine issues affecting life, liberty, or property of the citizens and the power to apply the law for that purpose.[30]

Some interplay among the branches is permitted in order to

---

24. U.S. CONST., art. I, § 1; art. II, § 1; art. III, § 2.
25. At the state level the doctrine has been recognized either by an express constitutional provision or by judicial implications. See *e.g.,* Langever v. Miller, 78 S.W. 2d 1025, 1035 (1974); Bailey v. Waters, 112 A. 818, 822 (1932).
26. T. Green, Jr., *To What Extent May Courts Under The Rulemaking Power Prescribe Rules of Evidence?,* 26 A.B.A.J. 482, 486 (1940).
27. No. 48, p. 330 (Heritage Press, 1945).
28. 289 U.S. 516, 530 (1933).
29. Fletcher v. Peck, 10 U.S. (6 Cranch) 87, 136 (1810); Benyard v. Wainwright, 322 So.2d 473, 475 (1975).
30. Rusch v. White, 166 N.E. 100, 106 (1929); City of Sapulpa v. Land, 101 Okla. 22, 27 (1924).

facilitate efficient governmental operation[31]—one of the goals of the separation doctrine mentioned above. However, it is an established principle that "no department is permitted either to exercise power belonging to another . . . or to interfere with another's administration of its own powers so as to impair its basic function in the constitutional scheme."[32] The issue then arises as to whether a shield law, which prevents a court from compelling testimony from a journalist, infringes upon the power of the judiciary. It clearly does if it erodes the "minimum functional integrity" of the judiciary.[33] The resolution of this issue hinges upon three questions: (1) Are shield laws primarily substantive or procedural? (2) Which branch has ultimate authority over these two spheres? (3) Even if shield laws are primarily substantive in nature, do they impair the "minimum functional integrity" of the courts?

TESTIMONIAL PRIVILEGES AND THE SUBSTANCE-PROCEDURE DICHOTOMY

Substantive law is that part of the law "which creates, defines, and regulates rights."[34] The enactment of substantive law is clearly within the power of the legislative branch.[35] The determination of broad principles or policies for social conduct is the legislature's primary function.[36] Therefore, if a journalists' testimonial privilege involves matters of public policy rather than the procedural aspects of the administration of justice, it is within the legislature's sphere of power.

On the other hand, if shield laws are deemed to be procedural, the issue becomes more complicated. The source and nature of rulemaking authority vary among the states.[37] Generally, state courts have claimed rulemaking authority upon one of three bases: (1) an historically existing, inherent judicial power to promulgate procedural rules; (2) an enabling act passed by the legislature authorizing the courts to make rules of procedure; or (3) a constitutional provision delegating to the Supreme

---

31. Youngstown Sheet and Tube Co. v. Sawyer, 343 U.S. 579, 635 (1952); Trybulski v. Bellows Falls Hydro-Electric Corp., 20 A.2d 117, 119-20 (1941).
32. Shomaker and Zesk, *supra* note 7, at 1279.
33. A. Levin and A. Amsterdam, *Legislative Control Over Judicial Rulemaking: A Problem In Constitutional Revision* 107 U. Pa. L. Rev. 1, 31-2 (1958).
34. Black's Law Dictionary (5th ed.), at 1281.
35. *See* Shomaker and Zesk, *supra* note 7, at 1280, note 43.
36. J. Sutherland, Statutes and Statutory Construction, § 1.03 (E.D. Sands, 4th ed., 1972).
37. For an analysis of the various approaches to rulemaking authority at the state level, see Shomaker and Zesk, *supra* note 7, at 1280-82, notes 45-54.

Court the right to create procedural rules for judicial proceedings.[38] Thus, the validity of a shield law may depend upon the degree of legislative involvement in the rulemaking process.

At the national level Congress has empowered the Supreme Court to promulgate procedural rules for federal courts in both civil and criminal cases.[39] However, these rules are subject to Congressional review.

Unfortunately, the substance-procedure dichotomy itself is not always clear-cut. "There may be areas in which procedural matters so closely border upon substantive rights and remedies that legislative enactments with respect thereto would be proper."[40] For example, certain evidentiary rules are "substantive declarations of policy because of their inextricable involvement with legal rights and duties."[41] A testimonial privilege is a kind of evidentiary rule. But to what extent is a shield law a "substantive declaration of policy"?

Although authorities disagree on the social wisdom of certain privileges, they appear to view testimonial privileges as imbued with certain public policy considerations that extend beyond the judicial concerns of evidence preservation. As has been noted:

> While framed as rules of evidence, [privileges] are not based upon policies concerned with the reliability or relevance of proof or the orderly dispatch of judicial business. Rather they are concerned with the interests to be served by encouraging uninhibited action within the particular situation or relationship. The advancement of the privileged interest is declared more important than the availability of one item of proof in the course of litigation.[42]

John Wigmore, in his authoritative treatise on the law of evidence, recognized the fundamental maxim that "the public . . . has a right to every man's evidence."[43] Other legal scholars tend to concur that "ordinarily the sanctity of confidence must yield to the necessity of getting all the facts" and that "it is only in a few rare relationships that the

---

38. *Note, Legislatively Enacted Newsman's Privilege Invalid As Infringement on Judicial Rulemaking Power,* 1977 BRIG. YOUNG U. L. REV. 493, 494 (1977). For a discussion of inherent judicial power to promulgate procedural rules, *see* R. Pound, *The Rule-making Power of the Courts,* 12 A.B.A.J. 599 (1926).
39. 28 U.S.C. § 2072 (1970); 18 U.S.C. § 3771 (1970).
40. Southwest Underwriters v. Montoya, 80 N.M. 107, 109 (1969).
41. Note 38, *supra,* at 497.
42. 3 J. HONIGMAN & C. HAWKINS, MICH. CT. RULES ANN. 403-04 (2d ed. 1965).
43. 4 WIGMORE, EVIDENCE, § 2192.

public policy of protecting the relationships overrides the public policy of unrestricted inquiry."[44]

Wigmore also felt that any exceptions to this rule were a legislative prerogative but that four fundamental conditions must exist as a prerequisite to the establishment of a privilege:

> (1) The communications must originate in a *confidence* that they will not be disclosed; (2) This element of *confidentiality must be essential* to the full and satisfactory maintenance of the relation between the parties; (3) The *relation* must be one which in the opinion of the community ought to be sedulously *fostered;* and (4) The *injury* that would inure to the relation by the disclosure of the communications must be *greater than the benefit* thereby gained for the correct disposal of litigation.[45]

Inherent in these conditions is the notion that the granting or withholding of an evidentiary privilege requires a balancing of competing policies.[46] And the weighing of competing policy interests is a legislative, not a judicial, function. As one legal scholar has noted:

> Privilege rules are not intended to regulate court procedure but rather to promote state social policy. In creating a privilege, society, working through the state legislatures, has decided that protecting a given relationship is more important than reaching the truth in a lawsuit.[47]

Even a cursory examination of the legal literature on this subject leaves little doubt that the debate concerning testimonial privileges for journalists usually centers around matters of public policy. The most substantial arguments generally involve policy issues dealing with (1) the public's interest in a free flow of news, (2) the impact on law enforcement and the administration of justice, (3) equality with other professions, and (4) the economic necessity of a statutory privilege for the reporter.[48]

States which have adopted modern evidence codes have recognized that privilege rules should be made by the legislature.[49] And most courts, despite their reluctance to recognize a common law privilege for reporters, have acknowledged the substantive nature of such privilege

---

44. 3 S. GARD, JONES ON EVIDENCE, CIVIL AND CRIMINAL, § 21:41 (6th ed. 1972).
45. WIGMORE, *supra* note 43, at § 2285.
46. *See In re* Grand Jury Impaneled January 21, 1975, 541 F.2d 373 (3rd Cir. 1976).
47. S. Garavito, *Separation of Powers and the Federal Rules of Evidence,* 26 HASTINGS L. J. 1059, 1072 (1975).
48. For a discussion of these policies, see Beaver, *supra* note 6, at 250-58.
49. Garavito, *supra* note 47, at 1073.

rules.⁵⁰ But these views notwithstanding, a separation of powers question might still exist if a privilege statute is constructed in such a way as to impair the "minimum functional integrity" of the court. A court might refuse to enforce such a law in order to preserve the separation of powers concept.

There are no established criteria for determining when this erosion of judicial authority occurs. Practices vary from state to state, depending upon how tolerant courts are of the intermingling of legislative and judicial prerogatives. Shield laws *per se* do not appear to interfere substantially with judicial power. But the "form" of a particular statute is crucial to a consideration of this question.

There are two primary kinds of shield laws: qualified (or divestitory) and absolute. Qualified statutes provide for a "divestible" privilege; that is, the court has the authority to divest the reporter of the privilege under certain circumstances. In such cases, the litigant must demonstrate that compulsory disclosure outweighs the public's interest in the free flow of information.⁵¹ States with qualified shield laws recognize the importance of the reporter's confidential sources but allow the courts some flexibility in the balancing of competing interests on a case-by-case basis.

Although states vary in the construction of their shield laws, several "tests" have been applied to resolve these competing values. The *reasonable likelihood test* rests upon the belief that the confidential information desired will be relevant to the subject of judicial inquiry. The *heart of the matter test* is predicated upon the belief that the desired information is crucial to the development of the case. The *miscarriage of justice test* requires a preliminary hearing at which the party desiring to compel a reporter to testify must prove that: (a) a probability exists that the reporter has information relevant to the investigation; (b) a subpoena is the only method by which the information can be obtained; (c) a miscarriage of justice would result if the information sought were not provided; and (d) there is a compelling need for the desired testimony.⁵²

Since qualified shield laws allow the judiciary to divest a reporter of the testimonial privilege, they appear to pose few threats to the separation of powers doctrine. But absolute laws interfere with the court's inherent power to compel testimony and thereby raise more serious separation of power questions.

---

50. *See* Branzburg v. Hayes, 408 U.S. 665 (1972); *In re* Wayne, 4 U.S.D.C. Hawaii 475 (1914); Republic Gear Co. v. Borg-Warner Corp., 381 F.2d 551, 555 "n." 2 (2d Cir. 1967) (dictum). *But see* 97 C.J.S. § 252, which states that a privileged communication "is not a rule of substantive law but a mere rule of evidence."
51. Shomaker and Zesk, *supra* note 7, at 1289.
52. The Council of State Governments, Shield Laws: A Report on Freedom of the Press, Protection of News Sources, and the Obligation to Testify (1973), at 5.

There are two forms of absolute shield statutes. Most states simply absolve reporters of any duty to reveal their sources.[53] However, three states[54] have established the privilege through removal of the court's contempt powers in such cases. But the contempt power is the judiciary's primary means of coercion. Hence, the abrogation of this authority has a drastic impact on the administration of justice. As one source has stated:

> By insulating a reporter from the general duty of every citizen to give his testimony, the legislature deprives the court of a source of information that may be vital to litigants in a particular case. The reporter, by refusing to testify, may substantially prejudice the rights of the parties before the court.[55]

Courts have tolerated some legislative interference with their contempt powers, subject to two conditions: (1) Any legislative regulation must preserve a penalty for disobedience to insure that the court's authority remains intact;[56] and (2) the legislature cannot determine what shall constitute contempt or declare that certain acts shall not be contemptuous.[57] Courts appear to be particularly reluctant to allow legislatures to insulate "classes" of offences from the threat of contempt. Thus, it is when privilege statutes incorporate a corollary removal of the judiciary's contempt powers that the separation of powers doctrine is most likely to be in jeopardy.

THE CALIFORNIA AND NEW MEXICO CASES

Courts in only two states, California and New Mexico, have examined the question of the application of the separation of powers doctrine to shield laws. New Mexico has a qualified statute and California has an absolute shield law. Courts in both states found their states' shield laws to be in violation of the separation of powers doctrine.

In the New Mexico case of *Ammerman* v. *Hubbard Broadcasting, Inc.*,[58] the plaintiffs sued several state broadcasters for allegedly

---

53. Shomaker and Zesk, *supra* note 7, at 1291, note 110.
54. California, Montana, and New York.
55. Shomaker and Zesk, *supra* note 7, at 1292.
56. See *In re* Garner, 177 P. 162 (1918); *In re* McKinney, 447 P.2d 972 (1968).
57. See *In re* San Francisco Chronicle, 36 P.2d 369 (1934). The U.S. Supreme Court has tended to take a conservative view of its own powers and has attempted to avoid an open conflict with Congress over legislative regulation of its powers. In fact, Congress has enacted legislation to regulate the contempt powers. *See Ex parte* Robinson, 19 Wall. 505 (1874); Toledo Newspaper Co. v. United States, 247 U.S. 402 (1918); Nye v. United States, 313 U.S. 33 (1941).
58. 551 P.2d 1354 (1976).

slanderous radio broadcasts and news reports. During the proceedings the trial court ordered the broadcasters to disclose their sources of information. The state's shield law provided, in part, that the trial court was not to order disclosure unless "it was essential to prevent injustice." If the trial court did order disclosure, the order could be appealed to the New Mexico supreme court and was to be heard *de nova* within twenty days of docketing.[59]

On the broadcasters' appeal, the court held that the statute creating the privilege was unconstitutional on the grounds that it intruded upon judicial power to develop rules of evidence given to the court by the state constitution.[60] But the court, without any significant discussion of the pros and cons of the substance-procedure dichotomy, summarily declared that all rules of evidence (apparently including testimonial privileges) are procedural:

> It is . . . true that rules of evidence are procedural, in that they are a part of the judicial machinery administered by the courts for determining the facts upon which the substantive rights of the litigant rest and are resolved. Rules of evidence do no more than regulate the method of proceeding by which substantive rights and duties are determined. Pleading, pretrial, all rules of evidence (including rules of presumption and privilege) and other trial and post-trial mechanisms designed to accomplish a just determination of rights and duties imposed by the substantive law, are traditionally considered to be "adjective law" or "procedural law."[61]

Having decided that the privilege was procedural, the court then ruled that the judiciary was the proper branch to promulgate procedural rules.[62] The court construed a provision of the state constitution granting it "superintending control over all inferior courts" as authorizing it to develop rules of procedure.[63]

The court was clearly correct in characterizing privileges as "rules

---

59. N.M.S.A. 1953 (supp. 1975), § 20-1-12.1.
60. Ammerman, *supra* note 2, at 1356-57. The court also ruled that (1) the requirement of a *de nova* hearing violated provisions of the state constitution that did not authorize *de nova* hearings in this type of case, and (2) the requirement of expedited review violated the constitutional principle that the court was to be in control of its own calendar and procedures. 551 P.2d at 1359.
61. *Id.* at 1357.
62. *Id.* at 1357 citing State v. Roy, 60 P.2d 646 (1936).
63. *Id.*

of evidence." But the court's conclusion that all rules of evidence are procedural is suspect. As one scholar who has examined the *Ammerman* case has stated: "In light of scholarly views noting the substantive nature of some rules of evidence, including privileges, it would have been proper for the court . . . to have entertained some doubt as to whether the newsman's privilege was a procedural rule."[64]

Two California cases considered the use of privilege by reporters during investigation of the violation of a court-imposed gag order.[65] The first case, *Farr v. Superior Court*,[66] grew out of the highly publicized Manson trial. When the grand jury returned indictments, superior court Judge William Keene entered a restrictive order prohibiting attorneys for the parties, court attaches, and witnesses "from releasing for public dissemination the content or nature of any testimony that might be given at trial or any evidence whose admissibility might have to be determined by the court."[67] The order, which clearly did not bind the press, remained in effect throughout the trial.

William Farr, a reporter for the *Los Angeles Herald-Examiner*, learned of a damaging statement made by a cellmate of one of the Manson codefendants. Farr obtained copies of the statement from two of the attorneys of record in the case in exchange for his promise not to reveal the source.[68]

Over a period of several months the trial judge held several hearings in an attempt to ascertain the sources of the "leaked" information. Farr testified that he had obtained copies from two attorneys of record in the case but refused to give their identity. His refusal was based on the California shield statute, which at the time stated:

> A publisher, editor, reporter, or other person connected with or employed upon a newspaper, or by a press association or wire service, cannot be adjudged in contempt by a court, the Legislature, or any administrative body, for refusing to disclose the source of any information procured for publication and published in a newspaper.[69]

64. Note 38, *supra* at 499. As the article notes, the authorities cited by the court to support its reasoning are not conclusive. In addition, the previous New Mexico case law does not support the result reached by the court in this case. See, e.g., Kreigh v. State Bank, 23 P.2d 1085 (1933), indicating that certain legislation modifying burden of proof requirements was valid.
65. For a discussion of the background of these cases and the California shield law, see Pickerell, *supra* note 6.
66. 22 Cal. App. 3d 60 (1971), *cert. denied*, 409 U.S. 1011 (1972).
67. *Id.* at 64.
68. *Id.*
69. CAL. EVID. CODE, § 1070 (1966). The California legislature has broadened the scope of the shield law in recent years.

At the time of the last hearing Farr was no longer a reporter but still refused to name his sources. The court cited him for direct contempt, holding that since Farr was no longer a newsman, he was not within the protective scope of the shield law. Farr was sentenced to jail, but the sentence was suspended pending appeal. The court of appeal affirmed.[70]

The state appellate court noted that courts have an inherent power to punish for contempt and that to grant Farr immunity "in the face of the facts here present would be to countenance an unconstitutional interference by the legislative branch upon an inherent and vital power of the court to control its own proceedings and officers."[71] In short, the legislature's efforts to immunize persons from punishment for violation of court orders contravened the separation of powers doctrine.

Farr was followed by *Rosato v. Superior Court*.[72] In this case, four employees of the *Fresno Bee* had obtained a copy of a secret grand jury report containing a series of bribery-conspiracy indictments. During a series of hearings the reporters were asked to reveal the sources of their information. They refused, and the trial judge initiated criminal contempt proceedings. Both the appellate court and the state supreme court refused to block the proceedings.[73] U.S. Supreme Court Justice William O. Douglas granted an order delaying the investigation,[74] but the full court later vacated the stay.[75]

Unlike the court in *Farr,* the *Rosato* appellate court, in upholding the contempt proceedings against the "Fresno Four," appeared to give deference to the legislative policy judgment represented by the shield law:

> ... we believe the Legislature in enacting [the shield law] recognized the importance of maintaining a free flow of information and intended that the statute be given a broad rather than a narrow construction. Accordingly, absent any constitutional or other limitation on the exercise of the privilege . . ., we believe it extends not only to the disclosure of any information, in whatever form, which may tend to reveal the source of the information, and, as in the case of the privilege against self-incrimination, the burden is upon the person claiming the privilege to show that the testimony

---

70. Note 66, *supra,* at 60. But this was not the end of the case. The state supreme court denied a hearing and the U.S. Supreme Court denied *certiorari.* The case dragged on for more than five years.
71. *Id.* at 69.
72. 51 Cal. App. 3d 190 (1975), *cert. denied,* 427 U.S. 912 (1976).
73. *Id.* at 223.
74. 420 U.S. 1301 (1975).
75. *Id.* (Douglas, W.O., dissenting).

may tend to lead to that source. Though the burden is on the person claiming the privilege, it is not a heavy one.⁷⁶

Nevertheless, the *Rosato* court ultimately reached the same conclusion as the *Farr* court, holding that the shield statute "if applied to immunize petitioner from contempt would unconstitutionally interfere with the power and duty of the court."⁷⁷ The court also justified its investigative power on the basis of its constitutional duty to insure a fair trial:

> ... any doctrinal tension between the First Amendment and the Sixth Amendment resulting in an impasse must be resolved in favor of the relatively unrestricted constitutional right to a fair trial rather than in favor of the relatively limited invasion on freedom of the press caused by the necessity of revealing a relatively restricted category of news sources .... Because the court's task is directed toward the protection of the constitutional right to a fair trial, *its investigative power should necessarily be broad* [emphasis added].

The *Farr* and *Rosato* cases represent a questionable application of judicial authority. Neither court exhausted alternative approaches before holding the reporters in contempt, and neither determined the exact nature of the danger to fair trial interests.⁷⁸ Nor did they accord adequate respect to the prerogatives of a coequal branch of government. The trial court "clearly infringed on the legislative policy more than was necessary to prevent unconstitutional interference with the judiciary."⁷⁹

CONCLUSION

The California and New Mexico decisions have raised the issue of the impact of state shield laws on the separation of powers doctrine. However, these cases may continue to be the exception rather than the rule. The weight of authoritative evidence suggests that testimonial privileges, including shield statutes, are primarily substantive or quasi-substantive. They involve matters of public policy that are primarily the prerogative of the legislative branch of government. And certainly the

---

76. Note 72, *supra*, at 217-18.
77. *Id.* at 222.
78. *See* Shomaker and Zesk, *supra* note 7, at 1298, notes 149-51.
79. *Id.* at 1299.

first amendment questions surrounding a "newsman's privilege" involve substantive policy considerations of great magnitude.

But since the separation of powers doctrine is construed differently within each jurisdiction, the issue cannot be considered moot. As more and more states enact privilege statutes and as existing laws increasingly undergo judicial construction, the chances of a judiciary-legislative confrontation are enhanced.

Apparently, qualified shield statutes are more likely to avoid this kind of confrontation, since judicial power and integrity remain virtually unimpaired. But absolute privilege laws, which restrict or abridge the courts' contempt authority, do indeed raise serious separation of powers questions. It is to be hoped that this lesson will not go unnoticed in the Congress if and when it enacts a federal shield law. If Congress decides that sound public policy requires a testimonial privilege for journalists, it must reconcile this policy with the commitment of the judiciary to the administration of justice. Both the press and the courts have a constitutional role to play. It may take the wisdom of Solomon to harmonize these competing interests, but it would be an inexcusable folly not to try.

F. DENNIS HALE

Attitudes of Media Attorneys Concerning Closed Criminal Proceedings[1]

F. Dennis Hale is Associate Professor at the School of Journalism at Bowling Green State University in Ohio. He received his BA from the University of Puget Sound in Tacoma, Washington, MS from the University of Oregon and Ph.D. from Southern Illinois University at Carbondale and was recipient of a fellowship from LEAA of the U.S. Justice Department for his dissertation on newspaper coverage of decisions of the California Supreme Court.

INTRODUCTION

In July 1976, 42-year-old Wayne Clapp went fishing with two other men on Seneca Lake in New York State. He never returned to his home in Henrietta, N.Y. Police discovered that his fishing companions had fled the state, his boat was laced with bullet holes, and Clapp's pickup truck was missing. Michigan police apprehended the two companions after they spotted the missing pickup in a Jackson County motel.

1. Presented to the Newspaper Division, Southeastern Regional Colloquium, Association for Education in Journalism, Memphis, Tennessee, January 20, 1981.

Efforts by Rochester, N.Y. newspapers to report the Clapp killing and the subsequent prosecution of the two fishing companions for second-degree murder resulted in a dramatic clash between the press and the courts. During late July and early August the two Gannett newspapers in Rochester each published seven routine stories about Clapp's disappearance, capture of accused persons, discovery of a buried gun, arraignment before magistrate, grand jury indictment, and formal arraignment. (Justice Blackmun, writing for four dissenters, characterized the articles as "placid, routine, and innocuous.")

For the next three months, Rochester newspapers published no stories about the crime. Then, on Nov. 4, the accuseds' attorneys requested that the press and public be excluded from a pretrial suppression hearing that would determine if the confession was voluntary that led to discovery of the gun. The prosecution did not object and trial judge Daniel A. DePasquale granted the closure because of reasonable probability of prejudice to the defendants.[2]

Gannett appealed the decision to state courts and finally the U.S. Supreme Court. On July 2, 1979, the Supreme Court upheld the closure of pretrial suppression hearings. The fragmented, 5-4 decision created as many questions as it answered. Three signers of the majority decision filed separate concurring decisions. And one judge filed a dissent that was joined by three others.[3]

The press feared that lower court judges would misuse the narrow holding of *Gannett* and close all phases of judicial proceedings. This proved to be the case. The Reporters Committee for Freedom of the Press studied state and federal courts for 15 months after *Gannett* and discovered 300 efforts to close criminal proceedings, with 175 successful.[4]

The intensity of the press-courts debate subsided after July 2, 1980, when the Supreme Court overruled Virginia courts which had permitted an entire criminal trial to be closed. The *Richmond* decision lacked clarity in its rationale. Although seven judges joined in the judgment and only one dissented, there were seven separate opinions.[5]

Gannett and *Richmond* underscore the continuing conflict between the press and judiciary concerning access to judicial proceedings. The

---

2. *Gannett Co., Inc. v. DePasquale*, 443 U.S. 368, 99 S.Ct. 2898, 61 L. Ed. 2d 608 (1979). See "Open Justice: The Threat of Gannett," *Communications and the Law*, vol. 1, no. 1 (Winter 1979): 3-13.
3. *Ibid.*
4. "Court Watch Summary Lists 300 Efforts to Close Court Doors," *The News Media & the Law*, 4, no. 4 (October-November, 1980): 34.
5. *Richmond Newspapers, Inc. v. Virginia*, 100 S.Ct. 2814, 65 L. Ed. 2d 973 (1980).

decisions demonstrate that lawyers and judges who generally have a high regard for civil liberties are less supportive of a liberty such as press freedom when it comes in direct conflict with judicial or attorney prerogatives.

This study examined attitudes on the open-courtroom question of attorneys who had been involved in press litigation. Some 86 attorneys who had appealed a libel case to a state or federal appellate court were questioned about press and public access to preliminary hearings and criminal trials. Attorneys merit study because of their influence in advising press clients, and their general influence in shaping press law as lawmakers.

METHODOLOGY

Questionnaires were sent to 200 law firms that had represented plaintiffs or defendants in 100 appeals or libel cases during the previous four years. The 100 appeals were final decisions of state or federal, intermediate or final, appellate courts that were reported in volumes two through five of *Media Law Reporter*.

Questionnaires, cover letters and stamped return envelopes were mailed out Feb. 8, 1980. Followup cover letters and identical questionnaires were mailed to the same 200 firms on March 3. The study was conducted after *Gannett* but before *Richmond*. Attorneys were aware that the Supreme Court had permitted closed, pretrial hearings; but they could not have been certain about whether the Court would extend the doctrine to closed, criminal trials.

Questionnaires were returned by 86 firms in 24 states and the District of Columbia. Some 50 responded to the first mailing, 36 to the second.

The four-page questionnaire consisted of 24 closed-ended and 5 open-ended items. Three questions concerned the right of the press to attend criminal trials; 19 concerned libel; and seven examined characteristics of attorneys and their practice such as years of experience, size of firm, political identification, and proportion of practice devoted to press law.

The three questions on access to criminal trial were:

> In *Gannet v. DePasquale* the Supreme Court ruled that pretrial evidentiary hearings may be closed to the press and public if there is a reasonable probability of prejudice to the criminal defendant. How do you feel about this decision? ____ strongly agree ____ agree ____ uncertain ____ disagree ____ strongly disagree
> How do you feel about expanding the *Gannett* doc-

trine to apply to entire criminal trials, as was done in *Richmond Newspapers v. Virginia* which currently is being reviewed by the Supreme Court? ____strongly agree ____ agree ____ uncertain ____ disagree ____ strongly disagree

What are your general thoughts about the public trial issue?

The two closed-ended questions were coded 0-4 with 0 the strongly agree and anti-press response, 4 the strongly disagree and pro-press response, and 2 the uncertain or neutral response.

Attitudes concerning preliminary hearings and criminal trials were compared using descriptive statistics and a T-test. The two attitudes also were correlated with attorney characteristics and some libel attitudes using nonparametric Spearman correlations. These libel variables were whether attorneys had represented persons suing the media, whether they perceived the press as cautious with facts prior to Burger Court decisions that limited libel protection, whether they saw the Burger Court as reducing libel protection, whether they perceived the press as understating Burger Court damage to press freedom, and whether Burger Court decisions permitted Watergate-type reporting.

FINDINGS

The attorneys differed significantly in their attitudes toward closed, pretrial hearings and closed, criminal trials. Some 45 disagreed or disagreed strongly with closed hearings, compared to 63 who objected to closed trials (Table 1). The means for the two attitudes were 3.04 and 2.28 on the 0-4 scale, which represented a statistically significant difference applying a T-test (T value = +6.39, df=81, p .001).

TABLE 1

ATTORNEY APPROVAL OF CLOSED HEARINGS AND TRIALS

Response	Hearings (N = 83)	Trials (N = 84)
	(percentages in parentheses)	
Strongly Agree	10 (12)	6 (7)
Agree	22 (27)	8 (10)
Uncertain	6 (7)	7 (8)
Disagree	23 (28)	13 (15)
Strongly Disagree	22 (27)	50 (60)

Attitudes concerning pretrial hearings and criminal trials were similarly associated with attorney characteristics and beliefs (Table 2). Both attitudes were positively and significantly associated with an attorney's press law practice, liberal political beliefs, perceiving the press as cautious with facts prior to Burger Court decisions that limited libel protection, and perceiving press commentary as understating Burger Court damage to press freedom. And the two closure attitudes were negatively and significantly associated with whether an attorney ever represented clients suing the media and whether the attorney perceived Burger Court decisions as not limiting press libel protection. Three variables unrelated to the pretrial and trial attitudes were years of legal experience, size of law firm, and opinion on whether Burger Court decisions permitted Watergate-type reporting.

TABLE 2

ASSOCIATION OF CLOSURE ATTITUDES WITH OTHER VARIABLES*

Variable	Hearings		Trials	
	Corr.	Sig.	Corr.	Sig.
Amount of Press Law Practice	.456	.001	.340	.002
Represent Persons Suing Media	−.366	.001	−.256	.019
Press Cautious With Facts	.399	.001	.339	.005
Not Limiting Libel Protection	−.362	.001	−.255	.019
Burger Damage Understated	.325	.003	.227	.040
Watergate Reporting Possible	−.054	.631	053	.636
Size of Firm	.170	127	.089	.426
Years of Legal Experience	−.030	.785	−.063	.570
Liberal Political Beliefs	.377	.001	.248	.025

*With the exception of two N's of 68, all statistics are based on N's of 81-84.

With the six pairs of significant correlations, the correlation with the criminal trial attitude was less significant and of a smaller magnitude than the correlation with the attitude on pretrial hearings.

Some 85 percent of the attorneys responded to the open-ended question about public trials. A handful rejected the concept:

> The press has overplayed the need to have public trials. I believe the defendant's right to a fair trial is far more important and heavily outweighs the public need to be assured that our judicial system will not operate a Star Chamber proceeding.

> Vital to our concept of justice but not ever at the expense of a defendant. No public right to know can ever outweigh an individual's right to a fair trial.
>
> A defendant's right to a fair trial must prevail—even over the public's interest in unfettered expression.
>
> The rule must be such that the criminal defendant is not deprived of a fair trial by an unbiased jury. Therefore evidence which is legally improper should not be presented to the jury through the press. Such restraints may, however, be removed after trial.

More representative were the following assertions:

> Access by the public is essential. The press is the public.
>
> Secret trials should not be allowed except under extraordinary circumstances which I cannot imagine at this time.
>
> It is constitutionally critical that trials be public.
>
> There is a great need to retain public trials. The alternative is to return to the days of Star Chamber proceedings. We see such abuses every day with the present grand jury system.
>
> It is a critical safeguard and must be protected at nearly all costs.
>
> The press has a duty to report on the trial, but also on the judge and the district attorney—both public officials.
>
> It is absolutely basic to a free society.
>
> There are no instances when the public or press should be excluded.

Some attorneys specifically criticized the *Gannett* decision:

> The *Gannett* decision permits abuse and misuse of trial judges.
>
> *Gannett* is the worst press decision of all. Only where the fairness of the trial will be placed in jeopardy should the press be barred—and that exception should be subject to strict guidelines, a hearing and findings subject to review.
>
> *Gannett* is disturbing enough, and its misinterpretation and misapplication by the lower courts is frightening. The fair trial-free press conflict can best be re-

solved by exercise of editorial discretion, venue change, and other devices rather than closing the door of the courtroom to the public.

DISCUSSION

The attorneys who participated in this survey apparently had given considerable thought to the question of public and press access to criminal proceedings. Most had definite opinions. Only 7 percent checked the "uncertain" response on the closed hearing question, and 8 percent on the closed trial question. And 84 percent volunteered remarks for the open-ended question about closed trials, a much higher rate than for the other four open-ended questions in the survey.

The attorneys appeared to be torn in their allegiance between the interests of their press clients and the independence of the judicial system. It was expected that some attitudes would be expressed that would be contrary to the press because 17 percent of the attorneys had primarily represented clients suing the media. However, a disproportionate 46 percent agreed or were uncertain concerning closing pretrial hearings merely because of a reasonable probability of prejudice to the defendant (*Gannett* doctrine), and 25 percent agreed or were uncertain concerning the closing of entire criminal trials. Being knowledgeable about a press right is no guarantee that a person will support that right.

This survey demonstrated that media attorneys differ substantially in their attitudes concerning specific press rights. Certain variables are associated with these attitudes including the amount of press law practice, whether an attorney primarily represented persons suing the media, and political identification. Members of the press should be aware of such factors when seeking advice from a member of the legal profession.

This study also offered evidence of the split between journalists and editors and attorneys and judges concerning the scope of press protection provided by the First Amendment. The split was most evident in the harsh press reaction in 1979 to *Herbert v. Lando*,[6] the so-called state-of-mind decision holding that in actual malice libel cases journalists are required to testify about their subjective conclusions and newsroom conversations involved in preparing a story.

The press demonstrated solidarity in publicly condemning the decision. Private opinions of journalists and editors were much the same. Briod interviewed 67 journalists and found that 74 percent disapproved

---

6. 441 U.S. 153, 99 S.Ct. 1635, 60 L.Ed. 2d 115 (1979).

of the decision even though 66 percent said they neither had been affected nor expected to be affected by the decision in any way.[7]

Attorneys and judges lined up on the opposite side. Attorneys generally interpreted the decision as reinforcing the status quo. The Supreme Court was more in agreement than its 6-3 vote indicated. None of the dissenters wanted to grant the press the immunity that was being sought by "60 Minutes" producer Barry Lando and CBS. And the Court's chief defender of press freedom, William Brennan, was on record as only "dissenting in part."

---

7. Briod, "Herbert v. Lando: Threat to the Press, Or Boomerang for Public Officials?" *Communications and the Law,* vol. 2, no. 2 (Spring, 1980): 59-92.

MARY KAY PLATTE

TV IN THE COURTROOM: RIGHT OF ACCESS?

Mary Kay Platte is a Ph.D. Candidate in Radio-Television-Film at Bowling Green State University, where she came on leave from her position as Assistant Professor of Mass Communications in regulation and management at Eastern Kentucky University. She is a writer/researcher/associate producer for public affairs and ITV at WBGU-TV.

INTRODUCTION

Stressing that the broadcaster must deal with public issues, the Federal Communications Commission in the 1948 Mayflower decision[1] emphasized the broadcaster's role as a guardian of the public interest. In the Red Lion case[2], the Supreme Court pointed out that the broadcaster's primary concern should be the interests of the viewer and the listener

1. See *The Mayflower Broadcasting Corporation and The Yankee Network, Inc. (WAAB)*, 8 FCC 333, 338 (January 16, 1941).
2. *Red Lion Broadcasting Co., Inc., et al. v. Federal Communications Commission et al.*, 395 U.S. 367 (June 9, 1969).

since the rights of the audience are protected by the First Amendment. If the broadcaster is to act as a fiduciary of the public, is he obligated to provide electronic coverage of public trials? Should television cameras be allowed in the courtroom?

Since the first televised trials in Oklahoma City in 1953 and in Waco, Texas, in 1955, the number of states allowing electronic coverage of trials has increased.[3]

In spite of the fact that most states do allow some electronic coverage in the courtroom, this coverage is limited by Canon 35, now 3A(7), which prohibits electronic or photographic coverage. All states, except Texas and Colorado, originally adopted Canon 35 as part of judicial procedure when the American Bar Association (A.B.A.) passed the rule in 1937. Canon 35 excluded photographic and radio coverage within the courtroom. In 1963, Canon 35 was changed to include the prohibition of television coverage. Then Canon 35 was replaced by Canon 3A(7) in 1972. Though allowing limited use of electronic coverage, this canon adheres to the same principle as Canon 35.

Many historians feel that Canon 35 was a direct result of the heavy media coverage of the trial of Bruno Richard Hauptmann. As Christopher H. Sterling and John M. Kittross pointed out:

> The trial was important not only for its titillating effect on American lives in 1935 but for what came out of it—severe restrictions on reporting of courtroom events by radio and photographers (after 1952 such rules included television).[4]

In fact, the special investigative committee of the A.B.A. waited a year after the Hauptmann execution to present its report. The report was adopted as Canon 35, but the A.B.A. disregarded the committee's recommendation that the question of photographic coverage should be decided by the trial judge with the consent of counsel. Instead, the A.B.A. prohibited photographic coverage altogether.[5]

The debate on the question of television coverage of courtroom proceedings continues. John M. Adams, past president of the Ohio State

---

3. As of 1981 some thirty states allow limited electronic coverage. Florida and Wisconsin have adopted a permanent policy which permits the judge alone to allow electronic coverage. See Martin Clark Bass, "Television's Day in Court," *New York Times Magazine*, 36 (February 15, 1981). Also see current summary tables prepared by the National Center for State Courts.
4. Christopher H. Sterling and John M. Kittross, *Stay Tuned*, at 179 (1978).
5. Alan Wurtzel, *Free Press/Fair Trial: Broadcast Access to Courtroom Proceedings*, (1978). Also see "Bar Outlines a Code of Ethics for Trials." *NY Times*, 2 (January 15, 1936).

Bar Association, explained the primary concern of many of the opponents of television coverage:

> I feel the necessity of having a fair trial over-rides any benefit which the public might receive from cameras in court. Our courts are in the justice business, not the entertainment business. The decorum of the court is very important.[6]

While some broadcasters would probably agree with Adams' concept of television as primarily an entertainment medium, perhaps most of them would accept Edwin Diamond's dismissal of this supposed major premise. Diamond, senior lecturer in political science at Massachusetts Institute of Technology, scoffed at the entertainment label and rejected it as a "show business myth."[7] He added that "newspapers and magazines seek to entertain as well as to educate or to sell ads."[8]

Though opposition to television coverage exists, various experiments have provided empirical data representing examinations of television's impact on the courtroom and the legal system. One research study done by Dr. James L. Hoyt of the University of Wisconsin found that—contrary to the Supreme Court's fear as expressed in the *Estes v. Texas* decision—responses from the subjects who were told they were being recorded and who saw the camera were more accurate than responses from subjects who were not recorded. Hoyt summarized:

> Far from being a danger and a potential hindrance to a fair trial, in this context television cameras can, in fact, lead to a fairer trial.[9]

Another study done by Dr. Gerald R. Miller and Dr. Norman E. Fontes of Michigan State University detailed four years of research into the use of video tape in trial proceedings. Miller and Fontes found that the use of video taped materials "did not produce any deleterious effect on juror response."[10]

Since Colorado and Texas have always permitted cameras in the courtroom, it is important to note some observations. Duane Silverstein, a former staff associate in the National Center for State Courts,

---

6. John M. Adams, Personal Letter, October 17, 1978.
7. Edwin Diamond, "Media Myths That Limit Free Speech," 25 *TV Guide*, 42 (November 5, 1977).
8. Id. at 42.
9. Wurtzel, at 22.
10. Gerald R. Miller and Norman E. Fontes, *Real Versus Reel: What's the Verdict?*, at 238 (1979).

applauded Colorado's success with cameras in the courtroom:

> Significantly, in Colorado there has not been one reversal due to television's alleged infringement of one's right to a fair trial.[11]

Silverstein described an investigation by the Colorado Supreme Court:

> Colorado Supreme Court Justice O. Otto Moore conducted a hearing on whether to allow cameras in the courtroom. During the hearing, hundreds of pictures were taken and a newsreel camera operated for half an hour without Moore's knowledge. Although he entered the hearing firmly opposed to allowing cameras in the courtroom, Moore wrote what has been referred to as a classic opinion destroying all opposing arguments.[12]

Justice Moore's conclusion was that neither the dignity nor the decorum of the court was in the least bit disturbed.

On the other hand, Texas was the scene for the notorious Billie Sol Estes trial. The heavy-handed media coverage of the Estes trial has been compared with the so-called carnival atmosphere of the Hauptmann trial by photojournalist Joseph Costa, founder and past president of the National Press Photographers Association:

> I covered the Bruno Richard Hauptmann trial for the *New York Daily News.* But the circus atmosphere did not exist *inside* that courtroom. However, the Estes trial was quite a different story. Unlike the judge for the Hauptmann trial, the presiding judge at the Estes trial did lose control of his courtroom.[13] (Emphasis added.)

Estes v. Texas was appealed to the Supreme Court on the ground that media coverage in the courtroom had interfered with the defendant's right to a fair trial. In 1965, the Estes conviction was overturned by the Court.

The opinion of the Court was delivered by Justice Tom Clark. After a review of the obtrusive media coverage, Justice Clark acknowledged the fact that the television and radio reporters have the same rights as

---

11. Duane Silverstein, "TV Comes to the Courts," *State Court Journal,* 53 (Spring 1978).
12. Id. at 17
13. Joseph Costa, Interview, (October 3, 1978).

the general public with regard to access. But he also indicated that the Court's conclusion was supported by the fact that forty-eight states consider the use of television in the courtroom improper.[14]

Chief Justice Earl Warren in his concurring opinion took the trial judge to task for his political use of television and his lack of control of the courtroom. Chief Justice Warren also pointed out the judge's casual approach towards the media coverage:

> The trial judge himself stated at the September hearing that if he wanted to see a ball game he would turn on his television set, so why not the same for a trial.[15]

Justice Potter Stewart, joined by Justices Black, Brennan and White, dissented. Though he felt that television coverage during a trial was not unconstitutional, Justice Stewart suggested that further experimentation was needed in order to determine the impact of television in the courtroom. He concluded:

> The suggestion that there are limits upon the public's right to know what goes on in the courts causes me deep concern.[16]

Justice John Harlan added a concurring opinion which has been echoed in a 1979 case, *Gannett Company, Inc., v. DePasquale*. Justice Harlan stated:

> Thus the right of 'public trial' is not one belonging to the public, but one belonging to the accused, and inhering in the institutional process by which justice is administered.[17]

Since the Estes trial, most states have allowed some form of electronic coverage. Moreover, in 1978, Ohio Chief Justice C. William O'Neill, as chairman of the National Conference of Chief Justices, appointed a committee to study the use of electronic media in the courtroom. With Chief Justice Ben F. Overton of Florida as the chairman, the committee proposed that Canon 3A(7) of the Code of Judicial Conduct should be amended to allow television, radio, and photographic coverage—provided certain guidelines are followed,[18] and in special

14. *Estes v. Texas* 381 U.S. 544 (1965).
15. Id. at 572.
16. Id. at 615.
17. Id. at 588.
18. See *Resolution I: Television, Radio, Photographic Coverage of Judicial Proceedings, Thirtieth Annual Meeting of the Conference of Chief Justices* (August 2, 1978).

cases such as "rape, custody of children, trade secrets, or where such coverage would cause a substantial increase in the threat of harm to any participant in a case, such coverage may not be desirable."[19]

This proposal was adopted at the thirtieth annual meeting of the National Conference of Chief Justices in Burlington, Vermont, on August 2, 1978. However, a similar proposal which was considered by the A.B.A. in Atlanta, Georgia, on February 12, 1979, was not passed.[20]

Nevertheless, several states have either dropped the ban on electronic coverage or encouraged experimental use of television in the courtroom. For example, the U.S. Court of Appeals in California has ruled that it is discriminatory to exclude television when print media is included.[21] Also, as of July 1, 1980, California ended its fourteen year ban on television in the courtroom.[22] Ohio has extended its experimental use of television in the courtroom;[23] and Florida, after a year of experimentation, has opened the courts to electronic and photographic coverage.

Ironically, Florida began its experimental use of television in the courtroom with the trial of a so-called television addict. A public television station (WPBT) in Miami, carried gavel-to-gavel coverage of the trial of Ronnie Zamora. Zamora's attorney, Ellis Rubin, proclaimed that television was responsible for his client's actions.

Zamora was accused of killing an elderly widow who surprised him in the act of robbing her home. Zamora was fifteen and an avid admirer of "Kojak."

In addition to the Florida distribution, WPBT provided video tape excerpts of the trial to outlets around the country. Even some foreign countries broadcast the tapes. Then, after the trial, WPBT produced a PBS program, "TV on Trial," which explored the ramifications of television coverage at trials.

Many observers of the Zamora trial found that cameras did not seem intrusive. In fact, most of the participants seemed to have ignored the presence of the cameras in the courtroom.[24] However, the jury re-

---

19. Id. at 3.
20. "Electronic and photographic coverage is not inconsistent with the right to a fair trial and should be permitted if it is unobtrusive and does not interfere with the conduct of the trial." From "Delegates Vote Disapproval of Courtroom Media Coverage," *The Blade* 3 (February 13, 1979).
21. See "TV in Court: Seven States Approve," *The News Media and the Law* 35 (December, 1977).
22. "California Courts to Allow Filming, Taping in Experiment," *The Blade* 4 (July 1, 1980).
23. "Camera Coverage in Court Extended," *The Blade* 6 (May 23, 1980).
24. "The Trials of TV," *Newsweek* 70 (October 10, 1977).

quested that they be allowed to see themselves later.[25]

Judge Paul Baker, who presided, called the WPBT experiment a success.[26] The only difficulty encountered by the photojournalists who were covering the trial was working out a pooling agreement for photographic and electronic coverage.[27]

Even Rubin felt that broadcasting the television coverage of the trial was a deterrent:

> I received hundreds of letters from kids who saw the trial on television and they said they were not aware of what happens when you commit a crime. And it gave them second thoughts.[28]

After the television experiment in Florida, the Ohio Supreme Court extended the one year rule that allowed television and camera coverage as designated by a trial judge "until further order of the court while the court studies the data collected."[29] Actually, a criminal trial in a specially designated courtroom was televised before the official experimental period began in Ohio. In a way, the Timothy Papp trial may have precipitated the experiment.

In 1978, Timothy Papp was tried in Akron, Ohio, for the murder and rape of Roxie Ann Keathley. As in the Hauptmann case, the victim was a child; Roxie Ann was nine. Also, as in the Hauptmann case, the trial had elements of sensationalism.

Five years had gone by since the afternoon Papp had led Lorain County sheriff's deputies to the area where the little girl's body had been left under a layer of leaves. But because of a reversal of Papp's original conviction, the United States District Court had ordered a new trial.[30]

Summit County Judge James Barbuto was assigned to the case. The pretrial publicity made it seem impossible for Judge Barbuto to find an unbiased jury in Lorain County. So he granted a change of venue request to the defense.[31]

Thus, the trial was moved to Judge Barbuto's Akron courtroom. At this point, the two trials, Papp and Hauptmann, become very different for the Papp trial marked a first in Ohio's history since Judge Barbuto's

---

25. See *TV on Trial*, transcript, at 29 (1978).
26. Id. at 48.
27. See "Photojournalism Stands Trial with Ronny Zamora in Florida." 32 *News Photographer* 10-14 (November 1977).
28. Ellis Rubin, Interview (October 26, 1978).
29. "Camera Coverage in Court Extended," supra note 23.
30. David A. Lieberth, "An Ohio Experiment: Television Coverage of the Timothy Papp Trial," 51 *Ohio Bar* 598 (May 15, 1978).
31. David A. Lieberth, Interview (October 4, 1978).

courtroom was specially equipped to provide for video taping.[32]

The Court Projects Director, Bill Kea, had designed the courtroom which included an adjacent control room. The television equipment had been installed in 1975 when Judge Barbuto had received a $93,000 grant from the federal Law Enforcement Assistance Administration to build a model courtroom in the old Summit County Courthouse.[33]

Initially, the television system had been set up so that trials could be video taped in order to make a record for appeals courts. However, the equipment had also been used in another way. One unruly defendant was disruptive, so he was placed under guard in the control room where he could hear and see his own trial without disturbing the judicial process.[34]

David A. Lieberth, an attorney with ten years of previous experience as news director for radio station WHLO in Akron, explained the unprecedented steps that followed the change of venue in the Papp case:

> In the fall of 1977, I wrote to Ohio Supreme Court Chief Justice C. William O'Neill, to ask the question, 'How might the bench, the bar, and the press of Ohio initiate an experiment to permit radio and television broadcasting and news photography of courtroom proceedings?'
>
> Prior to this, I met with Judge Barbuto to find out whether or not he would be willing to participate in any future experiments authorized by the Supreme Court. Any such trials in his courtroom could be televised *without intrusion* by broadcast reporters and photographers.[35]

Meanwhile, because of the possibility that Papp would be the first person to testify under hypnosis, Judge Barbuto realized the historic significance of this trial. As Lieberth stated:

> Barbuto foresaw wide interest in the Papp trial by reporters and in early March suggested that he would be willing to permit broadcasters to tap-in to the audio-video system of his courtroom *if* they could do so without violating the Ohio rule against cameras and tape recorders in the courtroom.[36]

32. One of Justice Harlan's concerns about the Estes trial was that the right to speak and print did not mean that the press could "bring the mechanical facilities of the broadcasting and printing industries into the courtroom." See *Estes v. Texas*, 381 U.S. 589 (1965).
33. See Lieberth, "Experiment," supra, at 599.
34. See Lieberth, Interview, supra note 31.
35. Id.
36. Lieberth, "Experiment," supra, at 601.

TV in the Courtroom: Right of Access?

Ohio Chief Justice O'Neill believed that television could be used as an aid to justice. Under Chief Justice O'Neill, the Ohio Supreme Court approved amendments to the Ohio Rules of Superintendence. These amendments permitted courts "to use electronic or photographic equipment for the presentation of evidence, the perpetuation of the record, or for other purposes of judicial administration."[37]

Television coverage of the Papp trial was carried as excerpts on the news. Radio station WHLO did gavel-to-gavel audio tape coverage in short segments which also included audio taped interviews with Judge Barbuto, the attorneys, and the jury.[38]

Judge Barbuto assigned Lieberth to act as media liaison[39] and allowed any radio or television station to use the audio and video equipment already in the courtroom.[40] ABC and CBS sent crews from Chicago to capture the testimony of the first person to testify under hypnosis, but they left when Papp changed his mind.[41]

Surprisingly, a video taped interview led to Papp's conviction. After the trial, David M. Powell, foreman of the jury, explained to reporters that the video tape showed Papp saying he didn't remember when he noticed the girl was dead. The tape was made by police following Papp's arrest on March 26, 1973. Powell said replaying and watching the video tape "actually did it."[42]

The sights and sounds of the Papp trial still remain. The television tapes and the radio tapes were given to the University of Akron School of Law Library on June 28, 1978, by television stations WEW and WKYC and by radio station WHLO.[43]

With so many states approving television coverage of trials, it seems likely that there should no longer be any constitutional question regarding equal access for the electronic press. In addition, the implications of three Supreme Court decisions should be considered carefully. The cases are *Gannett Company, Inc., v. DePasquale* (1979), *Richmond Newspapers, Inc., v. Virginia* (1980), and *Chandler, et al., v. Florida* (1981).

Gannett Co., Inc., v. DePasquale. Wayne Clapp disappeared in July, 1976. Clapp had gone fishing with two other men near his home in the suburbs of Rochester, New York. Later the same day, the two men

37. Lieberth, Interview, supra note 31.
38. Mary O'Neil, *New Service Information Summary* (June 28, 1978).
39. Rich Zarburgh, "Vast Media Army Covers Papp Trial," *Akron Beacon Journal*, 10 (March 19, 1978).
40. Lieberth, Interview, supra note 31.
41. William Kezziah, "Papp Won't Testify in Child-Slaying Trial," *Akron Beacon Journal*, (March 23, 1978).
42. William Kezziah, "Papp Convicted of Murder in Second Trial," *Akron Beacon Journal*, (March 25, 1978).
43. See *News Service Summary*, supra note 38.

returned in the boat and drove away in Clapp's truck. Clapp was never seen again, but bullet holes in the boat indicated that he was probably the victim of foul play.

The Gannett Company owned two Rochester newspapers, the morning *Democrat* and *Chronicle* and the evening *Times-Union*.[44] From July 16 to August 6, 1976, both papers ran about eight stories dealing with Clapp's mysterious disappearance, with state police appeals for help in locating the suspects, and with news of the suspects' arrest and arraignment. Included in this coverage were statements from the suspects concerning their guilt. Also, one story described the search for the body and murder weapon as well as the way one of the suspects led the police to a buried gun.

During the ninety day period prior to the pretrial hearing, defense attorneys asked Judge DePasquale to close the hearing to the public and the press in order to insure a fair trial. At the time the motion was considered, the district attorney did not oppose the motion, nor did the Gannett reporter.[45] The motion was granted.

The next day, Gannett reporter Carol Ritter did ask the court to set aside the order to close the hearing. Another hearing was scheduled to consider Ritter's petition. During the consideration of this petition, the judge indicated that he thought that the press had a constitutional right of access; but he felt that the defendant's right to a fair trial outweighed the right of press coverage.

> The judge thus refused to vacate his exclusion order or grant the petitioner immediate access to a transcript of the pretrial hearing.[46]

The Gannett Company began a series of appeals. The state appellate court

> ...held that the exclusionary orders transgressed the public's vital interest in open judicial proceedings and further constituted an unlawful prior restraint in violation of the First and Fourteenth Amendments. It accordingly vacated the trial court's orders.[47]

Then the New York Court of Appeals held that the case was technically moot since — under a plea bargaining arrangement — both

---

44. In 1978, the Gannett Company owned about 77 daily newspapers and several television stations. The company was vying for national circulation with other major publishing companies and faced crossownership action with the FCC. See "News Views," 33 *News Photographer*, 2 (June, 1978).
45. *Gannett Company, Inc. v. DePasquale*, 443 U.S. 375 (1979).
46. Id. at 376.
47. Id.

defendants had pleaded guilty; and a transcript had been released to the newspapers.[48] However, the Supreme Court disregarded the question of whether the case was moot or not and granted certiorari.[49]

The Court considered the question of whether a judge may exclude the public and the press from pretrial hearings because the defendants want to suppress newspaper accounts of confessions and material evidence. In a five-to-four majority, not only did the Court uphold the exclusion of the public and the press from pretrial hearings, but Justice Stewart, in his opinion for the Court, went even farther:

> The Constitution nowhere mentions any right of access to a criminal on the part of the public; its guarantee, like the others enumerated, is personal to the accused.[50]

It is interesting to note that Justice Stewart seems to have changed his mind about the public's right to know—as he expressed in his dissenting opinion in *Estes v. Texas*.[51] Not only that, but Justice Stewart in *Gannett Co., Inc., v. DePasquale* is echoing Justice Harlan's concurring opinion in the Estes case—the right of the public trial does not belong to the public, but to the accused.

In the Gannett case, Chief Justice Warren Burger concurred with the opinion of the Court and added:

> By definition a hearing on a motion before trial to suppress evidence is not a trial; it is a pretrial hearing.[52]

Justice Lewis Powell in his concurring opinion felt that although limitations should be considered carefully before closing a hearing:

> Because of the importance of the public's having accurate information concerning the operation of its criminal justice system, I would hold explicitly that petitioner's reporter had an interest protected by the First and Fourteenth Amendments in being present at the pretrial suppression hearing.[53]

---

48. Id.
49. Id. at 377.
50. Id. at 379-380.
51. In his dissenting opinion, Justice Blackmun cites Justice Stewart's change of mind.
52. See *Gannett Company, Inc., v. DePasquale*, supra, 443 U.S. at 394.
53. Id. at 397.

Justice William Rehnquist in his concurring opinion emphasized that:

> ...the court today holds, the Sixth Amendment does not require a criminal trial or hearing to be opened to the public if the participants to the litigation agree for any reason, no matter how jurisprudentially appealing or unappealing, that it should be closed.[54]

However, Justice Rehnquist went on to explain that the lower courts would not have to follow the Court's decision because it is up to each court to decide whether to open or close proceedings.[55]

Justice Harry Blackmun, joined by Justices Brennan, White, and Marshall, concurred with the Court on the question of whether the case was moot, but delivered the dissenting opinion. Noting that no stories appeared in either paper during the ninety days immediately preceding the hearing, Justice Blackmun questioned the depiction of the coverage in the Gannett newspapers as being excessive:

> Headlines were entirely factual. The stories were relatively brief. They appeared only in connection with a development in the investigation, and they gave no indication of being published to sustain popular interest in the case.[56]

Next, Justice Blackmun considered the explicit language of the Sixth Amendment. He concluded that though the accused is guaranteed a public trial this right

> ...is not sufficient to permit the inference that the accused may compel a private proceeding simply by waiving that right.[57]

After Justice Blackmun explored the common law basis of the right to a public trial, he cited *Sheppard V. Maxwell* and *Estes V. Texas* to show that both the print and electronic media representatives have the same rights as the public to attend trials and to report the proceedings.[58]

> Publicity is essential to the preservation of public confidence in the rule of law and in the operation of the courts.[59]

54. Id. at 404.
55. Id. at 405-406.
56. Id. at 408.
57. Id. at 418.
58. Id. at 445.
59. Id. at 448.

The *Gannett v. DePasquale* decision evoked many reactions. One article in the August 27, 1979, issue of *Newsweek* explained the frustrations caused by the fact "the Court and the press remain unsure of how to handle each other."[60] Even Chief Justice Burger suggested that the Court's ruling had been misunderstood.[61]

Syndicated columnist Anthony Lewis characterized the impact of the Gannett decision:

> Probably to the majority's surprise, judges around the country responded to the Gannett decision by closing courtrooms.[62]

Shortly before *Richmond Newspapers, Inc., v. Virginia* was adjudicated by the U.S. Supreme Court, James Kilpatrick wrote that perhaps it would be a good idea if the Supreme Court proceedings were televised. Kilpatrick felt that letting the public view the deliberations might improve the system. Citing attorney Alan B. Morrison's proposal to eliminate the secrecy of the Court, Kilpatrick said:

> During the term of court now ending every member but Justice Rehnquist has taken no part in at least one case. Justice Marshall sat on the sidelines in nine of the first 100 cases decided. Justices White, Powell, and Stewart were out for two each. When a $72,000-a-year justice declines to sit, maybe we should know why — and perhaps a system should be devised to designate substitute justices to fill in for the absent members.[63]

Richmond Newspapers, Inc., v. Virginia. A hotel manager was found stabbed to death on December 2, 1975. A suspect was arrested, tried and convicted. The Virginia Supreme Court reversed the conviction in October, 1977, because of the way evidence had been obtained.

After two previous mistrials in the same court, the third trial ended in a mistrial because a prospective juror had read newspaper accounts of the case and told the other prospective jurors about these accounts.

Just before the fourth trial, the counsel for the defendant moved that the trial be closed to the public. The trial judge asked if the prose-

---

60. See Diane Cooper and Emily Marshall, "Open and Shut Case," 94 *Newsweek*, 69 (August 27, 1979).
61. Id.
62. "Court Confounds Critics," *The Plain Dealer*, 7-8 (July 10, 1980).
63. James Kilpatrick, "High Court Should Lift Veil a Bit," *The Blade*, 12 (June 25, 1980). (Could be compared with citizen court watch groups which have been set up by the Fund for Modern Courts, the National Criminal Justice Reference Service, and the Federated Women's Clubs.)

cution had any objection. Neither the prosecutor nor the newspaper reporters, who were present in the courtroom at the time, had any objection. However, later that day, the reporters asked for a hearing to consider the motion. The judge granted the request.

The hearing was conducted as part of the closed trial. The counsel for the reporters argued that before the trial could be closed, the court should decide that the rights of the defendant could be protected in no other way. The court denied the motion to vacate, and the closed trial was to continue.

During the proceedings — without a jury present — the defendant was found not guilty by the court because of the lack of evidence. (The evidence was dismissed on a technicality.)[64]

The Richmond Newspapers appealed the court's closure order. The Virginia Supreme Court denied the petition. The Supreme Court granted certiorari:

> . . .here for the first time the court is asked to decide whether a criminal trial itself may be closed to the public upon the unopposed request of a defendant, without any demonstration the closure is required to protect the defendant's superior right to a fair trial, or that some other overriding consideration requires closure.[65]

In a seven-to-one majority, the Court reversed the Virginia Supreme Court. Chief Justice Burger delivered the holding which Justices White and Stevens joined. Chief Justice Burger outlined the common law tradition of the right of the public to attend trials and emphasized the importance of the print and electronic media "as surrogates for the public."[66] He concluded:

> We hold that the right to attend criminal trials is implicit in the guarantees of the First Amendment. . . .[67]

Clearly, he was opening the door not only to the public and the print media, but also to radio and television.

Justice John Paul Stevens concurred and labeled the case a "watershed."[68] Explaining that the First Amendment rights of the press and

---

64. *Richmond Newspapers, Inc., v. Virginia*, — U.S. —, 65 L Ed 2d 980, 100 S Ct (1981).
65. Id. at 981-982.
66. Id. at 987.
67. Id. at 991-992.
68. Id. at 993.

public are not absolute, he said:

> Today, however, for the first time, the Court unequivocally holds that an arbitrary interference with access to important information is an abridgment of the freedom of speech and of the press protected by the First Amendment.[69]

Justice Byron White concurred and reminded the Court that this case would not have been before the Court if the Sixth Amendment had been correctly applied to the Gannett case.

Justice William Brennan, joined by Justice Marshall, concurred and added:

> In advancing these purposes, the availability of a trial transcript is no substitute for a public presence at the trial itself. As any experienced appellate judge can attest, the 'cold' record is a very imperfect reproduction of events that transpire in the courtroom.[70]

However, Justice Brennan pointed out that the limitations imposed by a trial judge on the First Amendment rights of press and public are similar to time, place and manner restrictions.[71]

Expressing hope that the confusion caused by the Gannett decision would be clarified, Justice Blackmun concurred. Explaining that he was gratified to see that some of the "graffiti"[72] of the Gannett decision could be eliminated, Justice Blackmun again reaffirmed his belief that "the right to a public trial is to be found where the Constitution explicitly placed it—in the Sixth Amendment."[73]

Justice Powell did not take part in the consideration or decision of the case apparently because he had practiced law in Richmond.[74]

Justice Rehnquist dissented. He expressed dismay with the implications of the Court's holding because "it is basically unhealthy to have so much authority concentrated in a small group of lawyers who have been appointed to the Supreme Court and enjoy virtual life tenure."[75] Perhaps Justice Rehnquist's dismay was also tempered by the negative public and press reaction to the Gannett decision. Certainly, Justice Blackmun's listing of newspaper and magazine articles dealing with the

69. Id. at 994.
70. Id. at 1003.
71. Id. at 1002.
72. Id. at 1006.
73. Id. at 1007.
74. "High Court Bars Trials Held in Secret," 49 *Broadcasting* 27 (July 7, 1980).
75. See Justice Rehnquist, *Richmond Newspapers, Inc., v. Virginia*, supra— U.S.—at 1009.

Gannett decision shows that the Court is not completely isolated from public opinion.

Chandler, et al., v. Florida. Using walkie-talkies, two Miami Beach policemen discussed plans to burglarize a Miami Beach restaurant. Their conversation was picked up and recorded by a ham radio operator, John Sion. In July 1977, Noel Chandler and Robert Granger were arrested and charged with conspiracy to commit burglary, grand larceny, and possession of burglary tools.

Because of the nature of the crime, the trial attracted media attention. However, the defendants felt that such coverage violated their constitutional right to a fair trial. Through a pretrial motion, the counsel for the defense sought to have Florida's experimentally modified Canon 3A(7) declared unconstitutional. The trial court denied this, but certified the issue to the Florida Supreme Court.

The Florida Supreme Court declined to rule on this question since "it was not directly relevant to the criminal charges."[76] All of the additional attempts by the defense to prevent electronic coverage failed. Then, at *voir dire,* the defense counsel interrogated each juror on the question of whether or not the electronic coverage would prejudice him or her in any way. All responded that the media coverage would not affect them.[77]

Finally, a defense motion to sequester the jury because of the media coverage was considered by the court. This motion was denied, but the court instructed the jury not to watch or read anything about the case. Furthermore, the jurors were advised to view only the national news telecasts.[78]

Consequently, the defense counsel asked that the witnesses should also be instructed not to watch any televised accounts. The judge declined to give this instruction because he felt there was no electronic coverage of testimony.[79]

On the contrary, Sion's testimony was recorded as well as the prosecution's side of the case and the closing arguments. In all, two minutes and fifty-five seconds of the trial were broadcast.[80]

After the defendants were found guilty on all counts, the defense counsel moved for a new trial on the ground that a fair and impartial trial had been denied because of the electronic coverage. The Florida District Court of Appeal affirmed the convictions but did agree to cer-

---

76. *Chandler, et al., v. Florida,*—U.S.—(1981). *U.S. Law Week,* 26 January 1981, at 4143.
77. Id.
78. Id.
79. Id.
80. Id.

tify the question of the constitutionality of Experimental Canon 3A(7) to the Florida Supreme Court.[81]

The Florida Supreme Court denied review and held that the appeal was moot by reason of its decision in the *Petition of the Post Newsweek Stations, Florida, Incorporated* (1979).[82] However, the Supreme Court granted certiorari and considered

> [t]he question of whether, consistent with constitutional guarantee, a state may provide for radio, television, and still photographic coverage of a criminal trial for public broadcast, notwithstanding the objection of the accused."[83]

With Justice Stevens absent from the proceedings, the Supreme Court affirmed the Florida Supreme Court. Chief Justice Burger delivered the holding which Justices Brennan, Marshall, Blackmun, Powell, and Rehnquist joined.

Chief Justice Burger outlined the history of Canon 3A(7) and explained that the decision in the *Petition of the Post-Newsweek Stations, Inc.*, did not mean that electronic coverage is required under the Sixth Amendment.[84]

Since the appellants based most of their appeal on the decision in *Estes v. Texas,* he pointed out that though Chief Justice Warren's concurring opinion — joined by Justices Douglas and Goldberg — did support the appellant's position, the six separate opinions must be examined individually

> . . .to evaluate the claim that it represents a per se constitutional rule forbidding all electronic coverage.[85]

In particular, he examined Justice Harlan's opinion and determined that Estes did not prohibit electronic coverage of trials:

> . .Estes is not to be read as announcing a constitutional rule barring still photographic, radio, and television coverage in all cases and under all circumstances.[86]

---

81. Id.
82. This ruling allowed electronic coverage of trials to continue on a permanent basis in Florida. Although not meant as a mandate for electronic coverage, the decision specified that no consent was required. Only the presiding judge could prohibit coverage.
83. See *Chandler, et al., v. Florida,* supra.
84. Id. at 4144.
85. Id.
86. Id. at 4145.

Thus, there is no need to overrule a holding that does not exist.[87] Further,

> [i]t does not stand as an absolute ban on state experimentation with evolving technology, which, in terms of modes of mass communication, was in its relative infancy in 1964, and is, even now, in a state of continuing change.[88]

Considering the question of denial of due process because of photographic or broadcast coverage, Chief Justice Burger found that any criminal case gives rise to publicity. He admonished all trial courts to vigilantly protect the defendant's right to a fair trial with the "verdict based solely upon the evidence and the relevant law."[89] Moreover, he pointed out,

> Over the years, courts have developed a range of curative devices to prevent publicity about a trial from infecting jury deliberations.[90]

On the other hand,

> [t]he risk of juror prejudice in some cases does not justify an absolute ban on news coverage of trials by the printed media; so also the risk of such prejudice does not warrant an absolute constitutional ban on all broadcast coverage.[91]

Citing various studies which show that the presence of the electronic press does not interfere with the judicial process, he added that

> no one has been able to present empirical data sufficient to establish that the mere presence of the broadcast media inherently has an adverse affect. . . .[92]

While acknowledging modern technological advancements—though still troubled by the possibility that electronic coverage might even subtly interfere with the judicial process—Justice Stewart concurred and added:

> I have no great trouble in agreeing with the court today, but I would acknowledge our square departure from precedent.[93]

87. Id.
88. Id.
89. Id.
90. Id.
91. Id.
92. Id. at 4146.
93. Id. at 4148.

Justice White, in his concurring opinion, concluded:

> Although the Court's opinion today contends that it is consistent with Estes, I believe that it effectively eviscerates Estes.[94]

Conclusion. Several states have lifted the ban against television in the courtroom. Some states allow limited coverage. Others allow the use of video tape to record proceedings for educational, broadcast, and informational purposes. Video taped confessions and depositions may be used in some appeals courts. Gavel-to-gavel coverage as well as news excerpts of proceedings have been aired by broadcast stations.

The original 1937 report of the A.B.A. investigative committee recommended changes in the judicial procedure, but the recommendation that the judge consider the question of cameras in the courtroom with the consent of counsel was ignored. In his concurring opinion in *Richmond Newspapers, Inc., v. Virginia,* Justice Brennan suggested that a trial judge may limit access of the press and public to a certain extent. However, he also noted that a trial transcript is a poor replacement for media coverage. Moreover, after affirming that criminal trials are open to the press and the public, Chief Justice Burger, in the majority opinion, reiterated the idea from the Red Lion case that electronic media act as the fiduciary for the public. In addition, Justice Stevens emphasized the concept that any "arbitrary interference" with the public right to know "important information" is contrary to the freedom of the press under the First Amendment.

In *Chandler, et al., v. Florida,* the Supreme Court affirmed the right of each state to allow electronic and still photographic coverage of criminal trials without the consent of the accused. This holding denied that Estes prohibited all electronic coverage of trials. By not considering Estes as a precedent, the Court supported the concept that electronic coverage of a trial need not be considered obtrusive or prejudicial to the judicial process.

Thus, it would appear that the question of whether the electronic press should have access to the courtroom has received an affirmative reply.

---

94. Id. at 4149.

DAVID M. O'BRIEN

The Trials and Tribulations of Courtroom Secrecy and Judicial Craftsmanship: Reflections on Gannett and Richmond Newspapers*

David M. O'Brien is an Assistant
Professor in the Woodrow Wilson
Department of Government and
Foreign Affairs, University of Virginia.

"Justice must satisfy the appearance of justice."[1] —**Justice Felix Frankfurter**

Justice Felix Frankfurter reminds us that the symbols and rituals of the judicial process condition—and, hence are often as crucial as—the tangible consequences of judicial politics. Traditionally, the appearance of justice and public confidence in the judicial system was

---

*This paper was originally delivered at the Annual Meeting of the Southern Political Science Association, November 6-9, 1980, in Atlanta.

1. *Offutt v. United States,* 348 U.S. 11, 14 (1954)

thought to be undermined by secret trials and closed judicial proceedings.[2] Unlike other governmental institutions and processes,[3] courts and trials have historically been open to members of the public and the press, both at common law[4] and under the Sixth Amendment provision that "[i]n all criminal prosecutions the accused shall enjoy the right to a speedy and public trial."[5]

The common law and contitutional presumption of the openness of judicial proceedings notwithstanding, a bare majority in *Gannett Co. v. DePasquale*[6] ruled that neither members of the public nor the press may constitutionally claim access to pretrial hearings. Justice Potter Stewart's plurality opinion for the Court, moreover, provoked considerable controversy by suggesting that the Sixth Amendment permits closure of both pretrial proceedings and trials.[7] The ambiguity of Justice Stewart's opinion and the divisions within the Court not only prompted no less than five justices to attempt to clarify, explain and defend the ruling with "off-the-bench" comments.[8] *Gannett* also invited lower court judges to exercise their discretion in closing pretrial hearings, trials, and even post-trial arraignments. In the 52 weeks following the ruling there were no less than 272 motions to close judicial proceedings, resulting in 160 closures.[9]

2. See, e.g. Joseph Story, *Commentaries on the Constitution of the United States* (Boston: Little, Brown, 5th ed., 1891), at 662; and Thomas Cooley, *A Treatise on Constitutional Limitations* (Boston: Little, Brown, 8th ed., 1927), at 312.
3. See, e.g., *Greer v. Spock*, 428 U.S. 828 (1976) (military bases); *Adderly v. Florida*, 385 U.S. 39 (1967) (jails); *Pell v. Procuiner*, 417 U.S. 817 (1974), *Saxbe v. Washington Post Co.*, 417 U.S. 843 (1974), and *Houchins v. KQED*, 438 U.S. 1 (1978) (prisons).
4. See, e.g., Jeremy Bentham, *Treatise on Judicial Evidence* (London: 1827), at 67-68; and Sir William Blackstone, *Commentaries on the Laws of England* (Oxford: Clarendon Press, 1766), at 372-373.
5. U.S. Constitution, VI Amendment.
6. *Gannett Co. v. DePasquale*, 99 S.Ct., 2898 (1979).
7. Ibid., at 2914-2917
8. See, e.g., "Brennan Assails Media Criticisms of Court Decisions," *The Washington Post*, A 12, Col. 1 (October 18, 1979); "Justice Marshall Hits Colleagues on Rights," *Seattle Post-Intellegencer* B 2 (June 3, 1979); John Paul Stevens, "Some Thoughts on A General Rule," 21 *Arizona Law Review* 599 (1979), and *The New York Times*, A 14, col. 1 (September 9, 1979) (quoting Justice Stevens's view that "members of the general public, including the press, could not assert rights guaranteed to the accused by the Sixth Amendment"); *The New York Times*, A 17, col. 1 (August 9, 1979) (quoting Chief Justice Burger "that the opinion referred to pretrial proceedings only"); *The New York Times*, A 13, col. 1 (August 14, 1979) (reporting Justice Powell's address to a panel at the annual meeting of the American Bar Association and explanation that *Gannett* was based only on the Sixth Amendment); and *The New York Times*, A 15, col. 1 (September 4, 1979) (reporting Justice Blackmun's view that after *Gannett* closure of trials is permissible).
9. See, text to footnotes 84 to 88.

The Supreme Court subsequently accepted the challenge to the closure of a trial, in *Richmond Newspapers, Inc. v. Virginia*,[10] in order to clarify its ruling in *Gannett* and to again address claims by the press to a First and Sixth Amendment "right of access" or "public's right to know." The Court's 7:1 decision was in concurring Justice John Paul Steven's view a "watershed case."[11] Similarly, members of the press and communication lawyers celebrated the Court's vindication of the presumption of open trials and the public's "right of access." The decision was praised as "one of the two or three most important decisions in the whole history of the First Amendment."[12]

The enduring significance and precedential value of *Gannett* and *Richmond Newspapers* nonetheless remains unclear because of the divisions within the Court and the ambiguity of the rulings. In terms of constitutional politics, the failure to achieve consensus and relatively unambiguious opinions frustrates lower court compliance; indeed, renders discussions of "compliance" virtually meaningless. The trials and tribulations of the Court's treatment of the First and Sixth Amendments in *Gannett* and *Richmond Newspapers,* furthermore, brings to bear the perennially vexing issue of the parameters of judicial review and the contours of judicial creativity. After examining the presumption of open judicial proceedings rooted in common law practice and constitutional doctrine, the jurisprudence of *Gannett* and *Richmond Newspapers* is examined in terms of the ubiquitious demands of judicial craftsmanship[13] and the impact on lower court procedures. Contrary to some commentators,[14] the majority of the Court has not recognized a right of access per se, and, more generally, both cases significantly undermine the presumption of openness in judicial proceedings.

I. PUBLIC TRIALS AND THE PRESUMPTION OF OPENNESS

The presumption of openness rooted in the common law background of the Sixth Amendment underlies defendants' right to a "speedy and public trial." Open trial proceedings was established by the

---

10. *Richmond Newspapers, Inc. v. Virginia,* 100 S.Ct. 2814 (1980).
11. Ibid., at 2830 (Stevens, J., con. op.).
12. Dan Paul, quoted in "News Notes," "Richmond Decision Seen as Having Major Effect," 6 *Media Law Reporter* 11 (July 15, 1980).
13. See, David M. O'Brien, "The Seduction of the Judiciary: Social Science and the Courts," 64 *Judicature* 8-21 (1980), at 16-19.
14. See, e.g., James C. Goodale, "Gannett Is Burned by Richmond's First Amendment-'Sunshine Act,'" *The National Law Journal* 24 (September 29, 1980).

17th century in common law practice, stemming from earlier Anglo-Saxon customs. In 1612 Lord Edward Coke emphasized the "great importance" of the principle that "all causes ought to be heard, ordered and determined... openly."[15] So too, 17th and 18th century commentators—such as Jeremy Bentham and Sir William Blackstone—on English common law practice acknowledged both the tradition and salutary effects of publicity.[16]

The Sixth Amendment was thought to incorporate common law practice.[17] The most widely read and knowledgeable commentator on the Constitution and Bill of Rights within a generation of the founding period, Joseph Story observed that "in declaring that the accused shall enjoy the right to a speedy and public trial [the Sixth Amendment] does not but follow out the established course of the common law in all trials for crimes. The trial is always public."[18] In the 19th and 20th centuries, commentators like Thomas Cooley and John Wigmore also affirmed the tradition and auspicious policies underlying public trials.[19] In addition, all states recognize the right to a public trial: 41 states acknowledge that right in their constitutions, while in 7 states public trials are considered part of the common law tradition, and only in Massachusetts and Virginia does the right exist as a matter of statutory law.[20]

The policy considerations underlying common law practice and state and federal constitutional provisions for public trials are numerous. The publicity of trials is principally viewed as deterring judicial arbitrariness and thereby ensuring the accused's right to a fair trial. In 1827, for instance, Bentham argued: "[t]he knowledge that every criminal trial is subject to contemporaneous review in the forum of public opinion is an effective restraint on possible abuse of judicial power."[21] The presence of members of the public is also thought to reduce the possibility of a witness's perjury; while at the same time encouraging individuals, who possess relevant information, to come forth and

---

15. Lord Edward Coke, *Second Institutes of the Laws of England* (6th ed., 1681), at 103.
16. See, Bentham, supra note 4, at 67-68; and Cooley, supra note 2, at 372-373.
17. See, e.g., Story, supra note 2; and 1 The Debates in the *Several State Conventions on the Adoption of the Federal Constitution*, ed. by Jonathan Elliot (1881), at 328.
18. See, Story, supra note 2, at 662.
19. See, Cooley, supra note 2, at 312; and John Wigmore, *Evidence*, 3rd ed. (Mineola: Foundation Press, 1940), at §1823.
20. See, Seaton Siebert, *The Rights and Privileges of the Press* (New York: D. Appleton-Century, 1934), at 38-45.
21. Bentham, supra note 4, at 69.

testify.[22] Finally, open trials serve important public interests, as Lord Campbell in 1857 proclaimed: "It is of great consequence that the public should know what takes place in Court."[23] Publicity both educates people about the operation of the judiciary and provides an important opportunity for members of the public to scrutinize the administration of justice.

Although state and federal courts traditionally recognized the presumption of openness of judicial proceedings, members of the public and the press never possessed an unqualified legal right—regardless of whether that right was claimed as a common law, statutory or constitutional right—to attend criminal trials. While courts acknowledged, as the Ohio State Supreme Court put it in 1906, that "the people have the right to know what is being done in their court,"[24] fundamentally the right to a public trial was that of defendants and not the public. In other words, the "universal rule against secret trials"[25] primarily ensures procedural fairness, and only derivatively the public's interests in open judicial proceedings. Thus at common law and under the Sixth Amendment access neither the public nor the press could compel unconditional openness. Thomas Cooley, for example, reasoned that:

> "By this [provision that trials be public] is not meant that every person who sees fit shall in all cases be permitted to attend criminal trials; because there are many cases where, from the character of the charge, and the nature of the evidence by which it is to be supported, the motives to attend the trial on the part of portions of the community would be of the worst character, and where a regard to public morals and public decency would require that at least the young be excluded from hearing and witnessing the evidence of human depravity which the trial must necessarily bring to light. The requirement for a public trial is for the benefit of the accused; that the public may see he is fairly dealt with and not unjustly condemned."[26]

---

22. See, Note, "Trial Secrecy and the First Amendment Right of Public Access to Judicial Proceedings," 91 *Harvard Law Review* 1874 (1978); and Note, "The Right to A Public Trial in Criminal Cases," 41 *New York University Law Review* 1138 (1966).
23. *Davison v. Duncan,* 7 El. & Bl. 229, 231, 110 Rev. R. 572, 574 (Q.B. 1857).
24. *State v. Hensley,* 75 Ohio St. 255, 257, 79 N.E. 462, 463-464 (1906).
25. *In re Oliver,* 333 U.S. 257, 266 (1948).
26. Cooley, supra note 2, at 312.

At common law and under the Sixth Amendment, public and press access remains at the control of the court. Judges may permissibly limit public access in order to preserve the decorum of the courtroom or prevent prejudicial publicity. Moreover, under state statutes some limitations on public and press access are permitted per se. Several states, for instance, authorize judges to exclude journalists from juvenile courts and both minors and journalists from trials concerning matters deemed scandalous or obscene.[27]

II. PUBLIC TRIALS AND THE FAIR TRIAL/FREE PRESS CONTROVERSY

Although prior to *Gannett* and *Richmond Newspapers* the Supreme Court never directly ruled on the public's right to attend judicial proceedings, its rulings on the Sixth Amendment closely followed common law practice and policies recognizing the auspicious consequences of publicity. In the 1940s when the Court first turned to the issue of courtroom secrecy it acknowledged the interests of both defendants and the public in open trials:

> In view of this nation's historic distrust of secret proceedings, their inherent dangers to freedom, and the universal requirement of our federal and state governments that criminal trials be public, the Fifth Amendment's guarantee that no one shall be deprived of his liberty without due process of law means at least that an accused cannot be thus sentenced to prison.[28]

The Court further emphasized that "[w]hatever other benefits the guarantee to an accused that his trial be conducted in public may confer upon our society, the guarantee has always been recognized as a safeguard against any attempt to employ our courts as instruments of persecution."[29]

Albeit the Supreme Court recognized that the public has important interests in open trials,[30] it construed the Sixth Amendment to guarantee only the rights of the accused, and not of the press or the public. The Court, however, also ruled that "although a defendant can, under

---

27. See, Wigmore, supra note 19, at §1835, pp. 449-450.
28. *In re Oliver*, 333 U.S. 257 (1943).
29. Ibid.
30. See, *Barker v. Wingo*, 407 U.S. 514, 519 (1972) (right to speedy trial involves societal interest).

some circumstances, waive his constitutional right to a public trial, he has no absolute right to compel a private trial."[31] Thus under the Sixth Amendment members of the public and the press have no constitutional right to compel open trials, but neither do defendants have a constitutional right to a closed trial. Furthermore, because the Sixth Amendment guarantees an accused's rights, and only derivatively the public's interest, judges may restrict public access and publicity in order to ensure due process and procedural fairness.[32]

In the last three decades on precisely those occasions when judges restricted or constrained publicity about trials the press has increasingly asserted its interests under the First Amendment. First Amendment interests of the public and the press are distinguishable from those interests in publicity embraced by the Sixth Amendment. First Amendment claims to open trials are grounded on individuals' right of free speech and press and the public's interests in freedom of information and self-governance, rather than a concern about the fairness of a particular trial. Accordingly, in 1946 Justice Frankfurter declared that "trials must be public and the public [has] a deep interest in trials."[33] A year later his frequent interlocutor on the high bench, Justice William Douglas, likewise poignantly observed: "The trial is a public event. What transpires in the court room is public property."[34] Some years later Justice Frankfurter again reiterated that, "One of the demands of a democratic society is that the public should know what goes on in courts by being told by the press what happens there, to the end that the public may judge whether our system of criminal justice is fair and right."[35]

The First Amendment, unlike the Sixth Amendment, comprehends the public's broader interests in freedom of information and self-governance. Closed judicial proceedings may deprive the public of vital information, which in turn potentially diminishes citizens' effective exercise of their electoral powers and hence the accountability of judges, prosecutors and police officials. Nor are the public's interests adequately protected by the participants in a closed trial. The public's interests may be sacrificed when either prosecutors attempt to conceal police or prosectorial misconduct and ineptitude, or when defendants endeavor to keep proceedings secret in order to safeguard embarrassing facts or personal privacy.[36] The First Amendment therefore provides a basis for

---

31. *Singer v. United States,* 380 U.S. 24, 25 (1965).
32. See, e.g., *Illinois v. Allen,* 397 U.S. 337, 343 (1970).
33. *Pennekamp v. Florida,* 328 U.S. 331, 361 (1946) (Frankfurter, J., con. op.).
34. *Craig v. Harney,* 331 U.S. 367, 374 (1947) (Douglas, J.).
35. *Maryland v. Baltimore Radio Show, Inc.,* 338 U.S. 912, 920 (1950) (Frankfurter, J., dis. op. from denial of *certariori).*
36. See, discussion in text to footnotes 84 to 88.

the public and the press to challenge restraints on publicity and access to judicial proceedings, even though defendants find secrecy benign or demand trial closure to prevent publicity—publicity that might prove prejudicial or merely reveal personally embarrassing facts or other sensitive information such as the identity of witnesses or confidential governmental information.[37]

The competing interests of defendants and the public precipitated the so-called "fair trial/free press" controversy.[38] Sensational murder trials—such as as those of Dr. Sam Sheppard[39] and Charles Simants[40] — ostensibly necessitated judicial accommodation of the Sixth Amendment right of defendants with the First Amendment interests of the public and press. Actually, since constitutional rights are assertable only against the government and not other individuals,[41] the fair trial/free press controversy demanded that the Court balance the government's actions in limiting publicity in order to ensure due process and a fair trial with the First Amendment.[42] Although the fair trial/free press controversy does not involve balancing the First and Sixth Amendments per se, the controversy heightened the press's concern over "the public's right to know" and the availability and extent of information about judicial proceedings.

Prior to the 1960s the Supreme Court appeared reluctant to sanction restraints on pretrial and trial publicity, typically overturning contempt charges of the press for editorials and publicity concerning judicial proceedings.[43] But, publicity on occasion proved prejudicial and during the 1960s the Warren Court was eventually forced to insist that judges exercise their responsibility and powers to ensure fair trials. The Warren Court, however, remained sensitive to the public's First Amendment interests in the availability of information about the conduct of trials. In *Estes v. Texas,* for example, when holding that television broadcasting of a criminal trial jeopardizes due process and the defendant's right to a fair trial, the Court acknowledged that "the public has

---

37. See, discussion in text to footnotes 86 to 88.
38. See, generally, Report of the Twentieth Century Fund Task Force on Justice, Publicity and the First Amendment, *Rights in Conflict* (New York: McGraw-Hill, 1976); and Chilton Bush, ed., *Free Press and Fair Trial* (Athens: University of Georgia, 1970).
39. See, *Sheppard v. Maxwell,* 341 U.S. 350 (1951).
40. See, *Nebraska Press Association v. Stuart,* 427 U.S. 539 (1976).
41. See, e.g., *Burdeau v. McDowell,* 256 U.S. 465, 475 (1921); and David M. O'Brien, *Privacy, Law and Public Policy* (Praeger Publishers, 1979).
42. See, generally, Comment, "Gagging the Press in Criminal Trials," 10 *Harvard Civil Rights-Civil Liberties Law Review* 608 (1975).
43. See, e.g., *Pennekamp v. Florida,* 328 U.S. 331 (1946); *Craig v. Harney,* 331 U.S. 367 (1947).

a right to be informed as to what occurs in its courts."[44] Justice Stewart himself the author of several opinions denying a First Amendment-" right of access,"[45] wrote in a dissenting opinion in *Estes* that "[t]he suggestion that there are limits upon the public's right to know what goes on in courts causes me deep concern."[46] The following year when overturning the conviction of Sam Sheppard for the murder of his wife, the Warren Court again emphasized that "[t]he press does not simply publish information about trials but guards against the miscarriage of justice by subjecting the police, prosecutors, and judicial processes to extensive public scrutiny and criticism."[47] In both cases there was nationwide publicity and the problem was that lower courts failed to ensure the decorum essential to a fair trial. In the Sheppard case the press had a "Roman Holiday" with the live broadcasting of the coroner's inquest from the school gymnasium. At the trial the judge reserved three of the four rows of benches in the court room for reporters and permitted the erection of a press table inside the bar of the court, which allowed journalists to overheard all of Sheppard's conversations with his attorneys! Accordingly, Justice Thomas Clark, writing for the Court, indicated that trial judges should adopt rules governing reporters' access to the court room, and insulating witnesses from journalists; as well as barring police, witnesses and counsel from talking about trial proceedings.

The Warren Court's ruling in *Sheppard v. Maxwell*[48] intensified the fair trial/free press controversy. Immediately the American Bar Association adopted as part of its Canons of Professional Ethics the Reardon Report's proposal of rules limiting attorney's permissible statements about pending trials and recommending that judges use their contempt power to inhibit prejudicial publicity. The American Newspapers Publishers Association responded by contending both that such interference with news reporting thwarted First Amendment press freedoms and "the public's right to know," and that pretrial and intrial publicity in fact contributed to fair trial procedures and results.[49] The

---

44. *Estes v. Texas*, 381 U.S. 532, 541 (1965). In *Chandler v. Florida*, 101 S. Ct. 802 (Jan. 26, 1981), Chief Justice Burger, for a unanimous Court, ruled that photographic and broadcast coverage of criminal trials does not inherently deny due process.
45. See, e.g., *Pell v. Procuiner*, 417 U.S. 817 (1974); *Saxbe v. Washington Post Co.*, 417 U.S. 843 (1974); and *Gannett Co. v.DePasquale*, 99 S.Ct. 2898 (1979).
46. *Estes v. Texas*, 381 U.S. 532, 615 (1965) (Stewart, J., dis. op.).
47. *Sheppard v. Maxwell*, 341 U.S. 350 (1951).
48. Ibid.
49. See, generally, Alfred Friendly and Ronald L. Goldfarb, *Crime and Publicity; The Impact of News on the Administration of Justice* (New York: The Twentieth Century Fund, 1967).

ANPA's opposition notwithstanding, *Sheppard* and the Reardon Report encouraged judges to issue "gag orders" on counsel, witnesses and jurors in sensational trials.

In the 1970s the press vigorously contested judicially imposed gag orders as an abridgement of the First Amendment. Though declining to review several highly controversial gag orders,[50] the Burger Court continued to recognize the important and interdependent interests of defendants and the public. In the Burger Court's major treatment of the fair trial/free press controversy in *Nebraska Press Association v. Stuart,* the Chief Justice reaffirmed that "prior restraints on speech and publications are the most serious and least tolerable infringement of First Amendment rights."[51] In striking down the gag order, Chief Justice Burger suggested that judges employ other devices to safeguard against prejudicial pretrial and intrial publicity. He specifically listed as alternatives: (1) change of venue (i.e., moving the trial to another locality where there exists less public interest in or publicity about the trial); (2) postpone the trial so as to permit adverse publicity to die down; (3) permit rigorous voir dire examination of potential jurors to check against prejudice; (4) instruct juries emphatically as to its responsibility to only consider admitted evidence; and (5) sequester the jury.[52] Additionally, trial judges may grant mistrials for adverse publicity and convictions can be reversed on appeal.

Because the Court did not strike down the gag order as unconstitutional per se, Justice William Brennan, joined by Justices Potter Stewart and Thurgood Marshall, wrote a concurring opinion indicating that all gag orders are constitutionally impermissible.[53] However, none of the devices outlined by the Chief Justice seriously interferes with "the public's right to know,"[54] and the crucial remaining issue was whether the use of these devices would indeed ensure fair trials. The difficulties of controlling prejudicial publicity, however, led trial judges to not only continue the use of gag orders but to close pretrial hearings and trials.

---

50. See, e.g., *Farr v. Pitchess,* 96 S.Ct. 3200 (1976); *Rosato v. Superior Court,* 96 S. Ct. 3200 (1976); and *Evans v. Fromme,* 96 S.Ct. 1664 (1976).
51. *Nebraska Press Association v. Stuart,* 427 U.S. 539, 563-564 (1976). See also, *Oklahoma Press Publishing Co. District Court,* 430 U.S. 308 (1977).
52. Ibid.
53. Ibid.
54. For a further discussion, see: David M. O'Brien, *The Public's Right to Know: The Supreme Court and the First Amendment,* Chapter 4 (Praeger Publishers, 1981).

III. GANNETT AND ITS IMPACT

In 1978 the Supreme Court refused to hear three trial secrecy cases[55] but granted *certariori* in *Gannett v. DePasquale,*[56] presenting a challenge to the closure of a pretrial hearing. At a pretrial hearing on the suppression of allegedly involuntary confessions and certain physical evidence, the defendants requested that the public and the press be excluded on the grounds that adverse pretrial publicity would jeopardize their ability to receive a fair trial. The district attorney did not oppose the motion for closure, nor did a reporter, who was employed by Gannett Publishing Company and present at the hearing. The trial judge granted the motion. The following day, the reporter requested a copy of the trial transcript and asserted a constitutional right to cover the proceeding. The trial judge denied the request. On appeal, the reporter successfully challenged the closure as violative of the First, Sixth and Fourteenth Amendments, but the New York Court of Appeals reversed, upholding the exclusion of the public and the press from pretrial proceedings. Gannett Publishing Company petitioned the Supreme Court for review, arguing that the Sixth Amendment conferred a right of access on the public and press to attend pretrial hearings as well as trials, and urging the Court to narrow its holdings in *Pell v. Procuriner,*[57] *Saxbe v. Washington Post Co.,*[58] and *Houchins v. KQED*[59] by recognizing a First and Fourteenth Amendment right of access to pretrial proceedings.

Divided over the issues the Court's opinion was so broadly framed as to not only invite criticisms from the Court's commentators but prompt no fewer than five justices later publicly to discuss the ruling.[60]

---

55. See, e.g., *United States v. Gurney*, 558 F.2d 1202 (5th Cir. 1977) *(suppression of information during trial), cert. denied* 98 S.Ct. (1978), *Central South Carolina Chapter, Society of Professional Journalists v. Martin*, 556 F.2d 706 (4th Cir. 1977) (gag order on trial participants), *cert. denied* 434 U.S. 1022 (1978); and *State ex rel. Leach v. Sawicki, cert. denied,* 434 U.S. 1014 (1978).
56. *Gannett Co. v. DePasquale,* 99 S.Ct. 28998 (1979).
57. *Pell v. Procuriner,* 417 U.S. 817 (1974) (denying a press claim to a First Amendment constitutional right of access to interview individually designated prisoners in a state prison).
58. *Saxbe v. Washington Post Co.,* 417 U.S. 843 (1974) (denying press claims to a First Amendment right of access to interview prisoners in a federal prison).
59. *Houchins v. KQED,* 438 U.S. 1 (1978) (denying a First Amendment right of access to a portion of a prison). For a further discussion of claims to a First Amendment right of access, see, David M. O'Brien, "Reassessing the First Amendment and the Public's 'Right to Know' in Constitutional Adjudication," 26 *Villanova Law Review* 1-62 (1980).
60. See, supra note 8.

As in *Pell* and *Saxbe,* Justice Stewart wrote the opinion for a bare majority. Justices John Paul Stevens and Lewis Powell, however, now joined the Chief Justice and Justice William Rehnquist, the latter three writing concurring opinions.[61] Justices Brennan and Marshall, the staunchest supporters of a constitutional right to know,[62] were joined by Justice Harry Blackmun and Byron White in a dissenting opinion authored by Justice Blackmun. The line-up of the justices resulted from their giving precedence to the Sixth Amendment claim rather than the claim for a First Amendment right of access.

After summarizing the circumstances of the litigation, Justice Stewart observed that "[t]he Constitution nowhere mentions any right of access to a criminal trial on the part of the public; its guarantee, like the others enumerated, is personal to the accused."[63] Yet the issue in *Gannett* was "whether members of the public have an enforceable right to a public trial that can be asserted independently of the parties in the litigation."[64] Acknowledging that "there is a strong societal interest in public trials," he went on to emphasize that "[r]ecognition of an independent public interest in the enforcement of Sixth Amendment guaranteed is a far cry...from the creation of a constitutional right on the part of the public."[65] Under the Sixth Amendment any public interest involved is "protected by the participants in the litigation" because the amendment is fundamentally "a 'guarantee of an accused.'"[66]

---

61. Justices Stevens and Powell previously dissented from the majority's denial of claims to a First Amendment right of access in *Saxbe v. Washington Post Co.,* 417 U.S. 843, 873 (1974) (Powell, J., dis. op.); and *Houchins v. KQED,* 438 U.S. 1, 19 (1978) (Stevens, J., dis. op.).
62. Justice Brennan's broad interpretation of the First Amendment and endorsement of the consitutional legitimacy of the public's "right to know" under the amendment is grounded on his understanding, if not entirely faithful interpretation, of Alexander Meiklejohn's thesis on the First Amendment. See, A. Meiklejohn, *Political Freedom* (1965); A. Meiklejohn, "The First Amendment Is an Absolute," 1961 *Supreme Court Review* 26 (1950); and William Brennan, "The Supreme Court and the Meiklejohn Interpretation of the First Amendment," 79 *Harvard Law Review* 1 (1965). For a further discussion, see, David M. O'Brien, "The First Amendment and the Public's 'Right to Know,'" 13 *Hastings Constitutional Law Quarterly* 579-631 (1980), at 613-618.

    Justice Marshall apparently shares the interpretation of the First Amendment and the public's "right to know" advanced by Justice Brennan. See, *Saxbe v. Washington Post Co.,* 417 U.S. 843, 850 (1974) (Powell, J., dis. op., joined by Brennan and Marshall, JJ.); *Pell v. Procuiner,* 417 U.S. 817, 836 (1976) (Douglas, J., dis. op., joined by Brennan and Marshall, JJ.); *Rosenbloom v. Metromedia,* 403 U.S. 29, 78 (1971) (Marshall, J., dis. op.).
63. *Gannett Co. v. DePasquale,* 99 S.Ct. 2898, 2905 (1979).
64. Ibid., at 2907.
65. Ibid.
66. Ibid, at 2901-2905.

Justice Stewart differed from the dissenters in concluding that—notwithstanding common law practices, the importance of open criminal trials and authorities from William Blackstone to Thomas Cooley[67]—the Sixth Amendment's public trial guarantee did not grant the public or the press a right of access to pretrials or trials. Moreover, Justice Stewart though that any First Amendment right of access had been adequately considered in the trial judge's determination that publicity of the pretrial hearing would pose a "reasonable probability of prejudice to the defendants."[68] Justice Stewart found it significant that the trial judge had entertained the press's objections to closure and that, in any event, the denial of access had been only temporary, not absolute, since after the defendants pleaded guilty the press was permitted to obtain a copy of the suppression hearing transcript. Justice Stewart thus concluded: "We need not decide in the abstract... whether there is any such constitutional right. For even assuming, *arguendo,* that the First and Fourteenth Amendments may guarantee such access in some situations, a question we do not decide, this putative right was given all appropriate deference by the state *nisi prius* court in the present case."[69]

Because Justice Stewart stated no less than dozen times that the public and press have no constitutional right of access to either pretrials or trials, his opinion reached issues not raised by the instant case and invited confusion as to the Court's ruling. Accordingly, Chief Justice Burger added a concurring opinion to underline that *Gannett* dealt only with pretrial hearings, and to clarify the nature of such proceedings and their contemporary importance as the result of the exclusionary rule and motions to suppress evidence. He also reserved comment on whether the public and the press may claim a right under the First and Fourteenth Amendment to attend trials.[70]

Although Justice Powell joined the opinion of the Court on the Sixth Amendment issue, his concurrance addressed the First Amendment issues that Justice Stewart avoided. Justice Powell underscored "the importance of the public's having accurate information concerning the operation of its criminal justice system," and therefore would have held "explicitly that petitioner's reporter had an interest protected by the First and Fourteenth Amendments."[71] Remaining consistent with his concurring opinion in *Branzburg v. Hayes*[72] he thought that the

---

67. See, Ibid., at 2940 (Blackmun, J., dis. op.); Blackstone, supra note 4, at 372-373; Story, supra note 2 at 662; and Cooley, supra note 2, at 328.
68. Ibid., at 2912.
69. Ibid.
70. Ibid., at 2913 (Burger, C.J., con. op.).
71. Ibid., at 2914 (Powell, J., con. op.).
72. *Branzburg v. Hayes,* 408 U.S. 665 (1972).

Court should reach an accommodation of the First Amendment rights of the public and the press with those of the criminal defendant. He maintained that the right of access is not absolute and that "[i]t is limited both by the constitutional right of the defendants to a fair trial... and by the needs of government to obtain just convictions and to preserve the confidentiality of sensitive information and the identity of informants."[73] Justice Powell thus remained willing to legitimate "the public's right to know" as a limited but enforceable right in some circumstances.[74] Indeed, what particularly disturbed him in *Gannett* was that the Court failed to articulate a procedure or standard by which lower courts might balance the First Amendment against the interests of the government and criminal defendants. In joining the majority, however, Justice Powell, as Justice Stevens, abandoned his fellow dissenters in *Pell, Saxbe* and *Houchins* because he found the trial judge's balancing of the public's First Amendment interests against those of the government and criminal defendants acceptable and because he endorsed Justice Stewart's interpretation of the Sixth Amendment.

Justice Rehnquist wrote a concurring opinion to emphasize that "the public does not have *any* Sixth Amendment right of access to such proceedings"[75] and to address Justice Powell's understanding of the First Amendment issue. He emphasized that the Court's reservations on the First Amendment claims of access were more apparent than real, because "it is clear that this Court repeatedly has held that there is no First Amendment right of access in the public or the press to judicial or other governmental proceedings."[76] Justice Rehnquist's observation was not prompted by Justice Stewart's personal reservations on the First Amendment claims; but, rather by the fact that Justice Stewart was required to express public reservations in order to win the votes of Justices Stevens and Powell, since Justices Blackmun and White dissented over the Sixth Amendment issue. Justice Rehnquist reminds us

---

73. *Gannett Co. v. DePasquale,* 99 S.Ct. 2898, 2915 (1979) (Powell, J., con. op.).
74. Justice Powell neither shares the broad interpretation of the First Amendment advocated by Justices Brennan and Marshall (see supra note 62) nor would he give as extensive scope to the public's "right to know." For instance, he would not grant the press special privileges in order to fulfill the public's "right to know." However, he has indicated that he is not entirely opposed to the constitutional legitimacy of a "right to know" and apparently thinks that government policies must give reasonable consideration to the public's interest in knowing. See, *Gannett Co. v. DePasquale,* 99 S.Ct. 2898, 2914-2917 (1979) (Powell, J., con. op.); *Nixon v. Warner Communications,* 435 U.S. 589 (1978); and *Saxbe v. Washington Post Co.,* 417 U.S. 843, 873 (1974) (Powell, J., joined by Brennan and Marshall, JJ., dis. op.).
75. *Gannett Co. v. DePasquale,* 99 S.Ct. 2898, 2918 (1979) (Rehnquist, J., con. op.) (emphasis in original).
76. Ibid.

of Justice Stewart's position by quoting from his concurring opinion in *Houchins:* "The First and Fourteenth Amendments do not guarantee the public a right of access to information generated or controlled by government, nor do they guarantee the press any basic right of access superior to that of the public generally. The Constitution does no more than assure the public and the press equal access once government has opened its doors."[77] Justice Rehnquist's opinion thus was designed to publicly castigate Justice Powell, as well as Justices Brennan, Marshall and Stevens and the Court's commentators, for construing "the First Amendment [as] some sort of constitutional 'sunshine law' that requires notice, an opportunity to be heard and subsequent reasons before a government proceeding may be closed to the public and press."[78]

Justice Blackmun, author of the dissenting opinion, quarreled only with the majority's understanding of the Sixth Amendment public trial guarantee. He concluded that the amendment by "establishing the public's right of access to a criminal trial and a pretrial proceeding, also fixes the rights of the press..."[79] Like Justice Stewart, he did not reach the First Amendment issue, commenting merely that "[t]o the extent the Constitution protects a right of access to the proceeding, the standards enunciated under the Sixth Amendment suffice to protect that right."[80] That the dissenters also declined to address the First Amendment issue is understandable since Justices Blackmun and White reject the notion that the First Amendment guarantees either a "right to know" to the public or special privileges for the press to gather and publish materials so as to inform the public.[81] Remarkably, neither Justice Brennan nor Justice Marshall wrote separate dissenting opinions; yet, their broad interpretations of the First Amendment and "the public's right to know" appear in several earlier dissenting opinions.[82]

Inasmuch as *Gannett* turned on the Sixth Amendment the exclusion of the public and the press from pretrial hearings it did not deny any previously recognized constitutional right under the First or the Sixth

---

77. *Houchins v. KQED,* 438 U.S. 1, 16 (1978) (Stewart, J., con. op.), quoted in *Gannett Co. v. DePasquale,* 99 S.Ct. 2898, 2918 (1979) (Rehnquist, J., con. op.).
78. *Gannett Co. v. DePasquale,* 99 S.Ct. 2898, 2918 (1979) (Rehnquist, J., con. op.).
79. Ibid., at 2919 (Blackmun, J., dis. op., joined by Brennan, White and Marshall, JJ.).
80. Ibid., at 2940.
81. Justices Blackmun and White joined the majority opinions denying a First Amendment right of access in *Pell v. Procuiner,* 417 U.S. 817 (1976); *Saxbe v. Washington Post Co.,* 417 U.S. 843 (1974); and *Houchins v. KQED,* 438 U.S. 1 (1978).
82. See, supra note 62.

Amendment. *Gannett,* moreover, complements *Nebraska Press Association* by sanctioning another means of safeguarding against adverse pretrial publicity and enhancing the prospects for a fair trial.

Justice Stewart's opinion for the Court nevertheless raised more questions than it answered. No less than a dozen times he indicated that the ruling applied to both pretrial hearings and trials. Yet, in approving the lower court's treatment of First Amendment interests under a hypothetical right of access, Justice Stewart severely undercut the effect of his statement that the Court had never recognized such a right of access. His ambiguous treatment of the Sixth Amendment further frustrated lower courts' compliance in two important ways. On the one hand, it remained unclear whether *Gannett* applied to only pretrial hearings or to trials as well. On the other hand, lower courts construing the Court's opinion as implying an as yet undefined right of access were left without a standard by which to apply that right against competing interests of the government and defendants. The lack of judicial craftsmanship in narrowly formulating the ruling perpetuated confusion about the Court's decision, invited further litigation and thwarted the possibility of lower court compliance. The enduring significance of *Gannett* perhaps lies in its exposition of how to make bad law — "bad law" in that a fragmented Court producing ambiguous and broadly formulated opinions engenders uncertainty, unpredictability and renders lower court compliance virtually impossible.

Despite the justices' extra-judicial attempts to clarify, explain and defend *Gannett,* the press and the Court's commentators found the decision "cloudy," "confused," "mushy," and a "muddle."[83] As James Goodale summed it up: "Gannett Means What it Says; But Who Knows What it Says?"[84] The American Society of Newspaper Editors (ASNE) issued a "Media Alert" urging editors and publishers to challenge closures of preliminary hearings and trials, and suggesting that reporters carry wallet-sized cards to be used in the event that they are excluded from judicial proceedings.[85] Warning that "[u]ntil and unless the *Gan-*

---

83. See, *Birmingham Post-Herald,* A 4 (August 21, 1979); *Chicago Sun-Times,* A 56 (September 20, 1979); *Baltimore Sun,* A 14 (September 22, 1979); *The Washington Post,* A 15 (August 10, 1979); *Time* (September 17, 1979); and *Newsweek,* 69 (August 27, 1979).
84. See, James C. Goodale, "Gannett Means What it Says; But Who Knows What it Says?" *National Law Journal,* 14 (October 16, 1979). Before the Supreme Court's decision, Mr. Goodale analyzed the problem of *Gannett* in "Open Justice: The Threat of Gannett," 1 *Communications and the Law* 3 (Winter, 1979).
85. "Media Alert," American Society of Newspaper Editors, p. 1 (Summer, 1979).

nett decision is modified [the cards] will probably be needed," ASNE proposed that the cards read:

> "Your honor, I am _____, a reporter for the _____. I respectfully request the opportunity to register on the record an objection to the motion to close this proceeding to the public, including the press. Our legal counsel advises me that standards set forth in some recent federal and state court decisions require a hearing before the courtroom can be closed. Accordingly, I respectfully request such a hearing and a temporary recess so that I can report to my editor and so that our counsel can be present to make the appropriate arguments. Thank you."[86]

The ambiguity of *Gannett* indeed had considerable impact on public and press access to judicial proceedings. In the 52 weeks following the decision, defendants, prosecutors, witnesses and judges sought to close proceedings in no less than 13 federal courts and 259 state courts.[87] Tables I-IV (see Appendix) summarize the post-*Gannett* closure actions. Motions for closure were introduced in 214 pre-indictment and pretrial proceedings, and no less than 47 trials and 11 post-trial arraignments. Significantly in view of the traditional presumption of openness in judicial proceedings, motions for closure were successful in 122 pre-indictment and pretrial hearings, and resulted in 33 closed trials and 5 closed post-trial arraignments.

Defendants overwhelmingly initiated motions for closure in 220 cases, whereas prosecutors sought closure in 18 instances and joined defendants in 9 other motions. Judges initiated closure in 23 cases and in 2 sodomy cases witnesses unsuccessfully endeavored to close proceedings. Although all closures explicitly or implicitly deny First Amendment claims to "the public's right to know," in more than half of the cases (149 instances) judges did not record their reasons for approving or denying closure motions. When judges did publicly justify their actions the primary reason for closure was to prevent prejudicial publicity and ensure a fair trial. While the demands of securing a fair trial and an impartial jury justified closure in 122 cases, judges also entertained and

---

86. Ibid.
87. The data on the post-*Gannett* closure motions was gathered from summaries of motions reported by newspapers to the Reporters Committee for Freedom of the Press, a non-profit legal research and defense organization, based in Washington, D.C.

accepted as grounds for closure considerations such as personal privacy and embarrassment of defendants, witnesses and even counsel. The import of the latter considerations becomes clearer, if no more appropriate as the bases for closure, in terms of the kinds of cases in which parties sought court room secrecy. The majority of cases involved prosecutions for attempted murder or murder (150 cases); followed by cases involving rapes or other sexually-related crimes (38); and, then, violent crimes such as assault, battery and kidnapping (22); and, finally, the possession or sale of illegal drugs (15). The remaining 49 cases involved a variety of crimes, ranging from official misconduct, embezzlement, bank fraud and counterfeiting; to possession of firearms, extortion and terrorism; and to medical fraud, malpractice and abortion/manslaughter. The impact of *Gannett* on trial court practice, thus, appears to confirm Justice Blackmun's view that the public's interests in open trials are not adequately safeguarded by the immediate participants in a trial.[88]

Gannett substantially eroded the traditional presumption and practice of open court proceedings. The ambiguity of the ruling's applicability to preliminary hearings and trials, as much as the absence of constitutional standards for permissible closures, inevitably perpetuates litigation over closed judicial proceedings and necessitates that the Supreme Court eventually clarify its ruling.

IV. RICHMOND NEWSPAPERS AND THE FIRST AND SIXTH AMENDMENTS

Sensitive to both the problematic nature and the impact of *Gannett* the Supreme Court agreed on October 9, 1979, to hear a challenge to the closure of a trial in *Richmond Newspapers, Inc. v. Virginia.*[89] The case originated several years earlier, prior to *Gannett,* but involved the first constitutional challenge to the complete closure of a criminal trial.

The circumstances of *Richmond Newspapers* illustrate some of the problems of securing a fair trial. Here, the closure was requested by defense counsel in the fourth trial of John Paul Stevenson for the stabbing and murder of a hotel manager in 1975. Initially in 1976 Stevenson was promptly tried and convicted of second-degree murder in the Circuit Court of Hanover County, Virginia. A year later the Virginia State

---

88. See discussion in text to footnotes 33 to 43, and *Gannett Co. v. DePasquale,* 99 S.Ct. 2893, 2930 (1979) (Blackmun, J., dis. op.).
89. *Richmond Newspapers, Inc. v. Virginia,* 100 S.Ct. 2814 (1980).

Supreme Court reversed his conviction, finding that a bloodstained shirt purportedly belonging to Stevenson had been improperly admitted as evidence at his trial. Retried the following year, his second trial in the same court ended in mistrial when one of the jurors asked to be excused after the trial had begun and there was no available alternate juror. The third trial, in 1978, also ended in a mistrial because a prospective juror had read about Stevenson's previous trials and told the other jurors about the case before the retrial had even begun. At the outset of Stevenson's fourth trial his attorneys requested, and the prosecution did not object to, a closed trial on the grounds that they did not "want any information being shuffled back and forth when we have a recess as to what — who testified to what."[90] On the bench barely a year and presiding over two of the earlier mistrials, Judge Richard H.C. Taylor agreed to the closure and rebuffed the arguments of two reporters from Richmond Newspapers who were excluded from the trial. Judge Taylor found his authority to close the trial in the Virginia State Code and justified by the previous mistrials and the particularly small Hanover courtroom. Under Virginia law judges may exercise their discretion in closing a criminal trial or excluding "from the trial any person whose presence would impair the conduct of a fair trial, provided that the right of the accused to a public trial shall not be violated."[91]

Ironies abound in this rather routine murder trial. Judge Taylor's unprecedented closure occurred in a 200-year old court house where Patrick Henry once orated on the freedom of speech and press.[92] Yet, the closed trial which prompted the Richmond Newspapers' appeal to the Supreme Court had not even attracted the attention of the local weekly newspaper in Hanover County.[93] Moreover, Stevenson was found not guilty but not as the consequence of the jury's verdict. Judge Taylor affirmed a motion by the defense counsel for a dismissal since the case against Stevenson, without the evidence of the bloodstained shirt, was only circumstantial. Still, the details of both the evidence against Stevenson and the basis for his acquittal remain obscure because the trial was closed, no trial transcript was made and a tape-recording of the trial and Judge Taylor's ruling is largely inaudible.[94]

On appeal to the Supreme Court, Harvard Law Professor Laurence Tribe argued for the appellants that the First Amendment and the Sixth

---

90. Donald Baker, "Court to Rule on Secret Trial," *The Washington Post*, A 7 (June 25, 1980).
91. Code of Virginia, 2.1-240-2.1-346.1 (1950).
92. See, Brief of Appellants, *Richmond Newspapers, Inc. v. Virginia*, Supreme Court of the United States, Term, 1979, No. 79-243, p. 72.
93. See, Baker, supra note 90.
94. See, Brief for Appellants, *Richmond Newspapers, Inc. v. Virginia*, supra note 92, at 6-7, 42 n. 37.

Amendment independently and interdependently guarantee a constitutional right to attend trials.[95] The First Amendment secures a right of access, he reasoned, because trial secrecy deprives citizens of information vital to their self-governance; whereas the Sixth Amendment establishes a norm of openness and gives the public standing to challenge closure of trials. The right of access, Tribe further insisted, was implicit in the interdependence of the First and Sixth Amendments:

> The First Amendment . . . opens a constitutional window into a proceeding already identified by the Sixth Amendment as beyond such control—assuring that, even with the connivance of the accused, the state may not bar members of the public and press from a criminal trial without compelling justification . . . . The proceedings of criminal trials are the quintessential subjects of First Amendment protection against government interference with public access: public by tradition, public by function, and public as a matter of constitutional text and structure.[96]

Significantly, rather than imploring the Court to reconsider the line of cases running from *Pell* to *Gannett,* Tribe distinguished those cases on the ground that there access had been demanded and denied to places not traditionally or constitutionally recognized as public places or proceedings. Hence, he argued that while *Branzburg* had noted that the public and the press have no constitutional right or access to "grand jury proceedings, [the Supreme Court's] conferences, the meetings of other official bodies gathered in executive session, and the meetings of private organizations,"[97] the Court's prior rulings never implied that the public and the press are excluded from places and proceedings historically open to the public.

Relying on *Gannett* Virginia Attorney General Marshall Coleman defended closure of the trial, arguing that neither the Sixth Amendment nor common law practices establish a constitutional right of access for the public to attend criminal trials.[98] Considering the First Amendment claim, he quite properly pointed out that, "[t]he common thread of this Court's First Amendment decisions is the notion that freedom to *disseminate* ideas and information about public affairs is central to the

---

95. Ibid.
96. Ibid., at 36.
97. Ibid., at 31, quoting *Branzburg v. Hayes,* 408 U.S. 665, 684 (1971).
98. Brief for Appellees, *Richmond Newspapers, Inc. v. Virginia,* Supreme Court of the United States, October Term, 1979, No. 79-243, at 22.

purpose of the First Amendment."⁹⁹ He conceded that "[t]he free flow of information concerning our courts of justice is undoubtedly a vital concern in our system of democratic self-governance."¹⁰⁰ "But it is a wholly different proposition," Coleman observed, "to suggest that the First Amendment guarantees access to all sources of information that may be beneficial to informed public opinion."¹⁰¹

As in *Gannett,* no majority supported the opinion for the Court in *Richmond Newspapers.* A majority of the justices did appear to embrace Tribe's argument that the public and the press are constitutionally entitled to attend criminal trials because trials traditionally and under the Constitution constitute a "public forum."¹⁰² For over forty years when elaborating a functional analysis of the First Amendment, the Court acknowledged protection for public forums as essential to each individual's right to speak, to distribute publications and to assemble in public places, such as streets, sidewalks and parks. Accordingly, Chief Justice Burger's plurality opinion, joined by Justices White and Stevens, found the right of the public to attend trials in the intersection of the First and Sixth Amendments.¹⁰³ Justice Stewart likewise found the nexus between the amendments to create a constitutionally protected

---

99. Ibid. (emphasis in original).
100. Ibid.
101. Ibid.
102. The concept of a public forum was initially articulated by Justice Roberts in *Hague v. C.I.O.,* 307 U.S. 496, 515-516 (1937), wherein he observed: "Whatever the title of streets and parks may rest, they have immemorially been held in trust for the use of the public and, time out mind, have been used for purposes of assembly, communicating thoughts between citizens, and discussing public questions. Such use of the streets and public places has, from ancient times, been a part of the privileges, immunities, rights and liberties of citizens. The privilege of a citizen of the United States to use the streets and parks for communication of views on national questions may be regulated in the interest of all; it is not absolute, but relative, and must be exercised in consonance with peace and good order; but it must not, in the guise of regulation, be abridged or denied." The Court extended the concept of a public forum in *Thomas v. Collins,* 323 U.S. 516 (1945), *Niemotko v. Maryland,* 340 U.S. 268 (1951) (public parks); *Cox v. New Hampshire,* 312 U.S. 569 (1941), and *Cox v. Louisiana,* 379 U.S. 536 (1965) (public passages); and *Amalgamated Food Employees Union v. Logan Valley Plaza, Inc.,* 391 U.S. 308 (1968) (shopping centers). The court rejected extension of First Amendment protection for public forums in *Lehman v. City of Shaker Heights,* 418 U.S. 298 (1974) (bus placards); *Greer v. Spock,* 428 U.S. 328 (1976) (military bases); *Adderly v. Florida,* 385 U.S. 39 (1967) (jails); *Pell v. Procuiner,* 417 U.S. 817 (1974) (prisons). See, generally, Harry Kalven, Jr., "The Concept of the Public Forum," *Supreme Court Review* 23 (1965).
103. *Richmond Newspapers, Inc. v. Virginia,* 100 S.Ct. 2814, 2830-2831 (1980) (White and Stevens, JJ., con. ops.).

public forum, and thereby endeavored to distinguish the decision here from his opinion for the Court in *Gannett*.[104] Justices Stevens, White and Blackmun added brief concurrences celebrating the Court's decision because, in Justice Blackmun's words, it was "gratifying. . . to see the Court wash away at least some of the graffiti that marred the prevailing opinions in *Gannett*.[105] Justice Brennan's concurrence, joined by Justice Marshall, elaborated a more extensive theory of First Amendment protection for the public.[106] The sole dissenter, Justice Rehnquist, lamented the Court's activism and incursion on state's rights.[107]

Chief Justice Burger's opinion began by clarifying that *Gannett* applied only to pretrial hearings, dismissing Justice Stewart's earlier assertions as pure *dicta*. Affirming that the issue of public access to trials had not been previously decided, he turned to the history of the Sixth Amendment, surveying the "prophylactic purpose" and "therapeutic value"[108] of open trials. Reiterating that openness serves to assure fair proceedings and "satisfies the appearance of justice,"[109] he reaffirmed prior rulings that the Sixth Amendment's provision for public trials guarantees only the right of defendants. The Chief Justice, however, interpreted the "presumption of openness" in the Sixth Amendment as connoting that "the people retained a 'right of visitation' which enabled them to satisfy themselves that justice was in fact being done."[110] That is, although the Sixth Amendment does not guarantee an enforceable right of the public to attend trials, it conveys to the public a "right of visitation."[111] Turning, then, to the First Amendment, Chief Justice Burger reasserted the Court's broad functional analysis of freedom of speech, press and assembly: "expressly guaranteed freedoms share a common core purpose of assuring freedom of communication on matters relating to the functioning of government."[112] Quoting *Branzburg* and *Gannett,* he argued that "[i]t is not crucial whether we describe this right to attend criminal trials to hear, see, and communicate observations concerning them as a 'right of access,' . . . or a 'right to gather information,' for we have recognized that 'without some protection for

---

104. Ibid., at 2840 (Stewart, J., con. op.).
105. Ibid., at 2841 (Blackmun, J., con. op.).
106. Ibid., at 2832-2841 (Brennan, J., con. op.). See also, William Brennan, "Address," 32 *Rutgers Law Review* 173 (1979).
107. Ibid., at 2842-2844 (Rehnquist, J., dis. op.).
108. Ibid., at 2824-2825.
109. Ibid., at 2826-2827.
110. Ibid., at 2825.
111. Ibid.
112. Ibid., at 2826-2827.

seeking out the news, freedom of the press would be eviscerated.'"[113] He thus concluded that central to the First Amendment's protection for freedom of information is the concept of a public forum or arena in which individuals may collectively and freely discuss matters of personal and public interest. Chief Justice Burger found open trials analogous to other public forums in which members of the public and the press historically enjoyed access, and distinguishable from places not generally or constitutionally recognized as open to the public, e.g. prisons, jails and military bases.[114]

Significantly, Chief Justice Burger's opinion did not turn on a reconsideration of the Court's previous rulings in *Pell, Saxbe, Houchins* and *Gannett,* denying the constitutionality of claims to First Amendment affirmative rights. Instead, the Chief Justice expanded the concept of a public forum to include trials, and thereby recognized the constitutional presumption of public access to trials. He did not denominate a First Amendment affirmative right of access per se. Instead, he acknowledged the enforceability of First Amendment claims as contingent on the place or forum to which access is demanded. Underscoring this by expressly denying that the public possesses an unconditional right to open trials, the Chief Justice emphasized that "[j]ust as a government may impose reasonable time, place, and manner restrictions upon the use of its streets in the interests of such objectives as the free flow of traffic . . . so may a trial judge in the interest of the fair administration of justice, impose reasonable limitations on access to a trial."[115] Public forums differ as much as city streets and court rooms differ, and therefore the restrictions imposed on the public and the press vary from one forum to another. As Justice Frankfurter once eloquently pointed out:

> A trial is not a 'free trade in ideas,' nor is the best test of truth in a courtroom 'the power of the thought to get itself accepted in the competition of the market,' . . . A court is a forum with strictly defined limits for discussion. It is circumscribed in the range of its inquiry and in its methods by the Constitution, by laws, and by age-old traditions. . . . Of course freedom of speech and press are essential to the enlightenment of a free people and in restraining those who wield power.

---

113. Ibid., at 2827, quoting *Branzburg v. Hayes,* 408 U.S. 665, 681 (1972).
114. See supra note 102.
115. *Richmond Newspapers, Inc. v. Virginia,* 100 S.Ct. 2814, 2830 n. 18 (1980).

> Particularly should this freedom be employed in comment upon the work of courts, who are without many influences ordinarily making for humor and humility, twin antidotes to the corrosion of power. But the Bill of Rights is not self-destructive. Freedom of expression can hardly carry implications that nullify the guarantee of impartial trials.[116]

Similarly, Chief Justice Burger suggested that public access may be limited since judges must control the decorum of court rooms, but "the question in a particular case is whether that control is exerted so as to deny or unwarrantedly abridge . . . the opportunities for the commemoration of thought and the discussion of public questions immemorially associated with resort to public places."[117]

The Chief Justice was obviously troubled by a declaration of unenumerated constitutional rights.[118] Yet by grounding the Court's decision on the First Amendment's protection for public forums and the Sixth Amendment's presumption of openness, he assiduously and creatively justified the constitutionality of open trials without committing the Court to an independent affirmative right of access per se. In other words, as much as Chief Justice Burger exercised judicial creativity in extending First Amendment protection and the concept of a public forum to criminal trials, he cautiously eschewed impermissible creativity *cum* construction of a broad and undefined affirmative right of access under the First and Sixth Amendments.

The Chief Justice's tempered exercise of judicial creativity was not entirely appreciated by his colleagues. In Justice Stevens's view *Richmond Newspapers* stood as "a watershed case" because previous cases "never before . . . squarely held that the acquisition of newsworthy matter is entitled to any constitutional protection whatsoever."[119] Concurring Justice White aptly pointed out that "[t]his case would have been unnecessary had *Gannett* . . . construed the Sixth Amendment to forbid excluding the public from criminal proceedings except in narrowly defined circumstances."[120] Justice Blackmun's broad interpretation of the Sixth Amendment, however, was not acceptable to a majority of the Court. Chief Justice Burger's opinion therefore turned on the

---

116. *Bridges v. California,* 314 U.S. 252, 283 (1941) (Frankfurter, J., dis. op.).
117. *Richmond Newspapers, Inc. v. Virginia,* 100 S.Ct. 2814, 2830 n. 18 (1980), quoting *Cox v. New Hampshire,* 312 U.S. 569, 574 (1941).
118. See, Ibid. at 2828-2829.
119. Ibid. at 2831 (Stevens, J., con. op.).
120. Ibid., at 2830 (White, J., con. op.).

juxtaposition of the First and Sixth Amendments in order to both extend the concept of public forums to criminal trials and preclude further claims to a right of access to other governmental facilities and proceedings not traditionally open to the public. Hence, Justice Stevens mistakenly found it "somewhat ironic that the Court should find more reason to recognize a right of access today than it did in *Houchins.*"[121] For the Chief Justice and Justices White, Blackmun and Stewart there was no irony since the touchstone for the Court's narrow holding was that the First and Sixth Amendments run together in safeguarding access by members of the public and the press to criminal trials, subject to the conditions imposed by a judge to ensure a fair trial. The irony for Justice Stevens arises from his willingness to make exceptions to the "general rule"[122] that the First Amendment protects only freedom from restraints on the dissemination of information.

Justice Stevens, like Justices Powell, Brennan and Marshall, remains prepared to recognize First Amendment affirmative action.[123] Here, Justice Powell, the Virginian on the Court, did not participate in the decision; but Justice Brennan, joined by Justice Marshall, wrote a concurring opinion in order to emphasize their divergence from the majority when interpreting the First Amendment. Whereas the Chief Justice endeavored to narrowly define the Court's ruling, Justice Brennan gave a broad jurisprudential basis for *Richmond Newspapers,* stressing that "the Court has not ruled out a public access component to the First Amendment in every circumstance."[124] "Read with care and in context," he argued, "our decisions must therefore be understood as holding only that any privilege of access to government information is subject to a degree of restraint dictated by the nature of the information and countervailing interests in security of confidentiality."[125] In Justice Brennan's view, the amendment "embodies more than a commitment to free expression and communicative interchange for their own sake; it has a structural role to play in securing and fostering our republican system of self-government."[126] Accordingly, Justice Brennan, unlike the majority of the Court, would go beyond recognizing access to public forums to expressly denominate First Amendment affirmative rights and the constitutional legitimacy of a directly enforceable "public's right to know."

121. Ibid., at 2831 (Stevens, J., con. op.).
122. See, John Paul Stevens, "Some Thoughts About A General Rule," supra note 8; and O'Brien, supra note 54.
123. See supra notes 62 and 74.
124. *Richmond Newspapers, Inc. v. Virginia,* 100 S.Ct. 2814, 2832-2833 (1980) (Brennan, J., con. op.).
125. Ibid., at 2833.
126. Ibid.

V. CONSTITUTIONAL POLITICS AND JUDICIAL CRAFTSMANSHIP

Gannett and *Richmond Newspapers* considerably undermine the traditional presumption of open judicial proceedings. *Gannett* remains intact. Pretrial and pre-indictment proceedings may (and undoubtedly in the future frequently will) be closed to the public and the press, at least when there is a probability of prejudice and the prosecution and the judge find no objection. As post-*Gannett* closures indicate, judges may close proceedings in order to cover-up embarrassing facts or to safeguard interests in personal privacy. Judges may do so because the standards for closure are ill-defined and therefore permit considerable discretion in closing proceedings for reasons other than preventing prejudicial publicity.

Justice Powell's concurrence suggested that under the First Amendment judicial proceedings may be closed only when there exists a likelihood of prejudicial publicity if the proceedings were open and when there are no alternative means of dealing with such threats to securing a fair trial, e.g., change of venue.[127] Justice Powell's standard of the likelihood of prejudicial publicity, however, was not supported by any other justice. Moreover, it remains a weaker standard than that suggested by the four dissenters. Under the Sixth Amendment, Justice Blackmun argued, closures are permissible only when there would be irreparable damage to the defendant's right to a fair trial and there are no alternatives for dealing with adverse pretrial publicity.[128]

In sanctioning the closure of pretrial proceedings, *Gannett* at once expanded and left unstructured judges' discretion in balancing the competing interests of the public and the press against the government's and defendants' interests in court room secrecy. Judges may reach their closure determinations on (1) Justice Stewart's plurality opinion's view that closed proceedings are permissible under the Sixth Amendment when there exists a probability of prejudice; or (2) Justice Powell's First Amendment standard of the likelihood of prejudicial publicity; or (3) the dissenters' more rigorous standard of irreparable damage to the defendant's Sixth Amendment fair trial rights.

---

127. See discussion at supra note 50.
128. *Gannett v. DePasquale,* 443 U.S. 368, 441-442 (1979) (Blackmun, J., dis. op.).

Richmond Newspapers provides no further guidance for judges when ruling on pretrial and post-trial closure motions. Nor did a majority of the Court agree on a standard for guiding judges in closing trials. Chief Justice Burger's plurality opinion indicates that judges may close trials when the defendant demonstrates "an overriding interest"[129] in the closure of the courtroom. Other than suggesting that interests in courtroom secrecy will infrequently justify exclusion of the public and the press, he leaves undefined what the standard of "overriding interest" requires. Precisely because the overriding interest standard is too vague, Justices White, Blackmun, Brennan and Marshall refused to embrace the Chief Justice's opinion. Justices White and Blackmun would apply their Sixth Amendment standard, articulated in *Gannett*, of irreparable damage to fair trial proceedings. In contrast, Justices Brennan and Marshall find the First Amendment to "tip the balance strongly toward the rule that trials be open" so as to preclude the necessity of specifying "[w]hat countervailing interests might be sufficiently compelling to reverse this presumption of openness."[130] *Richmond Newspapers*, like *Gannett*, thus gives no clear guidance for lower courts in ruling on closure motions and accommodating the respective interests of the public, the defendants, and the government.

The Supreme Court's failure to achieve consensus on the basis and the standard for closing pretrial and trial proceedings reflects the deeper disagreements among the justices over the contours of a constitutional right of access to judicial and other governmental proceedings. Contrary to some commentators,[131] *Richmond Newspapers* does not represent the Court's acceptance of the constitutional legitimacy of the "public's right to know" or a First Amendment affirmative right of access. Instead, *Richmond Newspapers* registers the sharp divisions within the Burger Court that have developed in the 1970s over the denomination of First Amendment affirmative rights.[132]

In terms of constitutional politics, the Chief Justice and Justices Stewart and Rehnquist remain rather consistent in their denial of the constitutional legitimacy of an independent directly enforceable right

---

129. *Richmond Newspapers, Inc. v. Virginia*, 100 S.Ct. 2814, 2830 (1980).
130. Ibid., at 2839 (Brennan, J., con. op.).
131. See, Goodale, supra note 14, at 24, wherein he argues: "It is the first time in history that the court has found the 'right to know' in the Constitution ... In fact, after the *Richmond* case, there may at some point in time be no need for such an act (i.e., the Freedom of Information Act), or a sunshine act of any kind ..."
132. See, O'Brien, supra note 62, at 618-631.

of access under the First Amendment.[133] Justices Blackmun and White also rather consistently agree with them.[134] A majority of the Court thus interprets the First Amendment to only ensure the conditions for freedom of information and an informed public, rather than to mandate First Amendment affirmative action. As Justice Stewart succinctly put it: "the Constitution itself is neither a Freedom of Information Act nor an Official Secrets Act."[135] By contrast, Justices Brennan and Marshall endorse First Amendment affirmative action precisely because they hold that the amendment does not prohibit what it does not require, and that judicially-created First Amendment affirmative rights serve the important policy objective of enhancing the free flow of infor-

---

133. See, *Buckley v. Valeo,* 424 U.S. 1, 235 (1976) (Burger, C.J., con. and dis. op.); *New York Times Co. v. United States,* 403 U.S. 711, 749 (1971) (Burger, C.J., dis. op.). Chief Justice Burger has endeavored to adhere to the historical basis for and background of the First Amendment. Moreover, recognition of an enforceable constitutional "right to know" is at odds with his deference to congressional and state powers to regulate expression and punish some forms of expression. See, e.g., *Miller v. California,* 413 U.S. 15 (1973). Chief Justice Burger, however, has entertained the notion that the public's "right to know" has some constitutional legitimacy as an abstract or background right of the Constitution. His principal concern is that a "right to know" is not absolute or directly enforceable. Dissenting in *New York Times Co. v. United States,* 403 U.S. 713 (1971), he observed: "The newspapers make a derivative claim under the First Amendment; they denominate this right as the public 'right to know'; by implication . . . the right is asserted as absolute. . . . The First Amendment right itself is not an absolute." Ibid., at 749 (Burger, C.J., dis. op.). Again, in his concurring and dissenting opinion in *Buckley v. Valeo,* 424 U.S. 1 (1976), he addressed the political ideal of the public's "right to know" in order to underscore that "[t]he public right ought not be absolute when its exercise reveals private political convictions." Ibid., at 237 (Burger, C.J., con. and dis. op.).

Among the present members of the Supreme Court, Justice Rehnquist appears to be the least sympathetic to the political ideal of the public's "right to know" and its constitutional legitimacy. Dissenting from the Court's holding that the First Amendment offers some protection for commercial speech and, in particular, for advertisements listing the prices of prescription drugs, Justice Rehnquist candidly observed: "I cannot distinguish between the public's right to know the price of drugs and its right to know the price of title searches or physical examinations or other professional services for which standardized fees are charged." *State Board of Pharmacy v. Virginia Citizens Consumer Council,* 425 U.S. 748, 785 (1976) (Rehnquist, J., dis. op.). See, also *Gannett Co. v. DePasquale,* 99 S.Ct. 2898, 2917 (1979) (Rehnquist, J., con. op.).

134. See supra note 81.
135. Potter Stewart, "Or of the Press," 26 *Hastings Law Journal* 631, 636 (1975).

mation essential to an informed public.[136] While Justices Powell and Stevens agree that a right of the public to know about government operations is defensible in terms of vindicating the interests of an informed citizenry, they disagree with Justices Brennan and Marshall on the scope of judicial creativity in constitutional interpretation. Justices Powell and Stevens therefore may abandon Justices Brennan and Marshall, as they did in *Gannett* and *Richmond Newspapers,* when they find that the government has in a reasonable manner considered the interests of an informed public when denying access to particular materials, proceedings and facilities.[137]

Gannett and *Richmond Newspapers* fundamentally pose the central issue in judicial line-drawing,[138] namely, the legitimate scope of judicial creativity in constitutional interpretation. As Justice Rehnquist's concurence in *Gannett* and caustic dissent in *Richmond Newspapers* reminds his brethren and the Court's commentators: unlike common law judges, justices of the Supreme Court are bound by the plain language of parchment guarantees.[139] Judicial creativity differs not merely in degree, but in kind, when used to expand the scope of constitutional rights by broadly construing enumerated guarantees and when employed to construct new constitutional rights. The difference between construing constitutional provisions and the construction of new constitutional rights is largely what distinguishes legitimate and illegitimate exercises of judicial review. Still, Justice Rehnquist perhaps did not sufficiently appreciate the difference between permissible judicial creativity and extra-constitutional judicial ingenuity in fashioning constitutional rights from within the "shadows"[140] of the Constitution. In *Gannett,* the dissenters were willing to extend the plain language of the Sixth Amendment to pretrial hearings because of the prevailing practice of open judicial proceedings. More dramatically and creatively the Chief Justice in *Richmond Newspapers* sought to chart a course be-

---

136. See supra note 62, and O'Brien, supra note 62, at 614-631.
137. See supra note 74.
138. See, generally, Henry J. Abraham, *The Judiciary,* 185-204 (Boston: Allyn and Bacon, 5th ed., 1980).
139. See, *Gannett Co. v. DePasquale,* 99 S.Ct. 2898, 2917 (1979) (Rehnquist, J., con. op.), and *Richmond Newspapers, Inc. v. Virginia,* 100 S.Ct. 2814, 2841-2843 (1980) (Rehnquist, J., dis. op.). For a further discussion, see, Louis Lusky, "Public Trial and Public Right: The Missing Bottom Line," 8 *Hofstra Law Review* 273 (1980).
140. *Whalen v. Roe,* 97 S.Ct. 869, 876 n. 23 (1977).

tween ensuring the "requisite latitude"[141] of the First and Sixth Amendments and the extra-constitutional denomination of a novel, unenumerated right.

Gannett and *Richmond Newspapers* sharply divided the Burger Court over the contours of basic constitutional guarantees and with respect to the justices' perceptions of the proper scope of judicial review. The costs of fragmentation within the Court bear not only on the ubiquitous demands for judicial craftsmanship. The failure to agree on and articulate standards for guiding lower courts' closure of judicial proceedings permits trial judges to exercise broad discretion in closing judicial proceedings, invites further litigation and therefore promises to burden the Court's docket in the future.

---

141. See, Letter of James Madison to Thomas Jefferson (October 17, 1788), in The *Papers of Thomas Jefferson*, ed. by Julian Boyd (Princeton, New Jersey: Princeton University Press, 1958), Vol. 14, at 16-18. See also *Richmond Newspapers, Inc. v. Virginia*, 100 S.Ct. 2814, 2827-2829 (1980).

APPENDIX

POST-GANNETT CLOSURE ACTIONS

Table I*

Motions Made		Reversed on Appeal
1. Closure Motions Enforced	146	14
2. Closure Motions Denied or Withdrawn	112	1
3. Direct Prior Restraint on Publication	14	6
	272	21

Table II*
Type of Proceeding: Result of Motions

	Open	Closed	Total
1. Pre-Indictment	18	24	42
2. Pre-Trial	74	98	172
3. Trial	14	33	47
4. Post-Trial	6	5	11
	112	160	272

Table III**
Initiation of Closure Motions

Party	Motions
1. Defendant	220
2. Prosecution	18
3. Defendant and Prosecution	9
4. Witnesses	2
5. Judges	23
	272

Table IV**
Reason for Closure

1. No Reason Given	(149)	5. Statutory Basis	(4)	
2. Prejudice to Jurors	(112)	6. Embarrassment	(22)	
3. Jeopardize Fair Trial	(10)	a. victims	(8)	
4. Protection of Witnesses	(3)	b. witnesses	(7)	
		c. defendants	(2)	
		d. others	(5)	

*Source: "Court Watch Summary," Reporters Committee for Freedom of the Press (August 18, 1980).
**Compiled from summaries of motions reported to the Reporters Committee for Freedom of the Press.

EUGENIA ZERBINOS

The Right to Know: Whose Right and Whose Duty?*

Eugenia Zerbinos is
an Instructor at the
College of Journalism,
Marquette University.

Journalist Kent Cooper first used the phrase the "right to know" in the 1940s. Since then, the slogan has been adopted in the "cause of conserving and broadening the right . . . called 'press freedom.' "[1] But what is the right to know? Is it that the "public business is the public's business," as Harold Cross maintained?[2] Or is it a phrase "whose elegance is exceeded only by its vagueness," as Don Pember has observed?[3]

Several scholars have attempted to find a right to know within the meaning of the Constitution and the First Amendment. While Gellhorn

---

*The author wishes to thank Dr. Bruce L. Miller, professor of philosophy, Michigan State University, for his helpful comments in the preparation of this paper.

1. Kent Cooper, *The Right to Know: An Exposition of the Evils of News Supression* (New York: Farrar, Straus and Cuday, 1956), p. xiii.
2. Harold Cross, *The People's Right to Know* (Morningside Heights: Columbia University Press, 1953), p. xvii.
3. Don Pember, *Mass Media Law* (Dubuque, Iowa: Wm. C. Brown Company, Publishers, 1977), p. 438.

argues that the right to know principle is "so broadly and vaguely phrased that it cannot decide cases,"[4] the right to know has influenced judges' decisions. For example, in refusing to grant the U.S. government a permanent injunction to restrain *The New York Times* from publishing the Pentagon Papers, Federal District Judge Murray Gurfein said:

> A cantankerous press, an obstinate press, a ubiquitous press must be suffered by those in authority in order to preserve the even greater values of freedom of expression and the right of the people to know.[5]

Clearly, however, there is no phrase in the Constitution that states that the public has a right to know. Of course, there are those who would argue that the right to know is inherent in a democratic system of government. A self-governing people must know about the workings of their government so they may make informed decisions and exercise their franchise. In an oft-quoted passage, the "father of the Constituion" and author of the First Amendment, James Madison, underscored the importance of an informed electorate.

> A popular government, without popular information or the means of acquiring it, is but a prologue to a farce or a tragedy; or perhaps both. Knowledge will forever govern ignorance. And a people who mean to be their own governors, must arm themselves with the power knowledge gives.[6]

But if the people have a right to know, what is it that they have a right to know and who has the correlative duty to provide what the public has a right to know? Is the right to know a fundamental right derived directly from the Constitution, or is it a right that stems from a broader societal goal? This paper is an attempt to address these questions and determine the role of the press in fulfilling the right to know. To provide a framework for answering these questions, court decisions and scholarly arguments for a constitutional right to know will be examined within a philosophical definition of the meaning of rights.

---

4. Walter Gellhorn, "The Right to Know: First Amendment Overbreadth?" *Washington University Law Quarterly* 1976: 26.
5. New York Times v. United States, 403 U.S. 713 (1971).
6. James Madison to W.T. Barry, 1822, quoted in Saul Padover, ed., *The Complete Madison* (New York: Harper and Brothers, 1953), p. 337.

The Right to Know: Whose Right and Whose Duty?

THE MEANING OF RIGHTS

Philosophers speak of rights by making a distinction between those claims which are liberties and those which are rights.[7] A liberty means a freedom to choose between doing or not doing a given thing. There is no correlative duty in others specifically related to the exercise of that liberty. A right, on the other hand, entails the existence of a duty in another.

For example, an individual is at liberty to pursue any career that he or she wishes. If that individual chooses to be a physician, others have no duty to ensure that the desire to be a physician is fulfilled. Under the law, however, an individual who desires to be a physican has the right not to be discriminated against because of race when being considered for admittance to medical school. The medical school administrators have the duty to ensure that admissions policies are not racially discriminatory.

Certain liberties may be rights as well. Speaking freely is an example. An individual is at liberty to speak or not to speak. If the individual chooses to speak, no one has the duty to listen. But, the right to speak freely is guaranteed under the First Amendment. Therefore, the government has the duty not to interfere with that person's exercise of the right to speak freely.

Rights also have certain distinguishing attributes. A universal right accrues to all members of society, while a particular right is in force only for some members of society. For example, all individuals have a right to peaceful occupancy of their homes. A landlord has the particular right to collect rent from the tenants who occupy his building.

The correlative duty bearer may be *in rem* or *in personam*. *In rem* means that all persons have a duty with respect to the individual's right. For example, all persons have the duty not to interfere with an individual's right to peaceful occupancy of his home. *In personam* means that only some individuals or perhaps a government have a duty with respect to the individual's right. Only tenants of a particular building have a duty to pay rent to the owner of the building.

Rights may be exercise or non-exercise, general or specific, and positive or negative. An exercise right is the right to choose to do or to not do something such as speaking or voting. Exercise rights are not waived, but one may choose not to utilize them. For instance, one may choose not to vote. A non-exercise right is the right not to be or to be treated in a certain way. An individual has the right to privacy or the

---

7. See, for example, Joel Feinberg, *Social Philosophy* (Englewood Cliffs, NJ: Prentice-Hall, Inc., 1973).

right not to be injured, rights that are sometimes "waived." The right not to be injured, for example, is waived when an individual chooses to play rugby. The right may be negative in that an individual or a government may not interfere. No one may interfere with another person's right to vote. But the right to vote may also be positive in the sense that the government must provide the individual with a polling place, ballots, etc., so the individual may exercise this right.

The diagram of the attributes of rights illustrates these distinctions.[8] An alleged right can be tested for clarity and persuasiveness by analyzing it within this schema.

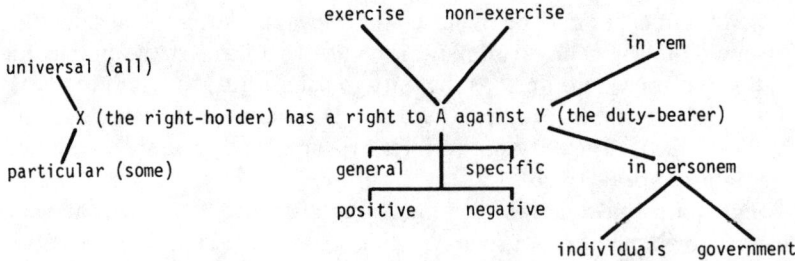

Dworkin, who has written extensively on philosophy of law, also makes a distinction between principles (rights) and policy (goals).[9] Principles are certain fundamental rights such as life, liberty and the pursuit of happiness from which constitutional rules have been derived. These rules yield certain specific rights such as those enumerated in the Bill of Rights. Policy, on the other hand, is related to societal goals, such as, it is desirable for the workings of government to be open for public inspection. These goals may be enumerated in statutes that also yield specific rights. The Freedom of Information Act is a statute that yields a right of access to government information.

8. The diagram is courtesy of Prof. Bruce Miller, Department of Philosophy, Michigan State University, East Lansing.
9. Ronald Dworkin, *Taking Rights Seriously* (Cambridge, Mass.: Harvard University Press, 1978).

> Justification of principle argues that a particular rule is necessary in order to protect an individual right that some person (or perhaps group) has against other people, or against the society of government as a whole.[10]

Individual citizens have a right to express themselves without government censorship, even if those citizens are members of the American Nazi Party who wish to march through a Jewish community.

> Justification of policy . . . argues that a particular rule is desirable because that rule will work in the general interest, that is, for the benefit of society as a whole.[11]

It may have been in the interest of the community in Skokie, Ill., to forbid the Nazis from demonstrating. However, when principle and policy are at odds, policy must yield to principle.

INTERPRETATIONS OF A RIGHT TO KNOW

When the Freedom of Information Act was signed into law, President Lyndon B. Johnson expressed a "deep sense of pride that the United States is an open society in which the people's right to know is cherished and guarded."[12] Indeed, the campaign for access to government, which began in the 1950s, was a campaign for the people's right to know. While the FOI Act was intended to assure maximum disclosure of government information and can be interpreted as a battle won in the name of the public's right to know, the Act does not require that the government give the public whatever information it desires. There are, in fact, nine exceptions to the type of information that is required to be made public.[13]

Nine years before passage of the FOI Act, Parks argued in favor of open government and applying a right to know under the Constitution He believed that access to government information was required "for

---

10. Ronald Dworkin, "The Rights of Myron Farber," *The New York Review of Books,* Oct. 26, 1978, p. 34.
11. *Ibid.*
12. Public Papers of the Presidents, Lyndon B. Johnson, 1966 II. p. 699, quoted in Harold L. Nelson and Dwight Teeter, Jr., *Law of Mass Communciation,* p. 420.
13. 5 U.S.C.A. §552, amended by Public Law 93-502, 88 Stat. 1561-1564.

our democratic system to function successfully."[14] The primary purpose of the speech-press clause, Parks said, was:

> ... to prevent the government from interfering with the communication of facts and views about governmental affairs, in order that all could properly exercise the rights and responsibilities of citizenship in a free society. *This clause was intended as one of the guarantees of the people's right to know.*[15]

In addition, the right to gather news and the right to impart news, Parks said, were "obviously" part of freedom of the press.[16]

Emerson also believes that the right to know is an integral part of the system of freedom of expression, "embodied in the First Amendment and entitled to support by legislation or other affirmative government action."[17] He maintains that the Supreme Court has recognized a constitutional right to know, although the contours of the right remain obscure. He reduces the right to know to: (1) the right to read, to listen, to see and to otherwise receive communications, and (2) the right to obtain information as a basis for transmitting ideas or facts to others, that is, the right to communicate.[18]

Similarly, Ivester believes that the right to know is a constitutional right that includes the "rights to receive information from willing or neutral sources, and to acquire information from a perhaps unwilling governmental source."[19] This right to know flows from an analysis of democratic systems of government.

> Self-government is possible only to the extent that the leaders of the state are responsible and responsive to the will of the people. But if the will of the people is to have validity, if the people are to function as a rational electorate, they must have adequate knowledge of what the government is doing.[20]

14. Wallace Parks, "The Open Government Principle: Applying the Right to Know Under the Constitution," *The George Washington Law Review* 26 (1957): 3.
15. *Ibid.*, p. 9.
16. *Ibid.*, p. 10.
17. Thomas I. Emerson, "Legal Foundations of the Right to Know," *Washington University Law Quarterly* 1 (1976): 2.
18. *Ibid.*
19. David Mitchell Ivester, "The Constitutional Right to Know," *Hastings Constitutional Law Quarterly* 4 (1977): 109.
20. *Ibid.*, p. 115. See also Alexander Meiklejohn, *Free Speech and Its Relation to Self Government* (New York: Harper & Brothers Publishers, 1948).

The Right to Know: Whose Right and Whose Duty?

The right to know is also implicit in the structure of a self-governing system, Ivester maintains. The theories of popular sovereignty and government by compact go beyond the notion that the right to know is inherent in these ideas.[21]

BeVier, however, concludes that a right to know "cannot be sustained as a matter of constitutional principle."[22] She suggests that inferring that there is a right to know within the meaning of the Constitution is like asking whether the Constitution guarantees that the public be well-informed.[23]

The claims by Parks, Emerson and Ivester of a right to know do not withstand analysis within the rights schema. While Parks believes the speech-press clause of the First Amendment was intended as a right to know guarantee, he fails to define what he means by a right to know. Emerson's definition of a right to know includes the right to read, to listen, to see and to otherwise receive communication, all exercise rights that are negative. No one should interfere with the exercise of those rights. The right to obtain information to transmit ideas to others, though, is unclear as a right. Certainly, it is an exercise right, but is it positive or negative? Is it that the government or individuals may not interfere with the right to obtain information, or is it positive in that the government or individuals must provide the information so that it may be communicated? The right to receive and gather information from willing sources, delineated by Ivester as a right to know, are negative exercise rights. Yet the right to acquire information from an unwilling government would seem to be a positive, exercise right.

Those who maintain that there is a constitutional right to know, or that there ought to be, would define the concept as a right to receive information or communication and the right to acquire or gather information. The latter notion has been argued as justifying a right to keep one's sources of information confidential. The following section explores the boundaries of these rights as interpreted by the U.S. Supreme Court and identifies the right-holders and the duty-bearers.

"RIGHT TO KNOW" CASES

There have been no "right to know" cases as such, but according to Emerson *Lamont v. Postmaster General*[24] was the first "clear expres-

---

21. *Ibid.*, p. 116.
22. Lillian BeVier, "An Informed Public, an Informing Press: The Search for a Constitutional Principle," *California Law Review* 68 (1980): 485.
23. *Ibid.*, p. 499.
24. *Lamont v. Postmaster General*, 381 U.S. 301 (1965).

sion of a 'right to know' " by the U.S. Supreme Court. At issue in this very narrow case was the constitutionality of a statute that required a written request for delivery of mail from abroad that contained Communist propaganda. The Court held that the statute violated the addressee's right of free speech. In a concurring opinion, Justice Brennan said:

> I think the right to receive publications is . . . a fundamental right. The dissemination of ideas can accomplish nothing if otherwise willing addressees are not free to receive and consider them. It would be a barren marketplace of ideas that had only sellers and no buyers.[25]

Within the context of attributes of rights, the following right emerges from *Lamont:* The public (the right-holder) has a right to receive (exercise) foreign Communist propaganda (specific) and the government (the duty-bearer) has a duty not to interfere (negative) with the delivery of that information. It is a principle derived from the First Amendment.

The right to receive information was also given support in *Red Lion.*[26] This case, which upheld the constitutionality of the personal attack rules and Fairness Doctrine that apply to broadcasters, asserted that the public has the right to "receive suitable access to social, political, esthetic, moral and other ideas and experiences."[27] The Court said it was the "right of the viewers and the listeners, not the right of the broadcasters, which is paramount."[28] Therefore, requiring broadcasters to air both sides of controversial issues would best serve the public interest. This right is derived through constitutional interpretation and from a societal goal and enumerated in statute. The public (the right-holder) has a right to hear (exercise) different viewpoints on controversial issues of public importance (specific) and it is the duty of broadcasters (duty-bearer) to fulfill that right (positive).

In *Miami Herald v. Tornillo,*[29] though, the Court rejected a similar right to receive different viewpoints. The Court declared unconstitutional a Florida right-of-reply statute which required newspapers to allow candidates for public office to publish replies when their personal

---

25. *Id.* at 308.
26. *Red Lion Broadcasting Co. v. FCC*, 395 U.S. 367 (1969).
27. *Id.* at 390.
28. *Id.*
29. *Miami Herald v. Tornillo*, 94 S. Ct. 2831 (1974).

The Right to Know: Whose Right and Whose Duty?

character or official records were attacked. The Court, it seems, was limiting the notion that there ought to be as much public discussion as possible on an issue if it meant infringing on the First Amendment. In this instance, freedom of the press, a right derived from the Constitution, took precedence over what might be construed as a right of the people to know, a right derived from policy. If the Court had upheld the statute, the right would be much like that described above in *Red Lion*.

A right to hear different viewpoints also did not extend to viewpoints disseminated by way of paid political advertising as ruled in *CBS v. Democratic National Committee*.[30] The Court upheld the right of broadcasters to refuse to sell time for advertising dealing with political campaigns and controversial issues. This is not a right but a liberty for which there is no duty-bearer. Broadcasters are at liberty to accept or not accept paid political advertising. But more recently, the Court ruled that broadcasters must sell air time to "legally qualified candidates for federal elective office" once a campaign has begun.[31] The case involved the networks' refusal to sell air time to the Carter-Mondale presidential committee. The Court said the rule giving federal candidates a right of access to broadcast stations "makes a significant contribution to freedom of expression by enhancing the ability of candidates to present, and the public to receive, information necessary for the effective operation of the democratic process."[32] Two specific exercise rights emerge from this case, one positive and one negative. First of all, candidates for federal office have the right to express themselves freely by using the public air waves and it is the duty of broadcasters to fullfill that right (positive). The second right is a qualified one. If federal candidates choose to exercise their right to use the public air waves, then the public has a right to hear their viewpoints and it is the duty of broadcasters not to interfere with that right (negative).

The public also has a right to receive price advertisements from pharmacists. In *Virginia State Board of Pharmacy et al. v. Virginia Citizens Consumer Council, Inc., et al.,* a Virginia statute which prohibited pharmacists from advertising the prices of prescription drugs was declared unconstitutional.[33] The Court reaffirmed an earlier decision[34]

---

30. *CBS v. Democratic National Committee,* 412 U.S. 94 (1973).
31. *CBS v. Federal Communications Commission,* 49 LW 4891 (1981).
32. *Id.* at 4899.
33. *Virginia State Board of Pharmacy v. Virginia Citizens Consumer Council, Inc.,* 425 U.S. 748 (1976).
34. *Kleindienst v. Mandel,* 408 U.S. 753 (1972).

in which it had acknowledged a First Amendment right to "receive information and ideas," a right derived from interpretation of the First Amendment. The public (the right-holder) has a right to receive consumer information (exercise and specific) and the government (the state of Virginia) has a duty not to interfere (negative) with that right.

Citizens also have a right to possess and use obscene materials in the privacy of their own homes and the government has a duty not to interfere, based on the decision in *Stanley v. Georgia*.[35] In *Stanley,* the police had a search warrant that allowed them to look for gambling evidence. Instead, they found three reels of pornographic film. While the Court maintained that "It is now well established that the Constitution protects the right to receive information and ideas,"[36] the right to receive information of this type is somewhat limited. For example, an individual cannot transport those films across state lines.[37] The films cannot be imported[38] nor can they be viewed in adult movie theatres.[39] Therefore, the right to possess obscene material in the privacy of one's home is protected by constitutional interpretation. The public is the right-holder and the government has the duty to not interfere. But, if there is no correlative right for someone to sell or give obscene materials to others, then this seems to be an empty right.

The right to receive information also does not extend to an individual who wishes to travel to a country when travel to that country has been banned. In *Zemel v. Rusk,*[40] a state department regulation banning travel to Cuba was challenged. Zemel wanted to satisfy his curiosity firsthand about the state of affairs in Cuba. It was argued that the regulation infringed on Zemel's right to know. The Court said that even though the policy inhibited the free flow of information, a First Amendment right was not involved. "The right to speak and publish does not carry with it the unrestrained right to gather information."[41]

It has been suggested that even though the individual's right to gather information may be limited, the press right to acquire information might be broader.[42] The Court, however, has consistently said "the First Amendment does not guarantee the press a constitutional right of

---

35. *Stanley v. Georgia*, 394 U.S. 557 (1969).
36. *Id.* at 564.
37. *U.S. v. Orito*, 413 U.S. 139 (1973).
38. *U.S. v. 12 200-ft. Reels of Super 8 mm Film*, 413 U.S. 123 (1973).
39. *Paris Adult Theatre v. Slaton*, 413 U.S. 49 (1973).
40. *Zemel v. Rusk*, 1 Med. L. Rptr. 2299.
41. *Id.* at 2305.
42. "The Rights of the Public and the Press to Gather Information," *Harvard Law Review* 87 (1974): 1506.

The Right to Know: Whose Right and Whose Duty?

special access to information not available to the public generally."[43]

Two decisions in 1974 involved special access rights of the press not generally available to the public. In *Pell v. Procunier,*[44] four prison inmates and three journalists brought suit challenging the constitutionality of California prison regulations barring media interviews with specific inmates. Although the case involved the free speech rights of inmates, the decision addresses the issue of access to information. The Court recognized that:

> Although the constitutional right of free speech has never been thought to embrace a right to require a journalist or any other citizen to listen to a person's views, let alone a right to require a publisher to publish those views in his newspaper, we proceed upon the hypothesis that under some circumstances the right of free speech includes a right to communicate a person's views to any willing listener, including a willing representative of the press for the purpose of publication by a willing publisher.[45]

This does not mean, though, that government has a duty to accord the press special access to information not available to members of the public generally.

In a similar case, *Saxbe v. Washington Post,*[46] the *Post* challenged the constitutionality of a policy statement of the Federal Bureau of Prisons which prohibited personal interviews between reporters and specific inmates. The *Post* contended that prohibition of all press interviews with prison inmates abridged the protection that the First Amendment accords the news gathering activity of a free press. Although the lower courts affirmed that the statement abridged the First Amendment, the Supreme Court said the policy did not place the press in a position any less advantageous than that held by the public generally. In fact, the Court said, the policy already accorded greater access to the press than it did to other members of the public.

The Court also said in *Branzburg v. Hayes*[47] that newsmen have no constitutional right of access to the scenes of crime or disaster when the general public is excluded. In a dissenting opinion, Justice Stewart

---

43. *Branzburg v. Hayes*, 408 U.S. 665, 684 (1972).
44. *Pell v. Procunier*, 1 Med. L. Rptr. 2379 (1974).
45. *Id.*
46. *Saxbe v. Washington Post*, 1 Med. L. Rptr. 2314.
47. 408 U.S. at 685.

noted that "A corollary of the right to publish must be the right to gather news."[48] The majority opinion did acknowledge the right of the press to gather information. "Without some protection for seeking out the news, freedom of the press could be eviscerated."[49]

In dissenting opinions in *Branzburg*, Justices Stewart and Douglas said that the right to gather news also implies a right to a confidential relationship between a reporter and his source. A case which involved a refusal by a reporter to reveal information to the court was that of *New York Times* reporter Myron Farber. Dworkin notes that the distinction between principle and policy are relevant in this case. Farber had refused to hand over his notes and other material he had gathered for a series of articles he had written about the deaths of hospital patients. The series led to the murder indictment of Dr. Mario Jascalevich, who was subsequently found not guilty. When Farber refused to comply with the court order, he was jailed for contempt.[50]

Dworkin notes that the core of the First Amendment is a matter of principle because individual citizens have a right to express themselves free from government censorship. The content of what they say may not be limited, even if the official believes he has good policy reasons for doing so, and even though he may be right. Dworkin argues, however, that arguments in defense of reporter's privilege to withhold information are arguments of policy. The arguments guaranteeing a reporter's privilege to keep sources confidential stems from the fact that informers might be deterred from talking to the reporter. The public interest would not be well served if this were to happen. But, says Dworkin, this argument of policy, must yield to the defendant's genuine rights to a fair trial, even at some cost to the general welfare. "It is both safer and more accurate to describe the privilege of confidentiality . . . as a privilege frankly grounded in efficiency."[51]

Although some states have passed laws to protect reporter's privilege, the rights of journalists under statutes are not uniform, and vary widely depending on the statute. So in some states a right derived from societal goals or policy has been established by statute to give journalists a right to keep their sources confidential. The right, then, may be interpreted as particular because it applies only to journalists in states that have such statutes, and it is a specific exercise right. It is negative in that government has a duty to not force reporters to divulge their confidential sources.

The U.S. Court of Appeals did recognize the public's right to know in

48. *Id.* at 727.
49. *Id.* at 681.
50. Dworkin, "Farber," p. 35. See also *In re Farber*, 4 Med. L. Rptr. 1360 (1978).
51. *Ibid.*

The Right to Know: Whose Right and Whose Duty?

United States v. Dickinson.[52] In this case, newspaper reporters were fined by the U.S. District Court for disobeying a court order. The reporters had been prohibited from reporting details of evidence taken at a hearing of a VISTA worker charged with conspiring to murder the mayor of Baton Rouge.

> . . . the public's right to know the facts brought out in this specific hearing was particularly compelling here, since the issue being litigated was a charge that elected state officials had trumped up charges against an individual solely because of his race and political civil rights activities.[53]

Nevertheless, the public's right to know was not compelling enough to persuade the court to overturn the contempt citations. The Court held, in effect, that the public's right to know was not an immediate right. It could wait until the appellate court had ruled.

The right to know matters of public interest was protected in *Landmark Communications v. Virginia.*[54] The Virginia *Pilot* had published an article which accurately reported a pending inquiry of the state's judicial review commission. Although a state statute required confidentiality of all commission proceedings, the Pilot's managing editor thought the information was a matter of public importance which should be brought to the attention of the Pilot's readers. The Court said the operation of the commission clearly involved interests served by "public scrutiny and discussion of government affairs which the First Amendment was adopted to protect."[55] In this instance, the right-holder could be said to be either the public or the press, and, therefore, does not fit neatly into the rights schema. The right is universal if it applies to all members of the public, but it is particular if it applies only to the press. It is an exercise right for both the press and the public, although it applies to each differently. It may be positive or it may be negative. If if is the public's right, then some institution or individual must provide that information to the public making it a positive right. But if it is a press right, the government has the duty to not interfere with that right. Finally, if it is a right that belongs to the press, then the government is the duty-bearer. But if it is a right that belongs to the public, who is the duty-bearer? Certainly, the government does not

---

52. *United States v. Dickinson,* 465 F. 2d. 496 (1972).
53. *Id.* at 508.
54. *Landmark Communications v. Virginia,* 3 Med. L. Rptr. 2153.
55. *Id.* at 2157.

have the duty to disseminate all information about matters of public interest to every citizen. Does the press have a duty to keep the public informed about matters of public interest? This, of course, runs counter to First Amendment interpretation that the press cannot be required to publish what it does not wish to publish.

Lofton maintains that the right to know was clearly rejected by the Court in *Houchins v. KQED*.[56] KQED, a San Francisco public television station, sought access to county jail facilities after an inmate had committed suicide. Two lower courts held that under the First Amendment, journalists have broader rights of access to prisons than does the general public. The Supreme Court, however, "flatly rejected the idea that there is a 'right to know' about government action and policy."[57] The Court emphasized that in earlier decisions, *Grosjean v. American Press* and *Mills v. Alabama,* it had "emphasized the importance of informed public opinion and the traditional role of a free press as a source of public information."[58] Nevertheless, while the Court was concerned with the freedom of the media to communicate information once it was obtained, it did not suggest that the Constitution compels government to provide the media with information or access on demand. In other words, the media have a right to communicate information freely, and the government has a duty not to interfere with that right. The right does not extend further because there is no correlative duty on the part of government to provide that information or access on demand.

In a dissenting opinion in *KQED,* Justice Stevens inferred that there ought to be a right to gather information.

> . . . information-gathering is entitled to some measure of constitutional protection . . . this protection is not for the private benefit of those who might qualify as representatives of the 'press' but to insure that the citizens are fully informed regarding matters of public interest and importance.[59]

Justice Stevens would have the right-holder be the public. But would the right be an exercise right in the sense that the public has a right to gather information and the government has a duty to provide the public with that information (positive)? Or is it that the media have a right to

---

56. *Houchins v. KQED,* 3 Med. L. Rptr. 2521 (1978).
57. John Lofton, *The Press as Guardian of the First Amendment* (Columbia, S.C.: The University of South Carolina Press, 1980), p. 273.
58. 3 Med. L. Rptr. at 2523.
59. *Id.* at 2533.

The Right to Know: Whose Right and Whose Duty?

gather information so that the public can receive it? In the latter instance there is a danger of putting the media in the position of duty-bearer.

The issue of a right to know was addressed a bit more directly in *Richmond Newspapers, Inc., et al., v. Commonwealth of Virginia et al.*[60] The question addressed by the court was whether the right of the public and the press to attend criminal trials is guaranteed under the Constitution. After three mistrials, a fourth trial was about to begin related to the killing of a motel manager. At the request of the defense, the judge ordered the courtroom closed to the public and the press, but the Supreme Court ruled against courtroom closure. It said the First Amendment expressly guaranteed "a common core purpose in assuring freedom of communication on matters related to the functioning of government."[61] The Court also noted that free speech carries with it some freedom to listen. This right is derived from constitutional interpretation. It is an exercise right that accrues to the public — the public has a right to attend criminal trials. The correlative duty on the part of the judiciary is not to interfere with that right, except in genuinely extraordinary circumstances.

CONCLUSION

Scholars can be found on both sides of the argument over whether a right to know can be found within the meaning of the Constitution. These scholars have relied primarily on historical interpretation of the meaning of the First Amendment as a basis from which to argue their point. This analysis was not undertaken to argue the point further. Rather, the purpose was to determine the parameters of the "right to know," if, indeed, there is such a right, within the philosophical definition of rights and their attributes.

The evidence leads one to conclude first of all that the right to know stems from a broader societal goal, that is, to ensure that a self-governing people be well informed. It cannot, however, be construed to be a right in and of itself. This becomes clear when one tries to fit the right to know into the rights schema. The right to know might be described as Feinberg described the right to life, that is, "a broad category in which a large miscellany of rights can be placed."[62] The category itself does not say what these rights are or what it means to

60. 40 CCH S. Ct. Bull. B4332.
61. *Id.* at 4349. See also, *Estes v. Texas*, 381 U.S. 532, "... the public has the right to be informed as to what occurs in the courts," at 541.
62. Feinberg, p. 71.

possess the universal right. "Commitment to this universal right is often best understood as an endorsement of a more or less vague ideal."[63]

At most, the right to know is a name for what Feinberg calls package rights, a set of discretionary rights that are in some way related to a particular subject.[64] For example, the "right to a fair trial" package includes the discretionary rights to call witness, to not incriminate oneself, to cross-examine, and so on. In this context, then one might be tempted to include in the right to know package the right to receive communciation, Emerson's definition of a right to know. But as noted earlier, the right to receive communication by itself does not withstand analysis within the rights schema. One would have to be more specific. Discretionary rights that might be included are the right to receive (or not receive) Communist propaganda, the right to hear different viewpoints about controversial issues, the right to hear from candidates to federal offices, the right to receive consumer price information, and the right to possess obscene materials in one's home. These are universal exercise rights that hold for all members of society.

The right to know package might also include the right to obtain government information. A right of access to government information exists through the federal Freedom of Information Act, similar state laws, and through the less-specified common law right of access to public records. There are some who hail *Richmond*[65] as the first step toward a constitutional right of access to information, and hence, a constitutional right to know.

A corollary to access to information is the right to keep one's news sources confidential. But not all states have statutes protecting reporter's privilege, and the right does not hold for all members of society. In view of this, it would seem inappropriate to include this particular right in the right to know package.

For those rights that one would apply under a right to know package, the right-holder is the public and not just a portion of the public such as the press. The press, of course, acts as an agent of the public in the sense that it provides information that no individual member of the public could obtain alone, or that could be obtained only with great difficulty. There is nothing in the Constitution, however, that mandates that the press inform the public, although it has assumed that responsibility throughout history. In a democratic society it has been expected that the press would keep a watchful eye on the workings of government and act as a champion of the public's right to know. The press has

63. *Ibid.*
64. *Ibid.*, p. 70.
65. 40 CCH S. Ct. Bull. B4332.

The Right to Know: Whose Right and Whose Duty?

not been required to fulfill an information-gathering role. To put the press in the position of duty-bearer would seem to infringe on its First Amendment freedoms. In the analysis herein, the duty-bearer in almost every instance is the government. Two exceptions arise in which the duty-bearers are broadcasters.

In short, then, unless one argues for the right to know being an umbrella name for several specific rights, the argument for a general right to know loses force. Unless defined as the specific rights mentioned, a right to know would be difficult to enforce. For those who wish to argue for a constitutional right to know, however, it is heartening to recall that the U.S. Supreme Court has found a right of privacy in the Constitution, which nowhere uses such a phrase.

ANTHONY GREEN

Government Lawyers and the Press

Anthony Green, recently graduated from the Villanova University School of Law, is clerk for Pennsylvania Supreme Court Justice James T. McDermott. Prior to attending law school, Mr. Green was an award-winning investigative reporter and an associate editor for *Philadelphia Magazine*. He has written for numerous other publications.

The Lindberg baby kidnap/murder trial of Bruno Richard Hauptmann in 1933 was probably one of the first big publicity 'carnival'[1] trials of any note in the days of modern technology. The parties, the few onlookers who could wangle themselves inside, and the press corps reporting to anxious readers all over the world, were all crammed into a quaint courtroom in a small New Jersey town called Flemington. One estimate put the press corps at about seven hundred, including the one hundred twenty-nine who were manning the rudimentary cameras and sound equipment. The event garnered millions of words in print.[2] Much of it was attributed to defense counsel who was promising 'bombshell' witnesses to exculpate his client, who proclaimed Hauptmann innocent throughout in live broadcasts, and who, upon defeat, attacked the 'mob justice' which was allegedly accorded his client.

According to reports, though, the prosecutor was not to be totally upstaged in the press. He carried on his own well-organized publicity campaign, holding daily press conferences.[3] At one point he was quoted as saying, "We have

1. "Carnival" as used in the precedent-setting case on the issue of denial of due process by prejudicial publicity. Sheppard v. Maxwell, 384 U.S. 333, 358 (1966).
2. Hallam, *Some Object Lessons on Publicity in Criminal Trials*, 24 MINN. L. REV. 453, 454 (1940).
3. Portman, *The Defense of Fair Trial from Sheppard to Nebraska Press Association: Benign Neglect to Affirmative Action and Beyond*, 29 STAN. L. REV. 393, 397 (1977).

ANTHONY GREEN

an iron-clad case against Hauptmann and will prove that he murdered the helpless infant."[4]

* * *

Leslie Irvin is not as widely remembered as Bruno Richard Hauptmann. Irvin was charged and convicted in the murder of six in a small town in Indiana. The worldwide press did not descend on the *Irvin* trial.[5] For Indiana, though, it was the big time. It was estimated that 95 percent of the homes in the county which was the site of the trial received the newspapers recounting the gritty case; radio and television also "blanketed that county."[6] When the Supreme Court reversed the conviction and remanded the case on due process grounds, Justice Frankfurter concurred, making a special point to attack the District Attorney's "collaboration" with the media campaign which fatally infected the trial of Leslie Irvin.[7]

* * *

Notably devoid of any blood or gore—save for the strange suicide of the wife of the government's star witness—the ABSCAM case was the crime story of the last decade. The F.B.I. "sting" operation—which caught a caucus of congressmen, local politicians, lawyers, and one U.S. Senator on videotape taking bribes from F.B.I. agents masquerading as Arab shieks—seriously embarrassed the United States Congress. At the very beginning, that crime story was plagued by charges of prejudicial publicity prompted by outspoken prosecutors.

The initial leaks to *The New York Times* and NBC News led to a near flood of unauthorized disclosures to other reporters around the country. In one episode, the United States Attorney for the Eastern District of Pennsylvania called the Philadelphia *Inquirer*'s federal courts reporter, advising her to play catch-up—that Philadelphia and south Jersey politicians would play a vital role in the penetrating ABSCAM story.[8]

* * *

From Hauptmann's trial to *Irvin* to ABSCAM, government lawyers have

4. Hallam, *supra* note 2, at 460.
5. See Irvin v. Dowd, 366 U.S. 717 (1961).
6. *Id.* at 725.
7. *Id.* at 730.
8. Department of Justice, *Unauthorized Disclosures Regarding ABSCAM, PENDORF, and BRILAB,* 7 (Jan. 14, 1981). (Hereinafter cited as *ABSCAM Report.*)

Government Lawyers and the Press

been implicated in noteworthy publicity campaigns, and there are many other instances illustrating the history of the relationship between government lawyers and the media, a sometime love affair which occasionally sullies the image of justice.

The mandate seems crystal clear: that the relationship between the lawyer, any lawyer—but especially the government lawyer—and the reporter should remain a superficial one, with the lawyer barred from speaking to a reporter about pending litigation except in a very few, very specific circumstances. As guidance, Disciplinary Rule 7-107 (DR 7-107) is the most pertinent proviso.[9] It severely limits a lawyer from making an extra-judicial statement reasonably likely to be disseminated publicly in criminal matters, civil litigation, professional disciplinary proceedings, juvenile matters or administrative actions. Scant information which would naturally be contained in public records can be disclosed but without any elaboration or explanation.

Along with the Disciplinary Rule, there have been countless writings on the ever-controversial Fair Trial/Free Press issue,[10] as well as a number of crucial Supreme Court cases.[11] The landmark case was *Sheppard v. Maxwell*,[12] considered to be the inspiration for Disciplinary Rule 7-107. *Sheppard* involved a prominent doctor accused and convicted of bludgeoning his wife to death. During the investigatory stage of the case, there was considerable sensational publicity, with editorials demanding an expeditious arrest and with front-page articles dripping with sexual innuendo, blood and gore. The trial judge and the prosecutor were both candidates for judgeships in an election to be held two weeks before the commencement of the trial. An army of reporters daily descended on the courtroom, where part of the press box was *inside* the bar of the courtroom only a few feet away from the jury box. The Court attacked the "carnival atmosphere" of the trial and reversed the conviction on due process grounds.[13]

---

9. Model Code of Professional Responsibility DR 7-107 (1981 as amended).
10. *Revised Report of the Judicial Conference on the Operation of the Jury System on the "Free Press-Fair Trial" Issue*, 87 F.R.D. 519 (1980); Reardon, *The Fair Trial-Free Press Standards*, 54 A.B.A.J. 343 (1968); Association of the Bar of the City of New York, Special Committee on Radio, Television, and the Administration of Justice, *Freedom of the Press and Fair Trial, Final Report with Recommendations* (1967); LEFTON, JUSTICE AND THE PRESS (1966); FRIENDLY & GOLDFARB, CRIME AND PUBLICITY (1967).
11. *E.g.*, Richmond Newspapers, Inc. v. Virginia, 448 U.S. 555 (1980) (Absent some overriding interest, criminal trials must be open to the public and the press); Gannett Co. v. DePasquale, 443 U.S. 368 (1979) (Pre-trial suppression hearings could be closed to the press at the court's discretion); Estes v. Texas, 381 U.S. 532 (1965) (Due process would be violated by the intrusion of television cameras during criminal trials. The Court most recently retreated from this position in Chandler v. Florida, 449 U.S. 560 (1981)).
12. 384 U.S. 333 (1966).
13. *Id.* at 358.

ANTHONY GREEN

The conflict between fair trial and free press is so fine a tightrope that the government lawyer should be wary of climbing the carnival ladder. But that has hardly been the case. The daily papers and six o'clock evening news broadcasts often turn the spotlight on an aggressive prosecutor or a vivacious public interest attorney at the center of—or at least lurking behind—a news story. Sometimes the lawyer will merely be an unnamed source who is "close to the investigation." Sometimes the lawyer will talk for the record. Sometimes the government lawyer will routinely issue a press release[14] about a complaint filed or an indictment returned or hold a press conference to discuss the case.[15] Many private firms are now retaining press agents to alert the media of their successes in the trenches, and most governmental agencies have a "public affairs" person on the payroll to handle inquiries from the media and, sometimes, to sell the agency's own story.[16]

The violations of the prophylactic rule imposed on attorney-media relations are so prevalent as to encourage immunity to them. Only in a rare case is there a *cause celebre*. One such case involved the leaks to the media right before the indictments were handed down in the F.B.I.'s ABSCAM, PENDORF and BRILAB "sting" operations.

   14. This, according to the ABA, is not unethical conduct. Its Committee on Professional Responsibility endorsed, for example, a legal aid society's practice of sending out press releases upon the initiation of a civil action. *See*, ABA Comm. on Professional Ethics, Opinions, Informal No. 1172 (1971); Formal Opinion No. 334 (1974). But such an office could not send out copies of the complaint unsolicited. *See*, ABA Comm. on Professional Ethics, Opinions, Informal No. 1230 (1972). The same rule was applied to state prosecutors and U.S. Attorneys. *See*, ABA Comm. on Professional Ethics, Opinions, Informal No. 1345 (1975).
   15. Whether the government lawyer should hold a press conference to announce an indictment or a complaint filed is a matter of taste. One prosecutor/commentator advised against it: "There is a tendency at the time of indictment for some prosecutors to have their cake and eat it too—to take a second blow at the defendants by holding a press conference or similar conclave to 'discuss' the charges. A few more ambitious prosecutors have elevated this tactic to something of an art form, complete with banks of microphones and charts. From my own experience, it is better for a prosecutor to issue an extremely sparse press release—it is safer in the long run—even if it leaves some reporters groping for a catch phrase or two to summarize the case.... Unless a prosecutor is running for office and wants the public to see how nicely he can smile, there is simply no good reason to announce an indictment with any fanfare." Hurson, *The Trial of a Highly Publicized Case—A Prosecutor's View*, 16 AM. CRIM. L. REV. 473 (1979). (Hereinafter cited as Hurson.)
   16. *See*, Brill, *How to Handle the Press*, 3 AM. LAW. 8 (January 1981); Brill, *Lawyers: Image Makers Join Legal Profession*, WASHINGTON POST, Sept. 10, 1979, at C-1, col. #1; Berreby, *Polishing the Firms' Staid Image*, NATIONAL LAW JOURNAL, March 15, 1982, at 1, col. 4.
      It is noteworthy that the *judge* presiding over the trial of Jack Ruby, Lee Harvey Oswald's killer, retained a public relations counselor to handle "the courtroom setting, the press [and] the trial publicity." Rubenstein v. Texas, 407 S.W.2d 793, 796 (Tex. Crim. App. 1966).

Government Lawyers and the Press

This is not a new problem. The news leak has always been a special problem plaguing government investigations and an ethical dilemma for the government attorney: How much can I say? How much should I say? Recognizing this predicament, this article will seek to delve into some of the pressures involved, investigating what makes a government lawyer and the reporters natural subjects for a love affair, what drives a prosecutor into the arms of a journalist. There are the factors of ego, blind ambition, and the prospect of making a living as a literary lawyer. There are political tugs, both within the confines of a bureaucracy and within the political animal of an elected government lawyer. There is sometimes the need for a government lawyer to legitimize his efforts in the public eye, and there is a constitutional need to satisfy the public's right to know. In analyzing the issue, it is important to keep in mind the distinction between the two broad categories of government lawyers: prosecutors, and most others, such as government-sponsored "consumer advocates."

I. THE FIRST AMENDMENT AND THE GOVERNMENT LAWYER

Before analyzing the various ethical conflicts raised, however, an initial question must be answered: Does the government lawyer, acting as such, have a First Amendment right of free speech possibly allowing him to fend off complaints about prejudicial or unethical statements with a copy of the Bill of Rights in hand? Such an argument has been employed.[17]

Lawyers are not stripped of their First Amendment rights when they are admitted to the bar. In one case, a defense attorney, speaking some 182 miles from the courthouse, criticized the presiding judge. The attorney was subsequently suspended from practice for his words. The Supreme Court reversed the decision, however, saying that lawyers are free "to criticize the state of the law." Even Justice Frankfurter, who dissented in that case acknowledged that right: "Of course, a lawyer is a person and he too has a constitutional freedom of utterance and may exercise it to castigate courts and their administration of justice."[18] In *Konigsberg v. State Bar*,[19] the Court acknowledged the importance of allowing the states to regulate their own lawyers but concluded that, "It is important both to society and the bar itself that lawyers be unintimidated—free to think, speak, and act as members of an Independent Bar."[20]

17. See, for example, Widoff v. Disciplinary Board, 54 Pa. Commw. Ct. 124, 420 A. 2d 41 (1980), aff.--Pa.--,--A. 2d.--(1981), *appeal dismissed, cert denied*,--U.S.--50 U.S.L.W. 3590 (1982). Brief for appellant at 14–18 (1981).
18. In re Sawyer, 360 U.S. 622, 666 (1958). He went on, though: "But a lawyer participating in a trial, particularly an emotionally charged criminal prosecution, is not merely a person and not even merely a lawyer." *Id*. at 666.
19. 353 U.S. 252 (1957).
20. See also, In re Primus, 436 U.S. 412 (1978). In that case the Court analogized

ANTHONY GREEN

A. As the Lawyer is an 'Officer of the Court', His Right to Speak May Be Abridged

An attorney is also an officer of the court.[21] This role does not necessarily gag him, however:

> [A] lawyer's responsibility to protect the fairness of the judicial process does not mean that lawyers and litigants surrender their First Amendment rights at the courthouse door. Even public officials who have special responsibilities to the court do not necessarily have a 'more curtailed' right to freedom of expression than the average citizen.[22]

Nevertheless, the 'officer of the court' designation has been determinative in allowing broad restrictions on an attorney's speech. Professor Tribe objects: "...(T)he label 'officer of the court' cannot be decisive; a *private* attorney cannot simply be assimilated into the category of government agents."[23]

B. As a Government Employee, the Government Lawyer May Lose His Right to Speak

Professor Tribe's distinction for private attorneys cannot be decisive either. For government employees also have First Amendment rights[24] — although restraints are feasible.[25]

Policemen present an interesting situation, somewhat analogous to a prosecutor's circumstance. "[P]olicemen, like teachers and lawyers, are not relegated to a watered-down version of constitutional rights."[26] Not only do law enforcement officials need to keep the officers quiet during ticklish investigations, but they also see a need to maintain a paramilitary-type *esprit de corps* in the ranks. Therefore, policemen's First Amendment rights may be contracted by their employers via a reasonable regulation which is tailored to fit a legitimate governmental purpose.[27]

---

litigation as a form of First Amendment free expression.
21. Goldfarb v. Virginia State Bar, 421 U.S. 773, 792 (1975).
22. *In re Halkin*, 598 F. 2d 176 (D.C. Cir. 1979); citing Wood v. Georgia, 370 U.S. 375, 393 (1962).
23. L. TRIBE, AMERICAN CONSTITUTIONAL LAW, 628 (1978) (emphasis added).
24. *E.g.*, Pickering v. Board of Education, 391 U.S. 563 (1968).
25. Wood v. Georgia, *supra* note 22; Tribe, *supra* n. 23, at 628, n. 26.
26. Garrity v. State of New Jersey, 385 U.S. 493, 500 (1967).
27. Gasparinetti v. Kerr, 568 F.2d 311 (3d cir. 1977); Muller v. Conlisk, 427 F. 2d 901 (7th Cir. 1970).

Government Lawyers and the Press

In the absence of a carefully designed regulation or law, though, a law enforcement official can discuss matters concerning his employment without inviting punishment by his superiors or the court.[28] In *Wood*, a grand jury was investigating allegedly racially motivated voter misconduct, and the local sheriff criticized a judge's actions in a press release. The Court held that for a judge to wield his contempt power, there must be an imminent threat to the administration of justice. Without that threat,

> The First Amendment envisions that persons be given the opportunity to inform the community of both sides of the issue under such circumstances. . . . (T)his privilege should not be curtailed. . . . Men are entitled to speak as they please on matters vital to them; errors in judgment or unsubstantiated opinions may be exposed, of course, but not through punishment for contempt for the expression. Under our system of government, counter argument and education are the weapons available to expose these matters, not abridgement of the rights of free speech and assembly.[29]

28. Wood, *supra* note 22.
29. *Id*., at 389.
    Another compelling issue in this area revolves around a lawyer's right to criticize a judge. Historically, most restrictions governing an attorney's right to attack a judge have been affirmed as not violating any First Amendment right of speech. *In re* Philbrook, 105 Cal. 471, 38 P. 884 (1895); People ex rel. Elliot v. Green, 7 Colo. 244, 3 P. 374 (1884); *In re* Thatcher, 80 Ohio St. 492, 89 N.E. 39 (1909); *In re* Gorsuch, 76 S.D. 191, 75 N.W. 2d 644 (1956); The Florida Bar, 284 So. 2d 686 (Fla. 1973). Regulations barring disparagement of the entire court were also allowed. *In re* Frerichs, 238 N.W. 2d 764, (Iowa 1976); State Board of Examiners v. Hart, 104 Minn. 88, 116 N.W. 212 (1908); *In re* Woodward, 300 S.W. 2d 385 (Mo. 1957); State ex rel. Hall v. Niewoehner, 116 Mont. 437, 155 P. 2d 205 (1944); *In re* Raggio, 87 Nev. 369, 487 P.2d 499 (1971) (Involving a district attorney who made critical statements about the Nevada high court). *Contra*, Polk v. State Bar of Texas, 374 F.Supp. 784 (N.D. Tex. 1974) (Where a lawyer successfully brought a § 1983 action for injunctive relief after his reprimand from the state bar; arrested on a drunk driving charge, the lawyer issued a jailhouse press release attacking the judge as "perverse" and the local District Attorney as "dishonest and unethical.") Sometimes, a lawyer's attack on a judge will mean a mistrial. Elder v. Commonwealth, 30 CRIM. L. RPTR. 2416 (Mass. Sup. Jud. Ct. Jan. 20, 1982) (After the District Attorney attacked the judge concerning a sentence in another case, the judge ordered a mistrial in the ongoing trial, remarking, "Given the present posture of the circumstances, circumstances created solely by the District Attorney, any decision of the Court will be perceived by some, perhaps many, as being suspect.")
    While sometimes the judicial immunity to such influences is taken for granted, a court's sensitivity to outside influences like press comment has been acknowledged. "Our judges are high minded men and women. But it is difficult to remain oblivious to the pressures that the news media can bring to bear on them both directly and through the shaping of public opinion." Estes v. Texas, 381 U.S. 532, 548–49 (1965); *see also* Pennekamp v. State of Florida, 328 U.S. 331, 348 (1946).

ANTHONY GREEN

Other cases have held, though, that a public employee may be discharged for his public statements without offending the First Amendment.[30] In another vital area, the government could validly limit its employees' First Amendment right of political activity based upon the Hatch Act.[31]

Another interesting line of cases involves the Central Intelligence Agency's literary 'bad boys'. At issue are not only the pertinent C.I.A. regulations regarding internal secrecy, the agency's fabled honor and *esprit de corps*, but especially contracts which bar former C.I.A. employees from publishing anything involved with agency business without agency right of perusal.[32]

In the *Snepp* case,[33] even though no classified or even non-public material was disclosed in his book *Decent Interval*, the pre-publication contract held firm and the proceeds from sales of the book were placed in a constructive trust. The Court found the pre-publication policy a reasonable means to protect secret information and therefore there was no violation of the First Amendment. In dissent, though, Justice Stevens saw a need to balance the interests of the government and its employee:

> Like an ordinary employer, the CIA has a vital interest in protecting certain types of information; at the same time, the CIA employee has a countervailing interest in preserving a wide range of work opportunities (including work as an author) and in protecting his First Amendment rights.[34]

C. Government May Limit Its Lawyers' Right to Speak

Just as a policeman or a C.I.A. agent may have his First Amendment rights limited, so may a government lawyer. The government lawyer must answer to a higher authority—more than an illusive ethical restraint. As the employer, the government may restrict its employee's speech by vigorously enforcing in-house no-comment regulations, which are generally more stringent than the Disciplinary Rule.

So a government lawyer is treated with, and lives under, a sharper sword by the courts than does the average lawyer. In a case where the District Attorney was held in contempt for extra-judicial statements in violation of a protective order, the Court talked about its power to shrink the First Amend-

30. *E.g.*, Arnett v. Kennedy, 416 U.S. 134 (1974).
31. 5 U.S.C. § 1501 *et seq.* (1940); United Public Workers v. Mitchell, 330 U.D. 75 (1947).
32. Snepp v. U.S., 444 U.S. 507 (1980); Alfred A. Knopf Co. v. Colby, 509 F. 2d 1362 (4th Cir. 1975), *cert. denied*, 421 U.S. 908 (1975); U.S. v. Marchetti, 466 F.2d 1309 (4th Cir. 1972), *cert. denied*, 409 U.S. 1063 (1973).
33. *Id.*
34. *Id.* at 520.

Government Lawyers and the Press

ment rights of a government lawyer:

> Prosecutors, of course, do not lose their First Amendment rights when they assume office.... They are, however, elected or appointed to prosecute criminal cases, rather than to talk about them. By taking office, they necessarily accept certain limitations. [In footnote:] So do all of us. No member of the court could hope to escape appropriate sanctions if he treated the press to a running commentary on our deliberations on a case which is under submission.... Surely, then, a state may try to preserve the integrity and efficiency of its administration of criminal justice by attempting to forestall the prejudicial effect of some prosecutor's fondness for publicly talking shop.[35]

Certainly, the cases make a distinction between criminal cases on the one hand and civil litigation and administrative proceedings on the other where, for example, the Free Press-Fair Trial strains are less onerous and where there is usually much more lag time between the filing of a complaint and the actual proceeding.[36]

The government lawyer is not just any lawyer; he is not just any officer of the court. The Code of Professional Responsibility makes a distinction between a government lawyer and the private attorney and implies a further distinction between prosecutors and other government lawyers. Generally, the rules encourage a higher quantum of restraint in the government attorney.

D. A Right to Speak Based on the Public's Right to Know

If attacked for his outspokenness, a government lawyer may argue that he needs to speak in order to serve the public's right to know, based on the First Amendment. Most recently, the Supreme Court recognized that right flowing from the First Amendment in *Richmond Newspapers, Inc. v. Virginia*,[37] saying, "Free speech carries with it some freedom to listen." This declaration, however, was not a new one.[38] "[T]he First Amendment goes beyond the protection of the press and the self-expression of individuals to

---

35. Younger v. Smith, 30 C.A. 3d 138, 157, 106 CAL. RPTR. 225, 237 (1973).
36. *E.g.*, Chicago Council of Lawyers v. Bauer, 522 F.2d 242, 258 (7th Cir. 1975), *cert denied* 427 U.S. 912 (1976).
37. 448 U.S. 555, 576 (1980).
38. *E.g.*, Kliendienst v. Mandel, 408 U.S. 753, 762, 775 (1972); Stanley v. Georgia, 394 U.S. 557, 564 (1969); *Thomas v. Collins*, 323 U.S. 516, 534 (1945); *Martin v. City of Struthers*, 319 U.S. 141, 143 (1943), But, *cf.* Gannett Co., Inc. v. DePasquale, 443 U.S. 368 (1979) (Where a closed pre-trial suppression hearing

prohibit government from limiting the stock of information which members of the public may draw."[39] In *Red Lion Broadcasting Co. v. FCC*,[40] where the Court upheld the Federal Commerce Commission's "fairness doctrine," it was observed,

> [I]t is the purpose of the First Amendment to preserve an uninhibited marketplace of ideas in which truth will ultimately prevail.... It is the right of the public to receive suitable access to social, political, esthetic, moral, and other ideas and experiences which is crucial here.[41]

It should not be hard to assert this right for the listeners as the plaintiffs did in the *Richmond Newspapers* case.[42]

It might be noted that the Court failed to buy the right-to-know/accountability argument in a trio of cases involving press access to prisons.[43]

While it is not conclusive that speech is a right of the government lawyer flowing from the First Amendment Right of Speech, it may be persuasive that there is a duty to speak resting in the First Amendment's implicit right to know which vests in the government lawyer's clients: the public. The government does not possess any rights as such. Government has only duties, only a role.[44] To fill that role, the government lawyer is required to speak.

II. REGULATING A GOVERNMENT LAWYER'S SPEECH

On the premise that a government lawyer's speech may be curbed, various means have been employed towards that end.

---

was sanctioned.) The right of the public and press to attend criminal trials, absent 'weighty' state justifications, was recently reaffirmed in Globe Newspaper Co. v. Superior Court, U.S. 102 S. Ct. 2613 (1982).
39. First National Bank of Boston v. Bellotti, 435 U.S. 765, 783 (1978).
40. 395 U.S. 367 (1969).
41. *Id.* at 390.
42. Richmond, *supra* note 37. (Although the issue was not actually argued in that case.)
43. Pell v. Procunier, 417 U.S. 817 (1974); Saxbe v. Washington Post, 417 U.S. 843 (1974); Houchins v. KQED, 438 U.S. 1 (1978). In *Houchins*, Justice Stevens wrote in dissent, "Without some protection for the acquisition of information about the operation of public institutions such as prisons by the public at large, the process of self-governance contemplated by the Framers would be stripped of its substance." *Id.* at 32. In those cases, it was crucial that the press bring the information as to prison conditions to the public; just as government lawyers deliver such information about the government to the public. Justice Stewart, who wrote for the majority, was insistent, though, that the press had no greater right of access to such information than the general public. Pell, *supra*, at 834.
44. See U.S. Const. amend. I.

Government Lawyers and the Press

A. DR 7-107—An Attempt to Limit Trial Publicity

Disciplinary Rule 7-107[45] is the threshold tool for gagging a government lawyer—or any lawyer for that matter. Its viability, however, is questionable. In two circuit court opinions, the rule has been attacked on constitutional grounds. In *Chicago Council Lawyers v. Bauer*,[46] the rule was found to be overbroad and "to stifle fundamental personal liberties." The Court hinted that it would be more sympathetic to a more concrete, "serious and imminent threat" test, rather than the more "amorphous," "reasonable likelihood" test. In *Hirschkop v. Snead*,[47] however, the Court held the rule valid as to criminal jury trials but overbroad as applied to criminal bench trials, the sentencing function, civil litigation, and administrative proceedings. As to the latter, the Court concluded that the rule restricted more comment than was necessary to protect such proceedings.[48] In both cases, the Courts were skeptical about broad rules which tended to deprive the public of the articulate voice of the attorney and of his knowledge and information, which should be in the public domain.

Aside from the criticism from the courts in the context of litigation, DR 7-107 has been hit with other blows. In a judicial review of the Free Press-Fair Trial issue, it was recommended that the rule not apply in the sentencing arena or during civil litigation.[49]

The *American Bar Association Commission on Evaluation of Professional Standards, Final Draft of Model Rules of Professional Conduct*[50] attempts to cope with the criticism of DR 7-107 in Rule 3.6.[51] It attempts specificity with

---

45. See note 9.
46. *Supra* note 36.
47. 594 F. 2d 356 (4th Cir. 1979).
48. See also Markfield v. Association of the Bar, 49.A.D.2d 576, 370 N.Y.S. 2d 82 (1974) *appeal dismissed*, 37 N.Y. 2d 794, 375 N.Y.S. 2d 106 (1975); Ruggieri v. Johns-Manville Products Corp., 503 F. Supp. 1036 (D.R.I. 1980).
    Other courts have endorsed the validity of the Rule. See *In re* Porter, 268 Or. 417, 521 P.2d 345 (1974) *cert denied* 380 U.S. 987 (1975); State of New Jersey v. Duyne 43 N.J. 369, 204 A.2d 841 (1964) (Where the Court expressed its approval of DR 7-107's predecessor Canon 20).
49. *Revised Report of the Judicial Conference Committee on the Operation of the Jury System on the "Free Press-Fair Trial" Issue*, 87 F.R.D. 519, 524 (1980).
50. May 30, 1981. The so-called Kutak Rules were again debated at the ABA's midyear meeting in New Orleans, and its sponsors are optimistic that it will be passed at the Bar's annual meeting in August 1983. There was no significant debate about the model rule's approach to lawyer-media relations. See, 69 A.B.A.J. 421-423 (April 1983).
51. Rule 3.6 is as follows:
    (a) A lawyer shall not make an extrajudicial statement that the lawyer knows or reasonably should know will have a substantial likelihood of materially prejudicing an adjudicative proceeding. An extrajudicial statement, other than one permitted by paragraph (b), ordinarily is likely to have such an effect when it

illustrations of conduct which would be deemed inappropriate. Like DR 7-107, though, it covers all types of litigation.

B. DR 2-101: An Attempt to Inhibit Lawyer Touting

Disciplinary Rule 2-101 seeks to discourage a lawyer from using "any form of public communication" to promote himself and thus attract business. The Bar had to retreat from a much more rigid position on the publicity issue in light of the Supreme Court's decision which permitted attorney advertising.[52]

At face value, DR 2-101 would seem not to apply to a government lawyer; however, the rule reflects the Bar's desire that its membership in general

---

refers to a civil matter triable to a jury, or a criminal matter or proceeding that could result in incarceration, and the statement relates to:

(1) the character, credibility, reputation or criminal record of a party, suspect in a criminal investigation or witness, or the identity of a witness, or the expected testimony of a party or witness;

(2) in a criminal case or proceeding that could result in incarceration, the possibility of a plea of guilty to the offense or the existence or contents of any confession, admission, or statement given by a defendant or suspect or that person's refusal or failure to make a statement;

(3) the performance or results of any examination or test or the refusal or failure of a person to submit to an examination or test, or the identity or nature of physical evidence expected to be presented;

(4) any opinion as to the guilt or innocence of a defendant or suspect in a criminal case or proceeding that could result in incarceration; or

(5) information the lawyer knows or reasonably should know is likely to be inadmissible as evidence in a trial and would if disclosed create a substantial risk of prejudicing an impartial trial.

(b) A lawyer involved in the investigation or litigation of a matter may state without elaboration:

(1) the general nature of the claim or defense;

(2) information contained in a public record;

(3) that investigation of the matter is in progress, including the general scope of the investigation, the offense or claim or defense involved and, except when prohibited by law, the identity of the persons involved;

(4) the scheduling or result of any step in litigation;

(5) a request for assistance in obtaining evidence and information necessary thereto;

(6) a warning of danger concerning the behavior of a person involved, when there is reason to believe that such danger exists; and

(7) in a criminal case:

(i) the identity, residence, occupation and family status of the defendant or suspect;

(ii) if the defendant or suspect has not been apprehended, information necessary to aid in apprehension of that person;

(iii) the fact, time and place of arrest, resistance, pursuit and use of weapons; and

(iv) the identity of investigating and arresting officers or agencies and the length of the investigation.

52. Bates v. State Bar of Arizona, 433 U.S. 350 (1977).

Government Lawyers and the Press

avoid further muddying the already muddy image of lawyers by trying to sell themselves to the public. This more general view could apply to a lawyer who takes a government position with the hope of making himself into a star and then profiting on the notoriety in the private sector.[53]

C. ABA Standards: Moving Towards Specificity

In addition to adhering to the Disciplinary Rules, lawyers involved in the criminal justice system must meet the demands of the *ABA Standards Relating to the Administration of Criminal Justice*.[54] The American Bar Association standards as to the prosecution function reinforce the general desire that a prosecutor "not exploit his office by means of personal publicity connected with a case...."[55] The ABA standards as to fair trial and free press are more specific and helpful. The standards specifically suggest that a lawyer—defense counsel or prosecutor—refrain from releasing the kind of information which creates the most problem from a prejudicial point of view—citing confessions, prior criminal records, opinions as to guilt of innocence and the like. The ABA standards leave room for the prosecutor to "discharge" his "official or professional obligations."[56]

D. Judicially Imposed rules

The *Sheppard* case encouraged the courts to take action to deal with the problem of prejudicial publicity. Many courts have used the *Sheppard* case as authority to set general rules of court and to act remedially in special circumstances. The ABA standards seem to have served as guidance for most judicial rules.[57] DR 7-107 has inspired other courts.[58]

---

53. That is not at all an unusual route for an ambitious attorney. See EULAU & SPRAGUE, LAWYERS IN POLITICS, 43 (1964).
54. *The Prosecution Function; Fair Trial and Free Press*, (2d. ed. 1980) (Hereinafter cited as *ABA Standards*.)
55. *Id.* at § 3-1.3.
56. Prosecutors are generally more sympathetic to the approach of the ABA Standards than to the more limiting Disciplinary Rules. In a letter to the Pennsylvania Bar committee studying the Final Draft of the Model Rules of Professional Conduct, the Deputy for Law of the Philadelphia District Attorney's Office criticized the revised rule as being too restrictive. Letter from Eric B. Henson to Michael Bloom, Chairman of the Committee on Professional Responsibility (Sept. 10, 1981).
57. The rule in Pennsylvania, for example, closely follows the ABA Standard. See Commonwealth v. Pierce, 451 Pa. 190, 303 A.2d 209 (1973), *cert denied*, 414 U.S. 878 (1973).
58. The Eastern District of Pennsylvania has also adopted a special rule for "widely publicized" cases, Federal Local Rules of Civil Procedure (E.D.) 43. It is more conservative, barring any comment beyond the public record. Rule 2 of the

ANTHONY GREEN

When rules of court become too broad in nature, they tend to invite trouble. In *County of Los Angeles v. Superior Court for County of Los Angeles*,[59] the local court sought to enjoin all law enforcement officials and lawyers from talking to the media from the time of arrest to the time of arraignment, except to tell the time and place of the arrest and of the offense charged. While recognizing that prosecutors and police officers sometimes go beyond the constitutional boundaries, the Superior Court ruled that, "No court can fairly determine in advance that such pretrial publicity will result in prejudice to the accused in *all* cases, no matter how much such publicity may be deplored."[60] Other judicial rules, on the other hand, have met with more success.[61]

E. In-House Rules: Strategies

As with judicially imposed rules, in-house no-comment rules mirror either DR 7-107 or the ABA standards.[62] Such rules characteristically allow the disclosure of the vital statistics as to name, age, charge, location of arrest and the like, and bar the release of highly prejudicial information.[63]

Local Rules of Criminal Procedure applies civil rule 43 to criminal matters. *See In re* Grand Jury Proceedings, 632 F.2d 1033 (3rd Cir. 1980) (Where the Court discusses the interaction of DR 7-107, the local rules, and the Justice Department regulations in terms of the request of an ABSCAM defendant for an evidentiary hearing to seek out the federal employees who leaked the material to the media.)

59. 253 Cal. App. 2d 670, 62 Cal Rptr. 435 (1967).
60. *Id.* 253 Cal. App. 2d at 681, 62 Cal. Rptr. 442. California, as with most other things, was a trendsetter in the field of pre-trial publicity and strong rules in reaction to that publicity. *See* Warren & Abel, *Free Press-Fair Trial: The "Gag Order," A California Aberration*, 45 CAL. L. REV. 53, 55 (1972).
61. *See* State v. Nelson, 210 Kan. 637, 504 P.2d (1972) (Where a rule was held not to offend First Amendment standards and would not chill speech where the lower court's call for discipline was rescinded); State, Angel v. Woodahl, 171 Mont. 13, 555 P. 2d 501 (1976) (Where a ban on speech surrounding an investigation met the 'clear and present danger' test); *In re* Oliver, 308 F. Supp. 1183 (N.D. Ill. 1970) (Where an attorney was reprimanded by the Court for violating the judicial conference's directive regarding speech in the midst of pending litigation; the attorney was advised that if he wished to talk about the case, he should simply withdraw as counsel).
62. *See* 28 C.F.R. § 50.2 (1975) for the Justice Department's approach.
63. In pertinent part, the Justice Department rule states:
   (3) Personnel of the Department of Justice, subject to specific limitation imposed by law or court rule or order, may make public the following information:
   (i) The defendant's name, age, residence, employment, marital status, and similar background information.
   (ii) The substance or text of the charge, such as a complaint, indictment, or information.
   (iii) The identity of the investigating and/or arresting agency and the length

Government Lawyers and the Press

During the Watergate affair, the Special Prosecution Force's annual report noted that Archibald Cox's decision to implement a public affairs office to deal with the press was a successful weapon in halting the kind of leaks which could have plagued his operation, more useful than the relevant regulations or Disciplinary Rules.[64] Security was tight and the lawyers knew that Cox (and later his successor, Leon Jaworski) and the public affairs director were the only ones authorized to talk to the press. It was largely suc-

---

and scope of the investigation.

(iv) The circumstances immediately surrounding an arrest, including the time and place of arrest, resistance, pursuit, possession and use of weapons, and a description of physical items seized at the time of arrest. Disclosures should include only incontrovertible, factual matters, and should not include subjective observations. In addition, where background information or information relating to the circumstances of an arrest or investigation would be highly prejudicial or where the release thereof would serve no law enforcement function, such information should not be made public.

(4) Personnel of the Department shall not disseminate any information concerning a defendant's prior criminal record.

(5) Because of the particular danger of prejudice resulting from statements in the period approaching and during trial, they ought strenuously to be avoided during that period. Any such statement or release shall be made only on the infrequent occasion when circumstances absolutely demand a disclosure of information and shall include only information which is clearly not prejudicial.

(6) The release of certain types of information generally tends to create dangers of prejudice without serving a significant law enforcement function. Therefore, personnel of the Department should refrain from making available the following:

(i) Observations about a defendant's character.

(ii) Statements, admissions, confessions, or alibis attributable to a defendant, or the refusal or failure of the accused to make a statement.

(iii) Reference to investigative procedures such as fingerprints, polygraph examinations, ballistic tests, or laboratory tests, or to the refusal by the defendant to submit to such tests or examinations.

(iv) Statements concerning the identity, testimony or credibility of prospective witnesses.

(v) Statements concerning evidence or argument in the case, whether or not it is anticipated that such evidence or argument will be used at trial.

(vi) Any opinion as to the accused's guilt, or the possibility of a plea of guilty to the offense charged, or the possibility of a plea to a lesser offense.

Also see guidelines issued by the prosecuting attorney of St. Louis, Missouri. *ABA Standards, supra* note 54 at 34. An in-house memorandum issued by Philadelphia District Attorney Edward G. Rendell sought to help office personnel "feel more confident in their dealings with the press." Memorandum to staff from Edward G. Rendell, 1 (Oct. 23, 1980). The memo "encouraged" the assistants to release anything to the press "presented on the record to the Court," with the caveat that they clear any other sorts of communications with his Deputy for Communications. The memo reminded the lawyers of DR 7-107 and even listed the names and numbers of the daily newspaper criminal justice beat reporters. Rendell stressed that with full information about the system, the "public would react in a manner that would make our job easier." *Id*. at 1.

64. Department of Justice, *Watergate Special Prosecution Force Report* (Oct. 1975). (Hereinafter cited as *Watergate Report*.)

cessful, save for one episode when *The Washington Post* got a story by rummaging through the Force's trash bin, prompting the office to requisition a paper shredder.[65] On the other hand, the ABSCAM leaks were attributed, at least in part, to the Department's public affairs personnel, and the leaks flowed in spite of the department regulations.[66]

In success or in failure, the in-house rules and the consequences of such have evoked some interesting reactions from the media, both positive and negative. In one case, a U.S. Attorney made some imprudent remarks prior to an indictment in a case.[67] *The New York Times* was moved to comment in an editorial:

> [T]he press cannot be expected to refrain from printing statements issued by public officials, as for example the United States Attorney, even though such statements may be prejudicial to a fair trial. The only way to stop this abuse is to stop it at the source.[68]

During the more recent case of the Watergate probe, though, one reporter frustrated by the absence of sources caused by Cox's stringent press policy was more cynical; the unidentified reporter was not moved by the legal arguments advanced for secrecy's sake:

> I think your office has put together one of the best bands of lawyers this town has ever known, but they are still government lawyers and they think like government lawyers, and other Washington lawyers got us into this mess in the first place. So I think in this area of cases above all, we need to know more about the way government lawyers think and why they decide to do things and not to do things. Lawyers don't like to talk about those things and over the years they have developed all sorts of fancy reasons not to. And since Congressmen (mostly) and judges (entirely) — the only ones with subpoena powers — are lawyers too, nobody can make them. But I think you ought to be prepared to explain your decisions. And if you're not, you ought to explain why you're not.[69]

---

65. *Id.* at 230
66. *ABSCAM Report, supra* note 8, at 8.
67. United States v. Dioguardi, 20 F.R.D. 33, 34 (S.D. N.Y. 1956).
68. N.Y. TIMES, Sept. 5, 1956, at 26, col. 1.
69. *Watergate Report, supra* note 64.

F. Bar-Court-Media Agreements: Untested and Maybe Unrealistic

Last but not least, some states have had interesting experiences with voluntary guidelines agreed upon by the local bar and the media. The success of these experiments has never really been studied; who knows how a circulation-hungry newspaper or a ratings-crazed television station really performs when that big story comes its way?[70]

III. TALKING TO THE PRESS: MOTIVES, PRESSURES

Despite the numerous mechanisms which would serve to chill a government lawyer's desire to talk to the press, there are other pressures at work when the reporter and the government lawyer get together—ephemeral strains which cause many a government lawyer to walk the tightrope.

A. Lawyers Want to Share Some of the Spotlight

First, there is ego; most lawyers have some desire to be in the spotlight. Some media attention helps to quench that thirst. One of the prosecutors in the *Mandel*[71] case in Maryland acknowledged this need:

> This interest [in the highly publicized] case is whetted, one suspects, when legal colleagues surface on the nightly news, captured in the dynamic sketches of courtroom artists, or simply standing in front of the courthouse explaining why their client has no comment. Every trial attorney yearns for that splendid moment in the courtroom....When combined with the vision of the courtroom packed with the press, of the artists laboring furiously to catch the gesture and of rapt attention from assorted courtroom observers invariably drawn to the scene of a major trial, any lawyer can conjure up a setting of high drama, and even perhaps a singular chance to stand in the shoes of Clarence Darrow.[72]

---

70. See American Bar Association, *Fair Trial/Free Press: Voluntary Agreements* (1974).
71. See U.S. v. Mandel, 591 F. 2d 1347 (4th Cir. 1979).
72. Hurson, *supra* note 15, at 473. *See also* the comments of Richard Kuh, the former District Attorney of New York County, who, in talking about the 'prosecution mentality', suggested that the forces of ego, self-righteousness and power sometimes win over consideration of fairness and ethics when dealings with the press come into play. GALSTON, PROFESSIONAL RESPONSIBILITY OF THE LAWYER: THE MURKY DIVIDE BETWEEN RIGHT AND WRONG, 104 (1977).

B. Publicity Used as a Weapon in Intra-Governmental Feuds

Publicity is used by government lawyers to wage wars against competing offices. For example, positive public opinion can help a government agency or prosecutorial office in its fight for appropriations at the expense of another, less publicity-conscious office.[73] The competitive factor was recognized as a motivating force in the ABSCAM disclosures:

> Investigators and attorneys working on [the probes] as well as media relations people, had a natural interest in assuring that their stories were told, and told well. Many of them perceived their respective offices as making special contributions to the investigation, and deserving particular credit in the competition for publicity that might follow. Rivalry and competition among offices and agencies occurred in each of these investigations. While natural, healthy, and inevitable to an extent, the tensions resulting from management of multi-district inquiries were conducive to unauthorized disclosures. In at least one instance, such disclosures may have been motivated by personal animus or bias resulting from past disputes.[74]

C. Publicity Used as a Tool to Propel a Lawyer's Career

Blind ambition is a further motivation. A lawyer might jump into the arms of the media, suspecting that some publicity would help advance his or her career. This pressure was also recognized in the ABSCAM report: "Enhancing institutional image may have verged on self-promotion to some degree.... Favorable publicity helps sell books and enhances employment opportunities."[75]

---

73. Such wars are frequent, for example, between the offices of the local U.S. Attorney and the Justice Department's Organized Crime Strike Forces. See Penn, *Justice on Trial*, WALL STREET JOURNAL, March 16, 1982, at 1, col. 4. The article critically examined the viability of the strike force concept, including the impact on the criminal justice system due to the feverish competition between local U.S. Attorneys and Strike Force Attorneys. The article commenced with a reference to the recent film "Absence of Malice" which centered on the consequences of a leak from a government lawyer for a Florida businessman played by Paul Newman. The article's subordinate headline read, "Federal Strike Forces Get Lots of Headlines, But Do They Work?"
74. ABSCAM Report, *supra* note 8, at 13.
75. *Id.* at 13.

Government Lawyers and the Press

D. Satisfying the Public's Right To Know

More substantially, the issue raises a conflict between the ethics of talking to the press and a First Amendment right to know belonging to the public. As analyzed above, the Supreme Court has declared that the First Amendment implicitly carries with it a right to know.[76] Much of what the public has a right to know about is in the work and minds of the government lawyer.

Furthermore, a lawyer generally has a duty to keep his clients informed about litigation fought on their behalf. The government lawyer's clients are usually the citizens. Generally, he should not be impeded in communicating with his clients in the most efficient manner—through the media. Further, he has a duty to deliver the best representation for his clients—that also might require media relations.

1. *The Prosecutor's Predicament*

The prosecutor's dilemma is perhaps the most compelling. On the one hand, he is to represent his clients zealously in fighting crime; but, on the other hand, he is charged with the duty of dispensing impartial justice rather than merely gaining convictions at all costs. "The prosecutor is both an administrator of justice and an advocate.... The duty of the prosecutor is to seek justice, not merely to convict."[77]

The demands might sometimes collide in practice, leaving the prosecutor neutral; he becomes an impotent advocate.

a. *Prosecutors Playing the Political Game Have to Play to the Press*

Many prosecutors have to cope with politics along with ethical strains; or, they choose to play politics. Even if they are not elected, prosecutors may owe their jobs to the political process and must bow to it. Serving the electorate often demands playing to the press:

---

76. *Supra*, at 11–12.
77. *ABA Standards*, supra note 54 § 3-1.1 (b) (c). The Court in Berger v. U.S., 295 U.S. 78 (1934), was at its most eloquent on this point in a case where an Assistant U.S. Attorney overstepped his bounds in a counterfeiting case: "[H]e is in a peculiar and very definite sense the servant of the law, the twofold aim of which is that guilt shall not escape or innocence suffer. He may prosecute with earnestness and vigor—indeed he should do so. But while he may strike blows, he is not at liberty to strike foul ones. It is as much his duty to refrain from improper methods calculated to produce wrongful convictions as it is to use every legitimate means to bring about justice." *Id.* at 88. *See also* Imbler v. Pachtman, 424 U.S. 409, 413 (1976).

Because the district attorney is elected, his reliance on the political system makes him particularly vulnerable to pressure by the press. There may be a natural inclination to publicize matters for reasons other than keeping the public informed.[78]

These pressures are not new. Dean Roscoe Pound wrote:

> Politics requires taking advantage of possibilities of publicity....The need for getting results puts pressure upon the prosecutors to use the 'third degree,' to suppress evidence, to bulldoze witnesses, and generally indulge in that lawless enforcement of law which produces a vicious circle of disrespect for law.[79]

Sometimes politics forces the prosecutor to assume the facade of the *macho* man; the easiest way to dress up in the disguise is to make bold, perhaps prejudicial statements about crime and the criminals he is prosecuting. It sells. It makes headlines. It woos voters. According to Professor Albert Alschuler, various factors, including political pressures:

> ...push prosecutors toward an impatient, crusading, 'gang-buster' self-image (that of the prosecutor of the mass media) rather than to a careful, impartial, quasi-judicial self-image (that espoused by the Code of Professional Responsibility).[80]

b. *A Brief Look at Prosecutorial Misconduct*

A chronicle of prosecutorial misconduct in the publicity area might commence with *People v. Stroble*,[81] a case involving the brutal murder of a

---

78. Schneider & Marks, *The Contrasting Ethical Duties of the Prosecutor and Defense Attorney in Criminal Cases*, 7 U.W.L.A. L. REV. 120, 126 (1975).
79. R. POUND, CRIMINAL JUSTICE IN AMERICA, 185–186 (2d ed. 1945). *See also* Note, *Prosecutorial Indiscretion: A Result of Political Influence*, 34 IND.L.J. 477, 484–485 (1959).
80. Alschuler, *Courtroom Misconduct by Prosecutors and Trial Judges*, 50 TEX. L. REV. 629, 676 (1976).
   This particular phenomenon is not solely found in the government lawyer who happens to be a politician but also in the politician who happens to be a lawyer. Maybe, sometimes, he just forgets about the basics like fair trial and due process that one learns in law school; or, maybe a little *macho* will win points with the voters. In one unforgettable instance, then President Richard Nixon pronounced Charles Manson guilty in the Sharon Tate/LaBianca murders before the jury had made their decision. The newspaper headline screamed, "Manson Guilty, Nixon Declares." Of course, Manson brought the paper into the courtroom for display to the jury. BUGLIOSI, HELTER-SKELTER, 326–27 (1974).
81. 36 Cal. 2d 615, 226 P. 2d 330 (1951); *aff'd*, 343 U.S. 181 (1952).

Government Lawyers and the Press

six-year-old girl. There was a hint of sex play, making the story even more sensational. The conviction held firm, despite the prosecutor's antics. The defendant's sanity was a crucial issue; the district attorney repeatedly affirmed the defendant's mental health to the press. Before trial, the district attorney testified before a quickly assembled gubernatorial conference and said that sex offenders such as the defendant should be disposed of in the same way as "mad dogs." The most unseemly episode, though, took place at the very beginning of the affair, when the District Attorney released details of the defendant's confession *while the interrogation was in process*. The California Supreme Court chided the him for his "play-by-play" bulletins.[82]

Sometimes a defendant and defense counsel are behind the publicity campaign,[83] which is not an easy task.[84] For, except in unusual cases—like political corruption cases where the defendant can easily arrange to fill a press conference hall[85]—it has usually been the prosecutor who has the media's ear. There are logical and practical reasons for that. "As is true throughout the criminal process, the principal source of potentially prejudicial statements...is the public official, whose words have the ring of authority and authenticity."[86]

Along with the prosecutor's supposed credibility, there is also the continuity of the prosecutor's relationship with the local reporter(s). There is usually only one district attorney and one criminal beat reporter in a town, while the defense attorney changes from defendant to defendant, from crime

82. *Id.* 36 Cal. 2d at 621, 226 P.2d at 334.
83. See TRIBE, AMERICAN CONSTITUTIONAL LAW, 406 (1978): "Indeed a defendant may have a very strong interest in gaining media attention in order to combat the stigma of a criminal indictment, expose abuses of prosecutorial *misconduct*, raise a defense fund, or discuss the political significance of the trial." *See also,* Note, *Silence Orders—Preserving Political Expression by Defendants and Their Lawyers,* HARV. C.R.-C.L. L. REV. 595 (1970-71).
84. *See* Younger, *Some Thoughts on the Defense of Publicity Cases,* 29 STAN. L. REV. 591 (1977); Ferber, *Beating Bad Press: Protecting the California Criminal Defendant from Adverse Publicity,* 10 U.S.F.L. REV. 391 (1976); *see also* an interesting analysis of how Clarence Darrow influenced public opinion during the Loeb and Leopold trial. I. STONE, CLARENCE DARROW FOR THE DEFENSE, at 178 (1941).
85. *E.g.,* Mandel v. U.S. 408 F. Supp. 673 (D.C. Md. 1975). The case was unusual in that the government sought a protective order. It is typically the other way around. "In the present case, it appears that the government is seeking the order because the defendants have ready access to the media and any frequent assertion in the press by the defendants of their innocence of the charges against them or the reporting of interviews which the defendants attack the *bona fides* of the prosecution or the motives of the prosecutors may effectively prevent unbiased consideration by a trial jury of the government's case." *Id.* at 676-77.
86. American Bar Association, *Project on Minimum Standards for Criminal Justice, Fair Trial and Free Press,* 26 (Tent. Draft Sept. 1966). Language not included in the second edition. *ABA Standards, supra* note 54.

to crime. A rapport naturally develops between reporter and prosecutor which only a rare defense attorney could hope to promote.

While there are no 'how-to' articles on prosecutorial public relations, the phenomenon is not new.[87] The prosecutor's peculiar penchant for trial-by-newspaper has even been acknowledged in modern literature:

> And the District Attorney may have been stretching the facts, too, when he mentioned cannibals. He also announced that some of the hearts were missing. The next day, the medical examiner, who should know, said the hearts were there. The so-called news became so loud that Costa's lawyers went to court about it, complained justly of publicity "fraught with images of sexual perversions, mutilations, diabolic mischief and suggestions of occultism." They asked the judge to stop the mouths of the prosecuting authorities. The judge complied. So it is quiet now—except for a few tiny leaks.[88]

c. *The Prosecutor's Legitimate Reasons for Talking to the Press*

Some of the public relations techniques which a prosecutor could use to gain personal advantage are inevitably attacked as carnival-like antics and thus unethical. There are some aspects of a prosecutor's job which *demand* the use of the media.

1. *The Duty to Satisfy the Public's Right to Know.* Feeding the public with information about prosecutions brought on their behalf and about the status of the criminal justice system is the most vital reason for a prosecutor to talk to the media.

But what is in the realm of information the public has a right to know?

---

87. *E.g.*, Griffin v. U.S., 295 F. 437 (3d Cir. 1924) (Where prosecutor boasted of having three confessions from the defendant as his "ace in the hole"); U.S. v. Leviton, 193 F. 2d 848 (2d Cir. 1951), *cert denied*, 343 946 (1952) (Where, after an interview with the prosecutor during the trial, a newspaper reported an unsubstantiated story that the defendant had tried to bribe a witness; copies of the newspaper were found in the jury room); U.S. v. Milanovich, 303 F. 2d 626, 630 (4th Cir. 1962) (Where the prosecutor, during a radio interview, talked about a defendant's past criminal record; while the statements amounted to a "gross violation of professional propriety meriting severe condemnation," a new trial was *not* called for); U.S. ex rel. Bloeth v. Denno, 313 F. 2d 364 (3d Cir. 1963) (Among other extrajudicial statements attributed to both sides, one by the prosecutor led to a *Newsday* headline which read: "Bloeth Must Go To The Chair: DA"); U.S. v. Pfingst, 477 F. 2d 177 (2d Cir. 1973) (On the eve of the defendant's bankruptcy trial, the U.S. Attorney and the County District Attorney held a joint press conference to announce a much more sensational bribery indictment of the defendant).

88. K. VONNEGUT, WAMPETERS FOMA & GRANFALLOONS, 7374 (1965).

Government Lawyers and the Press

And at what expense? Most prosecutors accept the premise that the public's right to know is limited where there is a "clear and present danger" of interfering with a defendant's right to a fair trial. The borderline is fuzzy, though, and some prosecutors have taken advantage of the doubt to promote themselves and their offices. A lively debate between Monroe Freedman and ex-New York Special Prosecutor Maurice Nadjari was especially telling.[89] Nadjari saw little problem and urged liberal disclosure. Freedman was not too receptive to what he later described as the prosecutor's "cavalier attitude":

> What one can get away with is not always what one should do, and I think this evening we're concerned with what one should do. A prosecutor can get away with using the most vicious of weapons, pre-trial publicity. The prosecutor is privileged legally to defame other citizens. The prosecutor who does so in my judgment is reprehensible. I am not suggesting that the indictment be hidden from the press. What I condemn is any prosecutor who calls press conferences, who invites in the television cameras and who proceeds before trial to smear another person's name and, for practical purposes, in a major part of the community, destroy the presumption of innocence.[90]

Later, away from Nadjari's earshot, Freedman urged disciplinary boards to look closely at such prosecutorial flamboyance.[91]

Doubtless Dean Freedman would have had little quarrel with Professor Archibald Cox's handling of the problem during the Watergate affair:

> Cox was mindful of the national concern over Watergate and of the public's right to be kept as fully informed as possible about the work of his office. "The public deserves as much accurate information as is consistent with the sometimes severe constraints placed on prosecutors as officers of the court," he said when he announced the establishment of the Public Affairs Office.[92]

California prosecutor Evelle Younger, like Nadjari, has been more generous with regard to a prosecutor's role in servicing the public's right to know. After the trial of the assassin of Senator Robert Kennedy, Younger wrote, in

---

89. Galston, *supra* note 72, at 60.
90. *Id.* at 60.
91. FREEDMAN, LAWYERS' ETHICS IN AN ADVERSARY SYSTEM, 94 (1975).
92. *Watergate Report, supra* note 64 at 227.

an article venting his frustration: "The muzzling of responsible sources of information creates a vacuum that will be filled by irresponsible sources."[93] He cited an episode from the midst of the trial of Sirhan B. Sirhan. A rumor surfaced that then Egyptian President Nasser was behind the assassination of Kennedy. The rumor was widely publicized. Because of an expansive gag order, the district attorney would only respond with a "no comment."

> Was the public entitled to responsible information that would end rumors and reduce public concern? Common sense says it was. The traditional duty of an elected official is to keep his electorate informed.... I don't suggest that the public, prior to trial, has an absolute right to know about the illicit love affairs of a medical practitioner charged with his wife's murder. But the public does have a right to know what investigations are being conducted and what rumors have been found to be untrue.[94]

Indeed the courts have had little to say with regard to prosecutor's need for leeway in satisfying the public's right to know. In one case, a criminal defendant brought a civil rights action,[95] complaining that the prosecutor's extrajudicial statements infringed on his right to a fair trial.[96] In talking about the arrest of the plaintiff, the district attorney suggested that the plaintiff had ties to the organized crime families of Trumanti and Columbo. The *New York Post* quoted him as calling the plaintiff a "vulture." While the court

---

93. Younger, *Fair Trial, Free Press and the Man in the Middle*, 56 A.B.A.J. 28 (1970).
94. *Id* at 129-130; referring to the facts of Sheppard v. Maxwell supra, 384 U.S. 333 (1966). Younger continued his fight to preserve the prosecutor's right to speak in the face of broad court-imposed rules and case-by-case judicial gag orders. See Younger v. Smith, 30 Cal. App. 3d 138, 106 Cal. Rptr. 225 (1973) (Where Younger, then the District Attorney of Los Angeles and, by the time the appeal was heard, the elected Attorney General of California, invited a contempt conviction by sending out an innocuous news release in violation of an expansive protective order. The news release outlined the testimony of a witness during the trial of a defendant in a double murder case. Younger was successful and his contempt conviction was annulled. It was a hollow victory, though, with the Court failing to address the issues in which Younger was interested).
    Years after his prosecution, Sirhan B. Sirhan remains a "victim," of prosecutorial publicity. The reversal of the California Parole Board to reduce his sentence on the basis of good behavior was attributed, at least in part, to publicity and public opinion. Los Angeles District Attorney John Van De Camp waged a vigorous war to reverse the decision and Sirhan, for his part, cited Van De Camp's ambitions as the reason for the reversal; e.g., Naugtie, *Politics Delays Possible Parole, Sirhan Claims*, WASHINGTON POST, August 28, 1981, at 1.
95. 42 U.S.C. § 1983 (1979 as amended.)
96. Martin v. Merola, 389 F. Supp 323 (S.D.N.Y. 1975); aff'd 532 F. 2d 191 (2d Cir. 1975) (*per curiam*).

was a bit taken aback by the "lurid and sensational" stories, they found that prosecutorial immunity protected the district attorney acting within the scope of his jurisdiction—which as far as they could ascertain at that point in the proceedings, the district attorney was doing in that case. As for the right to know:

> The District Attorney has wide discretion in the conduct of criminal prosecutions, and in deciding what matters to present to the grand jury. He is an important elected official of the County. His work is intimately connected with public good; diligent performance of his duties are [sic] matters of vital public interest concerning which the public has a right to know, and the media a legitimate interest in reporting, not only indictments and arrests, but their significance. Scope of the latter includes information about the extent and nature of the alleged loan sharking racket, its method of operation, the electronic means employed to detect it.... Apart from the right of the public to know it, it would seem that the prosecutor should enjoy some right of free speech so as to permit him to account through the media to the voting public for his stewardship of his important public trust.[97]

In a similar case, the Third Circuit reversed a lower court's decision to dismiss a civil rights action premised on violations of the First, Fourth, Fifth, and Sixth Amendments. In *Helstoski v. Goldstein*,[98] the U.S. Attorney was accused of "deliberate leaks" to destroy a former Congressman's political career. If true, the Court held, such actions would go beyond the scope of a prosecutor's job, and prosecutorial immunity would be extinguished.[99]

2. *Fulfilling His Duties: More Reasons for a Prosecutor to Talk to Reporters.* While no prosecutor would, at least publicly, endorse trial by newspaper, there are times when press attention can help a prosecutor fulfill his obligation to do justice. For example, in a public corruption case, publicity could be employed to compel a "target" to veer away from resting on

---

97. *Id.* 389 F. Supp. at 326. In that case, it should be noted, too, that while the circuit court affirmed in a *per curiam* decision, the two concurring judges saw the need, *when the time was ripe*, to air the question of the breadth of prosecutorial immunity as to possibly prejudicial public statements and whether it was indeed within the scope of a prosecutor's duties to discuss a criminal defendant's alleged ties to an organized crime family. 532 F. 2d at 196–97.
98. 552 F. 2d 564 (3d Cir. 1977).
99. *Id.* at 566

his Fifth Amendment rights when testifying before a grand jury. Publicity about such invocation of Fifth Amendment rights is predictably negative. Thus, publicity was helpful in the prosecution of former Governor Mandel in Maryland.[100] Also, especially with regard to public corruption and white-collar prosecutions, there is a manifest deterrent value in the heightened publicity surrounding such cases. Indeed, embarrassing headlines are considered part of the punishment in white-collar cases.[101]

Aside from trying to satisfy the public's right to know—sometimes legitimately, sometimes not—there are other occasions when the prosecutor's duties require him to take advantage of reasonable press relations. A prosecutor has a duty to ensure the smooth operation of the judicial process.[102] This might require beaming the spotlight of public attention on a particular problem or even a specific judge in a specific case. A prosecutor's attempt to harass a trial judge was discussed in *United States v. Cerilli*.[103] During a television show interview, a U.S. Attorney criticized the judge's decision on a motion. Of the attorney's actions, it was said:

> His television demonstrations could not have been for the purpose of fairly convicting the three defendants in the courtroom before a jury of twelve, but could have been only for the purpose of convicting the trial judge *ex parte* before the court of public opinion and coercing a leaning towards the prosecution's side.[104]

While the tactic obviously incensed the trial judge, he was not moved to order a dismissal of the indictment.[105]

The prosecutor also has a duty to warn the public of inherent dangers in the community. In most cases this duty can be served without any prejudice to a particular defendant, but consider a hypothetical case where a judge irresponsibly sets a dangerous criminal free with only nominal bail. To get the story printed might result in the release of information which could be prejudicial at trial and might not be allowed into evidence pursuant to the rules of evidence. The media is characteristically uninterested in sterile press releases and statements lacking in any detail. To get the word out, the prosecutor would have to give the media "good copy"—perhaps a flamboyant state-

---

100. Hurson, *supra* note 15, at 481–82.
101. See U.S. v. Bergman, 416 F. Supp. 496 (S.D.N.Y. 1976).
102. See Ethical Considerations 8-2, 8-9.
103. 428 F. Supp. 801 (W.D.Pa. 1977).
104. *Id.* at 805–06.
105. The defendant was later convicted. See 603 F. 2d (3d Cir. 1979), *cert denied*, 444 U.S. 1043 (1980).

ment depicting the defendant as an "animal." Or, it might mean releasing the defendant's past criminal record, which might not be allowed at trial. The question is a close one, requiring an on-the-spot balancing of the interests: public safety against the constitutional demand of a fair trial for the defendant.[106]

Finally, the prosecutor has to keep in mind his image and that of his office, not solely for selfish political reasons but also to serve the ends of justice, a need which was recognized by the Special Prosecution Force during the Watergate scandal:

> Even though the prosecutorial staff felt uneasy about it, the Special Prosecution Force depended heavily on public goodwill. The Special Prosecutor decided that it was important to court the press, so it was the press officer's job to keep the "hungry pirahnas" happy without giving them much to eat— not an easy task.[107]

Without the goodwill of the public, a prosecutor's efforts could be for naught:

> [A] thoughtful prosecutor wishes to develop and preserve public confidence in the work of his office and consequent public acceptance of guilty verdicts once obtained. There can be no more disastrous result from a prosecutor than to obtain a major prosecution but to fail to create public confidence in the validity of that conviction because of the manner in which it was obtained. The prosecutor must endeavor to rebut pretrial attacks against the indictment (and increasingly in these cases against the prosecutors themselves) in a clear, forceful but honorable fashion that not only succeeds in prevailing on various motions but winning the confidence of observers as well.[108]

---

106. This hypothetical became reality last summer in Philadelphia when a Judge released on $50,000 bail two men who allegedly attempted to kill an organized crime figure on the streets of the City. The two men quickly paid their bail and were not seen again for a few weeks until they surrendered themselves. Philadelphia District Attorney Edward G. Rendell excoriated the judge, and told one newspaper: "Hopefully we will find them. And hopefully we will find them alive.... We've got two very dangerous people out on the street where they shouldn't be." *Bail Boost Sought for Testa Suspects*, PHILA. DAILY NEWS, August 2, 1982 at 3, col. 1.
107. Frampton, *Some Practical and Ethical Problems of Prosecuting Public Officials*, 36 MD. L. REV. 1, 24–25 (1976).
108. Hurson, *supra* note 15, at 486–87.

ANTHONY GREEN

2. *Other Government Lawyers Join the Carnival*

Government lawyers in a civil practice do not have to face murky Free Press-Fair Trial issues to the same extent as do prosecutors. Civil litigation is much more drawn out. The chances are less likely that a civil jury will be tainted by prejudicial publicity.[109] Much of the work of the civil government lawyer never goes before a jury and is determined instead by a judge or an adjudicator who should be less susceptible to taint from publicity. Still, the government lawyer must live by the same disciplinary rules and ethical considerations which place them and government prosecutors on a different plane from their adversaries in the private sector, requiring greater restraint.[110] Hamstrung and gagged, other government lawyers face pressures similar to those the prosecutor confronts, making him want to talk to the media: ego, politics, ambition and competition. There are also analogous legitimate reasons for a civil government lawyer to talk to the press within the scope of his duties: legitimizing his role, satisfying the public's right to know, and warning the public of inherent dangers.

Consider the quandary which faced the government lawyer in *Widoff v. Disciplinary Board*.[111] The plaintiff was Pennsylvania's then consumer advocate, engaged to represent the public's position in contests with the state's public utilities. He considered keeping the public, his clients, abreast of litigation fought on their behalf involving public utilities to be a crucial element of his duties. Widoff unsuccessfully challenged the constitutionality of DR 7-107 on grounds that it unreasonably limited his First Amendment rights, hindered his ability to do his job, and was overbroad in scope. He took the action after the State Disciplinary Board cautioned him against making any statements to the press or distributing news releases in the midst of litigation or administrative deliberations. On the other side of the aisle, of course, the utilities could aggressively mount their own public opinion campaigns through their public relations departments. The lower court emphatically rejected Widoff's view that he needed to talk to the press in order to carry out his job as consumer advocate:

> He is not and cannot be merely a blind advocate for his client; he is an officer of the court with a duty to himself, to the legal community and the public to promote the integrity of the tribunal in which he is a participant and to avoid conduct that

---

109. *See* CBS, Inc. v. Young, 522 F. 2d (6th Cir. 1975) (Where order restricting speech surrounding civil litigation in the Kent State killing case was found to be constitutionally infirm). *See also Chicago Lawyers, supra* note 36.
110. *See* Ethical Consideration 7-13.
111. *Widoff, supra* note 17.

Government Lawyers and the Press

would be likely to prejudice that forum. His function requires him to represent his client in adversarial inquiries in the courtroom and not on the streets.[112]

There is certainly some support, however, for the argument that a lawyer needs to fight for his clients outside of the courtroom as well. During the impeachment trial of a judge, President James Buchanan, in his lawyering days, argued that it is "the imperative duty of an attorney to protect the interests of his clients out of court as well as in the court."[113]

Along with arguing that the rule interfered with his ability to keep his clients adequately informed, the consumer advocate in *Widoff v. Disciplinary Board* also expressed a concern over taking this "articulate spokesman" away from public debate.[114] While the cases dealt generally with private attorneys, some of the language in *Hirschkop* and the *Chicago Lawyers* case applies to the situation of a government lawyer such as a consumer advocate:

> Often actions are brought on behalf of the public interest on a private attorney general theory. Civil litigation in general exposes the need for governmental action or correction. Such revelations should not be kept from the public.[115]

> Since lawyers are considered credible in regard to pending litigation in which they are engaged and in one of the most knowledgable positions, they are a crucial source of information.[116]

> Civil actions may also involve questions of public concerns such as the safety of a particular stretch of highway, the need of government to exercise its power of eminent domain, or the means of racially segregating schools and colleges.[117]

Or, very easily, such actions may involve the petition of a utility for a substantial rate increase. The voice of someone like a government consumer advocate is vital to such public debate, if not a catalyst for it.

It is also vital that a government lawyer have enough free rein to inform his public that he is available to help them. Probably the most effective

112. *Id.* 54 Pa. Commw. Ct. at 131, 420 A. 2d at 44.
113. Stansbury, *Report of the Trial of James H. Peck*, 455 (1833); cited in L. TRIBE, *supra* note 23, at 628.
114. Brief for appellant, at 34.
115. Chicago Lawyers, *supra* note 36, at 258.
116. *Id.* at 258
117. Hirschkop, *supra* note 47, at 373.

means of demonstrating that the agency is meeting its mandate is to publicize actions presently in litigation. Such publicity proclaims, "Here I am. I did it for him. I can do it for you." Recent developments seem to permit this kind of self-promotion by an attorney acting on behalf of the public. With regard to disciplinary rules concerning the solicitation of business, a wider scope is allowed for an attorney working for the public good than for a private attorney. Such was the distinction drawn in cases decided back-to-back by the Supreme Court.[118]

IV. CONCLUSION

The issue is substantial. Two Circuit Courts of Appeals and the New York Court of Appeals have questioned the viability of the prevailing rule of professional responsibility, at least in part. Also, the ABA is still wrestling over a total revision of the current code of ethics, including the issue of press/lawyer relations.

Hopefully, the courts and the Bar will come to grips with the issue with the reality of the situation in mind: that lawyers do and always will talk to reporters; that the marriage is a healthy one for the many reasons cited in this article and indeed it should remain so. Government lawyers have been some of this country's most effective and articulate spokespeople and social warriors. No broad rule should mute that voice.

A lawyer charged with the duty of fighting for the consumer, such as a legislatively created consumer advocate, should not be muzzled by a broad disciplinary rule as in the *Widoff* case. In that case, the consumer advocate should have been allowed to argue his position as vociferously as did the utility companies. He also should have been allowed to keep his clients, the consumers of his state, adequately informed through the media. The chances that civil litigation, a bench trial, or an adjudicatory hearing would be swayed by a few news stories are slight. Our judges and adjudicators are, one hopes, made of stronger stuff.

No lawyer should seek to win his battles in the headlines and in front of microphones. "Legal trials are not like elections, to be won through the use

---

118. *In re* Primus, 436 U.S. 412 (1978) (Involving an ACLU attorney who, at a public gathering, told a group of women of their legal rights in light of a state law requiring sterilization before the receipt of further public assistance moneys); Ohralik v. Ohio State Bar Association, 436 U.S. 447 (1978) (Involving a private attorney who personally solicited auto accident victims in search of litigation and a fee). *See also* ABA Comm. on Professional Ethics, Opinions, Informal Opinion No. 334 (1974) (Where it was implied that gaining publicity for a community legal services program was vital to its role of providing legal services to the public).

Government Lawyers and the Press

of the meeting hall, the radio, and the newspaper."[119] It is only suggested that government lawyers need to keep their clients informed as to litigation brought on their behalf, that the public's right to know about such litigation is precious, and that government lawyers should be allowed to participate in public debate about an issue.

On the other hand, the balancing process must consider the chances of the media's influencing a criminal jury trial. *Sheppard*-type carnivals must be avoided. There, the more concrete "clear and present danger" test will suffice. The "reasonably likely" test, in comparison, is too broad, limiting too much speech. The restriction on speech should be no greater than necessary to accomplish the legitimate goal of the government.[120] In extraordinary situations, whether they be criminal or civil, remedial steps can be taken: continuances, protectice or so-called gag orders[121] or change of venue. Similarly, the Justice Department must vigilantly protect against the type of leaks which plagued the ABSCAM affair. Stringent regulations, complete with tough punishment for loose lipped government attorneys, must remain intact. While the standard must limit the prosecutor's seeking to enrich himself personally or politically, it must also leave the prosecutor enough room to do his duty and talk to his public.

To completely quiet the voice of the government lawyer, though, would be a mistake. Sometimes he or she is the lone soldier of a cause or position and thus a vital participant in this nation's daily debate—which must continue.

119. Bridges v. California, 314 U.S. 252, 271 (1941).
120. Procunier v. California, 416 U.S. 396, 413 (1974).
121. The Court in Nebraska Press Association v. Stuart 427 U.S. 539, 570 (1976), voided a gag order in that case but allowed that in an extraordinary case, such orders would be valid.

JACK A. GOTTSCHALK

"Consistent with Security"... A History of American Military Press Censorship

Jack A. Gottschalk is with the New Jersey law firm of Morahan & Coppola. He is a former Assistant Essex County (N.J.) Prosecutor, a former Captain U.S.A.R. and Field Press Censor. He is an adjunct professor at Fairleigh Dickinson University.

In 1649 Parliament passed a law permitting the Secretary of War to license all army news. If no other purpose was served by the act, it was a precedent for censorship in the American colonies that officially began on May 13, 1725, when a Massachusetts Order-In-Council required that:

> The printers of the newspapers in Boston be ordered upon their peril not to insert in their prints anything of the public affairs of this province relative to the war without the order of the government.[1]

Given these actions, it is surprising that no censorship occurred during the Revolution, a point recalled by Thomas Jefferson in an 1813 letter where he wrote:

> The first misfortune of the Revolutionary War induced a motion to suppress or garble the account of it. It was rejected with indignation.[2]

For whatever reason, although government-media relations in the nation's

---

1. JAMES RUSSELL WIGGINS, FREEDOM OR SECRECY, 94 (New York: Oxford University Press, 1964).
2. Ibid., 94–95.

early years were rocky (*e.g.*, the *Philadelphia General Advertiser's* publication of the 1795 peace treaty with England was the "Pentagon Papers" incident of the time), pure military censorship apparently did not occur during the War of 1812, or during the Mexican War (1846–1848), the last American conflict where the idea of press censorship was not entertained, possibly because the war came too soon for the telegraph system.

By 1856, however, when Great Britain was fighting in the Crimea, telegraph communication had given war reporting unprecedented speed and, as Phillip Knightley relates in *The First Casualty*, military press censorship came with it.[3] When the American Civil War began in 1861, both sides employed censorship widely, if not well.

Southern newspapers had more difficulties than did Northern ones. A lack of trained journalists, chronic paper shortages, and constant efforts to satisfy the Confederate government's stringent censorship created an enormous burden.[4] But, while Southern censorship was rigid, it was, at least, consistent—a trait badly lacking in the North where censorship policy shifted on a daily basis.

Early in the war the Union government suggested a voluntary, self-imposed newspaper censorship, but the idea went largely unheeded primarily because no government censorship guidelines were provided. The effort at voluntary censorship having failed, the government subsequently moved to enforce a compulsory system that essentially consisted of after-the-fact (of publication) suspension of offending newspapers and close supervision of what was transmitted by the press over the far-flung system of telegraph lines.

Military actions against the press were numerous in the North and included the cases of the *New York Journal of Commerce* and the *New York World*. Both newspapers were suspended from publication for two days in 1864 because they published what turned out to be a forged letter—purportedly written by President Lincoln—that called for a 400,000-man draft in that year.[5] On other occasions, several publishers were denied postal privileges by the government as a punishment for censorship violations, and General Ambrose Burnside shut down the *Chicago Times* for three days in 1864 because of its generally anti-administration editorial views. The suspension was lifted only after Lincoln countermanded Burnside's closing order.[6]

Censorship also generated among the media a distrust of government because of the use of censorship to stop the release of unfavorable news about

---

3. PHILLIP KNIGHTLEY, THE FIRST CASUALTY 16 (New York: Harcourt Brace Jovanovich, 1975).
4. JOHN HOHENBERG, FREE PRESS/FREE PEOPLE, 122–23 (New York: Columbia University Press, 1971).
5. *Ibid.*, 121.
6. *Ibid.*, 121–122.

American Military Press Censorship

command cowardice and bad judgment, a distrust not eased by the military's antipress attitudes. Early in 1862, for example, General Henry W. Halleck flatly refused to allow newspaper correspondents anywhere in his zone of command.[7] Halleck was not unique. General William T. Sherman consistently kept reporters at a distance. Sherman based much of his opposition to the press on security considerations. In his opinion, the Confederate government obtained more intelligence from Northern newspapers than from its espionage efforts, a point that cannot be disregarded after noting the log entry written by Captain William Semmes, commander of the *C.S.S. Alabama*, a famous Confederate commerce raider. After capturing the *S.S. Manchester*, bound for Liverpool from New York, and aboard which Semmes found a number of Northern newspapers, he wrote:

> "I learned from them [the newspapers] where all the enemy's gunboats were, and what they were doing.... Perhaps this was the only war in which the newspapers ever explained, beforehand, all the movements of armies and fleets to the enemy...."[8]

Despite harassment and obstruction from Burnside, Halleck, Sherman, and others, correspondents continued to report, and newspapers continued to print the news—both good and bad. *The New York Times* summed up the issue during the war by noting:

> More harm would be done to the Union by the expulsion of correspondents than those correspondents now do by occasional exposures of military blunders, imbecilities, peccadilloes, corruption, drunkenness, and knavery, or by their occasional failure to puff every functionary as much as he thinks he deserves.[9]

By April 1898, when William Randolph Hearst proudly took credit for war with Spain, better transportation enabled correspondents to reach places in days rather than weeks, and stories could be filed quickly because of ever faster communications. These journalistic capabilities created military censorship problems that were not properly addressed in the Spanish-American War, probably because of its brevity.

As in the Civil War, security was a problem. Correspondents aboard war-

---

7. *Ibid.*, 123.
8. JOURNALIST 3 & 2, RATE TRAINING MANUAL, NAVTRA 10294-C, Naval Training Command at 16–17 (Washington, D.C.,: U.S. Government Printing Office, 1973).
9. HOHENBERG, FREE PRESS/FREE PEOPLE, 123–124.

JACK A. GOTTSCHALK

ships during the early days of the war freely cabled news about American ship movements and combat intentions, news that was released to Madrid as soon as it appeared in the daily newspapers. Clearly, some censorship was necessary and the result was the formation of naval censorship units that were established at Key West, Florida, Washington, D.C., and in seven cable offices in New York City.[10] The nominal head of military censorship in New York by mid-summer of 1898 was Grant Squires, a former *New York Tribune* reporter who, as a civilian official, served in a liaison role between the military and news organizations. The Navy retained complete censorship control.

American naval censorship was imposed in 1914 at Vera Cruz following U.S. intervention there,[11] but no military censorship was used during the U.S. Army's expedition against the Mexican bandit-revolutionary, Pancho Villa, in 1916.

Once America entered the First World War in 1917, George Creel, a former newspaper editor (and a confidante of President Woodrow Wilson), was named to head the Committee on Public Information, the nation's newly formed propaganda and censorship agency headquartered on Jackson Place in Washington, D.C. Creel's management of domestic news censorship was based on a set of regulations prepared by the State, War, and Navy Departments before the United States entered the war.[12] These regulations, which the press voluntarily accepted, prohibited publication of such things as troop movements in the United States, ship sailings, and the identification of units being sent overseas.

Against the patriotic backdrop of the Creel Committee's activities appeared the Espionage Act of 1917 and the Sedition Act of 1918. The former was so broad that for the press not to have violated some portion of it would have been miraculous. Under its provisions, publishing any information that could be remotely considered as aiding the enemy or interfering with American military operations or war production was punishable by as much as twenty years in prison and a $10,000 fine.[13] And under the terms of the Sedition Act of 1918, any criticism of the conduct or actions of the American government or its military forces, including negative remarks about the flag, military uniforms, etc., could be similarly punished.[14]

Meanwhile, the chief American press censor serving in France with the American Expeditionary Force (AEF) was a former *New York Herald* reporter and Associated Press correspondent named Frederick Palmer, who had been personally recruited by General Pershing and directly

10. JOURNALIST 3 & 2, RATE TRAINING MANUAL, 15.
11. WIGGINS, FREEDOM OR SECRECY, 95.
12. *Ibid.*
13. HOHENBERG, FREE PRESS/FREE PEOPLE, 182–183.
14. *Ibid.*

commissioned as a major assigned to public relations.[15] Palmer was an excellent reporter, but his inability to handle the censorship problem quickly became clear. The correspondents accused him of not passing sufficient information, while the Army complained that he was not censoring enough.[16]

Palmer was soon replaced by a committee composed of ex-journalists, who had been commissioned as reserve officers for public relations duties, and Regular Army officers. The combination was chaotic and, in retrospect, it is amazing that only five journalists out of approximately sixty correspondents assigned to cover the war lost their AEF press credentials.[17] The war nevertheless ended with a major censorship incident, the "False Armistice" story.

The military censors passed for publication a United Press dispatch filed by Roy Howard announcing the armistice a full four days before the real one was actually signed. Howard had filed his story based on information given to him by a reliable source, an American admiral at Brest, France. But, as a result of that story, the censors blacked out contact between the United Press in New York and Howard in France for three hours, thus stopping any possibility of correction, addition, or explanation.[18] Interestingly, the end of the Second World War in Europe would involve another censorship blackout.

When war came to America in December 1941, some government censorship was already in operation. On December 31, 1940, Secretary of the Navy Knox formally requested the media to stop publishing any data about certain subjects (new ships, troop movements, etc.) without specific naval authorization; and in September 1941, both the Army and Navy announced that press censorship plans had been formulated to control information flowing from the United States in the event of a national emergency.

While the Roosevelt administration had formulated tentative censorship plans involving various executive departments and agencies including the Federal Bureau of Investigation and Federal Communications Commission, there was no central press censorship authority.

Pearl Harbor produced the jolt necessary for government action. On December 8, F.B.I. Director J. Edgar Hoover was given temporary powers to direct all news censorship and to control all other telecommunications traffic in and out of the United States. Simultaneously, President Roosevelt requested that the American news media voluntarily respect the Department of the Navy's censorship guidelines published a year earlier. Only eight days later, Roosevelt appointed Byron Price as Director of Censorship, relieving Hoover

---

15. KNIGHTLEY, FIRST CASUALTY 124.
16. HOHENBERG, FREE PRESS/FREE PEOPLE, 184.
17. *Ibid.*
18. KENT COOPER, THE RIGHT TO KNOW, 215–16 (New York: Farrar, Strauss & Cudahy, 1955).

of that responsibility; and on December 18, 1941, pursuant to the War Powers Act, the President created the Office of Censorship with Price as its chief.

Since the Office of Censorship could only issue guidance relevant to domestic news censorship, it relied on the power of persuasion linked to a voluntary news censorship system that was worked out with the full cooperation of the media. The product of these labors was the *Code of Wartime Practices*, which became effective January 15, 1942.

The nation was hungry for war news and looked anxiously toward Washington, particularly during the grim, early days of the conflict. The Office of War Information (O.W.I.), created in June 1942 as America's propaganda agency, stood between the government and the press and was bound to feel severe stings of criticism from all quarters. Elmer Davis, the highly respected newsman and Director of the O.W.I., was powerless to force government agencies (including the military) to supply more accurate and timely non-sensitive information to the public, a situation that made relations between the O.W.I. and the media extremely tense. And it was military news censorship that caused many of the problems.[19]

The only theater in which American forces were actually engaged early in the war was the Pacific. There, a combination of MacArthur's almost dictatorial censorship[20] and the overtly antipress attitudes of Chief of Naval Operations Admiral Ernest J. King[21] made attempts at news coverage difficult at best.

MacArthur's restrictive news media policy (*e.g.*, multiple censorship of correspondent's copy before release)[22] and his use of censorship for "image building"[23] were matched by the Navy's policy of delaying the news and then compounding the belated release by linking bad news with stories of combat success. While MacArthur got away with it, the Navy began suffering a loss of credibility.[24] The incidents of news management were not insignificant ones—*e.g.*, news of the American naval defeat off Savo Island was released almost nine weeks after the battle.[25]

The press, quick to recognize the government's heavy-handedness and suspicious that a lack of candor could mean a cover-up of military incompetence, bitterly complained of the Navy's attitude, particularly since the voluntary censorship program aided the Navy's attempts to manage the news. It fell to Davis to strike the delicate balance between picturing America's war

19. Lloyd J. Graybar, *Admiral King's Toughest Battle*, NAVAL WAR COL. REV., 40–43 (February 1979).
20. KNIGHTLEY, FIRST CASUALTY, 281–282.
21. Graybar, *Admiral King's Toughest Battle*, 39.
22. KNIGHTLEY, FIRST CASUALTY, 281.
23. *Ibid.*, 281–282.
24. Graybar, *Admiral King's Toughest Battle*, 40.
25. *Ibid.*, 40–41.

American Military Press Censorship

efforts in the best possible light while retaining the government's credibility with both press and public. Only after Davis successfully appealed to King (through Hanson Baldwin of *The New York Times*) did the Navy release news rapidly while remaining within reasonable security limits.[26] Davis's burden was, of course, not eased when early in 1942 Stanley Johnston, a *Chicago Tribune* correspondent who had learned of the Navy's ability to break the secret Japanese naval codes, inadvertently reported the names of Japanese ships involved in the Midway battle. When these names appeared in the newspaper the immediate fear was that the Japanese would know that their codes had been compromised. The fears were unfounded but, in the tenor of the times, the government referred the matter to a federal grand jury which refused to indict anyone concerned.[27]

U.S. naval censorship in the Pacific continued to remain rigidly effective throughout the war. It was (and still is, as shown by the Falkland Islands campaign) far easier to censor news correspondents aboard warships. They are limited in their movement, contacts, and communications, and can only report what they are told by a command that frequently does not have the full story itself.

Despite MacArthur, the Army recognized that press censorship in Europe would require a different approach, and a special observer group had been sent to England in late 1941 to study recent British experience and to reach agreement with the British on a censorship policy that would become effective once U.S. forces entered the European theater. By the time the first American troops arrived in the United Kingdom in January 1942, the British and American representatives had completed their work, and joint censorship was a reality.

Four American officers initially constituted the entire U.S. military press censorship group, which was housed with British censorship at the Ministry of Information. By October 1942, when some officers were transferred to provide censorship support for Operation TORCH (the code name for the invasion of North Africa), there were ten officers and one enlisted man assigned to the London censorship office of the American military forces.

Taken in chronological order, American censorship of large-scale ground actions began with TORCH. To accomplish its censorship mission, the joint American-British military command assigned four censorship teams composed of both U.S. and British officers to the operation. One team was assigned to each of the three invading task forces, and one additional team was stationed at the Gibraltar headquarters.[28]

26. *Ibid.*, 42.
27. *Ibid.*, 40.
28. PRESS CENSORSHIP IN THE EUROPEAN THEATRE OF OPERATIONS, 1942–1945 at 15 (Lodi, N.J.: 201st Field Press Censorship Detachment, USAR, reprint of SHAEF report, 1975).

JACK A. GOTTSCHALK

Censors went ashore with the landing troops, a necessity because accredited combat correspondents were also with the first assault waves and their news submissions had to be moved for censorship processing as quickly as possible.

The basic U.S. censorship guide during TORCH and the subsequent North African campaign was the previously noted *Code of Wartime Practices* as revised in June 1942 with supplements provided by the Office of Censorship and by the commanding officers of the various military theaters of operation.[29] Based on the procedures established in the *Code*, all new material was supplied in duplicate, first to public relations and then to the censors, a task that aggravated the media more than the censorship itself, particularly since the only alleged function of the military's public relations personnel was to transmit the copy once censorship had passed it for publication.[30]

In addition to delay, other problems resulted from the sheer volume of news material and the lack of a sufficient military transmission capability to move the censored news to London and then to the rest of the world. But even when the organizational and transmission difficulties were finally remedied, news was unreasonably held up, often for a week in the censorship process, at Gibraltar, later in Algiers, and then again in London.[31] Meanwhile, the correspondents noted that official press releases and communiqués were processed through censorship immediately and reached the homefront reading audience before the news reports.

But the single biggest problem to affect media-military relations in North Africa was the American use of field press censorship to block the release of political news. This "policy" censorship[32] arose because of the turmoil caused by French colonial policy combined with violent antagonisms involving the Free French and the Vichy leadership.

The American State Department was opposed to the French government-in-exile headed by Charles DeGaulle. The U.S. supported General Henri Giraud, who, it was felt, would be easier to handle than DeGaulle in working with the Allies to stabilize North Africa. When it appeared that Giraud was not reliable, the United States began secret negotiations with pro-German Admiral Darlan, who controlled the French armed forces in North Africa. On December 24, 1942, Darlan was assassinated.

Meanwhile both the American and British news media had become increasingly vocal about North African events. Consequently, top U.S. military and diplomatic officials felt the urge to impose censorship on all political news from North Africa until the situation stabilized. The military

29. *Ibid.*
30. *Ibid.*, 16.
31. *Ibid.*, 16–17.
32. Cooper, Right to Know, 201–202.

American Military Press Censorship

view was that the uncertain political situation would encourage pro-German underground movements, and the diplomats argued that a news blackout would permit a political arrangement to be negotiated without concurrent public speculation. Thus the stage was set for Eisenhower to impose a strictly political censorship (which he later excused) that endured for six weeks, during which time the necessary agreements were reached between Giraud and DeGaulle.[33]

In Europe, because of the lessons learned from North Africa, censorship training was emphasized and officers specially trained for censorship were assigned.[34] Gradually, along with the training of personnel, an updated censorship doctrine was developed, its basic thrust being that security was the prime news censorship consideration.

Organizational problems were also addressed as D-Day grew closer. A Joint Press Censorship Group composed of officers from the British, Canadian, and American forces was formed,[35] and an indoctrination course was held at the Chancellor's Hall in the Ministry of Information from April 10 to 21, 1944. Media and military notables, such as Edward R. Murrow, Brigadier General David Sarnoff and General Walter Bedell Smith, were in attendance.[36]

At these meetings four primary objectives were chosen as the foundation of Allied press censorship operations: (1) security, (2) speed, (3) consistency, (4) censorship guidance and assistance to war correspondents.[37] On April 25, 1944, Operational Memorandum Number 27 was issued by Supreme Headquarters, Allied Expeditionary Force, which set forth the governing principle for the employment of field press censorship: "...That the minimum amount of information will be withheld from the public consistent with security."[38]

There were over five hundred accredited combat correspondents in England by D-Day. Many went into France with the first landings. Others were dropped with the paratroopers behind German lines on the night of June 5, and still others were in bombers above the invasion or aboard the naval armada that bombarded the coast.

Submissions from bridgeheads established ashore reached censorship units located just behind the lines by courier, radio, and carrier pigeon. And censorship units at various levels had qualified linguists available to handle news copy that arrived in a dozen languages.[39] Three censorship teams, each including two Army, one Navy, and an Air Force officer, accompanied the

33. DWIGHT D. EISENHOWER, CRUSADE IN EUROPE, 153–54 (New York: Doubleday & Co., Inc., 1948; Garden City Books Edition, 1952).
34. PRESS CENSORSHIP, 37.
35. *Ibid.*, 43.
36. *Ibid.*, 46–50.
37. *Ibid.*, 55.
38. *Ibid.*
39. *Ibid.*, 60.

forces ashore on D-Day. Two teams were assigned to the U.S. forces and one to the British. A fourth team joined British forces several days after the initial assault on the beaches. Naval censorship was accomplished on the two command vessels of the invasion fleet.[40]

The amount of copy submitted in the first days of the invasion was staggering. Upwards of 700,000 words were filed in color or feature copy alone. And overseas material arriving from France once the forces were ashore did not really begin to hit the Ministry of Information offices until almost forty-eight hours after the invasion began.[41]

On July 25, 1944, prior to the liberation of the French capital city, a major test of censorship practices occurred. During the opening phases of the attack on a German strongpoint at St. Lo, American ground troops were bombed in error by U.S. planes. One of the many fatalities was Lieutenant General Lesley J. McNair, and one of the first stories processed by censorship was written by Ernie Pyle, who had personally witnessed the incident.[42] There was no attempt to cover the error, and thus censorship remained true to the policy stated before the invasion—that security was the only basis for censorship.

In August, Allied armies entered Paris and a new censorship headquarters was quickly established on the second floor of the Hotel Scribe,[43] although London remained the primary censorship clearinghouse for several weeks until Paris was completely secured. When that task was finally accomplished, London was officially designated as the "rear" censorship headquarters and Paris as the "main," an arrangement that continued for the rest of the European war.[44]

The closing days of European action saw the greatest failure of military press censorship operations when measured against the much heralded censorship principles. The incident took place on April 11, 1945, at Ninth U.S. Army headquarters. American troops assigned to Combat Command B of the Second Armored Division had reached the western bank of the Elbe River. They were ready to move toward Berlin when they were abruptly halted by Ninth Army's commander, Lieutenant General William Simpson.

Shortly after returning to his headquarters, Simpson held a news conference but took the unusual step of ordering his press censor to stop any reports of what he was about to tell the media.[45] The general then told the correspondents that, acting under orders from Eisenhower as relayed by Omar Bradley, his units were not moving on to Berlin. Policy censorship

40. *Ibid.*, 61.
41. *Ibid.*, 65.
42. Hohenberg, Free Press/Free People, 264.
43. Press Censorship, 81.
44. *Ibid.*, 84.
45. Cooper, Right to Know, 203–206.

under the guise of military security was thus employed as it would be a month later with the German surrender.

In his post-war writings, Eisenhower noted that:

> Under the terms of the surrender document the heads of the German armed services were required to appear in Berlin on May 9 to sign a ratification in the Russian headquarters. The second ceremony was, as we understood it, to symbolize the unity of the Western Allies and the Soviets, to give notice to the Germans and to the world that the surrender was made to all, not merely to the Western Allies. For this reason we were directed to withhold news of the first signing until the second could be accomplished.[46]

One American reporter, Edward Kennedy of the Associated Press, felt that there was a definite need to release the surrender news to a war-weary world. Kennedy avoided censorship by calling his story to London from SHAEF headquarters in Paris. London censorship passed the surrender news and the Associated Press in New York put it on the wire.[47]

After the Kennedy story was published, SHAEF suspended all Associated Press coverage in Europe for eight hours—and Kennedy was fired.[48]

The introduction of American military power onto the Korean peninsula in June 1950 caught the nation and its media off balance. Television was still in its infancy, but print, radio, and newsreel correspondents (eventually numbering over three hundred) arrived with the troops, often embarking from the same port—Tokyo. At first, press censorship was completely voluntary, a sort of gentlemen's agreement between the military and the press. This arrangement lasted from June 1950 until late December of that year when field press censorship was placed in effect.

It has been argued that the voluntary system failed because the competitive nature of the news business forced correspondents to commit serious security violations. Some of the military complaints during the voluntary censorship period were that news representatives, after being trusted by briefing officers, had prematurely announced the arrival of certain major American units in Korea, tactical troop movements, the initial recovery of American prisoners from the Chinese, and the use of the F-86 Sabrejet fighter for the first time in combat.[49] But the initial media restrictions were not solely based on security, and the guidelines were vague. When stories about panic,

46. EISENHOWER, CRUSADE IN EUROPE, 472.
47. COOPER, CRUSADE IN EUROPE, 211–212, 219.
48. *Ibid.*, 216, 221, 222–224, 231–233.
49. MELVIN B. VOORHEES, KOREAN TALES, 104 (New York: Simon and Schuster, 1952).

inferior U.S. equipment, and South Korean civil corruption were published, censorship became inevitable.

Once censorship headquarters was established at Eighth Army, the previous practice (under the voluntary system) of having correspondents file their copy and photos with Tokyo either by military communications channels or via cable directly to the United States was stopped. All news material, including film, had to be passed by the Eighth Army's censors. The Air Force followed the Army's lead, operating through a security division in its Korean public information office. Both the Army and Air Force censorship organizations were headed by lieutenant colonels.[50]

It did not take long for jurisdictional problems to develop. On January 11, 1951, Far East Command in Tokyo, which had been part of the censorship program along with Eighth Army, bowed out of the picture, leaving censorship completely to field army control. Apparently, during the ensuing sixty days, the field army did not censor enough, because on March 13, Tokyo headquarters announced that it was going to review all news material passed in the field for publication. This "multiple censorship" concept, which had been carefully avoided (except for MacArthur's South Pacific Theater) during the Second World War, remained in effect until Far East Command finally relieved the Eighth Army completely of its censorship duties in the spring of 1951.[51]

The final organizational structure of Korean military press censorship was based on a letter of instructions issued by Far East Command on January 6, 1953. In that document, a Joint Field Press Censorship Group (JFPCG), Far East Command (composed of military press censorship detachments of the Army, Navy, and Air Force) was created. The head of the group (the Chief Field Press Censor) was responsible to the Public Information Officer of the Far East Command and was assisted by deputy chief censors representing the Army, Navy, and Air Force. The chief censor's duties included supervision and implementation of field press censorship with regard to all United Nations and Far East Commands.[52] In order to carry out its function, the Joint Field Press Censorship Group stationed detachments at Far East Command, Eighth Army and Fifth Air Force Headquarters and at the Panmunjom armistice negotiation site.

Some examples of political censorship used in Korea were noted by Robert C. Miller, who wrote in the *Nieman Reports* that the news media were not permitted to:

50. FIELD PRESS CENSORSHIP, FM 45–25, OPNAVINST 5530.5, AFM 190–5, at 58 (Washington, D.C.: Departments of the Army, Navy, and Air Force, 1954).
51. VOORHEES, KOREAN TALES, 112–113.
52. FIELD PRESS CENSORSHIP, 45–50.

American Military Press Censorship

...mention the actions of South Korean police who blackmailed innocent farmers, threatening to arrest them as Reds unless they paid off. Hundreds fled into the mountains and joined guerrilla units because of police blackmailing tactics, but stories concerning this were killed....[53]

The Korean censorship was so political in tone and so rigidly enforced that deliberate covert efforts were made by some reporters to avoid it. In the book *Korean Tales*, Melvin B. Voorhees, who as a lieutenant colonel headed the Eighth Army's censorship operation, recalled how correspondents employed a technique called the "Twenty Questions Trick" (a telephone code used between Korea and Tokyo, where the news media bureau offices were located) to get past censorship.[54]

In July 1953 the armistice ending the Korean War was signed. The Army created a field press censorship capability in the reserve even before the conflict was over. At the Department of Defense level, the responsibility for supervising military press censorship was given to the Assistant Secretary of Defense for Public Affairs, and in August 1954 the Department of Defense published a joint service manual entitled *Field Press Censorship* with the following designations:

> Department of the Army Field Manual FM 45-25
> Department of the Navy OPNAV INSTRUCTION 5530-5
> Department of the Air Force Manual AFM 190-5

This joint service manual was to be the standard procedural document for censorship organization and operations should the military again be required to implement a media security program.

During this period each of the service departments moved ahead independently with information security planning. In the Air Force, an Office of Information, reporting directly to the Secretary of the Air Force, was designated as the top-level public relations authority, with censorship being accorded a minor role. The Navy's information program was set up within the Department of the Navy's Office of Information and headed by the Chief of Information, who was also the public affairs adviser to the Chief of Naval Operations. Neither the Air Force nor the Navy maintained a manned press censorship organization within their respective active or reserve components.

---

53. PAUL BLANSHARD, THE RIGHT TO READ, 120–21 (Boston: The Beacon Press, 1955).
54. VOORHEES, KOREAN TALES, 106–107.

JACK A. GOTTSCHALK

Public information planning and organization had been refined (with the Army having the only media censorship capability) by the time of the Cuban Missile Crisis in October 1962. Within an hour of President Kennedy's October 22 address to the nation in which he announced the presence of Soviet missiles in Cuba, the Army's field press censorship detachments were partially and quietly mobilized.[55]

In terms of manpower, these units included less than three hundred officers and men. Of that number, only five officers were requested to report for immediate active duty at Headquarters, Continental Army Command (CONARC), located at Fortress Monroe, Virginia. While all members of the units unquestionably would have been called to duty had hostile action occurred, only these five officers were initially contacted. Three of them remained on duty for the three days of the crisis and two stayed with CONARC for five weeks.[56]

The decision to alert these units was based on the determination of the Joint Chiefs of Staff that the Army be ordered to prepare for possible field press censorship in the southeastern United States. A headquarters had to be organized for this purpose together with field press censorship teams of sufficient size to meet the needs of an estimated two hundred fifty correspondents. In the final analysis, contingency plans were developed that envisioned only the southern half of Florida as an active combat area.[57]

Planning for this potential censorship task included the designation of Orlando, Florida, as the location for processing and censoring of still news photos, with motion picture and television film to be flown to the Department of Defense in Washington, D.C., for censorship action. All news copy submissions were to be handled by field press censorship teams located within the combat area. The reserve officers were ordered to prepare censorship plans for use by the Army of the Atlantic (ARLANT) and the air and naval forces in the area (CINCLANT).[58] Had these plans been used, military press censorship would have become a reality on American soil for the first time since the Civil War. The crisis ended, of course, and the censorship planning involved with it became a largely unknown part of history.

Almost as soon as the United States entered the Vietnam War on a massive scale in August 1964, media censorship for purposes of military security became a Pentagon planning consideration. Early in the war, the Army placed a colonel from its reserve field press censorship detachments on active duty and sent him to South Vietnam for the purpose of assessing the situation and reporting on the feasibility of implementing field press

55. Carl M. Justice, former Commanding Officer, 211th Field Press Censorship Detachment, USAR, Conversation with author, November 10, 1981.
56. Ibid.
57. Ibid.
58. Ibid.

American Military Press Censorship

censorship. Concurrently, discussions on the subject were held between the Department of Defense and General William Westmoreland, commander of U.S. forces in Vietnam.

Barry Zorthian, who later became a senior member of Time, Inc., served in Vietnam as director of the Joint United States Public Affairs Office (JUSPAO) and as minister-counsellor for information in the American embassy in Saigon. He has revealed that censorship was often considered in Vietnam and that the idea was rejected each time for practical reasons.[59] Zorthian is on record as having been personally opposed to media censorship there, although he acknowledges that his views may have represented the minority position.[60]

Zorthian's views seem justified by the fact that the press voluntarily observed the military security rules that were established even though the conflict was unpopular with the media and the public. In over four and one-half years and in dealing with approximately two thousand news media representatives, only six security violations were considered by the military to be serious enough to involve the loss of Department of Defense accreditation, Zorthian has noted.[61]

Obviously, given the government's desire for censorship as compared to its repeated decisions not to employ it, there had to be some very cogent reasons for the lack of implementation. It is submitted that these reasons were political and logistical.

During the Vietnam War, television film was shot, processed, and shown to American audiences within twenty-four hours. Even if all combat film had been censored by the military, the war—which was being fought without a clear purpose or goal—would eventually have become a target of severe public criticism. Censorship would simply have delayed an inevitable reaction.

In addition, the military did not control the movements of civilians in South Vietnam. Each day, airliners landed and took off from Saigon airport, and anyone with the desire (and money) could hire a private plane to fly over the country. Unless all movement and means of transportation had been stringently controlled by the military (as in the Second World War), nothing could have prevented news correspondents from going anywhere in South Vietnam on their own. Similarly, any media representative with a news story stopped by censors (had censorship been in effect) could have boarded a civilian plane for the United States (or any other place) and filed the story regardless of censorship. As long as the reporter was no longer individually subject to military jurisdiction, the only possible punishment was the loss of Department of Defense press accreditation.

59. Barry Zorthian, *The Dimension of Communication,* PERSPECTIVES IN DEFENSE MANAGEMENT, Industrial College of the Armed Forces, 5–6 (February 1969).
60. *Ibid.*, 5.
61. *Ibid.*, 4.

JACK A. GOTTSCHALK

In June 1971 the Department of Defense moved to disassociate itself with the word "censorship" when it issued Directive 5230.7 wherein the Pentagon replaced "censorship" with the less provocative term "Wartime Information Security Program" or "WISP." The directive defined both the National Wartime Information Security Program and the Field Press Wartime Information Security Program as follows:

> *National WISP.* The control and examination of communications entering, leaving, transiting, or touching the borders of the United States, and the voluntary withholding from publication by the domestic public media industries of military and other information which should not be released in the interest of the safety and defense of the United States and its Allies.

> *Field Press WISP.* The security review of news material subject to the jurisdiction of the Armed Forces of the United States, including all information or material intended for dissemination to the public.[62]

The document provided for the implementation of National WISP, *i.e.*, censorship, through the National Censorship Agreement entered into on October 1, 1963, between the Department of Defense and the Office of Emergency Planning (now the Federal Emergency Management Agency). Under its provisions, in any national emergency where domestic censorship was invoked, an Office of National WISP (similar to the Office of Censorship during the Second World War) would be activated. Initial personnel for this censorship organization would be provided by the Department of Defense and subsequently augmented by members of the National Defense Executive Reserve (NDER), civilian public information executives pre-assigned to perform the public media censorship task.[63]

In a letter dated May 15, 1978, from the Office of the General Counsel, Department of Defense, to William M. Nichols, General Counsel, Office of Management and Budget, the reasons were set forth for a modification of Executive Order 11490. Executive Order 11490, which had gone into effect on October 28, 1969, assigned the Department of Defense responsibilities under the terms of the National Censorship Agreement.[64] According to the letter, the House Committee on Government Operations heard testimony

---

62. Arthur J. Simpson, Jr., *Wartime Public Media Censorship* at 10 (Unpublished essay, Carlisle Barracks, Pa.: U.S. Army War College, 1971).
63. *Ibid.*, 11–14.
64. Letter from general counsel of the Department of Defense to William M. Nichols, general counsel, Office of Management and Budget, May 15, 1978.

during 1972 from representatives of the Office of Emergency Planning that cast official doubt on the need for WISP short of a nuclear attack. Because of that testimony and the nonemployment of WISP during both the Korean and Vietnam conflicts, the House Committee on Appropriations directed in its 1974 Report on the Department of Defense Appropriations Bill that the reserve WISP units of the Army, Navy, and Air Force be phased out by June 30, 1974.[65]

On January 30, 1975, the letter states, the Department of Defense asked the Federal Preparedness Agency (now also part of the Federal Emergency Management Agency) to rescind the National Censorship Agreement.[66] The Federal Preparedness Agency and the Department of Defense then became involved in discussions seeking to create another national WISP structure that could operate without the use of Department of Defense personnel, all national WISP units having been deactivated in fiscal year 1974 after appropriations for their existence were denied by Congress.[67]

Apparently, the discussions between the concerned government agencies were not productive because on June 3, 1981, William H. Taft, IV, general counsel, Department of Defense, wrote to David Stockman, director of the Office of Management and Budget, stating that the Department of Defense wanted to amend Executive Order 11490 in order to be relieved of responsibilities more appropriately assigned to civilian agencies.[68] Subsequently, on November 27, 1981, General Richard G. Stilwell, (Retired), Office of The Under Secretary of Defense, sent a memo to each service secretary and to the Chairman of the Joint Chiefs of Staff stating that:

> It should be noted that in 1974, the House and Senate Committees on Appropriations concurred that "it is unlikely *that any element of WISP* would be implemented in any contingency," and deleted all funds for participation by reserve personnel in WISP training. The WISP reserve units were subsequently disbanded in that same year.[69]

The Stilwell letter is most interesting, particularly depending on how one interprets the phrase *"any element of WISP,"* since the Army Reserve field press censorship detachments were operating until April 1977 and certainly funds were being expended for that purpose. In any event, it appears that the

65. *Ibid.*
66. *Ibid.*
67. *Ibid.*
68. Letter from William H. Taft IV, general counsel of the Department of Defense to David A. Stockman, Director, Office of Management and Budget, June 3, 1981.
69. Memo from General Richard G. Stilwell, USA (Retired), November 27, 1981.

use of military WISP in Korea and certainly in the Cuban Missile Crisis was ignored. There is no question that the 1972 hearings and the fiscal year 1974 appropriations decision, together with the Pentagon's questions (after Vietnam) as to whether field press censorship could again be effectively employed, led to the decision to eliminate America's only military censorship capability represented by the Army Reserve units in 1977. However, despite the Army's view that technology has made field press censorship obsolete, it has been used by Israel during its recent Lebanon campaign[70] and by the British during the Falkland Islands fighting.

These recent and clearly perceived needs for media censorship by military authorities in democratic nations may well indicate that our own history of military press censorship is not yet complete. America's global commitments and the possibility that despite (or because of) nuclear weapons a Third World War might be largely or totally conventional require that we still heed the Supreme Court's words in *Near v. Minnesota*:

> No one would question but that a government might prevent actual obstruction to its recruiting service or the publication of the sailing dates of transports or the number and location of troops.[71]

In summary, the media and the public, respectively, must remain determined to inform and be informed. The media and public also must be aware that our national interests may at some future time again require the use of media censorship "consistent with security" by military and civil authorities.

70. TV GUIDE, July 5, 1982, A–1.
71. Near v. Minnesota, 283 U.S. 697, 716 (1931).

ROBERT L. HUGHES

Abating Obscenity As a Nuisance: An Easy Procedural Road for Prior Restraints

An associate professor at Virginia Commonwealth University, Robert L. Hughes holds a J.D. from the University of Florida and an M.A. in Journalism from the University of Missouri. He has written for newspapers in Charlotte, North Carolina, and West Palm Beach, Florida.

Constitutional orthodoxy assumes that a system of prior restraints poses a far greater danger to First Amendment values than does a system of subsequent punishment.[1] Courts ordinarily put strong presumptions against the constitutionality of restrictions that bar speech from entering the marketplace of ideas.[2] A few classes of speech, however, are not considered to merit constitutional protection and may be suppressed.[3] Yet even in these instances, a prior restraint is usually tolerated only when it is accompanied by rigorous procedural safeguards to minimize the risk of suppressing protected speech along with the unprotected.[4]

An emerging exception to the general rule that government must prove the unprotected character of speech with a high degree of certainty is found in

1. Near v. Minnesota, 283 U.S. 697, 51 S. Ct 625, 75 L. Ed. 1357 (1931). See also, L. TRIBE, AMERICAN CONSTITUTIONAL LAW, 724–31 (1978).
2. E.g., New York Times v. United States, 403 U.S. 713, 91 S. Ct. 2140, 29 L. Ed.2d 822 (1971) (per curiam).
3. E.g., Chaplinsky v. New Hampshire, 315 U.S. 568, 62 S. Ct. 766, 86 L. Ed. 1031 (1942) (fighting words).
4. This is often expressed in terms of a "clear and present danger" Schenck v. United States, 249 U.S. 47, 39 S. Ct 247, 63 L. Ed. 470 (1919) or a "heavy presumption" against the prior restraint (New York Times v. United States, 403 U.S. 713, 91 S. Ct. 2140, 29 L. Ed.2d 822 (1971) (per curiam)). See also, Freedman v. Maryland, 380 U.S. 51, 85 S. Ct. 734, 13 L. Ed.2d 649 (1965).

the use of civil nuisance law to regulate obscenity. This article will examine the threat to speech interests inherent in the relaxed burden of proof common to ordinary nuisance litigation and the insensitivity of the U.S. Supreme Court to that threat.

I. BACKGROUND

Until fairly recently, most government authorities have preferred criminal prosecution as the primary tool for controlling obscenity. In the years since the 1957 landmark decision in *Roth v. United States*[5] declared obscene expression to be beyond the pale of First Amendment protection, a substantial body of law and commentary has developed concerning not only the boundary separating obscene and nonobscene expression but also the procedures for determining on which side of the border any given expression falls.[6] The substantive law has been debated extensively and, to a limited extent, modified.[7] One element of the calculus is hardly ever questioned: Whatever the prevailing definition of obscenity, the state may not impose criminal sanctions without demonstrating to an exceedingly high level of probability that the speech at issue does fit the definition.

The possibility of error is an inescapable part of any fact-finding process, including a trial. But because of the special dangers a defendant faces in a criminal prosecution, the judicial system shifts the risk of fact-finding error to minimize the possibility of an erroneous conviction. Legal and social principles agree that "... it is significantly worse for an innocent man to be found guilty than for a guilty man to go free."[8] To achieve this policy, the Constitution requires that in all criminal prosecutions the government has the formidable burden of proving each element of an offense "beyond a reasonable doubt."[9] In a criminal obscenity prosecution, the government must prove not just that the accused exhibited or sold the material. It must prove beyond a reasonable doubt that the material itself falls into a class of

---

5. 354 U.S. 476, 77 S. Ct. 1304, 1 L. Ed.2d 1498 (1957).
6. F. SCHAUER, THE LAW OF OBSCENITY (1976) provides an exhaustive analysis of the definitional problem and, though becoming dated, remains the best treatise on the topic.
7. Frequently the result has been less protection for sexually oriented material. *E.g.*, Miller v. California, 413 U.S. 15, 93 S. Ct. 2607, 37 L. Ed.2d 419 (1973) relaxed the previous requirement that material must be utterly without redeeming social value to be designated obscene.
8. C. MCCORMICK, EVIDENCE 798 (2d ed., 1972).
9. *See, In re* Winship, 397 U.S. 358, 90 S. Ct. 1068, 25 L. Ed. 368 (1970), particularly Justice Harlan's concurring opinion at 369 for an illuminating commentary on this standard.

Abating Obscenity as a Nuisance

unprotected expression. Thus, the elaborate safeguards attending a criminal trial serve to protect marginal material from erroneous classification as well as to protect the defendant.

A criminal prosecution is not the sole weapon against pornography. A menagerie of civil action is available to authorities.[10] *Kingsley Books v. Brown*,[11] decided the same day as *Roth* but largely overshadowed by it, accepted the principle of a noncriminal approach to obscenity regulation. The Court saw merit in a civil injunctive procedure that provided personal notice, prior to a criminal prosecution and its risk of imprisonment, of exactly what materials are not protected by the First Amendment and therefore subject to suppression.[12] For a merchant seeking to discover whether he can lawfully distribute a book, the Court suggested, the civil process is advantageous because, should he guess wrong, about the worst that can happen is the issuance of an order not to distribute any more copies of the book. On the other hand, if a criminal prosecution is possible and the merchant errs in construing the same obscenity doctrine which baffles the best legal minds and appears to confound the Court itself at times, he may go to jail. The severity of criminal penalties, as proponents of the civil approach suggest, cannot but deter some nonobscene matter from entering the marketplace.[13] The assumption, explicit or implicit, of these and related arguments is that the civil remedy will be exclusive and accompanied by stringent protections for both material and defendant. Neither has been the case. States have greatly increased the frequency of civil enforcement measures, especially during the last five years, but only as a supplement to prosecution. None have eliminated criminal remedies.[14]

During this same period, both courts and commentators have focused on the substantive questions. Too little attention has been paid to the procedures of the fact-finding process—and that which has, for the most part has been piecemeal or incidental.[15]

---

10. *E.g.*, seizure and destruction, zoning, public nuisance, licensing.
11. 354 U.S. 436, 77 S. Ct. 1370, 1 L. Ed.2d 1452 (1957).
12. *Id.* at 442. Justice Burger endorsed this view in Paris Adult Theater I v. Slaton, 413 U.S. 49, 51, 93 S. Ct. 2628, 37 L. Ed.2d 446 (1973).
13. *See*, Rendleman, *Civilizing Pornography: The Case for an Exclusive Obscenity Nuisance Statute*, 44 U. CHI. L. REV. 509, 513 (1977). *See also*, Hogue, *Regulating Obscenity Through The Power To Define and Abate Nuisances*, 14 WAKE FOREST L. REV. 1 (1978).
14. J. BARRON AND C. DIENES, HANDBOOK OF FREE SPEECH AND FREE PRESS 607 (1979). The authors also rebut the position that civil penalties are the preferable form of obscenity regulation.
15. Schauer's treatise, *supra* note 6, probably the most extensive modern work on the topic, fails to consider the proof problem in civil obscenity cases.

II. THE ROLE OF PROCEDURE

As the Court itself has pointed out, "[P]rocedures by which the facts of a case are determined assume an importance fully as great as the validity of the substantive law to be applied."[16] Given the vagueness of the Court's definitional approach to obscenity—what, for example, is "prurient," "patent," or "serious?"[17]—and the First Amendment values at stake, the reliability of the fact-finding in these cases is critical. A loose procedural standard here will undermine the most scrupulously protective substantive law.

Most civil suits are, in fact, resolved by a standard far less demanding than that mandated in criminal prosecutions. In the great majority of noncriminal cases, the law tolerates a substantial margin of fact-finding error or, to put it another way, wrongly decided cases. This is considered acceptable (1) because neither the loss of liberty nor the stigma of a conviction is risked; (2) because errors over time are likely to fall equally between the defendant and the plaintiff, and an error favoring one is no more odious than an error favoring the other[18]; and (3) because a less-than-exacting standard of factual accuracy allows cases to be decided more expeditiously.[19]

In the ordinary civil case, the fact-finder must be persuaded of the rightness of his verdict by a "preponderance of the evidence." One side of a controversy is said to have a preponderance of the evidence when its case is more convincing that the other's. Another explanation of this measure of persuasion is that it requires proof sufficient to make the existence of a contested fact more probable that its nonexistence.[20] It is, at bottom, case-by-case balancing. What is of special significance here is that the trier of fact may make a decision properly but at the same time entertain a reasonable doubt that it is the correct one.

A narrow range of civil cases has traditionally demanded a greater degree of certitude. These tend to be those cases in which policy disfavors a particular kind of claim.[21] For such cases, courts have fashioned an

---

16. Speiser v. Randall, 357 U.S. 513, 520, 78 S. Ct. 1332, 2 L. Ed.2d 1460 (1958). *See generally*, Morgan, *First Amendment Due Process*, 83 HARV. L. REV. 518 (1970).
17. In an obscenity trial, "[t]he basic guidelines for the trier of fact must be: (a) whether the 'average person, applying contemporary community standards', would find that the work, taken as a whole, appeals to the prurient interest, (b) whether the work depicts or describes, in a patently offensive way, sexual conduct specifically defined by state law, and (c) whether the work, taken as a whole, lacks serious literary, artistic, political or scientific value." Miller v. California, 413 U.S. 15, 24, 93 S. Ct. 2607, 37 L. Ed.2d 419 (1973).
18. MCCORMICK, *supra* note 8, at 798.
19. *Id.*
20. F. JAMES, CIVIL PROCEDURE 250 (1965).
21. *E.g.*, creation of an oral trust (MCCORMICK, *supra* note 8, at 796). *See also*, Chaunt v. United States, 364 U.S. 350, 81 S. Ct. 147, 5. L. Ed.2d 120 (1960).

intermediate test which is more exacting than that used in the run of civil proceedings but which stops short of the elevated standard required by criminal due process. It is generally described as proof by "clear and convincing evidence."[22]

All legal tests, including this one, lack mathematical precision and are vulnerable to semantic attacks. But the "clear and convincing" standard is more than easy rhetoric and doubtless makes the fact-finder more likely to resist persuasion than a "preponderance of the evidence" benchmark. The Court has found in several contexts a constitutional necessity that the "clear and convincing" standard be applied to protect particularly important interests present in some civil cases. At least once the interest was speech. In *New York Times v. Sullivan*,[23] the Court held that a libel plaintiff who is a public official must prove his case by a standard of "convincing clarity," a lesser gauge posing unacceptable risks to First Amendment goals. When a prior restraint—rather than subsequent punishment in the form of a civil judgment—has been imposed, the Court has gone much further: "Any system of prior restraints comes to this Court bearing a heavy presumption against its constitutional validity."[24] These principles and the implications of a lenient fact-finding process escaped the Court when it considered an obscenity case with potentially great ramifications.

III. *COOPER V. MITCHELL BROTHERS' SANTA ANA THEATER*

In *Cooper v. Mitchell Brothers' Santa Theater*,[25] the Court held that a film may be found obscene and suppressed as a public nuisance using only the relaxed standard of proof common to ordinary civil litigation. The case was one of first impression, and its importance lies not just in the rule announced but in the offhanded way the Court dealt with the issue.

The question was whether a civil action to abate the showing of obscene films as a public nuisance requires proof beyond a reasonable doubt that the films in fact are obscene. Long used to clear public sidewalks and abate the emission of noxious gases, general nuisance laws are today often applied in order to prohibit the exhibition or sale of obscene matter.[26] Some states have

22. McCormick, *supra* note 8, at 796.
23. 376 U.S. 254, 84 S. Ct. 710, 11 L. Ed. 686 (1964).
24. New York Times v. United States, 403 U.S. 713, 91 S. Ct. 2140, 1 L. Ed.2d 1498 (1957).
25. 454 U.S. 90, 102 S. Ct. 172, 70 L. Ed.2d 262, 7 Media L. Rep. 2223 (1981), *rev'g* People *ex. rel.* Gow v. Mitchell Bros.' Santa Ana Theater, 114 Cal. App.3d 923, 171 Cal. Rptr. 85 (1981).
26. *See generally*, W. Prosser, Law of Torts 571–91 (1974). This treatise provides a sound overview but does not deal especially with the suppression of speech as a nuisance.

enacted special nuisance laws to cope specifically with obscenity.[27]

Using a general nuisance statute, the city of Santa Ana alleged that seventeen specifically identified films were obscene and that their exhibition by the theater constituted a public nuisance. After the evidence was heard, the trial court instructed the jury it could find the films obscene only if persuaded of that designation "beyond a reasonable doubt." The jury found eleven films obscene and four not obscene. It was unable to reach a verdict in the case of two films. The trial court issued an injunction that, among other things,[28] prohibited the theater from again exhibiting the eleven films. Several appeals were filed, including that of the city, which claimed the trial court erred in requiring the issue of obscenity to be proved "beyond a reasonable doubt." The city argued the burden of persuasion should be that of "clear and convincing evidence."

The California Court of Appeals agreed with the trial judge that the beyond-reasonable-doubt burden was correct.[29] Referring with approval to Justice Brennan's concurring opinion in *McKinney v. Alabama*,[30] the court concluded that the pivotal importance of free speech prohibited its classification and subsequent suppression as obscenity by a less stringent standard.[31] Whether the California appellate court believed the Constitution required that conclusion — as contrasted with the court's merely being persuaded by the force of Brennan's argument — is unclear. If the state court did not reach its conclusion solely because it believed the Constitution required it to, there was no federal question to be resolved, and the principle that federal courts should abstain from meddling in strictly state affairs should have foreclosed consideration of the case by the Supreme Court.[32]

Despite its doubtful jurisdiction, the Court accepted the case. Then, in virtually summary fashion, without requiring or weighing full briefs on the question and without holding oral arguments, the Court, with a vote of six to three, reversed the lower court in a six-paragraph, unsigned opinion. Justice Stevens, in a dissent grounded on the Court's precarious jurisdiction, was distressed "to consider the Court considers novel questions of this

---

27. A representative list may be found in Comment, *A Nuisance Abatement Statute That, When Applied To Obscenity, Authorizes A Prior Restraint On The Future Exhibition Of Unnamed Films, Violates The Constitution*, 13 GA. L. REV. 1076, fn. 19 (1979).
28. None is relevant to this article. For the most part they involve the reach of the injunction.
29. *Mitchell Brothers'*, supra note 25, 454 U.S. 90 .
30. 424 U.S. 670, 678, 96 S. Ct. 1189, 47 L. Ed.2d 386 (1976) (Justice Brennan concurring).
31. *Mitchell Brothers'*, supra note 25, 454 U.S. 90. A North Carolina nuisance statute designed to control obscenity has been similarly construed. Fehlhaber v. North Carolina, 675 F.2d 1365 (4th, 1982).
32. C. WRIGHT, LAW OF FEDERAL COURTS 481-92 (2d ed., 1970).

Abating Obscenity as a Nuisance

character so easy as not even to merit argument."[33]

That consideration failed to preclude a majority of the Court's holding that the Constitution does not require proof beyond a reasonable doubt in a civil obscenity case. States may impose such a standard if they wish, the Court said, but the Constitution does not demand it.[34] The Court's rationale appears primarily in its assertion that it had never before insisted on such a burden in a civil case.[35] The majority focused only on the measure of procedural due process to be afforded a litigant in the ordinary civil case and ignored the decision's impact on the defendant's right to speak or an audience's right to receive information. Justice Brennan did not.[36]

In a dissent in which he was joined by Justice Marshall,[37] Brennan reiterated his view that the First Amendment requires a state seeking to censor otherwise constitutionally protected material to prove that material obscene beyond a reasonable doubt. Brennan cited his concurring opinion in *McKinney*, in which he said:

> In the civil adjudication of obscenity..., the bookseller has at stake...an "interest of transcending value"—protection of his right to disseminate and the public's right to receive material protected by the First Amendment. Protection of these rights demands that the fact-finder be almost certain— convinced beyond a reasonable doubt—that the materials are not constitutionally immune from suppression.[38]

Brennan charged that decision making, already prone to unacceptable error because of the "dim and uncertain" line that separates the protected from the obscene, will be pushed even further in that direction "if the fact-finder is only marginally confident that the material falls on the unprotected side of the line."[39] This unreliability, he added, creates substantial risk of self-censorship.

---

33. *Mitchell Brothers', supra* note 25, 454 U.S. 90, 94 (Justice Stevens dissenting).
34. *Id.* at 173.
35. Justice Stevens pointed out that this was far from clear and offered several cases, none recent, in support. *Id.* at 175, fn. 5.
36. *Id.* at 174.
37. Had he remained on the Court, former Justice Potter Stewart probably would have joined with Brennan, whose distaste for some aspects of obscenity regulation Stewart shared. *See, e.g.*, Paris Adult Theater I v. Slaton, 413 U.S. 49, 83–84, 93 S. Ct. 2628, 37 L. Ed.2d 446 (1973) (Justice Brennan, with whom Justices Stewart and Marshall join, dissenting).
38. McKinney v. Alabama 424 U.S. 670, 684, 96 S. Ct. 1189, 47 L. Ed.2d 386 (1976) (Justice Brennan concurring).
39. *Id.* at 685. In Avenue Bookstore v. Tallmadge, 456 U.S. —, 103 S. Ct. 356, 74 L. Ed.2d 393 (1982) (per curiam), the Court denied a writ of certiorari in a case

IV. ANALYSIS

Little can be added to Justice Steven's regret at the hasty, superficial treatment the majority of his brethren gave this case. No sanctions threatened were of such pressing gravity to justify the Court's short-circuiting the normal appellate procedure and taking this case when the jurisdictional question was not developed fully and ripe for review. How the Court decided the case determined only whether six more films might be added to the list of eleven the Santa Ana Theater was already prohibited from showing. In fact, it was the government, not the theater, that appealed this aspect of the case.[40] Certainly no danger of incurable harm to the government justified the Court's reaching to take this case. Once it had, though, the question presented was not so unimportant nor its resolution so transparent as to explain or excuse the Court's casual approach. This case simply deserved better.

Most cases that reach appellate courts are complex. Each side can muster some law and logic for its view, and usually something can be said for intermediate positions. This case was no exception. Due regard for a crucial and vexing problem should have led the Court away from a superficial analysis. The case held issues which, if faced at all, insisted on measured development and reasoned analysis. Yet its handling was almost perfunctory, a practice increasingly common in sensitive cases and one which several members of the court itself have condemned as a "patent abuse of our judicial power."[41]

None of this, of course, lessens the need to examine the opinion closely and see just what the court did. In its simplest terms, the case holds only that a beyond-reasonable-doubt standard is not required by the Constitution in a civil action seeking to suppress obscenity as a nuisance. The extremely limited character of the holding is consistent with the Burger Court's step-by-step approach to constitutional adjudication, deciding nothing more than that which absolutely must be decided.[42] While this is not without advantages,[43] it risks ultimate failure because a fragmented, particularistic methodology retards, and may prevent altogether, the doctrinal development necessary

---

that raised many of the issues pertinent to the use of nuisance law to regulate obscenity. Justice White, joined by Justices Brennan and Marshall, wrote a vigorous dissent arguing these questions ought to settled.

40. *Mitchell Brothers', supra* note 25, 102 S. Ct. 172 fn. 1.
41. Hutto v. Davis, 454 U.S. 370, 102 S. Ct. 703, 705, 70 L. Ed. 556 (1982) (per curiam) (Justice Brennan dissenting).
42. *See generally*, Cox, *Foreword: Freedom Of Expression In The Burger Court*, 94 HARV. L. REV. 1 (1980).
43. Primarily it avoids the adoption of a fallacious legal rule because the decision maker has not had the benefit of full arguments on the issue. The Court cannot anticipate every future dispute. An actual controversy must exist. Poe v. Ullman, 376 U.S. 497, 81 S. Ct. 1752, 6 L. Ed.2d 989 (1961).

Abating Obscenity as a Nuisance

for a coherent body of law. Put another way, the forest may be lost among the trees.

For example, if one seeks to discover among the Court's decisions a cohesive, constitutional attitude toward civil regulation of obscenity, one must analyze and attempt to reconcile several cases. One of them calls for special sensitivity when the civil process threatens First Amendment freedoms.[44] Another points out that injunctions are more akin to criminal, rather than noncriminal, law.[45] One states that a full adversary hearing is required before material may be banned as obscene[46]; another holds due process in those proceedings does not require a jury trial.[47] And now one must reckon with a case that does not distinguish between the abatement of a bonfire and the banishment of speech. There are others.[48] Just what the Court's position on obscenity is is conjectural. Certainly it cannot be found in any one case. Nor is it easily found as lying somewhere in between the cases or as an amalgamation of them. One fears the real position of the Court is all over the place.

It is not necessary to refute the premise that the primary role of the legislature is to set policy and that of the courts to resolve disputes to expect the Supreme Court, particularly when a dispute involves the meaning of the Constitution, to articulate its reasoning fully and describe how its decision fits with, or alters, established law. Failure to do that not only sows confusion about the meaning of the law—what is permitted and what is not; it also invites inconsistent results and the appearance of subjectivity in the decisional process. Eventually, the stature and moral authority of the Court itself are lessened.[49]

In *Mitchell Brothers'*, the insular approach was carried to the limit. The Court majority woodenly viewed the issue presented as one of the procedures required in the great bulk of civil cases. In doing so the Court ignored its own teachings and admonitions to be wary when speech may be

---

44. *McKinney*, 424 U.S. 669, 674, 96 S. Ct. 1189, 47 L. Ed.2d 386 (1976).
45. Hoffman v. Pursue Ltd., 420 U.S. 592, 95 S. Ct. 1200, 43 L. Ed.2d 492 (1975).
46. Freedman v. Maryland, 380 U.S. 51, 85 S. Ct. 734, 13 L. Ed.2d 649 (1965). The Court also has said that, "the regulation of a communicative activity such as the exhibition of motion pictures must adhere to more narrowly drawn procedures than is necessary of the abatement of an ordinary nuisance." Vance v. Universal Amusement Co., Inc., 445 U.S. 308, 315, 100 S. Ct. 1156, 63 L. Ed.2d 413 (1980) (per curiam).
47. Alexander v. Virginia, 413 U.S. 836, 93 S. Ct. 2803, 37 L. Ed.2d 993 (1973) (per curiam).
48. For many, *Media Law Reporter*, a weekly service that provides the texts of federal and state media law decisions and information about important legislative and administrative developments, is the most convenient way to keep abreast of changes. It is published by the Bureau of National Affairs, Inc., 1231 25th Street, N.W., Washington, DC 20037.
49. R. Berger, Congress v. The Supreme Court 163–209 (1969).

jeopardized. Absent from the majority opinion is even lip service to the special rights involved: the right to distribute and the right to receive information. That the rights in this case concern sexually oriented material and would likely be exercised only by a tiny minority is precisely the point. If the First Amendment is to offer a full measure of protection, it must reach marginal material that may well be distasteful to the majority.

This is not to argue that the First Amendment ought to shield pornography. That case has been made ably, but unsuccessfully, elsewhere.[50] It is to suggest that the Court's tunnel vision in viewing this case did violence to what many thought were established principles protecting marginal material. A majority of the Court, confronted with the substantive question, had never before held that nonobscene, erotic matter may be treated differently, consistent with the First Amendment, from other forms of protected expression.[51] Yet the Court's neglect in *Mitchell Brothers'* to remember that substance and procedure are of one cloth allowed what had not happened directly to be done indirectly.

One can only hypothesize why the majority perceived the procedural question as so divorced from substantive rights as to deserve not even token explanation. It may not have recognized the censorship aspect of the case.[52] The theory of nuisance law is not to suppress or abate an idea, but to suppress a condition: specifically here, the showing of obscene films. It is not the films themselves but their exhibition that constitutes the nuisance.[53] Acceptance of this notion allowed the Court to approve the channeling of arguably vulgar, but clearly nonobscene broadcast at a time when children would less likely be in a radio audience.[54] Similar considerations permit

50. *See, e.g.*, Paris Adult Theater I v. Slaton, 413 U.S. 49, 73–114, 93 S. Ct. 2628, 37 L. Ed. 446 (1973) (Justice Brennan dissenting).
51. Young v. American Mini-Theaters, 427 U.S. 50, 96 S. Ct. 2440, 49 L. Ed.2d 310 (1976) concerned another approach to obscenity regulation, a zoning ordinance. That case upheld the regulation, but not suppression, of adult theaters by zoning ordinances. Justice Stevens in that case wrote for only a plurality, not a majority. Justice Powell expressly disagreed with the part of the plurality opinion that held that "non-obscene erotic materials may be treated differently under First Amendment principles than other forms of protected expression." *Id.* at 73. *See also*, FCC v. Pacifica Foundation, 438 U.S. 726, 98 S. Ct. 3026, 57 L. Ed.2d 1073 (1978). There, Stevens's suggestion that speech may be regulated on the basis of its content again mustered only a plurality.
52. A prior restraint in the classic sense was arguably not involved, since obscene speech is not protected and a court, rather than an administrative agency, decided the issue of obscenity. Once the fact of obscenity is found, it is not speech at all, and there can be no prior restraint. J. BARRON AND C. DIENES, HANDBOOK OF FREE SPEECH AND FREE PRESS 33–61 (1979). *But see*, Near v. Minnesota, 283 U.S. 697, 51 S. Ct. 625, 75 L. Ed. 1357 (1931).
53. People *ex rel.* Gow v. Mitchell Brothers' Santa Ana Theater, 114 Ca. App. 3d 923, 931, 171 Cal. Rptr. 85, 90 (1981).
54. FCC v. Pacifica Foundation, 438 U.S. 726, 98 S. Ct. 3026, 57 L. Ed.2d 1073 (1978).

Abating Obscenity as a Nuisance

zoning ordinances to restrict adult theaters and bookstores.[55] But these restrictions are essentially on time, manner, and place, restrictions traditionally subject to far less exacting judicial scrutiny than content-based suppression. The relationship between these cases and one in which the effect of the restriction is to prohibit speech entirely is tenuous and consistent only with the most mechanical application of principle and the most crabbed of reasoning.

Viewed from a different perspective, *Mitchell Brothers'* will be seen to follow a line of cases that emphasizes the minimal protection provided defendants by the U.S. Constitution and that invites state courts and legislatures to craft their own protections. If possible, the Court will simply avoid any First Amendment issue. For example, the Court effectively reversed itself and allowed states to permit cameras in their courtrooms, not on the basis of any First Amendment right to know, but because the Court said interpreting the Sixth Amendment right to a fair trial in order to require the exclusion of broadcasting equipment was undue interference in state procedural experimentation.[56] In another case, the Court invited the states to construe their own constitutions or to enact laws to protect reporters from being compelled to reveal their sources, but refused to declare that such protection springs from the First Amendment.[57] Where the First Amendment plays a role in the outcome, the Court has emphasized that it establishes only a floor, and states remain free to experiment with standards above that. In *Gertz v. Robert Welch Inc.*,[58] for example, the Court held only that, in a libel action, the Constitution prohibits states from imposing liability without fault. States might, if they wish, adopt more rigorous protection for defendants in libel suits. Certainly in these and similar cases there is a strong element of states' rights and federal restraint. This was clearly not an unimportant factor in *Mitchell Brothers'*.

V. CONCLUSION

Mitchell Brothers' has provided a potent weapon permitting authorities to periodically sweep "filth" from theaters. Materials that could not be proscribed by criminal processes may be censored as a civil nuisance. Whatever the difference might mean to the defendant, the effect to the audience is identical. Once government claims material may fit into the rubric of obscenity, it is permitted to employ the slackest standard of proof known to

---

55. Young v. American Mini-Theaters, 427 U.S. 50, 96 S. Ct. 2440, 49 L. Ed.2d 310 (1976).
56. Chandler v. Florida, 449 U.S. 560, 101 S. Ct. 802, 66 L. Ed.2d 740 (1981).
57. Branzburg v. Hayes, 408 U.S. 665, 92 S. Ct. 2646, 33 L. Ed.2d 626 (1972).
58. 418 U.S. 323, 94 S. Ct. 2997, 41 L. Ed.2d 789 (1974).

the law—a touchstone foreign to all other content-based speech regulation—to prove the validity of its own classification.

The effect of this sort of boot-strapping should be self-evident. Borderline, but nonobscene, material will be erroneously banned. That goes hand in hand with a measure of proof that has a low error threshhold. Added to that built-in error is the likelihood that a fact-finder will be more willing to rule against a defendant in close cases, since the stigma and sanctions in a civil action are significantly less burdensome than those in a criminal prosecution. Finally, the expense of defending this kind of suit and the uncertainty of the result will deter distributors from handling some films and books near the boundary of protection.

The decision leaves ample room for the Court to someday put a more formidable barrier of protection around erotic, but nonobscene, speech than that provided by the "preponderance of the evidence" standard.[59] Strictly speaking, the Court held only that the "beyond-reasonable-doubt" standard was *not* required; it did not say what *was* required. A future defendant will no doubt ask the court to adopt the "clear and convincing" standard as that which best protects speech and serves the legitimate interests of government. Much can be said for that position.[60]

Still, one would not be well advised to translate the possibility of the Court's agreeing to take such a case into the probability that it will undertake to defend vigorously this sort of speech. The Burger Court's disposition to show great deference to state authority can no longer be disregarded, if indeed it still is. The time is gone when a litigant might comfortably base his appeal solely on the federal Constitution and rely upon it to protect speech interests. Only a bold or reckless defendant would now ignore state constitutional provisions in his appeal as well as making the customary citations to the U.S. Constitution. Both courtroom and classroom must give renewed attention to safeguards found in state law.

In a similar sense, the case is a reminder of the importance of procedure. For many outside courtrooms, it is only too easy to direct attention solely on the substantive law—how, for example, are we to define obscenity?—and forget that the procedure used to answer that question is every bit as important as the substantive problem. In this respect, if *Mitchell Brothers'* promotes a keener awareness of the importance of procedure and state law, particularly among laymen concerned with free speech interests, it will leave one bright corner in an otherwise dismal landscape.

59. *See generally*, Randleman, *Civilizing Pornography: The Case For An Exclusive Obscenity Statute*, 44 U. CHI. L. REV. 509 (1977).
60. *See, e.g.*, D. GILLMORE AND J. BARRON, MASS COMMUNICATION LAW (3d ed., 1979).

JOHN SOLOSKI
CAROLYN STEWART DYER

The Cost of Prior Restraint: *U.S. v. The Progressive*

John Soloski and Carolyn Stewart Dyer are assistant professors at the University of Iowa's School of Journalism and Mass Communication. Professor Dyer teaches courses in media law; Professor Soloski teaches media economics. Both have worked as professional journalists.

Multi-million-dollar damages awarded in recent libel cases have received much publicity; however, media defendants in such cases rarely pay large damage awards. A recent study of media libel cases between 1980 and 1982 found that in only seven cases did media defendants pay any damage award.[1] The largest award was $400,000, in *Gertz v. Welch*,[2] and the average award, excluding *Gertz*, was $71,585.[3] The study also found that media defendants lost forty-seven of fifty-three libel cases at the trial level, but only in seven cases were damage awards affirmed on appeal.[4] Similarly, in his study of libel cases decided by appellate courts between 1977 and 1980, Franklin found that plaintiffs were successful in only five percent of the cases, compared to sixty-six percent for media defendants.[5] By concentrating attention on the size of recent libel awards, news accounts of these cases have ignored other effects litigation costs have on a publication. Win or lose,

---

1. *Defamation Trials and Damage Awards—Updating the Franklin Study*, LIBEL DEF. RESOURCE CENTER BULL. NO. 4, at 3 [hereinafter cited as LDRC BULL.]
2. 94 S. Ct. 2997, 418 U.S. 323, 41 L. Ed. 789, 1 MED. L. RPTR. at 1642 (1974).
3. LDRC BULL. NO. 4, *supra* note 1, at 3. The six other damage awards were for $35,000, $50,000, $60,000, $65,000, $69,500 and $150,000.
4. *Id.*
5. Marc A. Franklin, *Suing Media for Libel: A Litigation Study*, 1981 AM. BAR FOUND. RESEARCH J. 802–803.

JOHN SOLOSKI and CAROLYN STEWART DYER

publications must pay attorneys' fees, court costs, and direct and indirect expenses of legal defenses.

The purpose of this paper is to consider the litigation costs of a particular media case. Using the case-study approach, we will address the following questions: What does it cost in money and time to engage in litigation? How did the publication under study meet these expenses? How did the litigation process affect the publication? The paper also addresses the adequacy of the existing means of financing media litigation. The case that will be examined is *U.S. v. The Progressive*,[6] a prior restraint case in which the government attempted to prevent the publication in 1979 of an article about the H-bomb.

THE INCREASE IN LITIGATION

During the last decade and a half, Americans have been turning to the courts in dramatically increasing numbers. Between 1965 and 1975, the number of cases heard by appellate courts rose by eighty-four percent; and—although there are no systematic records for state courts—between 1968 and 1976, the number of cases heard by California courts rose by ninety percent.[7] It is not known whether the number of media-related cases has risen at these rates, but it is generally assumed that the number of civil suits against the media—libel and invasion of privacy, primarily—has increased significantly in recent years. Furthermore, governmental action against the media—in the form of withholding information, subpoenaing of reporters and their notes and records, and restraining publication of information—has increased. As with everything else, the cost of litigation has risen. One report indicates that the cost of defending a libel case has tripled since 1960, with attorneys' fees now ranging between sixty and two hundred dollars an hour.[8] At one newspaper the cost of litigation and legal counsel increased from $7,400 to $74,000 between 1976 and 1980;[9] and a lawyer reported that his newspaper client spent $240,000 on legal fees in 1980.[10]

The cost of litigation has not gone unnoticed by individuals who want to harass or punish the media.[11] But perhaps a more important consequence of the increased frequency and cost of litigation is media self-censorship to

---

6. 467 F. Supp. 990 (1979).
7. JETHRO K. LIEBERMAN, THE LITIGIOUS SOCIETY at 5 (1981).
8. *Litigation Costs and Self-Censorship*, FREEDOM OF INFORMATION CENTER REP. No. 434, at 1 (February 1981).
9. Franklin, *supra* note 5, at 800.
10. *Id.*
11. BROADCASTING, November 17, 1980, at 63. What makes this of particular interest is that since 1976, no radio or television station has lost a libel decision in appellate court (Franklin, *supra* note 5, at 811).

The Cost of Prior Restraint

minimize the risks of libel and invasion of privacy suits and forestall government action. This "chilling effect" may result in the public's receiving less critical information from an overly cautious media. Also, to protect themselves, the media are increasingly relying on attorneys for prepublication advice and review of copy. Large media organizations have hired in-house First Amendment attorneys. And the publisher of a small, independently owned newspaper claimed he sold his paper to a newspaper chain because he could no longer afford the risks of litigation.[12] Some media observers believe that the cost of just one big case can cause the death of a small, independently owned medium.[13]

It is impossible to make generalizations about the impact of litigation on every medium by examining just one case, *U.S. v. The Progressive*; however, the case demonstrates the problems a small, independently owned publication faces when it becomes involved in potentially expensive litigation. Though the legal process and related expenses do vary from case to case, the costs of all cases are based on the same elements—legal and factual research, preparation of legal documents and arguments, court costs, and representation in court. Like other prior restraint cases, *The Progressive* case lacked the costly trial and damage awards that can make libel and invasion of privacy cases more expensive.

Figures from some media law cases indicate a range of litigation costs in recent years. In 1971 the Pentagon Papers case, which proceeded from New York and Washington, D.C., federal district courts through two appeals courts to the U.S. Supreme Court in just three weeks, cost the *New York Times* $150,000 for outside legal counsel alone; the *Washington Post*'s legal bills amounted to $70,000.[14] The *Nebraska Press Association* case, which involved the Association's challenge of a court order prohibiting publication of testimony and evidence presented in open court, cost about $125,000.[15] For eight months (1975–1976), that case bounced back and forth several times between state and federal courts. A more recent case—*Richmond Newspapers v. Virginia*—decided by the U.S. Supreme Court in 1980, cost between

---

12. DES MOINES REGISTER, July 14, 1979, at 6A. The publisher was Ken Johnson of the *Grand Junction Sentinel* (Colorado) who sold his paper to Cox.
13. PRESSTIME, May 1981, at 11.
14. New York Times v. U.S.; U.S. v. Washington Post, 403 U.S. 713, 91 S. Ct. 2140, 29 L. Ed. 2d 822 (1971). SANFORD J. UNGAR, THE PAPERS & THE PAPERS 306 (1972). The *Times*' legal bill from the firm of Cahill, Gordon and Professor Alexander Bickel came to $150,000. Another $50,000 was spent on preparatory legal work, in case "the newspaper or Neil Sheehan should be indicted on criminal charges in connection with the disclosure of the Papers" (UNGAR, at 306–307).
15. Nebraska Press Association v. Stuart, 427 U.S. 539, 96 S. Ct. 2791, 49 L. Ed. 2d 973 (1976). On cost, interview with Phil Berkebile, General Manager, Nebraska Press Association (March 9, 1979).

$75,000 and $100,000, according to the paper's publisher.[16] This case was a procedurally simple review by state and federal supreme courts of a judge's decision to close a trial to the press and public. In the well-publicized libel case involving Mobil Oil President William P. Tavoulareas and the *Washington Post*, litigation costs on both sides totalled over $2 million, with the *Post* spending between $500,000 and $750,000.[17] These figures represent the litigation costs at the trial level, and they are likely to grow significantly since Tavoulareas has vowed to pursue the case to the U.S. Supreme Court, if necessary.

The gross figures for the cost of a case tell only part of the story. For the New York Times Company, which had revenues of more than $290 million in 1971, $150,000 was a relatively minor expense.[18] And in the *Nebraska Press Association* case, several individuals devoted nearly full-time for several months to raising the funds for the case. Even then, the costs were spread out among many media in the state and region.[19] But for the independently owned *Progressive*, the final cost of its case reached $240,000 — a large sum compared to its 1979 operating budget of $600,000, which included a deficit of $126,000.

FINANCING *THE PROGRESSIVE*

Like many political journals, *The Progressive* has been a publication of commitment, not profit. Since its founding in 1909 by Robert LaFollette, the publication has had only one profitable year, 1954, when, though its circulation was only thirty thousand, it sold more than two hundred thousand reprints of an issue about Senator Joseph McCarthy. *The Progressive*'s publisher at the time of the case, Ron Carbon, characterized the magazine's economic history as "hard times and terribly hard times." When the H-bomb article was published in November 1979, he said the magazine was experiencing "desperate times."[20]

The Progressive is a subscription magazine with limited newsstand sales. Its national newsstand distributor was not even interested in more than the usual three thousand copies of the issue containing the then well-publicized

16. Richmond Newspapers v. Virginia, 100 S. Ct. 2814, 448 U.S. 555, 65 L. Ed. 2d 973 (1980). Quoted in Robert G. Picard, *The Might of the Media: Media Self-Censorship*, THE PRESS 17 (March 1981).
17. Tavoulareas v. Washington Post. 8 MED. L. RPTR. at 2262 (D.D.C. May 2, 1983) and WALL STREET J., July 7, 1982, at 1, col. 1.
18. NEW YORK TIMES CO., 1981 ANNUAL REPORT. According to Harrison E. Salisbury, the preparation of the Pentagon Papers stories cost about $250,000 (HARRISON E. SALISBURY, WITHOUT FEAR OR FAVOR 12, 213 (1980)).
19. Berkebile, *supra* note 15; G. Woodson Howe, *Fair Trial vs. Free Press: Who Won?*, THE NEBRASKA NEWSPAPER, August 1976, at 76.
20. Ron Carbon, *Bonanza*, THE PROGRESSIVE 66 (November 1979).

The Cost of Prior Restraint

H-bomb article.[21] At the time of the H-bomb case, the magazine's circulation was about forty thousand. The magazine has a net circulation increase of about fifteen hundred to two thousand a year, but Carbon said *The Progressive* will never circulate enough copies to attract substantial advertising. Besides, Carbon said, advertisers "recognize a hostile editorial climate when they see one."

At the beginning of the H-bomb case, syndicated columnist Jack Kilpatrick accused the magazine of provoking the government in order to generate publicity and thus boost circulation and profits. There is no doubt that the case did generate publicity—much of it incorrect and misleading—but it did not increase circulation, and the magazine continues to operate at a deficit. Pat Vander Meer, who replaced Carbon as publisher in 1982, estimates that of the current $1,096,185-a-year operating budget, circulation generates between seventy and seventy-five percent of the income, advertising less than five percent, and ancillary activities, particularly fundraising campaigns, the other twenty-five percent.

A budget deficit is a regular occurrence at *The Progressive*, but it has been reduced to nearly zero each year by contributions from subscribers. According to Gordon Sinykin, chairman of the board and *The Progressive*'s attorney, operating losses in 1978 were $92,000; in 1979, not counting legal expenses, losses were $126,000; and in 1980, the deficit reached $172,000. For 1983, the projected deficit is $186,105. Clearly, *The Progressive* is not in an economic position to engage in expensive litigation.

THE FACTS OF *THE PROGRESSIVE* CASE

The court case, *U.S. v. The Progressive*, involved an article by freelance writer Howard Morland entitled "The H-bomb Secret: To Know How Is to Ask Why."[22] The government contended that if the article were published, *The Progressive* would reveal secret "restricted data" about nuclear energy, in violation of the Atomic Energy Act of 1954.[23] The Department of Justice argued that, under the law, certain information is "born secret" and is automatically restricted from the moment an individual creates the information, even if the original sources of the idea are not secret.

The case—and the seven-month prohibition on publication of the article—began after *The Progressive* declined to submit the article to the Department of Energy for editing or to refrain from publishing it. The Department of

---

21. Data for this article were derived from the financial records of *The Progressive* and its attorneys. Additional information came from extensive interviews with Gordon Sinykin, Erwin Knoll, and Ron Carbon.
22. THE PROGRESSIVE 14–23 (November 1979).
23. 42 U.S.C. 2280.

Justice filed a motion in federal district court for a temporary restraining order against *The Progressive*. U.S. District Court Judge Robert Warren conducted a hearing in Milwaukee on the motion on March 9, 1979, and issued a temporary restraining order that expired on March 26. In a second hearing, the government argued for a preliminary injunction to extend the prohibition on publication. Judge Warren proposed that the article be submitted to a panel of scientists for review. *The Progressive* rejected that proposal, and Judge Warren entered a preliminary injunction on March 26. *The Progressive* appealed the injunction to the Seventh U.S. Circuit Court of Appeals in Chicago, but the court declined to hear the case quickly, as *The Progressive* had requested. A hearing was conducted by the Court of Appeals September 13, 1979, and a decision was anticipated late in September. But on September 16, a Madison, Wisconsin, newspaper published a letter by H-bomb hobbyist Charles Hansen, which revealed much of the same information about the H-bomb contained in Morland's *Progressive* article. The next day the Department of Justice announced it was abandoning the case. The Court of Appeals vacated Judge Warren's injunction on September 28, and *The Progressive* published the H-bomb article in its original form in its November 1979 issue. This was the longest prohibition on publication ever ordered by a federal court.

COST OF *U.S. V. THE PROGRESSIVE*

As a small journal perennially on the edge of financial oblivion, *The Progressive* managed to stay clear of the law until 1979. In the six years before the H-bomb case, the magazine's total legal expenses came to about $1,000, averaging about $165 a year. Most of the expenses were incurred for processing bequests from estates of subscribers. According to *The Progressive*'s editor, Erwin Knoll, the magazine had never been threatened with a libel suit. The only legal problem relating to editorial content that anyone associated with the magazine could remember was *Ms.* magazine's allegation of copyright infringement over the use of the department heading "No Comment," which appears in both publications. The problem was resolved in an exchange of letters between attorneys.

With this limited experience in media law, none of *The Progressive* staff anticipated that the actual costs of the H-bomb case would be as much as $240,000. Nor did they realize that it would take a year out of their lives and make publishing a monthly magazine extremely difficult. None of the staff realized how difficult it would be to raise funds to pay the legal bills. Even Gordon Sinykin, whose law firm represented not only *The Progressive* but also a daily newspaper and who *did* anticipate the case would be expensive, did not expect the case to cost as much as it did. At times during the litigation, he advised the editors that the case was jeopardizing the survival of the magazine, and he outlined alternative courses of action. Sinykin, who had been associated with the magazine for forty years, said that in his role as chairman of the board he would have abandoned the case if a choice had to be made between the magazine's survival and fighting the injunction.

As editor of the magazine, Knoll's priorities were the opposite of Sinykin's. Although Knoll said he never believed *The Progressive* would be destroyed, he would not have dropped the case just to save the magazine. But he admits, "We were blithely getting into something we didn't know the full scope of." When Sinykin advised Knoll that the case would be expensive, Knoll responded, "You worry about the law, and we'll worry about finding the money." Knoll said that when he contemplated an expensive case, he thought "maybe – if we had to so something *really* huge – $50,000."

The legal groundwork for the case was done by the law firm of LaFollette, Sinykin, Anderson and Munson in Madison,[24] a relatively small firm of fourteen attorneys. Morland, whose legal interests as author of the article were expected to differ from those of the magazine and its editors, was initially represented on a fee basis by Madison attorney Tom Fox. As it became evident that the case would be expensive, portions of the case were taken on a *pro bono* basis by the American Civil Liberties Union (ACLU) and by the Washington, D.C., office of the Wall Street law firm of White and Case.[25] In the final arrangement, LaFollette, Sinykin represented the magazine, coordinated the case, and developed the scientific argument; the ACLU represented the editors Knoll and Sam Day and developed the First Amendment argument; White and Case represented Morland; and Tom Fox served as Madison liaison for Morland.

After the second hearing in U.S. District Court, Carbon, along with Sinykin and the ACLU attorney, developed a proposed budget for the entire case (Figure 1). The budget included a four-week trial, a second appeal to the Court of Appeals and, finally, an appeal to the U.S. Supreme Court. The projected total cost for all of this was $285,000, including the $33,000 in attorneys' fees already incurred through the March 26 preliminary injunction. The projected budget had taken into account the *pro bono* representation of Knoll and Day but had not anticipated that Morland's representation would also be on a *pro bono* basis.

In fact, *The Progressive* case proceeded no further than the second phase of the projected six-phase budget. The cost estimates through the second phase had been $85,000 in attorneys' fees and $30,000 in out-of-pocket expenses.

---

24. Hereinafter cited as LaFollette, Sinykin.
25. HOWARD MORLAND, THE SECRET THAT EXPLODED 148–149, 190–191, 215–216 (1981).

Attorneys' Fees

Phase 1: Through preliminary injunction (actual cost)	$33,000
Phase 2: Through Court of Appeals hearing	52,000
Phase 3: Discovery and pretrial preparation	48,000
Phase 4: District Court trial	25,000
Phase 5: Second appeal to Court of Appeals	42,000
Phase 6: Appeal to U.S. Supreme Court	24,000
Subtotal	$224,000
Direct Costs, Expenses	60,000
TOTAL	$284,000

Figure 1. Projected Budget for The Progressive *Case from Appeal to the U.S. Supreme Court.*

1. *Nation, Columbia Journalism Review, Playboy, National Journal, New York, New West, Juris Doctor, Inquiry, Working Papers, New York Review of Books, New Republic, New Engineer, Focus, Midwest, Village Voice, St. Louis Journalism Review, Black Scholar, Rolling Stone, Editor and Publisher, The Witness, Sojourners, Texas Observer, American Lawyer, Cleveland Magazine, Seven Days, Transaction, I. F. Stone's Weekly,* American Booksellers Association, Inc., Council for Periodical Distributors Associations.
2. *Chicago Tribune,* Reporters Committee for Freedom of the Press, Freedom to Read Foundation.
3. *Scientific American.*
4. *New York Times,* American Society of Newspaper Editors, American Association of Publishers, National Association of Broadcasters, Association of American Presses, The Globe Newspaper Company.
5. Fusion Energy Foundation.
6. Committee for Public Justice, Pen American Center, Authors' League of America, Inc.

Figure 2. Parties Filing Amicus *Briefs with Court of Appeals in* The Progressive *Case.*

The Cost of Prior Restraint

But the actual costs reached $240,000 – or 109 percent more than anticipated. About $165,000 was for attorneys' services, and about $75,000 was for direct, out-of-pocket expenses.

LaFollette, Sinykin billed *The Progressive* $158,000 for 3,287 hours of services provided by three attorneys working full-time on the case and three attorneys working part-time. These figures represent a fee of about $48 an hour, a rate Sinykin said was twenty-five to forty percent below the firm's regular rate. LaFollette, Sinykin did not charge a premium for some eighteen-hour-a-day, seven-day weeks the staff worked; nor did Sinykin charge the magazine for about two hundred hours of his own time on the case. Carbon estimated that LaFollette, Sinykin billed *The Progressive* about $46,000 less than the going rate. Fox billed the magazine $6,500 for his services representing Morland.

All legal counsel submitted bills for out-of-pocket expenses, and *The Progressive* itself accumulated between $25,000 and $30,000 in direct expenses. LaFollette, Sinykin's expenses were $17,500; White and Case's were $16,300; the ACLU's were $15,000; and Fox's were about $500. The most detailed figures for expenses are available from LaFollette, Sinykin and may be considered representative of the other law firms' expenses in the case. The largest expenses incurred by LaFollette, Sinykin were for travel ($4,000), copying ($3,700), research ($3,000), printing ($2,700), telephone ($2,000), and transcripts ($800). In addition, there were smaller expenses for postage, express mail, binders, a safe deposit box, and miscellany.

Other than attorneys' fees, the most expensive part of *The Progressive* case was the development of evidence to demonstrate that Morland's article was based on information easily found in the public domain. A significant portion of the LaFollette, Sinykin expenses went to developing this argument, as did *The Progressive*'s own expenses and some of the ACLU's. The need to coordinate three or four different legal efforts resulted in some duplication of work, extra copying of materials, travel, and phone expenses. But duplication of effort is not uncommon in complex cases.

The argument that the information was available to the public was based on four elements. First, LaFollette, Sinykin had research done by physicists in Madison and in other parts of the country and abroad. One physicist, Theodore Postol of the Argonne National Laboratory, worked in the LaFollette, Sinykin offices for about two weeks advising lawyers, gathering scientific information, and developing a bibliography of published literature on the H-bomb. Second, Morland spent about a week in the LaFollette, Sinykin offices preparing an affidavit and being questioned on how he gathered information for the article. Third, the ACLU sent an independent researcher to the Los Alamos Scientific Laboratory's public library in New Mexico, where he successfully duplicated a critical part of Morland's research. *The*

JOHN SOLOSKI and CAROLYN STEWART DYER

Progressive's publisher and managing editor generated the fourth element of the argument by traveling and telephoning to negotiate with scientists to sign affidavits saying that the kind of information in the H-bomb article was available to the international scientific community and to the general public. Extraordinary expenses for trips to gather the signed affidavits included the employment of notaries public, who sometimes sat and waited for hours while scientists read the article and decided whether or not to sign affidavits.

As of the middle of 1983, Vander Meer said that the debts from the case had been reduced to about $7,200. The LaFollette, Sinykin bill was being paid on a schedule of monthly installments. Aggressive fundraising has long since ended, and for most people the issue is dead. Knoll said, "It was much easier, much more dramatic, for me to go around talking to people who might be contributors as the bound and gagged editor of *The Progressive* than the one who fought and waged a successful struggle to publish something."

Expenses are ready measures of the impact of a lawsuit on a publication, but what may be more important is the cost in time and energy. For *The Progressive*'s small staff, the extra time demands included assisting attorneys in preparation of defense arguments, responding to requests for information and interviews from other media, and, of course, raising money to pay the legal bills. These demands made the task of publishing the magazine much more difficult than it had been before the case.

Carbon estimated that he and the two editors devoted nearly full-time to the case during the first two and one-half months after the suit was filed. After that, the demands on the staff increased whenever there was court action. Knoll estimated that in the year after the case began, he spent nearly twenty-five percent of his time on the road speaking about the case. In the first eighteen months, he spoke in thirty states. But neither Knoll nor Carbon kept detailed records of how they spent their time or how much money each speaking engagement generated. Asked what the days were like, Knoll answered without hesitation, "Lunatic."

Morland, an otherwise unemployed freelance writer and antinuclear activist, had to spend time in Madison, New York, and Washington, D.C., consulting with attorneys. He also had speaking engagements and news interviews that took time away from other work he might have been doing. Except for some talk-show interviews and speeches, Morland was not paid for his activities related to the case, and only occasionally were his travel expenses paid.[26] To save money, he piggybacked necessary unpaid trips onto paid trips, resulting in some very hectic days. Once, during a two- or three-day period of about ten interviews a day, Morland literally fell asleep while answering a question, according to Carbon. The only pay Morland received

26. MORLAND, *supra* note 25 at 65, 111, 148, 203–204, 211–212, 216, 223.

The Cost of Prior Restraint

from *The Progressive* was $1,000 for two articles and another $350 for the right to publish the now valuable H-bomb article.[27] *The Progressive* did, however, accept financial responsibility for Morland's defense, something a freelancer cannot routinely expect.

The demands of the media caused the most interruptions in the normal activities of *The Progressive* staff. The staff decided at the beginning of the case to respond to every reasonable request for information and interviews. They wanted to counter the impression left by the judge and the government that the article did, indeed, reveal secret, dangerous information. Since the article was locked in a safe, the staff concluded that they needed to say as much as possible without violating the court order that prohibited them from discussing the scientific content of the article. At least indirectly, they wanted to show that they were not an "irresponsible bunch of crazies," in Knoll's terms, as they felt some media had portrayed them in stories and in editorials. And, Knoll said, the case was about access to information, and it would have been hypocritical to deny the media information they requested.

The consequence of trying to answer all the questions was that at times there would be several television crews waiting at the door when the staff arrived for work, and the principals in the case did nothing but talk to reporters "for a whole day, several days in a row," Knoll said. With first three, then four telephone lines into the office, Knoll said there were times when all of the phones would be busy for hours. And if he left the office for a few hours, Knoll would have twenty or thirty phone calls to return and he would spend the rest of the day on the phone. Staff members also tried to accommodate most requests for speeches. Eventually, a foundation was formed to help arrange speaking tours and other public relations activities.

Then there was the magazine to publish. The attention generated by the case resulted in a fifty-percent increase in the number of unsolicited manuscripts. Each of the two hundred fifty or so manuscripts that arrived each month had to be read to find the one or two usable ones. The one media contribution about which Knoll speaks most warmly and passionately was the donation of the services of a copy editor by the *Bergen Evening Record* in Hackensack, New Jersey. The *Record* sent a reporter to Madison for a few weeks during the summer of 1979. He worked through the large backlog of manuscripts and helped put out the magazine while the editors were busy on the case. Knoll said that his assistance "was worth thousands of dollars to us and it was a magnificent contribution."

The New Jersey newspaper was not the only volunteer to come to the aid of *The Progressive*, but it was the only direct media contribution. Knoll said that he and other staff members "called in every chip," every personal

---

27. *Id.* at 213.

due bill they had ever earned. They accepted nearly every offer to answer phones, to stuff envelopes, to house out-of-town visitors. In short, Knoll said, commenting on the time and energy that the case absorbed, "It was almost as if a year had been taken out of our lives, our work, to devote to this thing." Two years later, he said he was "still digging out, still catching up on some of the time we lost."

MEDIA SUPPORT FOR *THE PROGRESSIVE*

When Knoll first contemplated the case and what it would mean to the magazine, he thought that the American mass media would come to its aid by providing editorial support and contributing to the defense fund. "We thought this was a clear, open-and-shut First Amendment case, and the media organizations aren't going to let us go down the tube on an issue like this," Knoll said.

This expectation was not unreasonable if previous case histories were used as a guide. Not only was *The Progressive* case a First Amendment case, it involved an obvious prior restraint by the government. And the U.S. Supreme Court has said most clearly that if the First Amendment protects against anything, it protects the press against prior restraint, with very few exceptions.[28] In the few prior restraint cases before *The Progressive* case, the media supported the defendants. The conservative publisher of the *Chicago Tribune*, Colonel Robert R. McCormick, contributed $35,000 in legal services to Jay M. Near for his landmark prior restraint case in 1931. McCormick also convinced the American Newspaper Publishers Association to contribute $5,000 to Near's cause.[29] In the Pentagon Papers case, neither the *New York Times* nor the *Washington Post* needed financial assistance, but they did receive editorial support from most of the press in the United States.[30] In the *Nebraska Press Association* case, individual media and media organizations contributed most of the $125,000 needed to pursue the case, and editorial support for the Nebraska media was nearly unanimous.[31]

---

28. Near v. Minnesota, 283 U.S. 697, 51 S. Ct. 625, 75 L. Ed. 1357 (1931); Organization for a Better Austin v. Keefe, 402 U.S. 415, 91 S. Ct. 1575, 29 L. Ed. 2d 1 (1971); New York Times v. U.S.; U.S. v. Washington Post; and Nebraska Press Association v. Stuart.
29. Near v. Minnesota. A Talk with Fred Friendly, Author of *Minnesota Rag*, a press release circulated by Random House, at 3 (n.d.). N. D. PHILIP KINSLEY, LIBERTY AND THE PRESS 4 (1944).
30. JOHN LOFTON, THE PRESS AS GUARDIAN OF THE FIRST AMENDMENT 263 (1980). Of the eighty-two editorials published in EDITORIALS ON FILE 807–871 (1971), seventy-seven supported the *New York Times* and the *Washington Post*.
31. Howe, *supra* note 19, at 4. Lofton, *supra* note 30, at 271. EDITORIALS ON FILE 873–880 (1976). All twenty-two editorials published favored the Nebraska Press Association and the U.S. Supreme Court.

The Cost of Prior Restraint

Based on other media's experience with First Amendment cases, *The Progressive*'s editors were *certain* that the media would come to their aid. "In that expectation, we were catastrophically mistaken. As it turned out, the major media institutions, corporations, associations weren't terribly concerned about our First Amendment rights, lest we jeopardize theirs," Knoll said. Not only did the media fail to help the magazine financially; most opposed the magazine's position in editorials. A few, however, such as the *New York Times*, eventually supported the magazine editorially.[32]

The only individual mass medium to contribute money to *The Progressive*'s legal defense fund was *Playboy* magazine, which gave Knoll five thousand dollars and a Hugh M. Hefner First Amendment award. The Wisconsin Freedom of Information Council contributed one thousand dollars. A number of chapters of the Society of Professional Journalists/Sigma Delta Chi contributed twenty-five to fifty dollars each, and nearly two years after the case was completed, the national convention of SPJ/SDX endorsed *The Progressive*'s stand and contributed five hundred dollars.

The only other direct media support came in an offer of legal assistance from Clayton Kirkpatrick, publisher of the *Chicago Tribune*. The offer was declined because the attorneys were concerned about spreading the legal defense too thin and thus losing control over the arguments in the case. A number of magazines, weekly newspapers, professional organizations, and three daily newspapers did file joint *amicus curiae* briefs in support of *The Progressive* (Figure 2). Since Judge Warren had taken judicial notice of the editorial opposition to *The Progressive*'s stand in the case, the media participation in the *amicus curiae* briefs was important, but it did not help financially.

Due to the negative editorial reaction to the case, *The Progressive* staff did not engage in much formal fundraising among the media and were generally rebuffed when they did. Knoll was invited to speak at the American Society of Newspaper Editors convention a couple of weeks after the suit was filed. He was not invited, however, to the American Newspaper Publishers Association convention that was held about the same time in the same city, even though the convention's theme was the First Amendment.

The fundraising was rather informal and amateurish, both Knoll and Carbon admitted. The efforts included a direct mail campaign, speaking tours, and an appeal to subscribers, as well as meeting with foundation representatives and wealthy individuals. The largest single contribution was $25,000, which came out of one meeting with a small group of liberal philanthropists who together contributed $70,000. Carbon estimates that the magazine's subscribers contributed $70,000, in addition to the $100,000 they contributed

---

32. EDITORIALS ON FILE 304–311 (1979). Of nineteen editorials published, only three were supportive of *The Progressive*.

during 1979 to offset the magazine's yearly deficit. The direct mail campaign did not quite break even. Carbon and Knoll said that the speaking tours were not effective fundraisers either, but some speeches were indirectly responsible for contributions, including $5,000 contributed during a party after an ACLU chapter speech. The speeches by Knoll and Morland were more valuable in disseminating *The Progressive*'s position on the First Amendment and on nuclear development. The fees for many of the speeches just barely covered the speaker's travel expenses.

Although the magazine was accused of using the H-bomb case to boost circulation, in 1979 circulation increased by only about seven hundred, compared to the three to four thousand new subscribers anticipated from the annual circulation drive. The demands of the case made it impossible for the magazine to conduct its regular circulation drive in 1979. Though careful records were not kept, Carbon estimated that the magazine lost a few dozen subscriptions as a result of the case, and more were lost because the magazine accepted the *Playboy* award, which feminists in particular criticized.

REDUCING THE RISK OF LITIGATION

Given the political issues and the legal arguments of *The Progressive* case, it would seem that the failure of the mass media to come to the aid of the magazine was based on a rejection of *The Progressive*'s strong antinuclear stand and a fear that the U.S. Supreme Court would eventually rule in favor of the government and erode the protections of the First Amendment against prior restraint. The inaction and opposition of the media were clearly not the result of ignorance about the cost of media litigation. The media have been aware for some time of the high cost of litigation and of the impact it can have on a medium. Professional associations—especially the American Newspaper Publishers Association (ANPA) and the National Association of Broadcasters—have been actively developing means of reducing the costs of litigation and for sharing information about litigation, especially libel. The development of libel insurance and, more recently, First Amendment insurance is meant to minimize some of the risks of publishing and broadcasting. Of these, First Amendment insurance is most relevant to *The Progressive*'s situation, but it was not available when the case began, and *The Progressive* would not have been eligible for coverage because the insurance is only available to ANPA members.

First Amendment insurance was developed in 1979 by the Mutual Insurance Company of Bermuda at the request of the ANPA. It became available to ANPA members in April 1980, and by the summer of 1983, over three hundred media entities had purchased the insurance.[33] In November 1980,

33. Interview with representative of Mutual Insurance Co. (July 1983).

The Cost of Prior Restraint

First Amendment insurance was made available to members of the National Association of Broadcasters by the Media/Professional Insurance Company. Its protection is not as broad as the insurance offered by Mutual.[34] Mutual's First Amendment insurance covers prior restraint, access questions, reporter's privilege, statutory limitations on publication, antitrust involving "significant First Amendment issues, and other actions recognized as involving violations of the 'free press' guarantee of the First Amendment."[35] Coverage is limited to a maximum of one million dollars per incident.

The ANPA's objective in developing First Amendment insurance was to provide small- and medium-sized newspapers with the financial resources to undertake First Amendment cases. In announcing the insurance program, Allen Neuharth, chairman of Gannett and, at that time, the head of ANPA, called it "a great step forward in providing newspapers throughout the United States, particularly smaller newspapers, the opportunity and the means to fight for and to defend freedom of speech and the press."[36]

But an important question about First Amendment insurance is: Can the smaller media afford to buy the coverage? About half of the newspapers and broadcast stations in the United States do not carry libel insurance, which would indemnify against that more likely legal problem, and there is no reason to expect that these media will buy First Amendment insurance.[37] Even if *The Progressive* could afford to buy First Amendment insurance, Knoll said that he would oppose buying it on principle. "I don't think I need to insure myself for the exercise of rights granted me by the Constitution," he said.

The rates and deductibles for Mutual's First Amendment insurance increase on a sliding scale according to circulation and are based on Mutual's libel insurance rates. To buy First Amendment insurance a newspaper must also buy Mutual's libel insurance. For a newspaper with a circulation of 5,000 or less, the annual premium for First Amendment insurance is $247 for $100,000 of coverage and $504 for $1 million of coverage, with a deductible of $2,500. A newspaper with a circulation between 25,001 and 50,000 would pay a premium of $500 for $100,000 of coverage and $1,148 for $1 million of coverage, with a $7,500 deductible. For large newspapers, those with circulations between 150,001 and 200,000, the annual premium is $1,680 for $100,000 of coverage and $3,216 for $1 million of coverage, with a deductible of $15,000.[38]

34. BROADCASTING, November 17, 1980, at 63–64.
35. Letter from Arthur B. Hanson, U.S. General Counsel for Mutual Insurance Co., to interested First Amendment attorneys (September 28, 1979). *See also* Richard A. Ek, The Bermuda Connection: Lifeline to a Free Press, a paper presented to the Law Division at the annual convention of the Association for Education in Journalism, Michigan State University, East Lansing, Michigan (August 1981).
36. PRESSTIME, February 1980, at 52.
37. PRESSTIME, November 1980, at 4; BROADCASTING, November 17, 1980, at 63.
38. Representative of Mutual Insurance Co., *supra* note 33.

JOHN SOLOSKI and CAROLYN STEWART DYER

The First Amendment insurance offered to broadcasters by the Media/Professional Insurance Company is also tied to its libel coverage. For radio, the annual premiums for libel insurance are based on the advertising rate card and for television on the hourly programming rate. First Amendment insurance adds an additional fifty percent to the annual libel premium.[39]

Although Mutual has provided a list of the types of cases covered by its First Amendment insurance, payment of claims is not automatic under the policy. Mutual, not the publisher, makes the final decision on whether or not to pursue a case or to resist government action as *The Progressive* did. When First Amendment insurance was in the planning stages, Arthur B. Hanson, general counsel to the Mutual Insurance Company, said, "We will *tell* [the publisher] whether he is going to court or not." The decision to underwrite a case is made by a panel consisting of Mutual's attorney, the publisher's attorney, and at least three attorneys selected by the insurance company. A ruling by the majority is binding on both Mutual and the insured. But unlike Mutual's libel insurance, under which the publisher's attorney handles the case, First Amendment insurance permits the insurance company to select the attorney for the case.[40]

As an example of a case that would not be covered by Mutual's First Amendment insurance, Hanson said that it would not apply in a libel case when a reporter claims a First Amendment privilege to refuse to identify a source or to provide other information necessary to the newspaper's defense. "I don't care if the reporter goes to jail," Hanson said, "but I'm not going to pay out a million dollars just because some dummy thinks he's got a privilege when the court has said he doesn't."[41] This example raises the question of whether the insurance would have covered *The Progressive*, which was clearly proposing to violate the letter of the Atomic Energy Act of 1954. And would it have covered *The Progressive* if the staff had decided to violate the court order and publish the H-bomb article? That is an option *The Progressive*'s editors considered, as did some *New York Times* executives in the Pentagon Papers case.[42]

Opportunities and decisions to publish alleged H-bomb secrets or Pentagon Papers are rare, but accusations of libel are a common and costly problem for the media. Some media people expect that the publicity surrounding large damage awards in recent libel cases will result in more suits being filed against the media. James C. Goodale, former *New York Times* general counsel, said, "There is no question [that libel lawyers are going to file] more and more

39. BROADCASTING, *supra* note 34.
40. Ek, *supra* note 35, at 31.
41. Interview with Arthur B. Hanson (Fall 1979).
42. SALISBURY, *supra* note 18, at 290–291, describes a meeting in which violation of a court order was discussed.

The Cost of Prior Restraint

libel suits because they see that plaintiffs can be awarded a lot of money and it can be very lucrative."[43] But it is the defense costs that are the most debilitating and demoralizing, particularly when a medium wins a libel case. John K. Zollinger, publisher of the *Gallup Independent* (New Mexico) said his paper spend "nearly two percent of our net profit on legal costs. It's no joke any more [because] you win and still pay."[44]

Most libel insurance policies do not automatically cover the legal expenses that make even winning a case costly. One insurance company representative estimated that libel insurance for a magazine the size of *The Progressive* would cost about $650 a year for $100,000 of coverage and $1,200 for $1 million of coverage. There would be a $2,500 deductible, and legal fees would not be covered. Coverage of legal expenses adds thirty-five percent to the premium.[45] But not all insurance companies would be eager to write libel insurance for a politically active and editorially aggressive magazine such as *The Progressive*. A representative of one major insurance company said that his company likes to insure "nice publications," meaning those unlikely to be involved in controversy or litigation.[46] A study undertaken by the legal department of the National Association of Broadcasters (NAB) found that stations which broadcast news, editorials, talk or call-in programs, or public affairs programs are required to carry special deductibles up to four times the usual deductible.[47] The study reported that four percent of the stations responding to a questionnaire had "to modify or cancel types of programming or news coverage" because of possible pressure from their insurance companies.[48] The results of this study led the NAB to develop a more comprehensive insurance program for its members. Libel insurance without provisions for attorneys' fees and other legal expenses would seem to be a poor bargain for media without exceptional in-house counsel services. Although premiums and deductibles for libel and First Amendment insurance do not seem high compared to annual budgets, it is likely that the premiums will rise if the volume of claims and large damage awards continues to increase. Then, insurance will not be merely an incidental expense.

Insurance is just one of the resources available to the media to help offset the cost of litigation. If a media institution has neither insurance (or enough insurance to cover all expenses) nor individual funds to engage in litigation, it might turn to one of several organizations interested in media cases. These

---

43. PRESSTIME, *supra* note 13, at 10.
44. PRESSTIME, *supra* note 37, at 5.
45. Interview with a representative of Media/Professional Insurance Co. (July 1983).
46. Interview with a representative of a major insurance company that provides libel insurance to newspapers and broadcasters (March 1981).
47. BROADCASTING, March 10, 1980, at 68.
48. *Id.*

JOHN SOLOSKI and CAROLYN STEWART DYER

include the Reporters Committee for Freedom of the Press, the Libel Defense Resource Center, the American Civil Liberties Union, subcommittees of the American Newspaper Publishers Association, the American Society of Newspaper Editors (ASNE), and the Society of Professional Journalists/Sigma Delta Chi (SPJ/SDX).

The ACLU did provide valuable assistance to *The Progressive* and it has provided *pro bono* counsel for other media in First Amendment cases. But the ACLU's purpose is to promote and protect civil liberties, broadly defined, and the media and the First Amendment are not its only nor its primary concerns. In October 1982, the ACLU changed its policy on libel and said that it would be interested in libel cases involving public figures and public issues. Prior to that, the ACLU was not active in libel cases. The ACLU's policy change was in reaction to the apparent increase in the number of libel suits and large damage awards.[49] While the ACLU provides *pro bono* counsel, its clients generally have to pay out-of-pocket expenses, which amounted to $16,000 in *The Progressive* case.

The strictly journalistic organizations—ANPA, ASNE, and SPJ/SDX—do not have the resources and staffs to help finance cases. The more common contribution these organizations make is to file *amicus curiae* briefs in cases undertaken and underwritten by other media institutions. The *amicus* briefs provide moral support and sometimes they make important legal arguments, but they do nothing to help pay the bills. Although the executive committee of ASNE voted within a few weeks of the start of *The Progressive* case to support the magazine, the support came in the form of an *amicus* brief filed jointly with other media organizations. ANPA took no action. The national SPJ/SDX did not take any action until long after the case was finished.

The Reporters Committee was formed to provide legal aid to reporters and media, but it was of little assistance to *The Progressive*. When the case began, Knoll said that Jack Landau, head of the committee and former coworker with Knoll in the Newhouse newspaper chain, volunteered legal and financial assistance. Within a few days, however, Knoll said that Landau changed his position and advised Knoll to compromise with the government by submitting the article to "experts" who would decide what could be published without endangering national security. That was not the sort of aid *The Progressive* was expecting, and Landau's recommendation drew a bitter reaction from Knoll. "Whatever the Reporters Committee is," Knoll said, "it is not a committee for freedom of the press." In the end, the Reporters Committee did join the *Chicago Tribune* and the Freedom to Read Foundation in filing an *amicus* brief.

---

49. Gilbert Cranberg, *ACLU: Second Thoughts on Libel*, COLUMBIA JOURNALISM REV. 42–43 (January/February 1983).

The Cost of Prior Restraint

Even if the Reporters Committee had wanted to help *The Progressive*, it is unlikely that the committee would have had the financial resources to undertake an expensive case. Shortly before *The Progressive*'s case began, the Reporters Committee reported a $31,000 budget deficit.[50] The Reporters Committee is itself dependent on the largess of media institutions, foundations, and individuals for its funds. Although the committee cannot provide much in the way of direct legal help, it will attempt to arrange *pro bono* representation for a reporter or a medium if it becomes financially necessary.

The Libel Defense Resource Center (LDRC) did not exist at the time of *The Progressive*'s case, and even if it had, it would not have been of any help. The LDRC was formed in 1982 by media companies, professional organizations, libel insurance companies, and foundations to act as a clearinghouse for information about libel in the United States. The LDRC's budget in 1982 was about $70,000, of which about $10,000 was deficit; its projected budget for 1983 was about $80,000. The LDRC provides model briefs and pleadings, compiles reports on libel, and collects other information about libel of interest to the media and their attorneys, but it does not get involved in litigation.[51]

In short, none of the organizations with a specific interest in media law issues has the resources to do more than offer advice and information. The legal aid that is most frequently given is the filing of *amicus* briefs. But even when these organizations provide legal help, there are problems. Legal counsel provided by a third party and *amicus* briefs subject the media institution involved in the case to a possible loss of control over its legal arguments. The involvement of the ACLU in *The Progressive* case illustrates some of the problems that could arise with an *amicus* brief. Before the March 26 hearing on the preliminary injunction, the ACLU filed an *amicus* brief recommending that the court appoint a panel of scientists to review the H-bomb article. Sinykin said that when he learned of the ACLU's argument, "we were horror-stricken." Judge Warren read the ACLU's brief along with legal documents filed by *The Progressive*, the government, and other *amici*, and he initially adopted the ACLU's suggestion. Thus, a compelling *amicus* argument, which was contrary to the magazine's own position, supplanted *The Progressive*'s argument against *any* form of prior restraint. When the ACLU subsequently offered to represent Knoll and Day, Sinykin said that the ACLU's help was accepted on condition that the ACLU abandon the idea of an independent review of the article. In the Pentagon Papers case, outside counsel for both the *New York Times* and the *Washington Post* opposed

---

50. THE QUILL 13 (March 1979).
51. Interview with Henry R. Kaufman, General Counsel for the Libel Defense Resource Center (July 15, 1983).

publication of the documents. The *Times* had to find a new lawyer the night before its first court hearing, and, after the case was completed, the *Post* terminated its arrangement with its counsel because of his recommendation against publication and the *Post*'s dissatisfaction with his arguments in the case.[52]

CONCLUSION

One of the obvious results of the cost of litigation is that the media will avoid situations that may result in legal problems. Floyd Abrams, an attorney who helped to represent the *New York Times* in the Pentagon Papers case, said, "If things develop to the point where large jury verdicts or large counsel fees on a yearly basis are the norm and not the exception, then I don't have any doubts that publications will be obliged to trim their sails.... The real danger is that the public will never know."[53] Since it is difficult to know when the media engage in self-censorship, it is impossible to gauge how common a practice it is or what types of stories are not published.

Even Knoll and Carbon acknowledge that they would be more cautious if an issue comparable to the H-bomb secret came up again. They would plan their strategy ahead of time and raise defense money before publication. "I think we would have to go out and talk about the article with people and try and get [financial] commitments in advance," Sinykin said. The reactions of those solicited might well determine whether the article would be published. Knoll adds, however, that in the same circumstances, he would disobey what he thought was an unconstitutional court order and publish the article, on his own if necessary.

If a media organization cannot rely on the financial support of larger organizations and does not have insurance to cover the costs of litigation, what then are the medium's alternatives when faced with a potentially expensive case? The bottom line is that a small, independently owned medium may have to risk its own survival in order to pursue litigation that may actually benefit all media. *The Progressive* did not quite reach the point at which a decision had to be made between killing the magazine and dropping the case. If premiums for libel and First Amendment insurance increase as expected, then it is not inconceivable that some media may be forced to drop their insurance or accept less-than-adequate coverage. The cost of litigation poses a serious threat to the freedom of the press. The existing means of financing media litigation are inadequate, and there is a need for a comprehensive system of responding to media legal problems. The establishment of organizations

52. On the *Times'* losing its attorney and finding others, *see* SALISBURY, *supra* note 18, at 244–247. On *Post* and attorney, *see* UNGAR, *supra* note 14, at 306.
53. Quoted in Picard, *supra* note 16, at 16.

The Cost of Prior Restraint

such as the LDRC and the Reporters Committee and the holding of conferences for attorneys and journalists to discuss and share information about media law cases are a good first step, but more needs to be done. Whatever form a comprehensive system would take, it needs to provide: (1) information on how previous cases were managed and what successful and unsuccessful strategies were used, so media participants need not develop their own strategies in a vacuum when cases occur; (2) ready access to informed legal advice, tailored in strategy to the medium choosing to take or defend an unpopular action; (3) experienced legal counsel available on the short notice required in prior restraint cases; (4) money to pay direct expenses as well as attorneys' fees, or a guarantee of *pro bono* representation; and (5) voluntary assistance to help the medium continue to publish or broadcast while legal problems occupy the time of the staff.

F. DENNIS HALE

State Press Law Provisions and State Demographics

F. Dennis Hale is an associate professor
and is head of the News-Editorial
Sequence in the School of Journalism at
Bowling Green State University in Ohio.
He teaches journalism law and
newspaper reporting.

Despite the intensified federalization of freedom of expression during the 1960s by the U.S. Supreme Court and Chief Justice Earl Warren, many aspects of freedom of press today remain the province of the states. As the result of decisions by the Warren Burger Court during the 1970s that rebuffed efforts to further expand the First Amendment, state legislators and state appellate court justices define the limits of press freedom, particularly in areas related to the gathering as opposed to the disseminating of news.

State solons and state appellate judges enjoy significant discretion in formulating press law in six areas: libel, privacy, confidentiality of sources, obscenity, cameras and recorders in the courtroom, and access to government meetings and records. In the area of privacy, the states have retained jurisdiction primarily because of inactivity of the U.S. Supreme Court (the exception is the privacy tort of false light, which is governed by the federal actual malice rule[1]). In the other five areas of freedom of press, the Supreme Court has specifically reserved authority for the states. In 1972 in *Branzburg*[2] the Court said that the First Amendment does not protect journalists from being required to testify about confidential sources before grand juries. The 1974 *Gertz* decision[3] narrowed the definition of public figure, limiting the application of the actual malice rule and diminishing First Amendment protec-

---

1. Cantrell v. Forest City Publishing Co., 419 U.S. 245, 95 S. Ct. 465 (1974).
2. Branzburg v. Hayes, 408 U.S. 665, 92 S. Ct. 2646 (1972).
3. Gertz v. Robert Welch, Inc. 418 U.S. 323, 94 S. Ct. 2997 (1974).

tion in libel. The Court ruled in *Saxbe*[4] in 1974 that the Constitution does not grant journalists any more access than the general public to government. *Chandler*[5] left the states free to regulate photographing and recording in state courtrooms. And *Miller*[6] granted the states more discretion in controlling obscenity by eliminating the constitutional requirement that an obscene work must be utterly without redeeming social value.

The states do not enjoy continued or complete authority in these areas of press law. A future Supreme Court could create First Amendment limits in these six areas. Or, Congress could statutorily create national standards to protect the press as it did in regard to police searches of newsrooms.[7] Additionally, although the Court has granted the states considerable latitude in specific areas of press freedom, on several occasions the Court has ruled that such state authority has limits. For example, after strengthening the authority of states to prosecute for obscenity in *Miller*, the Court in *Jenkins*[8] prevented states from declaring films obscene unless they contain explicit portrayals of sexual acts. And in *Branzburg* the Court made it clear that it would not permit the government to harrass the press through the use of subpoenas unrelated to good-faith investigations of crime.

States, then, have a significant role in shaping press rights. The purpose of this study was to analyze the states to identify factors that are either positively or negatively related to press laws. Forty-three social, economic, cultural, and political characteristics were examined to determine whether they were statistically associated with eight measures of press rights in the states.

Political scientists have made extensive use of this methodology (1) to determine if state policy outcomes are related to environmental factors and inputs and (2) to study regionalism. As Dye pointed out, the variability of the states makes this practical: "Fortunately, if only for the sake of analysis, there are marked differences among the states in economic development levels."[9]

METHODOLOGY

The study was conducted by gathering sociological and census data on the fifty states and correlating those state characteristics with quantifiable

4. Saxbe v. Washington Post Co., 417 U.S. 843, 94 S. Ct. 2811 (1974).
5. Chandler v. Florida, 449 U.S. 560, 101 S. Ct. 802 (1981).
6. Miller v. California, 413 U.S. 15, 93 S. Ct. 2607 (1973).
7. M. Genovese, *New Law Bars Surprise Police Searches of Media*, 2 PRESSTIME 10–11 (November 1980).
8. Jenkins v. Georgia, 418 U.S. 153 (1974).
9. T. DYE, POLITICS, ECONOMICS, AND THE PUBLIC: POLICY OUTCOMES IN THE AMERICAN STATES 11 (1966); T. DYE AND V. GRAY, THE DETERMINANTS OF PUBLIC POLICY (1980); I. SHARKANSKY, REGIONALISM IN AMERICAN POLITICS (1970).

State Press Law Provisions and State Demographics

press law provisions of the states. Press law information came from dissertations and journals giving state-by-state breakdowns on such things as open meeting laws, retraction statutes, shield laws, and cameras in the courtroom. State sociological data came from *Statistical Abstracts of the United States* (1981 edition), *The Almanac of American Politics 1982, Newspaper Circulation Analysis* for September 1982, *The Book of the States* (1982-83 edition), and *The Book of American Rankings* (1979 edition).

Seven press law provisions primarily concerned statutes created by the state legislatures to protect the press in gathering information. An eighth, nonlegal provision was added — the presence of voluntary bench-bar-press guidelines. As with any empirical research, the quantifying and operational defining of information resulted in some potential distortion. For example, the dichotomous variable, shield laws, divided the states into those with and without shield statutes. This ignored major differences between statutes. It also ignored those few states in which judges — as opposed to the legislature — have created a qualified right of confidentiality for reporters. The eight press law variables were: financial disclosure,[10] public vote,[11] advanced notice,[12] bar-press guidelines,[13] shield laws,[14] courtroom cameras,[15] open meetings,[16] and retraction laws.[17]

The eight press law provisions were correlated with forty-three state characteristics, which fall into five broad categories: political, economic, sociological, cultural, and media. The eight political characteristics were: registered voters, federal employees, local taxes, years of statehood, tenure of judges, election of judges, Society of Professional Journalists, and appellate judges per population.[18] The six economic characteristics were: average income, blue collar workers, bank loans, stock ownership, poverty-level

10. Number of types of public officials required to publicly disclose their financial condition. THE BOOK OF THE STATES 1982–1983 32 (1982).
11. Number of legislative houses that require a recorded roll call on vote to report a bill to the floor. *Id.* at 116.
12. Number of legislative houses in which advanced public notice is required before a committee may consider a bill. *Id.*
13. States in which judges, attorneys, and journalists have approved voluntary guidelines for the reporting of crime. *Justices Allow Censorship Arguments*, 6 NEWS MEDIA & THE LAW 48 (June–July 1982).
14. States with statutes that protect reporters from disclosing confidential sources. J. Jackson, *Shield Laws Vary Widely*, 3 PRESSTIME 14–15 (May 1981).
15. Number of types of courts in which cameras and recorders are permitted. *Cameras in the Courts*, 6 NEWS MEDIA & THE LAW 48 (June–July 1982).
16. Strength of open-meeting statute, ranging from 0 to 9. J. ADAMS, STATE OPEN MEETING LAWS: AN OVERVIEW (University of Missouri, Freedom of Information Foundation, 1974).
17. Existence of retraction provision in state libel statute. D. Dickerson, A Challenge to the Constitutionality of Retraction Statutes, doctoral diss., Southern Illinois University at Carbondale (1977).
18. *Supra* note 10 at 150–51, 156–57; STATISTICAL ABSTRACTS OF THE UNITED STATES 518 (1981); C. JUDGE, THE BOOK OF AMERICAN RANKINGS 104, 255 (1979).

F. DENNIS HALE

residents, and jobless rate for 1980.[19] The fourteen sociological characteristics were: population, population density, population immobility, home ownership, blacks, ruralism, English natives, birth rate, crime rate, elderly, population between twenty-five and forty-four years old, population growth in last decade, central city population, and suburban population.[20] Eleven cultural characteristics were Northeastern states, Midwestern states, Southern states, Western states, church membership, lawyers, passports, artists, alcohol consumption, education level, and illiteracy.[21] And there were four media variables: per capita daily newspapers, per capita Sunday newspapers, television stations, and weekly newspapers.[22]

The association between the eight press law measures and the forty-three state characteristics was analyzed using the Pearson correlation coefficient program of the *Statistical Package for the Social Sciences*.[23] Also analyzed were the correlations between the press law variables. Because of the lack of hypotheses concerning the direction of resulting correlations, a two-tailed test of statistical significance was used at the .05 level.

RESULTS

There were twenty-five statistically significant correlation coefficients between the eight press law provisions and forty-three state characteristics (see Table 1). Five state characteristics were associated with two or more press laws and accounted for twelve of the twenty-five significant correlations.

Tenure, years for a term of office for state supreme court members, was negatively associated with two press laws ($-.35$, $-.42$). States with shorter judicial terms tended to be more supportive of press laws. This was an unexpected outcome. Support for press rights generally exists in a politically liberal, pro-civil liberties environment. Short terms for appellate judges should be associated with political conservatism—not liberalism—because short terms limit the independence of judges and make them more responsive to the popular beliefs of voters and judicial appointers.

Immobility was negatively associated with two press laws ($-.28$, $-.31$), indicating a positive association between population mobility and press protec-

---

19. STATISTICAL ABSTRACTS 382, 447, 467; AMERICAN RANKINGS 74, 277–78.
20. 64, no. 9 NEWSPAPER CIRCULATION ANALYSIS Part II, Sect. V, p. 3 (September 1982); STATISTICAL ABSTRACTS 12, 16, 20, 32, 36, 792; AMERICAN RANKINGS 31–32, 40–41, 151–52; M. BARONE AND G. UJIFUSA, THE ALMANAC OF AMERICAN POLITICS (1981).
21. Collapsed Regions of the U.S. Bureau of Census, STATISTICAL ABSTRACTS 20, 150; AMERICAN RANKINGS 47–48, 77–78, 179–80, 188, 235–36.
22. NEWSPAPER CIRCULATION ANALYSIS 3; STATISTICAL ABSTRACTS 588; '82 AYER DIRECTORY OF PUBLICATIONS 1231–74 (1982).
23. N. NIE, STATISTICAL PACKAGE FOR THE SOCIAL SCIENCES 276–300 (1975).

State Press Law Provisions and State Demographics

tion. It may be easier to pass laws favorable to the press in states with large numbers of non-natives who have shallow roots. State government may accede to more openness and accessibility in such an environment.

Ruralism was negatively associated with four press law provisions ($-.43$, $-.37$, $-.33$, $-.28$), and suburbanism was positively associated with two press law provisions (.35, .32). In addition, two of the strongest associations for characteristics with a single significant correlation were the population of the state (.40) and proportion of central city population (.52). These results of ruralism, suburbanism, population, and central city indicate that urbanism is conducive to the creation of laws that protect the press and provide access to government information.

The positive associations with per capita consumption of Sunday newspapers (.43, .29) also were consistent with the strength of urbanism. Sunday circulation is strongly related to state population and suburbanism.

Of the characteristics tested in this study, the social measures were the most influential. Political and economic variables, somewhat surprisingly, provided little explanation for differences in press laws. Such things as voter registration, level of taxation, strength of the Society of Professional Journalists, income level, loan activity and stock ownership—variables that reflect affluence, economic vitality, and progressivism—were largely unrelated to the existence of press laws. The cultural variables, also surprisingly, provided little explanation. Levels of education, illiteracy, and region of the country made little difference. And the concentration of lawyers, which could be related to litigiousness and the existence of laws protective of the press, was not significant.

Just as surprising was the lack of explanation for individual press law provisions. Half of the provisions appeared to exist in a vacuum, unrelated to their environment. There were no significant correlations for bench-bar-press guidelines and only one for cameras in the courtroom. And for two other press law variables—existence of shield statutes and prior notice for legislative hearings—each had only two significant correlations. This study provided little explanation for the existence of these four provisions in some states. Random events and historical accidents may explain their existence more than anything else.

Greater explanation was provided for two press law provisions—retraction laws and public vote requirement for the legislature—each of which had four significant correlations. Retraction statutes were negatively associated with judges' tenure and positively associated with the election of judges, home ownership, the Midwest, and level of education. More logical were the four correlations for public voting—negative for poverty and ruralism and positive for suburbs and Sunday newspapers.

Two press law provisions were more related to state characteristics than

F. DENNIS HALE

STATE CHARACTERISTIC	PRESS LAW PROVISIONS							
	FINANCIAL DISCLOSURE	PUBLIC VOTE	ADVANCED NOTICE	BAR-PRESS GUIDELINES	SHIELD LAW	OPEN MEETINGS	RETRACTION LAWS	COURTROOM CAMERAS
Political								
Registered voters	-.31							
Federal employees								
Local taxes								
Statehood						-.28		
Tenure of judges						-.35	-.42	
Elected judges							.28	
Soc'y of Prof. Journalists								
Appellate judges								
Economic								
Average income								
Blue collar								
Bank loans								
Stock ownership	-.30							
Poverty		-.29						
Jobless rate (1980)					.38			
Social								
Population	.40							
Population density						-.32		
Population immobility						-.28		
Home ownership							.31	
Blacks								-.31

State Press Law Provisions and State Demographics

Social (continued)					
Ruralism	−.43	−.37	−.33		−.28
English natives					
Birth rate					
Crime rate					
Elderly					
Population age 25–44					
Growth in last decade	.52				
Central city population		.35	.32	.34	
Suburban population					
Cultural					
Northeast					
Midwest					.28
South					
West					
Church membership					
Lawyers					
Passports					
Artists					
Alcohol consumption				.36	
Education level					
Illiteracy					
Media					
Per capita daily papers	.43				
Per capita Sunday papers		.29			
Television stations					
Weekly papers					

Table 1. Correlations Between Press Law Provisions and State Characteristics

the others. The two, strength of open meeting laws and disclosure of officials' finances, were correlated with six characteristics each. Open meetings appeared to be related to characteristics of younger states. There were negative correlations with length of statehood, judges' tenure, population immobility, and home ownership, and positive correlations with population growth in the 1970s and level of education. The logic behind the six correlates for financial disclosure was not as evident: negative associations for voter registration, stock ownership, and ruralism; positive associations for population, central city, and Sunday newspapers. Interestingly, these two press law provisions most strongly tied to their state environments only indirectly influence the press. Financial disclosure and open meetings most directly influence elected officials, legally mandating the release of government information to the public and the press. The press benefits indirectly.

Little explanation was provided by the test of associations between the eight legal provisions. Only two of the twenty-eight correlations were statistically significant: a .37 correlation between two requirements for the legislature, public voting, and notice for hearings, and a .35 correlation between retraction laws and financial disclosure. The conclusion: state press law provisions were largely unrelated to each other.

The twenty-seven statistically significant correlations in this study provided only *some* explanation for the existence of press law provisions. Although statistically significant, more correlations were not of *practical* significance because the strength of the association was modest at best. The quality known as variance measures the extent that one variable accounts for variation in another variable. Variance is computed by squaring the correlation coefficient. Thus a correlation of .707 is necessary if one variable is to explain fifty percent of the variation in another variable. None of the correlations in this study approached that level. Only six of the twenty-seven correlations surpassed .387, which is the minimum correlation if a variable is to explain fifteen percent of the variation in another variable.

More precise measures of press laws and additional state characteristics might generate stronger correlations. Shield laws could be ranked according to the amount of protection they provide. Better measures could be devised for political liberalism and journalist influence in the states. Liberalism could be measured by the percent of adults who belong to the American Civil Liberties Union or Americans for Democratic Action. Other measures of a state's liberalism are the percent who voted for presidential candidate George McGovern, or the average ACLU or ADA rating of a state's two U.S. senators. Per capita membership in the Society of Professional Journalists might be a better indicator of journalist lobbying power than the number of SPJ chapters for the population.

DEBRA M. ZIGELBAUM

Political Speech or Obscenity?

Debra M. Zigelbaum is a recent graduate of Syracuse University College of Law.

In October of 1983, Larry Flynt, publisher and editor of *Hustler* magazine, announced his candidacy for President of the United States. Mr. Flynt "vowed to use his presidential campaign to test the nation's obscenity laws by airing commercials featuring hard-core sex acts."[1]

Mr. Flynt's attempt caused considerable concern in the broadcast industry because the equal opportunity provision of the Communications Act of 1934 prohibits the censoring of any advertisement in which a candidate's voice or picture appears.[2] However, the U. S. Criminal Code prohibits the dissemination of obscene material.[3] Apparently, the two statutes are in direct conflict,[4] yet a violation of either statute could result in the revocation of a broadcaster's license.[5] The dilemma of choosing between violating the equal opportunity provision and violating the prohibition against the broadcast of obscenity—either of which might mean loss of license—is not only difficult

1. Washington Post, Nov. 9, 1983, at A2.
2. 47 U.S.C.A. § 315(a) (1958 & West Supp. 1983).
3. 18 U.S.C.A. § 1464 (1964 & West Supp. 1966–1983).
4. See *supra* notes 2 and 3.
5. Section 312(a)(4) of the Communications Act of 1934 states: "The Commission may revoke any station license for willful or repeated violation of, or willful or repeated failure to observe any provision of this chapter or any rule or regulation of the Commission authorized by this chapter. . . ." 47 U.S.C.A. § 312(a)(4) (1958 & West Supp. 1983). Section 312(a)(6) of the Communications Act of 1934 states: "The Commission may revoke any station license. . . for violation of section . . . 1464 of Title 18." 47 U.S.C.A. § 312(a)(6) (1958 & West Supp. 1983). Section 312(a)(7) of the Communications Act of 1934 states: "The Commission may revoke any station license for willful or repeated failure to allow reasonable access to or to permit purchase of reasonable amounts of time for the use of a broadcasting station by a legally qualified candidate for Federal elective office on behalf of his candidacy." 47 U.S.C.A. § 312(a)(7) (1958 & West Supp. 1983).

DEBRA M. ZIGELBAUM

for the licensee, it presents a dilemma for the Federal Communications Commission (FCC) as well.

The FCC was concerned that "if it ruled that station owners could refuse to run Flynt's ads, it might set a dangerous precedent for more ambiguous cases."[6] In particular, the FCC was concerned that the ruling could give broadcasters leeway to play politics and affect an election.[7] The matter was one of first impression for both the courts and the FCC. Until then, the FCC and the courts had interpreted the no-censorship provision in section 315(a) as absolute.[8]

This article will explore broadcasters' obligations when presented with political announcements by legally qualified candidates pursuant to 47 U.S.C.A. section 315(a) that contain obscene or indecent material, and will determine whether the equal opportunity doctrine supercedes the statutory bar against the broadcast of obscenity.[9]

THE BROADCAST MEDIA AS A POLITICAL OUTLET

Radio and television have become important sources of news and information for the American public. The obvious benefits of the ability to transmit voice and picture to the public contributed greatly to the broadcast media's rapid proliferation in our society.[10] Approximately eighty-five percent of the population receives its news from radio or television.[11] The tremendous impact of watching television film and listening to commentary cannot be compared

---

6. Washington Post, January 3, 1984, at A15.
7. Id.
8. See Farmer's Educ. & Coop. Union of America v. WDAY, Inc., 360 U.S. 525 (1959) (unanimously holding that a licensee was barred from censoring the comments of a speaker exercising rights under section 315(a) because such censorship was contrary to the basic purpose of section 315(a) to promote full and unrestricted discussion of political issues by legally qualified candidates); see also, NAACP v. F.C.C., 45 R.R.2d 378 (1979) (in which the FCC held that even if it were to find the word "nigger" obscene or indecent, under section 315(a), the legally qualified candidate could not be prevented from using the word during his use of the licensee's facilities).
9. In exploring the answers to these questions, the writer makes no attempt to set out a standard by which the licensee is to determine whether such content is, in fact, obscene or indecent. For purposes of these inquiries, it will be assumed that the political announcements are obscene or indecent.
10. In 1950, there were approximately forty-three million households served by a total of 2,867 radio stations and five million households served by a total of ninety-eight commercial VHF stations. See TELEVISION FACTBOOK 75-a, Services Volume No. 40 (1981–1982 ed.) and STATISTICAL ABSTRACT OF THE UNITED STATES 367, U.S. Dept. of Commerce, Bureau of the Census (100 ed. 1979). At the same time, there were approximately 1,772 daily newspapers with an estimated total circulation of 33,829,000. 49 Fed. Reg. 20,323 (Monday, May 14, 1984).
11. Id.

Political Speech or Obscenity?

with reading the printed page.[12] Radio and television have major influence on the personal, social and cultural habits of the nation;[13] thus, the broadcast media are important outlets through which the public can exercise its first amendment right of free speech. The preservation and protection of political speech has long been recognized as the core of our first Amendment rights.[14]

The high degree of protection afforded political speech and the obvious desirability of the broadcast media as political outlets compelled Congress to enact a plan to foster political debate.[15] Due to the pervasiveness of the broadcast media and its ability to confront the audience suddenly, Congress was greatly concerned that broadcasters would use the monopolistic nature of their industry to influence the public's political attitudes and exert an inordinate amount of control over the political system in this country.[16] Congress feared, for example, that broadcast licensees would support certain political candidates and refuse to air opponents' political messages, or alter the opposing political announcements for the benefit of the licensee-supported candidate. Congress feared that broadcasters would, in general, present unilateral views of the political arena in direct opposition to the very purposes of a democratic society.[17]

Therefore, Congress enacted section 315(a) of the Communications Act for the general purpose of fostering political debate and discourse over the radio.[18] Section 315(a) states:

> If any licensee shall permit any person who is a legally qualified candidate for any public office to use a broadcasting station, he shall afford equal opportunities to all other such candidates for that office in the use of such broadcasting station: Provided, That such licensee shall have no power of censorship over the material broadcast under the provisions of this section.[19]

---

12. Address by Spiro Agnew, Mid-West Regional Republican Committee, Des Moines, Iowa (November 13, 1969).
13. *Id.*
14. Professor Meikeljohn's first amendment theory embodies the belief that because political speech is essential to self-governing and to understanding the political arena, political speech deserves absolute protection from governmental interference. A. MEIKELJOHN, FREE SPEECH AND ITS RELATION TO SELF GOVERNMENT 65–66 (1948).
15. *See*1959 U.S. CODE CONG. & AD. NEWS 2564, 2566.
16. *Id.* at 2570–73; *see infra* note 64.
17. *See supra* note 15.
18. *Id.* at 2567.
19. The FCC's rule states, in substance, that a legally qualified candidate is a person who has publicly announced that he/she is a candidate and who meets the qualifications prescribed by the applicable laws to hold the office for which he/she

The language requiring the licensee to provide broadcast time to all other such candidates was included in the statute to prevent a legally qualified candidate from gaining unfair advantage over an opponent through favoritism of a station in selling or donating time or in scheduling political broadcasts.[20] Congress also feared that if a licensee could protect itself from liability in no other way but by refusing to broadcast opposing candidates' advertisements, the effect would be to hamper broadcasting as a political outlet rather than to foster it.[21] Therefore, the equal opportunity provision protects the licensee from susceptibility to offers of financial gain in exchange for refusing to air opposing candidates.[22] Although the regulations promulgated by the FCC do not require the licensee to provide the legally qualified candidate access to its facilities, the regulations do require that once it does provide access

---

    is a candidate, and who:
      1. Has qualified for a place on the ballot or
      2. Has publicly committed himself/herself to seeking election by the write-in method and is eligible under the applicable law to be voted for by sticker, by writing his/her name on the ballot, or other method, and makes a substantial showing that he/she is a bona fide candidate for nomination or office.
47 C.F.R. § 73.1940(g) (1982).
    A special situation arises in connection with candidates for President and Vice President, since they are running nationwide. Candidates for nomination to either of these offices must (1) make a public announcement of candidacy; (2) be eligible to hold the office under the Constitution and other applicable laws and (3) either the candidates or their proposed delegates must have qualified for the primary or Presidential preference ballot in the state in which they are running or have made a substantial showing of bona fide candidacy in that state, territory or the District of Columbia. Persons will be considered legally qualified candidates for nomination only in the state or states in which they qualify under the above standard, unless they qualify in ten or more states (or nine and District of Columbia), in which event they will be considered legally qualified candidates for nomination in all states, territories and the District of Columbia. 47 C.F.R. § 73.1940(a)(4) (1982).
    Thus, a presidential candidate who qualifies in less than ten states will be entitled to equal opportunities, freedom from censorship, lowest unit rates, reasonable access, etc., only in those states in which the candidate qualifies. Candidates who qualify in ten or more states will gain these rights in all states. *New Primer on Political Broadcasting and Cablecasting*, 69 F.C.C.2d 2,228 (1978).
    Therefore, depending upon whether Larry Flynt was a legally qualified candidate in less than ten states, he would have been entitled to equal opportunities only in those states in which he qualified. However, if he had qualified in more than ten states, he would have been entitled to equal opportunity in all states.
    For purposes of this article, the writer has assumed that Larry Flynt was a legally qualified candidate, in any or all states. It is irrelevant for purposes of this case study whether he qualified in less than or more than ten states; the problem and its solution are unchanged.
20.   U.S. CODE, *supra* note 15, at 2,571.
21.   Farmer's Educ. & Coop. Union of America v. WDAY, Inc., 360 U.S. 525 (1959).
22.   U.S. CODE, *supra* note 15.

Political Speech or Obscenity?

to one legally qualified candidate, the broadcaster must provide access to all others.[23]

The no-censorship provision in section 315(a) was designed to eliminate the licensee's potentially powerful political influence.[24] Congress recognized that if the licensee were given editorial discretion in determining the content of political announcements, it could delete portions of messages that were unfavorable to a particular candidate or to views of licensee owners or managers.[25] The result would be a complete contravention of the purposes behind the equal opportunity provision of section 315.[26]

THE LEGISLATIVE HISTORY OF SECTION 315(a) AND THE CENSORSHIP OF OBSCENITY

Section 312 of the Communications Act of 1934 empowers the FCC to impose administrative sanctions for certain violations enumerated in section 312.[27] In particular, section 312(a)(6) of the Act provides that, "[t]he Commission may revoke any station license or construction permit for violation of section 1304, 1343, or 1464 of Title 18."[28] Section 1464 of Title 18 states that, "[w]hoever utters any obscene, indecent, or profane language by means of radio communication shall be fined not more than $10,000 or imprisoned not more than two years, or both."[29]

The conflict arises when section 315(a) is read side by side with section 312(a)(6).[30] Section 315(a) prohibits censorship, yet section 312(a)(6) makes

23. The regulations promulgated by the FCC provide that,

> ...no station licensee is required to permit the use of its facilities by any legally qualified candidate for public office, but if any licensee shall permit any such candidate to use its facilities, it shall afford equal opportunities to all other candidates for that office to use such facilities. Such licensee shall have no power of censorship over the material broadcast by any such candidate.

47 C.F.R. § 73.1940(g) (1982).
24. *See, e.g.*, 67 CONG. REC. 5,483 (1926).
25. *See* U.S. CODE, *supra* note 15.
26. *Id.* at 2,568.
27. *See* 47 U.S.C.A. § 312(a)(6) (1958 & West Supp. 1983).
28. *Id.*
29. 18 U.S.C.A., *supra* note 3.
30. 47 U.S.C.A. §326 (1958 & West Supp. 1983) provides:

> Nothing in this chapter shall be understood or construed to give the Commission the power of censorship over the radio communications or signals transmitted by any radio station, and no regulation or condition shall be promulgated or fixed by the Commission which shall interfere with the right of free speech by means of radio communication.

the broadcast of obscene and/or indecent language a violation for which the FCC can revoke a licensee's license.[31]

Section 315(a) is silent on its face regarding exceptions to the no-censorship provision, and the section neither expressly empowers the FCC to impose sanctions for violations of section 1464 nor expressly shields broadcasters from such liability.[32] Yet, the courts have interpreted the no-censorship requirement of section 315(a) as creating an absolute privilege on political announcements.[33]

The language that evolved into section 18 of the Radio Act and ultimately into section 315(a) of the Communications Act was in response to fear that broadcasters would abuse their industry to exploit the public.[34] Despite the fears expressed by Secretary of Commerce Herbert Hoover, in 1926 the House approved a bill which provided that,

> [i]f a licensee permitted his broadcast station to be used by a candidate or candidates for any public office, or for the discussion of any question affecting the public, he shall make no discrimination as to the use of such broadcasting station, and with respect to said matters the licensee shall be deemed a common carrier in interstate commerce: provided, That such licensee shall have no power to censor material broadcast.[35]

Eventually, the bill passed the Senate, but only after Senator Clarence Dill proposed the following amendment, which came to be known as the Dill Amendment:

> If any licensee shall permit a broadcasting station to be used by a candidate or candidates for any political office, he shall afford equal opportunities to all candidates for such public office in the use of such broadcasting station: Provided, That such licensee shall have no power to censor the material broadcast under the provisions of this paragraph and shall not be liable to criminal or civil action by reason of any uncensored utterances thus broadcast.[36]

31. 47 U.S.C.A., *supra* note 27; note also that 18 U.S.C.A. section 1464 is a criminal statute and violations of it can result in fine or imprisonment as well as revocation of license.
32. 47 U.S.C.A., *supra* note 2.
33. See *supra* note 8.
34. U.S. CODE, *supra* note 15, at 2564, 2567.
35. See H.R. 9971 (S. REP. No. 772), 69th Cong., 1st Sess. § 4.
36. U.S. CODE, *supra* note 15.

Political Speech or Obscenity?

When the bill was considered by the conference committee, it placed the Dill Amendment dealing with the exemption from criminal liability in section 18. The conference committee subsequently eliminated the language relieving stations from criminal or civil liability by reason of any uncensored utterances under the provision.

The bill was then enacted as the Radio Act of 1927 with section 18 as recommended by the conference committee and provided that,

> [i]f any licensee shall permit a broadcasting station to be used by a candidate or candidates for any political office, he shall afford equal opportunities to all candidates for such public office in the use of such broadcasting station: PROVIDED, That such licensee shall have no power to censor the material broadcast under the provisions of this paragraph.

Upon the enactment of the Communications Act of 1934, section 18 of the Radio Act of 1927 was carried forward in a substantially unaltered form as section 315(a).[37]

As a result of Congress' refusal to exempt licensees from criminal or civil liability for the transmission by reason of any uncensored utterances, and because no other indication can be found in the legislative history, it can be inferred that Congress did not intend for broadcasters to be exempt from section 1464 violations.[38] Evidenced by the fact that section 315(a) was codified without protection for the broadcast of obscene or indecent speech, it is reasonable to conclude that Congress expected broadcasters to abide by all laws, including the prohibition against the broadcast of obscenity.[39] Thus, the no-censorship provision of section 315(a) is limited by section 1464.[40]

Although this result runs contrary to dictum in *Farmer's Educ. & Coop. Union of America v. WDAY, Inc.*[41] (that broadcasters have no power to censor material presented to them by a legally qualified candidate pursuant to section 315 (a)) and to subsequent case holdings,[42] any other result is inconsistent with the purposes of section 315(a). The very definition of obscenity elucidated by the Supreme Court is that "it lacks serious political value,"[43] and Justice

---

37. *Id.* at 2,566.
38. *See, e.g.*, H.R. REP. NO. 1886, 69th Cong., 2nd Sess. 10, 18.; Title 18 U.S.C.A. § 1464 (1964 & West Supp. 1966–1983) provides that, "[w]hoever utters any obscene, indecent, or profane language by means of radio communication shall be fined not more than $10,000 or imprisoned not more than two years, or both."
39. *See, e.g.*, H. R. REP., *supra* note 38.
40. *Id.*
41. Farmer's Educ. & Coop. Union of America v. WDAY, 360 U.S. 525 (1959).
42. *Id.* at 526; NAACP v. Button, 45 R.R.2d 378 (1979).
43. Miller v. California, 413 U.S. 15, 24 (1973).

Murphy, quoted in discussing the indecent language of *FCC v. Pacifica Foundation*, stated that "such utterances are no essential part of any exposition of ideas, and are of such slight social value... that any benefit that may be derived from them is clearly outweighed by the social interest in order and morality."[44]

Thus, by definition, political speech is not obscene or indecent[45] and is protected by the first amendment.[46] The purpose of section 315(a) is to provide equal opportunity for political speech over the nation's airwaves.[47] Therefore, the no-censorship provision of section 315(a) is limited by first amendment-protected speech.[48] This limitation on obscene broadcasts does nothing to foul either the public's access to essential political information or to insight into the political process, the very purposes for which the no-censorship provision of section 315 was enacted. Furthermore, this limitation protects the listener's first amendment rights as well.[49]

Section 326 of the Communications Act also proscribes censorship.[50] However, the Court in *Pacifica* concluded that the no-censorship provision in section 326 did not bar the FCC from restricting indecent broadcasts,[51] and the Court in *Illinois Citizens Commission for Broadcasting v. F.C.C.* extended this holding to include obscene programming.[52] In agreeing with the FCC, the *Pacifica* Court admitted that the section 326 prohibition against censorship unequivocally denied the FCC any power to edit proposed broadcasts in advance and to excise material considered inappropriate for the airwaves.[53] The Court reasoned, however, that the legislative history of section 326 made it perfectly clear that this section was not intended to limit the FCC's power to regulate the broadcast of obscene, indecent, or profane language.[54]

Section 29 of the Radio Act of 1927 was the predecessor to the present

---

44. FCC v. Pacifica Foundation, 438 U.S. 726, 746 (1978) (quoting Chaplinsky v. New Hampshire, 315 U.S. 568, 572 (1942)).
45. Miller v. California, 413 U.S. 15, 24 (1973).
46. Post Newsweek Standard-Connecticut, Inc. v. Travelers, 510 F. Supp. 81, 6 Med. L. Rep. 2,540 (1981).
47. See *supra* notes 15–17 and accompanying text.
48. See Post Newsweek Standard-Connecticut, Inc. v. Travelers, 510 F. Supp. 81, 6 Med. L. Rep. 2,540 (1981); see *supra* notes 15–17 and accompanying text.; see *also*, Roth v. United States, 354 U.S. 476 (1957) (Obscene materials have been denied the protection of the first amendment because their content is so offensive to contemporary moral standards).
49. See CBS v. DNC, 412 U.S. 94 (1973).
50. 47 U.S.C.A. § 326 (1958 & West Supp. 1983).
51. F.C.C. v. Pacifica Foundation, 438 U.S. 726, 737 (1977).
52. Illinois Citizens Commission for Broadcasting v. F.C.C., 515 F.2d 397 (D.C. Cir. 1975).
53. 47 U.S.C.A. § 326 (1958 & West Supp. 1983).
54. F.C.C. v. Pacifica Foundation, 438 U.S. 726, 737 (1977).

Political Speech or Obscenity?

section 326 and provided that,

> [n]othing in this Act shall be understood or construed to give the licensing authority the power of censorship over the radio communications or signals transmitted by any radio station, and no regulation or condition shall be promulgated or fixed by the licensing authority which shall interfere with the right of free speech by means of radio communications. No person within the jurisdiction of the United States shall utter any obscene, indecent, or profane language by means of radio communication.[55]

In 1934, this section was re-enacted as section 326 of the Communications Act of 1934[56] and continued to carry the ban on broadcasting obscene or indecent speech. However, this ban was removed from section 326 in 1948 and became 18 U.S.C. section 1464.[57] Now section 326 of the Communications Act states that,

> [n]othing in this Chapter shall be understood or construed to give the Commission the power of censorship over the radio communications or signals transmitted by any radio station, and no regulation or condition shall be promulgated or fixed by the Commission which shall interfere with the right of free speech by means of radio communication.[58]

Although the language of section 326 is very broad, the scope of the section is apparently limited by 18 U.S.C. section 1464.[59] The *Pacifica* Court reasoned that because section 29 of the Radio Act of 1927 was the source of both the anti-censorship provision and the FCC's authority to impose sanctions for the broadcast of indecent or obscene language,[60] quite plainly, Congress intended to give meaning to both provisions.[61] Respect for that intent requires that the censorship language be read as inapplicable to the prohibition on broadcasting obscene, indecent, or profane language. There is nothing in the legislative history to contradict this conclusion.[62]

---

55. Radio Act of 1927, ch. 169, § 29, 44 Stat. 1162, 1172, *repealed by* Communications Act of 1934, ch. 652, § 326, 48 Stat. 1064, 1091.
56. 47 U.S.C.A. § 326 (1958 & West Supp. 1983).
57. *Supra* note 3.
58. 47 U.S.C.A. § 326 (1958 & West Supp. 1983).
59. Pacifica Foundation v. FCC, 556 F.2d 9, 20 (1977).
60. *See supra* text accompanying note 55.
61. FCC v. Pacifica Foundation, 438 U.S. 726, 738 (1977).
62. *Id.* at 738.

The Court held, therefore, that section 326 did not limit the FCC's authority to impose sanctions on licensees who engaged in obscene, indecent, or profane broadcasting,[63] that the FCC was correct in restricting the broadcast, and that as a result, the FCC's actions did not abridge first amendment rights.[64] The *Pacifica* decision does not preclude the FCC from using the higher obscenity standard of *Miller v. California*[65] in imposing administrative sanctions on broadcasters if their programming is obscene.[66] Thus, the section 326 prohibition on censorship does not limit the FCC's authority to impose sanctions on licensees who engage in obscene broadcasting.

Judging from the similarities in the legislative histories of section 315(a) and section 326, it can be concluded that reasoning similar to that which the Court employed in *Pacifica* would also be applied to the situation at bar and a similar result obtained.[67] It can be inferred by analogy to section 326 that the no-censorship provision of section 315(a) is not a bar to the restriction of obscene political announcements. A licensee faced with an obscene political

---

63. *Id*. at 737–8.
64. *Id*. at 726, 741; Pacifica is narrowly construed to mean that broadcasters may broadcast "indecent" matter at times when children do not constitute a significant portion of the audience.

    The Pacifica Court went on to hold that section 1464 made the broadcast of indecent material a crime separate from the broadcast of obscene material. Further, it held that the Pacifica Foundation broadcast was indecent, accepting the FCC's definition of indecent as including the exposure of children to language that describes, in patently offensive terms, sexual or excretory activities and organs, at times of the day when there is a reasonable risk that children may be in the audience. Indecency, the Court noted, differs from obscenity mainly in that it does not appeal to prurient interest or sexual longing.

    A majority of the Pacifica Court held that application of a statutory standard less demanding than the obscenity standard of Miller (i.e. indecency) did not violate the first amendment rights of broadcasters because their media are: (1) unique in their pervasive presence in society and their ability to confront the audience suddenly with material it may not want to receive and (2) uniquely accessible to children, relying on the rational presented in *Ginsberg v. New York*.
65. In Miller v. California, 413 U.S. 15 (1973), Chief Justice Burger announced a new definition of obscenity:

    Material is obscene if (a) the average person, applying contemporary community standards would find that the work, taken as a whole, appeals to the prurient interest, (b) the work depicts or describes in a patently offensive way, sexual conduct specifically defined by the applicable state law; and (c) the work, taken as a whole, lacks serious literary, artistic, political or scientific value.

66. *See* Illinois Citizens Commission for Broadcasting v. F.C.C., 515 F.2d 397 (D.C. Cir. 1975); Roth v. United States, 354 U.S. 476 (1957) (Obscene materials have been denied the protection of the first amendment because their content is so offensive to contemporary moral standards).
67. *See supra* notes 21–44 and accompanying text.

Political Speech or Obscenity?

announcement would not be violating the equal opportunity provision by refusing to broadcast obscene material pursuant to section 1464.

CONCLUSION

The case law suggests that a legally qualified candidate for public office is free to say anything, whether or not it relates to the candidacy, and whether or not the material is scandalous or in any manner unsuitable for broadcast.[68] However, the *Pacifica* Court concluded that section 326 did not bar the FCC from restricting indecent broadcasts,[69] and *Illinois Citizens Commission for Broadcasting*[70] extend the *Pacifica* holding to include obscene programming. Therefore, the no-censorship provision of section 326 does not bar the FCC from restricting obscene broadcasts.

As the legislative history of the section 326 no-censorship provision closely parallels the legislative history of the section 315(a) no-censorship provision, then by analogy, licensees can censor obscene political broadcasts under section 315(a).

It can be inferred from Congress' refusal to exempt licensees from criminal or civil liability for the transmission by reason of any uncensored utterances, that Congress did not intend for broadcasters to be exempt from section 1464 violations.[71] It is not unreasonable to conclude that Congress expected broadcasters to abide by all laws, including the prohibition against the broadcast of obscenity.[72] The lack of protection for broadcasters from criminal liability for obscene political broadcasts suggests that Congress would not expect a broadcaster to violate a federal criminal statute in order to comply with another non-criminal federal statute.

Therefore, the equal opportunity provision of the Communications Act of 1934 does not supercede the statutes that normally bar the broadcast of

---

68. *See* Farmer's Educ. & Coop. Union of America v. WDAY, Inc., 360 U.S. 525 (1959) (unanimously holding that a license was barred from censoring the comments of a speaker exercising rights under section 315(a) because such censorship was contrary to the basic purpose of section 315(a) to promote full and unrestricted discussion of political issues by legally qualified candidates); *see also*, NAACP v. F.C.C., 45 R.R.2d 378 (1979) (in which the FCC held that even if it were to find the word "nigger" obscene or indecent, under § 315(a), the legally qualified candidate could not be prevented from using the word during his use of the licensee's facilities).
69. *See supra* notes 59–64 and accompanying text.
70. Illinois Citizens Commission for Broadcasting v. F.C.C., 515 F.2d 397 (D. C. Cir. 1975).
71. *See, e.g.*, H. R. REP., *supra* note 38. Section 1464 of Title 18 states that "Whoever utters any obscene, indecent, or profane language by means of radio communication shall be fined not more than $10,000 or imprisoned not more than two years, or both."
72. *See, e.g.*, H. R. REP., *supra* note 38.

obscenity. Broadcasters could have censored Mr. Flynt's obscene political announcements without violating section 315(a).

A limitation on obscene broadcasts does nothing to foul either the public's access to essential political information or to insight into the political process, the very purposes for which the no-censorship provision of section 315 was enacted. Furthermore, this limitation protects the listener's first amendment rights as well.[73]

The concerns of the FCC that such a precedent would be dangerous is minimized by the fact that in today's society, a political candidate is unlikely to run for elective office on an obscene political platform. It is possible that the FCC will be faced with ambiguous cases in which it is called upon to decide whether the content of a political message is, in fact, obscene (so as to merit censorship). However, in the sixty-three years since the enactment of the no-censorship provision of section 315(a), this is the first time that the provision has conflicted with section 1464.

Moreover, the concern that broadcasters will play politics is similarly minimized because broadcasters are forced to pass judgment with respect to obscenity in other aspects of their programming that are subject to the same restraints (i.e., section 1464 and fear of license revocation or non-renewal). Broadcasters are not novices in deciding whether programming is indecent or obscene.

73. *See* Post Newsweek Standard-Connecticut, Inc. v. Travelers, 510 F. Supp 81, 6 Med. L. Rep. 2,540 (1981); *see supra* notes 15-17 and accompanying text.

STEVE BACHMANN

The Irrelevant First Amendment

Steve Bachmann is a member of the bars of Arkansas, Indiana, Louisiana, New York and Washington, D.C. He received his B.A. from Harvard College, his J.D. from Harvard Law School and his M.F.A. from the University of New Orleans.

> The few cannot go on accumulating wealth unless they accumulate the power to manipulate the minds of the many. To expropriate manpower they have to expropriate the brain. What is being abolished in today's affluent societies, from Moscow to Los Angeles, is not exploitation, but our awareness of it . . . . The material pauperization of the last century is followed and replaced by the immaterial pauperization of today. Its most obvious manifestation is the decline in political options available to the citizen of the most advanced nations: a mass of political nobodies, over whose heads even collective suicide can be decreed, is opposed by an ever-decreasing number of political moguls. That this state of affairs is readily accepted and voluntarily endured is the greatest achievement of the mind industry.
>
> Hans Enzensberger[1]

In a recent book, the late Professor Ithiel de Sola Pool argued that first amendment jurisprudence has not kept up with the recent revolutions in communications technology. He suggested that if the trends continue, the first amendment will, for all practical purposes, be irrelevant to the supposedly democratic society it is meant to maintain.[2] However, observations from contemporary observers suggest that Pool's feared future is here today, if not

---

1. ENZENSBERGER, CRITICAL ESSAYS 11 (1982).
2. POOL, TECHNOLOGIES OF FREEDOM 226, 224-5 (1983).

STEVE BACHMANN

already yesterday: "Shopping malls, for example, are now the third most frequented space in our lives, following home and workplace."[3] And in the words of another commentator, "[M]all culture now dominates the nation's urban social and commercial life. . . . currently [shopping centers] produce more than one-half of the nation's annual retail sales, and serve as the homogenized community centers for beauty contests, art, boat and auto shows, and local craft fairs."[4] In other words, while Pool worried about capacity to communicate in 2020, the individual familiar with first amendment law as it presently stands could seriously question whether most people today enjoy any sort of meaningful access to their fellow citizens for the purposes of political discussion.

In the three places that Americans spend the brunt of their time, the right of access to their fellow citizens is limited—if not by first amendment law, then by laws of property that sanction exclusion from the means of access. For example, if Citizen Mary wishes to reach Citizen John at his home (either through door knocking, mail box drops, newspaper articles, or media programs), she is likely to encounter a number of impediments, some of which are absolute and subject to the arbitrary discretion of others.[5] The rights of access that Mary has to John at his workplace are comparably circumscribed, even if she wants to convince him to join a union.[6] If Mary opts for the third best alternative for encountering John, her chances are equally dismal, for the right of access to shopping centers exists only by the grace of a few state courts.[7]

The preceding strongly suggests that the first amendment will not have to wait for Pool's technological revolution in order to become irrelevant. It already is.

There are a number of reasons for bemoaning this situation. From one perspective, the grief involves a loss of capacity—and accordingly, humanity—on the part of citizens who can neither express themselves effectively nor ex-

---

3. NAISBITT, MEGATRENDS 45 (1982).
4. R. LOUV, AMERICA II 52 (1985).
5. *See, e.g.,* Hynes v. Mayor of Oradell, 425 U.S. 610 (1976); Troyer v. Babylon, 483 F. Supp. 1135 (E.D.N.Y., 1980), *aff'd*, 628 F.2d 1346, *aff'd sub nom*, Southampton v. Troyer, 449 U.S. 988 (1980); U.S. Postal Service v. Council of Greenburgh Civic Assoc., 453 U.S. 114 (1981); Red Lion Broadcasting Co. v. F.C.C., 395 U.S. 367 (1969); CBS v. DNC, 412 U.S. 94 (1973); Cullman Broadcasting Co., 40 F.C.C. 576 (1963); Miami Herald Publishing Co. v. Tornillo, 418 U.S. 241 (1974).
6. *See, e.g.,* Sears, Roebuck & Co. v. San Diego Cty. Dist. of Carpenters, 436 U.S. 180 (1978); Republic Aviation v. N.L.R.B., 324 U.S. 794 (1945) *reh. den.*, 325 U.S. 894.
7. Lloyd Corp. v. Tanner, 407 U.S. 551 (1972); Pruneyard Shopping Center v. Robins, 447 U.S. 74 (1980); State v. Schmid, 423 A.2d 615 (N.J., 1980), *appeal dismissed*, 102 S. Ct. 867 (1980; Alderwood Assoc. v. Wash. Environmental Council, 635 P. 2d 108 (Wash., 1981). *Contrast* State v. Felmet, 273 S.E.2d 708 (1981).

ercise a meaningful impact on their lives.[8] From another perspective, it represents the destruction of an elegant if not ingenious system political checks and balances as established by the founding fathers.[9] On the philosophical level of the Frankfurt School, it represents the triumph of the "mind industry."[10] On a more mundane level, the irrelevance of the first amendment intimates imminent social discord, if not civil war. At least one commentator has remarked that the more people are frustrated in their desire to be heard, the more radical will be the measures they adopt in order to be heard.[11] Ultimately, what is at stake is the government's legitimacy, for there is no consent of the governed if the consent derives from constrained discourse.[12] Without legitimacy, the reign of violence begins.[13]

That the relevance of the first amendment is important should be even more obvious than its contemporary state of irrelevance. At this point, though, the question becomes: How can the first amendment be brought back to the United States, and make this society a better—if not safer—place for living? What roles, if any, can judicial doctrine play in re-invigorating the promises of the first amendment? How did judicial doctrine get to the point where it applies the first amendment to every place except where it counts?

In attempting to address these issues, this article will adopt the following course: We will begin by trying to articulate what we want from the first amendment. Without such a moral explication, we cannot really identify "appropriate" interpretations of the first amendment. After our moral excursion, we will look to the historical background of the first amendment. If our view is consistent with those held by the Americans who passed the first amendment, we can rest assured that we continue to participate in a system of regularized rules that continue to restrain arbitrary power. Yet, we should also acknowledge the extent to which such an investigation is unnecessary, because the Constitution's framers determined that the people of 2020 should

---

8. This alienation is deplored morally by writers like Enzensberger, *supra* note 1. It reveals itself empirically in studies which indicate that worker productivity rises with worker control. *See, e.g.*, Work in America, Report of a Special Task Force to the Secretary of HEW (1973); BLUMBERG, INDUSTRIAL DEMOCRACY (1969); HUNNIUS, ET AL., WORKERS' CONTROL (1973).
9. ELY, DEMOCRACY AND DISTRUST (1982).
10. ENZENSBERGER, *supra* note 1.
11. Barron, *An Emerging First Amendment Right of Access to the Media*, 37 GEO. WASH. L. REV. 487 (1969). Unlike earlier members of the Supreme Court, some of that body's present members appear to have no appreciation of the fact that their exotic interpretations of the first amendment lead to even more exotic interpretations. *Cf.* Clark v. CCNV, 52 USLW 4986, 4989 n. 9, *and* 4989 (Burger, concurring), *to* Adderly v. Florida, 385 U.S. 39, 50-1 (1966) (Douglas).
12. *Cf.* ELY, *supra* note 9.
13. EMERSON, TOWARD A GENERAL THEORY OF THE FIRST AMENDMENT 12, 13 (1966). *Cf.* A. FORTAS, CONCERNING DISSENT AND CIVIL DISOBEDIENCE 63 (N.Y., 1968).

not be limited by the vision of white males in 1787.[14] We have not allowed the framers' thoughts concerning blacks, women, and elitism to limit us.[15] Furthermore, historical investigation would reveal that those who initially implemented the first amendment engaged in activities that would "clearly" violate what most of would conceive to be obvious first amendment limits.[16]

After our historical overview we will conclude by investigating the state of first amendment jurisprudence as it presently stands. We have already suggested that the courts have made some wrong choices. We will further suggest that there is little coherency to the sorts of choices they have made. We will note reasons that might explain why the doctrines have assumed the forms that they have. We will also look for ways out of the present welter.

PRINCIPLES UNDERLYING THE FIRST AMENDMENT

When we bemoaned the decline of the first amendment, we intimated some moral attitudes related to it. Ultimately, we would submit that our varying concerns merge into a unitary conception initially articulated by Hegel, and later developed by Feuerbach and Marx. The conception is one that involves a vision of individuals fulfilling themselves through society and history. From the perspective of these German philosophers, the Good is that which contributes to humanity's consummation in divinity—or, the ideal society. Through philosophical speculation, through scientific research, and through political debate and action, human beings, working individually and together, articulate Good, implement Good, and become Good.

---

14. Edmund Randolph, one of the five men charged with drafting the Constitution near the end of the 1787 Convention, observed in his notes that, "In the draught of a fundamental constitution, two things deserve attention: 1. To insert essential principles only, lest the operations of government should be clogged by rendering those provisions permanent and unalterable, which ought to be accommodated to times and events . . . ." C. ROSSITER, 1787: THE GRAND CONVENTION (1966). Jefferson shared a similar perspective: "[L]aws and institutions must go hand in hand with the progress of the human mind. As that becomes more developed, more enlightened, as new discoveries are made, new truths disclosed, and manners and opinions change with the change of circumstances, institutions must advance also, and keep pace with the times." JEFFERSON, THE PORTABLE THOMAS JEFFERSON 559 (Peterson ed. 1975). *See also* John Marshall: "[The Constitution is] intended to endure for ages to come, and, consequently, to be adapted to the various *crises* of human affairs." McCulloch v. Maryland, 4 Wheat. 316, 414 (1918).
15. As evidenced by the fifteenth, nineteenth, and seventeenth amendments to the Constitution, respectively.
16. *E.g.*, the Federalists passed the notorious Alien and Sedition Acts which outlawed criticisms of the government until the next inauguration date. BLUM, ET AL., THE NATIONAL EXPERIENCE 162, 168 (2d ed. 1968). For his part, Jefferson attempted to prosecute various newspaper editors for seditious libel. U.S. v. Hudson and Goodwin, 7 Cranch 32 (1812).

Irrelevant First Amendment

Given the preceding, our moral vision for the first amendment might be expressed along the following terms: The Good is the ascertainment and implementation of "divine" potentials in humanity, by individuals in particular and by humankind in general. History involves the realization of this Good through intellectual effort in philosophy and science, and political effort in societal interaction and history. The first amendment exists to insure that government shall not obstruct individuals when they try to implement the Good in thought—and in politics (which attempts to actualize the Good discovered in thought). Ultimately, government's role is to insure the establishment of a democratic system of societal discourse, to which all citizens will have meaningful access, so that the Good may be discovered and implemented, both individually and collectively.

Though we have emphasized the role German philosophy plays in underpinning this conception of the first amendment, we should also acknowledge the extent to which English thought also harmonizes with this conception. The first amendment traces more to Milton and his heirs than to Hegel and his. The point here is simply that underlying English conceptions of freedom of speech is a notion of historical development and humanistic consummation that is comparable to that of the Germans. Both postulate an evolutionary process that is ultimately positive and progressive, as long as there are no "artificial" interferences with the "natural" processes of discovery and advocacy of truth.[17] Both schools have a notion that truth is to be uncovered and implemented by human effort and experience, and that in this trial-and-error process, individuals and humanity will benefit.

If there is any difference between these two traditions that should be acknowledged, it is this: When the English talk about their market for ideas, they seem to assume that everyone in it enjoys equal capacity and that government needs to do nothing except ensure that the market is there and running. By contrast, the Germans (particularly Marx and his heirs) do not ignore how government constitutes the market. They are less ready to assume that government is playing a neutral role, either in the sustenance of the market or in the establishment of its various players.

How the preceding translates into first amendment concerns has very important implications. When the English say that government should not get

---

17. For instances of this vision, *see, e.g.*, MILTON, PARADISE LOST, AND SELECTED POETRY AND PROSE 490, 500-01 (Northrop Frye ed. 1964); JOHN LOCKE, *A Letter Concerning Toleration* in GREAT BOOKS OF THE WESTERN WORLD 15 (R.M. Hutchins ed. v. 35, 1952). JEFFERSON and RANDOLPH, *supra* note 14, and JEFFERSON, *supra* note 14, at 253; and JOHN STUART MILL, SELECTED WRITINGS OF JOHN STUART MILL 286, 296 (B. Wishy ed. 1959). To bridge the gap between Germans, radicals, and Englishmen, we might note that Mill opens his book *On Liberty* (see above) by acknowledging his debt to Wilhelm von Humboldt—also a hero of contemporary anarchist thinkers—and linguistic philosopher Noam Chomsky. CHOMSKY, FOR REASONS OF STATE 397 f (1973).

in the way of the individual as (s)he attempts to conceive and implement good, they think primarily in terms of the way government might obstruct such efforts through explicit prohibitions. By contrast, when Germans look for governmental obstructions, they ask things like: How do the property relations that government sustains interfere with the individual's attempt to ascertain and realize good? At this point, Germans will begin to say things like: If government is to make no law prohibiting freedom of speech, then what about laws of property that prohibit me from speaking to John in shopping malls in the workplace, or in John's newspapers and television programs? As at least one commentator has observed, property is sovereignty delegated.[18] Even the United States Supreme Court—at certain junctures, at least—has not been oblivious to factors such as these.[19]

Yet, this is not the place for investigating where judicial doctrine may or may not play role in effectuating a viable first amendment. The point to note at present is that a viable notion of the first amendment must take into account the role that property (and government's role in sustaining it) affects real freedom of speech. More importantly, we must note that government and the rules it enforces in regard to speech and property ultimately affect the Good that we would see implemented in our lives as individual and social beings. We are arguing that the first amendment has reason to exist because it can help us to the truth, which can make us free, enhance our capacities, and fulfill our lives and hopefully the destiny of humankind. The first amendment helps towards this by insuring that government will not interfere with the processes by which we discover and implement truth. From the German tradition, we emphasize that government can hinder one's capacity to discover, speak, and implement truth not only through explicit prohibition, but also through the systems of power that it engenders and sustains. Any first amendment which is to have any meaning will be one which protects the individual from not only the former interferences, but also the latter.

FIRST AMENDMENT HISTORY

At this point the issue becomes the extent to which our "Hegelian" vision of the first amendment comports with the vision held by the framers' generation.[20] Our position concerning this point is very simple: The Hegelian

---

18. Cohen, *Property and Sovereignty*, CORNELL L. Q. 8 (1927).
19. *See, e.g.*, Shelley v. Kramer, 334 U.S. 1 (1948); Marsh v. Alabama, 326 U.S. 501 (1946).
20. It seems best to talk about the *generation* that established the first amendment as opposed to any particular set of people, *e.g.*, the "Founding Fathers." For their part, the Fathers at best thought that a first amendment was irrelevant to the Constitution they had drafted, either because it was a matter for the states and/or because the new government had no power to deal with such (although John

Irrelevant First Amendment

vision is eminently consistent with the visions held by those Americans who promulgated the first amendment. We have also noted the progressive, evolutionary conceptions of Jefferson and Randolph.[21] Alexander Hamilton expressed similar sentiments when he argued that, "besides the advancement of truth, science, morality, and arts in general," the significance of freedom of the press inhered

> in its diffusion of liberal sentiments on the administration of government, its ready communication of thoughts between subjects, and its consequential promotion of union among them, whereby oppressive officers are shamed or intimidated into more honourable and just modes of conducted affairs.[22]

Anti-federalists, whose political pressure created the first amendment, also correlated personal and civil well-being with freedom of inquiry.[23] A few years later, Tunis Wortman summarized matters:

> By the very constitution of his nature, man is an intelligent Being: every object by which he is surrounded, every princi-

---

Marshall was prepared to say that if it was necessary "to satisfy the people at large," one might be punished for one's political opinions). Levy, ed. FREEDOM OF THE PRESS FROM ZENGER TO JEFFERSON liv–lv (Levy ed. 1966). P. SMITH, THE SHAPING OF AMERICA 91 (1980). It was the popular uproar that followed the Constitution's presentation to the populace that secured the passage of the first amendment. For example, in the case of James Madison, the passage of a Bill of Rights constituted a major issue when he stood for election to the First Congress. And thus when he attended the First Congress, he played a key role in ensuring the passage of the Bill of Rights. *Id.* at 166. As the federalist John Marshall put it,

> Serious fears were extensively entertained that those powers [which the Constitution gave the central government] . . . might be exercised in a manner dangerous to liberty . . . . In almost every convention by which the constitution was adopted, amendments to guard the abuse of power were recommended . . . . In compliance with a sentiment thus generally expressed, to quiet fears thus extensively entertained, amendments were proposed by the required majority in congress, and adopted by the states.

Barron v. Baltimore, 7 Peters 250 (1833). In short, the first amendment (as well as the whole Bill of Rights) is best seen as the product of "We the people." Popular demand created it, and that demand grew out of the revolutionary experiences of a generation that had shed blood over issues of power and its abuse.

21. *See supra* note 14.
22. *Cited in* LEVY, *supra* note 20, at 397.
23. *See, e.g.* THE ANTI-FEDERALISTS 21 (C. Kenyon ed. 1966).

ple which is presented to his understanding, necessarily become the subjects of his contemplation . . . . From all these considerations it has been maintained, that a liberty of investigation into every subject of thought, is not only the perfect and absolute right of civil society; but that the unrestricted exercise of that right, is indispensable to the progression and happiness of mankind.[24]

It should be clear that the first amendment generation believed in uninhibited exploration and expression for the sake of individuals, society, and humankind as a whole. It should be acknowledged, however, that when this generation worried over inhibitions of freedom of expression, it did not look to incredible concentrations of property as potential sources of obstruction to the progressive evolutionary processes that they celebrated.

There were a number of reasons for this oversight. First, the United States was a remarkably egalitarian society for the period (at least in terms of the white males who "counted"). In part, this was due to the diaspora of American Loyalists, who were many in number and generally more well-to-do than the revolutionary Americans who seized the nation.[25] In part, it was due to the fact that even the poorest white male could always avail himself of the frontier if he wished to better himself.[26] In the end, American society was remarkably middle class.[27] While there were differences in property distribution, these differences were never so radical as to undercut the concrete autonomy of every citizen. And thus every citizen could say what (s)he would without fear of devastating retaliation.

Second, technological considerations allowed almost any American citizen to multiply his/her words with a minimal to moderate amount of property. During this period, communication occurred through speeches, broadsides, sermons, pamphlets and newspapers.[28] Publishing one's sentiments was within the reach of nearly every enterprising individual.[29]

Third, the politics of the time caused the first amendment generation to focus its concerns over freedom of expression on the new government—and on the old church. Concerning the government, the great fear of many Americans over the establishment of the constitutional system was that it might establish "martial law," a military king, or a "masqued aristocracy."[30] One

24. LEVY, *supra* note 20, at 230–33.
25. SMITH, *supra* note 20, at 4. BROWN, THE GOOD AMERICANS 227 (1966).
26. HOFSTADTER, AMERICA AT 1750 172–3 (1973); *see also* the remarks of Pinckney in SMITH, *supra* note 20, at 77.
27. HOFSTADTER, *supra* note 26, at 132.
28. BURNS, THE VINEYARD OF LIBERTY 28 (1983).
29. POOL, *supra* note 2, at 11.
30. KENYON, *supra* note 23, at 17, 70, 72, 77.

recent observer has noted that the establishment of the Constitution—with its locked doors and dubious ratification procedure—had all the odors of a coup d'etat.[31] As for the church, the point to note here is that the first amendment was passed during the period encompassed by the "Great Awakening." "Its essential aspect was the internal reinvigoration of Protestantism through more popular styles of worship."[32] In political terms, the Great Awakening ended a system whereby value articulation and implementation was directed and co-ordinated by a ruling elite through local pastors supported by government. It encouraged a system where every individual might participate in that process, untrammeled by state or state-sponsored church. In the end, the first amendment's foci on both church and state make more sense when these historical considerations are acknowledged.

Fourth, the political doctrines and political experiences of revolutionary Americans did not lead them to fear concentrations of private property as a threat to liberty. Their concerns dealt with the Hegelian vision previously discussed, but in Whiggish fashion, they looked to government (and church) as the potential sources of threat to implementation of their Hegelian visions. The political struggles in North America from 1750 to 1800 were continuations of political struggles begun in England over a century before, during that country's first Civil War. During the English Civil War, the initial issue was the extent to which the government should be subject to the discretion of one man (the King). Over the years, however, matters extended into questions of how many people should have a say in running the nation (the franchise), and what forms such participation should assume (censorship, assembly, petition). Yet, during this epoch, the problem was still defined as one of government versus the citizen. In one sense, those without property had been defined out of the polity altogether by certain philosophers.[33] Thus the only question remaining for political theory at the time was what King Charles, King George II, or King/President Washington—not some grand property owner—might do.

In short, the revolutionary generation did worry itself over the integrity of Hegelian processes more in "English" than in "German" terms. But the point to note presently is that, at that juncture in American history, there was no reason to focus on implicit sources of governmental inhibition—as opposed to the explicit sources emphasized by the "English perspective." At that juncture, socio-economic, technological, historical and philosophical considerations all worked to underplay any potential contradiction between the two perspectives. The subsequent agitations over American racism—and, more-

---

31. WASSERMAN, AMERICA BORN AND REBORN 52 (1983).
32. HOFSTADTER, *supra* note 26, at 51.
33. John Locke, for example, denied humanity to those without property. C. B. MACPHERSON, THE POLITICAL THEORY OF POSSESSIVE INDIVIDUALISM Ch. 5 (1966).

over, industrial development—would bring out the contracictions, but only after the first amendment had been drafted and ratified. A number of years would pass before these tensions would begin to manifest themselves in judicial doctrine.

SALVAGING THE FIRST AMENDMENT

Over the past fifty years, the U.S. Supreme Court has been a relatively conscientious protector of first amendment rights when violation of such has occurred in areas under the direct jurisdiction of national and local governments. "Traditional public forums" like streets, sidewalks, and parks have come to enjoy a somewhat sacrosanct status.[34] With such forums, the government must regulate in the least obtrusive manner possible.[35] The results are less revolutionary in spaces like mail boxes, fairgrounds, and utility poles.[36] But a commentator like Naisbitt might suggest that you might as well be talking about first amendment rights of access to the moon when you talk about such locations, because citizens are spending most of their time at home, at work, and in the shopping centers—and not at the fairgrounds and parks. Pool might add that one should also focus on the primary arteries of discourse and that though today those might include the television, radio, telephone, mails, books, and newspapers, tomorrow all of those media will be concentrated into one vast network of computer-type consoles, which will be tied together by various wires and electro-magnetic waves. The "traditional public forum" where meaningful discourse occurred in St. Paul's time was the "agora."[37] Now it is something else.

Of course, once one starts to focus on the realities of the *wheres* of reaching people, then one will start to acknowledge the realties of the *hows* of reaching people. The hows are not easy. As we have noted, means of access to home, work, and shopping malls range from the limited to the non-existent.[38] Whether the technological revolution envisioned by Pool is going to change anything is open to question. While Pool fears trammels established by the government, advocates for the cablecasters are already equating "American freedom"

---

34. U.S. v. Grace, 103 S. Ct 1702 (1983), Hague v. CIO, 307 U.S. 496 (1939). *Contra*, Davis v. Massachusetts, 167 U.S. 43 (1897).
35. U.S. v. Grace, 103 S. Ct. 1702 (1983).
36. U.S. Postal Service v. Council of Greenburgh Civil Association, 453 U.S. 114 (1981); Heffron v. Iskcon, 452 U.S. 640 (1981); City Council v. Taxpayers for Vincent, 80 L. Ed2d 772 (1984).
37. THE INTERLINEAR GREEK-ENGLISH NEW TESTAMENT 545 (Acts 17:17) (Marshall ed. 1958). An "agora" is a forum/marketplace, a place of assembly. LIDDELL AND SCOTT, GREEK-ENGLISH LEXICON 7 (1967).
38. *See supra* notes 5–7.

with the right of the cablecaster to do with "his" cable network what he pleases.[39]

Governments potentially threaten Hegelian processes of progress because they represent past and temporary achievements of progress. They have a vested interest in retarding Hegelian processes because such processes imply transcending the present government. Hence, governmental threats to first amendment processes should never be underestimated or ignored. But while the courts seem to have acknowledged these principles to a degree, they have all but ignored entirely the threat to Hegelian processes that emanate from less obvious activities of government—e.g., those which sustain enormous concentrations of "private" property. It is on the basis of private ownership that one's access to the important media of today and tomorrow has been restricted. The question therefore becomes: On what legal bases might we care for the trammels erected by laws of private property, and again institute the Hegelian processes of value discovery and implementation which the first amendment contemplates?

In answering this question, the first point to note is the extent to which the Supreme Court has, in fact, acknowledged that first amendment rights are public rights:

> [The First] Amendment rests on the assumption that the widest possible dissemination of information from diverse and antagonistic sources is essential to the welfare of the public, that a free press is a condition of a free society . . . . Freedom of the press from governmental interference under the First Amendment does not sanction repression of that freedom by private interests.[40]

> [T]he people as a whole retain their interest in free speech by radio and their collective right to have the medium function consistently with the ends and purposes of the First Amendment. It is the right of the viewers and listeners, not the right of the broadcasters, which is paramount . . . . It is the purpose of the First Amendment to preserve an uninhibited marketplace of ideas which will ultimately prevail, rather than to countenance monopolization of that market, whether it be by the Government itself or a private license.[41]

---

39. Bachmann, Book Review, 6 COMMUNICATIONS AND THE LAW 81 (October 1984) (reviewing CABLESPEECH).
40. Associated Press v. U.S., 326 U.S. 1, 20 (1945).
41. Red Lion Broadcasting Co. v. F.C.C., 395 U.S. 367, 390 (1968).

However, not only in the special cases of cabals (who violate antitrust laws) or of broadcasters (who employ publicly owned air waves) has the Supreme Court countenanced societal first amendment rights. In contexts with more explicit situations of private ownership, the Supreme Court has ratified the principle that rights commonly associated with private property must yield to constitutional considerations. For example, in *Marsh v. Alabama*,[42] involving the case of a company-owned town, the Court stated:

> Ownership does not always mean absolute domination. The more an owner, for his advantage, opens up his property for use by the public in general, the more do his rights become circumscribed by the statutory and constitutional rights of those who use it. [citations omitted] Thus, the owners of privately held bridges, ferries, turnpikes and railroads may not operate them as freely as a farmer does his farm . . . . When we balance the Constitutional rights of owners of property against those of the people to enjoy freedom of press and religion, as we must here, we remain mindful of the fact that the latter occupy a preferred position.

More recently, in the case of a shopping center, the Court stated:

> It is true that one of the essential sticks in the bundle of property rights is the right to exclude others . . . . And here there has literally been a "taking" of that right to the extent that the California Supreme Court has interpreted the State Constitution to entitle its citizens to exercise free expression and petition rights on shopping center property. But it is well established that "not every destruction or injury to property has been held to be a 'taking' in the Constitutional sense." *Armstrong v. United States*, 364 U.S. 40, 48 (1960). Rather, the determination whether a State law unlawfully infringes a landowner's property in violation of the taking Clause requires an examination of whether the restriction on private property "forc[es] some people along to bear public burdens which, in all fairness and justice, should be born by the public as a whole." Id., at 49. This examination entails inquiry into such factors as the character of the governmental action, its economic impact, and its interference with reasonable investment-backed expectations . . . .

---

42. Marsh v. Alabama, 326 U.S. 501, 506, 509 (1946).

> There is nothing to suggest that preventing appellants from prohibiting this sort of activity will unreasonably impair the value or use of their property as a shopping center . . . . [43]

Given the preceding, the notion that rights of exclusion traditionally associated with private property must sometimes yield to the human rights of citizens to self-determination should not be viewed as a particularly revolutionary proposition. As *Shelley v. Kramer*[44] has acknowledged, there are instances where the state must choose between supporting "private" rights and constitutional rights.[45] The cases of *Shelley, Pruneyard,* and *Marsh*, at least, acknowledge that there are instances where the choice does not automatically favor "private" property. In his *Marsh* decision, Black used the common carrier analysis to justify state incursions on private property rights for the sake of national commerce.[46] If the state can do that for the sake of production and distribution, why not the same for the sake of information dissemination? We have been emphasizing the importance of information dissemination for the sake of human liberation, following Hegel. Following Naisbitt, however, we might observe that information dissemination now constitutes our nation's primary commercial activity.[47] If such is the case, then "incursions" on "private" property rights become justified not only from the perspective of the first amendment, but also from the perspective of the commerce clause,[48] as well as the common law of the common carrier.

Of course, once one has acknowledged these notions, then new questions arise. Where does one draw the line? Under what circumstances does one favor societal discourse, and at what point does one sustain the "private" right to stifle it? (Or at the very least, choose not to be made party to views that one does not espouse?) If one's television facility might become designated as a common carrier, what about one's door? Can a Hare Krishna advocate pound on one's door between midnight and dawn?

At one end of the spectrum, near the extreme of outright governmental seizure, lies the law of the common carrier. It requires that the owner of a facility allow all members of the public to avail themselves of his facility at reasonable, non-discriminatory rates. We have already noted how a common carrier analysis might be employed by first amendment advocates through the back door with the commerce clause sign posted on it. But whether the justification derives from economic or metaphysical human fulfillment, it should be noted that the field of societal discourse in America is not oblivious

43. Pruneyard Shopping Center v. Robins, 447 U.S. 74, 82–85 (1980).
44. Shelley v. Kramer, 334 U.S. 1 (1948).
45. *See also* Reitman v. Mulkey, 387 U.S. 369 (1967).
46. Marsh v. Alabama, 326 U.S. 501, 506 (1946).
47. NAISBITT, *supra* note 3, chapter 1. *See also supra* note 4.
48. *Cf.* Associated Press v. U.S., 326 U.S. 1, 20 (1945).

to common carrier requirements. As Pool has observed, the telegraph never "enjoyed" the laissez faire "protections" of the first amendment.[49] Given that precedent, neither did the telephone company.[50] Indeed, when radio technology first appeared in the United States, AT&T's initial approach was to treat radio as a common carrier.[51] Though Pool in general embraces a faith in private market forces, his ultimate conclusion concerning cable is that it, too, should become subject to common carrier responsibilities.[52]

Though resorting to common carrier analyses might democratize a number of the critical media in our society, one problem with relying on it too heavily is that the analogy begins to strain with some media. Carrying messages over a phone wire makes some intuitive sense. One begins to wonder when one thinks about a corporate bulletin board or the walks in the middle of a shopping mall. At this point, allusion to the doctrine of the "public forum" becomes more appropriate.

One of the more recent formulations of the public forum doctrine was contained in *Perry Education Assn. v. Perry Local Educators' Assn.*[53] The Court noted that "in places which by long tradition . . . have been devoted to assembly and debate, the rights of the state to limit expressive activity are sharply circumscribed."[54] A second category of places are those which have not been forums by "long tradition," but which have been postulated as such by the government (e.g., school board meetings, university meeting facilities).[55] While the state apparently may withdraw the designation of "public forum" from such places, as long as it does designate the places as such, its right to regulate access to such spaces is as limited as in the case of traditional public forums. In a third category are spaces possessed by the government and which the government may use like any "private" owner.[56]

The unfortunate aspect of the *Perry* decision is its reliance on wooden conceptions of property: The government either owns something like a private party and can do anything with it, or it does not. It is this sort of reasoning that leads to *Davis v. Massachusetts.*[57]

The better aspect of the *Perry* decision is its acknowledgement that a public forum can be something other than the "traditional" street, park, or sidewalk. What ought to be done with *Perry* and the public forum doctrine is this: The more a particular medium in society assumes the characteristics

---

49. Pool, *supra* note 2, at 91–2, 98.
50. *Id.* at 102–3.
51. *Id.* at 34–5.
52. *Id.* at 172.
53. Perry Education Assn. v. Perry Local Educators' Assn., 74 L. Ed2d 794 (1983).
54. *Id.* at 804.
55. *Id.* at 805.
56. *Id.*
57. *See* Davis v. Massachusetts, 167 U.S. 43 (1897).

of a public forum, then the more the public forum doctrine should be applied to it. If a medium begins to assume the characteristics of a public forum, then the court should recognize that fact and enforce dissolution of barriers to access. For example, in the case of many large, metropolitan daily newspapers, they have now assumed the role played by the eminently traditional "agora." They are sustained by ad revenues, and they are where people go to shop and gain commercial information, as well as "news."[58] It would not seem inappropriate to require some right of access to this public forum.[59]

While one could argue that such a requirement might abridge the newspaper publisher's right to freedom of the press, the appropriate reply would be that the right of the citizen to press freedom is being restricted by the market power enjoyed by the publisher.[60] The publisher would not have to be prevented from saying what s/he pleased. S/he would only be required to open some space in his/her agora for alternative points of view. As cost considerations begin to grow, the state can sanction some access fees, just as it presently sanctions fees for access to the streets for certain public demonstrations.[61] Other media would be subject to similar, albeit flexible analyses. While cable might be conducive to a purer public forum analysis to the point of being labelled a common carrier, corporate production facilities might entail more restrictions. Two feet next to the blast furnace might never qualify as an appropriate space for societal discourse. The same cannot be said for the company cafeteria or water cooler. Since the objective is to promote societal discourse, the rights of owners of those facilities to discourage discourse at such places would be circumscribed.

That such an approach to these questions is necessary should be apparent. The technology of the first amendment's speech and assembly has been changing more and more radically, to the point where Pool fears for its imminent irrelevance. Of course, we have previously noted that the first amendment might already be irrelevant. The point, though, is that something should be done to re-establish its relevance. A creative application of the public forum doctrine might help accomplish such a goal.

Certainly, one of the primary problems with such an approach is the complexity of its application. Is the church newsletter a public forum like the *New York Times*? How does one determine the appropriate fee for access to the

58. See POOL, *supra* note 2, at 18 f., 206 f.
59. While we are arguing that the large metropolitan daily might best be analogized to the traditional "agora," it is not inappropriate to note that it might also be analogized to a "fairgrounds," which seems to entail some first amendment aspect. *Cf.* Heffron v. Iskcon, 452 U.S. 640 (1981).
60. See, *e.g., infra* note 75.
61. See, *e.g.,* Cox v. New Hampshire, 312 U.S. 569 (1941); *but see* Goldberger, *A Reconsideration of* Cox v. New Hampshire: *Can Demonstrators Be Required to Pay the Costs of Using America's Public Forums?* 62 TEX. L. REV. 403 (1983–84). *Cf.* 2 U.S.C. 431 f.

satellite connection? The answer to the objection of "complexity" is that you either value meaningful first amendment discourse or you do not. If courts can determine what affects interstate commerce and what does not, then a court can conceivably determine at what point a flyer resembles an agora more than a personalized expression of opinion. If courts can ascertain what is an appropriate fee for access to the streets, then courts can conceivably judge the propriety of a minimal access fee for space in the *New York Times*. Perhaps the complexity objection calls for extension of the jurisdiction of the Federal Communications Commission (FCC), with supervisory jurisdiction exercised by the courts.[62] But whether the complexity calls for action by the judiciary, the legislature,[63] or the legislature's administrative agencies, the point remains: the first amendment calls for no restrictions on the part of free speech by government. Today, those restrictions derive as much if not more from governmentally promoted systems of property as they do from direct governmental interference. If the first amendment means the right of a citizen to meaningful impact on societal discourse, then the courts (and other branches of government) are going to have to acknowledge reality and take the difficult steps required to assure real capacity for speech, petition, and assembly.[64]

Of course, we must acknowledge that while the U.S. Supreme Court has from time to time taken tentative steps towards embracing the vision we are advocating, it has also taken emphatic steps in the opposite direction. In the case that finally quenched even the right of labor unions to engage in free speech in shopping centers,[65] the Court stated flatly: "[I]t is, of course, a commonplace that the constitutional guarantee of free speech is a guarantee only against abridgement by government, federal or state."[66]

The arguments that citizens must have some right of access to newspapers was confronted directly by the Court in *Miami Herald Publishing Co. v. Tornillo*.[67] In this case, the Florida legislature granted political candidates a right

62. *Cf.* U.S. v. Midwest Video Corp., 406 U.S. 649 (1972).
63. Much of our discussion has concerned the federal level. *Cf.* 2 U.S.C. 431 f. However, the role of the state legislatures should note be ignored. Recall Pruneyard Shopping Center v. Robins, 447 U.S. 74 (1980) and Miami Herald Publishing Co. v. Tornillo, 418 U.S. 241 (1974). *Cf. also* LA. CONST. art. 1, sec. IV, which suggests that property must be used responsibly: "Every person has the right to acquire, own, control, use, enjoy, protect and dispose of private property. This right is subject to reasonable statutory restrictions and the reasonable exercise of the police power."
64. *Cf.* ELY, *supra* note 9.
65. The case is Hudgens v. NLRB, 424 U.S. 507 (1976). Originally, labor unions had been given the right to picket in shopping centers in the context of a labor dispute in Food Employees Union Local 590 v. Logan Valley Plaza, Inc., 391 U.S. 308 (1968). In Lloyd v. Tanner, 407 U.S. 551 (1972), war protestors attempted to extend the right to advocates not involved in a labor dispute. They lost, and in Hudgens, what was lost by the war protesters was lost by the labor unions.
66. Hudgens v. NLRB, 424 U.S. 507, 513 (1976).
67. Miami Herald Publishing Co. v. Tornillo, 418 U.S. 241 (1974).

of access to answer newspaper attacks, and made it a misdemeanor for those newspapers which failed to comply. The Court squarely acknowledged a number of the points we have already raised, but in the end it invalidated the Florida statute.[68]

Through Justice Burger, the Court adduced three justifications for rejecting the arguments of the right-of-access proponents: (1) stare decisis; (2) the argument that the marketplace of ideas would be sterilized even more if the right-of-access statute were implemented; and (3) a variation on our Hegelian notions, i.e., that big newspapers are players in that Hegelian process, too, and government should not squelch them.[69]

The stare decisis argument is easily disposed of. First, if the precedents are bad, one does not improve upon a mistake by sustaining it. The Supreme Court's turnabout in *Hudgens v. NLRB*[70] illustrates the extent to which this court is prepared to make a fetish of stare decisis. But whatever arguments there are that justify honoring precedent, they are in a sense irrelevant in this case. "Traditional approaches to the first amendment" is an argument which either side can advance. There is Justice Burger's laissez faire version. There is also the Hegelian version we have discussed. There are the cases cited by the right-of-access people in the *Tornillo* case and rejected by Chief Justice Burger.[71] Finally, there is the whole history of governmental subsidy of the press.[72] In short, it is easy to argue that our "tradition" of the first amendment calls for acknowledgement of government's role in structuring societal discourse and an affirmation of government's responsibility to ensure that the discourse promotes individual and social interests.[73]

As for the second argument that enforcement of a right-of-reply access would make newspapers all the more cautious, such a point may in fact justify rejection of the Florida statute as written.[74] Yet, it does not obliterate a general right-of-access concept. The Florida statute stated that, in particular circumstances, a newspaper would have to give access to viewpoints it would otherwise not wish to publish. A more generalized right of access could make certain monopolistic newspapers acknowledge that part of their general course of business would include the responsibility to provide some space to some would-be advocates (again, possibly at a modest price). The problem now is that some advocates are boxed out of the monopolist newspapers altogether, and their proffers of payment are refused.[75] The adverse nature of the present

68. *See, e.g., id* at 247–58.
69. *Id.*
70. Hudgens v. NLRB, 424 U.S. 507 (1976).
71. *See* Miami Herald Publishing Co. v. Tornillo, 418 U.S. 241, 247 f (1974).
72. *See* POOL, *supra* note 2, 16 f., 78.
73. *See also* Red Lion Broadcasting Co. v. F.C.C., 395 U.S. 367, 390 (1968).
74. *See* Miami Herald Publishing Co. v Tornillo, 418 U.S. 241, 244 n.2 (1974).
75. *See, e.g.,* CIRINO, DON'T BLAME THE PEOPLE 302 f. (1971); "Donahue" Transcript #03054, 13; *and* Bachmann, *supra* note 3.

situation should be manifest. It can be cared for with a simple declaration to the effect that certain holders of certain forms of "agorae" are going to have to keep some "booths" open for opinions they might not normally entertain.[76] In short, the second objection might respond to the particular Florida statute, but it does nothing to respond to a right-of-access obligation in general.

As for the third point—that big newspapers have rights like everyone else—it simply ignores two major issues. The first is that these newspapers are basically enjoying their rights at the expense of everyone else. The fact that ten parties out of a million enjoy freedom does not necessarily speak well for the state of freedom in a system that supposedly supports it generally. The second ignored issue is that newspapers are more than newspapers. The press of today is not the press of 1789. Again, our argument has been that many large newspapers and media outlets might better be analogized to St. Paul's agora. They are less personalized expressions of opinion than they are centers where people come together for the sake of commerce and information. The entities that resemble such public enterprises should be held to certain levels of responsibility to the public, as was the company town in *Marsh v. Alabama*, and as was the shopping center in *Pruneyard*. Requiring television stations, cablecasters, and monopolistic newspapers to hold some areas open for outside advocates would not preclude them from advocating what they please. It would involve no confiscation of property. It should involve an ultimate benefit for everyone in society (including, possibly, the agora holders, who will be sponsoring a more exciting marketplace).

Of course, when and if Chief Justice Burger or any group constituting a majority of the Supreme Court is going to embrace the concepts informing our points is open to doubt. Indeed, other members of the court have intimated an even greater solicitude for traditional notions of private property than have Chief Justice Burger.[77]

The question at this point thus becomes why the present Supreme Court majority is so intensely wedded to these traditional notions. With the minimal leap of logic suggested by Justice Rehnquist in his *Pruneyard* analysis,[78] the Court could salvage most all of the property tradition, and yet at the same time, ratify an equally fundamental American tradition—viz., universal democracy.

---

76. *Cf. supra* notes 37, 59.
77. *See* White, Pruneyard Shopping Center v. Robins, 447 U.S. 74, 96, *and* Powell, *id.* at 96–7.
78. Justice Rehnquist suggests that as long as investment-based expectations are not undercut, there is no taking of property. Miami Herald Publishing Co. v. Tornillo, 418 U.S. 241, 82 f (1974). As we have suggested, a combination of universal access requirements and minimal access fees (when necessary) could easily establish a stable system for investment considerations. *Cf.* note 61.

Irrelevant First Amendment

The nastier answer to this question would allude to Hans Enzensberger's remarks and suggest that the Supreme Court is simply part of a totalitarian establishment, the goal of which is the totally administered state, i.e., a society wherein everyone fits into a particular system of production, consumption, and hierarchy, with minimal protest. Herr Enzensberger might observe that the many advances in first amendment theory that I applauded at the beginning of this section were not implemented by the Supreme Court until their significance had become attenuated by the development of mass media. In other words, during the 19th and early 20th centuries, the right to the streets, parks, and sidewalks was of paramount concern, because they constituted major media for the period. Yet, during such eras, the Supreme Court sustained the right of the government to act as a private property owner when it did not want particular actors to speak on its "property." Hence in 1897, for example, an individual's conviction for passing out leaflets on the Boston Commons was sustained.[79] Not until 1939 was this decision overturned.[80] By this time, of course, the significance of access to parks, streets, and sidewalks for the purposes of societal discourse had become significantly diminished. Radio had become a mass medium, and television was not far in coming.[81]

Yet, to try to explain the Supreme Court majority's recalcitrance in such conscientious, instrumentalist terms smacks of an analysis that credits the Court with a conscientiousness that our historical sense balks at according.[82] It is quite likely that if a member of that majority were confronted with the instrumentalist analysis, he or she would begin to respond with justifications for his or her position in terms sounding something like the following: We cannot use the first amendment to limit property rights, because if the state can begin to use parts of the constitution to encroach upon rights of property, where will it all end? Will one's security in property then become subject to the whim of who is in government? Then we would be back to a variation on the situation which our English civil warriors would have condemned, viz., one where one's livelihood would be subject to the whim of some bureaucrat, if not one king. One motivating factor behind the framing of the constitution (if not the bill of rights) was protection of property rights. That is not necessarily a bad thing, when the individual can rest secure in a province where the state cannot reach him/her. That is why we have the fourth and eighth amendments—as well as the due process clause that protects one in one's possession of property. Security in the possession of property is a

---

79. Davis v. Massachusetts, 167 U.S. 43 (1897).
80. Hague v. CIO, 307 U.S. 496 (1939).
81. *See, e.g.,* BRINKLEY, VOICES OF PROTEST (1982).
82. However, there are times when some members of the Court come to the bench with a particular political agenda in mind, e.g., when Chief Justice Taft assumed his office with an eye to "reverse a few decisions," and to "hit every little while" the labor "faction." BERNSTEIN, THE LEAN YEARS 191 (1960).

good thing because it retains for an individual the just fruits of labor and thereby encourages productivity. It affords a modicum of security against the whims of others, whether they be in government or in the private sector. With such security, the individual can plan and live a life worthy of a human being.[83]

The preceding disquisition may or may not be a fair imputation to those who would defend traditional notions of property, but it does set out a not uncommon line of argument. In part, we appreciate the sacrosanct nature of property because it stands for certain notions of human dignity: you deserve the fruits of your work. Human beings are more attractive in contexts of comfort than they are in contexts of deprivation. People deserve protection from unwarranted abuse by others.

When the argument is expressed in such abstract terms, one grows to appreciate the value inherent in the preceding perspective. Yet, those abstract terms serve as the perspective's critique as well as its justification. Once one turns from the theory to look at present reality, one notes that the system of property being justified by the theory does not always implement the notions of dignity that the theory promises. In a market where some people own factories and other people do not, the people without factories are going to get for their labor what they can extract from the owners of factories. Whether it will be a fair or living wage will in part depend upon minimum wage laws that limit a factory owner from using the factory as s/he pleases. In a zero sum society[84] where some individuals can accumulate as much as they please, with no regard to the consequences for others, it may mean comfort for some. But it is likely to imply deprivation for many. When some people lack access to essentials of a decent life, they are more subject to domination than they would be if they were securely possessed of life's essentials. In short, when one looks to the practical implications of the property theory outlined above, one finds that it does not live up to its pretentions. Analysis of its presuppositions reveal many of them to be hollow.

At this point the question becomes: What alternatives are there? To answer, we would begin by looking to the conceptions of freedom and security celebrated by our property advocate. We would begin by noting that human good has to be conceived in terms other than mere independence from others. The state of "freedom" is one of capacity as well as independence. To ensure achievement of a happy state of capacity a society might try to guarantee one access to particular quanta of material goods so that one might purchase means to capacity in various fields.[85] Alternatively a society might simply note that

---

83. *Cf.* RAWLS, A THEORY OF JUSTICE 407 f. (1971).
84. *Cf.* THUROW, THE ZERO SUM SOCIETY (1980).
85. This notion is a variation on the "voucher" concept promulgated by many market theorists.

there are some capacities that no individual can be denied: e.g., work, housing, education, clothing, food, etc.[86] In one sense, the alternative approaches might be viewed as similar, in that they both can be construed as "property" systems.[87] However, by expressing the vision in terms of direct entitlements instead of material goods, the latter vision opens the door to a more community-oriented perspective on human life.[88] Instead of being viewed as an atom in an exchanging marketplace, the human being is viewed as a person with capacities to be developed through experiences with other people. At such a point, the individual suddenly becomes viewed as an entity more dependent upon and integrated into society—which seems to be a more realistic view of what the human being is, when compared to the asocial monad postulated by more traditional property theories.[89]

When we reach a conception that looks to achieving human dignity through means beyond mere atomistic possession, a conversion to our vision of the first amendment becomes an easier step to take. Instead of ratifying a newspaper publisher's right to exclude, we begin to ratify the right of all citizens to be included in the process of social discourse and self-transformation. The newspaper publisher's humanity is not necessarily diminished. Like the Pruneyard Shopping Mall owner, (s)he is not being robbed. Hopefully, (s)he will find his/her experience enriched—like that of the less-blessed citizens.

Of course when one formulates the arguments to the Supreme Court majority in the terms of Hegelian vision, the question remains whether or not they will find it any more or less compelling than alternatives already advanced. On the one hand, as lawyers, we must continue to essay such approaches. As historians, however, we must acknowledge that more may be required. One historically minded lawyer, who has helped shift the courts from one set of principles to another, has observed that historical circumstances might be as much responsible for inducing court shifts as his own eloquence or rhetoric.[90] His experience dealt with the civil rights struggles, and to an extent, the value shifts he helped to implement involved incursions on tradi-

---

86. Cf., e.g., Reich, The New Property, 73 YALE L.J. 733 (1964); see also Unger, The Critical Legal Studies Movement, 98 HARV. L. REV. 563, 599 (1983).
87. See Reich, supra note 86.
88. Cf., e.g., the medieval notion of the "commons," resources to which every individual in the community enjoyed access rights. THOMPSON, WHIGS AND HUNTERS (1975). Similar concepts were also employed by the American Indians. L. HYDE, THE GIFT 121 f., 268 (1983).
89. See DALLMAYR, TWILIGHT OF SUBJECTIVITY (1981), and MACPHERSON, supra note 33.
90. KINOY, RIGHTS ON TRIAL 146–47 (1983). See also Bachmann, Book Review, 62 TEX. L. REV. 1601 (1984) (reviewing RIGHTS ON TRIAL).

tional notions of property.[91]

However, it is more instructive to view the more radical shifts concerning property that occurred during the 1930s. Prior to the 1930s, the Supreme Court was all but rabid in its support of traditional property conceptions. The Court declared that it was an "arbitrary restraint of [liberty]" for a jurisdiction to attempt to establish wage rates for women.[92] It was a violation of "the right to contract" and of constitutionally secured "liberty" for a state to try to regulate the number of hours worked in a day.[93] When the government tried to regulate employment contracts dealing with the right to unionize, the Court characterized such as "an arbitrary interference with the liberty of contract which no government can legally justify in a free land."[94] The Supreme Court finally shifted from the positions in 1937 with the *West Coast Hotel Co. v. Parish*[95] and *N.L.R.B. v. Jones & Laughlin Steel Corp.*[96] cases. But these decisions were rendered in a context of unprecedented social upheaval, labor unrest, and threats from Franklin Roosevelt that he would "pack" the court.[97] The primary "swing" justice admitted that he changed his vote because of his reading of the political situation in the country.[98]

---

91. One victory won during the civil rights struggles was the right of black people to be served in "public" accommodations like lunch counters and hotels, even though these facilities were the "private" property of particular owners. See, e.g., Heart of Atlanta Motel, Inc. v. U.S., 379 U.S. 241 (1964). See also RAINES, MY SOUL IS RESTED 435–45 (1977).
92. Adkins v. Children's Hospital, 261 U.S. 525, 561 (1922). See also Morehead v. New York, 298 U.S. 587 (1936).
93. Lochner v. N.Y., 198 U.S. 45, 53 (1905).
94. Adair v. U.S., 208 U.S. 161, 174–5 (1908).
95. West Coast Hotel Co. v. Parish, 300 U.S. 379 (1937).
96. N.L.R.B. v. Jones & Laughlin Steel Corp., 301 U.S. 1 (1937).
97. BERNSTEIN, THE TURBULENT YEARS (1969). See also Bachmann, *Lawyers, Law and Social Change*, 12 N.Y.U. REV. L. & SOC. CHANGE 1 (1984).
98. Some years after the fact, Justice Roberts stated:

> Looking back, it is difficult to see how the Court could have resisted the popular urge for uniform standards throughout the country—and for what in effect was a unified economy . . . . An insistence by the Court on holding federal power to what seemed its appropriate orbit when the Constitution was adopted might have resulted in even more radical changes in our dual structure than those which have been gradually accomplished through the extension of the limited jurisdiction conferred on the federal government.

A. T. MASON, THE SUPREME COURT, FROM TAFT TO WARREN 122 (1968). Another way of viewing Roberts' statement is to note that he wanted to preclude a revolution—and adjusted his legal opinions accordingly.

Irrelevant First Amendment

The point, of course, is that it is open to question whether or not the relevance of the first amendment is going to rise or fall with the Supreme Court's "natural receptivity" to good argument. The first amendment will become relevant when larger masses of people begin to take such arguments seriously and begin to press for their implementation. Of course, for that to occur, the courts may or may not have to take our arguments seriously to some degree (otherwise, the populace will never hear of them). When we come to that point, we must again begin to explore the questions that Enzensberger raises.

JAMES C. HSIUNG

Indecent Broadcast: An Assessment of *Pacifica*'s Impact

James C. Hsiung is an assistant professor in the Department of Communication at Purdue University.

It was a shock to the broadcast industry when the U.S. Supreme Court upheld the Federal Communications Commission's (FCC) decision on *FCC v. Pacifica Foundation*[1] (*Pacifica*) in 1978. The industry and many critics were afraid that this newly created FCC rationale to regulate indecent programming would increase censorship of broadcast content, chill broadcast licensees, and curtail the first amendment rights of broadcasters. *Broadcasting* wrote, "There are fears that door has been opened for commission interference in numerous programming areas."[2] *Publishers Weekly* indicated that this case "has brought cries of censorship from broadcasters and a warning from dissenting Justices that it could set a precedent for banning genuine works of literature from the airwaves if they contained 'four-letter words.' "[3] One critic asserted:

> By banning the broadcast [George Carlin's monologue], the Court embarked on a new era in first amendment controversies: 1) it set a precedent for the Supreme Court to be

1. FCC v. Pacifica, 438 U.S. 726 (1978). The Supreme Court ruled that the FCC did not violate the first amendment rights of the station WBAI by holding George Carlin's monologue entitled "Filthy Words" was indecent.
2. WBAI Ruling: Supreme Court Saves the Worst for the Last, BROADCASTING 20–22 (July 10, 1978).
3. Wagner, *"Seven Dirty Words": Supreme Court Ruling Raises Fear of Censorship,* 214 PUBLISHERS WEEKLY 84–85 (July 17, 1978).

the judge of the value of words and 2) it prohibited the expression of an idea about attitudes of the public over a public medium without a showing of a significant countervailing public interest [citations omitted].[4]

Others were also concerned that the Supreme Court, by ignoring precedents, authorized the FCC to regulate protected speech based on its content, even though the speech was not considered obscene.[5]

Former FCC Chairman Charles D. Ferris responded to the concerns and criticism by indicating that "the particular set of circumstances in the *Pacifica* case is about as likely to occur again as Halley's Comet."[6] Following, the *Pacifica* decision, however, there has been no clear indication of how the courts will rule on similar cases in the future and of how the FCC might react to enforce the new doctrine of broadcast indecency.

The objective of this article is to investigate the implications of *Pacifica* by examining subsequent FCC actions and court cases related to indecency in electronic media.[7] The result of this examination will

---

4. Parish, *Casenotes of FCC v. Pacifica Foundation*, 57 U. DET. J. URB. L. 95, 121 (Fall 1979).
5. White, *Pacifica Foundation v. FCC: "Filthy Words": the First Amendment and the Broadcast Media*, 78 COLUM. L. REV. 164 (1978). Wolff, *Pacifica's Seven Dirty Words: A Sliding Scale of the First Amendment*, 79 U. ILL. L. F. 969 (1979). Wolff indicated that prior cases had held that "the objectionable content of offensive speech is not a constitutionally cognizable excuse for its suppression." These cases included

> Erzonznick v. City of Jacksonville, 422 U.S. 205 (1975) (display of nudity on drive-in movie screen); Eaton v. City of Tulsa, 415 U.S. 697 (1974) (indecent language by trial witness on cross-examination); Lewis v. City of New Orleans, 415 U.S. 130 (1974) (utterance of vulgar epithet); Hess v. Indiana, 414 U.S. 105 (1975) (utterance of vulgar remarks advocating violence); Papish v. University of Missouri Curators, 410 U.S. 667 (1973) (indecent remarks in campus newspaper); Cohen v. California, 403 U.S. 15 (1971) (wearing of a jacket imprinted with vulgar language); Brandenberg v. Ohio, 395 U.S. (1965) 444 (utterance of racial slurs).

Id. at 1002, note 252.
6. *Which Way the Wind Blows at the FCC after WBAI*, BROADCASTING 31-32 (July 24, 1978). The quote was the speech made by Ferris to the New England Broadcasters Association.
7. In order to conduct this research in a systematic approach, a computer citator search of WESTLAW database was conducted in April 1986. As the result of the search, there were ninety-nine references citing *Pacifica* consisting of sixty-eight cases. Among these, only four cases related to the electronic media and were relevant to our present discussion. Additionally, an extra case, *Home Box Office, Inc., v. Wilkinson*, 531 F. Supp. 986 (1982), was included due to its relevancy, although it did not cite *Pacifica*. As far as the FCC's actions are concerned, there were also seven cases related to *Pacifica*, which will be discussed in this article.

An Assessment of *Pacifica's* Impact

demonstrate whether the concerns about and fears of the *Pacifica* ruling were correctly presented nearly a decade ago, or whether the "narrowness" of *Pacifica* has been adhered to by the FCC and the courts. This article will begin with a brief history of how the FCC handled broadcast indecency before *Pacifica;* how the FCC has reacted to the ruling in its succeeding cases will follow. The litigations over indecency and obscenity in electronic media after *Pacifica* will then be examined. Finally, the implications of *Pacifica* will be generalized.

I. INDECENCY: A BRIEF HISTORICAL REVIEW OF FCC ACTIONS

Broadcast regulation has always been complex and paradoxical, especially in the area of obscene and indecent broadcasts. On the one hand, the FCC is prohibited from censoring broadcast signals and from interfering with the first amendment rights of broadcasters.[8] On the other hand, the FCC is empowered to regulate "any obscene, indecent, or profane language by means of radio communication" under 18 USC 1464.[9] The FCC has constantly found itself on a collision course with these statutory mandates. In the 1960s, however, the FCC seemed willing to regulate "offensive" programming under the term of indecency instead of obscenity.[10] Although it had little success in creating judicial precedent prior to *Pacifica,* the FCC had regulated and defined indecent broadcasts.[11]

The first case indirectly related to indecent broadcast was *Palmetto Broadcast Co.* (WDKD),[12] albeit the issue of an offensive program was

---

8. Communications Act of 1934, 47 U.S.C. 326 (1982). "Nothing in this Act shall be understood or construed to give the Commission the power of censorship over the radio communications or signals transmitted by any radio station, and no regulation or condition shall be promulgated or fixed by the Commission which shall interfere with the right of free speech by means of radio communication."
9. Crime and Criminal Procedures, 18 U.S.C. 1464 (1982). "Whoever utters any obscene, indecent, or profane language by means of radio communication shall be fined not more than $10,000 or imprisoned not more than two years, or both." Originally, this sentence was under Section 326 of the Communication Act and was lifted and placed in United States Code by Congress in 1948. Both the Department of Justice and the FCC have the authority to enforce it.
10. *See infra* notes 17 and 18 and accompanying text.
11. These cases included *In re* Applications of E.G. Robinson, Jr., TR/AS Palmetto Broadcast Co. (WDKD), Kingstree, S.C., 33 F.C.C. 250 (1962); *In re* WUHY-FM Eastern Education Radio, 24 F.C.C.2d 408 (1970); and In the Matter of Sonderling Broadcasting Corp., WGLD-FM, Oak Park, ILL., 41 F.C.C.2d (1973).
12. *In re* Applications of E.G. Robinson, Jr., TR/ Palmetto Broadcast Co. (WDKD), Kingstree, S.C., 33 F.C.C. 250 (1962), *recon. den.,* 34 F.C.C. 101 (1963). *E.G. Robinson, Jr. v. FCC,* 334 F.2d 584, *cert. den.* 379 U.S. 843 (1964).

considered only as a part of license renewal. In 1960, the FCC received complaints that the Charlie Walker show, broadcast between January and April, 1960, over station WDKD, consisted of "vulgar, suggestive material susceptible of double meaning with indecent connotations."[13] During the investigation, the station owner, Robinson, tried to conceal the problem of Walker's show from the FCC by claiming he was not familiar with the nature of and the statement of the program.[14] When WDKD came up for license renewal, the FCC denied the renewal because Robinson lacked candor and did not exercise supervision over programming.[15] Although the issue of the case was not concerned with indecent broadcast, the Commission stressed that it had the authority under the public interest standard to deal with programming "obviously offensive or patently vulgar."[16] Otherwise,

> radio could become predominantly a purveyor of smut and patent vulgarity—yet unless the matter broadcast reached the level of obscenity under 18 USC 1464, the Commission... would be powerless to prevent this perversion or misuse of a valuable national resource [note omitted].[17]

This case marked the beginning of a period in which the FCC was willing to impose sanction on any indecent broadcast under the public interest standard, if not under obscenity law which, in its view, lacked clarity and applicability.[18] However, it should be noted that the FCC rejected a similar complaint regarding offensive programming in renewing licenses of the Pacifica Foundation two years later.[19] The Commission indicated that it was not "concerned with individual programs—nor is it at any time concerned with matters essentially of licensee taste or judgment."[20]

---

13. *Id.,* 33 F.C.C. 250 (1963).
14. *Id.,* at 252.
15. *Id.,* at 257–258.
16. *Id.,* at 257.
17. *Id.,* at 256 n.7. The FCC indicated that "the legal considerations applicable to 18 U.S.C. 1464 are not clear because of the dearth of court decisions."
18. *Id.* And *see* supra note 12, 34 F.C.C. 101, 103 (1964).
19. *In re* Applications of Pacifica Foundation for Initial License of Station KPFK, etc., 36 F.C.C. 147 (1964). The FCC found that two of the five programs complained about were offensive. But it indicated that these were isolated incidents different from the *Robinson* case two years prior. For historical discussion of this case, see Richard L. Barton's *The Lingering Legacy of Pacifica: Broadcasters' Freedom of Silence.* 53 JOURNALISM QUARTERLY 429 (1976).
20. *Id.* at 148.

An Assessment of *Pacifica*'s Impact

The two subsequent cases directly involving indecent and obscene broadcasts were *WUHY-FM, Eastern Education Radio*[21] and *WGLD-FM, Sonderling Broadcasting Corp.*[22] In *WUHY-FM,* the noncommercial education station broadcast a taped interview with Jerry Garcia, leader of "The Grateful Dead." Garcia expressed his views by "frequently interspersing" offensive words "as adjectives, or simply as an introductory expletive or substitute for the phrase, et cetera."[23] Although the FCC agreed that the broadcast was not obscene and admitted that there were no precedents for this case, it continued to define indecency as follows: "the material broadcast is (a) patently offensive by contemporary community standards; and (b) is utterly without redeeming social value."[24] Under these standards, the FCC determined that the recorded Garcia interview fell within the meaning of "indecent." The FCC imposed a forfeiture of $100 and encouraged the station to file for judicial review. The station paid the forfeiture and did not appeal the case.

In *Sonderling,* the FCC received complaints about WGLD-FM's popular call-in talk show known as "topless radio" and determined the station violated both indecency and obscenity standards of 18 USC 1464.[25] The FCC fined WGLD-FM $2,000 and again urged judicial consideration. Although WGLD-FM denied liability, it sent a check of $2,000 to the FCC, which indicated the payment was considered "an admission of liability."[26] Ironically, two citizen groups appealed the decision to the D.C. Circuit Court when their petition for remission of the fine imposed on WGLD-FM was denied by the FCC.[27] The D.C. Court upheld the FCC's decision, yet left the definition of "indecent" untouched.[28]

Finally, the FCC found itself a test of indecent broadcast when the Pacifica Foundation decided to appeal the case which involved "social satirist" George Carlin's album of "Filthy Words."[29] Following a complaint about the program, the FCC issued an Order regarding the broadcast of Carlin's monologue. In its Order, the FCC reiterated the concept

---

21. *In re* WUHY-FM, Eastern Education Radio, 24 F.C.C.2d 408 (1970).
22. In the matter of Sonderling Broadcasting Corp., WGLD-FM, Oak Park, ILL., 41 F.C.C.2d 777 (1973).
23. *In re* WUHY-FM, Eastern Education Radio, 24 F.C.C.2d at 409 (1970).
24. *Id.* at 412. These two criteria were based on rulings of three cases: Jocobellis v. Ohio, 378 U.S. 184 (1965); Memoirs v. Massachusetts, 383 U.S. 413 (1963); and Roth v. U.S., 354 U.S. 476 (1956).
25. In the matter of Sonderling Broadcasting Corp., WGLD-FM, Oak Park, Ill., 41 F.C.C.2d 777 (1973).
26. *Id.* at 780.
27. *Id.* The two groups were the Illinois Citizens Committee for Broadcasting and the Illinois Division of the American Civil Liberties Union.
28. Illinois Citizens' Committee for Broadcasting v. F.C.C., 515 F.2d 397 (1975).
29. Pacifica Foundation v. F.C.C., 556 F.2d 9 (D.C. Cir. 1977), *aff'd,* 438 U.S. 726 (1978).

of "indecent"[30] and determined that, although the show "lacks the element of appeal to the prurient interest," it was "patently offensive," especially when children were present.[31] The FCC, however, did mention that different considerations would be given to a program's "literary, artistic, political or scientific value" if the program were aired in late evening "when the number of children in the audience is reduced to a minimum."[32] The FCC imposed an administrative sanction on the licensee of WBAI-FM which was kept in the station's file for future license renewal consideration.[33]

On appeal, the D.C. Circuit Court reversed the FCC's decision. It indicated that the Order was both overbroad and vague, and that the broadcast was not obscene under *Miller*.[34] The U.S. Supreme Court reviewed the case and upheld the FCC's Order with no majority. The Court articulated three pertinent reasons for supporting the FCC decision. First, the FCC did not violate the Section 326 anticensorship provision of the Communications Act because it had "power to review the content of completed broadcasts in the performance of its regulatory duties."[35] Second, the FCC had the authority to "impose sanctions on licensees who engage in obscene, indecent, or profane broadcasting," even though indecent language lacked "prurient appeal."[36] Third, the Court stated that, among all forms of communication, "it is broadcasting that has received the most limited First Amendment protection."[37] This is because broadcasting is "a uniquely pervasive presence" and "uniquely accessible to children."[38] And based on the narrowness of this "specific factual context," the FCC's programming regulation of "indecent" was valid.

---

30. In the Matter of a Citizen's Complaint Against Pacifica Foundation Station WBAI-FM, New York, N.Y., 56 F.C.C.2d 94, 98 (1975). The FCC stated that "the concept of 'indecent' is intimately connected with the exposure of children to language that describes, in terms patently offensive as measured by contemporary community standards for the broadcast medium, sexual or excretory activities and organs, at times of the day when there is a reasonable risk that children may be in the audience [note omitted]."
31. *Id.* In making the decision, the FCC relied on two precedents, which were Miller v. California, 413 U.S. 15 (1973) (formulated the definition for obscenity) and Ginsberg v. State of New York, 390 U.S. 629 (1968) (prohibited the distribution for obscene material among children).
32. *Supra* note 30, at 98, 100. Although the standards of "indecent" are the same, the FCC applied the "channeling" approach of nuisance law to the case by which, in its view, the material could be broadcast at late night with minimum children present and considered less offensive.
33. *Id.* at 99.
34. *Supra* note 29, at 21–22. For a detailed discussion, see White, *supra* note 5.
35. *Id.*, 438 U.S. 726, at 734–737.
36. *Id.* at 738–741.
37. *Id.* at 747.
38. *Id.* at 748–749.

An Assessment of Pacifica's Impact

In this case, the Court not only created a new rationale—pervasiveness—for broadcast regulation, but also gave the FCC a separate jurisdiction to regulate indecent broadcast material that was not legally obscene.[39] It was a two-fold triumph for the FCC. First, the FCC could now impose sanctions on indecent broadcast, avoiding the clash between its statutory mandates and the first amendment rights of broadcasters, and avoiding close judicial review. Second, it now had the regulatory flexibility to apply either the obscenity definition under *Miller* or the indecent rationale under *Pacifica*.

II. FCC RESPONSES AFTER PACIFICA (1978-86)

Less than three weeks later, the FCC, in a license renewal decision,[40] rejected a similar complaint about indecent programming and seemed to hold back from the decision of *Pacifica*. When noncommercial educational station WGBH-TV came up for a license renewal, Morality in Media of Massachusetts, Inc. (Morality) filed a petition to deny the application and asserted that WGBH-TV "has failed in its responsibility to the community by consistently broadcasting offensive, vulgar and otherwise material harmful to children without adequate supervision or parental warnings."[41] The FCC denied the allegations and granted the license renewal.

The Commission stressed that it could not deny a license because certain materials were "offensive to some or even a substantial number of listeners,"[42] and had to weigh a licensee's "overall" programming performance. It also seemed to retreat from its position in *Pacifica* by stating that there was no hard evidence supporting that these programs were "harmful to children."[43] Furthermore, it believed that it did not have the

---

39. For discussion, *see* GILLMOR & BARRON, MASS COMMUNICATION LAW: CASES & COMMENT 930-33 (4th ed. 1984); Denise M. Trauth and John Huffman, "The Pacifica Case: The Supreme Court's New Regulatory Rationale for Broadcasting," paper presented at 1979 ICA convention; and White, *supra* note 5.
40. *In re* Application of WGBH Educational Foundation, 69 F.C.C.2d 1250 (1978).
41. *Id.* at 1250-251. Morality singled out four programs, including a "Masterpiece Theater" series (adulterous relationships); "The Thin Edge" (adultery and fornication); "Monty Python's Flying Circus" (materials about scatology, immodesty, vulgarity, nudity, profanity); and "Rock Follies" (vulgar, profane, and obscene materials), which it believed were vulgar and profane.
42. *Id.* at 1252-253. The FCC cited two cases, which were *Pacifica* (1964) and *Sonderling* (1973), *supra* notes 19 and 22.
43. *Id.*, and see In the Matter of a Citizen's Complaint Against Pacifica Foundation station WBAI-FM, New York, N.Y., 56 F.C.C.2d 94, 100 (1975). In *Pacifica*, the FCC indicated that its "failure to set forth its position could lead to widespread use of indecent language on the public's airwaves, a development which would (1) critically impair broadcasting as an effective mode of expression and communication, (2) ignore the rights of unwilling recipients, and (3) ignore the danger of exposure to children."

prerogative "to intervene in any case where words similar or identical to those in *Pacifica* are broadcast over a licensed radio or television station." The FCC stressed that it intended "to observe the narrowness of the *Pacifica* holding" unless the indecent language had been "repeated over and over as a sort of verbal shock treatment."[44]

Shortly after WGBH-TV, another incident involved a gubernatorial candidate, J.B. Stoner, who used the word "nigger" in his political spot announcements.[45] The Atlanta NAACP, citing the month-old *Pacifica* case, sent a telegram to the FCC and requested that actions be taken. The Commission declined the complaint based on three reasons. First, the Communications Act Sections 315 and 326 prohibited the FCC from regulating political speech made by a legally qualified candidate and from censoring broadcast content.[46] Second, the word "nigger" did not fall within the meaning of "indecent" utterance set forth in *Pacifica*.[47] Third, the first amendment restricted the FCC from imposing content-based regulation unless the broadcast was "obscene, profane or indecent language" within the holding of *Pacifica* and the obscene definition of the Supreme Court.[48] A similar case also occurred during the 1980 presidential election when a political radio spot used the word "bullshit" to express dissatisfaction with three Presidential candidates.[49] The FCC made clear that precedents inhibited it from censoring any political speech on radio or television delivered by a legally qualified candidate. Only if the speech creates "a clear and present danger of riot or violence,"[50] could the FCC intervene.

The FCC did not deal with the question of indecent broadcast until 1982 when it received complaints about alleged interference from an amateur radio KB6TG licensed to Kenneth Gilbert in California.[51] The investigator found that Gilbert deliberately interfered with the frequencies used by other amateur operators on two occasions and employed four-letter words repeatedly during the transmission.[52] The FCC determined

---

44. *Ibid*, at 1254. The Commission cited the Concurring Opinions of Justices Powell and Blackmun. *Supra* note 1, at 757.
45. *In re* Complaint by Julian Bond Atlanta NAACP Atlanta, Georgia, 69 F.C.C.2d 943 (1978).
46. *Id.* at 944.
47. *Id.*
48. *Id.*
49. *In re* Complaints of Barry Commoner and LaDonna Harris "Against NBC Radio," 87 F.C.C.2d 1, 2 (1980).
50. CARTER, FRANKLIN & WRIGHT, THE FIRST AMENDMENT AND THE FIFTH ESTATE 269-70 (1986).
51. In the Matter of Revocation of License of Kenneth L. Gilbert, 92 F.C.C.2d 130 (1982).
52. *Id.* at 132-34.

An Assessment of *Pacifica*'s Impact

that Gilbert violated two sections of the FCC's rules intended to prevent willful or malicious interference with "any radio communications or signals" and "communications containing obscene, indecent or profane words, language or meaning."[53] The FCC revoked the license of KB6TG and suspended Gilbert's radio operator license. Although the main concern here was interference, it was the first time that the FCC applied *Pacifica*. It ruled that Gilbert's "bad language" was indecent within the definition of *Pacifica*.[54]

A year later, the FCC declined to accept a complaint filed by Decency in Broadcasting, Inc. (Decency) which accused station WFBQ-FM of broadcasting certain "obscene, indecent and profane material."[55] Decency claimed that the morning drive show called "Bob and Tom Show" of WFBQ-FM consistently made "off color" comments and its language was profane. In rejecting this complaint, the FCC issued a two-page Order and concluded that, based on *Miller* and *Pacifica,* the alleged language was not profane within the meaning defined by the Court and "any sanction imposed by the Commission for the broadcast of profane language in this situation would [not] be judicially upheld."[56]

Once again, the Pacifica Foundation found itself under attack in 1983 when its station WPFW-FM applied for a license renewal. Along with other allegations, the American Legal Foundation (ALF) accused WPFW-FM's programming of being "flagrantly offensive and vulgar"[57] and filed a petition to deny. ALF indicated that indecent language such as "motherfucker" and "shit" occurred repetitively in WPFW's programs. Based on the definition set forth in *Pacifica,* ALF claimed that the station violated 18 USC 1464.[58]

The FCC asserted that ALF failed "to make a prima facie case" and showed nothing more than "isolated use [of alleged language] in the course of a three year license term."[59] It also stressed that words similar or identical to *Pacifica* did not "amount to the repetitious 'verbal shock treatment.' "[60] Additionally, the FCC reiterated that it could not deny a renewal application based on the "subjective determination" of the

---

53. *Id.* at 136. Telecommunications, 47 C.F.R. 97.119 and 97.125 (1985).
54. *Id.* at 138–39.
55. In the Matter of Application for Review Filed by Decency in Broadcasting, Inc., of a Denial of Its complaint against Rahall Broadcasting of Indiana, Inc., Licensee of Station WFBQ(FM) Indianapolis, Indiana, 94 F.C.C.2d 1162 (1983).
56. *Id.* at 1163.
57. *In re* Application of Pacifica Foundation for Renewal of License for Noncommercial Station WPFW(FM), Washington, D.C., 95 F.C.C.2d 750 (1983).
58. *Id.* at 760.
59. *Id.*
60. *Id.*

petitioner, who viewed the programming as "offensive and vulgar."[61]

These cases seem to suggest that the FCC was reluctant to take action unless it was sure that its decisions could stand up under judicial scrutiny and that alleged language fell clearly within the definitions of *Pacifica*. In some cases, such as WGBH and WPFW, the circumstances and similarities were not so discernible in comparison with *Pacifica*. The FCC, however, decided to stay within the narrow guidelines established in *Pacifica* and not pursue the issue of indecent broadcast vigorously. Although the FCC did apply *Pacifica* in the case of KB6TG amateur radio station, it did not revoke the station's license solely because of the indecent language used in the broadcast, but also because of deliberate interference.

In the next section, the focus will center around the court cases related to indecent matter in electronic media chronologically. But it should be noted here that, although they were not broadcasting, these cases all cited *Pacifica* and can provide an insight to how the courts reacted to the new rationale for rulings involving indecency.[62]

III. LITIGATIONS AFTER PACIFICA (1978–86)

A. Amplified Speech

Houston city ordinances were challenged in 1980 by Gary Reeves, who intended to use sound amplification equipment for the purpose of disseminating his political and educational views.[63] Pursuant to the city ordinances, Reeves had to obtain a permit and comply with "specific restrictions on the use of sound amplification equipment outside of buildings or residential property."[64] Reeves challenged these ordinances on constitutional grounds in Texas Southern District Court, and the court ruled these restrictions were overbroad and vague. The city of Houston appealed the case.

In its appeal, the city asserted that it "could properly prohibit amplification of words or sounds that were 'obscene' and that such prohibition was not limited to specifically 'erotic' speech."[65] The Texas Southern District Court struck down this restriction because it was "unconstitution-

---

61. *Id.* at 761. The two cases the FCC based its decision on were *Sonderling* and *WGBH*. See *supra* notes 22 and 40.
62. *Supra* note 7. One extra case was discussed because it was used as a precedent for two later cases which cited *Pacifica*.
63. Gary Reeves v. Jim McConn, 631 F.2d 377 (5th Cir. 1980).
64. *Id.* at 380.
65. *Id.* at 379.

An Assessment of *Pacifica*'s Impact

ally overbroad" and failed to specify that "only 'erotic' sounds could be prohibited under *Miller* (citations omitted)."[66]

However, the Fifth Circuit Court disagreed and reversed the ruling by quoting *Pacifica*. In its view, because amplified speech was similar to broadcasting in that it

> exposes the public to uninvited or even unwelcome speech in a manner that often gives the listener no completely effective means of avoidance, the state may act to impose sanctions on those who use 'obscene, indecent or profane language' during broadcasts.[67]

In this regard, amplified speech would not have the same first amendment protection usually given to "printed or unamplified speech."[68] Therefore, the city had the authority to regulate all amplified speech content and sounds, even though they were not "erotic" as specified under *Miller*.

Subsequently, Reeves argued on the rehearing that reliance on *Pacifica* was misplaced because "the broader governmental power over broadcast media is based upon the fact that radio and television intrude into the privacy of the home, where 'the individual's right to be left alone plainly outweighs the First Amendment rights of an intruder.' "[69] Again, the Circuit Court ruled that "amplified speech also intrudes into the home" and "*Pacifica* does not draw a rigid line at the front door of the home."[70] It also stated that the protection against obscene and indecent speech afforded by the state did not "completely vanish" because "the unwilling listener and his family leave home and enter the public streets."[71]

Although this was a case unrelated to broadcasting, the Circuit Court employed the new broadcast rationale—pervasiveness—created by *Pacific* as a basis to justify content-based regulation for "obscene, indecent or profane" speech. In addition, it broadened the meaning of *Pacifica* and extended the government's authority to regulate not only indecent broadcasting, but also amplified speech.

---

66. *Id.* at 387.
67. *Id.*
68. *Id.*
69. Reeves v. McConn, 638 F.2d 762, 763 (5th Cir. 1981).
70. *Id.*
71. *Id.* at 764.

B. Cable Indecency: State Statute and City Ordinance

Three subsequent cases dealt with material distributed by cable and defined indecent by a state or a city ordinance. By distinguishing cable and broadcasting as different media, the courts invalidated all three cases and concluded that the reasoning of *Pacifica* was not appropriate in cable. Although the court did not cite *Pacifica* in *HBO v. Wilkinson*,[72] this case set the precedent for the following two.

In *HBO v. Wilkinson*, HBO initiated an action against a Utah statute that made it a crime "for any person to knowingly distribute by wire or cable any pornographic or indecent material to its subscribers." The state law defined indecent material as "description or depictions of illicit sex or sexual immorality."[73] District Court Judge Jenkins held that the statute was unconstitutionally overbroad because it tried to deal with speech other than hard-cord pornography and went beyond the mandates of *Miller* without any safeguards.[74]

Although Jenkins was sympathetic with the state's good intention in protecting children, precedents dictated that "only in relatively narrow and well-defined circumstances may government bar public dissemination of protected materials to them [minors] (citations omitted)."[75] In this case, Utah's statute was not "narrow and well-defined" and did not exclude protected speech from the criminal sanctions. In addition, because the statute did not mention children, it would be "equally applicable to cable TV programming reaching homes and environments having no children at all," and was too broad.[76]

During the same year (1982), an identical suit, also in Utah, was brought by a local cable system in *Community Television of Utah, Inc. v. Roy City (Roy City)*.[77] The challenge was against a Roy City ordinance which prohibited the local cable system from distributing indecent programming. But this time Roy City relied on *Pacifica* as the principal rationale in defending the ordinance.

Again Judge Jenkins presided in the case and, based on the reasoning in *HBO v. Wilkinson*, ruled the ordinance was overbroad. However, to illustrate the inapplicability of *Pacifica* in this case, he went to great lengths in comparing the differences between cable and broadcasting and

---

72. HBO v. Wilkinson, 531 F. Supp. 986 (1982).
73. *Id.* at 987.
74. *Id.*
75. *Id.* at 996-97. The court cited three cases: Erzonznick v. City of Jacksonville, 422 U.S. 205 (1975); Ginsberg v. New York, 390 U.S. 629 (1968); and Tinker v. Des Moines School Dist., 422 U.S. 205 (1975).
76. *Id.*
77. Community Television of Utah Inc. v. Roy City, 555 F. Supp. 1164 (1982).

An Assessment of *Pacifica*'s Impact

examined the rationales for regulation behind these two media.[78]

He stressed that cable is not broadcasting; does not use the radio spectrum; requires subscription; is privately owned without advertising; and can be cancelled by subscribers.[79] On the other hand, broadcast media, such as radio and television, use public airwaves; do not require subscription; and are "free" with extensive advertising. Based on these differences, Roy City failed to distinguish between these two media, and the "pervasiveness" rationale of *Pacifica* was not applicable here.[80] Thus, if *Pacifica* was irrelevant here, the city ordinance in regulating indecent material carried by cable was "obviously and facially beyond *Miller*.[81]

Another similar case dealing with indecent programming on cable was *Cruz v. Ferre* in Miami, Florida. The Florida District Court applied the same comparison and rationales used in *Roy City* and *HBO v. Wilkinson* and adjudicated that a Miami city ordinance was overbroad "where it applied to more than just obscenity."[82] It also indicated that precedent prohibited the imposition of programming regulation on cable because "theory—physical interference and scarcity requiring an umpiring role for government—is absent (citation omitted)."[83] The City of Miami appealed the decision, and the Eleventh Circuit Court upheld the ruling, pointing out that the "pervasiveness" component of *Pacifica* was not found in cable television—besides over-the-air signals carried by cable systems are still subject to *Pacifica*.[84]

C. Regulation of "Dial-A-Porn"

"Dial-It," also know as "dial-a-porn," is a telephone service offered by Carlin Communications, Inc., which provides prerecorded tapes of actual or simulated sexual activities. Since it is a telephone service, anyone can get access to the service and no mechanism is employed to prevent minors using it. "Dial-It" has drawn public attention due to parental complaints and has received millions of calls every year since its inception.

Congress, in order to keep minors away from the service, passed an amendment which later became law when the President signed the legisla-

---

78. *Id.* at 1166–169.
79. *Id.* at 1167. Judge Jenkins listed nine differences between cable and broadcast. For present discussion, only five were relevant.
80. *Id.* at 1169–170.
81. *Id.* at 1171.
82. Cruz v. Ferre, 571 F. Supp. 125 (1983).
83. *Id.* at 132. The court cited HBO v. FCC, 567 F.2d 9 (D.C. Cir. 1977), *cert. den.*, 434 U.S. 829 (1977), in which the FCC was prohibited from imposing programming regulation on subscription-type services, such as HBO.
84. Cruz v. Ferre, 755 F.2d 1415, 1420, 1422 n.10 (11th Cir. 1985).

tion on December 8, 1983.[85] The amendment was included in the Communications Act Section 223 and instructed the FCC to formulate regulation for "obscene or harassing telephone calls."[86] Under the Congressional mandate, the FCC issued a *Report And Order* in June of 1984, which required "Dial-It" service to be operated only between the hours of 9:00 p.m. and 8:00 a.m. Eastern Standard Time and to be paid by credit card before transmission of the messages.[87] Carlin Communications, Inc. filed suit in the Second Circuit Court and challenged the FCC's time-channeling Order as violating the first amendment and overbroad in proscribing "any obscene or indecent communication."[88]

In adjudicating the case, the court held that telephone service was not "uniquely pervasive" and "uniquely accessible to children, even those too young to read."[89] Thus, *Pacific* could not be applied to telephone service which "transmits the spoken word, not photographs, moving pictures, or live performances."[90] The court quoted a recent Supreme Court case holding that *"Pacifica* is inapplicable outside the broadcast context."[91]

In terms of time-channeling regulation, the Circuit Court rejected the FCC's argument because "the FCC has failed adequately to demonstrate that regulatory scheme is well tailored to its ends or that those ends could not be met by less drastic means."[92] It could not understand why the FCC barred "Dial-It" service during the daytime hours when children are more likely to be in school. In addition, the court indicated that the FCC did not fashion an appropriate mechanism for protecting children.[93] The court, however, did suggest that approaches such as blocking or access numbers might be more suitable as a less restrictive scheme to protect children.

85. Carlin Communication, Inc. v. FCC, 749 F2d 113, 115–116 (2d Cir. 1984).
86. 47 U.S.C. § 223, amended December 8, 1983 (Public Law 98-214). Section 223 subsections (a) (1) (A) and (b) (1) (A) (B) stipulate that "Whoever—by means of telephone—makes any comment, request, suggestion or proposal which is obscene, lewd, lascivious, filthy, or indecent; . . .Whoever knowingly makes (directly or by recording device) any obscene or indecent communication for commercial purposes to any person under eighteen years of age. . . shall be fined not more than $50,000 or imprisoned not more than six months, or both."
87. "Enforcement of Prohibitions Against the Use of Common Carriers for the Transmission of Obscene Materials," 49 Fed. Reg. 24,996, 25,000–5,002 (1984).
88. Carlin Communication, 749 F.2d 113, 117 (2d Cir. 1984).
89. *Id.* at 120.
90. *Id.*
91. *Id.* The court cited Bolger v. Youngs Drug Products Corp., 463 U.S. 60, 103 S. Ct. 2875 (1983), in which the Supreme Court reiterated the "narrowness" of *Pacifica* and indicated that "special interest of the federal government in [broadcast] regulation does not readily translate into a justification for regulation of other means of communication," at 103 S. Ct. 2884.
92. *Id.* at 121.
93. *Id.* at 122.

An Assessment of Pacifica's Impact

It is interesting to note that the FCC did take the suggestion and adopted a Personal Identification Number (PIN) as a means to access "Dial-It" service. The Second Circuit Court struck down the rules again because a PIN access code would not work in New York due to technical reasons. However, the FCC plan is allowable in other states. The FCC now has either to reformulate the existing rules to a national workable plan or to impose another set of rules only suitable for New York in dealing with obscene and indecent phone calls.[94]

IV. CONCLUSION

From the foregoing discussion, several observations can be drawn regarding *Pacifica* and its future. First, *Pacifica* is limited to narrowly defined incidents in broadcasting and does not apply to other "means of communication." The outcome of future cases will be difficult to predict because *Pacifica* will be interpreted differently by various levels of courts and its applicability will depend on the medium involved.

Second, although the Supreme Court gave the FCC a broader authority to regulate not only obscene but also indecent broadcast, the FCC has not expanded its regulatory jurisdiction in indecency-related issues. On the contrary, it seems to have backed away from the precedent and been reluctant to apply *Pacifica* vigorously. But this does not mean that the FCC has discarded that regulatory power. With the existence of *Pacifica,* the FCC has the freedom or the obligation to apply it when it deems necessary. As Krasnow and Longley indicate: "The continual threat of judicial review thus tends to have an impact on the policies of the FCC even when these policies are not formally adjudicated."[95]

Third, the review of subsequent cases has shown that the great fear of censorship and the concern about first amendment protection when *Pacifica* was first handed down were unwarranted. Nevertheless, one could argue that *Pacifica* could have created a hidden chilling effect resulting in the avoidance of broadcasting indecent material over the air. Thus, the examination of subsequent cases cannot evaluate the true effect of *Pacifica.*

Additionally, several problems could rise in the future. Although the Supreme Court has reiterated the narrowness of *Pacifica* and stressed that government's "special interest" in a specific medium cannot be used to justify regulation for other types of communication,[96] other new media, such as Direct Broadcast Satellite (DBS) and Multichannel Multipoint

---

94. *NY Court Kills FCC Strictures on Dial-A-Porn,* COMMUNICATIONS WEEK 1, 37 (April 21, 1986).
95. KRASNOW & LONGLEY, THE POLITICS OF BROADCAST REGULATION 52 (2d ed. 1978).
96. Bolger v. Youngs Drug Products Corp., 103 S. Ct. 2875, 2884 (1983).

JAMES C. HSIUNG

Distribution Service (MMDS) which have characteristics similar to broadcasting, could become the judicial testing ground for *Pacifica*.[97] Arguments for cable may not be suitable for MMDS and DBS in fencing themselves off from regulation based on *Pacifica*. Moreover, even though the U.S. Attorney General's Commission on Pornography recently voted not to recommend that the FCC enforce rules against "indecent" programming on cable,[98] the draft documents of the Commission on Pornography originally proposed that the FCC "use its full regulatory powers and impose appropriate sanctions against cable television programmers which transmit obscene and indecent programs."[99] Therefore, although *Pacifica* is seemingly inactive, it is far from dead. A trend has emerged from attempts to keep obscene and indecent materials out of subscription-type services such as cable. The trend may well build pressure on the FCC for stepped-up programming restrictions, which inevitably will result in *Pacifica*-type judicial testing.

97. Both DBS and MMDS use radio spectrum and broadcast over the air.
98. *Cable Spared in Porn Panel Vote,* BROADCASTING 40 (May 5, 1986).
99. *Draft Obscenity Report Urges FCC to Act on Pornography,* BROADCASTING 88 (April 21, 1986).

JON DILTS

Open Meetings in Higher Education

Jon Dilts is an associate dean and assistant professor in the Indiana University School of Journalism, a member of the Indiana Bar, and director of the Higher Education Reporting Project, a program of research and training for education reporters in Indiana.

After a dramatic legislative effort in the 1960s and 1970s to open the formal processes of government to public observation, every state now has either revised or devised statutes to require open meetings.[1] During the past decade, those statutes have produced a sizable amount of litigation that continues to produce a sizable amount of controversy, particularly as they apply to higher education.[2]

While several important studies have examined and monitored open meeting legislation,[3] there has been less analysis of court interpretation. This is partly because it is difficult and dangerous to try to generalize about cases that do not share a common statutory text. Yet, insofar as there are similarities, it is useful to compare and discuss decisions of various jurisdictions. This study examines state appellate court decisions as they apply to higher education open meeting cases. It focuses on the almost universal notion in the state statutes that the target of the openness requirement is the "governing body," and considers the implications of that for news reporters.

---

1. ALA. CODE tit. 14, sec. 13-5-1 (1975); ALASKA STAT. sec. 44.62.310-.312 (Supp. 1975); ARIZ. REV. STAT. ANN. sec. 38-431 to -431.08 (Supp. 1979); ARK. STAT. ANN. sec. 12-2801 to -2807 (1979 Replacement Vol.); CAL. GOV'T. CODE sec. 11120-31 (Supp. 1979) and sec. 54950-61 (Supp. 1979); COLO. REV. STAT. ANN. sec 29-9-101 (Supp. 1978); CONN. GEN. STAT. REV. Sec. 1-21 to -21A (Supp. 1979); DEL. CODE ANN. tit. 29, sec. 10001 to 10005 (Supp. 1977); FLA. STAT. ANN. sec. 286,011 (Supp. 1981); GA. CODE ANN. sec 40-3301 to -3303 (Supp. 1979); HAWAII REV. STAT. sec. 92-1 to -13 (1976 Replacement Vol.); IDAHO CODE sec 67-2340 to -2347 (Supp. 1979); ILL. ANN. STAT. ch. 102, sec 41-46 (Smith-Hurd Supp. 1979); IND. CODE sec. 5-14-1.5-

JON DILTS

I. OPEN SCHOOLS

When state legislatures began to insist on open meetings, the public schools most immediately affected were local elementary and secondary public institutions.[4] That was partly because local schools constituted a big chunk of what the press covered and, at least from the press' point of view, were among the greatest offenders.[5] Of less immediate interest to the news media were public col-

---

1 to -7 (Supp. 1979); IOWA CODE ANN. sec. 28A.1 to 28A.8 (Supp. 1979); KAN. STA. ANN. sec. 75-4317 to -4320 (1977 and Supp. 1978); KY. REV. STAT. ANN. 61:805-.991 (1975); LA. REV. STAT. Sec 42.5 to .8 (Supp. 1979); ME. REV. STAT. ANN. tit. 1 sec. 402 – 06 (1964), *as amended,* (Supp. 1979) MD. ANN. CODE, art. 41, sec. 14 (1978 Replacement Vol.); MASS. ANN. LAWS ch. 30A, sec. 11A (1979); MICH. COMP. LAWS ANN. sec. 15.261-273 (Supp. 1979); MINN. STAT. ANN. sec. 471.705 (1977); MISS. CODE sec. 25-41-1 to -15 (Supp. 1978); MO. ANN. STAT. sec. 610.010-.030 (1979); MONT. REV. CODE ANN. sec. 82-3401 to -3406 (Supp. 1977); NEB. REV. STAT. sec. 84-1408 to -1414 (1976 Reissue Vol.); NEV. REV. STAT. sec. 241.010 to .040 (1973); N.H. STAT. ANN. sec. 91A:1 to A:8 (Supp. 1977); N.J. STAT. ANN. sec. 10:4-7 to -21 (1976); N.M. STAT. ANN. sec. 10-15-1 to -4 (Supp. 1979); N.Y. PUBLIC OFFICERS LAW sec. 95 to 106 (Supp. 1979); N.C. GEN. STAT. sec. 143-318.1 (1978 Replacement Vol.); N.D. CENT. CODE sec 44-04-19 (1960); OHIO REV. STAT. sec. 121.22 (1978); OKLA. STAT. ANN. tit. 25, sec. 301-14 (Supp. 1979); OR. REV. STAT. 192.610 to -.690 (1981); PA. STAT. ANN. tit. 65 sec. 261-269 (1981); GEN. LAWS R.I. sec. 42-46-1 to -10 (1977 Reenactment Vol), *as amended* (Supp. 1978); S.C. CODE ANN. sec. 30-3-10 to -50 (1981); S.D. COMP. LAWS ANN. sec. 1-25-1 to -5 (1974); TENN. CODE ANN. sec. 8-44-101 to -107 (1981); TEX. REV. CIV. STAT. art. 6252-17 (Supp. 1978); UTAH CODE ANN. sec. 2.1-340 to -346.1 (1979 Replacement Vol.); WASH. REV. CODE sec. 42.30.010-.920 (1974) *as amended* (Supp. 1979); W. VA. CODE sec. 6-9A-1 to -7 (1979 Replacement Vol.); WIS. STAT. ANN. sec. 19.81 to .98 (Suppl. 1979); WYO. STAT. ANN. sec. 9-11-101 to -107 (1977).
2. Gellhorn and Boyer, *Government and Education: The University as a Regulated Industry,* 1977 Ariz. St. L. J. 569.
3. Sharon Hartin Iorio, *How State Open Meeting Laws Now Compare with Those of 1974,* JOURNALISM QUARTERLY 741 – 749 (1985); Pat Keefe, *State Open Meetings Activity,* FREEDOM OF INFORMATION CENTER REPORT NO. 378. Columbia: University of Missouri, 1977; JOHN B. ADAMS, STATE OPEN MEETING LAWS: AN OVERVIEW, Columbia, MO: Freedom of Information Foundation, 1974.
4. Private schools are not subject to government-imposed requirements that meetings or records be open to the public. *But see* Simon, *The Application of State Sunshine Laws to Institutions of Higher Education,* 4 J.C. & U.L. 82 (1977); Hendrickson, "State Action" and Private Higher Education, 2 J.L. & EDUC. 52 (1973).
5. In Indiana, for example, impetus for the legislation came largely as a result of efforts by Jack Howey and John Mitchell of Nixon Newspapers Inc. Howey, then editor of the *Peru Tribune,* and Mitchell, then publisher of the *Frankfort Times* and a former Indiana legislator, expressed frustration about their newspapers' inability to cover closed school board meetings. Local education still is perceived as a major offender, as reflected in the results of a survey conducted by the Higher Education Reporting Project at Indiana University in 1986. More than half (53.1 percent) of the daily newspaper reporters covering education who responded said they have had occasion while working on a story to believe Indiana's open-meeting law was violated by school officials.

leges. Press interest in higher education was for many years so deflected by sports and the dullness of the college bureaucracy that only a dozen papers developed any reputation at all for covering colleges.[6] Even today, only a handful of newspapers have a reporter covering higher education full time.[7]

Some of this disinterest may have contributed to an attitude in academia that the rules of openness did not apply with force on a college campus. At any rate, higher education largely escaped the inconvenience of openness. Even scientific research conducted on the university campus and supported by federal money managed to avoid much of the inconvenience of federal legislation requiring freedom of information.[8]

However, those halcyon days are disappearing. College and university administrators, concerned that open-meeting requirements cause widespread damage to decision making, have been inconvenienced enough that they now are seriously discussing the possibility of a concerted effort to push for legislative protection.[9]

That there has long been an argument for secrecy in government is beyond dispute.[10] Aside from democratic rhetoric, secrecy has a firm tradition in the United States.[11] The English common law practice of private governmental

---

6. Roger Yarrington, in a 1984 study of higher education writers, identified reporters from the following papers as writers with a national reputation for covering higher education: the *Portland Oregonian,* the *New York Times, The Christian Science Monitor, The Boston Globe, The Lincoln* (Neb.) *Journal,* the *St. Petersburg Times, The Milwaukee Journal,* the *Los Angeles Times,* the *Chicago Tribune,* the *Baltimore Sun,* and the *San Francisco Chronicle.* Roger Yarrington, *Meet the Education Press,* CASE CURRENTS 36 – 40 (February 1984).
7. Les Tanzer, *Details at 11: How the Media View Higher Education,* CASE CURRENTS 34 – 36 (September 1980).
8. David Pritchard, Freedom of Science Information under Federal Law. Paper presented to the Mass Communications and Society Division and the Science Writers Educators Group, Association for Education in Journalism annual convention, Athens, Ohio, July 1982.
9. *"Sunshine" Laws Harming Public Colleges' Decision Making, Report Says,* THE CHRONICLE OF HIGHER EDUCATION, Oct. 3, 1984, 11; *Trustees' Group Weighs Plan to Press for Closed Meetings,* THE CHRONICLE OF HIGHER EDUCATION, Oct. 10, 1984, 18. Some of the perceived inconveniences of mandated openness is summarized in a research report prepared for the Association of Governing Boards of Universities and Colleges. They include (1) the discouragement of applications from highly qualified people for the presidencies of public colleges and universities; (2) the loss of candor in the evaluation of faculty members and administrators; (3) the chilling of free speech by those intimidated by the public spotlight; and (4) an overall decline in the quality of decision making by governing boards. *See also Sunshine Laws Said to Hinder Search Process,* THE CHRONICLE OF HIGHER EDUCATION, Dec. 11, 1985, 1.
10. S. BOK, SECRETS (1982).
11. For a general discussion of the history of public access to governmental meetings, see H. CROSS, THE PEOPLE'S RIGHT TO KNOW (1956); F. THAYER, LEGAL CONTROL OF THE PRESS (4th ed. 1962); A. WIGGINS, FREEDOM AND SECRECY (1956); Note, *Open Meeting Statutes, The Press Fights for the "Right to Know,"* 79 HARV. L. REV. 1199 (1962).

meetings continued in the United States well after the American Revolution. The Constitutional Convention of 1787 conducted its sessions in secrecy, and debate during the early years of the Senate were in closed session.[12]

On the other hand, advocates of open meetings have often hotly argued that the public's right to attend meetings is implicit in the first two articles of the Constitution as well as the first amendment.[13] American courts, while hesitant to interpret the Constitution so broadly, have nevertheless recognized some validity in the constitutional appeal. In cases involving protection for confidential news sources,[14] access to court proceedings,[15] and the polling of voters exiting voting sites,[16] courts have repeatedly found some constitutional support for news gathering.[17]

Nevertheless, the Supreme Court has not found a constitutional mandate for access to legislative or administrative information,[18] and in the absence of such a mandate, both Congress and the states have adopted statutes in support of the principle of open government. Since 1953, with the pioneering passage of Indiana's Hughes Anti-Secrecy Act and California's Brown Act, open meeting requirements have become a part of the legal literature of every state government.[19]

---

12. M. FARRAND, THE RECORDS OF THE FEDERAL CONVENTION OF 1787 xi, 15 (rev. ed. 1937).
13. Comment, *Open Meeting Laws: An Analysis and Proposal*, 45 MISS. L. J. 1151, 1159 (1974); Comment, *Ambiguities in Oregon's Open Meeting Legislation*, 53 ORE. L. REV. 339, 341 (1974). For arguments supporting a constitutional right of access, see Parks, *The Open Government Principle: Applying the Right to Know under the Constitution*, 26 GEO. WASH. L. REV. 1 (1957); Note, *Access to Official Information: A Neglected Constitutional Right*, 27 IND. L. J. 209 (1952).
14. Branzburg v. Hayes, 408 U.S. 665 (1972).
15. Richmond Newspapers, Inc. v. Virginia, 448 U.S. 555 (1980); Globe Newspaper v. Superior Court, 457 U.S. 596 (1982); Press-Enterprise v. Superior Court, 464 U.S. 501 (1984).
16. Daily Herald Co. v. Munro, 758 F. 2d 350 (9th Cir. 1984); Clean-up '84 v. Heinrich, 759 F. 2d 1511 (11th Cir. 1985).
17. Wiggins offers a number of reasons why public access is important: (1) taxpayers have an absolute interest in legislative deliberations; (2) citizens have not yielded sovereignty and must be informed of their representatives' actions; (3) open proceedings draw upon the intelligence of the whole community; (4) open proceedings encourage public participation in government; (5) open proceedings protect against fraud and mistake; (6) open proceedings protect honest officials from unfounded rumors; (7) open proceedings increase the accuracy of fact-finding. J. WIGGINS, FREEDOM OR SECRECY (1964).
18. Pell v. Pecunier, 417 U.S. 817 (1974); Saxbe v. Washington Post Co., 417 U.S. 843 (1974); Houchins v. KQED, Inc. 438 U.S. 1 (1978).
19. Dilts, *The "Open Door" Laws: An Appraisal of Open Meeting Legislation in Indiana*, 14 VAL. U. L. REV. 296 (1980); for a general discussion of federal efforts to open government meetings and information, see Hunter, *Statutory and Judicial Responses to the Problem of Access to Government Information*, 79 DET. COLL. L. REV. 51 (1979).

That statutory literature of openness is a literature of experience and compromise rather than one of democratic logic. While logic might conclude that the most vigorous debate, the most sensible decisions, and the greatest consensus are necessarily achieved in a public forum, experience suggests that this is not always so. Public officials, like everyone else, can be intimidated, reticent, or embarrassed in a public forum. It is no surprise that the candor and robust debate that thrives in gossipy private discussion sometimes withers in public.

Statutory compromises are also a function of common sense. Conducting some public business in public could be a disservice to the public. For example, strategy sessions concerning active litigation or collective bargaining in the presence of the opposition would be self-defeating. Planning of security measures in the presence of those determined to steal or kill could be disastrous.[20]

So, when school officials complain that open meeting laws can sometimes interfere with government, they speak from a reality familiar to legislatures and courts. There are costs to openness that the statutes attempt to ameliorate with exceptions and definitions.

How, then, have the courts reacted to those complaints? If there is a message in the judicial response, it is this: public higher education carries no special portfolio. In so far as governing bodies within academia exist, those governing bodies are subject to statutorily mandated openness. But there is the rub. It is often difficult to tell who governs academia.

II. THE LYNCHPIN: WHO GOVERNS?

The applicability of open meeting statutes to higher education has been litigated in at least twenty-one states.[21] The results vary, of course, according to what courts perceive as the legislative intent, but a key factor in all of the litigation has been the question: who governs? Because open meeting statutes are aimed at governing bodies of public agencies, the question of whether the target body actually exercises governmental power is sometimes the first and only

---

20. Indeed, these are common exceptions to openness in state statutes. For example, see INDIANA CODE 5-14-1.5-6(a), which allows for executive sessions where strategy or security are involved.
21. Alaska, Arizona, Arkansas, Colorado, Florida, Georgia, Illinois, Indiana, Iowa, Kentucky, Louisiana, Michigan, Mississippi, Missouri, Montana, North Carolina, North Dakota, Oklahoma, Tennessee, Texas, and Washington. During 1986, UCLA avoided litigation by agreeing to permit public access to university committee meetings as a matter of university policy without acknowledging the applicability of California's open meeting act.

question. States such as Indiana,[22] Washington,[23] North Dakota,[24] and Alaska,[25] for example, have been willing to trace governing power well into the ranks of the faculty. Other states, such as Florida,[26] Tennessee,[27] and North Carolina[28] have not.

Courts have been asked to decide whether trustees,[29] faculty,[30] administrators,[31] students,[32] athletic councils[33] and fund-raising foundations[34] are or are not governing bodies. In all of these situations, the courts have proved willing to probe beyond self-assertions of authority or lack of authority, to evidence of the groups' actual power as a governor.

Evidence of governance comes in a number of different forms: (1) as a formal delegation of decision-making authority from an already recognized governing body; (2) as the ability to function as an alter ego for the governing body; or (3) as the de facto ability to make binding decisions of policy. The cases in which governance has been an issue indicate a common judicial approach notwithstanding all of the differences of statutory language. The common approach has two related branches: analyses of remoteness and analyses of autonomy.

III. REMOTENESS FROM POWER

Of critical concern to applicability of open-meeting legislation is the problem of drawing the line of responsibility from the principal governing body of an

---

22. Riggin v. Board of Trustees of Ball State University, 489 N.E. 2d 616 (Ind. App. 1986).
23. Cathcart v. Andersen, 85 Wash. 2d 102, 530 P. 2d 313 (Wash. 1975).
24. Stensrud v. Mayville State College, 368 N.W. 2d 519 (N.D. 1985).
25. University of Alaska v. Geistauts, 666 P. 2d 424 (Alaska 1983).
26. Marston v. Wood, 425 So. 2d 582 (Fla. 1983).
27. Fain v. Faculty of the College of Law of University of Tenn., 552 S.W. 2d (Tenn. App. 1977).
28. Student Bar Association Board of Governors v. Byrd, 293 N.C. 594, 239 S.E.2d 415 (N.C. 1977).
29. Arkansas Gazette Co. v. Pickens, 258 Ark. 69, 522 S.W.2d 350 (Ark. 1975); Phillips v. Board of Supervisors of Louisiana State University, 391 So.2d 1217 (La. App. 1980).
30. Student Bar Association Board of Governors v. Byrd, *supra* note 28.
31. Bennett v. Warden, 333 So.2d 97 (Fla. App. 1976); Tribune Publishing Co. v. Curators of the University of Missouri, 661 S.W.2d 575 (Mo. App. 1983).
32. McLarty v. Board of Regents of the University System of Georgia, 200 S.E.2d 117 (Ga. 1973). The Georgia committee was made up of students and faculty. In Virginia, State Attorney General Gerald Baliles issued an opinion in 1985 that the student government at Old Dominion University was subject to the Virginia open-meeting law because the students used public funds. *Are Student Government Meetings Open?* 6 (1) STUDENT PRESS LAW CENTER REPORT 30 (Winter 1984–85).
33. Green v. Athletic Council of Iowa State University, 251 N.W.2d 559 (Iowa 1977).
34. Courier-Journal & Louisville Times Co. v. University of Louisville Board of Trustees, 596 S.W.2d 374 (Ky. App. 1979).

organization to the subgroup which is the immediate target of statutory application. In Student Bar Association v. Byrd,[35] the Supreme Court of North Carolina ruled that the faculty of the law school, while a component of the school, was not a delegated component of the governing body because the faculty as *employees* possessed no inherent or delegated power. While the faculty had been authorized to make certain determinations about the day-to-day operation of the school, those determinations were wholly subject to modification and reversal by the board of governors. "The fact that such superior power is rarely used by the holder of it does not abrogate it. Thus the faculty of the School of Law is not the 'governing body' of the School of Law. The 'governing body' is the Board of Governors."[36]

The idea that an employee—whether faculty member or administrator[37]—is too remote from the power source to be considered a governor for open-meeting purposes was crucial in two earlier cases: *McLarty v. Board of Regents of the University System of Georgia* and *Bennett v. Warden*.[38]

In *McLarty*, the dean of student affairs organized a student/faculty committee to review student government's recommendations for allocation of student activity funds derived from a mandatory $4 per student fee. The committee advised the dean, who then advised the president, who then advised the chancellor of the university system. Only the chancellor had any authority to approve the use of the funds. The court found no delegation of decision-making power to the advisory committee.[39] Official action, said the court, was action "taken by virtue of power granted by law, or by virtue of the office held, to act for and in behalf of the State."[40] While the committee, the dean, and the president may all have had influence, they did not have the authority to act beyond their roles as executors and advisers.

That also was the case in *Bennett*. In that case, the president of a junior college met periodically with college employees to discuss problems and suggestions related to working conditions, wages, and hours. President Bennett was neither a board nor a commission, said the court, but merely the executive

---

35. Student Bar Association v. Byrd, *supra* note 28.
36. *Id.* at 421.
37. In Cahn v. Antioch University, 482 A.2d 120 (D.C. App. 1984), the court held that law school deans were not only employees but were agents of the university owing a fiduciary duty to the university which paid their salaries. In Institute for Professional Development v. Regis College, 536 F.Supp. 633 at 634 (D. Colo. 1982), the district court in a fraud case noted that faculty members "are deemed employees and agents of the institution."
38. McLarty v. Board of Regents of the University System of Georgia, *supra* note 32; Bennett v. Warden, *supra* note 31.
39. *Accord,* Pope v. Parkinson, 48 Ill.3d 797, 363 N.E.2d 438, 440 (1977). (Assembly Hall Advisory Committee's sole function is to advise.)
40. McClarty v. Board of Regents of University System of Georgia, *supra* note 32, at 119.

officer of a board and so outside the reach of an open-meeting law aimed at governing bodies. Moreover, the court found no evidence that the trustees exercised any control over the employee committee, or that either the president or the committee had any authority to determine policy. At most, they could make recommendations to an administrative council.

However, the court also implied that had the president and administrative officials actually exercised decision-making functions amounting to the making of policy, their meetings would have been included in the scope of the open-meeting statute.[41]

That situation occurred in *Cathcart v. Andersen*.[42] The court found that the faculty was not only the designated governing body by virtue of the statute establishing the law school, but also that the faculty exercised "considerable power over the governing of the school."[43] The faculty, sitting as a decision-making body, unilaterally approved the curriculum, set the scholastic standards, and exercised quasi-legislative authority delegated by the president. As for the ability of a higher governing body to overrule faculty action, the court said the "decisions of the faculty are 'conditional' only in an abstract, hypothetical sense and the board of regents adopts faculty actions almost as a matter of course."[44]

In contrast was *Fain v. Faculty of the College of Law*.[45] The faculty was not given governing power either formally by statute or informally by the exercise of power. Faculty input into decision-making came through committees created and controlled by the dean, an administrative officer, who, like President Bennett, was an individual executive and not independently making policy. Under these facts, the court in *Fain*, as in *Bennett* and *Byrd*, recognized that faculty governance was so limited and remote from power that it was not governance at all.

A remoteness analysis, then, seems to look for two things: (1) whether there is clear delegation of authority from a recognized group empowered to govern, and (2) whether the subordinate committee makes policy. If there is no delegation or there is delegation but no policy-making power, the body is likely to be too remote from governance to be covered by open meeting laws.

---

41. The court noted that meetings of the Administrative Council, comprised of supervisory and executive administrative officials under the president, were open to the public because the council made decisions amounting to the formulation of policy. Bennett v. Warden, *supra* note 31, at 100.
42. Cathcart v. Andersen, *supra* note 23.
43. *Id.* at 316.
44. *Id.*
45. Fain v. Faculty of the College of Law of the University of Tennessee, *supra* note 27.

IV. AUTONOMOUS POWER

Contrasting with the idea of remoteness is the notion of autonomous public power. While a group—such as a tenure committee—may be demonstrably remote from the formal source of power or lack the ability to set policy, it may nevertheless exercise governing power of its own. That can happen in at least three ways. First, an autonomous group may possess governing power because, regardless of form, it is an alter ego of a governing body.[46] Second, some states have specifically included advisory power as a function of governing power, and so subject autonomous units to the same openness standards as policy-making units.[47] And a third category of autonomy is possible—the imposition of openness upon a group whose expertise is so complete that it is deferred to consistently and regularly by a governing body.[48]

The autonomous group operating as alter ego is most clearly demonstrated in cases where members of the governing body regroup as a committee or as a fund-raising foundation to conduct public business.[49] In *Louisville,* for example, the trustees of the University of Louisville created a private, nonprofit corporation, The University of Louisville Foundation. The purpose of the foundation was to receive and hold property, grants, and other funds. Under Kentucky law, such a foundation is not a public agency because it has not been created by statute or executive order. Nevertheless, because the board of directors of the foundation consisted of the entire membership of the board of trustees of the university, and because whenever they met as foundation directors a quorum of trustees was present, the meetings of the private foundation were subject to Kentucky's open meeting law. The power of government resides in the people who make the decisions. "Their membership in another corporation does not remove them from public scrutiny...," said the court.[50]

Like the trustees in *Louisville,* the trustees in *Arkansas* regrouped into closed committees to conduct business. One such group, The Student Affairs Committee, met in closed session to discuss a proposed change that would permit students of legal age to possess and consume intoxicating beverages in university facilities. As in *Louisville,* the group was comprised of a majority of the trustees. The court said that such a group was subject to the Arkansas open

---

46. *See* Courier-Journal & Louisville Times Co. v. University of Louisville Board of Trustees, *supra* note 34.
47. *See* Riggin v. Board of Trustees of Ball State University, *supra* note 22; University of Alaska v. Geistauts, *supra* note 25.
48. Carl v. Board of Regents of the University of Oklahoma, 577 P.2d 912 (Okla. 1978); Green v. Athletic Council of Iowa State University, *supra* note 33.
49. Courier-Journal & Louisville Times Co. v. University of Louisville Board of Trustees, *supra* note 34; Arkansas Gazette Company v. Pickens, 533 S.W.2d 350 (Ark. 1975).
50. Courier-Journal & Louisville Times Co. v. University of Louisville Board of Trustees, *supra* note 34, at 376.

meeting law. Moreover, said the court, that decision was not predicated on the number of trustees present. The imperative of the legislation was that public business must be performed in a public manner. "Where is the basic difference in the nature of the business conducted by the board and the committee? Both are dealing with public business—both are dealing with problems that confront the institution which they represent."[51]

The Arkansas court found the intent of the legislature was to "cover the field," to reach any center of government power where public business was being conducted.[52] Not only was the committee operating as an alter ego of the trustees, but it was operating under a statute intended to reach any autonomous group dealing with the public's business. That same approach is reflected in a recent Indiana case.

The Court of Appeals of Indiana found that under Indiana law, an ad hoc disciplinary committee was required to follow open meeting requirements because, as in Arkansas, the statute captured autonomous groups, even if the group was remote from policy making.[53] "It is our view," said the court, "that the Act is massive and all inclusive by itself, and needs no expansion by us."[54]

In one sense, statutory all-inclusiveness works to make a remoteness analysis irrelevant. The external source of power becomes unimportant. What becomes important is the inherent power of the group to become a part of the decision-making process. The notion of autonomous power as an approach to determining governance does something fundamentally different from a remoteness analysis. It reaches beyond the seminal notion that openness is a requirement applicable to policy-making bodies to a further notion that openness is a requirement also applicable to any group brought under government's tent, regardless of its delegation.[55] The spirit of openness from this point of view is to provide citizens with first-hand knowledge about the reasons for decisions. As Justice Harris asked in *Arkansas Gazette Company v. Pickens*, "Is not the public entitled to know *why* a board adopts certain rules or regulations? The 'why' is the essence of the action taken."[56]

---

51. Arkansas Gazette Company v. Pickens, *supra* note 49, at 353.
52. *But see* Phillips v. Board of Supervisors of Louisiana State University, *supra* note 29. Committee meetings of the Board of Supervisors were not subject to the Louisiana open meetings law because 1) legislative intent was to not include committees, and 2) committees were advisory only. This was so even when committees were comprised solely of board members.
53. Riggin v. Board of Trustees of Ball State University, *supra* note 22.
54. *Id.* at 623.
55. In Rosenberg v. Arizona Board of Regents, 118 Ariz. 489, 578 P.2d 168 (Ariz. 1978), the court quoted A.R.S. sec. 38-43 and noted there was little doubt that a tuition appeal committee was a body within the meaning of that section: "'Governing Bodies' mean the governing bodies of the state... and all agencies, boards and commissions of the foregoing, or any committee or subcommittee thereof, which are supported in whole or in part by tax revenues or which expend tax revenues."
56. Arkansas Gazette Company v. Pickens, *supra* note 29, at 353.

Autonomous power may derive not only from the function of an alter ego or the reach of a statutory definition, but also by the delegation of decision making to an expert group. For example, in *Carl v. Board of Regents of the University of Oklahoma*, the court held that an admissions board which selected medical students for the College of Medicine exercised decision-making authority for the Board of Regents.[57] The court quoted from *Sanders v. Benton, Director of the State Board of Corrections*, 579 P.2d 815 (Okla. 1978): "If the subordinate entity in the performance of its assigned duties and responsibilities exercises actual or de facto decision-making authority, it must comply with the open meeting law."[58]

Likewise, in *Green v. Athletic Council of Iowa State University*, the court held that an athletic council organized by the regents to run intercollegiate athletics at the state university was subject to the open meeting law. The council decided, among other things, the contracts for contests, the selection of coaches, and the awarding of letters and scholarships for athletes. "Obviously," said the court, "the athletic council exercises governmental power. It is a powerful decision-making and policy-making body which acts for the public .... It is not a mere study or advisory group."[59]

In general, if a group exercises real power, the courts have found ways to include them under open meeting legislation. The most common theories have been that the group operates as an alter ego of a governing body, that the group is statutorily included, or that the group exercises de facto power derived from a governing body. There is some overlap in these theories, but they are nevertheless distinct from a remoteness analysis, which is concerned primarily with the formal structure of the chain of command.

V. IMPLICATIONS FOR REPORTERS

The implications of open-meeting litigation in the higher education context are several. The most important is that the question of governance is fact driven. The courts are interested in who governs, who delegates authority, and who makes decisions and takes actions.

The second implication of the cases is that the courts will examine the inclusiveness of the statutory language in an attempt to determine to what extent autonomous academic bodies are included. Where statutes specifically include nondecision-making groups, such as advisory or fact-finding committees, the courts will not bother to finesse the issue by entertaining a remoteness analysis.

---

57. Carl v. Board of Regents of the University of Oklahoma, *supra* note 48.
58. *Id.*
59. Green v. Athletic Council of Iowa State University, *supra* note 33, at 561.

And finally, the courts will not weigh competing concerns about governmental efficiency. Costs to governmental efficiency, in the courts' view, already have been weighed during the legislative process or will be weighed again later in a subsequent legislative session.

For reporters, that means it is important to know and understand the formal and informal governing structure of a particular college as well as the language of a particular statute. Gaining access to a meeting is as much a reportorial as a legal question. Because the courts pay attention, at least within the confines permitted by a particular open meetings statute, to the reality of governance, reporters can greatly improve their chances of access if they can articulate how a particular body exercises governing power. Certainly relevant are questions about lines of delegation: Was the target committee created by a governing body or a single administrator? To what extent does a governing body maintain the right to modify or reverse decisions by the target committee? Also relevant are questions of authority: Is the target committee's mission limited to factfinding and advice? And even if limited in that way, does the committee nevertheless make policy because of deference paid it by the governing body? And finally, how do those facts interlace with the language of a particular statute? The more a reporter knows about the functions and operations of a group, the better the reporter will be able to determine the chances of requiring compliance with open meeting laws.

The attachment of open meeting laws to higher education varies from state to state, partly because of statutory language and partly because of perceptions by the courts about who actually governs. Reporters would do well to investigate carefully how governance works informally as well as formally if they hope to edge courts and themselves toward a better understanding of what open government means and why it is worth seeking. Certainly the courts have not attempted to exclude colleges and universities from openness requirements, but they have paid critical attention to distinctions about who governs.

F. DENNIS HALE

Freedom of Expression: The Warren and Burger Courts

F. Dennis Hale is a professor in the School of Mass Communication at Bowling Green State University.

It was inevitable that comparisons would be made between the two Supreme Courts headed by Chief Justices Earl Warren and Warren Burger. Under the leadership of Earl Warren, the Court established an unprecedented record of activism and liberalism. This record included landmark decisions in such speech areas as libel, obscenity, fair trial, pamphleting, and picketing. Then Richard Nixon appointed Burger as chief justice and three other conservatives as associate justices—all within two and one-half years—with the avowed purpose of reversing the Court's judicial activism and political liberalism.

In the specific area of free speech, comparisons of the two courts resulted very early in press criticism of the Burger Court. In 1971, during Burger's second year in office, the Court strengthened freedom of press when it ruled that the president could not restrain the *New York Times* from publishing the classified Pentagon Papers. Three judges dissented from the decision, including Burger, who objected to the haste of the Court in deciding the case. While newspaper editorialists enthusiastically embraced the majority decision on the Pentagon Papers, various newspapers criticized the participation of the chief justice. The *Louisville Times* sarcastically observed that Burger's dissent "could have come straight from the typewriter of a Spiro Agnew ghostwriter."[1]

---

* Some of the data in the Burger portion of this article was coded by four students in the author's graduate class, Media Law Dynamics: Paul Kostyu, Terry Lueck, Jim Knepp, and Oliver Wang. The author acknowledges their assistance. This article is similar to a paper, "A Comparison of the Warren and Burger Courts on Freedom of Expression," delivered at a joint session of the Law Division and History Division of the Association for Education in Journalism and Mass Communication at San Antonio, Texas, in August 1987.
1. 2 *Editorials on File* 808 (1971).

F. DENNIS HALE

Seven months later, press criticism of Burger escalated after the Court ruled in *Branzburg v. Hayes* that the constitution does not protect journalists from being required to testify about confidential sources. This time Burger voted with an antipress majority. The *Oakland Tribune* called the decision a "serious blow at freedom of the press," and the *Dallas Times Herald* said the Court had "dimmed the light of knowledge for all of the people."[2]

The most shrill criticism of Burger Court policies on press freedom concerned three decisions in 1978 and 1979 that came in the middle of the chief justice's seventeen-year term. First, in *Zurcher v. Stanford,* the Court refused to expand the first amendment to protect newsrooms against warranted searches by police. The *Washington Post* called *Zurcher* a "staggering blow to freedom of the press," the *Miami Herald* accused the Court of "an appalling display of muddleheadedness," and the *Indianapolis Star* described *Zurcher* as "an opening wedge for a police state."[3]

The second controversial case of 1978-9, *Herbert v. Lando,* brought even harsher criticism from the nation's editorialists. And some critics mentioned a trend of antipress sentiment on the nation's highest court. The *Indianapolis Star* referred to "an ugly procession of anti-press-freedom decisions," and the *Miami Herald* said that "Under Chief Justice Burger, the U.S. Supreme Court has been systematically dismantling the First Amendment protections."[4]

The third decision of 1978-9 to attract harsh criticism was *Gannett v. DePasquale,* which allowed criminal courts to bar the press and public from pretrial hearings. The *Oregon Journal* observed, "Human liberties are not in good hands with the the Burger Court." And the *Evening Gazette* in Worchester, Massachusetts, concluded that "another piece of constitutional cloth was ripped from the public's back."[5]

During its last seven years the Burger Court ruled in favor of the press more frequently, and by the time the chief justice announced his retirement in the summer of 1986, press assessment was more balanced and less strident. The *Pittsburg Press* said that under the Burger Court, "free press guarantees of the First Amendment were reenforced." The *Rocky Mountain News* in Denver made similar observations. And the *Baltimore Sun* said that despite his feuds with broadcasters, the "retiring chief justice's First Amendment record is a good one."[6]

Now that Warren Burger has retired and another modern Court era has ended, it is appropriate to assess the Burger and Warren Courts' records on freedom of expression. When both of the Courts' speech decisions and all

---

2. *Id.*, Volume 3 (1972), at 887–88.
3. *Id.*, Volume 9 (1978), at 691, 696, and 699.
4. *Id.*, Volume 10 (1979), at 437 and 444.
5. *Id.* at 739 and 743.
6. *Id.*, Volume 17 (1986), at 686–689.

of the justices' votes are analyzed, what kind of record emerges? What did individual justices contribute, how did the Courts divide, and how did justices align themselves with one another? Those are the concerns of this study, which compares the voting of the Burger and Warren Courts on freedom of speech and press cases.

I. COURT PERSONNEL

The appointment of a new chief justice does not automatically change the complexion of a Supreme Court and herald a new era. Thus it is not always accurate to use the name of the chief justice to characterize a particular Supreme Court. However, with the Court from 1953 to 1969 under Earl Warren, and the Court from 1969 to 1986 under Warren Burger, such a characterization was appropriate.

The contrasting chief justices were symbolic of significant change within the Supreme Court. Seventeen justices served on the Warren Court, of which 70 percent were appointed by Democrats. And none of the Warren Court members was appointed by a Republican who was an ideological conservative. By comparison, of the thirteen justices on the Burger Court, 70 percent were appointed by Republicans. One Burger Court justice was appointed by a conservative ideologue, Ronald Reagan, and four justices were appointed by Nixon, who was not an ideologue but who was committed to appointing strict constructionists or judges who would interpret and not make the law.

Galloway described how the change in Court membership radically modified the composition of the Supreme Court between Warren and Burger. During the last two years of the Warren Court, 1967-9, he concluded that "the Court had attained another unprecedented historic plateau with six liberals, two moderates, and one conservative."[7] Galloway called what happened between the summer of 1969 and the fall of 1972 "one of the most dramatic short-term changes of judicial personnel in the entire history of the United States Supreme Court."[8] Within thirty months, the Court changed from a configuration of six liberals, two moderates, and one conservative to a configuration of three liberals, two moderates, and four conservatives: "By January 7, 1972, it was difficult for the liberals to win any controversial case before this bench."[9]

Most of this change occurred because of the fortuitous series of events that allowed Nixon to make four appointments to the Supreme Court. First, Nixon named a new chief justice to replace the most liberal chief justice in

---

7. R. GALLOWAY, THE RICH AND THE POOR IN SUPREME COURT HISTORY 1790–1982 160 (1982).
8. *Id.* at 168.
9. *Id.* at 169.

the history of the Court. Next, Nixon was allowed to replace liberals Hugo Black and Abe Fortas, and moderate John Harlan, with three conservatives: Harry Blackmun, Lewis Powell, and William Rehnquist.

Following are the ten members of the Warren Court who left the Court prior to the retirement of Warren. (The ten appear in the order in which they were appointed to the Court.)[10]

- Stanley Reed, a Kentucky native and a Justice Department attorney, was appointed by Franklin Roosevelt. He served only four years on the Warren Court.
- Felix Frankfurter, a Harvard law professor, also was appointed by Roosevelt. He and Warren served together for nine years.
- Robert Jackson, a U.S. attorney general, remained on the Court only one year while Warren was chief justice. He was a Roosevelt appointee.
- Harold Burton, a Cleveland mayor and U.S. senator, served during the first five years of the Warren Court. He was appointed by Harry Truman.
- Tom Clarke, a U.S. attorney general and U.S. Court of Appeals Judge, served thirteen years with Warren. He was appointed by Truman.
- Sherman Minton, a U.S. senator and U.S. Court of Appeals judge, served only three years with Warren. He also was nominated by Truman.
- Earl Warren, a Republican and a state attorney general and governor from California, was appointed chief justice by a Republican president, Dwight D. Eisenhower.
- Charles Whittaker, a federal trial court judge from Kansas and a member of the U.S. Court of Appeals, served nine years on the Warren Court. He was appointed by Eisenhower.
- Arthur Goldberg, a U.S. secratary of labor, only served three years on the Warren Court after his appointment by John F. Kennedy.
- Abe Fortas, a federal attorney during Roosevelt's New Deal, served four years on the Warren Court after an appointment by Lyndon Johnson.

The following seven justices served on the Supreme Court under both chief justices, Warren and Burger:

- Hugo Black, appointed by Franklin Roosevelt, served during the entire sixteen years of the Warren Court and the first two years of the Burger Court.
- William Douglas, also a Roosevelt appointee, served during the entire Warren Court and six years of the Burger Court.
- John Harlan, an Eisenhower appointment, served fourteen years on the Warren Court and just two on the Burger Court.

---

10. THE SUPREME COURT: JUSTICE AND THE LAW 166–69 (3d ed. 1983).

- William Brennan was an appellate court judge in New Jersey and a registered but inactive Democrat when he was appointed by Republican Eisenhower. He served thirteen years on the Warren Court and all seventeen of the Burger Court.
- Potter Stewart, Eisenhower's fifth and last appointment to the Court, served eleven years on the Warren Court and twelve years on the Burger Court. The Republican from Cincinnati previously served on the U.S. Court of Appeals.
- Bryon White, an appointment of Democrat John F. Kennedy, served seven years on the Warren Court and the duration of the Burger Court.
- Thurgood Marshall, a Lyndon Johnson appointment and the only black ever to serve on the Court, also served the entire duration of the Burger Court after two years on the Warren Court.

The following are the six justices who served excusively on the Burger Court:

- Warren Burger, Nixon's chief justice from St. Paul, Minnesota previously served thirteen years on the U.S. Court of Appeals.
- Harry Blackmun, a Nixon appointee from Minneapolis, served during all except the first year of the Burger Court.
- Lewis Powell—a Southern Democrat, American Bar Association president, and Nixon appointee—served the last fourteen years of the Burger Court.
- William Rehnquist, the last of the four Nixon appointments, also served fourteen years on the Court. He worked in Arizona politics and for the Nixon Justice Department.
- John Paul Stevens, the sole appointee of Gerald Ford, served the last eleven years of the Burger Court. He previously served on the U.S. Court of Appeals.
- Sandra Day O'Connor, Reagan's first appointment and the first woman on the Court, served during the last five years of the Burger Court.

II. METHODOLOGY

Various social scientists have analyzed the U.S. Supreme Court by comparing how individual justices vote on related cases. An underlying premise is that the philosophical, political, and jurisprudential background of justices influences their voting so that they may arrive at contrasting conclusions about a case based on the same set of facts.

Spaeth, a political scientists and a pioneer in this methodology, pointed out that conservative Supreme Court justices Frankfurter and Whittaker upheld state regulations of labor unions over 90 percent of the time. Liberal justices Douglas and Warren upheld the same state regulations less than 10 percent

F. DENNIS HALE

of the time. Spaeth concluded: "Frankfurter and associates are simply good economic conservatives—probusiness and antilabor. Just as clearly, Black, Douglas and Warren are economic liberals—antibusiness and prolabor."[11] Spaeth constructed cumulative scales representing justices' support for value systems. For example, he combined votes on civil liberties cases from 1958-77 for a "freedom" value and arrived at the following scores for Burger Court members:[12]

Douglas	.73
Black	.53
Marshall	.45
Brennan	.38
Stewart	.09
Stevens	.05
Powell	-.26
Harlan	-.30
Blackmun	-.34
White	-.40
Burger	-.49
Rehnquist	-.58

Two researchers have used comparative voting records specifically to examine the performance of the Supreme Court on freedom of expression cases. Stempel took advantage of the unprecedented stability of the Court during the ten terms, 1971 through 1980, to create a Guttman scale from the voting of eight justices on forty-seven press cases. The study excluded cases in which a justice excused himself, as well as cases concerning speech and not press.[13]

Padgett examined the voting of justices on 166 speech and press cases during the fifty-year period 1931-81. His list of cases was compiled from summaries published by *Editor & Publisher* magazine in 1976 and 1979, and from the directory of a media law textbook.[14] Thus the Padgett study was not based on a comprehensive list of press cases, and it significantly underrepresented speech cases. Padgett examined the extent to which the Court and its members favored press organizations or individual speakers, as well as opinion authorship, dissent, and interjudge agreement.[15]

---

11. H. SPAETH, SUPREME COURT POLICY MAKING 78-79 (1979).
12. *Id.* at 123.
13. Stempel, *A Guttman Scale Analysis of the Burger Court's Press Decisions*, 59 JOURNALISM Q. 256-259 (1982).
14. Padgett, *The Voting Record of Justice Stewart on First Amendment Cases*, 59 JOURNALISM Q. 554-559 (1982).
15. *Id.* at 555.

This study of the Burger and Warren Courts differed from those of Stempel and Padgett in a number of respects. Most obviously, because this study was conducted shortly after Chief Justice Burger retired, it was possible to analyze every year of the Burger Court. Second, this study was comprehensive and included every vote of every justice for all press and speech cases during the thirty-three years of the Burger and Warren courts.

A comprehensive list of cases was obtained by examining the civil liberties, copyright, libel, obscenity, records, and telecommunications entries of the yearly indexes of *Supreme Court Reporter.* The list included speech as well as press cases, and unsigned *per curiam* decisions as well as signed decisions. For the most recent eleven years, case names from *Supreme Court Reporter* were double-checked against the Supreme Court cases reported in *Media Law Reporter.* This resulted in an N of 198 for Burger cases and an N of 63 for Warren cases.

Each case was coded for the year it was filed by the Court, the communications medium (newspaper, magazine, radio, television, book, spoken word, newsletter or memo, film, other), and the major category of expression (prior restraint, libel, privacy, privilege, access to government, fair trial, media access, obscenity, copyright, advertising, broadcasting, speech, other).

Padgett's method was used in deciding whether the Court or justices supported or rejected free expression. If the decision as a whole supported the press organization or person invoking speech rights, it was considered a "pro" decision. If the specific exercise of free expression was restricted by the Court, either in part or entirely, it was considered an "anti" decision.[16] In those few cases in which personal speech rights clashed with press rights, such as private access to the new media, decisions favoring the press were coded as "pro" expression. The freedom-of-speech category included freedom-of-thought cases in which individuals were attempting to shield personal beliefs from government influence or disclosure.

The participation of each of the twenty-three members of the Warren and Burger Courts was coded for every case. Most of the time a judge participated in one of twelve ways. First, there were three types of opinions—majority, concurring, and dissenting. (Majority opinions announce the result for the parties to the case and, more importantly, the underlying rule and rationale. Concurring opinions support the result of the majority, but not the rule of law used to arrive at that result. And dissenting opinions reject the result, rule, and rationale of the majority decision.) For each of the three types of opinions, there were four forms of participation: author supporting expression, author limiting expression, signer supporting expression, and signer limiting expression. There were four other forms of participation, making

---

16. *Id.*

a total of sixteen: author of decision dissenting in part, signer of decision dissenting in part, disqualified and did not participate in case, and not on the Court at the time of the case.

Subsequently, statistical results were obtained for frequencies of variables and for cross-tabulations between pairs of variables. For some of the analysis, the justices' participation was collapsed from sixteen to three responses: support free expression, reject free expression entirely or in part, or nonparticipant in case. Two-by-two agreement tables were computed for pairs of justices to determine how often they agreed to either support or reject freedom of expression. Lastly, comparisons were made between the two Courts.

III. RESULTS AND DISCUSSION

During its seventeen years, the Burger Court decided 198 cases concerning speech and the mass media, or 11.6 per year. The Court wrote a mean of 140 formal decisions a year; thus free expression cases represented 8.3 percent of the Court's output. The Warren Court wrote sixty-three free expression decisions, or 3.9 per year, representing only 3.6 percent of the Court's average of 109 opinions a year (see Table 1). Not until the last five of its sixteen years did the Warren Court write more than five free expression opinions a year.

If the Burger Court slighted free speech, it was not in the quantity of formal decisions that the Court wrote about the subject. In volume of free speech opinions, the Burger Court was active and the Warren Court passive.

Parties invoking free expression rights won 48 percent of the time under Burger and 73 percent under Warren. Under both Courts, mass media litigants—newspapers, radio, television, books, magazines, and film—won somewhat less often than traditional speech litigants, such as picketers and public speakers. These 48 and 73 percent success levels compared with 58 percent for Padgett's sample of free expression cases for 1931–81.[17] Thus, in the percentage of cases won by free expression litigants, the Burger Court was less supportive than previous courts, and the Warren Court was significantly more supportive.

There were both differences and similarities in the kinds of cases decided by the two Courts. Both Courts devoted considerable time to obscenity and libel. However, the favorable win-loss record of media litigants in these cases under Warren was reversed under Burger. In addition, the categories of advertising and access to government received major attention from the Burger Court and almost no attention from the Warren Court (see Table 1).

Members of both Courts frequently disagreed with one another in deciding these cases (see Table 2). Some 37 percent of Warren decisions were unanimous, only slightly more than 30 percent for the Burger Court. This amounted to 2.0 dissents per opinion under Burger and 1.7 under Warren.

---

17. *Id.*

These figures are similar to the 1.24 to 2.34 dissents per case for all opinions during the sixteen years of the Warren Court, and the 2.14 and 2.10 dissents per case for all of the 1970 and 1973 decisions of the Burger Court.[18] The Burger and Warren Courts were no more divided in speech cases than either of the Courts were for all types of cases.

TABLE 1. FREE EXPRESSION CASES OF BURGER AND WARREN COURTS

Characteristics	Warren	Burger
Years	16	17
Freedom of expression opinions	63	198
Free expression opinions per year	3.9	11.6
Mean number of opinions per year	108.7	140
Dissents per free expression opinion	1.7	2
Freedom of press cases	39	114
Percent of all free expression cases	62%	58%
Freedom of speech cases	24	84
Percent of all free expression cases	38%	42%
Success of free expression parties	73%	48%
Success of free press parties	64%	43%
Success of free speech parties	88%	52%
Obscenity cases	16	36
Percent of all free expression cases	25%	18%
Success of free expression parties	63%	39%
Libel cases	14	15
Percent of all free expression cases	22%	8%
Success of free expression cases	87%	47%
Access to government	3	42
Percent of all free expression cases	5%	21
Success of free expression parties	67%	29%
Advertising	0	16
Percent of all free expression cases	0	8%
Success of free expression parties	0	75%

18. R. HODDER-WILLIAMS, THE POLITICS OF THE U.S. SUPREME COURT 95, 140 (1980).

TABLE 2. DISSENTING VOTES ON THE BURGER AND WARREN COURTS

Dissents	Number of Cases	Percent	Cumulative Percent
Burger Court			
None	60	30.3	30.3
One	19	9.6	39.9
Two	28	14.1	54.0
Three	51	25.8	79.8
Four	40	20.2	100.0
Warren Court			
None	23	36.5	36.5
One	9	14.3	50.8
Two	8	12.7	63.5
Three	10	15.9	79.4
Four	13	20.6	100.0

The dissent rates of individual justices were noteworthy because they also indicated the converse of dissent, or agreement with the majority rulings of the Courts. The most dissentient justices were the three liberals who frequently were in the minority on the Burger Court—Douglas, Brennan, and Marshall—who dissented 47, 38, and 35 percent of the time while on that Court (see Table 3). The leading dissenters on the Warren Court were two conservatives and a liberal—Harlan, Black, and Clark—who dissented from 25 to 31 percent of the time. Conversely, the two justices who dissented the least and most agreed with the Burger Court majority were Sandra O'Connor and Lewis Powell, who only dissented 10 and 11 percent of the time. Thus, conservatives Powell and O'Connor were most representative of the Burger Court's first amendment policies. Liberals Marshall, Brennan, and Warren, with low dissent rates ranging from 0 to 11 percent, were most representative of the Warren Court's first amendment policies.

When analyzing the performance of individual justices, it should be noted that Black and Harlan were marginal members of the Burger Court and only

TABLE 3. PARTICIPATION OF BURGER AND WARREN COURT MEMBERS*

Justice	Favor Expression	Opinion Author	Majority Author	Dissent Rate	N of Cases
Burger Court					
Black**	73	67	13	20	15
Douglas**	92	58	0	47	66
Harlan**	43	57	7	21	14
Brennan**	75	43	9	38	195
Stewart**	65	31	9	20	145
White**	43	32	14	13	198
Marshall**	74	26	6	35	191
Burger	36	36	18	14	198
Blackmun	46	26	5	14	195
Powell	46	34	15	11	171
Rehnquist	26	37	16	24	178
Stevens	58	42	6	30	125
O'Connor	42	31	13	10	52
Warren Court					
Black**	79	52	8	29	62
Reed	75	25	25	0	4
Frankfurter	50	38	0	19	19
Douglas**	88	45	5	23	60
Jackson	100	50	0	50	2
Burton	57	0	0	0	7
Clark	55	34	2	25	44
Minton	75	0	0	0	4
Warren	71	27	6	11	63
Harlan**	49	46	8	31	61
Brennan**	76	36	19	10	59
Whittaker	54	0	0	15	13
Stewart**	72	26	4	13	53
White**	62	29	4	20	45
Goldberg	88	35	12	18	17
Fortas	60	27	3	23	30
Marshall**	80	27	27	0	15

*Numbers represent percentages for those cases in which the justices participated.

**Justices who served on both courts.

served for two years; Douglas served for six of the seventeen years, and O'Connor served for the last five years. On the Warren Court, four justices—Reed, Jackson, Burton, and Minton—participated in fewer than eight of the Court's sixty-three free expression cases. And four other Warren Court justices—Frankfurter, Whittaker, Goldberg, and Marshall—participated in fewer than twenty opinions.

Six Burger Court justices supported free expression more often than the 48 percent for the Court as a whole (see Table 3). Douglas stood alone on the top with a rating of 92 percent. Next came Brennan, Marshall, and Black with ratings of 73 to 75, Stewart with 65, and Stevens with 58. In the middle of the ranking were Powell, Blackmun, and Harlan in the mid-50s, and O'Connor and White with 42 and 43. The chief justice's rating was 36. Rehnquist occupied the bottom position with a 26. This ordering resembled the results for Spaeth's freedom value constructed from 1958-77 cases: Douglas, Black, Marshall, and Brennan were clustered together at the top, followed by Stewart and Stevens, with Burger and Rehnquist at the bottom.[19] Burger and Rehnquist were not equivalent entities. Rehnquist was significantly less supportive of speech rights, which could pose a problem for the mass media during future years of the Rehnquist Court.

Quite a different pattern emerged on the Warren Court. Seven justices—led by Marshall, Goldberg, and Douglas with records in the 80s—scored in the liberal range in excess of 70 percent. Five justices achieved intermediate rankings: White and Fortas were in the 60s and Frankfurter, Clark, and Whittaker were in the 50s. Harlan's support, at 49, was the lowest for the Warren Court. In contrast, seven members of the Burger Court had lower percentage scores than Harlan's low score for the Warren Court.

Casting a vote for or against a right is one way to influence civil liberties law. Another method is for a judge to take the time to write a separate opinion. Opinion authorship included majority, concurring, and dissenting opinions. Douglas was the leader on the Burger Court, writing opinions for 58 percent of the cases he participated in (see Table 3). Of these, 29 percent were concurring opinions and 71 percent were dissenting opinions. The next most active authors were Brennan with 43 percent and John Paul Stevens with 42 percent. Brennan and Stevens apparently were striving to make an impact on first amendment law.

Douglas also was the third most active writer of free expression opinions on the Warren Court, writing them for 45 percent of the cases. The most conservative judge, Harlan, was second with 46 percent; and Black was first with opinions for 52 percent of the cases. Harlan may not have supported free speech, but he and liberals Black and Douglas wished to make an impact on that field of the law.

---

19. SPAETH, *supra* note 11, at 121.

Results were quite different when the analysis of authorship was narrowed to majority opinions. The influence of the chief justice—who voted with the majority in 86 percent of Burger cases and 89 percent of Warren cases—was evident. When he votes with the majority, the chief justice decides who will write the opinion of the Court. If majority opinions were equally divided, each judge would write 11 percent. Rehnquist, Powell, and Burger each wrote 15 to 18 percent of majority opinions (see Table 3) on the Burger Court. Liberals Brennan and Marshall, along with Blackmun, each wrote only 6 or 9 percent. And Justice Douglas, who served six years on the Burger Court, was locked out and was not assigned any majority opinions. Surprisingly, liberals Douglas, Black, and Warren wrote fewer than expected majority opinions for the Warren Court. The leaders were Brennan, Marshall, and Goldberg.

Authorship of a majority opinion provides visibility that a justice may or may not welcome. Free speech cases receive more thorough news coverage and editorial discussion than other Court cases. Thus a judge who is concerned about a public image might be more willing to author a prospeech than an antispeech opinion. A judge could exaggerate his or her prospeech position by actively authoring prospeech opinions, and by restricting involvement in anitspeech decisions to the mere signing of opinions.

The existence of this strategy was variously tested by examining the justices' participation as authors and signers of majority decisions. Burger exaggerated his proexpression stance by writing 30 percent of the proexpression majority opinions that he participated in; the expected percentage was 18 percent. Next on the Burger Court came Brennan (23), Powell (20), and Rehnquist (19). Burger, however, did not hide his participation in antiexpression opinions and wrote 23 percent of the opinions that he joined. Brennan and Blackmun appeared to be hiding their participation in antipress opinions, writing such majority opinions only 5 and 7 percent of the time when they agreed with them. Just the opposite, Rehnquist seemed to revel in his association with antispeech opinions, writing them 26 percent of the time. And when Rehnquist rejected speech in a dissent, 67 percent of the time it was as an author and not as a signer.

On the Warren Court, the five justices—Brennan, Black, Harlan, Goldberg, and Marshall—all authored majority prospeech opinions more than 25 percent of the time when they agreed with them. However, the judges were equally visible when they participated in antispeech opinions.

Rehnquist illustrates the analysis of agreement between pairs of justices. He and Burger together participated in 178 cases. Burger favored expression 11 percent of the time when Rehnquist rejected it; and Rehnquist favored expression 2 percent of the time when Burger rejected it. The two rejected speech 63 percent of the time, and they both supported speech 25 percent, for a total agreement of 88 percent. Quite a different pattern appeared when conservative Rehnquist was paired with liberal Brennan. The two rejected speech 18 percent and supported speech 20 percent, for 38 percent agreement. (Table 4 gives the agreement values and N for all pairs of justices.)

TABLE 4. AGREEMENT OF BURGER COURT MEMBERS ON EXPRESSION CASES*

	Harlan	Brennan	Stewart	White	Marshall	Burger	Blackmun	Powell	Rehnquist	O'Connor
Black	57	80	80	87	80	80	80	100	100	
	(14)	(15)	(15)	(15)	(15)	(15)	(15)	(01)	(01)	
Douglas	62	85	69	47	83	38	41	41	25	
	(13)	(66)	(65)	(66)	(65)	(66)	(66)	(46)	(48)	
Harlan		71	79	64	71	71	71			
		(14)	(14)	(14)	(14)	(14)	(14)			
Stevens		74	75	63	75	69	70	71	63	60
		(122)	(73)	(125)	(119)	(125)	(122)	(119)	(124)	(52)
O'Connor		58		77	59	83	78	84	85	
		(52)		(52)	(49)	(52)	(51)	(49)	(52)	
Brennan			75	61	91	50	63	61	38	58
			(142)	(195)	(188)	(195)	(192)	(169)	(175)	(52)
Stewart				74	77	68	73	76	58	
				(145)	(141)	(145)	(143)	(121)	(125)	
White					62	81	77	78	77	77
					(191)	(198)	(195)	(171)	(178)	(52)
Marshall						51	64	62	42	59
						(191)	(190)	(165)	(171)	(49)
Burger							83	81	88	83
							(195)	(171)	(178)	(52)
Blackmun								81	73	78
								(168)	(175)	(51)
Powell									75	84
									(169)	(49)
Rehnquist										85
										(52)

*Numbers in parentheses are the N of cases.

Results of the agreement analysis for the Burger Court are similar to the clusterings based on the justices' level of support of free speech (see Table 4). The three justices who supported free expression the most—all more than 73 percent—were Douglas, Brennan, and Marshall. Agreement between the three liberals equalled the agreement between the three conservatives and ranged from 83 to 91 percent.

At the other end of the spectrum were the three conservatives—Burger, Rehnquist, and O'Connor. Agreement within the conservative bloc also was high, ranging from 83 to 88 percent. Only slightly less conservative were three moderate conservatives—White, Powell, and Blackmun—who agreed with each other and with members of the conservative bloc from 73 to 84 percent of the time.

Between the three liberals and the three moderate conservatives were two independents, Stevens and Stewart. Neither exceeded 77 percent agreement with any other justice. And both had associations in the 70s with liberals as well as with moderate conservatives, but stronger associations with the liberals.

TABLE 5. AGREEMENT OF WARREN COURT MEMBERS ON EXPRESSION CASES*

	Douglas	Clark	Warren	Harlan	Brennan	Stewart	White	Fortas
Black	81 (59)	49 (43)	73 (62)	57 (60)	75 (59)	74 (53)	71 (45)	70 (30)
Frankfurter	33 (15)	93 (15)	56 (16)	86 (14)	42 (12)	78 (9)		
Douglas		49 (43)	82 (60)	49 (59)	86 (57)	78 (51)	67 (43)	68 (28)
Clark			66 (44)	86 (43)	59 (41)	62 (37)	74 (27)	69 (13)
Warren				61 (61)	92 (59)	79 (53)	78 (45)	87 (30)
Harlan					58 (59)	68 (53)	69 (45)	67 (30)
Brennan						85 (53)	84 (45)	73 (30)
Whittaker	46 (13)	83 (12)	54 (13)	77 (13)	54 (13)	78 (9)	100 (1)	
Stewart							79 (42)	69 (29)
White								67 (30)
Goldberg	100 (17)	56 (16)	94 (17)	53 (17)	88 (17)	81 (16)	75 (16)	71 (14)
Marshall	93 (14)		93 (15)	73 (15)	100 (15)	100 (15)	73 (13)	71 (14)

*Numbers in parentheses are the N of cases. Table omits four justices (Reed, Jackson, Burton, and Minton) who participated in seven or fewer cases.

Liberals Douglas, Brennan, and Marshall had equally high levels of agreement on the Warren Court, ranging from 86 to 100 percent (see Table 5). The liberal bloc also included three other Court members: Warren, Goldberg, and Black. Three justices—Stewart, White, and Fortas—agreed most of the time with the six liberals and were classified as independent liberals. A moderate bloc was formed by Clark, Harlan, and Frankfurter, who agreed 86 to 93 percent of the time. Whittaker was a fourth member of that bloc. (Justices Reed, Jackson, Burton, and Minton did not participate in enough cases to be classified.) There was not a true conservative bloc on the Warren Court comparable to the one on the Burger Court.

The seven justices who served on both Courts voted differently on the two Courts (see Table 3). For the seven, the mean support for free expression cases dropped by 6 percent after Burger became chief justice. One justice, Douglas, became more supportive and six became less supportive. White made the most dramatic change, dropping by 19 percent and changing from an independent liberal to a moderate conservative. This downward shift could indicate that the Burger Court was faced with more cases than the Warren Court that concerned the outer limits of protected speech.

IV. CONCLUSIONS

By combining two measures of the justices' behavior—level of support for free speech and agreement in voting—it was possible to characterize the participation of Burger and Warren Court members in free speech cases. On the Burger Court, Black and Harlan each participated in fewer than sixteen cases and could not be accurately classified. However, Black resembled the liberals and moderate conservatives, and Harlan resembled the moderate conservatives and conservatives. Not surprisingly, Douglas was the lone superliberal and Brennan and Marshall were liberals. Stevens and Stewart were independent liberals, and Powell, White, and Blackmun were moderate conservatives. The conservative bloc of Rehnquist, Burger, and O'Connor was just as cohesive as the liberal bloc of Douglas, Brennan, and Marshall.

The Warren Court was more liberal in a variety of respects. There was a large liberal bloc consisting of six justices; and two other justices, Stewart and White, consistently voted with the liberal bloc. There was no conservative bloc. Clark, Harlan, and Frankfurter formed a cohesive moderate bloc.

Well before the announced retirement of Warren Burger, scholars were characterizing the Court as moderate and conservative but not as reactionary or right-wing. In 1985, Abraham observed that appropriate titles for books on the Burger Court were "Neither Conservative Nor Liberal" and "The Counter-Revolution That Wasn't."[20] In 1979, Spaeth used the words "modera-

20. H. J. ABRAHAM, JUSTICES AND PRESIDENTS: A POLITICAL HISTORY OF APPOINTMENTS TO THE SUPREME COURT 294 (2d ed., 1985).

tion" and "moderate conservative" to describe the Burger Court: "The liberal policies of the Warren Court have not been overturned; nor have they been expanded."[21]

In 1982, two first amendment scholars largely agreed. Howard concluded that the Burger Court did not turn out to be the "Nixon Court," that it had not repealed doctrines of the Warren Court.[22] And prominent first amendment attorney Floyd Abrams concluded that, "In many areas, however, freedom of expression has triumphed under the Burger Court and is likely to again."[23]

This statistical analysis of the aggregate voting of the Warren and Burger Courts on speech cases is consistent with this characterization of the Burger Court as moderate or middle-of-the-road and not as right-wing or reactionary. During the Warren Court, often called the most liberal Court in the nation's history, parties exercising their speech rights did not win all of the time or even 90 percent of the time. They won about three-fourths of the time. This compared to one-half of the time for the Burger Court. This difference between the two fractions, one-half and three-fourths, does not justify the characterization of one Court as prospeech and the other as the opposite, antispeech. Also, the volume of speech cases decided by the two Courts does not justify this characterization. The Burger Court decided about three times as many speech cases per year as the Warren Court.

The more activist nature of the Burger Court in accepting free expression cases for review is documented in this study. Free expression simply did not receive as much attention from the Warren Court as such civil liberties as racial equality and the rights of the criminal accused. With the exception of obscenity and libel, the two Courts differed sharply in the types of speech cases they reviewed. At the top of the Burger Court agenda were access-to-government cases. These included Freedom of Information Act appeals and open-courtroom cases. Such cases were largely absent from the Warren Court agenda. Similarly, the commercial speech doctrine and advertising received significant attention from the Burger Court and almost no attention from the Warren Court. This entry of the Burger Court into unchartered areas, and the Burger Court's consideration of the expansion of Warren Court doctrines into more sensitive and extreme regions, may have contributed to the diminished success rate of speech parties before the Burger Court. It is one thing, as the Warren Court did, to decide whether to protect the press from libel suits of elected city commissioners and univerity athletic directors. It

---

21. SPAETH, *supra* note 11, at 93.
22. Howard, *The Burger Court and the First Amendment: Pulling a Decade into Perspective* in THE FIRST AMENDMENT RECONSIDERED 131 (Bill Chamberlin and Charlene Brown eds. 1982).
23. Abrams, *An Analysis*, in THE BURGER COURT, *id.*, at 143.

is quite another thing, as the Burger Court did, to decide whether to protect the press from libel suits from dealers of nudist magazine and persons cited for contempt of court.

The aggregate statistics from this study indicate that in the areas of speech and press, the Burger Court was moderate and not reactionary. Why, then, have some commentators and scholars described the Burger Court as an adversary of the press? One explanation is that these commentators and scholars who analyzed the Burger Court during the 1970s were weaned on the Warren Court of the 1960s. To a person weaned on the Warren Court, judicial activism and judicial liberalism are the norm. It is the natural state of affairs for the Supreme Court to decide the major social, economic, political, and legal issues of the day. To a student of the Warren Court, it is standard jurisprudence for the Court to draft a veritable statute, as it did in the *New York Times v. Sullivan* libel case, when it could have decided the case in favor of the press on the one narrow ground of insufficient identification. (Admittedly, the Burger Court engaged in the same form of excessive law-making in the *Gertz v. Welch* case.) A student weaned on Warren is not bothered by the limited capacity of appellate courts to conduct investigations and commission research as a prelude to major policy-making. From the action-oriented perspective of the Warren Court, it is abnormal for the nation's highest court to defer to the other branches of the federal government or to the states, or to delay until another day the expansion of a civil right. Shapiro sensed some of this when he observed that "each generation of critics is likely to be happier with the Court that shaped its intellectual adolescence than with the one it confronts when it reaches maturity."[24]

During various periods in its history, the U.S. Supreme Court has experienced fragmentation and dissension. The second half of the twentieth century has been one of those periods. However, the dissent rate of the Burger and Warren Courts on speech cases was no different than the overall dissent rates for the two Courts.

In conclusion, any study of how the last two Supreme Courts interpreted freedom of expression amounts to much more than just a study of the most recent thirty-three years of two centuries of U.S. constitutional history. Most of existing constitutional law on speech and press was created during those thirty-three years. "Significant Supreme Court enforcement and interpretation of the constitutional principle of freedom of speech and press really dates only to the second decade of this century."[25] This one study relying on one

---

24. Shapiro, *Fathers and Sons: The Court, the Commentators, and the Search for Values,* in THE BURGER COURT: THE COUNTER-REVOLUTION THAT WASN'T 236 (Vincent Blasi ed. 1983).
25. L. BOLLINGER, THE TOLERANT SOCIETY: FREEDOM OF SPEECH AND EXTREMIST SPEECH IN AMERICA 3 (1986).

The Warren and Burger Courts

methodology and one perspective is neither the first nor the last word about the comparative contributions of the Warren and Burger Courts to freedom of expression. In April of 1987, the magazine of the Society of Professional Journalists, *The Quill,* published a laudatory summary of the Burger Court record on freedom of press. Written by a journalism faculty member at Northwestern University, the article was entitled "Warren Burger Reconsidered."[26] In the June issue under the heading, "Burger Bunk," *The Quill* published a lively rebuttal written by a journalism faculty member at Ohio State University.[27] The debate about Warren Burger and the press, which began in 1971, two years into his term as chief justice, has just begun.

---

26. Protess, *Warren Burger Reconsidered,* THE QUILL 24-26 (April 1987).
27. Schwartz, letter, THE QUILL 6-8 (June 1987).

TRACIEL V. REID

An Affirmative First Amendment Access Right

Traciel V. Reid is an assistant professor in
the Department of Political Science and
Public Administration at North Carolina
State University.

An affirmative right of access is currently evolving in first amendment caselaw. This is an extremely important development in modern law. It indicates that governmental officials may be constitutionally barred from routinely concealing information from the public. Yet, this new first amendment policy is emerging with little notice because it is resulting from lower court decisions, which rarely receive the extensive media attention accorded to rulings rendered by the United States Supreme Court.

The right of access was first recognized by the Supreme Court in its 1980 decision in *Richmond Newspapers Inc. v. Virginia.*[1] In invalidating the closure of a Virginia murder trial, seven justices agreed that a first amendment right of access prohibited trial judges from excluding the public and press from criminal trials. The Court has subsequently applied the new first amendment right very restrictively; the right of access has become a right of admission to criminal trials, *voir dire* proceedings, and preliminary hearings.[2] This article argues that the lower federal and state courts are expanding the right's scope beyond the Court's limited interpretation. These courts are gradually transforming the access right into an affirmative first amendment right whereby communications and press litigants may gain access to a variety of governmental and nongovernmental processes.

Proponents of an affirmative first amendment access right maintain that it is essential to confront current threats to republican government. The system of free expression established by the framers was intended to ensure unlimited and open discussion of public affairs; under the speech and press freedoms, governmental institutions were prohibited from suppressing or coercing public expression. Modern governments no longer engage in direct

---

1. 448 U.S. 555 (1980).
2. *See* Press-Enterprise Co. v. Superior Court, 52 L.W. 4113 (1984); Press-Enterprise Co. v. Superior Court, 54 L.W. 4869 (1986).

suppression or coercion of expression, however. Instead, they have instituted policies designed to manipulate public opinion by controlling the flow of information about official activities. Representative of such policies are the deliberate dissemination of false information, the reclassification of official documents to prevent public inspection, and the obstruction of press access to news events.[3] An affirmative access right provides press and communications plaintiffs with a strong constitutional weapon to challenge policies that limit the disclosure of information possessed by the government. The first amendment would impose an affirmative duty upon government officials to open their decision-making processes to public inspection.

Furthermore, the thesis articulated here challenges the prevailing pessimism surrounding the right's role in modern law. Despite initial enthusiasm within the academic and journalistic communities, first amendment scholars have concluded that "the media's hope that *Richmond* would generate a broad constitutional newsgathering right has been scuttled. . . . "[4] Analyses appearing in law and communications journals have largely underestimated the right's impact upon traditional first amendment doctrine. This article argues that the right's underestimation springs from the approach employed in these articles. By primarily concentrating upon Supreme Court decision-making, most studies' conclusions reflect decisional patterns exhibited by a small, albeit important, part of the American judiciary. A nonhierarchical perspective that encompasses the access decisions rendered by the lower courts allows for a very comprehensive assessment of the adjudication of the access right.

This study begins by briefly discussing the Court's formulation of its access policy. The bulk of the article is devoted to an extensive examination

---

3. Emerson, *The Affirmative Side of the First Amendment*, 15 GEORGIA L. REV. 795 (Summer 1981); Criley, *The Public's Right to Know*, 42 THE HUMANIST 45 (Sept./Oct. 1986).
4. McLean, *The Impact of* Richmond Newspapers JOURNALISM QUARTERLY 789 (Winter 1984). See also Lewis, *A Public Right to Know about Public Institutions: The First Amendment as Sword*, SUPREME COURT REVIEW 1 (1980). Analyses that cite the lower courts have been largely impressionistic rather than empirical. Note, *Confusion in the Courthouse: The Legacy of the* Gannett *and* Richmond Newspapers *Public Right of Access Cases*, 59 SOUTHERN CALIFORNIA L. REV. 620 (March 1986); Plamondon, *Recent Developments in Law of Access*, JOURNALISM QUARTERLY (Spring 1986). See also Leeper, Richmond Newspapers, Inc. v. Virginia *and the Emerging Right of Access* JOURNALISM QUARTERLY 615 (Autumn 1984); Cohen, *Access to Pretrial Documents under the First Amendment*, 84 COLUMBIA L. REV. 1813 (November 1984); Note, *The First Amendment in the Classroom: Library Book Removals and the Right of Access to Information*, 23 BOSTON COLLEGE L. REV. 1417 (September 1982); Comment, *Is the Right of Access to Trials an Instance of a First Amendment Right to Know?* 42 OHIO STATE L. J. 831 (1981); Fenner and Koley, *Access to Judicial Proceedings: To* Richmond Newspapers *and Beyond*, 16 HARVARD CIVIL RIGHTS AND CIVIL LIBERTIES L. REV. 415 (Fall 1981); Note, *Access to Judicial Proceedings: After* Gannet *and* Richmond, 12 TEXAS L. REV. 663 (1981); Note, Richmond Newspapers Inc. v. Virginia: *A Demarcation of Access*, 34 U. MIAMI L. REV. 937 (July 1980).

An Affirmative First Amendment Access Right

of how federal and state courts have applied the access right in ways not condoned by the Supreme Court. The article concludes with several observations about the evolution of an affirmative first amendment right of access.

I. THE SUPREME COURT'S ACCESS POLICY

In developing the first public access right, the Supreme Court rejected its own structural approach to the first amendment. A structural analysis holds that the first amendment, in maintaining an open channel of communication between the citizenry and government, is an essential prerequisite for republican government. The amendment's protections perform an important structural function in a free society because, without speech and press freedoms, the public would be unable to oversee intelligently the activities of their elected representatives. The justices have also suggested that the first amendment has a broader responsibility than simply protecting "unfettered" public discussion; it has an equally demanding role in ensuring that public discussion remains "informed."[5] In recognizing the importance of an informed citizenry to a functioning republic, the Court, in *dicta*, has alluded to the existence of affirmative first amendment right, such as a right to receive information and a right to listen.[6]

Therefore, the right of access has legitimate roots in a structural interpretation of the first amendment.[7] The Court could have plausibly maintained that the first amendment provided the public with an enforceable right to

---

5. Saxbe v. Washington Post, 417 U.S. 843, 862–3 (1974).
6. *See* First National Bank of Boston v. Bellotti, 435 U.S. 765 (1978); Kleindeinst v. Mandel, 408 U.S. 753 (1972); Red Lion Broadcasting Co. v. FCC, 395 U.S. 367, 390 (1969); Mills v. Alabama, 384 U.S. 214 (1966); Lamont v. Postmaster General, 381 U.S. 301 (1965); Martin v. City of Struthers, 319 U.S. 141, 143 (1943); Grojean v. American Press Co., 297 U.S. 233 (1936).
7. Justice Lewis Powell has maintained that an access right stemmed from the societal function of the first amendment (443 U.S. 368 [1979]). In his dissent in *Saxbe v. Washington Post* (417 U.S. 843 [1974]), Powell held that "official restraints on access to news sources" were within the purview of the first amendment. In a number of decisions, the Court had held that the first amendment performed an important structural role in a democratic society by "preserving free public discussion of governmental affairs." Consequently, "governmental inhibitions of press access to newsworthy information warrants constitutional scrutiny" because, Powell argued, these restrictions prevented the press from informing the public about information to which it was entitled. 417 U.S. at 850, 860, 860–61, 861–75.

Also, Justice William Brennan intimated in *dicta* that the creation of an access right promoted the amendment's structural role. "[I]t has a structural role to play in securing and fostering our republican system of self-government. Implicit in this structural role is not only 'the principle that debate on public issues should be uninhibited, robust, and wide-open,' but also the antecedent assumption that valuable public debate as well as other civic behavior must be informed. The structural role model links the first amendment to that process of communication necessary for a democracy to survive, thus entails solicitude not only for communication itself, but also for the indispensable conditions of meaningful communications. 448 U.S. at 587, 587–88.

challenge official restrictions upon the availability of information controlled by the government. Under this perspective, claims for constitutional access should consequently be resolved by appealing to an affirmative first amendment right.

A. Historical Analysis and the Access Right

Despite its traditional structural argument, the Court relied instead upon historical analysis to determine the scope of the access right. This approachced by Justice Harry Blackmun. In his 1979 dissent in *Gannett Co. v. DePasquale*,[8] Blackmun urged his colleagues to apply legal history in determining the propriety of closing judicial proceedings.[9] One year later, the *Richmond Newspapers* Court adopted Blackmun's recommendation.[10] In his concurring opinion, Justice Brennan argued that contemporary requests for constitutional access should be adjudicated by appealing to historical practices.

> [T]he case for a right of access has special force when drawn from an enduring and vital tradition of public entree to particular proceedings or information. Such a tradition commands respect in part because the Constitution carries the gloss of history. More importantly, a tradition of accessibility implies the favorable judgment of experience. . . .
> To resolve the case before us, therefore, we must consult historical . . . practice with respect to open trials. . . .[11]

By adopting the "traditional access" trigger, the Court has allowed history to determine the scope of the access right. Historical analysis requires first examining the historical record to determine whether access has traditionally been provided the public and, secondly, allowing those past practices to be determinative in resolving current access issues. In short, the Court has developed a decision rule in which contemporary requests for access are rejected or granted based upon whether or not a tradition of access characterized the pertinent governmental process. This decision rule deprives the right of its affirmative potential because very few agencies outside of the judiciary have a legacy of openness similar to that of the courts.

Former Chief Justice Warren Burger was the chief architect of the Court's access policy. Arguing that "history is instructive" in applying the

---

8. 443 U.S. 368 (1979).
9. *Id.* at 405–6.
10. 448 U.S. at 601, 601–02 (1980): "[T]he Court in *Gannett* gave a modicum of lip service to legal history. . . . The Court's return to history is a welcome change in direction."
11. *Id.* at 587.

An Affirmative First Amendment Access Right

access right,[12] Burger diminished the force of the first amendment in increasing public access to governmental processes. He contended that the historic practice of keeping certain judicial proceedings accessible to the public required that the right of access apply only to these traditionally open proceedings.

Building upon Brennan's *Richmond Newspapers* concurrence, Burger consistently used a two-pronged test to resolve access cases. The first criterion is whether the "place . . . has historically been open to the press and general public."[13] Accordingly, the "historical evidence" demonstrated conclusively to Burger that "criminal trials both here and in England had long been presumptively open" and that pretrial suppression hearings were never as accessible as trials.[14] Furthermore, Burger rejected the Court's decision to invalidate a Massachusetts statute requiring the closing of trials involving minor victims of sexual assaults by citing the "long history of exclusion of the public" from trials concerning this subject.[15] This first feature of the access test has had a profound effect upon the scope of the access right; it effectively limits the right's force so that it serves only as a right to attend criminal proceedings that have a demonstrated tradition of openness.

The second criterion involves a determination of the benefits accrued from a grant of access. Here again, Burger relied on history in deciding the value of public access to a particular institutional process. Drawing extensively from the works of common-law jurists, Burger noted that criminal trials remained open because it was thought that the presence of interested yet uninvolved spectators produced important social benefits. Public attendance at trials educated the community about the way courts resolve criminal cases, served as a check on judicial behavior, increased the likelihood that relevant information would be available to the courts, and ensured that the court system treated all persons fairly and properly.[16] All of these reasons, which supported open criminal trials under the common and early American law, also supported the creation of a public access right in contemporary law.

Similarly, the ideas and practices of the past also support the Court's refusal to extend the access right to pretrial suppression hearing. The Court has never overturned its holding in *Gannett*. Despite the important function these proceedings perform in the modern criminal justice system, the Court,

---

12. *Id.* at 564, 564–75.
13. Press-Enterprise Co. v. Superior Court, 54 L.W. at 4871 (1986); 448 U.S. at 589 (1980).
14. 448 U.S. at 569 (1980).
15. See Globe Newspapers Co. v. Massachusetts, 457 U.S. 596 (1981). Speaking for the majority, Justice Brennan argued that the mandatory closing of all trials involving sexual assaults to minor victims conflicted with the public right of access to criminal trials. Burger dissented, citing the historical practice of closing such trials. 457 U.S. at 614.
16. 448 U.S. at 569, 571, 572, 572–75 (1980).

led by Burger, concluded that since open pretrial suppression hearings were never considered to promote important systemic values, then their openness was not mandated by the first amendment right.[17] Therefore, historical analysis was used by the Court to determine whether benefits accrued from a grant of access warranted first amendment protection.

The Court's most recent decision to prohibit the closing of preliminary hearings is illustrative of how historical analysis has been instrumental in developing the access right.[18] Here, Burger, in speaking for the majority, applied the two-prong test. Finding that preliminary hearings have been traditionally open to the public and that there was a demonstrated and established value accruing from their public nature, Burger concluded that the access right applied to this stage of the criminal justice system.[19]

Therefore, in rejecting its own structural interpretation, the Court has essentially ruled that the access right secures only those benefits historically enjoyed by the public. Historical analysis makes the access right a defender of the status quo rather than an innovative and useful tool to compel governmental openness. Under this approach, the Supreme Court has precluded the first amendment access right from ensuring that information pertinent to self-government would always remain available to the citizenry.

The Court's access policy has made communications and press plaintiffs understandably pessimistic about the access right's impact on law and policy. However, such pessimism is unwarranted because the lower courts have been very receptive to claims for constitutional access. An empirical analysis of federal and state court decisions indicates that these judges have been less enamored of historical practices than their judicial superiors. As a consequence, unlike the Supreme Court, the lower courts have adopted an expansive interpretation of the right of access.

II. LOWER COURT INTERPRETATION OF THE ACCESS RIGHT

The remainder of the article is an empirical examination of how the lower courts have applied the first amendment access right. This study

---

17. *Id.* at 569; 443 U.S. at 394–95; 956–97 (1979). Burger argued that under the common and early American law, "there was a very different presumption for proceedings which preceded trials." Public access was limited because "there was an awareness of the untoward effects that could result from the publication of information before an indictment was returned or before a person was bound over for trials." In creating and applying the right of access, the second prong of Burger's analysis was a modified functional analysis. Although he examined the value accrued from access to a particular governmental process, the former chief justice nevertheless held that the value must be historically recognized. Contemporary benefits resulting from access were insufficient to demand the application of the constitutional right.
18. 54 L.W. 4869 (1986).
19. *Id.* at 4871, 4872–83.

An Affirmative First Amendment Access Right

includes both unanimous and nonunanimous decisions rendered by trial and appellate courts within the federal and state judiciaries. It covers a seven-year period beginning after *Richmond* was decided in 1980 and extending through 1987. Two hundred and sixty-four cases, which were read in their entirety, were culled from *Sheppard's Citations*, the *Media Law Reporter*, and various law reviews and law journals.

It is important to emphasize that only decisions raising first amendment access arguments were included in this study. The careful inclusion and exclusion of cases were necessary to provide a reliable indicator of lower court interpretation of the access right, and not the amount of access granted by lower courts. Therefore, decisions grounded upon state law or state constitutional provisions were omitted. For example, a state court decision which ruled that a *state law* requires the televising of a criminal trial would not be counted in this study; however, a similar ruling grounded upon the first amendment right of access would be included.

The following examines how the lower courts have adjudicated access claims to judicial and nonjudicial processes. The cases will be discussed according to whether physical, informational, or technological access was requested from the courts.

A. Physical Access to Courts

Like the Supreme Court, the lower courts have applied the access right as a right of attendance. Approximately 69 percent of all cases involving claims to attend judicial proceedings were granted by federal and state judges. In contrast to their judicial superiors, however, inferior judges have employed the right to ensure openness throughout the judicial process. Rather than applying the access right to criminal trials, jury selection, and preliminary hearings only, the lower courts have permitted public attendance at a variety of proceedings held at different stages of the criminal justice, juvenile justice, and civil processes.[20]

---

20. Criminal proceedings: Idaho v. Bainbridge, 13 MEDIA L. REP. 1655 (Idaho Dist. Ct. 1986); Times-Picayune Publishing v. Marullo, 11 MEDIA L. REP. 1885 (La. Sup. Ct. 1985); Hort v. Gaylord Broadcasting, 11 MEDIA L. REP. 1511 (Fla. Dist. Ct. App. 1985); Delaware v. Shipley, 12 MEDIA L. REP. 1274 (Del. Super. Ct. 1985); Tennessee v. Drake, 10 MEDIA L. REP. 2038 (Tenn. Ct. Crim. App. 1984).
  Civil processes: Publicker Industries v. Cohen, 10 MEDIA L. REP. 1777 (3d Cir. 1984); Newman v. Graddick, 9 MEDIA L. REP. 1104 (11th Cir. 1983); Arkansas TV Co. v. Tedder, 10 MEDIA L. REP. 1617 (Ark. Sup. Ct. 1983); United States v. Angiulo, 10 MEDIA L. REP. 1324 (Dist. Ct. Mass. 1983).
  Juvenile proceedings: Tribune Newspapers West v. Superior Court, 218 Cal. Rptr. 505 (Cal. App. 2 Dist. 1985); Taylor v. Indiana, 8 MEDIA L. REP. 2287 (Ind. Sup. Ct. 1982); In re Chase, 8 MEDIA L. REP. 1496 (NY Fam. Ct. 1982); Connecticut v. Sheppard, 7 MEDIA L. REP. 1140 (Conn. Sup. Ct. 1980).

Table 1: Physical Access to the Courts

	Granted	Denied
Pretrial Proceedings(n = 82)	72.0%	28.0%
Criminal and Civil Trials(n = 19)	57.9%	42.1%
Other Judicial Hearings(n = 10)	70.0%	30.0%
Juvenile Proceedings(n = 13)	61.5%	38.5%

In granting access to a variety of judicial proceedings, the lower courts have been reluctant to make historical practices determinative in applying the first amendment right. Perhaps the willingness of federal and state judges to extend the right to pretrial evidentiary hearings is illustrative. Under the Supreme Court's view of first amendment access, pretrial hearings have historically been distinguished from the criminal trials. Arguing that the tradition of openness that characterized criminal trials was never accorded to pretrial proceedings, the Court has refused to extend the right to evidentiary hearings held prior to criminal trials.[21] In contrast, federal and state courts have accorded historical practices little relevance when adjudicating press and public demands to attend pretrial suppression hearings. One circuit court judge declared that reliance upon historic traditions "promotes form over substance."[22] Concluding that evidentiary hearings constituted a "critical stage" in the modern criminal justice system, judges have reasoned that public proceedings promoted the same "societal interests" fostered by open criminal trials.[23]

Furthermore, several state courts have extended the access right to juvenile proceedings. Since their inception, juvenile justice proceedings have been statutorily closed to the public. It has long been presumed that confidentiality in the adjudication of young offenders was essential to their rehabilitation. However, in a number of cases, state judges have suggested that confidentiality no longer outweighs first amendment concerns. They have argued that "for constitutional reasons, the presumption cannot be conclusive."[24] Rather than assuming the validity of barring noninvolved

---

21. *Supra* note 17. In fact, Burger, in writing the majority opinion in *Press-Enterprise II*, did not mention *Gannett* in any of his substantive arguments. A discussion of *Gannett* was unnecessary in considering the propriety of closing preliminary hearings. Preliminary hearings and pretrial hearings are very different proceedings in the criminal justice process. A preliminary hearing is held to determine whether or not the state has compiled sufficient evidence to warrant a trial. Conversely, pretrial hearings primarily occur after the preliminary hearing/grand jury, and their function is primarily to resolve evidentiary issues.
22. United States v. Brooklier, 685 F.2d 1162, 1171 (9th Cir. 1982).
23. United States v. Criden, 675 F.2d 550, 555 (3d Cir. 1982).
24. Florida Publishing Co. v. Morgan, 322 SE.2d 233, 238 (Ga. 1984).

spectators from these proceedings, state court judges, it has been held, must decide whether the "state's interest in a closed hearing is overriding or compelling."[25] For example, in *In re Roberts*,[26] an Ohio court, in ordering an open hearing to determine whether a juvenile defendant should be tried as an adult, concluded that the juvenile offender has to demonstrate how the presence of spectators in the courtroom would impede his fair trial right.[27]

In sum, most lower courts have not been persuaded by the Court's reliance upon history in assessing access claims. Instead, these tribunals have observed that "the First Amendment must be interpreted in the context of current values and conditions."[28] Accordingly, "historic tradition of open hearings" is insufficient grounds for upholding or invalidating a public exclusion order.[29] Federal and state court judges, therefore, have adopted a decision rule which demands structural rather than historical analysis in resolving physical access cases.

B. Informational Access to the Courts

Physical access to the courtroom represents only one dimension of constitutional access. Also, it is arguable that the first amendment houses a strong informational component. The central justification for protecting speech and press freedoms is to ensure the unrestricted exchange of information and ideas, not only among the citizenry but also between the electorate and its government. If an access right also emanates from the first amendment, then it should impose at least a limited duty upon public officials to provide all interested parties with materials pertinent to governmental decision making.

Furthermore, historical practices hardly support informational access to the courts. Unlike maintaining open criminal trials, judges have never been compelled to keep their files open for public inspection. They have always possessed absolute discretion in determining the circumstances under which court records were made available to interested parties.[30] The attachment of an informational component to the first amendment would significantly diminish traditional judicial discretion. Judges would be constitutionally obligated to disclose records and materials in their possession. In contrast to physical access to court proceedings, informational access imposes a duty upon current courts that had never been imposed upon their predecessors.

However, the Supreme Court has strongly opposed such an affirmative role for the first amendment. The Warren Court noted that the imposition of a constitutional duty to accede to public requests for information would

---

25. *Id.*
26. 13 MEDIA L. REP. 1427 (Ohio Ct. Crim. Pleas 1986).
27. *Id.* at 1428–30.
28. United States v. Chagra, 701 F.2d 354, 363 (5th Cir. 1983).
29. *Id.*
30. *See* Nixon v. Warner Communications, 435 U.S. 589 (1978).

disrupt governmental processes.[31] Prior to *Richmond Newspapers*, requests to copy President Nixon's "Watergate" tapes,[32] to enter prison facilities,[33] and to observe a pretrial suppression hearing[34] were all dismissed by the Burger Court on the grounds that "the First and Fourteenth Amendments do not guarantee the public a right of access to information generated or controlled by the government. . . ."[35] The creation of the access right was never intended to overrule any of these precedents. In its 1984 ruling in *Seattle Times Co. v. Rhinehart*,[36] the Court ruled that the access right could not be activated to provide the public with access to materials acquired during the civil discovery process. These decisions demonstrate that the Supreme Court has strongly opposed the creation of any constitutional right that allows the public to demand information controlled by the government.

Despite the Court's opposition, the lower courts have been receptive to public demands for judicially held information. Table 2 indicates that the first amendment has been successfully employed to compel disclosure of court documents in approximately 61 percent of these cases. There is little doubt that these courts have balanced the access right with other important considerations such as privacy interests, fair trial considerations, and commercial interests.[37] The impressive percentage of rulings supporting access reveals a strong presumption favoring disclosure, however. Consequently, "only the most compelling circumstances" override the public right of access to information.[38]

Table 2: Informational Access to the Courts

Granted	Denied
61.1%	38.9%
(n = 55)	(n = 35)

Furthermore, the data additionally show that a wide range of materials may be secured under the first amendment. Contrary to current perceptions, the access right has been activated against judicial orders sealing a host of documents and records pertinent to the resolution of civil and criminal cases.

31. Zemel v. Rusk, 381 U.S. 1, 16–17 (1965).
32. 435 U.S. 589 (1978).
33. Houchins v. KQED, 438 U.S. 1 (1978); Pell v. Procunier, 417 U.S. 817 (1974); 417 U.S. at 862–3 (1974).
34. 443 U.S. 368 (1979).
35. 438 U.S. at 16 (1978).
36. 52 L.W. 4612 (1984).
37. Plamondon, *supra* note 4, at 68.
38. *In re* Application NBC, 635 F.2d 945, 952 (2d Cir. 1980).

For example, the lower courts have granted access not only to discovery materials but also to evidentiary documents, bills of particulars, and affidavits for search warrants.[39]

Several arguments have been advanced to justify this first amendment interpretation. One position holds that informational access flows from physical access. The freedom to enter courtrooms is intended to inform or educate the public about the adjudicative process. Yet, open admission alone may be inadequate for the public to acquire a full understanding of why cases were settled the way they were. For example, evidentiary documents may be introduced in court but never carefully scrutinized in open court; recordings may be played in a courtroom filled with spectators, but those who were not in attendance would never have the opportunity to hear them. Since materials associated with particular litigation become a part of the trial process, arguably, they are covered by a strong presumption against their concealment. Perhaps the Second Circuit Court best explained the nexus between informational and physical access in its decision to allow press access to videotapes played during the criminal prosecution of Congressman Michael Myers.

> Once the evidence has become known to the members of the public, including representatives of the press, through their attendance at a public session of court, it would take the most extraordinary circumstances to justify restrictions on the opportunity of those not physically in attendance at the courtroom to see and hear the evidence. . . .[40]

Similarly, the ninth circuit court, in ruling that the first amendment right of access extended to documents filed in connection with criminal pretrial proceeding, concluded that "there is no reason to distinguish between pretrial proceedings and the documents filed in regard to them."[41]

A closely related defense of informational access notes "significant public interests."[42] The disclosure of information pertaining to the adjudication of cases before the courts promotes the public's interest in knowing about important societal issues. Public interest arguments have been employed in cases involving allegations of misconduct by public officials. The several prosecutions arising from the Federal Bureau of Investigation AB-

---

39. United States v. Smith, 12 MEDIA L. REP. 1345 (3d Cir. 1985) (bill of particulars); Rhode Island v. Cianci, 11 MEDIA L. REP. 2403 (RI Sup. Ct. 1985) (discovery material); *Affidavit for Search Warrant*, 12 MEDIA L. REP. 1904 (Pa. Ct. Com. Pleas 1986) (search warrant).
40. 635 F.2d at 952 (2d Cir. 1980).
41. Associated Press v. United States District Court, 705 F.2d 1143, 1145 (9th Cir. 1983).
42. 635 F.2d at 953 (1980).

SCAM operations are illustrative.[43] In these cases, federal judges, in permitting access to audio-video tapes introduced at judicial proceedings, essentially adopted the argument articulated by the judges of the United States Circuit Court in the District of Columbia. This appeals court outlined the public interests that warranted disclosure of the tapes.

> [T]his case involves issues of major public importance—a high government official has been charged with, and convicted of, betraying the public trust, and law enforcement agencies have been accused of employing tactics which subvert the constitutional rights of the citizenry. Thus, although the public's First Amendment right of access to the trial itself was fully respected in this case, and although the case was reported by the press and broadcast media, we believe that following the trial "there remains a legitimate and important interest in affording members of the public their own opportunity to see and hear evidence that records the activities of a member of Congress . . . as well as agents of the FBI."[44]

The public interest argument was also used to circumvent the force of *Seattle Times*. In *Prescott v. Public Register*,[45] the Massachusetts Supreme Judicial Court denied motions to seal materials submitted to the court pertaining to the divorce of the Norfolk County treasurer, who was also chairman of the Retirement Board. The High Court ruled that *Seattle Times* was inapplicable because "a different standard must be applied when the deposition of testimony at issue concerns a public official, and when that interest is relevant to allegations of misconduct in office." Informational access was granted to promote the "public's vital interest in acquiring information about official wrongdoing."[46]

Finally, lower court judges who have in the past favored informational access to the courts have relied upon common-law right of access. The creation of a constitutional access right may have prompted these judges to ground their traditional preference for public access upon the impregnable fortress of the first amendment. A number of federal and state judges may have been inclined to cite the first amendment access right in granting requests to examine and copy materials possessed by the judiciary. Indeed, Table 3

---

43. *In re* Application NBC, 635 F.2d 945 (2d Cir. 1980); United States v. Carpentier, 7 MEDIA L. REP. 2332 (Dist. Ct. 1981); *In re* Application NBC, 7 MEDIA L. REP. 1193 (DC Cir. 1981).
44. *In re* Application NBC, 653 F.2d 609, 614 (DC Cir. 1981).
45. 11 MEDIA L. REP. 2331 (Mass. Sup. Jud. Ct. 1985).
46. *Id.* at 2333.

An Affirmative First Amendment Access Right

indicates that the constitutional access right has been as successful in supporting claims for informational access as the common-law right of access.[47]

Table 3: Common Law/Constitutional Info. Access

	Granted	Denied
First Amendment (n=51)	66.7%	33.3%
Common Law (n=40)	65.0%	35.0%

The first amendment has secured public access to a variety of judicial documents. The data demonstrate that among the lower echelons of the judiciary, the right of access has provided significant protection against the sealing of court materials. The right of access has been used to ensure informational access to the courts, and as such it endows the first amendment with an affirmative role in modern law.

C. Technological Access to the Courts

Consititutional access may also encompass technological access to the judiciary. Technological access allows individuals and the press to bring audio, video, and other equipment into judicial proceedings as a means of copying and recording the proceedings or materials associated with those processes. Technological access amplifies physical and informational access because it allows individuals who were unable to attend judicial trials and hearings to have direct access to the adjudicative process.

Perhaps the televising of proceedings is the most intrusive form of technological access. The Supreme Court, in its 1981 *Chandler*[48] ruling, softened its earlier prohibition against the broadcasting of trials. Yet, the judtices have never accorded technological access constitutional status.

The lower courts have complied with this particular directive from the Court. On the federal level, federal judges have consistently refused to permit

---

47. The forty cases decided exclusively upon common-law grounds were not included in the 264 cases that raised first amendment claims. These common-law decisions occurred during the same 1980–1986 time period as the collected first amendment cases. Additionally, the first amendment cases counted in Table 3 represent federal and state court rulings that were decided purely upon first amendment grounds. The judges refused to address common-law arguments. For example, in adjudicating a motion to obtain a court record, a judge may cite both the first amendment right of access as well as the common-law right of access. Cases that were based upon both access rights were not included in Table 3, but comprised the 264 originally counted cases. Only twenty-seven common-law/first amendment cases were collected.
48. Chandler v. Florida, 449 U.S. 560 (1981); Estes v. Texas, 381 U.S. 532 (1965).

the media to televise federal judicial processes. They have argued that neither *Richmond Newspapers* nor the first amendment has any bearing on federal court rules prohibiting the operation of broadcast equipment in federal courts. The Fifth Circuit Court was restating a well-established policy when it dismissed motions to televise the fraud-and-racketeering trial of Lousiana governor, Edwin W. Edward; this appeals court concluded that "no case suggests that this right of access includes a right to televise, record or otherwise broadcast trials."[49] Similarly, states have been reluctant to apply the first amendment access right to justify the televising of judicial proceedings; instead, statutes allowing the broadcasting of trials and hearings have been enacted by several state legislatures. Consequently, the first amendment has had a very limited impact upon broadcasting of judicial proceedings.

Less intrusive forms of technological access have received varying judicial support. On the one hand, several courts have cited the first amendment in granting members of the public and press the privilege of using devices to record what transpired in court proceedings.[50] Prohibitions against the drawing of sketches during criminal trials have been overturned.[51] Furthermore, a Florida circuit court ruled that by allowing the press to photograph a juvenile detention hearing, the court was accommodating first amendment demands with the state policy requiring confidentiality in juvenile proceedings.[52] On the other hand, judges have been reluctant to permit the press simultaneous access to copy tapes as they are played in open court.[53]

The small number of cases raising first amendment claims for technological access to the court severely limits statistical analysis. Only seventeen cases involving technological access to the courts were collected. Of these cases, twelve (66.7 percent) denied and six (33.3 percent) granted access. However, an overview of the data indicates that the lower court judges, like their superiors on the Supreme Court, have largely refused to view technological access to the court as a component of any first amendment right.

---

49. United States v. Edwards, 12 MEDIA L. REP. 1997, 1998 (5th Cir. 1986); Westmoreland v. CBS, 596 F. Supp. 1166 (NY 1984); United States v. Hastings, 9 MEDIA L. REP. 1582 (11th Cir. 1983).
50. State ex rel. Cosmos Broadcasting v. Brown, 471 NE.2d 874 (Ohio App. 1984); Wisconsin v. Tande, 11 MEDIA L. REP. 1935 (Wis. Cir. Ct. 1985); United States v. Saunders, 11 MEDIA L. REP. 2247 (Dist. Ct. Fla. 1985); United States v. Kerley, 753 F.2d 617 (7th Cir. 1985); United States v. Yonkers, 10 MEDIA L. REP. 2521 (2d Cir. 1984).
51. KPNY v. Maricopa County Superior Court, 10 MEDIA L. REP. 1289 (Ariz. Sup. Ct. 1984); KTTC-TV v. Foley, 7 MEDIA L. REP. 1094 (Minn. Sup. Ct. 1981).
52. *In re* B.P., 9 MEDIA L. REP. 1151 (Fla. Cir. Ct. 1983).
53. United States v. Beckham, 12 MEDIA L. REP. 2073 (6th Cir. 1986); United States v. Torres, 11 MEDIA L. REP. 1661 (Dist. Ct. Ill. 1985); Fla. *ex rel.* Harte-Hanks v. Austin, 9 MEDIA L. REP. 1170 (Fla. Cir. Ct. 1983).

An Affirmative First Amendment Access Right

D. Nonjudicial Access

The lower courts have been ambivalent about applying the access right outside of the judicial process. Examples of nonjudicial access cases include requests to observe a county commissioners' pretermination hearing,[54] to inspect records submitted at a proceeding of a judicial inquiry and review board,[55] and to record a school board meeting.[56] Only an impressionistic analysis may be gleaned from the few compiled cases involving nonjudicial access. Of the thirty-two cases compiled in this study, 50 percent supported extending the right beyond the court system, while 50 percent held that the first amendment had no impact upon governmental or private decisions limiting public access.

The lower courts were most receptive to claims for physical access to noncourt processes. Although these courts have consistently refused to apply the first amendment right to private places,[57] they nevertheless have cited the access right to invalidate closures of governmental agencies. In eight cases arising from the closure of governmental bodies, only two upheld the closure. The right has successfully challenged policies restricting admission to unemployment insurance compensation hearings,[58] jails,[59] coroner's inquests,[60] school board hearings,[61] and even presidential news conferences.[62]

The 1985 decision in *Society of Professional Journalists v. Secretary of Labor*[63] is illustrative. The federal district court in Utah granted motions presented by press to enter and observe a Mine Safety and Health Administration fact-finding hearing investigating the causes of a coal mine fire. In enjoining the secretary of labor from holding the hearing unless members of the public and press were present, the district court noted that the right of access was "more of a procedural right than a substantive right."[64] Unlike substantive rights, procedural guarantees mandate the procedures and processes to which governmental bodies must strictly adhere. Accordingly, the

---

54. Nelson v. Boundary County, 9 MEDIA L. REP. 1855 (9th Cir. 1983).
55. First Amendment Coalition v. Judicial Inquiry and Review Board, 12 MEDIA L. REP. 1753 (3d Cir. 1986).
56. Dean v. Guste, 414 So.2d 862 (La. App. 1982).
57. State v. McCormack, 682 P.2d 742 (N.M.App. 1984); Stahl v. Oklahoma, 9 MEDIA L. REP. 1945 (Okla. Ct. Crim. App. 1983); Anderson v. WROC-TV, 7 MEDIA L. REP. 1987 (NY Sup. Ct. 1981).
58. Herald Co. v. Weisenberg, 8 MEDIA L. REP. 2450 (NY Sup. Ct. App. Div. 1982).
59. Copley Press v. Aurora, 11 MEDIA L. REP. 1679 (Ill. Cir. Ct. 1985).
60. Courier-Journal v. Gash, 9 MEDIA L. REP. 1735 (Ky. Cir. Ct. 1983).
61. *In re* Carter, 10 MEDIA L. REP. 1935 (Alas. School Bd. 1984).
62. CBS v. Reagan, 518 F. Supp. 1238 (11th Cir. 1981); see also WPIX v. League of Women Voters, 10 MEDIA L. REP. 2433 (Dist. Ct. NY 1984). Although the federal district court denied the request of a cable network to set up its own cameras at the presidential debates, the district court judges recognized a "limited right of access to newsworthy events" (at 1489).
63. 616 F. Supp. 569 (Dist. Ct. Utah 1985).
64. *Id.* at 577.

access right demands that, absent countervailing interests, formal administrative fact-finding hearings must be held in the open. Further, the procedurally mandated access must be met even if practical reasons prevent the press and public from physically entering the room where the hearing is convened. The court recommended that in these instances, the agency has a constitutional duty to provide a "room or area adjacent to the hearing room" for the press and the public to hear and observe (through electronic means, if necessary) the administration proceeding.[65]

Additionally, the district court observed that admission to governmental processes was consistent with established first amendment policy. Noting that ample precedent confirmed the access right's application to the fact-finding hearing, the court reasoned:

> The First Amendment guarantees of free speech and free press protect our right to freely criticize the government without fear of censorship by the government. But censorship in speaking and publishing is not the only form of censorship that must be prevented. The process of filtering information—selectively releasing some information while withholding other information—can be effectively used to prevent criticism and hide mistakes. The First Amendment guarantees apply to both forms of censorship.[66]

Given the limited number of cases, it would be unwise to conclude that constitutional access extends to all governmental proceedings. And yet, as suggested by the federal district court, "it means, instead, that [a public official] does not have the unfettered right to decide whether the hearings conducted by him are public or not."[67]

In contrast to physical access, informational access to nonjudicial proceedings has divided the lower courts. A few rulings have compelled governmental bodies such as police departments and city agencies to provide requested documents to parties.[68] However, an equally low number of decisions have rejected claims for informational access to nonjudicial agencies.[69]

The federal appeals court decision in *Capital Cities Media v. Chester*[70] is controlling. This 1986 ruling represents the most recent ruling involving

---

65. *Id.* at 578.
66. *Id.* at 576.
67. *Id.* at 578.
68. Baltimore v. Burke, 12 MEDIA L. REP. 1244 (Balt. Cir. Ct. 1985); Sheridan Newspapers v. Sheridan, 9 MEDIA L. REP. 2393 (Wyo. Sup. Ct. 1983); The Rake v. Gorodetsky, 452 A.2d 1144 (RI Sup. Ct. 1982).
69. Capital Cities Media v. Chester, 55 L.W. 2073 (3d Cir. 1986), 609 F. Supp. 494 (Dist. Ct. Pa. 1985); First Amendment Coalition v. Judiciary Inquiry and Review Board, 12 MEDIA L. REP. 1753 (3d Cir. 1986).
70. 55 L.W. 2073 (1986).

An Affirmative First Amendment Access Right

informational access to a nonjudicial body. *Capital Cities Media* arose from an investigation conducted by the Pennsylvania Department of Environmental Resources into the possibility that an outbreak of intestinal illness resulted from contaminated drinking water. News reporters requested all records and documents compiled by the department. The department provided the media with several documents but refused to disclose internal memoranda. The media challenged the constitutionality of the department's denial of access on first amendment grounds; it argued that the public had a "right to that information which is part of the public record and the government has the burden of establishing the nonpublic nature of the information sought."[71] Since the withheld information involved official response to a public concern, the department's refusal to provide access to the memoranda, the press reasoned, violated the first amendment.

The federal district court in Pennsylvania rejected the press' argument. In 1985, the district court ruled that neither *Richmond Newspapers* nor subsequent rulings rendered by the Supreme Court held that "the public or the media has a carte blanche right of access under the First Amendment to governmental information."[72]

On appeal, the Third Circuit Court of Appeals upheld the lower court's decision. Sitting *en banc*, the circuit court argued that decisions governing the disclosure of governmentally controlled information "historically have been regarded as political" and that "the people's representatives have not been unresponsive to political pressure when increased public access is needed."[73] Furthermore, the court dismissed the press' analysis of the first amendment and relied upon the Supreme Court's interpretation of the access right.

> It requires some straining of the First Amendment's text to construe its explicit preclusion of government interference as conferring upon each citizen a presumptive right of access to any government held information that may interest him or her. . . . These cases (*Richmond* et al.) hold no more than the government may not close government proceedings that historically have been open unless public access contributes nothing of significant value to the process or unless there is a compelling state interest in closure and a carefully tailored resolution of the conflict between that interest and the First Amendment concerns.[74]

71. 609 F. Supp. at 495 (Dist. Ct. Pa. 1985).
72. *Id.* at 497.
73. 55 L.W. 2073 (1986).
74. *Id.*

Finally, technological access to places outside the judiciary remains beyond the protection of the first amendment. There have been lower court rulings which have cited *Richmond Newspapers* and the first amendment when permitting individuals to tape record or video tape agency or school board meetings.[75] However, the number of these cases is so small that even tentative conclusions are unwise.[76]

An overview of the cases involving nonjudicial access demonstrates that the right of access is not confined to the courts. Although the lower courts have divided over the applicability of the access right beyond the judicial process, a significant proportion of federal and state decisions have supported claims for access to governmental processes. The access right has been successfully activated to keep governmental hearings public. Lower court judges have also cited the first amendment right of access in supporting requests for informational and technological access to nonjudicial agencies.

III. FIRST AMENDMENT ACCESS AND AN AFFIRMATIVE RIGHT

Federal and state court judges have refused to adopt the limited application accorded the right by the Supreme Court. As indicated by Table 4, litigants bringing access cases that extend the first amendment right beyond the narrow application condoned by the Supreme Court have convinced the lower courts to grant their requests in approximately 62 percent of all access claims resolved between 1980 and 1987.

---

75. North Broward Hospital District v. ABC, 13 MEDIA L. REP. (1986); Maurice River Board of Education v. Maurice River Teachers, 475 A.2d 59 (N.J. Super. A.D. 1984); Belchi v. Mansi, 9 MEDIA L. REP. 2203 (Dist. Ct. RI 1983).
76. Johnson v. Adams, 13 MEDIA L. REP. 1973 (Dist. Ct. Tex. 1986); Dean v. Guste, 414 So.2d 862 (La. App. 1982); Post Newsweek v. Traveller Insurance, 6 MEDIA L. REP. 2540 (Dist. Ct. Conn. 1981).

An Affirmative First Amendment Access Right

Table 4: Court Extension of First Amendment Access[77]

	Granted	Denied
Physical Access to Courts (n = 105)	70.5%	29.5%
Info. Access to Courts (n = 90)	61.1%	38.9%
Tech. Access to Courts (n = 18)	33.3%	66.7%
Access to Nonjud. Agencies (n = 32)	50.0%	50.0%
Total (n = 245)	61.6%	38.4%

The first amendment access right has been effectively used by press and the public to secure governmentally controlled information. Despite the narrow interpretation accorded the right by the Supreme Court, the access right has been extensively cited in lower court decisions invalidating official attempts to restrict public access to governmental decision-making process. These courts have argued that, like all first amendment freedoms, the access right must be adjudicated in light of its current structural responsibilities in a democracy. Therefore, federal and state judges have cited the right of access in prohibiting the closing of almost every court proceeding, in instructing judges to acquiesce to demands for materials controlled by their courts, and in compelling nonjudicial agencies to ensure that their processes remain accessible to the public.

The enlarged scope of the access right endows the first amendment with its affirmative right. For the lower courts, constitutional access hardly springs from historical practices. Federal and state courts have acknowledged the importance of history in adjudicating the right; however, they have refused to make the past practices and ideas controlling. Instead, cases were decided based upon the amendment's structural role along with a contemporary reading of public interests. In so doing, the right of access has been interpreted to compel the exercise of governmental power. Rather than preventing public officials from blocking information to which the citizenry was long entitled, state (and to a lesser extent, federal) judges have currently ordered officials to provide information to the public. Therefore, lower court application of the right of access has reflected an affirmative interpretation of the first amendment.

---

77. Cases collected in this table extended the right of access beyond that recommended by the Supreme Court. Decisions which held that the access right applied to agencies outside of the judiciary, to pre- and post-trial proceedings, and, before 1984 and 1986, *voir dire* proceedings and preliminary hearings, respectively.

IV. CONCLUSIONS

Lower court interpretation of the access right signals a new direction for the first amendment. The Supreme Court has not adopted the view articulated by a significant percentage of federal and state courts; however, judicial policy-making studies indicate that the Court's policies have often reflected decisions previously rendered by the lower courts.[78] It is not unlikely that the justices of the highest tribunal would mold their views in accordance to those articulated by their organizational subordinates. Therefore, it is plausible that the lower courts' access policy may eventually represent the access policy adopted by the Supreme Court.

Judicial recognition of an affirmative and enforceable right of access has profound legal and policy implications. Rather than only invalidating direct governmental attempts to intrude upon free expression, the amendment's protections require officials to comply with citizen demands for information. Such an interpretation of the first amendment, which springs from lower court application of the access right, creates a strong constitutional presumption favoring open governmental decision making. Official attempts to block or deny public access to institutional processes may be effectively challenged under the first amendment. Indeed, a vigorous interpretation of the access right has the potential of transforming the first amendment into a constitutional Freedom of Information Act and a constitutional Sunshine Law.

---

78. *See* C. A. Johnson & B. C. Canon, Judicial Policies: Implementation and Impact (1984); R. J. Richardson & K. N. Vines, The Politics of Federal Courts (1970).

Readings from COMMUNICATIONS AND THE LAW, 1

The articles collected in *Defamation: Libel and Slander* were published in the following issues of COMMUNICATIONS AND THE LAW.

"Herbert v. Lando: No Cause for Alarm," by Howard E. Goldfluss, originally appeared in vol. 1, no. 3, pp. 61-68, © 1979.

"Herbert v. Lando: Threat to the Press, Or Boomerang for Public Officials?" by Andre E. Briod, originally appeared in vol. 2, no. 2, pp. 59-92, © 1980.

"Fashioning a New Libel Defense: The Advent of Neutral Reportage," by Donna Lee Dickerson, originally appeared in vol. 3, no. 3, pp. 77-86, © 1981.

"The Future of Strict Liability in Libel," by F. Dennis Hale, originally appeared in vol. 5, no 2, pp. 23-37, © 1983.

"Protecting Confidential Sources in Libel Litigation," by Anthony Green, originally appeared in vol. 6, no. 3, pp. 39-51, © 1984.

"Retraction's Role Under the Actual Malice Rule," by Donna Lee Dickerson, originally appeared in vol. 6, no. 4, pp. 39-51, © 1984.

"Libel and the Long Reach of Out-of-State Courts," by Donna Lee Dickerson, originally appeared in vol. 7, no. 4, pp. 27-43, © 1985.

"Problems in Libel Litigation," by Erik L. Collins, Jay B. Wright and Charles W. Peterson, originally appeared in vol. 7, no. 5, pp. 41-57, © 1985.

"Avoiding the Chilling Effect: News Media Tort and First Amendment Insurance," by Robert L. Spellman, originally appeared in vol. 7, no. 6, pp. 13-27, © 1985.

"'Innocent Construction' Rule Survives Challenge," by Kyu Ho Youm and Harry W. Stonecipher, originally appeared in vol. 7, no. 6, pp. 43-60, © 1985.

"'Single Instance' Rule as a Libel Defense," by Kyu Ho Youm, originally appeared in vol. 9, no. 4, pp. 49-65, © 1987.

"Libel as Communication Phenomena," by Jeremy Cohen and Albert C. Gunther, originally appeared in vol. 9, no. 5, pp. 9-30, © 1987.

"Fact or Opinion: Where to Draw the Line," by Robert L. Spellman, originally appeared in vol. 9, no. 6, pp. 45-61, © 1987.

"Constitution Provides Limited Libel Protection to Broadcast Commentators," by Don Sneed, Whitney S. Mandel, and Harry W. Stonecipher, originally appeared in vol. 10, no. 2, pp. 19-30, © 1988.

Readings from COMMUNICATIONS AND THE LAW, 2

The articles collected in *Privacy and Publicity* were published in the following issues of COMMUNICATIONS AND THE LAW.

"The Public and the Fair Credit Reporting Act," by Blair C. Fensterstock, originally appeared in vol. 2, no. 1, pp. 31-43, © 1980.
"Resolving the Press-Privacy Conflict: Approaches to the Newsworthiness Defense," by Theodore L. Glasser, originally appeared in vol. 4, no. 2, pp. 23-42, © 1982.
"Motor Vehicle Records: Balancing Individual Privacy and the Public's Legitimate Need to Know," by Leslie G. Foschio, originally appeared in vol. 6, no. 1, pp. 15-20, © 1984.
"The Television Docudrama and the Right of Publicity," by Deborah Manson, originally appeared in vol. 7, no. 1, pp. 41-61, © 1985.
"The Big Dan's Rape Trial: An Embarrassment for First Amendment Advocates and the Courts," by Susanna R. Barber, originally appeared in vol. 7, no. 2, pp. 3-21, © 1985.
"The Freedom of Information Act Privacy Exemption: Who Does It Really Protect?," by Kimiera Maxwell and Roger Reinsch, originally appeared in vol. 7, no. 2, pp. 45-59, © 1985.
"Privacy Invasion Tort: Straddling the Fence," by Deckle McLean, originally appeared in vol. 7, no. 3, pp. 5-30, © 1985.
"Unauthorized Use of Deceased's Persona: Current Theories and the Need for Uniform Legislative Treatment," by Valerie B. Donovan, originally appeared in vol. 7, no. 3, pp. 31-63, © 1985.
"Press and Privacy Rights Could Be Compatible," by Deckle McLean, originally appeared in vol. 8, no. 2, pp. 13-25, © 1986.
"Photojournalism and the Infliction of Emotional Distress," by Michael D. Sherer, originally appeared in vol. 8, no. 2, pp. 27-37, © 1986.
"Recognizing the Reporter's Right to Trespass," by Deckle McLean, originally appeared in vol. 9, no. 5, pp. 31-42, © 1987.
"The 1978 Right to Financial Privacy Act and U.S. Banking Law," by Roy L. Moore, originally appeared in vol. 9, no. 6, pp. 23-44, © 1987.
"Unconscionability in Public Disclosure Privacy Cases," by Deckle McLean , originally appeared in vol. 10, no. 2, pp. 31-44, © 1988.
"Docudramas and False-Light Invasion of Privacy," by Tim A. Pilgrim originally appeared in vol. 10. no. 3, pp. 3-37, © 1988.

Readings from COMMUNICATIONS AND THE LAW, 3

The articles collected in *Censorship, Secrecy, Access, and Obscenity* were published in the following issues of COMMUNICATIONS AND THE LAW.

"Open Justice: The Threat of *Gannett*," by James C. Goodale, originally appeared in vol. 1, no. 1, pp. 3-13, © 1979.

"Introduction: The *Snepp* Case—Government Censorship Through The 'Back Door,'" by Henry R. Kaufman, originally appeared in vol. 1, no. 2, pp. 1-27, © 1979.

"First Ammendment Implications For Secondary Information Services," by Paul G. Zurkowski, originally appeared in vol. 1, no. 2, pp. 49-64, © 1979.

"Obscene/Indecent Programming: The FCC and WBAI," by Stanley D. Tickton, originally appeared in vol. 1, no. 3, pp. 15-27, © 1979.

"Heightened Judicial Scrutiny: A Test for the First Ammendment Rights of Children," by Denise M. Trauth and John L. Huffman, originally appeared in vol. 2, no. 2, pp. 39-58, © 1980.

"Obscenity and the Supreme Court: A Communication Approach to a Persistent Judicial Problem," by John Kamp, originally appeared in vol. 2, no. 3, pp. 1-42, © 1980.

"Shield Laws and the Separation of Powers Doctrine," by Louis A. Day, originally appeared in vol. 2, no. 4, pp. 1-15, © 1980.

"Attitudes of Media Attorneys Concerning Closed Criminal Proceedings," by F. Dennis Hale, originally appeared in vol. 3, no. 1, pp. 3-10. © 1981.

"TV in the Courtroom: Right of Access?," by Mary Kay Platte, originally appeared in vol. 3, no, 1, pp. 11-29, © 1981.

"The Trials and Tribulations of Courtroom Secrecy and Judicial Craftsmanship: Reflections on Gannett and Richmond Newspapers," by David M. O'Brien, originally appeared in vol. 3, no. 2, pp. 3-33, © 1981.

"The Right to Know: Whose Right and Whose Duty?," by Eugenia Zerbinos, originally appeared in vol. 4, no. 1, pp. 33-49, © 1982.

"Government Lawyers and the Press," by Anthony Green, originally appeared in vol. 5, no. 3, pp. 3-23, © 1983.

"'Consistent with Security' . . . A History of American Military Press Censorship," by Jack A. Gottschalk, originally appeared in vol. 5, no. 3, pp. 35-53, © 1983.

"Abating Obscenity As a Nuisance: An Easy Procedural Road for Prior Restraints," by Robert L. Hughes, originally appeared in vol. 5, no. 4, pp. 39-50, © 1983.

"The Cost of Prior Restraint: *U.S. v. The Progressive*," by John Soloski
  and Carolyn Stewart Dyer, originally appeared in vol. 6, no. 2,
  pp. 3-23, © 1984.
"State Press Law Provisions and State Demographics," by F. Dennis Hale,
  originally appeared in vol. 6, no. 3, pp. 31-38, © 1984.
"Political Speech or Obscenity," by Debra M. Zigelbaum, originally
  appeared in vol. 7, no. 3, pp. 3-14, © 1985.
"The Irrelevant First Amendment," by Steve Bachman, originally
  appeared in vol. 7, no. 4, pp. 3-25, © 1985.
"Indecent Broadcast: An Assessment of *Pacifica*'s Impact," by James C.
  Hsiung, originally appeared in vol. 9, no. 1, pp. 41-56, © 1987.
"Open Meetings in Higher Education," by Jon Dilts, originally
  appeared in vol. 9, no. 3, pp. 31-42, © 1987.
"Freedom of Expression: The Warren and Burger Courts," by F. Dennis
  Hale, originally appeared in vol. 9, no. 6, pp. 3-21, © 1987.
"An Affirmative First Amendment Access Right," by Traciel V. Reid,
  originally appeared in vol. 10, no. 3, pp. 39-58, © 1988.

Readings from COMMUNICATIONS AND THE LAW, 4

The articles collected in *Advertising and Commercial Speech* were published in the following issues of COMMUNICATIONS AND THE LAW.

"The First Amendment Protection of Advertising in the Mass Media," by Bradford W. Scharlott, originally appeared in vol. 2, no. 3, pp. 43-58, © 1980.

"Comparative Advertising Law and a Recent Case Thereon," by Patricia Hatry and Jeffrey C. Katz, originally appeared in vol. 3, no. 2, pp. 35-47. © 1981.

"Implications of First Amendment Doctrine on Prohibition of Truthful Price Advertising Concerning Alcoholic Beverages," by Gary B. Wilcox, originally appeared in vol. 3, no. 2, pp. 49-66, © 1981.

"False and Comparative Advertising Under Section 43(a) of the Lanham Trademark Act," by A. Andrew Gallo, originally appeared in vol.. 8, no. 1, pp. 3-29, © 1986.

"Alcoholic Beverage Advertising and the Electronic Media," by Gary B. Wilcox, Dorothy Shea and Roxanne Hovland, originally appeared in vol. 8, no. 1, pp. 31-41, © 1986.

"The Future of Alcoholic Beverage Advertising," by Roxanne Hovland and Gary B. Wilcox, originally appeared in vol. 9, no. 2, pp. 5-14, © 1987.

"The Commercial Speech Doctrine: *Posadas* Revisionism," by Denise M. Trauth and John L. Huffman, originally appeared in vol. 10, no. 1, pp. 43-56, © 1988.

"The First Amendment Defense to Negligent Misstatement," by Robert L. Spellman, originally appeared in vol. 10, no. 3, pp. 59-72, © 1988.

"The Tobacco Advertising Debate: A First Amendment Perspective," by David D. Vestal, originally appeared in vol. 11, no. 1, pp. 53-67, © 1989.

KF 4775 .A75 C46 1990

DATE DUE